Learning Classical Tibetan

Learning Classical Tibetan

A Reader for Translating Buddhist Texts

WITH GRAMMATICAL ANNOTATIONS AND TRANSLATIONS

Paul G. Hackett

SNOW LION
Boulder
2019

Snow Lion
An imprint of Shambhala Publications, Inc.
4720 Walnut Street
Boulder, Colorado 80301
www.shambhala.com

9 8 7 6 5 4 3 2 1

First Edition
Printed in the United States of America

♾ This edition is printed on acid-free paper that meets the American National Standards Institute Z39.48 Standard.
Shambhala Publications makes every effort to print on recycled paper. For more information please visit www.shambhala.com.
Snow Lion is distributed worldwide by Penguin Random House, Inc., and its subsidiaries.

Designed by Paul G. Hackett

LIBRARY OF CONGRESS CATALOGING-IN-PUBLICATION DATA

Names: Hackett, Paul G., author.
Title: Learning classical Tibetan: a reader for translating Buddhist texts / Paul G. Hackett.
Description: Boulder: Snow Lion, 2019. | Includes bibliographical references and index.
Identifiers: LCCN 2018022091 | ISBN 9781559394567 (hardcover: alk. paper)
Subjects: LCSH: Tibetan language—Textbooks for foreign speakers—English. | Tibetan language—Readers—Buddhism.
Classification: LCC PL3613 .H25 2018 | DDC 495/.486421—dc23
LC record available at https://lccn.loc.gov/2018022091

Dedicated to the memory of
the Venerable Geshe Jampel Thardo
of Drepung Loseling Monastic University

Contents

Preface

Introduction

Close to sixty years have passed since the Tibetan uprising against the Chinese invasion and occupation of Tibet. During that time, the fields of Tibetan and Buddhist Studies have changed radically and irrevocably. Until the time of the Tibetan diaspora, access to Tibetan literature was the purview of the few and the priviledged, the domain of a leisure class of scholars and diplomats with private libraries and the means to make use of them. With the commercial publishing of Tibetan works in India in the early 1960s, and their subsequent accession by the United States Library of Congress, all that began to change.

Today, there are more than a dozen public and private university libraries housing collections of Tibetan literature. Electronic text initiatives geared towards building Tibetan corpora abound, and digital scans of texts are now readily available from the Tibetan Buddhist Resource Center (http://www.tbrc.org/) courtesy of the man whose name is almost synonymous with Tibetan literature in the twentieth century, the legendary E. Gene Smith.

Despite the relative ease of availability of Tibetan literature today, however, formal training in reading Tibetan literature is still difficult to come by. This textbook was written to fill this need—to be the sort of textbook I wished I had had when I began my studies. It is intended as a companion volume to Joe Wilson's *Translating Buddhism from Tibetan*, and supplemented by the author's *A Tibetan Verb Lexicon*.

The Premise and Purpose of This Book

This book is based on the approach to foreign language instruction currently known as "Content and Language Integrated Learning" (CLIL). It is thus both a primer in the Tibetan language and a sourcebook on the subjects of religion and religious education. This book has been compiled for students and teachers of classical Tibetan language and literature—for anyone who wishes to learn classical Tibetan and expose themselves to aspects of the traditional Tibetan Buddhist educational curriculum. While there are several programs of study offering Tibetan throughout the United States, Europe, and Asia, there has previously been no attempt to offer a systematic CLIL primer in Tibetan Buddhist Studies in its primary language for nonnative speakers. This *Reader* is intended to rectify that situation and is designed to be used either in the classroom or for private study.

The Structure of This Book

This book is designed to function as a primer on several different levels. On the level of language, the texts contained in this *Reader* are organized in increasing complexity both in terms of vocabulary and grammar. In the Introductory Texts section, the student encounters simple sentential grammar and formulaic constructions, techniques of commentarial exegesis, occasional complex phrases, a first introduction to philosophy in poetic verse, and an example of historical narrative. In the Intermediate Texts section, the student is presented with five texts representing the formal introduction to the traditional Tibetan education system (see introduction, 7ff). In these texts, a greater variety of sentence styles are encountered stemming from poetic concerns, the emulation of more complex Sanskrit grammatical structures, and stylistic idiosyncrasies on the part of individual authors. In the final, Advanced Texts section, the student is presented with complex and/or abbreviated grammatical structures in exemplary texts in the genres of translated verse works, "Means of Accomplishment" (*sādhana; sgrub thabs*) and "Prayers" (*pranidhāna; smon lam*). Here, standard formulaic constructions are seen with grammatical infelicities that have arisen out of the idiosyncratic nature of these literary traditions.

On the level of content, this *Reader* is likewise organized into progressive readings designed to introduce the student to the Tibetan and Buddhist worldview. The texts contained in the first section are simple readings designed to provide an introduction to some of the basic genres of classical Tibetan literature: Buddhist sūtras, commentarial explanations, Buddhist narrative literature, poetic treatises, and historical narrative. The texts contained in the second section, however, cover the basic subjects encountered by a novice student entering the traditional educational system and constitute the first substantive introduction to Buddhist philosophy. In this section the focus is less on narrative style and genre and more on recognizing formulaic grammatical constructions and developing familiarity with foundational vocabulary and core concepts. Without this, any subsequent narrative, biographical, or poetic treatises will prove only partially comprehensible. To attempt to read more dynamic Tibetan narrative literature without command of the materials in this section would be like attempting to read the works of Dante Alighieri, John Milton, or Herman Melville without any basic knowledge of the Judeo-Christian religious tradition: it is possible to do so, but the subtlety of thought and cultural references contained within those works would be utterly lost on such a reader. The final section of the *Reader* contains texts of esoteric content and vocabulary. These texts reflect many of the core concepts in the esoteric literature of Indo-Tibetan Buddhism, including issues such as meditations at the time of death, complex meditative visualizations, and the behavior and manipulation of subtle bodily energies during yogic practices.

Finally, this book presents a third, intentional challenge to the reader. Throughout the three sections of the *Reader*—Introductory, Intermediate, and Advanced—the texts presented have been annotated to clarify difficult points of grammar as they occur; an index to these notes is given in appendix 2. In general, only the first instance of a new or difficult construction is noted, and once a given point of grammar has been addressed, it is not revisited. Consequently, these annotations decrease in frequency over the course of the book with presumed familiarity with the content of prior notes. In addition, since the need for knowledge of Sanskrit for advanced studies in Tibetan Buddhism becomes more obvious as progress is made, points of comparison to Sanskrit grammar are also given in the annotations as appropriate.

It is intended, moreover, that the grammatical annotations will not be merely consulted but rather learned and employed in subsequent reading. To aid in this approach, at the end of every grammatical annotation, a brief summary of "WHAT TO REMEMBER" is provided. It should be reiterated that these notes contain grammatical aids to reading the texts and for the most part are *not* content annotations; students desiring additional content information should consult with a scholar versed in the subject matter or refer to one or more of the published reference works cited in the introduction to each text.

What this reader is also not is a primer in different text formats (the traditional woodblock-printed "pecha" format being difficult to reproduce in Western book format) or different Tibetan scripts. The texts provided here have all been electronically typeset in the scholastic "U-jen" (*dbus can*) typeface. While training in alternate scripts such as "U-may" (*dbus med*) and "Kyuk" (*'khyug*) is a desideratum, such a task is sufficiently complex as to merit its own treatment in a separate work. As an aid in that direction, however, appendix 4 contains three duplicate texts: Tsongkhapa's *Three Principal Aspects of the Path*, chapter one of Śāntideva's *Engaging in the Deeds of a Bodhisattva*, and the *Long-Life Prayer for His Holiness the Dalai Lama* in three different scripts—Dru-tsa (*'bru tsha*), Bam-yik (*'bam yig*), and Kyuk-yik (*'khyug yig*), respectively; a secondary aid is provided in appendix 3 in the form of sets of tables of characters and combinations in different scripts.

How to Use This Book

In general, each student should engage the materials in accordance with their own skill level. Nonetheless, the intended use of this primer is as follows. In brief, the purpose of the study of these texts should not be interpreted as an exercise in tedium but rather as one of informative and progressive growth in language capability. Therefore, the student should initially attempt to produce a translation of each passage of each text independently, without consultation of the either the notes or the accompanying translation. Having produced a translation, one should then consult any notes accompanying the passage and memorize the grammatical points in the process of revising the translation. Finally, the student should compare their translation with the translation provided and attempt to understand the rationale behind and differences between the two. In this way, one experiences the struggle of working with a previously unseen text (the goal of this process), the discovery of new grammatical principles, and finally an example of an end product. In a classroom setting, this textbook can be used in two ways: as a six-semester course or as an abbreviated four-semester course. Sample syllabi for each are provided in appendix 6 with reference to this *Reader*, Wilson's *Translating Buddhism from Tibetan*, and the author's *A Tibetan Verb Lexicon*.

Finally, a part of education in literary Tibetan involves developing familiarity with basic rules of spelling and euphony, knowledge of which can provide a means of detecting typographical errors and omissions. To this end, appendix 1 provides the text and a summary of Yangjen Gaway Lodrö's mnemonic poem on grammar indicating their approximate Latinate categories.

Acknowledgments

It is with a mixture of amusement, humility, and chagrin that I note that now, more than twenty years *after* the "due date" of my original contract for this book with Snow Lion Publications, this *Reader* is finally in print. I can honestly say that is solely due to the consistent (and persistent) encouragement from Sidney Piburn that I continued to work on this project throughout these years. While many scholars have translated core works on Tibetan Buddhism over the previous forty years, it was only with the tireless efforts of Sidney Piburn that many of them were ever published. The same holds true of this textbook, and I cannot thank and praise Sid enough.

The materials initially chosen for study and presented here represent a variation on the graduate training course initially developed by Jeffrey Hopkins, which I adapted and modified over the course of several years teaching Classical Literary Tibetan at Columbia and Yale Universities. Several of the works chosen were initially translated by Hopkins himself or by others working in conjunction with him. To the extent that my own understanding would not be possible without their efforts, I gratefully acknowledge the following students and scholars who have both directly and indirectly aided me in my understanding of the Tibetan language and the Buddhist educational system: (beginning at the University of Virginia) Jeffrey Hopkins, William Magee, Karen Lang, Elizabeth Napper, Joe Wilson, Anne Klein, Daniel Perdue, Georges Dreyfus, Jules Levinson, Craig Preston, and Christopher Wilkinson, and (subsequently at Columbia University) Robert Thurman, Gen. Lozang Jamspal, and Gary Tubb.

Hopkins's program of studies at the University of Virginia that inspired this *Reader* began with the proposition that scholars of Tibetan religion and culture should not attempt to "reinvent the wheel" with regard to education in the subjects of Tibetan Buddhism but rather should look to those preexisting educational structures and teachers in the intellectual traditions under investigation. To these scholars as well—several of whom I had the good fortune to study with, either in person or through the proxy of audio tapes and transcripts—I would like to give acknowledgement, not only for their wisdom, but as their students will testify, for their exceptional kindness and patience in revealing the full embodiment of their learning: Geshe Jampel Thardo, Geshe Lhundup

Sopa, Laṭi Rinpoche Jangchup Tsultrim, Denma Lochö Rinpoche, Gyüme Khensur Losang Wangdu, Gyü-me Khensur Lobsang Jampa, Khensur Yeshey Tupden, Geshe Tenzin Rapgye, Geshe Ngawang Jangchup, Khensur Lobsang Tenzin Wangdak, Geshe Gelek Chodak, Ven. George Churinoff, and last but certainly not least, His Holiness Tenzin Gyatso, the Fourteenth Dalai Lama, fountain of wisdom and compassion.

In addition, as no books are ever produced in isolation, while many people have provided their assistance and support throughout the composition of this *Reader*, I would like to specifically thank Thomas Creamer, from whom I learned an immense amount about lexicography and language primer construction, Sidney Piburn (again) and Jeff Cox of Snow Lion Publications, and Susan Kyser, Liz Shaw, Lora Zorian, Casey Kemp, Audra Figgins, and Nikko Odiseos at Shambhala Publications, whose feedback greatly improved its structure and content and whose continued encouragement enabled me to bring this book to completion.

Paul G. Hackett
New York, New York, November, 2018

PART ONE

Introduction

Introduction

For over five centuries, until the Chinese invasion of Tibet in the 1950s, the three main monastic universities of the Lhasa Valley trained many of the greatest luminaries of the Buddhist intellectual tradition, from the Buriat regions of Siberia to the Kalmuk regions along the Volga River near the Caspian Sea. During this period of time, from the fifteenth to the twentieth century, the subtleties and intricacies of Śākyamuni Buddha's teachings set forth two thousand years earlier were elucidated, debated, and meditated upon in a rigorous course of training like no other on the planet.

In the midst of the physical and cultural genocide enacted upon the Tibetan Plateau under Chinese occupation, the entire corpus of these teachings was nearly lost. It was only through the extraordinary efforts and dedication of the Tibetan people that these teachings continue to exist. The texts included in this book are but a small introductory sample of the rich literary and philosophical heritage of Tibet, a heritage in service of whose preservation a great many people suffered and died.

Overview of the Texts

Despite the hardships presented by life in exile, the three great monastic universities of the Lhasa Valley—Drepung, Sera, and Ganden[1]—reestablished themselves in southern India, where they continue to function today. A vignette of life during these times illustrates the commitment on the part of Tibetans toward their traditions:

> The library of the original Sera Mey Monastic University in Lhasa suffered complete destruction at the hands of the invading Chinese army and subsequent "Cultural Revolution." Copies of the monastery textbooks were pieced together by the refugee monks in the years following their flight to India, and a valiant effort was made to republish sufficient quantities to continue the study tradition. During a twelve-year ordeal at the Buxa Dur refugee camp in northern

1. The "Three Great Seats" (*gdan sa gsum*): *'bras spungs*, *se ra*, and *dga' ldan*.

> India, teams of monks from Sera Mey rewrote the entire textbook series out by hand. Desperately poor, they obtained flimsy Indian paper and printed the early volumes on flat stones (a genuine lithograph) using cow's urine and charcoal for ink. These issues were, for the most part, carefully edited and are still often seen in the hands of older scholars.[2]

Recognizing the centrality of knowledge in the Buddhist endeavor, a basic course of training in epistemology, logic, and the sciences of the mind was laid out and honed in an educational tradition for over five centuries in both the debate-style (*rtsod grwa*) and commentary-style (*bshad grwa*) schools. It is this basic educational training that has produced the many geshes and lamas now scattered throughout the world.

In the course of training for the degree of Geshe (*dge bshes*), over twenty years may be spent on the major subjects such as Middle Way philosophy (*madhyamaka; dbu ma*), Valid Cognition (*pramāṇa; tshad ma*), the Perfection of Wisdom, and so forth. Following this, some students would go on to more advanced study in one of the tantric colleges. A streamlined version of this curriculum—from the basic subjects of logical reasoning up to and including tantra—was devised by His Holiness the Dalai Lama in the 1970s,[3] and although complete coverage of such a curriculum is beyond the scope of a textbook such as this, some elements of this basic course of training are included here.

Introductory Texts

It is easy for novice students of Tibetan to forget that they are attempting to enter a fully developed philosophical and religious tradition with over 2,500 years of intellectual and literary history. Consequently, the strength of the Tibetan intellectual tradition has always been its religious philosophy, and so the selection of texts presented here follows in that tradition. The texts chosen for inclusion in this section thus reflect: (a) their coverage of basic vocabulary and normative literary style, (b) the ease of comprehension of their grammar and vocabulary within their genres, and (c)

2. Ser-smad Thos-bsam-nor-bu'i-gling 1990, vol. 1, vi.
3. Tenzin Dorjee 1989, 33–46.

without compromising their intellectual content, a means of entering into the larger body of literature from which they come.

In their original published form, these texts were printed in a format that maximized the use of each printed page with only occasional excess "white space" between sections of text to indicate their internal structure. In formatting these texts for publication here, paragraph breaks have been inserted to break the text into coherent sections (reflected in the English translations, with occasional parenthetical Tibetan) for ease of reading.

The Heart Sūtra

Revered, studied, and recited by Buddhists all around the world, *The Bhagavātī, The Heart of the Perfection of Wisdom Sūtra* is one of the most well known of all Buddhist scriptures. It gives a pointed and concise presentation of both the doctrine of emptiness and the structure of the Buddhist path. Commonly known in Tibetan as "*Shé-rap nyíng-bo*" (*Shes rab snying po*), the *Heart Sūtra* is one of several texts commonly committed to memory and recited daily both for study and ritual purposes. Most notably, the sūtra contains the oft-quoted quatrain concerning the relationship between emptiness and the aggregates—as illustrated by the first aggregate, form (*rūpa; gzugs*): "These five aggregates, also, are to be purely and thoroughly seen as empty of own-nature (*svabhāva; rang bzhin*): form is empty [of its own nature]; emptiness [of own-nature] is [the mode of subsistence of] form. Emptiness is not other than form; form is not other than emptiness." In addition, the sūtra also presents one of the most famous mantras found in Buddhist literature: *Oṃ gate gate pāragate pārasaṃgate bodhi svāhā*. Both of these passages have elicited detailed exegeses on the part of subsequent generations.

The text is comprised of simple grammar and illustrates many of the key features of the Tibetan language documented in Wilson's presentation.

Jñānamitra's *Explanation of the Heart Sūtra*

Of the many canonical Indian commentaries written on the *Heart Sūtra*, the one by Jñānamitra is a clear and straightforward commentary on the words and phrases found in the sūtra. The inclusion of this text is to provide the student with experience in reading a root text—in this case, the *Heart Sūtra*—in conjunction with a commentary, and to introduce the idiosyncracies of the genre of classical Indian commentary in translation.

The Sūtra Called "The Wise and the Foolish"

The collection of stories known as *The Sūtra Called "The Wise and the Foolish"* contains numerous *jataka* tales, or narrative accounts of the previous lives of the Buddha. Among them, the story of Prince Mahāsattva giving his body to feed a hungry tigress has been one of the most popular stories over the centuries. Although translated from Chinese, this text adheres to normative Tibetan grammar and phrasing and replicates the formulaic opening of many other sūtras.

This text introduces the student to a more narrative form of literature, including some subtle aspects of Tibetan grammar, while remaining within the well-defined bounds of the genre of canonical scriptures.

Tsongkhapa's *Three Principal Aspects of the Path*

This text belongs to one of the most popular genres of Tibetan literature: verse poetry. The topic of exposition in this work is the "Stages of the Path" (*lam rim*) to enlightenment. Written by the founder of the Geluk (*dge lugs*) school, Tsongkhapa Losang Drakpa (*tsong kha pa blo bzang grags pa*, 1357–1419), to one of his patrons, the Lord of Tshakho, and although brief and undifferentiated from the rest of the letters in his collected writings, this work has been singled out by subsequent generations of scholars as a concise and pointed presentation of the Buddhist path because of its description of the three requisite features of the path to enlightenment: (1) the complete thought of renunciation of life in cyclic existence (*saṃsāra*), (2) the "mind of enlightenment" (*bodhicitta*), and (3) the exalted wisdom realizing emptiness. It is considered both an easily memorized mnemonic for the advanced student and an excellent summarized introduction for the beginner.

This text thus introduces the student to postcanonical composition and the idiosyncracies of reading verse poetry with its concise and constrained grammar.

Paṇchen Sönam Drakpa's *New Red Annals (selection)*

As the final text in this section, this selection covers the history of the Tibetan Empire (ca. 618–842) and the early stage of introduction of the Buddhist teachings to Tibet. The text selection is taken from within the larger historical work written by the textbook author for the Loseling College of Drepung Monastic University, Paṇchen Sönam Drakpa (*paṇ chen bod nams grags pa*, 1478–1554).

This text provides the student with an exercise in reading historical narrative and in recognizing proper names and new topic-specific vocabulary.

Intermediate Texts

In this section of the *Reader*, the student is presented with five texts of progressively deeper content and more complex grammatical structures. In terms of topics, these texts offer foundational concepts, terminology, and formal grammatical structures that enable the serious study of more advanced topics. In terms of grammatical structure, a greater variety of sentence styles are encountered stemming from poetic concerns, the emulation of more complex Sanskrit structures, and stylistic idiosyncrasies on the part of the author. Although ideally a sixth text should be included in this section—a presentation of "Grounds and Paths" (*sa lam*) to enlightenment, one of the two traditional summary textbooks for the study of the Perfection of Wisdom literature—texts that present this subject matter tend to be highly repetitious in terms of vocabulary and redundant in terms of grammar in relation to the other texts in this section. Nonetheless, since the concepts and core vocabulary presented in such texts are important for full comprehension of the implications of their later reference in other texts, a condensation of this material into sets of philosophical definitions is presented in appendix 7.

Purbujok's *"Introductory Path of Reasoning"*

The literature of "Collected Topics," generally referred to as "*du-dra*" (*bsdus grwa*), covers many key issues without an understanding of which no further progress can be made in the higher systems of thought. Written in formulaic Tibetan debate format, this genre of literature serves the dual purpose of both informing and training the student in the rudiments of logical thought. As part of a comprehensive presentation of Buddhist philosophy, it is asserted that a conceptual and logically grounded "inferential" understanding of the ultimate doctrine, emptiness, precedes direct realization. In addition, it is also held that without training the mind in logic, a practitioner might not be able to differentiate between valid and invalid interpretations of their meditative experiences, and hence would fall into error and mistaken views. Consequently, an understanding of logical inference is advocated as a necessary prerequisite to both the study and practice of Buddhism. The selection from the text presented here covers the first topic: colors and other external forms. A sample debate for practice is also provided in appendix 5.

In terms of grammar, the text offers a systematic introduction to the subtleties and variations of declarative statements, syllogisms, and consequences, as well as the variety of pronouns and formulaic expressions that can be used to abbreviate arguments (a style seen throughout all literary genres).

Jampel Sampel's *Presentation of Awarenesses and Knowers*

The second text in this section covers the subject known as "*lo-rík*" (*blo rig*), or "Awarenesses and Knowers," and is by the twentieth-century geshe Jampel Sampel (*'jam dpal bsam 'phel*, d.1975); it is used by the Loseling (*blo gsal gling*) College of Drepung Monastic University. This text is a primer in the Chaba system's presentation of Dharmakīrti's epistemology and introduces core vocabulary by means of which a broader understanding of his system may be approached. On the level of practice, the text is envisioned as providing an understanding of the various states of mind in terms of their status as valid or invalid perceivers; implicitly, it also allows one to understand the progression from mistaken to unmistaken states of consciousness along the path to enlightenment.

In terms of grammar, the text is a mixture of debate-style and commentarial explanations and demonstrates the manner in which formulaic structures can be integrated within a larger narrative structure.

Könchok Jikmé Wangpo's *Precious Garland: A Presentation of Tenets*

The third text included in this section is on the subject of "Tenets" (*siddhānta; grub mtha'*), literally "established conclusions." As part of the educational curriculum, it is held that a thorough understanding of tenets allows the student to differentiate the various disparate and oftentimes apparently contradictory teachings of the Buddha into meaningful, internally consistent systems. In addition, the tradition holds that this understanding clears the way in the student's mind for progress on the path; as stated in *The Descent into Laṅka Sūtra* (*Laṅkāvatāra-sūtra*):

> My Doctrine has two modes,
> Advice and tenets.
> To children I teach advice;
> To yogis, tenets.[4]

Such is said because it is held that while advice and stories can keep a practitioner from engaging in the sort of destructive actions that bring about more suffering, it is only an understanding of tenets that allows the practitioner to develop an internal force capable of counteracting one's own innate adherence to the misapprehensions of ordinary, everyday life and replace them with well-founded perspectives. In support of this, the text presents eight topics on the tenets of the philosophical systems in an ascending hierarchy of subjects surveying both non-Buddhist and Buddhist systems of tenets.

In terms of grammar and vocabulary, the text provides near-comprehensive coverage of the core vocabulary required for the study of Buddhist philosophy. It draws on the previous texts in this section (as well as the materials in appendix 7) and their vocabulary, presenting many of the topics covered from each philosophical system's perspective. On a grammatical level, the text combines some elements of debate-style presentation with explanatory narrative that employs more complex sentence structures.

Yangjen Gaway Lodrö's *Lamp Illuminating the Three Bodies*

The fourth text in this section introduces the student to the concepts and terms of the tantric death literature. As a text related to the "Unsurpassed Yoga" (*anuttara-yoga; bla med rnal 'byor*) tantric systems, its presentation of the Tibetan Buddhist system of subtle body physiology provides an essential understanding of the three bases to be purified during the course of practice of the tantric path: death, intermediate state, and rebirth. The text also discusses issues such as meditations at the time of death and the behavior and manipulation of subtle bodily forces at the time of death.

In terms of grammar and vocabulary, the text introduces a new set of core vocabulary related to esoteric content and tantric exegesis. The grammatical structures encountered in the text are on an intermediate reading level with occasional complex constructions and both intratextual and intertextual references.

4. *Laṅkāvatāra-sūtra; Lang kar gshegs pa'i mdo*, D 107, fol. 123b.7.

The Fourth Paṇchen *Lama's Prayer for Release from the Dangerous Bardo*

The final text in this section exposes the student to the terse and near-cryptic levels that some compositions take. Written in verse, the text offers an abbreviated presentation of the preceding text by Yangjen Gaway Lodrö.

The text draws on the vocabulary and concepts encountered in the previous text but presents the same material in the form of a poetic verse with omitted grammar and oblique references to material covered at length in the previous text. This text thus introduces the student to the genre of "aspirational prayers" (*gsol 'debs*) through familiar vocabulary.

ADVANCED TEXTS

In this section of the reader, the student is presented with four texts of challenging and complex grammatical structures. In terms of content, these texts reflect some of the core concepts in the esoteric literature of Tibetan Buddhism. In terms of grammatical structure, the texts in this section exemplify the literary categories of philosophical poetry, the formulaic constructions of "Means of Accomplishment" (*sādhana; sgrub thabs*) texts, and "Prayers" (*pranidhāna; smon lam*) written in high honorific style. In these texts, there are numerous grammatical infelicities, which have arisen as a result of their idiosyncratic literary traditions.

Chapter One of *Śāntideva's Engaging in the Deeds of a Bodhisattva*

One of the most famous of the Indian Buddhist treatises, Śāntideva's text presents techniques and methods designed to inspire the student to embrace the spiritual ideals of the perfections of generosity, patience, ethics, effort, concentration, and wisdom, and to employ them in one's daily life. Here is the first chapter, on the subject of the altruistic intention to attain enlightenment.

There have been a number of translations of this text into English over the past thirty years, each with their strengths and weaknesses. The advanced nature of this and the next text lies in their terse construction and the challenge to render elegant poetry.

Aśvaghoṣa's *Fifty Verses on the Guru*

Aśvaghoṣa's work is a short text on devotion to a tantric guru. Addressing a concept that is often misunderstood, Aśvaghoṣa's text lays out the characteristics of a suitable tantric guru as well as the mutual responsibilities of a student and a teacher. Hearkening back to the judgement of the Second Buddhist Council at Vaiśāli that reproached simple blind devotion to one's teacher, the text presents an informed and intelligent approach to relating to one's spiritual master. Written in verse form, the text is cited by Tsongkhapa as a prerequisite to the study of his *Great Exposition of Secret Mantra* (*Sngags rim chen mo*), as well as by Atīśa, Nāropā, and others as a prerequisite to entering upon tantric practice. In the Kalacakra system, moreover, failure to adhere to the teachings contained within the text is considered a violation of tantric vows. The text covers several key points, including how to investigate a potential teacher to see if he or she is suitable, how to conduct oneself properly in the teacher's presence, and the consequences of failing to. The text also covers more complex issues such as the mental disposition and visualizations which the student should enter into when studying with a tantric master.

His Holiness the Dalai Lama's *The Yoga of the Inseparability of the Guru and Avalokiteśvara*

This text was composed by His Holiness the Dalai Lama when he was nineteen years old at the request of one of the cabinet ministers of Tibet. In terms of grammar it introduces students to the idiosyncratic form of practice texts; in terms of content, it introduces the terminology of a meditation text, in this case, focused on Avalokiteśvara—the embodiment of compassion—of whom His Holiness the Dalai Lama is considered a manifestation.

Long-life Prayer for His Holiness the Dalai Lama

The final text included here is a standard prayer recited at teachings around the world for the continued health and well-being of His Holiness the Dalai Lama.

Composed in a highly ornate style with superlatives and honorifics, the text offers a number of vocabulary and grammar challenges to the student.

Taken as a whole, these texts represent a basic course of study for the would-be student of Tibetan Buddhism both in terms of subject matter and grammatical complexity in the Tibetan language. As one works through the selections in this *Reader*, it is important to keep in mind that the purpose of the study of these texts is progressive growth in language capability. Therefore, as the student progresses through each section of the texts, once the vocabulary and basic grammatical structures are mastered and a certain amount of progress with the material is made, the student should strive to develop a general reading ability by learning to recognize previously seen constructions as they are encountered, adding new vocabulary and grammatical structures to their repertoire of linguistic skills. In this way, the student can add an emphasis on content comprehension and begin to learn the art of crafting a smooth, coherent translation. This approach of initial translation, grammatical paradigm familiarity, and content comprehension should be employed for each section of each text as the vocabulary changes and new grammatical structures are introduced.

Throughout this process the student should keep in mind, especially in the early stages of study, that although some of the subjects presented here may not be as exciting as others within the field of Tibetan Buddhism, the subjects and vocabulary remain nonetheless crucial to both the practice and understanding of more advanced topics. As stated in the *Ornament for the Mahāyāna Sūtras* attributed to Maitreya:

> Without making effort in the five fields of knowledge,
> Even a supreme ārya [bodhisattva] will not become omniscient.
> Therefore, in order to subdue [difficult students], care for [them], and
> Realize omniscience for oneself, one must persevere in study.[5]

Keeping this in mind, the student is therefore encouraged to perservere in the study of this material. If one masters the basic concepts and grammatical structures presented here, the more advanced topics will be more easily accessible and serve as a proper base for subsequent study and practice.

5. Maitreya, *Ornament for the Great Vehicle Sūtras* (*Mahāyāna-sūtrālaṃkāra; Theg pa chen po mdo sde'i rgyan*) 12.60; Toh. 4020 fol. 15b.4.

Study Aids and Advice

The primary grammatical reference book for this reader is Joe Wilson's *Translating Buddhism from Tibetan*. The primary dictionary references for this book are the author's *A Tibetan Verb Lexicon* (2019) and Jeffrey Hopkins's *Tibetan-Sanskrit-English Dictionary* (2016). Although there is no single comprehensive Tibetan dictionary (print or electronic), there have been many dictionaries of the Tibetan language published in the past one hundred fifty years, each with their own strengths and weaknesses. Three of the most widely used and recommended for reading classical Tibetan literature are: Chandra Das, *A Tibetan-English Dictionary* (1902), Tsepak Rigzin, *Tibetan-English Dictionary of Buddhist Terminology* (1993), and J.S. Negi, *Tibetan-Sanskrit Dictionary* 16 vols. (1993–2005).

Though not a necessity at the initial level, it has been the experience of many students that an increased proficiency in spoken Tibetan facilitates the formation of a working vocabulary and an increased comprehension of literary Tibetan. Moreover, as the student progresses on to more complex texts and subjects, the necessity of consultation with native speakers and scholars becomes paramount. Hence, in many instances, oral commentary on a text of the student's interest can only be obtained through knowledge of spoken Tibetan. Preparatory materials toward this end were developed under the auspices of a grant from the U.S. Department of Education and are available publicly in William A. Magee's *Fluent Tibetan* (1993).

During the early stages of studying the Tibetan language, every form of working with a text has advantages. Hand copying passages for translation with sufficient space for grammatical notation and translation is one approach that many have found useful. This approach has the advantage of familiarizing the student with letter shapes as well as forcing the student to engage the text and its contents in a "hands on" manner. In the monastic setting it was traditionally expected that the student actually memorize the texts rather than merely hand copy them. Any student desiring an additional challenge should consider doing likewise. At the very least, however, it is strongly recommended that, as a preliminary exercise, students familiarize themselves with the grammatical paradigm sentences provided by Joe Wilson in the fourth and fifth appendices to *Translating Buddhism from Tibetan*.

For example, beginning with Wilson's appendix 5, the first paradigm sentence provided by Wilson to illustrate the marking of the agent of Class V and VI verbs (see Wilson, 636) is: སངས་རྒྱས་ཀྱིས་ཆོས་བསྟན།. Parsing this sentence for translation, annotating and glossing each word to be able to visualize the structure of the sentence, and marking them with Wilson's grammatical annotations would look like this:

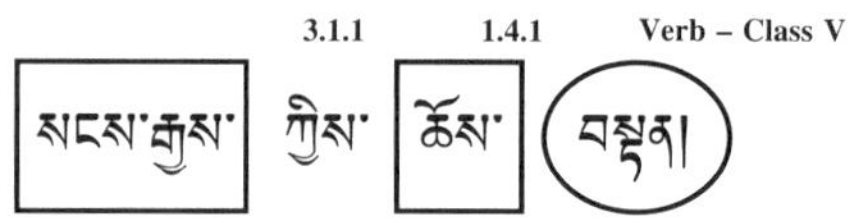

"Buddha" + 3rd case marker + "Dharma" + "to teach"

Having learned (if not memorized) the grammatical paradigms given in that appendix, one can apply knowledge of the categories to the example sentences found in Wilson's appendix 4. For example, one of the "Rhetorical Verbs" example sentences given by Wilson (also occurring in this *Reader*, 293 lines 14–15) is:

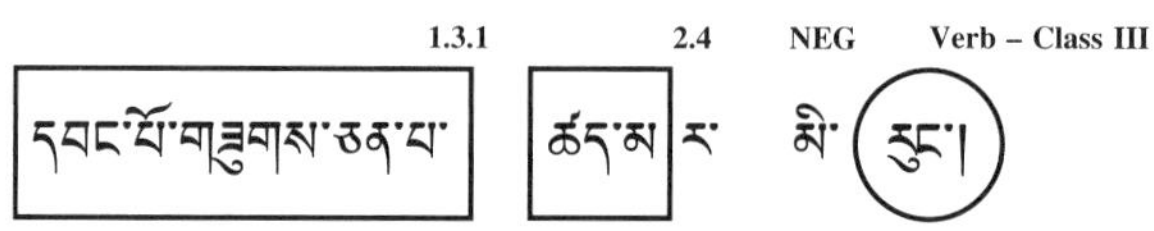

"physical sense power" + "valid cognition" (in 2nd case) + negative + "to be suitable"

While this process will eventually become unnecessary, many students have found it to be a useful excercise at the beginning stages of Tibetan language study.

Grammar Summary

The presentation of Tibetan grammar used and referred to throughout this *Reader* is derived from Joe Wilson's *Translating Buddhism from Tibetan* (1992) and the associated verb dictionary by the author, *A Tibetan Verb Lexicon* (2019). Of the various presentations of Tibetan grammar available in English, only Wilson's textbook presents different classes of Tibetan verbs in terms of their correspondence with requisite patterns of syntax. In addition, Wilson describes the modular composition of Tibetan sentences in terms of noun phrases and/or verb phrases either explicitly or implicitly terminated and those phrases that are connected to other sentences by means of a variety of connecting particles. In this way, Wilson's textbook pedagogically presents the relationship between Tibetan grammatical constructions and their comparable English forms. All grammatical annotations to the texts contained in this *Reader* refer to the grammatical system presented in the Wilson and Hackett volumes. For these reasons, the study of these texts in conjunction with this *Reader* is strongly encouraged (see the sample syllabi in appendix 6).

Nouns

Noun phrases occurring in sentences are "declined," or marked with case-marking particles in one of the eight cases described in Sanskrit and other Indo-European languages. This last point merits emphasis. Although so-called Old Tibetan (pre-eighth century) appears to have had some form of an alphabet and grammar in common with the current form of the language, since the eighth century, the language has been presented and conceived of in terms of a Sanskritic model. Although this may have been initially true only of those documents translated from Sanskrit into Tibetan, these Sanskritic features eventually pervaded all aspects of the literary culture of Tibet—in no short part due to the efforts of Rinchen Sangpo (*rin chen bzang po*) in the tenth century—such that they became part of the preferred narrative style of the educated classes of Tibet. For this reason, the terms used when discussing features of Tibetan grammar throughout this *Reader* reflect their usage in presentations of Sanskrit grammar to underscore the significance of the relationship between the grammar of the two languages. A notable example is the distinction made in verbal nouns between participles and gerunds in Sanskrit—a distinction preserved in Tibetan. The category of "participles" in Sanskrit and Tibetan refers to verbal nouns and verbal adjectives—that is, nouns and adjectives derived from a verb (present participles in English are easily recognized since they take the *-ing* ending). By contrast, a Sanskritic "gerund" (also called an "ablative absolute") is a verb form that is "used generally as an adjunct to the logical subject of a clause, denoting an accompanying or (more often) a preceding action to that signified by the verb of the clause" (Whitney, §989); gerunds are easily recognized in English since they take the form of a dependent clause "*having done X.*" These and other derivative forms will be discussed in the annotations to the texts.

The eight cases found in Tibetan are parallel to the eight cases for Sanskrit; they are given in a simple numbered form (*prathamā* = རྣམ་དབྱེ་དང་པོ་, *dvitīyā* = རྣམ་དབྱེ་གཉིས་པ་, etc.) but also have descriptive names as can be seen in the following chart:

Tibetan	Translation	Wilson	Latinate
མིང་ཙམ།	"mere names"	Nominative	Nominative
ལས་སུ་བྱ་བའི་སྒྲ།	"object terms"	Objective	Accusative
བྱེད་སྒྲ།	"agent terms"	Agentive	Instrumental
དགོས་ཆེད་ཀྱི་སྒྲ།	"purpose & benefit terms"	Beneficial & Purposive	Dative
འབྱུང་ཁུངས་ཀྱི་སྒྲ།	"source terms"	Originative	Ablative
འབྲེལ་བའི་སྒྲ།	"connection terms"	Connective	Genitive
རྟེན་གནས་ཀྱི་སྒྲ།	"dependence & place terms"	Locative	Locative
བོད་སྒྲ།	"vocative terms"	Vocative	Vocative

In addition to the varieties of purely syntactic (i.e., "non-case") uses of the particles, these case-marking particles (both explicitly and implicitly) can be illustrated as follows (drawn from Wilson, appendix 5).

I. Nominative མིང་ཙམ། རྣམ་དབྱེ་དང་པོ།
   A. Endings: none / optionally ནི་
   B. Uses:
      SUBJECT of a verb of predication (1.1.1):
         བུམ་པ་མི་རྟག་པ་ཡིན། A <u>pot</u> is impermanent.
      COMPLEMENT of a verb of predication (1.1.2):
         བུམ་པ་མི་རྟག་པ་ཡིན། A pot is <u>impermanent</u>.
      SUBJECT of verbs of existence (1.2.1), living (1.2.2), or dependence (1.2.3):
         བུམ་པ་ཡོད། <u>Pots</u> exist.
         གྲྭ་པ་དགོན་པ་ལ་བཞུགས། <u>The monks</u> live in a monastery.
         འབྲས་བུ་རྒྱུ་ལ་བརྟེན། <u>Effects</u> depend on causes.
      NOMINATIVE SUBJECT of a verb of action (1.3.1), or of motion (1.3.2):
         འཁོར་ལོ་འཁོར་རོ། The <u>wheel</u> turns.
         པདྨ་འབྱུང་གནས་བོད་ལ་ཕེབས། <u>Padmasambhava</u> went to Tibet.
      NOMINATIVE OBJECT of a verb or verbal (1.4.1):
         སངས་རྒྱས་ཀྱིས་ཆོས་བསྟན། Buddha taught the <u>doctrine</u>.

NOMINATIVE OBJECT of a verb of possession (1.4.2), or necessity (1.4.3):

ང་ལ་བུམ་པ་ཡོད། I have a pot.

སྨྱུ་གུ་ལ་ཆུ་དགོས། Sprouts need water.

TOPICAL nominative (indicates subject matter, often followed by ནི་) (1.5):

དང་པོ་ནི། བློས་རིག་པར་བྱ་བ་ཡུལ་གྱི་མཚན་ཉིད། With respect to the first, that which is to be known by an awareness is the definition of an object.

II. Accusative ལས་སུ་བྱ་བའི་སྒྲ། རྣམ་དབྱེ་གཉིས་པ།

A. Endings: སུ་ ར་ རུ་ དུ་ ན་ ར་ ལ་ Basic translation: "to," "in," "at"

B. Uses:

PLACE OF ACTIVITY (in, at) (2.1):

སངས་རྒྱས་ཀྱིས་རྒྱ་གར་ལ་ཆོས་བསྟན། Buddha taught the doctrine in India.

OBJECT of verb or verbal (2.2):

གཟུགས་ལ་ལྟ། looking at the body.

DESTINATION of a verb of motion (to) (2.3.1):

ཙོང་ཁ་པ་ལྷ་སར་ཡོང་། Tsongkhapa came to Lhasa.

METAPHORICAL DESTINATION (2.3.2):

གཞན་རྣམས་ལ་རིགས་འགྲེ། The reasoning extends to the others.

COMPLEMENT of a nominative verb (2.4):

ཐག་བཅད་པ་ལ་ཡིད་བརྟན་མེད་དུ་ཆུག [We] concede [our] decisions [as] lacking in reliability.

COMPLEMENT of an agentive verb (2.5):

སེམས་ཅན་ཐམས་ཅད་མར་ཤེས། [They] know all sentient beings as [their] mothers.

RECIPIENT (where benefit is not obvious) (2.6):

བླ་མ་ལ་མཆོད་པ་ཕུལ། [They] offer worship to the guru.

ADVERBIAL IDENTITY (-ly) (2.7.1):

འགྲོགས་པོར་ཕྱིན། [She] went quickly.

EXISTENTIAL IDENTITY (-ly) (2.7.2):

ལམ་དེ་ནི་ཐར་པའི་རྒྱུར་མི་རུང་། That path is not admissible as a cause of liberation.

TRANSFORMED IDENTITY (-ly) (2.7.3):

སངས་རྒྱས་ཀྱི་མདོ་བོད་སྐད་དུ་བསྒྱུར། The Buddha's sūtras were translated into Tibetan.

III. Instrumental བྱེད་སྒྲ། རྣམ་དབྱེ་གསུམ་པ།

A. Endings: གིས་ ཀྱིས་ གྱིས་ འིས་ ཡིས་ Basic translation: "by"

B. Uses:

AGENT of an agentive-nominative (3.1.1) or agentive-objective (3.1.2) verb:

སངས་རྒྱས་ཀྱིས་ཆོས་བསྟན་ཏོ། The Buddha taught the doctrine.

བཟང་སྐྱོང་གིས་བཅོམ་ལྡན་འདས་ཀྱི་ཞབས་ལ་གཏུགས། Bhadrapāla touched the feet of the Bhagavān.

INSTRUMENT of agentive (3.2.1, 3.2.2) or nominative verbs (3.2.3) :

བརྩོན་འགྲུས་ཀྱིས་ལམ་སྒྲུབ་ནས།

Once the path has been achieved by means of effort …

གཞན་རྣམས་ཀྱིས་མིག་གིས་ལྟ། Others gaze with [their] eyes.

མ་ཤེས་པའི་དབང་གིས་འཁོར་བར་འཁོར། [One] cycles in saṃsāra through the force of ignorance.

REASON (3.3):

མོ་ལ་བརྩོན་འགྲུས་ཡོད་པས་ལམ་བསྒྲུབ། Because she had effort, [she] achieved the path.

C. Non-case uses:

ADVERBIAL (-ly):

རང་བཞིན་གྱིས་གྲུབ་པ། inherently established

ABSENCE:

བདེན་པར་གྲུབ་པས་སྟོང་པ། empty of true establishment

CONJUNCTION (and, but) (said to be improper but frequently used):

མེད་པ་ཡིན་གྱིས། … is nonexistent, but

INCLUSION (within):

རྒྱུད་ཀྱིས་བསྡུས་པ། included within the [psychophysical] continuum

IV. Dative དགོས་ཆེད་ཀྱི་སྒྲ། རྣམ་དབྱེ་བཞི་པ།

A. Endings: སུ་ རུ་ ཏུ་ དུ་ ན་ ར་ ལ་ Basic translation: “for”

B. Uses:

BENEFIT (for, to) (4.1):

སྨན་པས་ནད་པ་ལ་སྨན་སྟེར། The doctor gave medicine to the sick.

PURPOSE (in order to) (4.2):

འབྲས་བུ་ཐོབ་པ་ལ་རྒྱུ་བསགས་དགོས།

One must accumulate the causes to obtain the effect.

SUBJECT of a verb of necessity (4.3):

མྱུ་གུ་ལ་ཆུ་དགོས། Sprouts need water.

V. Ablative འབྱུང་ཁུངས་ཀྱི་སྒྲ། རྣམ་དབྱེ་ལྔ་པ།

A. Endings: ལས་ ནས་ Basic translation: "from"

B. Uses:

ORIGIN/SOURCE (5.1.1, 5.1.2):

བ་ལས་འོ་མ། [It is] milk from a cow.

རྩ་ཚིག་ལས་.... [As is said] in the root text ....

INSTRUMENTAL (5.2):

རྩོལ་བ་ལས་ཐོབ་པ། [It is] achieved through effort.

ISOLATION (5.3):

གསུམ་ལས་དང་པོ་ནི། From among the three, the first is as follows ...

REMOVAL (5.4):

སྡུག་བསྔལ་ལས་སྐྱོབ་པ། Providing refuge from suffering.

COMPARISON (5.5):

དེ་ལས་ཆེ་བ། greater than that

INCLUSIVE sequence (5.6.1), locale (5.6.2), time (5.6.3): only ནས་

གཅིག་ནས་བརྒྱའི་བར། from one to one hundred

ལྷ་ས་ནས་རྒྱལ་རྩེའི་བར་དུ། from Lhasa to Gyantse

ཐོག་མ་མེད་པ་ནས། from beginningless time

REASON (5.7):

དུ་བ་ལས་མེར་ཤེས། Knowing [it] as fire due to smoke.

C. Non-case uses:

ADVERBIAL (-ly):

རེ་རེ་ནས། individually

GERUND marker:

ཐོས་ནས་བསམས། Having heard [this], [he] thought [about it].

DISJUNCTIVE GERUND (whereas; although having been):

དེ་བདེ་བ་ཡིན་པ་ལས། Whereas that is bliss, ...

VI. Genitive འབྲེལ་སྒྲ། རྣམ་དབྱེ་དྲུག་པ།

A. Endings: གི་ ཀྱི་ གྱི་ འི་ ཡི་ Basic translation: "of"

B. Uses:

POSSESSIVE (6.1.1):

རྒན་གྱི་དཔེ་ཆ། the teacher's book

TYPE (between nouns) (6.1.2):

ཆོས་ཀྱི་རྒྱལ་པོ། king of doctrine

དེ་རིང་གི་ལས་ཀ today's work

FIELD OF ACTIVITY (of) (6.1.3):

བོད་ཀྱི་རྒྱལ་པོ། king of Tibet

APPOSITIONAL (6.2.1):

དགོངས་འགྲེལ་ལ་སོགས་པའི་གཞུང་། Texts, the *Saṃdhinirmocana*, and so forth, …

COMPOSITIONAL (of) (6.2.2):

མདོའི་དཔེ་ཆ། a book of sūtras

METAPHORICAL (of) (6.2.3):

སྙིང་རྗེའི་ཆུ། water of compassion

POSTPOSITIONAL (of) (6.3):

དམར་པོ་ཡིན་པའི་ཕྱིར། because of being red

རང་གི་མདུན་དུ། in front of him

AGENTIVE (6.4.1):

སངས་རྒྱས་ཀྱི་བསྟན་པ། teachings of [i.e., by] the Buddha

OBJECTIVE (indicates object) (6.4.2):

བུམ་པའི་རྒྱུ pot's cause

DESTINATION (6.4.3):

བྱང་ཆུབ་ཀྱི་ལམ། path to enlightenment

SEPARATIVE (6.4.4):

ལམ་ལྔའི་གཉིས་པ། the second of five paths

ཀུན་གྱི་མཆོག the supreme of teachers

ORIGIN (6.4.5):

སྦྱིན་པའི་བསོད་ནམས། the virtue of/from giving

ADJECTIVAL (6.5):

དམར་པོའི་རས་ཆ། red cloth

CLAUSE CONNECTIVE TO THE SUBJECT/AGENT (6.6.1):

སྣང་བའི་ཡུལ། the object that appears

ཆོས་སྟོན་པའི་སངས་རྒྱས། the Buddha who teaches the doctrine

CLAUSE CONNECTIVE TO THE OBJECT (6.6.2):

སངས་རྒྱས་ཀྱིས་བསྟན་པའི་ཆོས། the Dharma which was taught by the Buddha

CLAUSE CONNECTIVE TO THE QUALIFIER (6.6.3):

རྣལ་འབྱོར་པས་ཆོས་སྒྲུབ་པའི་ཡུལ། a place where a yogi attains the Dharma

CLAUSE CONNECTIVE TO THE COMPLEMENT (6.6.4):

མི་རྟག་པ་ཡིན་པའི་ཆོས་ phenomena that are impermanent

C. Non-case usage of the genitive particles:

CONJUNCTION/RHETORICAL CONTINUATIVE (and, but):

དེ་དམར་པོ་ཡིན་གྱི that is red, but …

VII. Locative རྟེན་གནས་ཀྱི་སྒྲ། རྣམ་དབྱེ་བདུན་པ།

A. Endings: སུ་ རུ་ དུ་ ཏུ་ ན་ ར་ ལ་ Basic translation: “in,” “at”

B. Uses:

PLACE OF DEPENDENCE (7.1):

རྩོལ་བ་ལ་བརྟེན་ནས། in dependence on effort

PLACE OF LIVING OR EXISTING (7.2.1):

བོད་ལ་རི་མང་པོ་ཡོད། There are many mountains in Tibet.

INCLUSION (7.2.2):

བོད་མི་ལ་མཁས་པ་མང་པོ་ཡོད། Among Tibetans there are many scholars.

POSSESSIVE (7.3):

ང་ལ་དཔེ་ཆ་ཡོད། I have a book.

TIME (7.4):

ཆུ་ཚོད་བདུན་པ་ལ་ལས་ཀ་བྱེད། [We] work at seven o’clock.

TOPICAL (7.5):

དང་པོ་ལ། གཟུགས་ལ་དབྱེ་ན། First, if forms are divided …

REFERENCE (7.6):

དེ་ལ་གསུམ་ཡོད། Regarding that, there are three.

LOCATIVE ABSOLUTE (7.7):

རང་དོན་མ་རྫོགས་པར་་་ Without completing one’s own purpose ...

VIII. Vocative བོད་སྒྲ། རྣམ་དབྱེ་བརྒྱད་པ།

A. Endings: none Basic translation: “O,” “Hey”

no explicit case ending but sometimes preceded by the particles ཀྱེ and ཀྭ་ཡེ་

B. Uses:

ཀྱེ་ལྷའི་ལྷ། O god of gods!

ཤཱ་རིའི་བུ་འདི་ལྟ་སྟེ། O Śāriputra, consider this: ...

Verbs

As for the verb system in Tibetan, both similarities and differences with Sanskrit can be seen. While Tibetan shares many features with Sanskrit, such as the use of participles in lieu of a finite verb form and the formation of verbal collocations with Sanskritic adverbs, a crucial difference between the languages lies in the functional classification of verbs. In Sanskrit, verbs are grouped by conjugation paradigm; in Tibetan, however, verbs are most usefully grouped by requisite syntax.

The first level of knowledge necessary for understanding the function of Tibetan verbs is the syntax-based classification system. As described by Wilson, Tibetan verbs can be placed into one of eight classes as summarized in the following chart:

Verb Class	Descriptive Name	Tibetan Category
I	Nominative-Nominative Verbs	རྗེས་མཐུན།
II	Nominative-Locative Verbs	
	Simple Verbs of Existence	རྗེས་མཐུན།
	Verbs of Living, Dependence, or Attitude	ཐ་མི་དད།
III	Nominative-Objective Verbs	ཐ་མི་དད།
IV	Nominative-Syntactic Verbs	
	Verbs of Separation, Containment, and Disjunction	ཐ་མི་དད།
	Verbs of Conjunction	རྗེས་མཐུན།
V	Agentive-Nominative Verbs	ཐ་དད།
VI	Agentive-Objective Verbs	ཐ་དད།
VII	Purposive-Nominative Verbs	ཐ་མི་དད།
VIII	Locative-Nominative Verbs	
	Verbs of Possession	རྗེས་མཐུན།
	Verbs of Attribution	ཐ་དད།

As can be seen, Wilson's system offers a more nuanced classification system than traditional categories. Some examples of verbs in each class and their usage are presented below:

I. Nominative-Nominative Verbs

  A. Endings: none / optionally ནི་

  B. Examples of Verbs in this Class:

   SENTENCE WITH BOTH SUBJECT AND COMPLEMENT:

    བུམ་པ་མི་རྟག་པ་ཡིན། Pots are impermanent.

   SENTENCE WITH ONLY A COMPLEMENT:

    མི་རྟག་པ་ཡིན། [It] is impermanent.

II. Nominative-Locative Verbs

  A. Endings: SUBJECT: none / optionally ནི་; QUALIFIER: locative ལ་, etc.

  B. Examples of Verbs in this Class:

   Simple Verbs of Existence.

    SENTENCES WITH BOTH A SUBJECT AND A QUALIFIER:

     རི་རྣམས་བོད་ལ་ཡོད། Mountains exist in Tibet.

     ཀུན་བཏགས་བདེན་པར་མེད། Imputational natures do not truly exist.

   Verbs of Living.

    SENTENCE WITH BOTH SUBJECT AND QUALIFIER:

     ཁོང་ཡུལ་དེ་ལ་བསྡད། He lived in that area.

     བཅོམ་ལྡན་འདས་བྱ་རྒོད་ཀྱི་ཕུང་པོའི་རི་ལ་བཞུགས། The Tathāgata was dwelling on Vulture Peak.

    SENTENCE WITH ONLY A QUALIFIER:

     ཁྲི་ལ་བཞུགས། [He] is seated on a throne.

   Verbs of Dependence.

    SENTENCE WITH BOTH SUBJECT AND QUALIFIER:

     འབྲས་བུ་རྒྱུ་ལ་བརྟེན། Effects depend on causes.

   Attitude Verbs.

    SENTENCE WITH BOTH SUBJECT AND QUALIFIER:

     སྟོན་པ་ཐབས་ལ་མཁས། The teacher is skilled in methods [of liberation].

III. Nominative-Objective Verbs

  A. Endings: SUBJECT: none / optionally ནི་; COMP./QUAL.: objective ལ་, etc.

  B. Examples of Verbs in this Class:

   Verbs of Motion.

SENTENCES WITH BOTH A SUBJECT AND A QUALIFIER:

རང་ཉིད་གཅིག་བུ་འཇིག་རྟེན་ཕ་རོལ་དུ་འགྲོ། One alone goes to the next world.

རྭ་ཟམ་པར་འགྲོ། [Like] a goat walking over a bridge.

Generic Action Verbs.

SENTENCES WITH BOTH A SUBJECT AND A QUALIFIER:

འོད་ཟེར་རང་ལ་ཐིམ། Light rays dissolve into us.

ལམ་གཉིས་མཉམ་བཞག་ཐུན་གཅིག་ལ་སྐྱེ། Both paths are generated in one session of meditative equipoise.

Rhetorical Verbs.

SENTENCES WITH BOTH A SUBJECT AND A COMPLEMENT:

དབང་པོ་གཟུགས་ཅན་པ་ཚད་མར་མི་རུང་། A physical sense power is not suitable as a valid cognition.

IV. Nominative-Syntactic Verbs

A. Endings: SUBJECT: none / optionally ནི་

QUALIFIER: syntactic particle ལས་, དང་, ཀྱིས་ / གྱིས་ / གིས་ / ཡིས་ / –ས་

B. Examples of Verbs in this Class:

Separative Verbs.

SENTENCES WITH BOTH A SUBJECT AND A QUALIFIER:

རང་ཉིད་འཁོར་བ་ལས་ཐར། [They] themselves are free from cyclic existence.

སེམས་ཅན་རྣམས་མྱ་ངན་ལས་ག་ལ་འདའ། How can sentient beings pass beyond suffering?

SENTENCES WITH JUST A QUALIFIER:

མི་དལ་ཀུན་ལས་ཐར། [They] are freed from all states of nonleisure.

Verbs of Containment.

SENTENCES WITH BOTH A SUBJECT AND A QUALIFIER:

ཆོས་ཐམས་ཅད་རང་བཞིན་གྱིས་སྟོང་པའོ། All phenomena are empty of own nature.

བཀའ་གདམས་པའི་དགོན་སྡིང་དེ་ཀུན་ཕལ་ཆེར་མཆོད་རྟེན་གྱིས་གང་། Most all of the ancient Kadampa monasteries are filled with stūpas.

Conjunctive Verbs.

SENTENCES WITH BOTH A SUBJECT AND A QUALIFIER:

ང་རང་མི་སྡུག་པ་དང་ཕྲད་ན་... If we meet with the unpleasant ...

SENTENCES WITH JUST A QUALIFIER:

བཀུར་སྟི་དང་བཅས། [He] was treated with respect.

Disjunctive Verbs.

SENTENCES WITH BOTH A SUBJECT AND A QUALIFIER:

བློ་དེ་འདྲ་ཆགས་པ་དང་བྲལ། Such a mind <u>is free</u> of attachment.

SENTENCES WITH JUST A QUALIFIER:

སྐྱེ་བ་དང་འགག་པ་དང་བྲལ་བས་… Since [it] <u>is free</u> of production and cessation, ...

V. Agentive-Nominative Verbs

A. Endings: AGENT: agentive marker ཀྱིས་ / གྱིས་ / གིས་ / ཡིས་ / –ས་

OBJECT: none / optionally ནི་

B. Examples of Verbs in this Class:

SENTENCES WITH BOTH AN AGENT AND AN OBJECT:

སངས་རྒྱས་ཀྱིས་ཆོས་བསྟན། The Buddha <u>taught</u> the Dharma.

SENTENCES WITH AN OBJECT AND A QUALIFIER:

སེམས་ཅན་གཞན་གཏན་གྱི་བདེ་བ་ལ་འགོད། [One] <u>will establish</u> other sentient beings in final happiness.

SENTENCES WITH JUST A COMPLEMENT:

དཔེར་བཀོད་… Stating [this] as an example, ...

SENTENCES WITH JUST A QUALIFIER:

སྡུག་བསྔལ་ལས་སྒྲོལ་བའི་ཐར་པ་དང་ཐམས་ཅད་མཁྱེན་པའི་སར་འགོད། [We] <u>will establish</u> [them] in a state of omniscience and liberation, which is the emancipation from suffering.

VI. Agentive-Objective Verbs

A. Endings: AGENT: agentive marker ཀྱིས་ / གྱིས་ / གིས་ / ཡིས་ / –ས་

OBJECT: objective ལ་, etc.

B. Examples of Verbs in this Class:

SENTENCES WITH BOTH AN AGENT AND AN OBJECT:

ཁོས་གཟུགས་ལ་བལྟས། He <u>looked</u> at forms.

VII. Purposive-Nominative Verbs

A. Endings: SUBJECT: purposive ལ་, etc.

OBJECT: none / optionally ནི་

B. Examples of Verbs in this Class:

SENTENCES WITH BOTH A SUBJECT AND AN OBJECT:

མྱུ་གུ་ལ་ཆུ་དགོས། Sprouts <u>need</u> water.

VIII. Locative-Nominative Verbs

A. Endings: SUBJECT: locative ལ་, etc.; OBJECT: none / optionally ནི་

B. Examples of Verbs in this Class:

SENTENCES WITH BOTH A SUBJECT AND A COMPLEMENT:

དགྲ་བཅོམ་པ་ལ་ཉོན་མོངས་མེད། Arhats do not have afflictions.

དེ་ལ་ཆོས་མངོན་རྟོགས་ཞེས་བརྗོད། That is called "a clear realization of the Dharma."

Remarks on Tibetan Block-print Eccentricities

Eventually, as a person progresses in their study of Tibetan literature, they will begin reading Tibetan woodblock prints. The tradition of wooden block printing in Tibet dates back close to a thousand years, and wooden block printing was used for producing everything from thangkas (*thang ka*), maṇḍalas (*dkyil 'khor*), and prayer-flags (*rlung rta*) to, of course, books. The carving of these woodblocks (*dpar shing*) for printing books became the specialty of a certain subset of the monastic community, though, of course, some carvers were not as good as others and mistakes were made. If these mistakes were detected at the time of carving, an effort was usually made to correct them. These corrections take various forms.

One form of error correction—if the error was discovered while the block was still being carved—was to insert the omitted or corrected text interlinearly with a dashed line indicating the insertion point. For example:

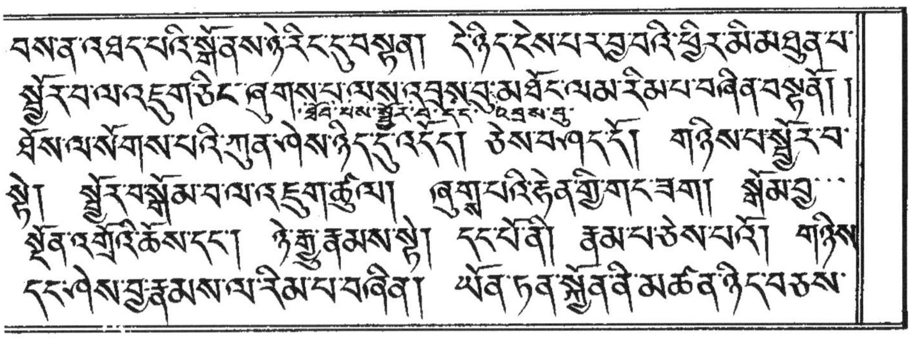

Fig. 1

Here the original Tibetan text reads: ཞུགས་པ་ལས་འབྲས་བུ་མཐོང་ལམ་, but with the correction: ཐོབ་པས་སྦྱོར་བ་དང་འབྲས་བུ་, the resulting corrected text reads: ཞུགས་པ་ལས་འབྲས་བུ་ཐོབ་པས་སྦྱོར་བ་དང་འབྲས་བུ་མཐོང་ལམ་.

A second form, similar to a footnote—and seen in one of the texts in this *Reader*—is to mark the text with a *svasti* (卍) or similar symbol and then carve the missing text at the bottom of the page. For example:

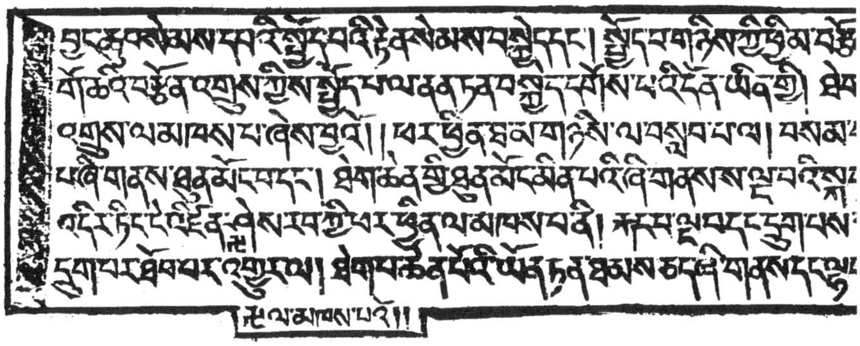

Fig. 2

This passage beginning on the fifth line of the Tibetan text reads: འདིར་དེང་ངེའི་ཛོན་ཤེས་རབ་ཀྱི་ཕར་ཕྱིན་ལ་མཁས་པ་ནི།, with the correction: ལ་མཁས་པའོ།།, resulting in a corrected text reading: འདིར་དེང་ངེའི་ཛོན་ལ་མཁས་པའོ།། ཤེས་རབ་ཀྱི་ཕར་ཕྱིན་ལ་མཁས་པ་ནི།.

Sometimes if a mistake was very small, or either of the above two methods was not an option, a new piece of wood would be carved, the old section chiseled out, and the new one inserted in its place. For example:

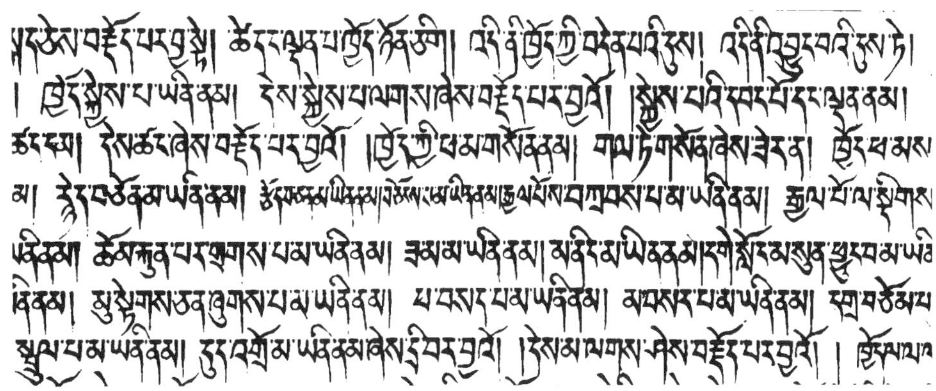

Fig. 3

The resultant, different text can clearly be seen in the third line. This method was used extensively in the Ch'ien-lung redaction of the Peking Tripiṭaka (ca.1737).

In addition, Tibetan woodblock carvers developed certain forms of shorthand notation (*bsdu yig*) to expedite carving. For example, one shorthand notation is the use of the Tibetan rendering of the retroflex *ḍa*, ཊ་ to indicate a གས་ suffix—that is, rendering for example, ལ་སོགས་ as ལ་སོཊ་. Another Sanskrit derivative notation, the *anusvāra*, is occasionally used for the letter "m" when space limitations arise. An instance of this would be to render the number three, གསུམ་, as གསུཾ་, or ཐམས་ཅད་ as ཐཾད་. However, the Sanskrit *visarga* would only be used in Sanskrit transliterations, such as in the word *duḥka*, དུཿཁ་ (see fig. 4, below).

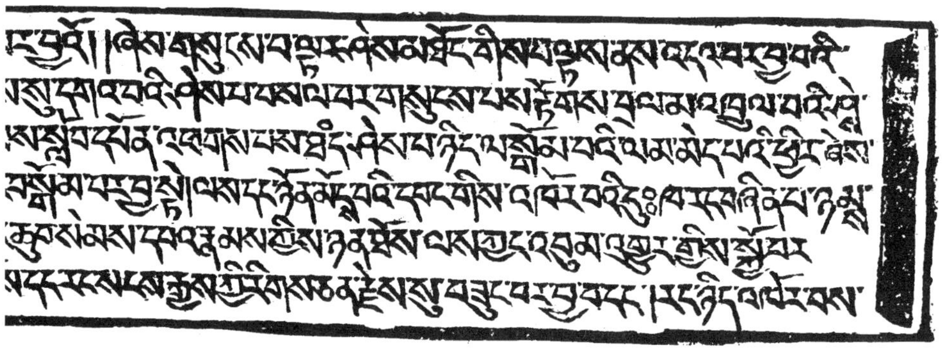

Fig. 4

Occasionally, a carver will omit letters and compress two syllables into one. This is seen more commonly with terminating particles, as in "this concludes the sūtra" མདོ་རྫོགས་སོ།, where the རྫོགས་སོ། becomes རྫོགསོ།. In other instances, usually less literary ones, words such as "Buddha" སངས་རྒྱས་ might be compressed into a single ligature such as སངྒྱས་, and the like. An example of this can be seen in figure 4 at the end of the second line, where the word ཤེས་ has been compressed into ཤྶེ་, at the end of the fourth line, where the word ཉམས་ has been compressed into ཉྨྶ་, and on the previous page (fig. 2, line five), where དེའི་ འཛིན་ was given as དེའིཛིན་.

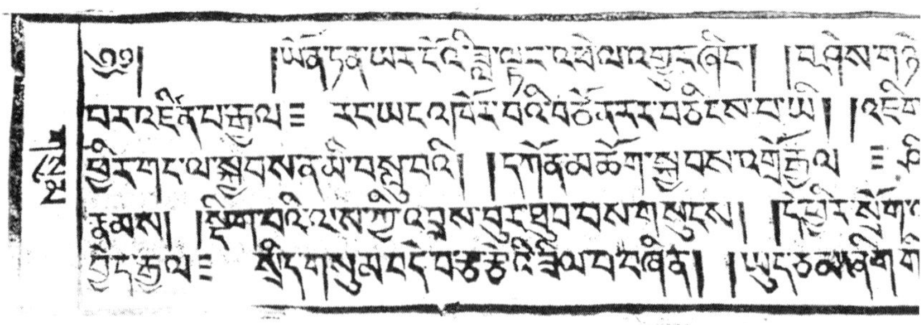

Fig. 5

Other instances arise, not out of illiteracy on the part of a carver, but merely out of this wish to conserve space or avoid carving repetitive phrases. Examples of just this can be seen in the use of the symbol ≡ (see fig. 5) or X, in several texts—such as Tsongkhapa's *Concise Exposition of the Stages of the Path* (*Lam rim mdor bsdus*)—where a repetitive set of phrases occur:

> རྣལ་འབྱོར་ངས་ཀྱང་ཉམས་ལེན་དེ་ལྟར་བགྱིས།
> ཐར་འདོད་ཁྱེད་ཀྱང་དེ་བཞིན་བསྐྱང་འཚལ་ལོ།

> I, a yogi, engage in such practices;
> You who desire liberation, need to do likewise.

In subsequent occurrences of these phrases, they are given simply as:

> རྣལ་འབྱོར་ངས་ཀྱང་ ≡ །
> ཐར་འདོད་ཁྱེད་ཀྱང་ ≡ །

with the ≡ indicating the intentionally omitted passages. This can also be seen in two of the texts in this book, the Fourth Paṇchen Lama's *Prayer for Release from the Dangerous Bardo* and the *Long-Life Prayer for His Holiness the Dalai Lama*.

Idiosyncracies such as these and others will be found by the student in various texts as their studies progress. Having seen nonstandard glyphs such as these, the student will gradually learn to recognize and negotiate their way through these textual variations and printing styles.

PART TWO

Tibetan Texts, Annotations, and Translations

The Heart Sūtra

The Perfection of Wisdom sūtras are divided into categories referred to as the mothers and sons. The six "mother" sūtras teach all eight subjects of clear realization, while the "sons" are said to teach only a portion of these.[1] There are eleven "son" sūtras: the *Seven Hundred Line*, the *Five Hundred Line*, the *Three Hundred Line* ("*Diamond Sūtra*"), the *Methods [of the Perfections in] One Hundred Fifty Lines*, the *Fifty Line*, the *Twenty-five Doors*, the *Questions of Suvikrāntavikrāmin*, the *Questions of Kauśika*, the *Perfection of Wisdom in One Letter*, *A Few Words*, and the *Heart Sūtra*.

The *Heart Sūtra* has received attention from generations of scholars as a particularly pointed presentation of key themes in the larger Perfection of Wisdom body of literature. It has played a large role in many Buddhist cultures both inside and outside of Tibet. In the Tibetan Buddhist canon, there are eight commentaries on this sūtra alone, while in the corpus of Tibetan literature in general, there are more than a hundred.

The *Heart Sūtra* is said to present both the explicit teaching on emptiness (*śūnyatā; stong pa nyid*) of "own nature" (*svabhāva; rang bzhin*) and the implicit teaching on the five "paths" (*mārga; lam*). The former refers to the statements made during the first three-quarters of the text, while the latter is taken to refer to the *Heart Sūtra* mantra;[2] the clear realizations (*abhisamāya; mngon par rtogs pa*), however, are not taught.

On a grammatical level, the *Heart Sūtra* is a relatively easy text to read in Tibetan and serves as a suitable introduction to foundational grammatical constructions as well as the genre of Tibetan translated sūtras in general. The text consists predominantly of grammatically simple sentences and repetitious and formulaic structures, which typify the genre. Like many other texts found in the canon, and as noted in its colophon, this text was translated during the time of the "early transmission" (*sngar dar*) of Buddhism into Tibet (ca. 750–850 C.E.) during which time translation activities were strongly regulated, yielding a high degree of consistency in terminology and sentence structures.

Further information on the *Heart Sūtra* can be found in Donald Lopez (1988, 1996) and in Geshe Sonam Rinchen (2003). Gareth Sparham also has published an extensive treatment of the subject in two multivolume series of translations (2006–

2012, 2008–2013), while Karl Brunnhölzl (2010, 2012) has published several books exploring the subject as it is treated in the later Kagyu and Nyingma traditions. Nonetheless, since much of the major research on the Perfection of Wisdom literature is hidden in academic journals or in unpublished dissertations, students wishing to pursue these topics in greater depth are encouraged to begin by consulting these more readily available works.

1. Paṇchen Sönam Drakpa, 1982–1983, vol. 3.

2. While many commentators discuss this issue, the eighteenth-century author Gungtang Tenpay Drönmay (*gung thang dkon mchog bstan pa'i sgron me*, 1762–1853) felt it significant enough to write an entire treatise devoted exclusively to the mantra. The text, *An Explanation of the Heart Sūtra Mantra, the Lamp Illuminating the Hidden Meaning* (*Shes rab snying po'i sngags kyi rnam bshad sbas don gsal ba sgron me*), was translated and published by Donald Lopez in *The Heart Sūtra Explained* (1988).

༄༅།།ཤེས་རབ་ཀྱི་ཕ་རོལ་ཏུ་ཕྱིན་པའི་སྙིང་པོ་ཞེས་བྱ་བ་བཞུགས་སོ།།

༄༅།། རྒྱ་གར་སྐད་དུ།[1] བྷ་ག་བ་ཏི་པྲ་ཛྙཱ་པཱ་ར་མི་ཏཱ་ཧྲྀ་ད་ཡ།།[2] བོད་སྐད་དུ། བཅོམ་ལྡན་འདས་མ་ཤེས་རབ་ཀྱི་ཕ་རོལ་ཏུ་ཕྱིན་པའི་སྙིང་པོ།། བཅོམ་ལྡན་འདས་མ་ཤེས་རབ་ཀྱི་ཕ་རོལ་ཏུ་ཕྱིན་པ་ལ་ཕྱག་འཚལ་ལོ།[3] འདི་སྐད་བདག་གིས་ཐོས་པ་དུས་གཅིག་ན།[4] བཅོམ་ལྡན་འདས་རྒྱལ་པོའི་ཁབ་ན་བྱ་རྒོད་ཀྱི་ཕུང་པོའི་རི་ལ་[5]དགེ་སློང་གི་དགེ་འདུན་ཆེན་པོ་དང་། བྱང་ཆུབ་སེམས་དཔའི་དགེ་འདུན་ཆེན་པོ་དང་ཐབས་གཅིག་ཏུ་[6]བཞུགས་ཏེ། དེའི་ཚེ་བཅོམ་ལྡན་འདས་ཟབ་མོ་སྣང་བ་ཞེས་བྱ་བའི་ཆོས་ཀྱི་རྣམ་གྲངས་ཀྱི་ཏིང་ངེ་འཛིན་ལ་སྙོམས་པར་བཞུགས་སོ།

ཡང་དེའི་ཚེ་བྱང་ཆུབ་སེམས་དཔའ་སེམས་དཔའ་ཆེན་པོ་འཕགས་པ་སྤྱན་རས་གཟིགས་དབང་ཕྱུག་ཤེས་རབ་ཀྱི་ཕ་རོལ་ཏུ་ཕྱིན་པ་ཟབ་མོའི་སྤྱོད་པ་ཉིད་ལ་རྣམ་པར་ལྟ་ཞིང་། ཕུང་པོ་ལྔ་པོ་དེ་དག་ལ་ཡང་རང་བཞིན་གྱིས་སྟོང་པར་[7]རྣམ་པར་ལྟའོ།[8] དེ་ནས་སངས་རྒྱས་ཀྱི་མཐུས། ཚེ་དང་ལྡན་པ་ཤཱ་རིའི་བུས། བྱང་ཆུབ་སེམས་དཔའ་སེམས་དཔའ་ཆེན་པོ་འཕགས་པ་སྤྱན་རས་གཟིགས་དབང་ཕྱུག་ལ་འདི་སྐད་ཅེས་[9]སྨྲས་སོ། རིགས་ཀྱི་བུ་གང་ལ་ལ་[10]ཤེས་རབ་ཀྱི་ཕ་རོལ་ཏུ་ཕྱིན་པ་ཟབ་མོའི་སྤྱོད་པ་སྤྱད་པར་འདོད་པ་དེས་ཇི་ལྟར་བསླབ་པར་བྱ།[11]

དེ་སྐད་ཅེས་སྨྲས་པ་དང་། བྱང་ཆུབ་སེམས་དཔའ་སེམས་དཔའ་ཆེན་པོ་འཕགས་པ་སྤྱན་རས་གཟིགས་དབང་ཕྱུག་གིས་ཚེ་དང་ལྡན་པ་ཤཱ་ར་དྭ་ཏིའི་བུ་ལ་འདི་སྐད་ཅེས་སྨྲས་སོ། ཤཱ་རིའི་བུ། རིགས་ཀྱི་བུའམ་རིགས་ཀྱི་བུ་མོ་གང་ལ་ལ་ཤེས་རབ་ཀྱི་ཕ་རོལ་ཏུ་ཕྱིན་པ་ཟབ་མོའི་སྤྱོད་པ་སྤྱད་པར་འདོད་པ་དེས་འདི་ལྟར་རྣམ་པར་བལྟ་བར་བྱ་སྟེ། ཕུང་པོ་ལྔ་པོ་དེ་དག་ཀྱང་།[12] རང་བཞིན་གྱིས་སྟོང་པར་ཡང་དག་པར་རྗེས་སུ་བལྟའོ། གཟུགས་སྟོང་པའོ།[13] སྟོང་པ་ཉིད་གཟུགས་སོ།[14] གཟུགས་ལས་སྟོང་པ་ཉིད་གཞན་མ་ཡིན། སྟོང་པ་ཉིད་ལས་ཀྱང་གཟུགས་གཞན་མ་ཡིན་ནོ། དེ་བཞིན་དུ་ཚོར་བ་དང་། འདུ་ཤེས་དང་། འདུ་བྱེད་དང་། རྣམ་པར་ཤེས་པ་རྣམས་སྟོང་པའོ།

ཤཱ་རིའི་བུ་དེ་ལྟ་བས་ན་ཆོས་ཐམས་ཅད་སྟོང་པ་ཉིད་དེ། མཚན་ཉིད་མེད་པ། མ་སྐྱེས་པ། མ་འགགས་པ། དྲི་མ་མེད་པ། དྲི་མ་དང་བྲལ་བ་མེད་པ། བྲི་བ་མེད་པ། གང་བ་མེད་པའོ། །ཤཱ་རིའི་བུ་དེ་ལྟ་བས་ན། སྟོང་པ་ཉིད་ལ་གཟུགས་མེད། ཚོར་བ་མེད། འདུ་ཤེས་མེད། འདུ་བྱེད་རྣམས་མེད། རྣམ་པར་ཤེས་པ་མེད། མིག་མེད། རྣ་བ་མེད། སྣ་མེད། ལྕེ་མེད། ལུས་མེད། ཡིད་མེད། གཟུགས་མེད། སྒྲ་མེད། དྲི་མེད། རོ་མེད།

རེག་བྱ་མེད། ཆོས་མེད་དོ། མིག་གི་ཁམས་མེད་པ་ནས། ཡིད་ཀྱི་ཁམས་མེད། ཡིད་ཀྱི་རྣམ་པར་ཤེས་པའི་ཁམས་ཀྱི་བར་དུ་ཡང་མེད་དོ།[15] །མ་རིག་པ་མེད། མ་རིག་པ་ཟད་པ་མེད་པ་ནས། རྒ་ཤི་མེད། རྒ་ཤི་ཟད་པའི་བར་དུ་ཡང་མེད་དོ། དེ་བཞིན་དུ་སྡུག་བསྔལ་བ་དང་། ཀུན་འབྱུང་བ་དང་། འགོག་པ་དང་། ལམ་མེད། ཡེ་ཤེས་མེད། ཐོབ་པ་མེད། མ་ཐོབ་པ་ཡང་མེད་དོ།

ཤཱ་རིའི་བུ་དེ་ལྟ་བས་ན། བྱང་ཆུབ་སེམས་དཔའ་རྣམས་ཐོབ་པ་མེད་པའི་ཕྱིར། ཤེས་རབ་ཀྱི་ཕ་རོལ་ཏུ་ཕྱིན་པ་ལ་བརྟེན་ཅིང་གནས་ཏེ།[16] སེམས་ལ་སྒྲིབ་པ་མེད་པས་སྐྲག་པ་མེད་དེ། ཕྱིན་ཅི་ལོག་ལས་ཤིན་ཏུ་འདས་ནས། མྱ་ངན་ལས་འདས་པའི་མཐར་ཕྱིན་ཏོ། དུས་གསུམ་དུ་རྣམ་པར་བཞུགས་པའི་[17] སངས་རྒྱས་ཐམས་ཅད་ཀྱང་། ཤེས་རབ་ཀྱི་ཕ་རོལ་ཏུ་ཕྱིན་པ་ལ་བརྟེན་ནས། བླ་ན་མེད་པ་ཡང་དག་པར་རྫོགས་པའི་བྱང་ཆུབ་ཏུ་མངོན་པར་རྫོགས་པར་སངས་རྒྱས་སོ།།

དེ་ལྟ་བས་ན་ཤེས་རབ་ཀྱི་ཕ་རོལ་ཏུ་ཕྱིན་པའི་སྔགས། རིག་པ་ཆེན་པོའི་སྔགས། བླ་ན་མེད་པའི་སྔགས། མི་མཉམ་པ་དང་མཉམ་པའི་སྔགས།[18] སྡུག་བསྔལ་ཐམས་ཅད་རབ་ཏུ་ཞི་བར་བྱེད་པའི་སྔགས།[19] མི་བརྫུན་པས་ན་[20] བདེན་པར་ཤེས་པར་བྱ་སྟེ། ཤེས་རབ་ཀྱི་ཕ་རོལ་ཏུ་ཕྱིན་པའི་སྔགས་སྨྲས་པ། ཏདྱ་ཐཱ། ཨོཾ་ག་ཏེ་ག་ཏེ་པཱ་ར་ག་ཏེ་པཱ་ར་སཾ་ག་ཏེ་བོ་དྷི་སྭཱ་ཧཱ། ཤཱ་རིའི་བུ། བྱང་ཆུབ་སེམས་དཔའ་སེམས་དཔའ་ཆེན་པོས་དེ་ལྟར་ཤེས་རབ་ཀྱི་ཕ་རོལ་ཏུ་ཕྱིན་པ་ཟབ་མོ་ལ་བསླབ་པར་བྱའོ།

དེ་ནས་བཅོམ་ལྡན་འདས་ཏིང་ངེ་འཛིན་དེ་ལས་བཞེངས་ཏེ། བྱང་ཆུབ་སེམས་དཔའ་སེམས་དཔའ་ཆེན་པོ་འཕགས་པ་སྤྱན་རས་གཟིགས་དབང་ཕྱུག་ལ་ལེགས་སོ་ཞེས་བྱ་བ་བྱིན་ནས།[21] ལེགས་སོ་ལེགས་སོ། རིགས་ཀྱི་བུ་དེ་དེ་བཞིན་ནོ། རིགས་ཀྱི་བུ་དེ་དེ་བཞིན་ཏེ། ཇི་ལྟར་ཁྱོད་ཀྱིས་བསྟན་པ་དེ་བཞིན་དུ།[22] ཤེས་རབ་ཀྱི་ཕ་རོལ་ཏུ་ཕྱིན་པ་ཟབ་མོ་ལ་སྤྱད་པར་བྱ་སྟེ། དེ་བཞིན་གཤེགས་པ་རྣམས་ཀྱང་རྗེས་སུ་ཡི་རང་ངོ་།

བཅོམ་ལྡན་འདས་ཀྱིས་དེ་སྐད་ཅེས་བཀའ་སྩལ་ནས། ཚེ་དང་ལྡན་པ་ཤཱ་རིའི་བུ་དང་། བྱང་ཆུབ་སེམས་དཔའ་སེམས་དཔའ་ཆེན་པོ་འཕགས་པ་སྤྱན་རས་གཟིགས་དབང་ཕྱུག་དང་། ཐམས་ཅད་དང་ལྡན་པའི་འཁོར་དེ་དག་དང་། ལྷ་དང་། མི་དང་། ལྷ་མ་ཡིན་དང་། དྲི་ཟར་བཅས་པའི་འཇིག་རྟེན་ཡི་རངས་ཏེ། བཅོམ་ལྡན་འདས་ཀྱིས་གསུངས་པ་ལ་མངོན་པར་བསྟོད་དོ།

འཕགས་པ་བཅོམ་ལྡན་འདས་མ་ཤེས་རབ་ཀྱི་ཕ་རོལ་ཏུ་ཕྱིན་པའི་སྙིང་པོ་ཞེས་བྱ་བ་ཐེག་པ་ཆེན་པོའི་མདོ་རྫོགས་སོ།། །།

རྒྱ་གར་གྱི་མཁན་པོ་བི་མ་ལ་མི་ཏྲ་དང་། ལོ་ཙཱ་བ་དགེ་སློང་རིན་ཆེན་སྡེས་བསྒྱུར་ཅིང་། ཞུ་ཆེན་གྱི་ལོ་ཙཱ་བ་དགེ་སློང་ནམ་མཁའ་ལ་སོགས་པས་ཞུས་ཏེ་གཏན་ལ་ཕབ་པའོ། དཔལ་བསམ་ཡས་ལྷུན་གྱིས་གྲུབ་པའི་གཙུག་ལག་ཁང་གི་དགེ་རྒྱས་བྲེ་མ་གླིང་གི་རྩིག་ངོས་ལ་བྲིས་པ་དང་ཞུ་དག་ལེགས་པར་བགྱིས་སོ།།[23]

① Introduction to a Canonical Text

Page 35, Line 4

Canonical texts can be easily recognized by a formulaic opening construction in which the language of the source text and original title are provided, followed by a statement of the title in its Tibetan translation. Although some early Tibetan authors adopted this style for their own compositions, here that is not the case.

WHAT TO REMEMBER

Canonical texts—with the exception of texts whose source title has been lost—are introduced by a phrase indicating the source language followed by the title of the text in that language transliterated into Tibetan. This is followed by the Tibetan-language title similarly introduced. Some examples of these are:

རྒྱ་གར་སྐད་དུ། — "In the language of India," usually meaning Sanskrit

རྒྱ་ནག་སྐད་དུ། or རྒྱ་ཡི་སྐད་དུ། or རྒྱའི་སྐད་དུ། — "In the language of China"

ཧོར་གྱི་སྐད་དུ། — "In the language of Mongolia"

བོད་སྐད་དུ། — "In the language of Tibet"

② Transliteration of Sanskrit in Tibetan Letters

Page 35, Line 4

Because the Tibetan alphabet—at least in the historical account—was derived from the Sanskrit alphabet, it is relatively easy to render Sanskrit words in Tibetan script. Here, the title of the text, the *Bhagavatī-prajñāpāramitā-hṛdaya*, was transmitted that way. A few things are immediately obvious from looking at the title rendered in Tibetan script: བྷ་ག་བ་ཏཱི་པྲ་ཛྙཱ་པཱ་ར་མི་ཏཱ་ཧྲྀ་ད་ཡ།. The first is that while some syllables could be mistaken for valid

Tibetan words, many others are not, and violate syllabic composition rules. The preponderance of long vowels (indicated by subjoined འ་ letters) and invalid consonant stacks are all clues that this is a transcription of Sanskrit. Those who know Sanskrit may notice that the Sanskrit letters "ja" (ज) and "va" (व) are represented by the Tibetan letters "dza" (ཛ) and "ba" (བ), respectively. One possible reason for this lies in the fact that there was a strong connection between Tibet and Kashmir, and Kashmiri pronunciations affected letter choices. Similarly, by extension, given the Kashmir connection with the tantric tradition of Bengal, the fact that in Bengali the letters "va" (व) and "ba" (ब) are conflated may have also contributed to these alignments between scripts. Nonetheless, the transliteration scheme is fairly standard and can be followed rather easily once it is learned.

WHAT TO REMEMBER

When the Sanskrit alphabet is represented in Tibetan transliteration, classical literature uses—more or less consistently—the following system:

Devanāgari:	अ	आ	इ	ई	उ	ऊ	ऋ	ॠ	ए	ऐ	ओ	औ	अं	अः	ॐ
Romanized:	a	ā	i	ī	u	ū	ṛ	ṝ	e	ai	o	au	aṃ	aḥ	oṃ
Tibetan:	ཨ་	ཨཱ་	ཨི་	ཨཱི་	ཨུ་	ཨཱུ་	ཨྲྀ་	ཨྲཱྀ་	ཨེ་	ཨཻ་	ཨོ་	ཨཽ་	ཨཾ་	ཨཿ	ཨོཾ་

Devanāgari:	क	ख	ग	घ	ङ	च	छ	ज	झ	ञ	ट	ठ	ड	ढ	ण	त	थ
Romanized:	k	kh	g	gh	ng	c	ch	j	jh	ñ	ṭ	ṭh	ḍ	ḍh	ṇ	t	th
Tibetan:	ཀ་	ཁ་	ག་	གྷ་	ང་	ཙ་	ཚ་	ཛ་	ཛྷ་	ཉ་	ཊ་	ཋ་	ཌ་	ཌྷ་	ཎ་	ཏ་	ཐ་

Devanāgari:	द	ध	न	प	फ	ब	भ	म	य	र	ल	व	श	ष	स	ह
Romanized:	d	dh	n	p	ph	b	bh	m	y	r	l	v	ś	ṣ	s	h
Tibetan:	ད་	དྷ་	ན་	པ་	ཕ་	བ་	བྷ་	མ་	ཡ་	ར་	ལ་	བ་	ཤ་	ཥ་	ས་	ཧ་

Note that the Tibetan letters ཙ་, ཚ་, ཛ་, and ཛྷ་ are used to represent the Sanskrit letters "ca" (च), "cha" (छ), "ja" (ज), and "jha" (झ) rather than the letters ཅ་, ཆ་, ཇ་, and ཇྷ་ as might be expected. Second, note that although some authors will use the Tibetan letter ཝ་ to represent the Sanskrit letter "va" (व), more commonly the Tibetan letter བ་ is used to represent both the Sanskrit letters "ba" (ब) and "va" (व)—likely a reflection of the Bengali roots of Tibetan Buddhist tantra.

These two features give rise to certain oddities in Tibetanized Sanskrit, such as the transliteration of the Sanskrit word *vajra* (**वज्र**) being rendered as བཛྲ་ (reflecting "bajra" in Bengali, and typically pronounced "bendzra" in colloquial Tibetan).

③ Opening Homage in a Canonical Text

Page 35, Line 5

In the early ninth century in Tibet, as Sanskrit Buddhist texts were beginning to be translated into Tibetan in a systematic manner, a series of royal decrees were issued by the Tibetan king prescribing standard vocabulary and conventions for translations. Among these proclamations was the decree that statements of homage should be standardized across the different categories of literature. Most sūtra texts contain either the standard homage to "all buddhas and bodhisattvas," or the more extensive one to the "Noble Three Jewels," that is the Buddha, his teachings (the Dharma), and his community of followers (the Saṅgha). The Perfection of Wisdom sūtras, however, have idiosyncratic homages—like the one here, which pays homage to the embodiment of the wisdom of all the buddhas, the Bhagavatī.

In terms of grammar, the sentence hinges on the final verbal collocation (or phrasal verb) ཕྱག་འཚལ་, meaning "to pay homage." The verb itself is formed from the root verb འཚལ་ (syntactic Class V, "to offer") with an honorific verbal prefix ཕྱག་. The verb is preceded by the indirect object, marked with a ལ་ particle (Wilson, case 2.6). In structural form the sentence can be mapped out as:

APP	2.6	VP()	
བཅོམ་ལྡན་འདས་མ་ ཤེས་རབ་ཀྱི་ཕ་རོལ་ཏུ་ཕྱིན་པ་	ལ་	ཕྱག་འཚལ་	ལོ།

WHAT TO REMEMBER

When reading the opening passage of a text, watch for common verbs of homage, offering, and praise, such as ཕྱག་འཚལ་, འདུད་, འབུལ་, མཆོད་, etc., that are preceded by a ལ་

and that sometimes occur at the end of multiples of four lines of fixed-length verse. Occasionally, homages will also contain an adverbial phrase such as གུས་པས་ ("respectfully") or མགོ་ནས་ ("with [my] head"), or similar expressions.

Formulaic Opening to a Sūtra

④

Page 35, Line 6

These are the famous words that open nearly every sūtra in the Tibetan Buddhist canon. Although they occur in Sanskrit *sūtra*s and Pali *sutta*s alike, there has been some debate over how they should be rendered. The phrase, in Sanskrit, is *evaṃ mayā śrutam ekasmin*, often rendered as "thus have I heard at one time." It is followed by a description of the circumstances of the teaching that follows. The subject of the debate is whether or not the time clause ("at one time") refers to the act of hearing ("at one time I heard ...") or to the situation that follows ("on one occasion the Bhagavān was dwelling ..."). The decision by the Tibetan tradition—and consensus of current scholars based on the Indian commentarial tradition—is that the former interpretation is the correct one.

WHAT TO REMEMBER

The import of the statement འདི་སྐད་བདག་གིས་ཐོས་པ་དུས་གཅིག་ན། is not to present hearsay testimony ("I heard that once it happened that ...") but rather that the person recounting the teachings is doing so in accordance with an unbroken oral transmission of the lineage ("at one time I heard thus").

Sanskrit Proper Names

⑤

Page 35, Line 6

The Tibetan tradition handled the translation of Sanskrit proper names in an idiosyncratic fashion. Depending upon the uniqueness (or correspondingly, the ambiguity) of Sanskrit proper names, a combination of syllable-by-syllable etymological translation and transliteration was used. The result is often a phrase that bears little or no literal sense in the context of the larger sentence. For example, the name of the great Indian scholar-siddha Nāgārjuna was rendered etymologically as *nāga* + *arjuna* (ཀླུ་སྒྲུབ་—"Nāga accomplishing"), while the name of one of the Buddha's main disciples—seen later in this text—Śāriputra, was rendered in a mixture of transliteration and translation as *śāri* + *putra* (ཤཱ་རིའི་བུ་ "son of Śāri," and later, ཤཱ་ར་དྭ་ཏིའི་བུ་ "son of Śāradvati"). The two proper names that occur here—place names, in fact—were translated etymologically from Sanskrit: *rājagṛha* (རྒྱལ་པོའི་ཁབ་) and *gṛdhrakūṭa* (བྱ་རྒོད་ཀྱི་ཕུང་པོའི་རི་).

WHAT TO REMEMBER

A phrase that appears semantically and syntactically unconnected to the rest of the sentence has a strong likelihood of being part of a proper name.

6 Syntactic Particle དང་ and Postpositional Phrases

Page 35, Line 7

The majority of postpositional phrases identified by Wilson (660) attach to their nouns and pronouns with a sixth-case particle (Wilson, case 6.3). The phrase encountered here, ཐབས་གཅིག་ཏུ་, likewise connects to its subordinate phrase using the sixth case in certain circumstances, or occasionally the possessive suffix བཅས་ in other circumstances, but more commonly uses the syntactic particle དང་. Each conveys a slightly different meaning and can be rendered differently in English.

WHAT TO REMEMBER

The translation of the postpositional phrase ཐབས་གཅིག་ཏུ་ can vary depending on the manner in which it connects to its subordinate phrase. Hence, "…དང་ཐབས་གཅིག་ཏུ་ can be translated as "together with"; "…པའི་ཐབས་གཅིག་ཏུ་ as "in the company of"; and "…དང་བཅས་ཐབས་གཅིག་ཏུ་ as "in one group together with."

Recognizing Class IV Verbs

⑦

Page 35, Line 11

One of the most important lessons for novice students of Tibetan language to learn is that not everything that looks like a case-marking particle is one. A perfect example is the variety of particles that can accompany Class IV verbs. Class IV verbs (nominative-syntactic verbs) are a subclass of nominative verbs (verbs whose subjects occur in the nominative case) but whose qualifiers are marked by a syntactic particle (see Wilson, 603–605). Four types of Class IV verbs can be distinguished in terms of their semantic dimension: separative verbs, verbs of containment, conjunctive verbs, and disjunctive verbs. Separative, conjunctive, and disjunctive verbs typically take their qualifiers marked by the syntactic particles དང་ or ལས་, while verbs of containment typically take their qualifiers marked by the third-case particles (ཀྱིས་, གྱིས་, གིས་, etc.) used syntactically (i.e., *not* marking the third case). Of the roughly four dozen Class IV verbs in the Tibetan language, one of the most common is the verb seen here, སྟོང་ ("to be empty (of)").

A common mistake when encountering Class IV verbs of containment is the tendency to try to force an instrumental reading on the qualifier ("empty *by way of* X"). This is simply wrong. While such a reading can be forced on some Class IV verbs (such as སྟོང་), the mistaken nature of this grammatical reading is evident when attempted with other Class IV verbs of containment, such as གང་ ("to be filled (with)").

> WHAT TO REMEMBER
>
> Not everything that looks like a case-marking particle is one, and it is the requisite grammar of different classes of verbs—not a presumed independent identity of particles—that determines the correct reading of a sentence.

Complements and Qualifiers

⑧

Page 35, Line 11

This short sentence demonstrates a number of compositional principles in Tibetan literature: assumed and omitted components (in this case, an agent), requisite and optional sentence components (in this case, an object and a complement), and the modular use of a sentence fragment as a single phrase. Recall (Wilson, 255ff., 465) that an agentive verb can take a number of basic components in forming a sentence: an agent, an instrument, an object, a complement, a qualifier, and a verb. In this sentence, since it is a continuation of the previous sentence (and indeed repeats the same final verb), the same agent is assumed and hence omitted. Since the final verb in the sentence, རྣམ་པར་ལྟ།, is a Class VI verb, we know that it must take its object marked in the "objective" (second) case. There are two candidates for possible objects in this sentence: the phrase ending with དེ་དག་ལ་ and the phrase ending with སྟོང་པར་. Since the phrase ending with དེ་དག་ལ་ is a simple noun phrase, we can reasonably conclude that it is the object. Interpreting the phrase རང་བཞིན་གྱིས་ as either a new agent or an instrument yields a nonsensical translation (see ཤེས་རབ་སྙིང་པོ note 7, above); it makes more sense as the syntactic qualifier of the Class IV verb that follows it, སྟོང་. Since the entire sentence fragment རང་བཞིན་གྱིས་སྟོང་པ་ likewise makes no sense as a verbal qualifier, one can conclude that it is functioning as a complete unit as a complement (something that provides additional information about the object) in the sentence.

WHAT TO REMEMBER

An agentive verb can take a number of basic components in forming a sentence:

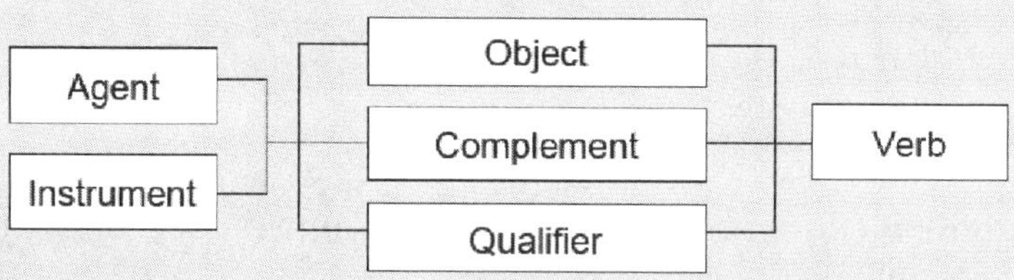

In addition to an agent (that which performs the activity of the verb) and an object (that which receives the action of the verb), often one or both of these will be accompanied by a complement (something that—with an agentive verb—provides additional information about the object) and/or one or more qualifiers (something that *qualifies* the activity of the verb by modifying it or restricting its scope of application).

Sanskrit Word *evaṃ* and the Tibetan འདི་སྐད་[ཅེས་] and དེ་སྐད་[ཅེས་] 9

Page 35, Line 12

The Sanskrit word *evaṃ* is most famously known in Buddhist contexts as the opening word of nearly every sūtra, as seen in the phrase *evaṃ mayā śrutam* (see ཤེས་རབ་སྙིང་པོ་ note 4, above). As in that context, here the word *evaṃ* (translated as འདི་སྐད་) is a demonstrative pronoun meaning "thus." Here, however, despite its co-occurence with the quote marker (ཅེས་), the word should not be taken as an explicit quotation but rather as the lead-in to what follows, as in "Śāriputra spoke thus to Avalokiteśvara: ..." (ཤཱ་རིའི་བུས་... སྤྱན་རས་གཟིགས་དབང་ཕྱུག་ལ་འདི་སྐད་ཅེས་སྨྲས་སོ།), and later in the text (where it is translated as དེ་སྐད་), "thus he spoke" (དེ་སྐད་ཅེས་སྨྲས་པ་) as the conclusion to what precedes it.

WHAT TO REMEMBER

With or without a quote marker, the words འདི་སྐད་ and དེ་སྐད་ should be taken as demonstrative pronouns indicating that a quotation (of speech) follows.

Relative and Correlative Pronouns 10

Page 35, Line 13

In contemporary English, simple relative pronouns mark adjectival clauses and function as connectives linking a clause and the main part of a sentence—for example, the word *whom* in the sentence, "He wrote to the person with *whom* he met last week." In Tibetan (and Sanskrit), such constructions require both a relative and a correlative pronoun. To illustrate, were the above example sentence rendered in such a form, it would read something like "To *that* person he met last week, to *him* he wrote" using the relative pronoun *that* and the correlated ("correlative") pronoun *him*.

Here the relative pronoun གང་ལ་ལ་ ("whosoever") similarly introduces the subordinate clause ཤེས་རབ་ཀྱི་ཕ་རོལ་ཏུ་ཕྱིན་པ་ཟབ་མོའི་སྤྱོད་པ་སྤྱད་པར་འདོད་པ་ ("wishing to engage in the practice of the profound perfection of wisdom"), while the correlative pronoun དེ་ ("him," "her," or as a gender-neutral singular pronoun, "they") relates the subordinate clause to the main sentence, དེས་ཇི་ལྟར་བསླབ་པར་བྱ། ("how should he/she/they train?").

WHAT TO REMEMBER

In classical Tibetan—like Sanskrit—complex subjects often use relative-correlative pairs of pronouns and phrases. Some relative-correlative pairs are:

> གང་ལ་ལ་ ("whosoever") ⇔ དེ་ ("him," "her," etc.)
> གང་ ("that," "whatsoever")⇔ འདི་/དེ་ ("[just] this"/"[just] that")
> གང་ཞིག་ ("whosoever") ⇔ དེ་/དེ་དག་ ("him," "her"/"those two," "them altogether")
> ཇི་སྲིད་དུ་ ("for so long as") ⇔ ད་དུང་ ("for just that long")
> ཇི་ལྟར་ ("just as ...") ⇔ དེ་ལྟར་/དེ་བཞིན་ ("just so, ... "/"like that ...")
> གང་ཡིན་པ་ ("whatsoever") ⇔ དེ་ཉིད་ ("just that," "that very thing," etc.)

and so forth.

11 Auxiliary Verbs: Optative Construction

Page 35, Line 13

Auxiliary constructions are a way of modifying the agency or scope of a verb without altering its basic meaning. For example, some auxiliary verbs are used merely to disambiguate verb tense or create causative constructions (i.e., "to cause to do [something]"), while others alter the temporal dimension of the verb (i.e., changing the past tense into the perfect). The construction seen here, *verb* + བར་བྱ་, is one way of conveying either the emphatic future ("[I] will do [something]") or the optative mood ("[something] should be done" or "[you] should do X"). It is typically formed by combining the future tense of the main verb (*verb* + བར་; Wilson, 614–616) with the future-tense form of the generic action verb བྱེད་ (བྱ་).

WHAT TO REMEMBER

The use of certain auxiliary verbal constructions, such as *future-tense verb* + བར་བྱ་, conveys the optative mood ("[something] should be done" or "[you] should do X").

The Syntactic Particles ཀྱང་, etc., Eliding Case Markers

12

Page 35, Line 17

The syntactic particles ཀྱང་, ཡང་, and འང་ have a variety of uses (see Wilson, 674–676). With nouns and adjectives, they are used to indicate emphasis—in the sense of *also*, *even*, *moreover*, or *however*—depending on context. In the process of doing so, however, they can occasionally elide the case-marking particle that would normally follow the word that precedes them. Here, for example, the sentence ཕུང་པོ་ལྔ་པོ་དེ་དག་ཀྱང་། རང་བཞིན་གྱིས་སྟོང་པར་ཡང་དག་པར་རྗེས་སུ་བལྟའོ། echoes a similar sentence previously seen, ཕུང་པོ་ལྔ་པོ་དེ་དག་ལ་ཡང་རང་བཞིན་གྱིས་སྟོང་པར་རྣམ་པར་ལྟའོ། (see ཤེས་རབ་སྙིང་པོ་ note 8, above).

Although one could make reference to the underlying Sanskrit (the object-complement pairs are the same), one can understand this from the standpoint of parallel grammar. In general, Tibetan compositions rely on parallel constructions to lend coherence and ease of comprehension to a work through slight variations in phrasing. Here, the ཀྱང་ has elided the ལ་ that would normally indicate the object of the verb བལྟ་.

WHAT TO REMEMBER

The syntactic particles ཀྱང་, etc., can occasionally elide a case-marking particle.

Verbal Participles: Past Passive Participles

13

Page 35, Line 17

The extent to which the Tibetan language bears the influence of Sanskrit cannot be overstated, and this sentence attests to that. Central to understanding this point is an understanding of the role of the past passive participle in Sanskrit. A "past passive participle," simply stated, is a derived form of a verb that expresses a past action in relation to an object. It is often used as an adjective, but more importantly, in Sanskrit, it can function in place of a conjugated verb. The same holds true in Tibetan.

To illustrate this with an English example, the past passive participle of "to give" is "given." It can be used as an adjective ("The given book was *Moby Dick*"), as part of a verbal phrase [a predicate adjective] ("The book was given"), or as a substantive ("The given [i.e., that which was given] was a book"). All of these uses are seen in Tibetan as well, where the participle (and verbal noun) is formed with the lexical suffix particles པ་ and བ་ (Wilson, 167ff.). Wilson describes this difference in usage in terms of "open" verbs (verbal participles that indicate verbal activity within a sentence) and "final" verbs (verbs that terminate sentences; cf. Wilson, 129–130); verbal nouns and adjectives (Wilson, 156–157) are similarly constructed. For example, the past-tense verb བསྟན་ (present tense སྟོན་, "to teach") is used to form the participle བསྟན་པ་ ("taught," or "that which was taught," i.e., "the teaching"). Here, the sentence གཟུགས་སྟོང་པའོ། follows from the previous one in which the five aggregates "are empty of their own nature" (རང་བཞིན་གྱིས་སྟོང་།). Hence, the first of the five aggregates, form (གཟུགས་), is similarly characterized, but rather than fully restating this as གཟུགས་རང་བཞིན་གྱིས་སྟོང་། the participial form of the verb has been used. Since many verbs in Tibetan (such as སྟོང་) are treated as predicate adjectives in English ("empty"), the resulting English translation remains the same: "Form is empty."

WHAT TO REMEMBER

The use of a verbal participle (an "open" verb) in lieu of a "final" verb is very common in Tibetan and mirrors the same practice in Sanskrit. Verbal participles are often used to express the idea that the individual sentences are part of a larger series of statements that form a complete thought. Since many verbs in Tibetan (such as སྟོང་) are treated as predicate adjectives in English ("to be empty"), the resulting English translation is not changed by the verb occurring in its participial form.

14 Omitted Verbs

Page 35, Line 18

The most basic sentence in Tibetan is one of simple declarative predication in the form "A is B." Often, when the identity of the subject (Wilson, case 1.1.1) and complement (Wilson, case 1.1.1) are unambiguous, the final verb of predication, usually ཡིན་, will be omitted. Such is the case here, and although གཟུགས་ is also the rarely seen future tense of the verb འཛུགས་ ("to touch" or "to set up"), in this context its identity as the first of the five aggregates, "form," is unambiguous. Consequently, because there is no ambiguity concerning its import, the final verb of predication, ཡིན་, has been omitted with the predication being implied. This does, however, underscore the necessity of contextual understanding when reading Tibetan in order to properly disambiguate the meaning of words. Even when the point of demarcation between subject and complement is ambiguous, the verb ཡིན་ may still be omitted, but the subject and predicate will be delimited by the use of the punctuation particle ནི་ to explicitly mark the nominative subject, as in ལྷམ་པ་ནི་གྲུ་བཞི། ("a square [is that which has] four corners").

WHAT TO REMEMBER

Simple statements of predication ("A is B") often occur as self-contained phrases of two items, with the subject occasionally marked by ནི་ and the verb ཡིན་ omitted. Other verbs—the simple verb of existence ཡོད་ or the generic action verb བྱེད་—may also be omitted in sentences, but only in specific unambiguous contexts.

The ...ནས་...བར་དུ་ ("From ... Up To ...") Construction 15

Page 36, Line 2

This sentence utilizes the ...ནས་...བར་དུ་ construction to indicate a list of items (assumed to be known by the reader) by providing only the first and last elements of the list. Here, the first and last two items in the list of the eighteen "elements" (Skt. *dhātu*; Tib. ཁམས་)—that is, the three sets of elements of sense faculty, object, and associated consciousness that constitute a cognitive event—are given. This structure is repeated in the sentence that follows as well, with the first and last items in the list of the "twelve links" of dependent origination (Skt. *pratītyasamutpāda*; Tib. རྟེན་ཅིང་འབྲེལ་བར་འབྱུང་བ་) along with their cessations.

WHAT TO REMEMBER

The ...ནས་...བར་དུ་ construction is a simple way to indicate a list of items by providing only the first and last elements of the list, occasionally followed by a quantifying number.

16 Distributed Verbs within a Single Sentence

Page 36, Line 6

This sentence demonstrates the distribution of two verbs to the same qualifier. Consequently, the sentence ཤེས་རབ་ཀྱི་ཕ་རོལ་ཏུ་ཕྱིན་པ་ལ་བརྟེན་ཅིང་གནས་སོ། should be understood as reading: ཤེས་རབ་ཀྱི་ཕ་རོལ་ཏུ་ཕྱིན་པ་ལ་བརྟེན་ཅིང་། ཤེས་རབ་ཀྱི་ཕ་རོལ་ཏུ་ཕྱིན་པ་ལ་གནས་སོ།.

Although in this case, the two verbs (བརྟེན་ and གནས་) are of the same class (Class II) and both take the associated phrase as their qualifier, such need not be the case.

WHAT TO REMEMBER

When an author wishes to apply two or more verbs to the same subject, object, complement, and/or qualifier, the verbs are simply given sequentially, usually (but not always) joined by the conjunctive syntactic particles ཅིང་, etc. This approach can be used in standard sentence constructions as well as in clauses.

17 Types of Clause Connectives

Page 36, Line 7

The sentence encountered here opens with the clause construction དུས་གསུམ་དུ་རྣམ་པར་བཞུགས་པའི་སངས་རྒྱས་ཐམས་ཅད་. When attempting to parse the grammar of a clause, the best approach is to restate the entire phrase as if it were a sentence. Since བཞུགས་ is a Class II verb, it is expected to take a subject in the nominative (first case) and a qualifier in the locative (seventh case). Since the noun that precedes the verb can be seen to be in the seventh case, what follows the verb, སངས་རྒྱས་ཐམས་ཅད་ "all the buddhas," would appear to be the "subject" of the verb. This can be verified by restating the entire phrase as if it were a sentence: སངས་རྒྱས་ཐམས་ཅད་དུས་གསུམ་དུ་རྣམ་པར་བཞུགས། "All the buddhas dwell in the three times." Hence, the construction is a clause connective to the agent/subject.

Although this is a particularly easy instance of a clause connective, some instances are more difficult to identify (such as clause connectives to complements and qualifiers—see ཁྱབ་མཐའ་ note 16 for such an example), but their correct identification remains central to producing a correct translation.

WHAT TO REMEMBER

When attempting to parse the grammar of a clause, the best approach is to restate the entire phrase as if it were a sentence. In most cases it is obvious what role the noun is playing in the phrase, but in other, less obvious instances this can clarify the grammar (see Wilson, 418–419, 649–651).

Clause Connective to an Agent/Instrument/Subject

These clauses connect to a subject or agent of what would be the main verb of the sentence. For example, with the agent of a Class V verb:

ཆོས་བསྟན་པའི་སངས་རྒྱས། ⇨ སངས་རྒྱས་ཀྱིས་ཆོས་བསྟན།

"The Buddha, who taught the Dharma" ⇨

"The Buddha taught the Dharma"

Or with the instrument of a Class V verb:

བདག་གི་མ་འདིས་མངལ་དུ་བསྐྱངས་པའི་བརྩེ་བ། ⇨ བདག་གི་མ་འདིས་མངལ་དུ་བརྩེ་བས་བསྐྱངས་།

"The love, by means of which this mother of mine sustained [me] in the womb" ⇨

"This mother of mine sustained [me] in the womb with love"

Similarly, with the subject of a Class II verb:

བསམ་གཏན་དང་པོ་ལ་གནས་པའི་འཕགས་པ། ⇨ བསམ་གཏན་དང་པོ་ལ་འཕགས་པ་གནས།

"A superior (*ārya*), who remains in the first concentration" ⇨

"A superior (*ārya*) remains in the first concentration"

Or with the subject of a Class VII verb:

ཟས་དང་ཆུ་དགོས་པའི་སེམས་ཅན། ⇨ སེམས་ཅན་ལ་ཟས་དང་ཆུ་དགོས།

"Sentient beings, who need food and water" ⇨

"Sentient beings need food and water"

CLAUSE CONNECTIVE TO A OBJECT

These clauses connect to the object of what would be the main verb of the sentence:

སངས་རྒྱས་ཀྱིས་བསྟན་པའི་ཆོས། ⇨ སངས་རྒྱས་ཀྱིས་ཆོས་བསྟན།
"The Dharma that was taught by the Buddha" ⇨
"The Buddha taught the Dharma"

CLAUSE CONNECTIVE TO A QUALIFIER

These clauses connect to words that qualify the action of what would be the main verb of the sentence; it specifies the time or place where the action takes place, or the reason:

སངས་རྒྱས་ཀྱིས་ཆོས་བསྟན་པའི་རྒྱ་གར། ⇨ སངས་རྒྱས་ཀྱིས་རྒྱ་གར་ལ་ཆོས་བསྟན།
"India, where the Buddha taught the Dharma" ⇨
"The Buddha taught the Dharma in India"

Or, rarely, with the qualifier of a Class I verb:

དེ་ཤེས་བྱ་ཡིན་པའི་སྤྱི། ⇨ དེ་ཤེས་བྱ་སྤྱི་ནས་ཡིན།
"A generality of that which is an object of knowledge, ..." ⇨
"That is an object of knowledge in terms of [its] generality."

CLAUSE CONNECTIVE TO A COMPLEMENT

These clauses connect to words that provide additional information about either the object (of Class V and VI verbs) or the subject (of Class I, II, III, and IV verbs) of what would be the main verb of the sentence. For example, with a Class V verb:

སངས་རྒྱས་ཀྱིས་ཆོས་བསྟན་པའི་ངེས་པ། ⇨ སངས་རྒྱས་ཀྱིས་ཆོས་ངེས་པར་བསྟན།
"The definitiveness of the Dharma that was taught by the Buddha ..." ⇨
"The Buddha taught the Dharma as definitive."

Or with the complement of a Class I verb:

ཆོས་དུང་དཀར་པོའི་ཁ་དོག་ཡིན་པའི་དཀར་པོ། ⇨ ཆོས་དུང་དཀར་པོའི་ཁ་དོག་དཀར་པོ་ཡིན།
"White, which is the color of a white religious conch, ..." ⇨
"The color of a white religious conch is white."

Translation Hint

18

Page 36, Line 11

The internal grammar of this phrase—one of a series of otherwise similar appositional phrases—is a little ambiguous. The Tibetan verb མཉམ་ is a Class IV verb, meaning that it takes its qualifier marked by a syntactic particle—specifically, དང་. Consequently, the subordinate clause modifying སྔགས་ could be read as a verb and its qualifier ("... that is equal to the unequaled"), or as two verbs distributed in the clause ("... that is unequaled and equal"). Only commentary—or the original Sanskrit text—can resolve the ambiguity.

Auxiliary Verbs: Causative Construction—བྱེད་, མཛད་, and བགྱིད་

19

Page 36, Line 11

As noted previously (ཤེས་རབ་སྙིང་པོ་ note 11), auxiliary constructions can be used to create causative constructions (i.e., "to cause to do [something]"). The construction seen here as part of a clause, *verb* + བར་བྱེད་, is one way of forming the causative construction. It is typically formed by combining the present tense of the main verb with the present-tense form of the generic action verb བྱེད་ (or the honorific forms, མཛད་ and བགྱིད་). With nominative verbs (Class II, III, and IV verbs), the construction *present-tense verb* + བར་བྱེད་ forms the causative; with agentive verbs (Classes V and VI), it forms either the reflexive causative or emphasizes the active voice.

WHAT TO REMEMBER

The causative construction is formed by combining the present tense of a verb with the present-tense form of the generic action verb བྱེད་ (or the honorific form, བགྱིད་) in the form: *verb* + བར་བྱེད་.

The Alternate Reason Clause Marker –ས་ན་

20

Page 36, Line 11

In addition to the reason clause marker ཕྱིར་, the logical syntactic particles ཀྱིས་ན་, གིས་ན་, གྱིས་ན་, ཡིས་ན་, and –ས་ན་ (and even the hybrid –ས་ཕྱིར་) can be used to mark reasons or indicate logical sequence in a sentence. The former (ཕྱིར་) functions as a postposition that connects to what precedes it with a sixth-case connective particle (Wilson, case 6.3) and specifies a logical reason. The logical syntactic particles ཀྱིས་ན་, etc., however, do not require such a connective and tend to convey a more loose attributive "reason" such as is seen here. Of these logical syntactic particles, the most commonly seen is the agglutinative form, –ས་ན་, which attaches to the participial form of a verb (as it does here).

WHAT TO REMEMBER

While the reason clause marker ཕྱིར་ marks a logical reason, the syntactic particles ཀྱིས་ན་, གིས་ན་, གྱིས་ན་, ཡིས་ན་, –ས་ན་, and –ས་ཕྱིར་ can be used to mark reasons in an attributive sense or to indicate a logical sequence in a sentence ("because (of) ..." or "since ...").

21 Sanskrit Word *sādhu* and the Tibetan ལེགས་སོ་[ཞེས་བྱ་བ་]

Page 36, Line 16

The Sanskrit word *sādhu* is taken in most contexts as a general exclamation of praise, as in *sādhu! sādhu!* (translated in Tibetan as ལེགས་སོ། ལེགས་སོ།)—"Good! Good!" However, when used as part of the expression ལེགས་སོ་ཞེས་བྱ་བ་བྱིན།, it connotes something more akin to the use of *evaṃ* (see ཤེས་རབ་སྙིང་པོ་ note 9, above). As with that phrase, the word should not be taken as an explicit quotation but rather as part of the lead-in to what follows, taking the entire phrase ལེགས་སོ་ཞེས་བྱ་བ་བྱིན། as a verbal expression meaning "to bestow benediction," as in "the Bhagavān ... bestowed his benediction to ... Avalokiteśvara."

WHAT TO REMEMBER

Free-standing and without a quote marker, the word ལེགས་སོ་ should be taken as a general exclamation; when it occurs as part of the idiomatic verbal expression ལེགས་སོ་ཞེས་བྱ་བ་བྱིན། ("to bestow benediction"), it conveys the lead-in to what follows.

Tibetan Modular Sentence Structures

22

Page 36, Line 17

This phrase introduces the "modular" nature of Tibetan sentences—that is, the way in which Tibetan sentences are composed of nested parts. Here, the subordinate clause ཇི་ལྟར་ཁྱོད་ཀྱིས་བསྟན་པ་དེ་བཞིན་དུ། contains within it another sentence that has been nominalized:

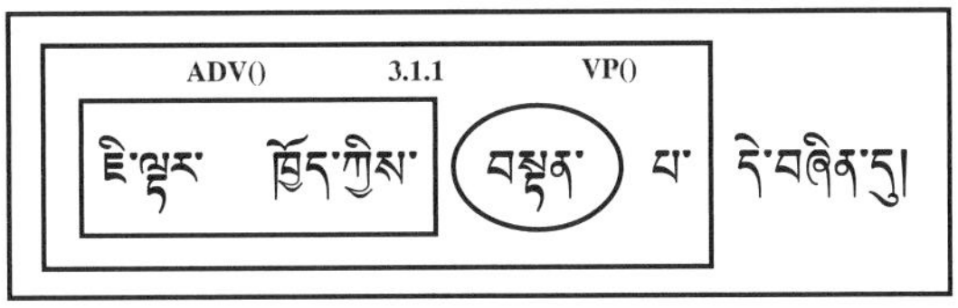

The sentence contained in the phrase is built around the Class V verb བསྟན་ and could be translated as "You taught in just this way." When the sentence is nominalized, it yields a noun phrase—"the teaching by you in this manner," or more colloquially, "just how you have taught"—associated with a postpositional clause marker, དེ་བཞིན་དུ་ ("in accordance with"). A similar construction is seen near the end of the text in the sentence བཅོམ་ལྡན་འདས་ཀྱིས་གསུངས་པ་ལ་མངོན་པར་བསྟོད་དོ།.

WHAT TO REMEMBER

The key concept in understanding the grammar of a complex Tibetan sentence is the modular nature of those sentences. Complex sentences in Tibetan are constructed modularly; that is, they are built up out of smaller units—phrases, clauses, and sentences—that have been nominalized.

Translation Hint

23

Page 37, Line 6

As with all colophons, a number of proper names can be found that, as noted above (see ཤེས་རབ་སྙིང་པོ་ note 5), are phrases that appear semantically and syntactically unconnected to the rest of the sentence. This applies to Tibetan proper names as well. Thus, in addition to the names of the translators and editors of the text, the final sentence in the colophon provides locations and associated information about the translation.

Translation of *The Heart Sūtra*

In Sanskrit: *Ārya bhagavatī-prajñā-paramitā-hṛdaya*
In Tibetan: *'Phags pa bcom ldan 'das ma shes rab kyi pha rol tu phyin pa'i snying po*
[In English: *The Superior, the Bhagavatī, the Heart of the Perfection of Wisdom*]

Homage to the Perfection of Wisdom, the Bhagavatī!

Thus have I heard at one time: the Bhagavān was dwelling in Rājagṛha on Vulture Peak together with a great community of monks and a great community of bodhisattvas. At that time, the Bhagavān entered into the samādhi called "Perception of the Profound" on the enumeration of phenomena.

Also at that time, the Bodhisattva, the Mahāsattva, the Superior, Avalokiteśvara looked at the practice of the profound perfection of wisdom and saw those five aggregates also as empty of inherent existence. Then, through the power of the Buddha, the Venerable Śāriputra spoke thus to the Bodhisattva, the Mahāsattva, the Superior, Avalokiteśvara. "Whosoever is a son of good family wishing to engage in the practice of the profound perfection of wisdom, how should he train?"

Thus he spoke, and the Bodhisattva, the Mahāsattva, the Superior, Avalokiteśvara replied thus to the Venerable Śāriputra. "O Śāriputra, whosoever is a son of good family or daughter of good family wishing to engage in the practice of the profound perfection of wisdom, they should adopt a view like this:

"Even those five aggregates should be seen as empty of their own nature. Form is empty; emptiness is form. Emptiness is not other than form. Form, also, is not other than emptiness. Similarly, feeling, discrimination, compositional factors, and consciousnesses are empty. Thus, Śāriputra, all phenomena are emptiness.

"There are no characteristics. No production. No cessation. No defilement. No freedom from defilement. No diminishment. No fulfillment.

"Thus, Śāriputra, in emptiness there is no form. No feeling. No discrimination. No compositional factors. No consciousnesses.

"No eye. No ear. No nose. No tongue. No body. No mind.

"No form. No sound. No smell. No taste. No object of touch. No phenomena. From no eye constituent, to no mental consciousness constituent; from no ignorance, and no extinction of ignorance, to no aging and death, and no extinction of aging and death. There is no suffering, origination, cessation, and path. No exalted wisdom. No attainment, also no nonattainment.

"Therefore, Śāriputra, since there is no attainment, bodhisattvas depend on and abide in the perfection of wisdom with minds without obstruction and hence without fear, and having thoroughly transcended the erroneous, have gone to final nirvāṇa. Moreover, all the buddhas who dwell in the three times have directly and perfectly awakened to unsurpassed, perfect, complete enlightenment in dependence upon this perfection of wisdom.

"Therefore, the mantra of the perfection of wisdom, the mantra of great knowledge, the unsurpassed mantra, the mantra that is unequaled and equal, the mantra that thoroughly pacifies all suffering, since it is not false, should be known as truth. The mantra of the perfection of wisdom is proclaimed: TADYATHĀ OṂ GATE GATE PĀRAGATE PĀRASAṂGATE BODHI SVĀHĀ! Śāriputra, a bodhisattva mahāsattva should learn the profound perfection of wisdom like this."

Then, the Bhagavān arose from that samādhi and having bestowed his benediction on the Bodhisattva, the Mahāsattva, the Superior, Avalokiteśvara, said, "Well done! Well done! O son of good family, it is like that; O son of good family, it is like that. One should engage in the profound perfection of wisdom just as you have taught, and even the tathāgatas will rejoice!"

The Bhagavān having spoken thus, the Venerable Śāriputra, the Bodhisattva, the Mahāsattva, the Superior, Avalokiteśvara, all those surrounding them, and the world together with its gods, men, demigods, and celestial musicians rejoiced and praised the word of the Bhagavān.

This completes the Great Vehicle sūtra called "Bhagavatī, the Heart of the Perfection of Wisdom."

[This text] was translated [into Tibetan] by the Indian abbot Vimalamitra and the translator-monk Rinchende, and edited and finalized by the great editor-translator monk Namkha, and others. It was written on the face of the wall of the Gyege Jemaling Temple at the Glorious Samye Monastic Complex and the editing was done well.

Jñānamitra's *Explanation of the Heart Sūtra*

Of the many canonical Indian commentaries written on the *Heart Sūtra*, the one by Jñānamitra[1] is a clear and straightforward commentary on the sūtra. The text is one of only two compositions attributed to him in thc *Commentarial Treatises* (*bstan 'gyur*) section of the Tripiṭaka, and no additional information is given about him in their colophons. Nonetheless, there are indications in his treatise that Jñānamitra (ca. late eighth century) adheres to some of the ideas espoused by the late Indian Yogācāra-Mādhyamika school,[2] such as referring to subject-object duality, phenomena as "natures," etc.

Although the novice student of Indian religious traditions may wish to focus exclusively on a root text as an avenue to understanding the foundational concepts of a tradition or its putative founder, the premise behind that approach is inherently flawed. The philosophical treatises (*śāstra*) and aphoristic statements (*sūtra*) "standing at the head of several of the philosophical schools are essentially signposts in a line of oral argument" and in the absence of that oral commentary, or as an alternate form of it, "the *sūtra*s often have meaning for us only as they are expounded in a full scholastic commentary."[3] Consequently, it is imperative for a student to learn how to read this literature in order to mature as a scholar.

As an example of commentarial exegesis, Jñānamitra's *Explanation* is fairly typical of the genre in terms of structure. Generally speaking, Tibetan commentaries can be classified into several different categories: word commentaries, annotations, meaning commentaries, and decisive analyses.[4] Word commentaries provide exegesis on a text in a word-by-word manner and can vary from intersyllabic interpolation[5] to extensive narratives. Annotations appear in the form of intersyllabic interpolation but also as what might be thought of as footnotes. Meaning commentaries provide an analysis of a text thematically and are not necessarily linked to—or even quoting—the original text in its entirety, while decisive analyses are one form that typifies monastic textbook literature, being comprised almost exclusively of debate-style narratives.

In classical Sanskrit commentarial literature there are similar though distinct self-proclaimed categories as well: *ṭīkā, vṛtti, pañjikā, bhāṣya, ṭippaṇī*, etc. Jñānamitra's *Explanation*—self-proclaimed as a *vyākhyā* (meaning simply "explanation")—falls into the first of these categories. Although there are differences between them,[6] sūtra commentaries often present the following traditional structures:[7]

- the meaning and significance of the title and homage
- the opening of the sūtra, establishing its authenticity in a varying number of categories, including in terms of the opening words, the occasion, the audience, the location, and the teacher
- the body of the sūtra often taking the form of a citation and an explanation, followed by restatement of the explicated term

Jñānamitra's *Explanation* follows this pattern as well, though he divides his exegesis into seven categories particular to the *Heart Sūtra*: the setting, the entry into wisdom, the defining characteristic of emptiness, the sphere of wisdom, the qualities of wisdom, the fruition of wisdom, and the *dhāraṇī* of wisdom.

When reading this text, however, it is important to keep in mind the fact that even related texts within the canon—such as a root text and a commentary—were more often than not translated by different translators and so a passage in the root text—the *Heart Sūtra* in this case—will inevitably be rendered slightly differently. Such will be seen in this text when the *Heart Sūtra* is quoted.

---

1. The full title is *The Explanation of the Heart of the Perfection of Wisdom* (*Ārya-prajñāpāramitā-hṛdaya-vyākhyā*). See Lopez 1996.
2. The so-called Yogācāra-Svātantrika-Mādhyamika School is an artifact of later Tibetan doxographies, intended to group together a number of authors during the eighth to tenth centuries in India (most notably Śāntarakṣita and Kamalaśīla, who visited Tibet) who asserted a hybrid philosophical system and relied on Yogācāra vocabulary and concepts in their explanations of points of Madhyamaka philosophy.
3. Tubb and Bose 2007, 1.
4. That is, *tshig 'grel, mchan 'grel, spyi don rnam bzhag*, and *mtha' dpyod*, respectively.
5. For an example of this style of commentary, refer to the two sample pages on p. 462.
6. Of these styles of commentary, *ṭīkā* or *vārttika* refers to a generic commentary, a *vṛtti* is a simple running commentary in prose, a *bhāṣya* is a full-length commentary including a formulaic treatment of each topic, a *ṭippaṇī* provides footnotes or annotations, while a *pañjikā* literally means "register" or "notebook" and is a self-deprecating term.
7. In other commentarial forms (such as a *bhāṣya* or *pañjikā*) there are other formulaic structures, such as the four "intentions" (*anubandha; rjes su 'brel pa*) of the commentary: (1) the "subject" (*viṣaya* or *abhidheya; brjod bya*), (2) "purpose" (*prayojana; dgos pa*), (3) "intended audience" (*adhikārin; ched du bya ba*) or alternately, the "purpose of the purpose" (*prayojana-prayojana; dgos pa'i dgos*) or "ultimate purpose" (*mūloddeśya; nying dgos*), and (4) the "connection" (*sambandha; 'brel pa*) between the subject and the commentary.

༄༅།།འཕགས་པ་ཤེས་རབ་ཀྱི་ཕ་རོལ་ཏུ་ཕྱིན་པའི་སྙིང་པོའི་རྣམ་པར་བཤད་པ།

༄༅།རྒྱ་གར་སྐད་དུ། ཨཱརྱ་པྲཛྙཱ་པཱ་ར་མི་ཏཱ་ཧྲི་ད་ཡ་ཊཱི་ཀཱ།
བོད་སྐད་དུ། འཕགས་པ་ཤེས་རབ་ཀྱི་ཕ་རོལ་ཏུ་ཕྱིན་པའི་སྙིང་པོའི་རྣམ་པར་བཤད་པ།

བཅོམ་ལྡན་འདས་མ་ཤེས་རབ་ཀྱི་ཕ་རོལ་ཏུ་ཕྱིན་པ་ལ་ཕྱག་འཚལ་ལོ། །

དེ་ལ་[1]བཅོམ་ལྡན་འདས་མ་ཤེས་རབ་ཀྱི་ཕ་རོལ་ཏུ་ཕྱིན་པའི་སྙིང་པོའོ་ཞེས་བྱ་བ་ནི་མདོའི་མཚན་ཉིད་བརྗོད་པས་ན་བཅོམ་ལྡན་འདས་མ་ཤེས་རབ་ཀྱི་ཕ་རོལ་ཏུ་ཕྱིན་པའི་སྙིང་པོ་ཞེས་བྱའོ། །ཐོག་མ་ཁོ་ནར་མིང་མ་བཏགས་ན་མདོ་གང་ཡིན་གཏོལ་མེད་པའི་ཕྱིར་མིང་སྨོས་སོ། །མིང་བཏགས་པ་འབའ་ཞིག་ཏུ་མ་ཟད་ཀྱི།[2] ཤེས་རབ་ཀྱི་ཕ་རོལ་ཏུ་ཕྱིན་པའི་སྙིང་པོ་འདིའི་མདོ་ཐམས་ཅད་ཀུང་འདིར་མ་འདུས་པ་མེད་པས་མདོའི་ཡང་མདོ་ཞེས་བྱའོ།[3] །

[4]དེ་ལ་བཅོམ་ལྡན་ཞེས་བྱ་བ་ནི་[5]བདུད་བཅོམ་པ་སྟེ། ཕུང་པོའི་བདུད་ལ་སོགས་པ་[6]ཤེས་རབ་ཀྱི་ཕ་རོལ་ཏུ་ཕྱིན་པའི་དོན་འདིས་བདུད་བཙལ་དུ་མི་རྙེད་ཅིང་བདུད་ཐམས་ཅད་མི་གནས་པའི་ཕྱིར་བཅོམ་པའོ། །ལྡན་ཞེས་བྱ་བ་ནི་ལེགས་པ་དྲུག་དང་ལྡན་པ་སྟེ། མཁྱེན་པའི་ཡོན་དན་ཐམས་ཅད་ཀུང་ཤེས་རབ་ཀྱི་ཕ་རོལ་ཏུ་ཕྱིན་པའི་བྱིན་གྱི་བརླབས་ལས་བྱུང་བས་ན་ལྡན་པའོ། །འདས་ཞེས་བྱ་བ་ནི་མི་གནས་པའི་མྱ་ངན་ལས་འདས་པའོ། ཤེས་རབ་ཀྱི་ཕ་རོལ་ཏུ་ཕྱིན་པའི་དོན་གྱིས་སེམས་དང་ཡིད་དང་རྣམ་པར་ཤེས་པ་ཐམས་ཅད་བཟློག་སྟེ། བག་ཆགས་ཐམས་ཅད་དང་བྲལ་བས་ན་འདས་ཞེས་བྱའོ། །མ་ཞེས་བྱ་བ་ནི་དུས་གསུམ་གྱི་སངས་རྒྱས་ཐམས་ཅད་ཀུང་ཤེས་རབ་ཀྱི་ཕ་རོལ་ཏུ་ཕྱིན་པའི་དོན་སྒྲུད་པ་ལས་བྱུང་། ཤེས་རབ་ཀྱི་ཕ་རོལ་ཏུ་ཕྱིན་པའི་དོན་གྱིས་བསྐྱེད་པས་ན་ཤེས་རབ་ཀྱི་ཕ་རོལ་ཏུ་ཕྱིན་པ་ནི་སངས་རྒྱས་ཐམས་ཅད་ཀྱི་ཡུམ་དུ་གྱུར་པས་ན་མ་ཞེས་བྱའོ། །ཤེས་རབ་ཅེས་བྱ་བ་ནི་ཐོས་པ་དང་། བསམས་པ་དང་། བསྒོམས་པའི་ཤེས་རབ་རྣམ་པ་གསུམ་གྱིས་ཡང་དག་པར་ཇི་ལྟ་བ་བཞིན་དུ་ཤེས་པས་ན་ཤེས་རབ་ཅེས་བྱའོ། །ཕ་རོལ་ཏུ་ཕྱིན་པ་ཞེས་བྱ་བ་ནི་ཤེས་རབ་ཀྱིས་ཆོས་གང་ཡང་རྗེས་སུ་མ་མཐོང་བའི་ཕྱིར་མཚན་མ་དང་མཐའ་གཉིས་དང་སྐྱེ་ཤི་ལས་འདས་པའི་ཕྱིར་ཕ་རོལ་ཏུ་ཕྱིན་པ་ཞེས་བྱའོ། །སྙིང་པོ་ཞེས་བྱ་བ་ནི་ཤེས་རབ་ཀྱི་ཕ་རོལ་ཏུ་ཕྱིན་པ་སྟོང་ཕྲག་བརྒྱ་པ་[7]ལ་སོགས་པའི་ནང་ནས་ཟབ་མོ་མཆོག་ཐམས་ཅད་མདོ་ཉུང་ངུ་འདིའི་ནང་དུ་མ་

འདུས་པ་མེད་པས་ན་སྙིང་པོ་ཞེས་བྱའོ། །བཅོམ་ལྡན་འདས་མ་ཤེས་རབ་ཀྱི་ཕ་རོལ་ཏུ་ཕྱིན་པ་ལ་ཕྱག་འཚལ་ལོ་ཞེས་པ་ནི་ཤེས་རབ་ཀྱི་ཕ་རོལ་ཏུ་ཕྱིན་པ་འབུམ་པའི་མདོ་ལས་ཀྱང་ཤེས་རབ་ཀྱི་ཕ་རོལ་ཏུ་ཕྱིན་པ་ལ་ཕྱག་འཚལ་ན། དུས་གསུམ་གྱི་སངས་རྒྱས་ཐམས་ཅད་ལ་ཕྱག་འཚལ་བ་དང་འདྲའོ་ཞེས་འབྱུང་བའི་ཕྱིར་བསོད་ནམས་ཀྱི་ཚོགས་བསགས་པ་དང་། མཆོད་པའི་ཕྱིར་ཕྱག་འཚལ་བའོ། །

ད་ནི་གཞུང་སྟེ། ཤེས་རབ་ཀྱི་ཕ་རོལ་ཏུ་ཕྱིན་པ་འདི་ལ་མགོ་མཇུག་ཏུ་དོན་རྣམ་པ་བདུན་གྱིས་བསལ་བར་བཤད་དེ། དེ་ཡང་གང་ཞེ་ན།[8] གླེང་གཞི་དང་། ཤེས་རབ་ལ་འཇུག་པ་དང་། སྟོང་པ་ཉིད་ཀྱི་མཚན་ཉིད་དང་། ཤེས་རབ་ཀྱི་སྤྱོད་ཡུལ་དང་། ཤེས་རབ་ཀྱི་ཡོན་ཏན་དང་། ཤེས་རབ་ཀྱི་འབྲས་བུ་དང་། ཤེས་རབ་ཀྱི་གཟུངས་སོ། །དེ་ལ་གླེང་གཞི་ནི་འདི་སྐད་བདག་གིས་ཐོས་པ་ཞེས་བྱ་བ་ནས། ཐབས་ཅིག་ཏུ་བཞུགས་ཏེ་ཞེས་བྱ་བའི་བར་དུའོ། །ཤེས་རབ་ལ་འཇུག་པ་ནི་ཕུང་པོ་ལྔ་ཡང་རང་བཞིན་གྱིས་སྟོང་པར་བལྟའོ་ཞེས་བྱ་བའི་བར་དུའོ། །སྟོང་པ་ཉིད་ཀྱི་མཚན་ཉིད་ནི་ཐོབ་པ་ཡང་མ་ཡིན། མ་ཐོབ་པ་ཡང་མ་ཡིན་ཞེས་བྱ་བའི་བར་དུའོ། །ཤེས་རབ་ཀྱི་སྤྱོད་ཡུལ་ནི་ཐོབ་པ་མེད་པར་[9]ཤེས་རབ་ཀྱི་ཕ་རོལ་ཏུ་ཕྱིན་པ་ལ་གནས་ཤིང་སྤྱོད་དེ་ཞེས་བྱ་བའི་བར་དུའོ། །ཤེས་རབ་ཀྱི་ཡོན་ཏན་ནི་མྱ་ངན་ལས་འདས་པའི་མཐར་ཕྱིན་ཏོ་ཞེས་བྱ་བའི་བར་དུའོ། །ཤེས་རབ་ཀྱི་འབྲས་བུ་ནི་བྱང་ཆུབ་ཏུ་མངོན་པར་རྫོགས་པར་སངས་རྒྱས་སོ་ཞེས་བྱ་བའི་བར་དུའོ། །ཤེས་རབ་ཀྱི་གཟུངས་ནི་མཇུག་གི་སྔགས་ཡན་ཆད་དོ། །

ད་ནི་གླེང་གཞིའི་དོན་བཤད་དེ།[10] འདི་སྐད་བདག་གིས་ཐོས་པ་ཞེས་བྱ་བ་ནི་ཐེག་པ་ཆེན་པོའི་མདོ་སྡེ་ཐམས་ཅད་འཕགས་པ་འཇམ་དཔལ་གྱིས་གསན་ཏེ། བསྡུས་པས་ན་བདག་གིས་ཐོས་པ་ཞེས་བྱའོ། །དེ་ལ་འདི་སྐད་ཅེས་བྱ་བ་ནི་ཤེས་རབ་ཀྱི་སྙིང་པོའི་རྣམ་གྲངས་ཇི་སྙེད་བརྗོད་པ་ཉིད་དོ། །བདག་གིས་ཐོས་པ་ཞེས་བྱ་བ་ནི་བཅོམ་ལྡན་འདས་ཀྱི་ཞབས་དྲུང་ནས་མཉན་ཏེ། དཔལ་གྱི་མགུར་ནས་གསུངས་པ་མངོན་སུམ་དུ་རྣ་བའི་དབང་པོས་ཐོས་པའོ། །དུས་གཅིག་ན་ཞེས་བྱ་བ་ནི་ཤེས་རབ་ཀྱི་སྙིང་པོ་དུས་གཞན་བཤད་པ་ལ་མི་བྱའི།[11] །བཅོམ་ལྡན་འདས་ཀྱིས་རྒྱལ་པོའི་ཁབ་ན་འཁོར་འདི་རྣམས་ལ་ལན་གཅིག་ཁོ་ན་ཞིག་བཤད་པའི་དུས་ལ་བྱའོ། །

བཅོམ་ལྡན་འདས་ཞེས་བྱ་བ་ནི་དེ་ལ་སྟོན་པ་[12]ནི་སུ་ཞིག་ཡིན། ཡུལ་ནི་གང་ཞིག་ཡིན། འཁོར་ནི་གང་གང་ཡིན། འདུས་ནས་དོན་ཅི་ཞིག་མཛད་དེ། སྟོན་པ་ནི་སངས་རྒྱས་བཅོམ་ལྡན་འདས། ཡུལ་ནི་རྒྱལ་པོའི་ཁབ་ཀྱི་བྱ་རྒོད་ཕུང་པོའི་རིའོ། འཁོར་ནི་དགེ་སློང་གི་དགེ་འདུན་ཆེན་པོ་དང་། བྱང་ཆུབ་སེམས་དཔའ་སེམས་དཔའ་ཆེན་པོ་རྣམས་སོ། །འདུས་ནས་དོན་ཅི་ཞིག་མཛད་ཅེ་ན། ཤེས་རབ་ཀྱི་ཕ་རོལ་ཏུ་ཕྱིན་པའི་སྙིང་པོ་འདི་སྟོན་ཏོ། །དེ་ལ་

ཚིག་གཉེར་བཤད་པ་ནི་གོང་མ་དང་འདྲ། རྒྱལ་པོའི་ཁབ་བྱ་རྒོད་ཀྱི་ཕུང་པོའི་རི་ལ་ཞེས་བྱ་བ་ནི་རྒྱལ་པོ་གཟུགས་ཅན་སྙིང་པོའི་ཡོན་དན་ལས་གྲགས་ཏེ།[13] ཡུལ་ལྗོངས་ཀྱི་གྲོང་ཁྱེར་སྤྱིའི་མིང་དུ་བཏགས་པའོ། །

བྱ་རྒོད་ཀྱི་ཕུང་པོའི་རི་ཞེས་བྱ་བ་ནི་ཡུལ་ལྗོངས་དེ་ཀྱ་ཆེ་བས་བྱ་རྒོད་ཕུང་པོའི་རི་སྤེ་མཐོ་ལ་བྱ་མང་པོ་འདུ་བའི་ཕྱིར་མིང་དུ་བཏགས་པའོ། །དགེ་སློང་གི་དགེ་འདུན་ཆེན་པོ་ཞེས་བྱ་བ་ནི་མཐུ་ཆེ་བ་དང་གྲངས་མང་བའོ། །བྱང་ཆུབ་སེམས་དཔའི་དགེ་འདུན་ཆེན་པོ་ཞེས་པ་ནི་ཐམས་ཅད་ཀྱང་ཤེས་རབ་ཀྱི་ཕ་རོལ་ཏུ་ཕྱིན་པའི་དོན་ཕུན་སུམ་ཚོགས་པ་མངོན་སུམ་དུ་ཆུད་ཅིང་གཞན་ཡང་ཤེས་རབ་ཀྱི་ཕ་རོལ་ཏུ་ཕྱིན་པ་ལ་འཇོག་པའི་བྱང་ཆུབ་སེམས་དཔའ་མང་པོའོ། །ཐབས་གཅིག་ཏུ་བཞུགས་ཏེ་ཞེས་བྱ་བ་ནི་བཅོམ་ལྡན་འདས་འཁོར་མང་པོས་བསྐོར་ཏེ་བཞུགས་པའོ། །འདི་ཡན་ཆད་ནི་གླེང་གཞིའོ། །

ད་ནི་ཤེས་རབ་ལ་འཇུག་པའི་དོན་གྱིས་བཤད་དེ། དེའི་ཚེ་བཅོམ་ལྡན་འདས་ཆོས་ཀྱི་རྣམ་གྲངས་ཟབ་མོ་སྣང་བ་ཞེས་བྱ་བའི་ཏིང་ངེ་འཛིན་ལ་སྙོམས་པར་ཞུགས་སོ་ཞེས་བྱ་བ་ནི། དེ་ལ་བཅོམ་ལྡན་འདས་འཁོར་དེ་དག་དང་། སེམས་ཅན་ཐམས་ཅད་ལ་ཐུགས་བརྩེ་ཞིང་བྱིན་གྱིས་བརླབ་པའི་ཕྱིར་སྙོམས་པར་ཞུགས་པའོ། །དེ་ལ་ཆོས་ཀྱི་རྣམ་གྲངས་ཟབ་མོ་སྣང་བ་ཞེས་བྱ་བ་ནི་ཆོས་ཀྱི་གཞུང་འདིས་ཆོས་ཐམས་ཅད་དམིགས་པ་དང་མཐའ་ཐམས་ཅད་ལས་འདས་པར་སྟོན་ཅིང་མཁྱེན་པའི་ཕྱིར་ཟབ་མོ་སྣང་བ་ཞེས་བྱའོ། །ཏིང་ངེ་འཛིན་ལ་སྙོམས་པར་ཞུགས་ཞེས་བྱ་བ་ནི་ཟབ་མོ་དེ་ཉིད་ལ་མཉམ་པར་གཞག་པའོ། །

ཡང་དེའི་ཚེ་བྱང་ཆུབ་སེམས་དཔའ་སེམས་དཔའ་ཆེན་པོ་འཕགས་པ་སྤྱན་རས་གཟིགས་ཀྱི་དབང་པོ་ཤེས་རབ་ཀྱི་ཕ་རོལ་ཏུ་ཕྱིན་པ་ཟབ་མོ་སྤྱོད་པ་འདི་ཉིད་ལ་རྣམ་པར་རྟོག་ཅིང་། ཕུང་པོ་ལྔ་པོ་དེ་དག་ཉིད་ལ་ཡང་རང་བཞིན་གྱིས་སྟོང་པར་ལྟའོ་ཞེས་པ་ལ། ཡང་དེའི་ཚེ་ཞེས་པ་ནི་འཁོར་འདུས་པ་དང་སྙོམས་པར་ཞུགས་པའི་དུས་ནའོ།[14] །

སྤྱན་རས་གཟིགས་ཀྱི་དབང་པོ་རང་བཞིན་གྱིས་སྟོང་པར་ལྟའོ་ཞེས་པའི་བར་དུ་ནི་འཕགས་པ་སྤྱན་རས་གཟིགས་ཀྱི་དབང་པོ་འཁོར་དེ་རྣམས་དང་། སེམས་ཅན་ཐམས་ཅད་ལ་ཐུགས་བརྩེ་བའི་ཕྱིར་ཤེས་རབ་ཀྱི་ཕ་རོལ་ཏུ་ཕྱིན་པ་ཟབ་མོ་ཉིད་ལ་རྣམ་པར་རྟོག་ཅིང་ཕུང་པོ་ལྔ་པོ་དེ་དག་ཀྱང་མི་དམིགས་པའི་རང་བཞིན་གྱི་སྟོང་པ་སྟོང་པ་ཉིད་ལས་གཞན་དུ་གྱུར་པ་གང་ཡང་མེད་དོ་ཞེས་བྱ་བར་དགོངས་པའོ།[15] །ཕུང་པོ་ལྔ་ཞེས་བྱ་བ་ནི་གཟུགས་ཀྱི་ཕུང་པོ་ནི་དབུ་བའི་གོང་བུ་ལྟ་བུའོ། །ཚོར་བ་ནི་ཆུ་བུར་ལྟ་བུའོ། །འདུ་ཤེས་ནི་སྨིག་རྒྱུ་ལྟ་བུའོ། །འདུ་བྱེད་ནི་ཆུ་ཤིང་ལྟ་བུའོ། །རྣམ་པར་ཤེས་པ་ནི་སྒྱུ་མ་ལྟ་བུའོ། །རང་བཞིན་གྱིས་སྟོང་པ་ཞེས་པ་ནི་ཕུང་པོ་ལྔ་པོ་དེ་དག་རང་གི་རང་བཞིན་གྱི་

མཚན་ཉིད་ཀྱིས་སྟོང་པ་ཉིད་དེ། མཐའ་ཐམས་ཅད་ལས་འདས་ཤིང་མཚན་ཉིད་མེད་པའི་ཕྱིར་སྟོང་པ་ཉིད་དོ། །

དེ་ནས་ཚེ་དང་ལྡན་པ་ཤཱ་རིའི་བུས་སངས་རྒྱས་ཀྱི་མཐུས་བྱང་ཆུབ་སེམས་དཔའ་སེམས་དཔའ་ཆེན་པོ་འཕགས་པ་སྤྱན་རས་གཟིགས་ཀྱི་དབང་པོ་ལ་འདི་སྐད་ཅེས་སྨྲས་སོ་ཞེས་པ་ནི་ཉན་ཐོས་ཆེན་པོའི་ནང་ན་ཤེས་རབ་ཀྱི་མཆོག་ཏུ་གྱུར་པའི་ཤཱ་རིའི་བུས་དེ་བཞིན་གཤེགས་པའི་བྱིན་གྱི་རླབས་ཀྱིས་འཕགས་པ་སྤྱན་རས་གཟིགས་ཀྱི་དབང་པོ་ལ་དྲིས་པའོ།[16] །རིགས་ཀྱི་བུ་གང་ལ་ལ་ཤེས་རབ་ཀྱི་ཕ་རོལ་ཏུ་ཕྱིན་པ་ཟབ་མོ་སྤྱོད་པ་སྤྱད་པར་འདོད་པ་དེས་ཇི་ལྟར་བསླབ་པར་བྱ་ཞེས་བྱ་བ་ལ། རིགས་ཀྱི་བུ་ཞེས་བྱ་བ་ནི་ཐེག་པ་ཆེན་པོའི་གསུང་རབ་ལས་སྐྱེས་ཏེ། དེ་བཞིན་གཤེགས་པའི་སྲས་སུ་གྱུར་པའོ། །གང་ལ་ལ་ཞེས་པ་ནི་ཐེག་པ་ཆེན་པོ་ལ་ཞུགས་པ་གང་སུ་ཡང་རུང་བའོ། །ཤེས་རབ་ཀྱི་ཕ་རོལ་ཏུ་ཕྱིན་པ་ལ་སྤྱོད་པ་ཞེས་བྱ་བ་ནི་ཤེས་རབ་ཀྱི་ཕ་རོལ་ཏུ་ཕྱིན་པ་སྤྱོད་པས་ཆོས་ཐམས་ཅད་ཀྱི་དེ་བཞིན་ཉིད་ཟབ་མོ་བརྗོད་དུ་མེད་པར་སྤྱོད་པའོ། །སྤྱད་པར་འདོད་པ་དེས་ཇི་ལྟར་བསླབ་པར་བྱ་ཞེས་པ་ནི་ཤེས་རབ་ཀྱི་ཕ་རོལ་ཏུ་ཕྱིན་པའི་དོན་སྤྱད་པར་འདོད་པ་དེས་ཇི་ལྟ་བུ་ཞིག་ཏུ་ཤེས་པར་བྱ་ཞིང་བསླབ་པར་བྱ་ཞེས་དྲིས་པའོ། །

དེ་སྐད་ཅེས་སྨྲས་པ་དང་། བྱང་ཆུབ་སེམས་དཔའ་སེམས་དཔའ་ཆེན་པོ་འཕགས་པ་སྤྱན་རས་གཟིགས་ཀྱི་དབང་པོས་ཚེ་དང་ལྡན་པ་ཤཱ་རིའི་བུ་ལ་འདི་སྐད་ཅེས་སྨྲས་སོ་ཞེས་པ་ནི་དྲིས་པའི་ལན་སྨྲས་པའོ། །ཤཱ་རིའི་བུ་རིགས་ཀྱི་བུའམ་རིགས་ཀྱི་བུ་མོ་གང་ལ་ལ་ཤེས་རབ་ཀྱི་ཕ་རོལ་ཏུ་ཕྱིན་པ་ཟབ་མོ་སྤྱད་པ་སྤྱོད་པར་འདོད་པ་དེས་འདི་ལྟར་བརྟག་པར་བྱ་སྟེ་ཞེས་པ་ནི། ཤེས་རབ་ཀྱི་ཕ་རོལ་ཏུ་ཕྱིན་པ་ལ་སྤྱད་པར་འདོད་པ་དེས་འོག་ཏུ་བཤད་པའི་དོན་བཞིན་དུ་བརྟག་པར་བྱའོ་ཞེས་པའོ། །

ཕུང་པོ་ལྔ་པོ་དེ་དག་ཀྱང་རང་བཞིན་གྱིས་སྟོང་པར་ཡང་དག་པར་རྗེས་སུ་བལྟའོ་ཞེས་པ་ནི་ཕུང་པོ་ལྔ་པོ་དེ་དག་ནི་རང་བཞིན་གྱིས་སྟོང་པ་ཉིད་དེ། །མཚན་ཉིད་མེད་པས་སྔོན་གྱི་དུས་ནས་མ་སྐྱེས། ད་ལྟར་གྱི་དུས་ན་མི་གནས། མ་འོངས་པའི་དུས་ན་མི་འགག་སྟེ། དུས་ཐམས་ཅད་དུ་སྐྱེ་བ་དང་། གནས་པ་དང་། འགག་པར་མ་གྱུར་པས་མི་གནས་པའི་རང་བཞིན་བརྗོད་དུ་མེད་པས་ན་སྟོང་པ་ཉིད་དོ། །བལྟའོ་ཞེས་པ་ནི་ཡང་དག་པ་ཇི་ལྟ་བུ་བཞིན་དུ་བལྟའོ། དེ་ལས་གཞན་པ་གང་དུ་ཡང་མི་བལྟའོ་ཞེས་པའོ། །འདི་ཡན་ཆད་ནི་ཤེས་རབ་ལ་འཇུག་པའོ། །

ད་ནི་སྟོང་པ་ཉིད་ཀྱི་མཚན་ཉིད་ཀྱི་དོན་གྱིས་བཤད་དེ། གཟུགས་སྟོང་པའོ། །སྟོང་པ་ཉིད་ཀྱང་གཟུགས་སོ་ཞེས་པ་ལ། དེ་ལ་གཟུགས་སོ་ཞེས་པ་ནི་སྟོང་པ་ཉིད་ཀྱི་རང་བཞིན་ཁོང་དུ་མ་ཆུད་པས་འཁྲུལ་པའི་སེམས་ཀྱིས་གཟུགས་སོ་མཐོང་ཞིང་རྟོག་པའམ། ཚིག་གིས་ཐ་སྙད་དུ་འདོགས་པའོ། །སྟོང་པའོ་ཞེས་བྱ་བ་ནི་གཟུགས་ཀྱི་རང་

བཞིན་སྟོང་པ་ཉིད་ཡིན་པས་སྔ་མ་འདས་པའི་དུས་ན་ཡང་མཚན་ཉིད་མེད་པས་དམིགས་སུ་མེད།[17] ད་ལྟར་དང་མ་འོངས་པའི་དུས་ན་ཡང་མཚན་ཉིད་མེད་དེ། དམིགས་སུ་མེད་པས་མཐའ་ཐམས་ཅད་དང་དངོས་པོ་ཐམས་ཅད་མི་གནས་པའི་ཕྱིར་སྟོང་པ་ཉིད་ཅེས་བྱའོ། །སྟོང་པ་ཉིད་ཀྱང་གཟུགས་སོ་ཞེས་བྱ་བ་ནི་སྟོང་པ་ཉིད་ཀྱང་དམིགས་སུ་མེད་པའི་རང་བཞིན་ལ་གཟུགས་སོ་ཞེས་ཚིག་གི་ཐ་སྙད་དུ་བཏགས་ལ།[18] དེ་ཀྱུད་ན་མི་གནས་པའི་ཕྱིར་སྟོང་པ་ཉིད་ཀྱང་གཟུགས་སོ། །

གཟུགས་ལས་སྟོང་པ་ཉིད་གཞན་མ་ཡིན། སྟོང་པ་ཉིད་ལས་ཀྱང་གཟུགས་གཞན་མ་ཡིན་ནོ་ཞེས་པ་ནི་གཟུགས་གང་ཡིན་པ་དེ་ཉིད་བརྗོད་དུ་མེད་པའི་སྟོང་པ་ཉིད་ཡིན་གྱི།[19] གཟུགས་སྤངས་ཏེ་སྟོང་པ་ཉིད་བཙལ་དུ་མི་རྙེད་པས་ན་གཟུགས་ལས་སྟོང་པ་ཉིད་གཞན་མ་ཡིན་ཞེས་བྱའོ། །བརྗོད་དུ་མེད་པའི་སྟོང་པ་ཉིད་གང་ཡིན་པ་དེ་ཉིད་ལ་གཟུགས་སོ་ཞེས་ཚིག་གི་ཐ་སྙད་དུ་བཏགས་པ་ཀྱུད་ན་མི་འདུག་ཅིང་མི་རྙེད་པའི་ཕྱིར་སྟོང་པ་ཉིད་ལས་ཀྱང་གཟུགས་གཞན་མ་ཡིན་ཞེས་བྱའོ། །དེ་བཞིན་དུ་ཚོར་བ་དང་། འདུ་ཤེས་དང་། འདུ་བྱེད་དང་། རྣམ་པར་ཤེས་པ་རྣམས་སྟོང་པའོ་ཞེས་པ་ནི་གཟུགས་ལ་ཇི་ལྟར་བཤད་པ་བཞིན་དུ་ཕུང་པོ་ལྷག་མ་རྣམས་ཀྱང་དེ་དང་འདྲ་བར་བལྟའོ། །ཤཱ་རིའི་བུ་དེ་བཞིན་དུ་ཆོས་ཐམས་ཅད་ཀྱང་སྟོང་པ་ཉིད་དེ་ཞེས་བྱ་བ་ལ། ཤཱ་རིའི་བུ་ཞེས་པ་ནི་མ་ཡིངས་པར་ལེགས་པར་ཉོན་ཅིག་ཅེས་བོད་པའི་ཚིག་གོ།[20] །

དེ་བཞིན་དུ་ཆོས་ཐམས་ཅད་སྟོང་པ་ནི་ཕུང་པོ་ལྔ་ལ་ཇི་ལྟར་བཤད་པ་ལྟར་གཞན་ཡང་སྐྱེ་མཆེད་དྲུག་ནས། རྣམ་པ་ཐམས་ཅད་མཁྱེན་པའི་བར་དུ་འཇིག་རྟེན་ལས་འདས་པའི་ཆོས་ཐམས་ཅད་ཀྱང་སྟོང་པ་ཉིད་དུ་ཤེས་པར་གྱིས་ཤིག་པའོ།[21] །མཚན་ཉིད་མེད་པ་ཞེས་པ་ནི་ནམ་མཁའ་ལ་མཚན་ཉིད་མེད་པ་ལྟར་ཉོན་མོངས་པའི་མཚན་ཉིད་ཀྱང་མེད་རྣམ་པར་བྱང་བའི་མཚན་ཉིད་ཀྱང་མེད་པའོ། །མི་སྐྱེ་མི་འགག་པ་ཞེས་པ་ནི་ད་ལྟར་སྐྱེས་པ་ནི་སྔོན་མེད་པ་ལས་ཕྱིས་ཡོད་པར་གྱུར་པའོ།[22] །འགག་པ་ནི་སྔོན་ཡོད་པ་ལས་ཕྱིས་མེད་པར་གྱུར་པའོ། །སྟོང་པ་ཉིད་ནི་དམིགས་སུ་མེད་པས་སྔོན་ནས་མ་སྐྱེས་པའོ། །མ་སྐྱེས་པས་ན་ཕྱིས་མི་འགག་པའོ། །

དྲི་མ་མེད་པ་དང་། དྲི་མ་དང་བྲལ་བ་མེད་པ་ཞེས་བྱ་བ་ལ། དྲི་མ་ཞེས་བྱ་བ་ནི་རྣམ་པར་ཤེས་པ་རྣམས་ཀྱིས་གཟུང་འཛིན་[23]དུ་སྤྱོད་པའོ། །སྟོང་པ་ཉིད་ནི་རྣམ་པར་ཤེས་པ་ལས་འདས་པས་དྲི་མ་མེད་པའོ། །དྲི་མ་དང་བྲལ་བ་མེད་པ་ནི་དྲི་མ་མེད་པས་བྲལ་བ་ཡང་མེད་པའོ། །བྲི་བ་མེད་པ་གང་བ་མེད་པའོ་ཞེས་བྱ་བ་ལ། བྲི་བ་ཞེས་བྱ་བ་ནི་སེམས་ཅན་ནོ། །གང་བ་ཞེས་བྱ་བ་ནི་སངས་རྒྱས་སོ། །མེད་པ་ཞེས་བྱ་བ་ནི་སེམས་ཅན་དང་སངས་རྒྱས་བཙལ་དུ་ཡང་མི་

སྙེད་པས་བྲི་བ་དང་གང་བ་མེད་པའོ། །

དེ་ལྟར་ན་སྟོང་པ་ཉིད་ནི་གཟུགས་མ་ཡིན་ཞེས་བྱ་བ་ལ། གཟུགས་ནི་གཞིག་པར་བྱ་བའི་[24]མཚན་ཉིད་ཡིན་གྱི། སྟོང་པ་ཉིད་ལ་མཚན་ཉིད་མེད་པའི་ཕྱིར་སྟོང་པ་ཉིད་ནི་གཟུགས་མ་ཡིན་ནོ། །ཚོར་བ་མ་ཡིན། དེ་བཞིན་དུ་ཚོར་བ་ནི་མྱོང་བའི་མཚན་ཉིད། འདུ་ཤེས་མ་ཡིན། འདུ་ཤེས་ནི་འཛིན་པའི་མཚན་ཉིད། འདུ་བྱེད་མ་ཡིན། འདུ་བྱེད་ནི་མངོན་པར་འདུ་བྱེད་པའི་མཚན་ཉིད། རྣམ་པར་ཤེས་པ་མ་ཡིན། རྣམ་པར་ཤེས་པ་ནི་སོ་སོར་བྱེ་བྲག་འཛིན་པའི་མཚན་ཉིད་ཡིན་གྱི། སྟོང་པ་ཉིད་ནི་དམིགས་སུ་མེད་པས་རྣམ་པར་ཤེས་པ་རྣམས་མ་ཡིན་ནོ། །རྣམས་མ་ཡིན་ཞེས་པ་ནི་ཕུང་པོ་ལྔ་རྣམས་ནི་ཟག་པ་དང་བཅས་པའི་མཚན་ཉིད་ཡིན་གྱི། སྟོང་པ་ཉིད་ནི་ཕུང་པོ་ལྔ་རྣམས་མ་ཡིན་ནོ། །

མིག་མ་ཡིན། དེ་ལ་མིག་ནི་མཐོང་བའི་མཚན་ཉིད་ཡིན་གྱི། སྟོང་པ་ཉིད་ལ་མཚན་ཉིད་མེད་པས་སྟོང་པ་ཉིད་མིག་མ་ཡིན་ནོ། །རྣ་བ་མ་ཡིན། དེ་བཞིན་དུ་རྣ་བ་ནི་ཐོས་པའི་མཚན་ཉིད་དོ།[25] །སྣ་མ་ཡིན། སྣ་ནི་སྣོམ་པའི་མཚན་ཉིད། ལྕེ་མ་ཡིན། ལྕེ་ནི་རོ་མྱང་བའི་མཚན་ཉིད། ལུས་མ་ཡིན། ལུས་ནི་རེག་པའི་མཚན་ཉིད། ཡིད་མ་ཡིན། ཡིད་ནི་བྱེ་བྲག་གཅོད་པའི་བདག་ཉིད་ཡིན་གྱི། སྟོང་པ་ཉིད་ནི་མཚན་ཉིད་མེད་པས་ཡིད་མ་ཡིན་ནོ། །དེ་ལྟར་དབང་པོ་དྲུག་པོ་ནི་འཛིན་པའི་མཚན་ཉིད་ཡིན་གྱི། སྟོང་པ་ཉིད་ནི་མཚན་ཉིད་མེད་པས་དབང་པོ་དྲུག་རྣམས་མ་ཡིན་ནོ། །

གཟུགས་མ་ཡིན། གཟུགས་ནི་ཁ་དོག་དང་དབྱིབས་ཀྱི་མཚན་ཉིད་ཡིན་གྱི། སྟོང་པ་ཉིད་ནི་མཚན་ཉིད་མེད་པས་གཟུགས་མ་ཡིན་ནོ། །སྒྲ་མ་ཡིན། དེ་བཞིན་དུ་སྒྲ་ནི་སྙན་མི་སྙན་[26]གྱི་མཚན་ཉིད། དྲི་མ་ཡིན། དྲི་ནི་སྣོམ་པའི་མཚན་ཉིད། རོ་མ་ཡིན། རོ་ནི་བྲོ་བའི་མཚན་ཉིད། རེག་བྱ་མ་ཡིན། རེག་བྱ་ནི་རེག་པ་འཇམ་རྩུབ་ཀྱི་མཚན་ཉིད། ཆོས་མ་ཡིན། ཆོས་ནི་བྱེ་བྲག་གི་རྣམ་པའི་མཚན་ཉིད་ཡིན་གྱི།[27] སྟོང་པ་ཉིད་ནི་མཚན་ཉིད་མེད་པས་ཆོས་མ་ཡིན་ནོ། །དེ་ལྟར་ན་ཡུལ་རྣམས་ནི་དམིགས་པར་བྱེད་པའི་རྐྱེན་གྱི་མཚན་ཉིད་ཡིན་གྱི། སྟོང་པ་ཉིད་མཚན་ཉིད་མེད་པས་ཡུལ་རྣམས་མ་ཡིན་ནོ། །

མིག་གི་ཁམས་མ་ཡིན་པ་ནས། ཡིད་ཀྱི་ཁམས་མ་ཡིན། ཡིད་ཀྱི་རྣམ་པར་ཤེས་པའི་ཁམས་ཀྱི་བར་དུ་ཡང་མ་ཡིན་ནོ། །དེ་ལ་ཁམས་བཅོ་བརྒྱད་ནི་གདུག་པའི་མཚན་ཉིད་ཡིན་གྱི། སྟོང་པ་ཉིད་ནི་མཚན་ཉིད་མེད་པས་ཁམས་བཅོ་བརྒྱད་མ་ཡིན་ནོ། །མ་རིག་པ་མ་ཡིན་པ་ནས་རྒ་ཤི་མ་ཡིན། མ་རིག་པ་ཟད་པ་མ་ཡིན་པ་ནས་རྒ་

ཤི་ཟད་པའི་བར་དུ་མ་ཡིན་ནོ། །མ་རིག་པ་ནས་རྒ་ཤིའི་བར་དུ་རྟེན་འབྲེལ་བཅུ་གཉིས་ནི་འཁོར་བ་འཛིན་པའི་མཚན་ཉིད་ཡིན་གྱི། སྟོང་པ་ཉིད་ནི་མཚན་ཉིད་མ་ཡིན་པས་མ་རིག་པ་ནས་རྒ་ཤིའི་བར་དུ་མ་ཡིན་ནོ། །མ་རིག་པ་ཟད་པ་ནས། རྒ་ཤི་ཟད་པའི་བར་དུ་རྣམ་པར་བྱང་བའི་མཚན་ཉིད་ཡིན་གྱི། སྟོང་པ་ཉིད་ནི་མཚན་ཉིད་མེད་པས་མ་རིག་པ་ཟད་པ་ནས་རྒ་ཤི་ཟད་པའི་བར་དུ་མ་ཡིན་ནོ། །

སྡུག་བསྔལ་བ་དང་། ཀུན་འབྱུང་བ་དང་། འགོག་པ་དང་ལམ་ཡང་མ་ཡིན་ནོ། །སྡུག་བསྔལ་ནི་ཉོན་མོངས་པའི་མཚན་ཉིད། ཀུན་འབྱུང་བ་ནི་ཉེ་བར་ལེན་པའི་མཚན་ཉིད། འགོག་པ་ནི་ཞི་བའི་མཚན་ཉིད། ལམ་ནི་ཤེས་པའི་མཚན་ཉིད་ཡིན་གྱི། སྟོང་པ་ཉིད་ལ་མཚན་ཉིད་མེད་པའི་ཕྱིར་སྟོང་པ་ཉིད་བདེན་པ་བཞི་མ་ཡིན་ནོ། །

ཡེ་ཤེས་མ་ཡིན། ཡེ་ཤེས་ནི་ཆོས་ཐམས་ཅད་མངོན་སུམ་དུ་གྱུར་པའི་མཚན་ཉིད་ཡིན་གྱི། སྟོང་པ་ཉིད་ལ་མཚན་ཉིད་མེད་པས་ཡེ་ཤེས་མ་ཡིན་ནོ། །ཐོབ་པ་མ་ཡིན། མ་ཐོབ་པ་ཡང་མ་ཡིན་ནོ། །ཐོབ་པ་ནི་བླ་ན་མེད་པ་ཡང་དག་པར་རྫོགས་པའི་བྱང་ཆུབ་བོ། །མ་ཐོབ་པ་ནི་སེམས་ཅན་གྱིས་བླ་ན་མེད་པ་མ་ཐོབ་པའོ། །མ་ཡིན་ནོ་ཞེས་པ་ནི་སྟོང་པ་ཉིད་ཀྱི་མཚན་ཉིད་ལ་བླ་ན་མེད་པའི་བྱང་ཆུབ་ཀྱང་མེད། སེམས་ཅན་ཡང་མེད་པས་ཐོབ་པ་ཡང་མ་ཡིན། མ་ཐོབ་པ་ཡང་མ་ཡིན་ནོ། །རྣམ་གྲངས་དེས་ན་ཆོས་ཐམས་ཅད་ནི་རང་བཞིན་གྱིས་སྟོང་པ་ཉིད་དེ། སྟོང་པ་ཉིད་ནི་དེ་ལྟ་བུ་ཡིན་ནོ་ཞེས་བསྟན་པའི་ཕྱིར་རོ། །འདི་ཡན་ཆད་ནི་སྟོང་ཉིད་ཀྱི་མཚན་ཉིད་དོ།

ད་ནི་ཤེས་རབ་ཀྱི་སྤྱོད་ཡུལ་གྱི་དོན་གྱིས་བཤད་དེ། ཤཱ་རིའི་བུ་དེ་ལྟར་བྱང་ཆུབ་སེམས་དཔའ་ཐོབ་པ་མེད་པར་ཤེས་རབ་ཀྱི་ཕ་རོལ་ཏུ་ཕྱིན་པ་ལ་གནས་ཤིང་སྤྱོད་དེ་ཞེས་པ་ལ། མ་ཆུད་པ་ལ་ཆུད་དོ་སྙམ་པ་[28]འབྱུང་བའི་ཕྱིར་ཤེས་རབ་ཀྱི་ཕ་རོལ་ཏུ་ཕྱིན་པའི་སྤྱོད་ཡུལ་འདི་ཙམ་ཞིག་དང་ལྡན་ན་སྟོང་པ་ཉིད་དུ་སྤྱོད་པའི་མཚན་མར་བཤད་པ་[29]དེ་ལྟར་ཞེས་པ་ནི་ཆོས་ཐམས་ཅད་སྟོང་པ་ཉིད་དུ་གྱུར་པའི་ཕྱིར་རོ། །བྱང་ཆུབ་སེམས་དཔའ་རྣམས་ཐོབ་པ་མེད་པར་ཤེས་རབ་ཀྱི་ཕ་རོལ་ཏུ་ཕྱིན་པ་ལ་སྤྱོད་ཅེས་པ་ནི་ཐེག་པ་ཆེན་པོ་ལ་ཞུགས་པའི་བྱང་ཆུབ་སེམས་དཔའ་རྣམས་ཀྱིས་ཕུང་པོ་ལྔ་ནས་ཐམས་ཅད་མཁྱེན་པའི་བར་དུ་ཅི་ཡང་ཐོབ་པ་མེད་པར་ཤེས་ཤིང་ཆོས་གང་ཡང་རྡུལ་ཙམ་རྗེས་སུ་མི་མཐོང་བར་ཤེས་རབ་ཀྱི་ཕ་རོལ་ཏུ་ཕྱིན་པ་ལ་སྤྱོད་པར་བྱའོ། །

ཆོས་ཐམས་ཅད་སྟོང་པ་སྟེ། མི་གནས་པའི་རང་བཞིན་ཡིན་ཡང་དེ་ལྟར་མི་ཤེས་པའི་མ་རིག་པའི་འཁྲུལ་པའི་སེམས་ཀྱིས་མུན་པར་གྱུར་པས་[30]སྲིད་པའི་རྒྱ་མཚོར་འཁོར་ཞིང་འཁྱམ་མོ། །འཁྲུལ་པའི་སེམས་དེ་ཉིད་ཅི་ཡིན་ཞེས་ཤེས་རབ་རྣམ་གསུམ་གྱིས་བརྟགས་ན། སེམས་ནི་དམིགས་སུ་མེད་པས་ཉོན་མོངས་པ་ཡང་མི་མཐོང་།

རྣམ་པར་བྱང་བར་ཡང་མི་མཐོང་། ཕུང་པོ་ལྔ་ནས་རྣམ་པ་ཐམས་ཅད་མཁྱེན་པའི་བར་དུ་ཡང་མི་མཐོང་ངོ་། །སྟོང་པ་ཉིད་དང་། མཚན་ཉིད་མེད་པ་དང་། མི་སྐྱེ་བ་དང་། མི་འགག་པ་ལ་སོགས་པ་ཡང་མི་མཐོང་། ཤེས་རབ་ཉིད་ཀྱང་ཡང་དག་པར་རྗེས་སུ་མི་མཐོང་། ཅི་ཡང་མཐོང་བ་མེད་པ་དེ་ནི་སེམས་ཀྱི་ངོ་བོ་ཉིད་མཐོང་བའོ། །དེ་ལྟར་སེམས་ཀྱི་ངོ་བོ་ཉིད་མཐོང་བ་དེ་ནི་བྱང་ཆུབ་མཐོང་བའོ། །གང་བྱང་ཆུབ་མཐོང་བ་དེ་ནི་ཆོས་ཉིད་ཀྱིས་སངས་རྒྱས་མཐོང་བའོ། །ཆོས་ཉིད་ཀྱིས་སངས་རྒྱས་མཐོང་བ་དེ་ནི་བདག་ཉིད་བླ་ན་མེད་པའི་བྱང་ཆུབ་ཏུ་མངོན་པར་རྫོགས་པར་སངས་རྒྱས་སོ། །

སྐབས་འདིར་ནི་ཐེ་ཚོམ་པས་སྨྲས་པ། དེ་ལྟར་ཅི་ཡང་མེད་པ་ཤ་སྟག་ཏུ་བཤད་པས་སྤྱི་སྡེགས་ཅན་ཆད་པར་ལྟ་བ་དང་། ཉན་ཐོས་ཞི་བའི་འགོག་པའི་ནང་དུ་ལྟུང་བར་མི་འགྱུར[31]རམ་ཞེ་ན། ལན་དུ་སྨྲས་པ། དེ་ལྟར་མི་འགྱུར་དེ་མི་དམིགས་པའི་ཚུལ་གྱིས་སེམས་ཅན་གྱི་དོན་བྱེད་ཅིང་བླ་ན་མེད་པའི་བྱང་ཆུབ་ཏུ་བསྔོ་བ་དང་། ཕ་རོལ་ཏུ་ཕྱིན་པ་དྲུག་ལ་སོགས་པ་མི་དམིགས་པའི་ཚུལ་གྱིས་སྤྱོད་པར་བྱེད་པས[32]དེ་ལྟར་སྐྱོན་དུ་མི་འགྱུར་རོ། །འདི་ཡན་ཆད་ནི་ཤེས་རབ་ཀྱི་སྤྱོད་ཡུལ་ལོ། །

ད་ནི་ཤེས་རབ་ཀྱི་ཡོན་ཏན་གྱིས་བཤད་དེ། །སེམས་ལ་སྐྱག་པ་མེད་པས་སྒྲིབ་པ་མེད་དེ།[33] ཕྱིན་ཅི་ལོག་ལས་ཤིན་ཏུ་འདས་ནས་མྱ་ངན་ལས་འདས་པའི་མཐར་ཕྱིན་ཏོ་ཞེས་བྱ་བ་ལ། ཤེས་རབ་ཀྱི་ཕ་རོལ་ཏུ་ཕྱིན་པའི་སྟོང་པ་ཉིད་དོན་ལ་ཐོས་པ་དང་། བསམས་པ་དང་། བསྒོམ་པའི་བར་དུ་མི་སྐྱག་པས། སེམས་པ་དང་། ཡིད་དང་། རྣམ་པར་ཤེས་པ་དང་། བག་ཆགས་ཐམས་ཅད་ཟློག་པར་བྱེད་པས་ན། སེམས་ཀྱི་སྒྲིབ་པ་མེད་ཅེས་བྱའོ།

ཐེག་པ་ལྔ་བུའི་སྤྱོད་པ་མུ་སྟེགས་ཅན་དང་། ཉན་ཐོས་དང་། རང་སངས་རྒྱས་ཀྱི་སྤྱོད་ཡུལ་ལས་ཤིན་ཏུ་འདས་ནས་ཉོན་མོངས་པའི་སྒྲིབ་པ་དང་། ཤེས་བྱའི་སྒྲིབ་པ་ཐམས་ཅད་ཟད་དེ། མྱ་ངན་ལས་འདས་པ་ཆེན་པོར་ཕྱིན་ཏོ། །འདི་ཡན་ཆད་ནི་ཤེས་རབ་ཀྱི་ཡོན་ཏན་ནོ། །

ད་ནི་ཤེས་རབ་ཀྱི་འབྲས་བུའི་དོན་གྱིས་བཤད་དེ། དུས་གསུམ་དུ་རྣམ་པར་གཤེགས་པའི་སངས་རྒྱས་ཐམས་ཅད་ཀྱང་ཤེས་རབ་ཀྱི་ཕ་རོལ་ཏུ་ཕྱིན་པ་ལ་གནས་ནས། བླ་ན་མེད་པ་ཡང་དག་པར་རྫོགས་པའི་སངས་རྒྱས་སུ་མངོན་པར་སངས་རྒྱས་སོ་ཞེས་པ་ལ། ཕྱོགས་བཅུའི་འཇིག་རྟེན་གྱི་ཁམས་ནས་དུས་གསུམ་དུ་གཤེགས་པའི་སངས་རྒྱས་ཐམས་ཅད་ཀྱང་ཤེས་རབ་ཀྱི་ཕ་རོལ་ཏུ་ཕྱིན་པ་ཟབ་མོ་འདི་འཛིན། ཀློག །ཁ་དོན་བྱེད། སྒོམ། གཞན་ལ་སྟོན་ཅིང་ཤེས་རབ་ཀྱི་ཕ་རོལ་ཏུ་ཕྱིན་པ་ལ་སྤྱོད་པས་བླ་ན་མེད་པའི་བྱང་ཆུབ་ཏུ་མངོན་པར་སངས་རྒྱས་སོ།

།དུས་གསུམ་གྱི་སངས་རྒྱས་ཐམས་ཅད་ཀྱང་། ཤེས་རབ་ཀྱི་ཕ་རོལ་ཏུ་ཕྱིན་པས་བསྐྱེད་ཤེས་རབ་ཀྱི་ཕ་རོལ་ཏུ་ཕྱིན་པ་ལས་བྱུང་བས་ན་ཤེས་རབ་ཀྱི་ཕ་རོལ་ཏུ་ཕྱིན་པ་ནི་སངས་རྒྱས་ཐམས་ཅད་ཀྱི་ཡུམ་དུ་གྱུར་པའོ། །འདི་ཡན་ཆད་ནི་ཤེས་རབ་ཀྱི་འབྲས་བུའོ། །

ད་ནི་ཤེས་རབ་ཀྱི་གཟུངས་ཀྱི་དོན་གྱིས་བཤད་དེ། དེ་ལྟ་བས་ན་ཤེས་རབ་ཀྱི་ཕ་རོལ་ཏུ་ཕྱིན་པའི་སྔགས་ནི་བདེན་དེ་མ་ནོར་བའོ་ཞེས་པ་ལ། དེ་ལྟ་བས་ན་ཞེས་བྱ་བ་ནི། གོང་དུ་གསུངས་པ་ཡིན་པས་ན་[34]དེ་ལྟ་བས་ན་ཞེས་བྱའོ། །ཤེས་རབ་ཀྱི་ཕ་རོལ་ཏུ་ཕྱིན་པའི་སྔགས་བདེན་དེ་མ་ནོར་བ་ཞེས་བྱ་བ་ནི་ཤེས་རབ་ཀྱི་ཕ་རོལ་ཏུ་ཕྱིན་པའི་དོན་རིག་པར་སྤྱོད་པ་ནི་སྔགས་ཞེས་བྱ་སྟེ། འཇིག་རྟེན་གྱི་ཆོས་ཐམས་ཅད་ཀྱང་བླ་ན་མེད་པའི་བྱང་ཆུབ་ཀྱི་ཐེག་པ་ཆེན་པོར་འགྱུར་ཞིང་། བདག་དང་གཞན་ཡང་བླ་ན་མེད་པའི་བྱང་ཆུབ་ཏུ་འཚང་རྒྱ་བས་ན་བདེན་དེ་མ་ནོར་བ་ཞེས་བྱའོ། རིག་པ་ཆེན་པོའི་སྔགས་ཞེས་བྱ་བ་ནི་ཤེས་རབ་ཀྱི་ཕ་རོལ་ཏུ་ཕྱིན་པའི་དོན་རིག་པའི་སྔགས་ནི་འདོད་ཆགས་ཞེ་སྡང་གཏི་མུག་དང་། འཁོར་བའི་སྡུག་བསྔལ་ཐམས་ཅད་བཟོད་པ་མེད་པའི་[35]རང་བཞིན་མེད་པར་སྟོན་པས་ན་ཤེས་རབ་ཀྱི་ཕ་རོལ་ཏུ་ཕྱིན་པ་ནི་རིག་པ་ཆེན་པོའི་སྔགས་སོ། །བླ་ན་མེད་པའི་སྔགས་ཞེས་པ་ནི། ཤེས་རབ་ཀྱི་ཕ་རོལ་ཏུ་ཕྱིན་པ་ནི་བླ་ན་མེད་པའི་བྱང་ཆུབ་ཏུ་འགྲུབ་པར་བྱེད་པས་ན། བླ་ན་མེད་པའི་སྔགས་སོ། །མི་མཉམ་པ་དང་མཉམ་པའི་སྔགས་ཞེས་པ་ནི། ཤེས་རབ་ཀྱི་ཕ་རོལ་ཏུ་ཕྱིན་པ་ནི་འཇིག་རྟེན་པ་དང་། ཉན་ཐོས་དང་། རང་སངས་རྒྱས་ཀྱི་སྤྱོད་པ་དང་མི་མཉམ་ཞིང་། སངས་རྒྱས་ཐམས་ཅད་ཀྱི་ཡེ་ཤེས་དང་མཉམ་པར་བྱེད་པས་ན་མི་མཉམ་པ་དང་མཉམ་པའི་སྔགས་སོ། །སྡུག་བསྔལ་ཐམས་ཅད་རབ་ཏུ་ཞི་བར་བྱེད་པའི་སྔགས་སུ་ཤེས་པར་བྱ་སྟེ་ཞེས་བྱ་བ་ལ་ཤེས་རབ་ཀྱི་ཕ་རོལ་ཏུ་ཕྱིན་པ་འཆང་། ཀློག །ཁ་དོན་བྱེད་པ་དང་། ཚུལ་བཞིན་དུ་ཡིད་ལ་བྱེད་ཅིང་། གཞན་ལ་འཆད་པས་ནི་[36]མིག་ནད་ལ་སོགས་པ་ནད་ཐམས་ཅད་མེད་པར་འགྱུར་ཞིང་། ཕྱོགས་བཅུའི་སངས་རྒྱས་དང་། ལྷ་ཀླུ་ལ་སོགས་པས་སྐྱོབ་པས་སྐྱོབ་པར་བྱེད།

ཤེས་རབ་ཀྱི་ཕ་རོལ་ཏུ་ཕྱིན་པ་སྤྱོད་པས་ངན་འགྲོ་དང་འཁོར་བའི་རྒྱ་མཚོ་ཐམས་ཅད་ཟློག་པར་བྱེད་པས་ན་སྡུག་བསྔལ་ཐམས་ཅད་རབ་ཏུ་ཞི་བར་བྱེད་པའི་སྔགས་སོ། །ཤེས་རབ་ཀྱི་ཕ་རོལ་ཏུ་ཕྱིན་པའི་སྔགས་སྨྲས་པ། ཏད་ཡ་ཐཱ། ག་ཏེ། ག་ཏེ། པ་ར་ག་ཏེ། པ་ར་སཾ་ག་ཏེ། བོ་དྷི་སྭཱ་ཧཱ་ཞེས་པ་ལ། ཤེས་རབ་ཀྱི་ཕ་རོལ་ཏུ་ཕྱིན་པའི་སྔགས་འདི་ནི་ཟབ་མོའི་མཆོག་ཐམས་ཅད་ཀྱི་དོན་བསྡུས་པ་རང་བཞིན་གྱིས་གྲུབ་པར་བྱེད་པས་བྱིན་གྱིས་བརླབས་པའི་སྔགས་སུ་གསུངས་པའོ། །

ཤཱ་རིའི་བུ་བྱང་ཆུབ་སེམས་དཔའ་སེམས་དཔའ་ཆེན་པོས་དེ་ལྟར་ཤེས་རབ་ཀྱི་ཕ་རོལ་ཏུ་ཕྱིན་པ་ཟབ་མོ་ལ་བསླབ་པར་བྱའོ་ཞེས་པ་ནི་དུས་གསུམ་གྱི་སངས་རྒྱས་ཐམས་ཅད་ཀྱང་ཤེས་རབ་ཀྱི་ཕ་རོལ་ཏུ་ཕྱིན་པ་སྤྱད་པ་ལས་སངས་རྒྱས་པས་ན་ཐེག་པ་ཆེན་པོ་ལ་འཇུག་པའི་བྱང་ཆུབ་སེམས་དཔའ་རྣམས་ཀྱིས་ཀྱང་ཤེས་རབ་ཀྱི་ཕ་རོལ་ཏུ་ཕྱིན་པ་ལ་བསླབ་པར་བྱའོ། །དེ་ནས་བཅོམ་ལྡན་འདས་ཏིང་ངེ་འཛིན་དེ་ལས་བཞེངས་ཏེ་ཞེས་པ་ནི། བཅོམ་ལྡན་འདས་ཟབ་མོའི་ཏིང་ངེ་འཛིན་ལ་ཞུགས་པའི་མཐུས་ཤཱ་རིའི་བུས་དྲིས་ཏེ། སྤྱན་རས་གཟིགས་ཀྱིས་བཤད་ནས་དེའི་དོན་རྫོགས་པ་དང་ཏིང་ངེ་འཛིན་ལས་བཞེངས་སོ། །བྱང་ཆུབ་སེམས་དཔའ་སེམས་དཔའ་ཆེན་པོ་སྤྱན་རས་གཟིགས་ཀྱི་དབང་པོ་ལ་ལེགས་སོ་ཞེས་བྱ་བ་བྱིན་ནས། ལེགས་སོ་ལེགས་སོ་ཞེས་པ་ནི་ཤེས་རབ་ཀྱི་ཕ་རོལ་ཏུ་ཕྱིན་པའི་སྙིང་པོའི་དོན་སྨྲས་པ། སངས་རྒྱས་ཐམས་ཅད་ཀྱིས་གསུངས་པ་དང་མཐུན་ཏེ། མ་ནོར་བའི་ཕྱིར་ལེགས་སོ་ཞེས་བསྔོད་པའོ། །རིགས་ཀྱི་བུ་དེ་དེ་བཞིན་ནོ། །རིགས་ཀྱི་བུ་དེ་དེ་བཞིན་ཏེ། ཇི་ལྟར་ཁྱོད་ཀྱིས་ཤེས་རབ་ཀྱི་ཕ་རོལ་ཏུ་ཕྱིན་པ་ཟབ་མོ་བསྟན་པ་བཞིན་དུ་སྤྱད་པར་བྱ་སྟེ་ཞེས་པ་ནི་སྤྱན་རས་གཟིགས་ཀྱིས་ཇི་སྐད་སྨྲས་པ་དེ་སངས་རྒྱས་ཐམས་ཅད་ཀྱིས་གསུངས་པ་དང་མཐུན་པས་ན་དེ་བཞིན་ནོ། །འཕགས་པ་སྤྱན་རས་གཟིགས་ཀྱིས་ཤེས་རབ་ཀྱི་ཕ་རོལ་ཏུ་ཕྱིན་པ་བསྟན་པ་དེ་བཞིན་དུ། ཐེག་པ་ཆེན་པོ་ལ་ཞུགས་པའི་བྱང་ཆུབ་སེམས་དཔའ་རྣམས་ཀྱིས་ཀྱང་སྤྱད་པར་བྱའོ། །དེ་བཞིན་གཤེགས་པ་ཡང་རྗེས་སུ་ཡི་རང་ངོ་ཞེས་པ་ནི། སྤྱན་རས་གཟིགས་ཀྱི་བཤད་པ་ལ་དེ་བཞིན་གཤེགས་པ་རྗེས་སུ་ཡི་རང་བར་མཛད་ན། གཞན་གྱིས་ཐེ་ཚོམ་མི་ཟ་བ་ལྟ་ཅི་སྨོས་ཞེས་པའོ།[37] །བཅོམ་ལྡན་འདས་དགྱེས་ཤིང་དེ་སྐད་ཅེས་བཀའ་སྩལ་ནས་ཞེས་པ་ནི་ཤེས་རབ་ཀྱི་ཕ་རོལ་ཏུ་ཕྱིན་པ་སྨྲས་པ་དེས་འཁོར་ཐམས་ཅད་ཀྱང་ཤེས་རབ་ཀྱི་ཕ་རོལ་ཏུ་ཕྱིན་པའི་དོན་རྟོགས་པར་གྱུར་ནས། ཐེག་པ་ཆེན་པོ་ལ་སྒྲིབ་པ་མེད་པའི་ཕྱིར་དགྱེས་ཤིང་དེ་སྐད་ཅེས་བཀའ་སྩལ་པའོ། །ཚེ་དང་ལྡན་པ་ཤཱ་རིའི་བུ་དང་། བྱང་ཆུབ་སེམས་དཔའ་སྤྱན་རས་གཟིགས་ཀྱི་དབང་པོ་དང་། ལྷ་དང་། མི་དང་། ལྷ་མ་ཡིན་དང་། དྲི་ཟར་བཅས་པའི་འཁོར་ཐམས་ཅད་བཅོམ་ལྡན་འདས་ཀྱིས་གསུངས་པ་ལ་མངོན་པར་དགའོ། །

བཅོམ་ལྡན་འདས་མ་ཤེས་རབ་ཀྱི་ཕ་རོལ་ཏུ་ཕྱིན་པའི་སྙིང་པོའི་འགྲེལ་པ་སློབ་དཔོན་ཛྙཱ་ན་མི་ཏྲས་མཛད་པ་རྫོགས་སོ། །

ANNOTATIONS TO JÑĀNAMITRA'S *EXPLANATION OF THE HEART SŪTRA*

Opening of a Canonical Commentary

1

Page 61, Line 8

Canonical commentaries form their own unique genre of literature in Sanskrit and that uniqueness is carried over in their Tibetan translations. The Tibetan representation of highly formulaic commentarial structures in Sanskrit entails a slightly different use of case-marking and syntactic particles. The opening of this text exemplifies this. Here the phrase དེ་ལ་ replicates the Sanskrit term *tatra*, which refers to a recently mentioned quotation and conveys the sense "in that [passage]," "in that case," or "with regard to that," and so on. Here, as the opening statement of the text, the phrase indicates that the entire composition is a work that stands in reference to another text; that is, it indicates that the text is a commentary.

WHAT TO REMEMBER

The phrase དེ་ལ་ in Tibetan replicates the Sanskrit term *tatra*, which refers to a recently mentioned quotation and conveys the sense "in that [passage]," "in that case," or "with regard to that," and so on. It indicates that what follows is an explanation of the preceding quotation or must be understood in reference to another text.

Case Marker ཀྱི་ as Syntactic Particle

2

Page 61, Line 10

Although the particle ཀྱི་ is most commonly seen as a sixth-case marker, when occurring at the end of a sentence (i.e., following a verb), it functions as a syntactic particle (see Wilson, 676–677). Given its conjunctive/disjunctive function, this passage could then be translated as "[This] is not limited to the mere imputation of a name, however, ..."

WHAT TO REMEMBER

Non-case syntactic particles applied to verbs and sentences are used to qualify a statement or segué to a related idea. The most common of these non-case syntactic particles in Tibetan literature is the particle ལ་ ("although ...," "but ...," etc.) used to segué from one sentence to another that qualifies it, and ནས་ ("having [done] ...") used to mark the end of a gerund (see introduction, 15 and 19). Seen somewhat less frequently are ཀྱི་, གྱི་, གི་, etc. ("but," "even though," "however," etc.), which are likewise used to segué to a related though disjunct statement.

3

Translation Hint

Page 61, Line 11

This sentence employs a grammatical feature that we have seen already, a modular sentence structure (see ཤེས་རབ་སྙིང་པོ་ note 22). It demonstrates the necessity of identifying the syntactic class of verbs to properly understand the role of the components of a sentence and the need to remain aware of the fact that different homographs of a verb can exist and may have different syntactic classes.

To read this sentence correctly, one can begin by identifying the natural break-points (that is, following syntactic particles, case markers, and nominative words and phrases) in the sentence:

ཤེས་རབ་ཀྱི་ཕ་རོལ་ཏུ་ཕྱིན་པའི་སྙིང་པོ་འདིའི་མདོ་ཐམས་ཅད་ / ཀྱང་ / འདིར་མ་འདུས་པ་ / མེད་པས་ / མདོའི་ཡང་མདོ་ཞེས་བྱའོ།

We can work from the end of the sentence backward. The final verb, བྱ་, when occurring in the collocation ཞེས་བྱ་, functions as a Class VIII phrasal verb meaning "to be called." When we look at the sentence as a whole, there does not appear, however, to be a subject marked in the seventh (locative) case as required by a Class VIII verb (although the syntactic particle ཀྱང་ could be eliding it—see ཤེས་རབ་སྙིང་པོ་ note 12). Next, the verb མེད་ occurs as a participle (མེད་པ་) marked in the third case. Since the third case marks agents, instruments, and reasons, and because the third case is attached to a verbal participle, it is reasonable to assume that this marks the end of a reason clause. Whether the verb མེད་ is functioning as a Class II verb of existence or a Class VIII verb of possession remains to be determined (although since we have not encountered any human actors in the narrative thus far that might "possess" something, it is a safe working assumption to take it as a Class II verb). The next point—and what might be considered the key to understanding the overall structure of the sentence—is to recognize that the nominative subject of the verb མེད་ is not merely the nominalized verb འདུས་ but a nominalized sentence built around the verb འདུས་. Since འདུས་ ("to gather," "to unite," "to subsume") is a Class II (nominative-locative) verb, we can see that everything that precedes it forms a grammatically complete sentence:

Nom. Subject (1.2.1)	SP	Loc. qualifier (7.2.2)	VP()
ཤེས་རབ་ཀྱི་ཕ་རོལ་ཏུ་ཕྱིན་པའི་སྙིང་པོ་འདིའི་མདོ་ཐམས་ཅད་	ཀྱང་	འདིར་	མ་འདུས།

As a sentence, it could be translated as: "All the aphoristic statements (*sūtra*) of this *Heart of the Perfection of Wisdom*, moreover, do not include [something] here." When nominalized and taken as the subject of the verb མེད་, the resulting new sentence becomes: "There is nothing that all the aphoristic statements of this *Heart of the Perfection of Wisdom* do not include." Taking this as a reason clause, the remainder of the sentence becomes clear: "[It] is called 'the sūtra of sūtras,'" i.e., a superlative.

Formulaic Commentarial Structures

Page 61, Line 12

Classical Indian scholastic exegesis is very "user friendly"; that is, it is structured in such a way as to make its content comprehensible. One way in which it achieves this is through the repetition of formulaic grammatical structures. Given the complexities of the Sanskrit language, classical Indian commentaries were envisioned as performing five basic functions: separating passages into individual words, providing the meaning of the words, specifying the grammatical relationship between words, indicating the structure of the sentence as a whole, and answering objections to the ideas being conveyed. When this literature was translated into Tibetan, some of these purposes became irrelevant—such as explaining points of Sanskrit grammar, which no longer applied to the translated text. In such instances, some translators felt free to simply ignore these passages and omit them from their translations, while others rearranged parts of the text to reflect the new Tibetan translation and its grammar.

Since the Sanskrit original for this text appears to be no longer extant, we cannot say what may have been omitted or changed, but some basic elements have clearly been preserved. For example, this sentence and the ones that follow replicate the basic pattern of a "grammatical analysis" (*vigraha*). In this scheme, the word being explained is first given as a quotation, followed by a paraphase of its meaning. A more detailed discussion follows that explains the larger idea being conveyed and that closes with a reason clause marker (either ཕྱིར་ or –ས་ན་). The entire passage then concludes with a restatement of the word or syllable being explained.

The first such "grammatical analysis" encountered here is slightly more complex in that the word being explained, བཅོམ་ལྡན་, is a two-syllable word, with each syllable explained separately. Nonetheless, this same basic pattern of analysis is followed:

Word: བཅོམ་ལྡན།

Detailed Analysis:

First Syllable: བཅོམ།

Paraphrase: བདུད་བཅོམ་པ།

Detailed Analysis: ཕུང་པོའི་བདུད་ལ་སོགས་པ་ཤེས་རབ་ཀྱི་ཕ་རོལ་ཏུ་ཕྱིན་པའི་དོན་འདིས་བདུད་བཙལ་དུ་མི་སྐྱེད་ཅིང་བདུད་ཐམས་ཅད་མི་གནས་པའི་ཕྱིར་བཅོམ་པ།

Second Syllable: ལྡན།

Paraphrase: ལེགས་པ་དྲུག་དང་ལྡན་པ།

Detailed Analysis: མཁྱེན་པའི་ཡོན་ཏན་ཐམས་ཅད་ཀྱང་ཤེས་རབ་ཀྱི་ཕ་རོལ་ཏུ་ཕྱིན་པའི་བྱིན་གྱི་བརླབས་ལས་བྱུང་བས་ན་ལྡན་པ།

WHAT TO REMEMBER

Classical Indian commentaries often follow a standard pattern of explanation of a root text. One of the most common forms of grammatical analysis (*vigraha*) entails the initial quotation of the word or phrase to be explained, followed by a paraphrase of its meaning, a detailed explanation of the larger idea or implication as a reason clause, and a final restatement of the word just explained.

Closing Quotation Marker ཞེས་[བྱ་བ་] ⑤

Page 61, Line 12

The syntactic particles ཞེས་, ཅེས་, and ཤེས་ mark the termination of a quotation and flag that quotation as a self-contained unit, signaling that the grammar of the sentence or phrase within the quotation is independent from the grammar of the larger sentence enclosing it. Unfortunately, Tibetan has no special marker for the start of a quotation. In some cases, however, the start of a quotation is clear, where it is preceded either by a textual source citation (see བློ་རིག་ note 13) or a lead-in to narrative (see ཤེས་རབ་སྙིང་པོ་ note 9).

In translation, the varieties of closing quotation markers (e.g., ཞེས་, ཞེས་པ་, ཞེས་བྱ་བ་, etc.) can be represented merely by English-style quotation marks. An alternate strategy, which can prove contextually more helpful, is to translate the marker with a phrase such as "the statement '...,'" or "the so-called '...,'" and similar such constructions.

WHAT TO REMEMBER

A variety of syntactic particles are used to mark the termination of a quotation. Depending upon the last letter of the preceding syllable, they are:

- ཞེས་, following words that end in the suffixes ང་, ན་, མ་, འ་, ར་, and ལ་
- ཅེས་, following words that end in the suffixes ག་, ད་, and བ་ (including the secondary suffix, ད་)
- ཤེས་, following words that end in the suffix ས་

Depending on context, such phrases may be left untranslated and represented by quotation marks or translated as "the statement '...,'" and so forth.

Discrete Lists and the Particle སོགས་ ⑥

Page 61, Line 12

Lists of things—often, of a known set of entities or qualities—are a common feature of Buddhist philosophy. Far less common is for a text to provide a complete enumeration of such lists. Unlike instances where a partial subset of a list is referred to (see ཤེས་རབ་སྙིང་པོ་

note 15), when a complete list is referred to it is far more common to find only the first one or two elements of a list given. Such is the case here, where it is presumed that the reader recognizes the reference to the list in its entirety. In such instances, the syntactic phrase ལ་སོགས་པ་ is used to indicate that the remainder of the list has been omitted. It is typically translated as "and so forth," or simply "etc."

In this case, the first item in the list, ཕུང་པོའི་བདུད་ ("the demon of the aggregates"), refers to a known list of four "demons" (*māra*; བདུད་)—the remaining three being: ཉོན་མོངས་པའི་བདུད་ ("the demon of the afflictions"), འཆི་བདག་གི་བདུད་ ("the demon who is the Lord of Death"), and ལྷའི་བུའི་བདུད་ ("the demon of [taking rebirth as] a divine child (*devaputra*)"). Such lists have been documented in the genre of literature known as "enumerated lists of phenomena" (*dharmasaṃgraha*; ཆོས་ཀྱི་རྣམ་གྲངས་; see bibliography).

WHAT TO REMEMBER

The syntactic phrase ལ་སོགས་པ་ is used to indicate that the remainder of a list has been omitted. It is typically translated as "and so forth" or simply "etc." See also སྨོ་རིག་ note 5 and སྐབ་མཐའ་ note 19.

⑦ Translation Hint: Canonical Text Titles

Page 61, Line 23

When text titles are cited in the body of a text, it is seldom that the full bibliographic title of a work will be given by an author. Instead, an abbreviated, alternate, or poetic title will be used. The title of the text cited here—*The Perfection of Wisdom in One Hundred Thousand Lines* (ཤེས་རབ་ཀྱི་ཕ་རོལ་ཏུ་ཕྱིན་པ་སྟོང་ཕྲག་བརྒྱ་པ་)—is a rare example of proper citation. The same text is later cited with a slight variation (འབུམ་པའི་མདོ་ instead of སྟོང་ཕྲག་བརྒྱ་པ་).

⑧ Commentarial Style: Rhetorical Questions

Page 62, Line 6

The Indian tradition of commentarial exegesis has a long and rich history, in which certain stylistic and formulaic approaches were developed and subsequently followed by authors over the centuries. By the time that Sanskrit Buddhist literature was beginning to be translated into Tibetan, a number of these styles had concretized and Tibetan translators were faced with the challenge of replicating these literary forms in Tibetan.

One such commentarial style came to be known as the *kathaṃ bhūtinī* approach, or rhetorical questioning, after one of the most frequent rhetorical questions used, *kathaṃ bhūta* ("how is it?"). In this style, the author proceeds by stating portions of the original (*mūla*; "root") text and expounding on the meaning through the use of rhetorical questions. The phrase དེ་ཡང་གང་ཞེ་ན། in Tibctan is one such example.

WHAT TO REMEMBER

A number of rhetorical statements are used in Tibetan to replicate similar formulaic constructions in Sanskrit. Although most can be translated literally, they should be recognized as specific rhetorical devices. Some examples are:

དེ་གང་ཞེ་ན། :: *kiṃ tat* : "What is that?" :: (Tib.) "If you ask, 'What is that?' "
ཇི་ལྟ་བུ་ཞེ་ན། :: *kīdṛśam* : "How is it?" :: (Tib.) "If you ask, 'How is it?' "
ཅིའི་ཕྱིར་ཞེ་ན། :: *kiṃ artham* : "For what purpose?" :: (Tib.) "If you ask, 'For what purpose?' "
ཅི་ཞིག་བྱ་ཞེ་ན། :: *kiṃityāha* : "What is [to be done]?" :: (Tib.) "If you ask, 'What is to be done?' "

Locative Absolute

9

Page 62, Line 11

As noted in the introduction to this text, the translators of Jñānamitra's commentary were different from those who translated the *Heart Sūtra*. As a result, there are slight divergences in renderings of passages between the root text and the text as it is quoted in the commentary (see also ཤེར་སྙིང་རྣམ་བཤད་ note 33). This is one such passage. In the *Heart Sūtra*, the passage being referred to here reads: སྒྲིབ་པ་མེད་པའི་ཕྱིར། ཤེས་རབ་ཀྱི་ཕ་རོལ་ཏུ་ཕྱིན་པ་ལ་བརྟེན་ཅིང་གནས་ཏེ།. Here, however, the reason clause སྒྲིབ་པ་མེད་པའི་ཕྱིར། has been rendered instead as a locative-absolute construction: སྒྲིབ་པ་མེད་པར།.

A locative-absolute construction is a complete or partial sentence that expresses (a) a condition in which something takes place or (b) some type of accompanying circumstance. The most common form is an expression of absence, typically with a negated verb or the existential verb of absence, མེད་, as seen here. Although a reason clause often indicates a direct causal connection to what follows, a locative-absolute construction can convey similar generic information in a less causal sense and merely as an accompanying circumstance or condition.

In terms of translation, the construction with མེད་ (as a Class VIII verb of possession) is typically translated as "without ...," but in this case མེད་ is functioning as a Class II verb of existence and hence is more accurately translated as a generic condition "there being no ..."

WHAT TO REMEMBER

A locative-absolute construction is a complete or partial sentence that expresses a condition in which something takes place or some type of accompanying circumstance. It is formed with an often negated verb + པར་ (indicating a condition of absence), although its translation can depend on the class of the verb itself as well as any accompanying agents, objects, complements, or qualifiers.

10 First-Person Statements

Page 62, Line 14

Since a substantial amount of Buddhist literature is written in an abstract and impersonal manner, it is easy to forget that an author may occasionally interject an opinion or speak directly to the reader in the first person. Here is precisely such an instance, a clue to this being the use of the free-floating adverb ད་ ("now")—bringing the narrative out of the abstract and into the present—to introduce the passage that follows.

WHAT TO REMEMBER

First person statements can be identified by a variety of features that indicate that the author is speaking directly to the reader, such as temporal phrases (ད་; "now"), vocatives (བུ་; "O my child"), or certain verbs (སྙམ་; "to think (that)," etc.).

Agglutinative Sixth Case as a Syntactic Particle

11

Page 62, Line 18

As noted (see ཤེར་སྙིང་རྣམ་བཤད་ note 2), after a verb or sentence, the non-case usage of the sixth-case marker indicates a break between the sentence that precedes it and the sentence that follows. The selection of the particular sixth-case marker to be deployed, however, still follows the rules prescribed for normative use. Here, since the sentence ends with a suffixless syllable (བུ་), the agglutinative form (–འི་) occurs.

WHAT TO REMEMBER

When following a verb at the end of a sentence, all the sixth-case particles (ཀྱི་, གྱི་, གི་, ཡི་, and –འི་) can serve as conjunctive and disjunctive syntactic particles.

Agent Nouns from Verbs

12

Page 62, Line 20

As previously mentioned (see ཤེས་རབ་སྙིང་པོ་ note 13), in addition to forming participles to be used in lieu of a finite verb, it is possible to form a noun or noun phrase from a nominalized verb or sentence using པ་ or པོ་ (བ་ or བོ་ after ང་, ན་, ར་, and ལ་) and མ་ or མོ་ in the feminine. It is also possible, however, to make a more subtle distinction between the types of nouns formed in reference to the tense of the verb that is nominalized. Previously, the past-tense verb བསྟན་ ("to teach") was nominalized to produce བསྟན་པ་ as the object-noun, "teaching." Here, it is the present-tense verb སྟོན་ that has been nomimalized, resulting in the agent-noun, སྟོན་པ་, "teacher." This general pattern holds for other verbs as well. See also བར་དོ་འཕྲང་སྒྲོལ་ note 2.

WHAT TO REMEMBER

When verbs are nominalized to form nouns, the nominalized past tense forms the object-noun, while the nominalized present tense forms the agent-noun.

13

Translation Hint

Page 63, Line 2

Recall that the Tibetan tradition handled the translation of Sanskrit proper names in a unique fashion (see ཤེས་རབ་སྙིང་པོ་ note 5). This sentence contains three proper names, two that have been seen before in the *Heart Sūtra* text—རྒྱལ་པོའི་ཁབ་ (*Rājagṛha*) and བྱ་རྒོད་ཀྱི་ཕུང་པོའི་རི་ (*Gṛdhrakūṭa*; "Vulture Peak")—and a third one, རྒྱལ་པོ་གཟུགས་ཅན་སྙིང་པོ་, that has not. As noted, a phrase that bears little or no literal sense in the context of the larger sentence is often a clue that a proper name has been encountered. Here, another clue is the lead-in adjective རྒྱལ་པོ་ (*rāja* or "king"), indicating that གཟུགས་ཅན་སྙིང་པོ་ is a proper name. Even with knowledge of common Sanskrit equivalents to Tibetan words, some proper names are difficult to reconstruct and an authoritative dictionary (see bibliography) must be relied upon. For example, although གཟུགས་ is a common rendering of the Sanskrit *rūpa*, and སྙིང་པོ་, a common rendering of the Sanskrit *garbha* ("heart" or "essence"), here གཟུགས་ཅན་ translates the Sanskrit *bimba* ("having a form" or "image") and སྙིང་པོ་ translates *sāra* ("pith" or "quintessence"), and hence གཟུགས་ཅན་སྙིང་པོ་ is "Bimbasāra" (or "Bimbisāra"), who was the king of Magadha and whose capital was Rājagṛha.

14

Commentarial Style: Glossing

Page 63, Line 17

Although grammatically complete sentences are the norm for the majority of Tibetan literature, in some genres, such as classical commentarial exegesis, simple glossing of words with equivalents or explanatory phrases is often considered sufficient. Here, because the passage in the root text being explained (ཡང་དེའི་ཚེ་; "also at that time") is temporal, a simple gloss ending with a locative of time (···དུས་ན་; "at the time (of) ...") is all that is given, although the author clearly indicates the end of the gloss with a terminating suffix (–འོ).

WHAT TO REMEMBER

In highly formulaic commentarial literature, grammatically complete sentences are not necessarily provided in glosses of the meaning of words and phrases, which may consist of phrases in the same case (locative, etc.). Such glosses are often explicitly terminated with sentence-terminating markers, but even these may be omitted if the glosses are short enough and sequential glosses are being given for the text as a whole.

Run-on Sentences without Punctuation

15

Page 63, Line 21

Recall that verbal participles can be used in lieu of a conjugated verb in the construction of "run-on" sentences (see ཤེས་རབ་སྙིང་པོ་ note 13)—that is, in sentences that are thematically connected to each other and form a complete thought as a whole. Here, we have an instance of the same sort of construction, although to avoid ambiguous grammar, the translator has resolved the syntactic qualifier to a genitive. Hence the sentence:

> ཕུང་པོ་ལྔ་པོ་དེ་དག་ཀུང་མི་དམིགས་པའི་རང་བཞིན་གྱི་སྟོང་པ་སྟོང་པ་ཉིད་ལས་གཞན་དུ་གྱུར་པ་གང་ཡང་མེད་དོ་
> ཞེས་བྱ་བར་དགོངས་པའོ།

should be understood as equivalent to reading the sentence as:

> ཕུང་པོ་ལྔ་པོ་དེ་དག་ཀུང་[ནི།] མི་དམིགས་པའི་རང་བཞིན་གྱི[ས]་སྟོང་པ། སྟོང་པ་ཉིད་ལས་གཞན་དུ་གྱུར་པ་གང་ཡང་མེད་དོ་
> ཞེས་བྱ་བར་དགོངས་པའོ།

WHAT TO REMEMBER

Run-on sentences occasionally omit separating punctuation for a variety of reasons—when they are part of a longer quotation, or when they are part of a sentence with distributed subjects, etc.

Commentarial Style: Paraphrased Restatement

16

Page 64, Line 5

Another approach to explaining the meaning of a sentence is to expand or restate the entire sentence, adding or substituting terms as needed. This style, known as *padārthokti* ("statement of the meaning of the words"), provides alternate or additional information to allow the reader to understand the contextual meaning of the statement. When a paraphrase is given in addition to a gloss or other explanation, the paraphrase can be marked by the phrase ཞེས་བྱ་བའི་དོན་ཏོ། ("has the meaning of …") or ཞེས་བྱ་བའི་ཐ་ཚིག་གོ། ("has the standard meaning of …"). Here, since only a paraphrase is given to explain the quotation, it is assumed to be understood as such.

WHAT TO REMEMBER

When a commentary explains complete sentences, sometimes the sentence under consideration is restated as a paraphrase providing alternate or additional information. In some instances, the paraphrase is marked by the phrase ཞེས་བྱ་བའི་དོན་ཏོ། ("has the meaning of …") or ཞེས་བྱ་བའི་ཐ་ཚིག་གོ། ("has the standard meaning of …").

17 The Verb དམིགས་

Page 65, Line 1

In Indian philosophical treatises, both Buddhist and non-Buddhist, vision and the perceptual act are used as exemplars of sensory experience in general. Even when used literally in a perceptual context, different verbs of perception convey subtly different shades of meaning. The three most common Tibetan verbs used in talking about the act of perception are མཐོང་ ("to see"), ལྟ་ ("to look (at)"), and finally, དམིགས་ ("to take as a perceptual object," "to visualize," or simply "to observe" or "to objectify"). Thus, when nominalized, དམིགས་པ་ is typically translated as "object of observation." Here, the verb དམིགས་ is being used as a "simple infinitive" (Wilson, 611, 614, and མདོ་མཛངས་བླུན་ note 11) in the passive sense ("to be objectified"). Consequently, the phrase དམིགས་སུ་མེད་ can be translated as "there is nothing to be objectified."

WHAT TO REMEMBER

The verb དམིགས་ conveys a unique dimension of the act of perception, emphasizing its objectifying aspect.

Translation Hint 18

Page 65, Line 4

This sentence demonstrates a number of syntactic features seen previously, including the ལ་ particle as a syntactic continuative (ཤེར་སྙིང་རྣམ་བཤད་ note 2 and བློ་རིག་ note 14), an omitted verb (ཤེས་རབ་སྙིང་པོ་ note 14), and the elision of a case marker by the syntactic particle ཀྱང་ (ཤེས་རབ་སྙིང་པོ་ note 12). One unique feature of the sentence here is that, in addition to the final syntactic ལ་, this sentence contains a second sentence similarly marked but with an omitted verb:

> སྟོང་པ་ཉིད་ཀྱང་གཟུགས་སོ་ཞེས་བྱ་བ་ནི་ / སྟོང་པ་ཉིད་ / ཀྱང་ / དམིགས་སུ་མེད་པའི་རང་བཞིན་ལ་ / གཟུགས་སོ་ཞེས་ཚིག་གི་ཐ་སྙད་དུ་བཏགས་ལ།

Although one could attempt to read the three noun phrases (སྟོང་པ་ཉིད་, …རང་བཞིན་ལ་, and …ཐ་སྙད་དུ་) as components of a sentence grammatically connected to the verb བཏགས་ (that is, as an object, complement, and qualifier, respectively), such a reading yields a translation whose meaning is unclear. Rather, taking the first two components as expressing a complete thought with an omitted ཡོད་ verb and elided locative subject marker:

> སྟོང་པ་ཉིད་[ལ་]ཀྱང་དམིགས་སུ་མེད་པའི་རང་བཞིན་[ཡོད་]ལ།

the sentence can be read as "even though emptiness [has] a nature that lacks objectification, ..." This sentence then segués nicely to the passage that follows: "[it] is designated conventionally [by the phrase] "is form."

Translation Hint 19

Page 65, Line 7

Like the relative-correlative phrase seen previously (see ཤེས་རབ་སྙིང་པོ་ note 10), this pair of phrases གང་ཡིན་པ་…དེ་ཉིད་ can be translated nearly literally as "whatsoever is [something] ... just that ..."

Technical Terms of Grammar 20

Page 65, Line 13

There is a technical vocabulary to Tibetan grammar that is occasionally seen in commentaries. Although the traditional declensions (nominative, accusative, etc.) are represented as numbered cases ([རྣམ་དབྱེ་]དང་པོ་, etc.) or occasionally in descriptive terms (as Wilson renders them—objective, agentive, purposive, etc.) that are similar to the Latinate categories, the eighth declension, the vocative (བོད་སྒྲ་), is occasionally abbreviated as simply བོད་—a homonym with the name of Tibet. Many others are homonyms as well.

WHAT TO REMEMBER

Some basic grammar terms to be familiar with are:

རྣམ་དབྱེ། : case declension	འབྲེལ་སྒྲ། : connective particle	བྱ་ཚིག : verb
གསལ་བྱེད། : consonant	འབྱེད་སྡུད་སྒྲ། : disjunctive particle	སྔོན་འཇུག : prefix
སྤྱི་སྒྲ། : relative pronoun	ལྷག་བཅས། : continuative particle	རྗེས་འཇུག : suffix
ཡང་འཇུག : secondary suffix	བྱེད་པའི་སྒྲ། : instrumental particle	དབྱངས་ཡིག : vowel
མཐའ་རྟེན། : final consonant	རྫོགས་ཚིག : terminating particle	བོད།/འབོད་སྒྲ། : vocative
འབྱུང་ཁུངས། : originative case	རྒྱན་སྡུད། : ornamental particle	ཚེག : syllabic punctuation
ཚིག་འཕྲད། : phrase terminator	དགག་པའི་སྒྲ། : negation particle	ཤད། : phrase punctuation
ད་ལྟ་བའི་ཚིག : present tense	མ་འོངས་པའི་ཚིག : future tense	འདས་ཚིག : past tense

21 Auxiliary Verbs: Exhortative

Page 65, Line 16

Recall that auxiliary constructions modify the modal aspect of a verb without altering its basic meaning (see ཤེས་རབ་སྙིང་པོ་ note 11). The construction seen here, *verb* + པར་གྱིས་ཤིག, is used to convey an exhortative mood ("[you] really should do X"). It is formed by combining the imperative form of the strong auxiliary verb (Wilson, 619) བགྱིད་ (གྱིས་) and the imperative marker ཤིག. It is important to note that the exhortative is easily confused with a similar construction, the precative (see མདོ་མཛངས་བླུན་ note 14).

WHAT TO REMEMBER

The use of certain auxiliary verb constructions, such as གྱིས་ཤིག, བྱེད་ཅིག, མཛོད་ཅིག, etc., conveys an exhortative mood ("[you] really should do X"). The construction can also occur in the negative, as *verb* + པར་མ་བྱེད་ཅིག ("[you] really should not do X").

Auxiliary Verbs: Subjunctive

22

Page 65, Line 18

The subjunctive mood is used to express a hypothetical situation, a situation that is contrary to facts, or one that expresses a hope or wish. Such is the purpose of the auxiliary construction seen here: *verb* + བར་གྱུར་. It combines the main verb with the past-tense form of the weak auxiliary verb (Wilson, 620) འགྱུར་ (གྱུར་). It is often seen with the conditional marker ན་ (see also བར་དོ་འཕྲང་སྒྲོལ་ note 10).

WHAT TO REMEMBER

The use of the auxiliary construction *verb* + བར་གྱུར་ conveys the subjunctive mood ("[something] *would be* X" or "[if something] *were to be* X ..."). See also མདོ་མཛངས་བླུན་ note 17 and གྲུབ་མཐའ་ note 20.

Translation Hint

23

Page 65, Line 21

The phrase གཟུང་འཛིན་ is a stock expression in Buddhist philosophy meaning "object and subject," or "apprehended and apprehender," in the sense of dualistic perception.

Verbal Participles: Gerundives

24

Page 66, Line 2

We have already encountered examples of nouns and noun phrases derived from verbs (including participles; see ཤེས་རབ་སྙིང་པོ་ note 13) and nominalized sentences used modularly (see ཤེས་རབ་སྙིང་པོ་ note 22). Here, however, is a very specialized form of a nominalized verb: the gerundive.

Recall that the optative (or emphatic future) construction—of *verb* + བར་བྱ་ (see ཤེས་རབ་སྙིང་པོ་ note 11)—conveys the sense of "[I] will do [something]" or "[something] should be done." When this construction is nominalized (i.e., turned into a noun phrase) through the addition of a nominalizing lexical particle (བ་), it forms the gerundive, or "future passive participle," and the resulting construction, *verb* + བར་བྱ་བ་, conveys the sense of "that which is to be done." For example, when the verb ཤེས་ ("to know") occurs in this construction, the phrase ཤེས་པར་བྱ་བ་ comes to mean "that which is to be known." Many such phrases have become concretized in the language, abbreviated, and treated as nouns. Hence, in this example, the phrase ཤེས་པར་བྱ་བ་ has been abbreviated over time as ཤེས་བྱ་ ("that which is to be known," or simply, "object of knowledge").

Here, the construction is seen with the verb གཞིག་ ("to destroy"/"to disintegrate"), and hence གཞིག་པར་བྱ་བ་ conveys the sense of being the object of the verbal activity—"that which is to be destroyed," or "that which disintegrates."

WHAT TO REMEMBER

The gerundive, or future passive participle, is formed by adding པར་བྱ་བ་ to the bare verb and conveys the sense of "that which is to be done." The more common constructions are often abbreviated as *verb* + བྱ་ and treated as fixed words ("object of [verb]").

25 Omitted Verb of Predication, ཡིན་

Page 66, Line 10

In this section of the text, the vast majority of statements are simple declarative sentences ending in the verb ཡིན་. Beginning here, with the passage རྣ་བ་ནི་ཐོས་པའི་མཚན་ཉིད་དོ།, the final verb ཡིན་ is omitted, while the ornamental terminating particle དོ་ is provided to signal the end of the sentence (although even this is abandoned in subsequent sentences). Given the previous use of this grammatical construction there is no ambiguity concerning its import, and hence the verb ཡིན་ has been omitted, although because the grammar of these phrases could still be misinterpreted, the subject and predicate are delimited by the use of ནི་ marking the subject.

WHAT TO REMEMBER

Simple statements of predication ("A is B") often occur as self-contained phrases of two items with the subject marked by ནི་ and the verb ཡིན་ omitted.

The Either-Or Construction

26

Page 66, Line 16

The passage here, སྒྲ་ནི་སྙན་མི་སྙན་གྱི་མཚན་ཉིད།, contains the phrase སྙན་མི་སྙན་. This repetition of a term in the negative is one means of indicating an "either-or" construction. Hence, the passage would be translated as "sound [is that which has] the defining characteristic of being either pleasant or unpleasant."

WHAT TO REMEMBER

One means of indicating an "or" or "either ... or" construction is through the duplication of the same word in the negative, for example, གཅིག་མི་གཅིག་ meaning "the same or not the same" and ཡིན་མ་ཡིན་ meaning "is or is not," etc.

Translation Hint

27

Page 66, Line 18

There is a substantial portion of technical vocabulary in Tibetan Buddhism—occurring across all genres and domains of Tibetan literature—drawn from the tradition of Buddhist epistemology. Terms such as རྣམ་པ་ ("aspect"), བྱེ་བྲག་ ("particular"), and མཚན་ཉིད་ ("definition" or "defining characteristics") are just such examples of terms and concepts to be found in the literature. To fully understand the significance of these terms, familiarity with the works of Dignāga and Dharmakīrti (and their intellectual successors) is required. The text included here as selection number six (Purbujok's *Introductory Path of Reasoning*) is intended as a first step in that direction. Additional reading recommendations are provided in the introduction to that text.

Closing Quotation Marker སྙམ་[པ་/དུ་]

28

Page 67, Line 15

In addition to the previously seen closing quotation marker ཞེས་ (see ཤེར་སྙིང་རྣམ་བཤད་ note 5), there is another closing quotation marker that occurs within Tibetan literature: the phrase སྙམ་[པ་/དུ་]. However, this closing quotation marker does not indicate the end of a literary or spoken quotation but rather is the closing quotation marker for thoughts and dreams. Hence, just as the closing quotation marker ཞེས་ may be left untranslated depending on context, so too may སྙམ་ be left untranslated, as when it occurs with verbs like བསམ་ ("to think") or is translated as "the thought '...,'" etc., with other verbs (as here). Alternately, it can appear as a final verb ("to think," "to wonder"), in which case it takes a sentence (without any additional marker) as its object.

WHAT TO REMEMBER

While other syntactic particles are used to indicate the end of a literary or spoken quotation, the closing quotation marker for thoughts is སྙམ་, which may be left untranslated or rendered with the expression "the thought '...,'" or similar such phrases.

29

Translation Hint

Page 67, Line 17

This is a run-on sentence without punctuation (see ཤེར་སྙིང་རྣམ་བཤད་ note 15); the sentence should be broken at this point, after the verbal participle བཤད་པ་ (see ཤེས་རབ་སྙིང་པོ་ note 13). The same holds true for the passage a few lines later beginning with the sentence མི་གནས་པའི་རང་བཞིན་ཡིན་ (page 67, line 21).

30

Multiple Verbal Modifiers

Page 67, Line 22

This phrase highlights the ability of the Tibetan language to "pile on" multiple modifying clauses. Here the three clause connective constructions utilizing the verbs ཤེས་, རིག་, and འཁྲུལ་ each modify the noun སེམས་ and take the frozen adverb དེ་ལྟར་ as their qualifier.

WHAT TO REMEMBER

The flexibility of the Tibetan language allows authors to create very compact sentences with more than one clause modifying the same noun. In some instances the complete clause-connective construction may be repeated, while in other instances verbs may be joined by the appropriate connector (ཅིང་, ཞིང་, etc.).

Translation Hint

31

Page 68, Line 8

The verb འགྱུར་ ("to become"), when occuring as an auxiliary verb in translations from Sanskrit, emphasizes the passive voice and often connotes a reflexive dimension to the verbal activity. More will be said about this later (see also བླ་མ་ལྔ་བཅུ་པ་ note 4).

Translation Hint

32

Page 68, Line 10

The use of བྱེད་ as an auxiliary verb with a nominative verb to create a causative construction (X་པར་བྱེད་ "to cause to X") was previously seen (see ཤེས་རབ་སྙིང་པོ་ note 19). A second usage of བྱེད་ in an auxiliary construction—commonly seen in translations from Sanskrit—is simply to emphasize the active voice and not to mark a causative. More will be said about this later (see བླ་མ་ལྔ་བཅུ་པ་ note 9).

Differences between Root Texts and Commentaries

33

Page 68, Line 12

It is not unusual for a commentary to contain readings that vary slightly from those found in the root text. This can occur for a number of reasons. The two texts could be the products of different translators (in the case of canonical texts), the two texts could come from different editorial recensions (such as the earlier [Old] Nartang recension and the later Derge recension), or the difference in reading could reflect a genuine difference in the original texts.

Already in this commentary there have been minor differences in readings between the root text and the commentary. For example, where the root text renders "Avalokiteśvara" as སྤྱན་རས་གཟིགས་ཀྱི་དབང་ཕྱུག་, the commentary renders it as སྤྱན་རས་གཟིགས་ཀྱི་དབང་པོ་; similarly, where the root text states གཟུགས་མེད་, the commentary states གཟུགས་མ་ཡིན་. All of these can be attributed to differences in style between the different translators of the root text and the commentary.

There have been numerous printings of the Buddhist canon in Tibet at various locations over the past seven hundred years, each with varying degrees of editing. There are two main groups of recensions of the canon: the so-called Tempangma (*thems spangs ma*) or "reference" edition (i.e., books that were not to pass beyond (*spangs*) the threshold (*thems*) of the library), and the Tsalpa (*tshal pa*) group, which appears to have undergone extensive editing over the centuries. Consequently, one of the most readily available and most often cited recensions of the Tibetan Buddhist canon—the Derge (*sde dge*; ca. 1734) recension within the Tsalpa group—diverges substantially from readings found in the earlier, Old Nartang (*snar thang*)/Tempangma (ca. 1431, and its alleged reprint, the "new" Nartang, ca. 1741). More to the point, because of this extensive editing, the readings found in the Derge recension of canonical texts often disagree with the commentaries on those same texts written in central Tibet prior to the eighteenth century, which referenced the more accurate Nartang recension—that is, the recension that contained readings closer to the original Sanskrit. Although all the canonical texts contained in this textbook reflect the Nartang recension, this issue is an important one to remember when working with canonical materials.

Finally, in some cases, one must consider the possibility that divergences in readings between root texts and their canonical commentaries reflect actual differences in the Indian Sanskrit originals. The passage encountered here appears to be one such instance. While the sūtra reads སེམས་ལ་སྒྲིབ་པ་མེད་པས་སྐྲག་པ་མེད་དེ།, Jñānamitra's commentary reads སེམས་ལ་སྐྲག་པ་མེད་པས་སྒྲིབ་པ་མེད་དེ།—a reading that is subsequently validated by his explanation. This difference in reading could reflect a genuine difference in interpretation by the author of the commentary or be indicative of a different (or possibly preferential) version of the root text that Jñānamitra based his commentary upon.

WHAT TO REMEMBER

Differences in readings between a root text and a commentary may be attributable to different translators (in the case of canonical texts), to different editorial recensions, or could reflect a genuine difference in interpretations or reading of the original text.

34

Translation Hint

Page 69, Line 5

Previously, the formation of verbal nouns and adjectives were discussed in the context of verbal participles (see ཤེས་རབ་སྙིང་པོ་ note 13). Here, the verb གསུངས་ (honorific for "to say" or "to speak") appears as one such verbal noun ("that which was said" or "what was said"). It should be noted that this construction—a verbal participle with a verb of predication, such as ཡིན་—has another possible reading that will be seen later (see ལམ་གཙོ་རྣམ་གསུམ་ note 9).

Commentarial Syntax: Use of ཀྱི་, etc., to Mark Apposition

Page 69, Line 10

Although up to this point in the text the grammatical structures have been normative, it is important to note that Indian commentaries can contain certain unique grammatical constructions. The idiosyncratic use of case-marking particles to indicate apposition—as we see here with the phrase བརྗོད་པ་མེད་པའི་རང་བཞིན་མེད་པར་—is one such construction.

Under normal circumstances, the passage བརྗོད་པ་མེད་པའི་རང་བཞིན་མེད་པར་ would be read as containing a clause-connective construction ("as lacking an own nature that is inexpressible"), but doing so would substantially deviate from the basic meaning of the text (since all phenomena have been established as *both* lacking an own nature *and* being inexpressible). Rather, the sixth-case marker –འི་ is being used as an apposition marker, joining two similarly descriptive phrases ("as lacking an own nature—that is, [as] inexpressible"). In Tibetan canonical translations that attempt to replicate the formulaic structures of classical Indian scholastic commentaries (*śāstra*), the translators use a range of case-marking particles in this manner; this practice can be so extreme in some cases as to render the text otherwise unintelligible to someone versed only in normative Tibetan grammar.

WHAT TO REMEMBER

In Tibetan canonical translations that attempt to replicate the formulaic structures of classical Indian scholastic commentaries (*śāstra*), the translators use a range of case-marking particles as apposition markers to join the words of the root text with synonyms or descriptive phrases.

36 Use of ནི་ to Disambiguate Grammar

Page 69, Line 17

Wilson (671) notes that "ནི་ sets off a word or noun phrase, but does not change the declension of the word or phrase before it" and that, in general, "ནི་ may follow any syntactic element in a sentence." In longer, more complex sentences, the particle ནི་ performs the critical function of disambiguating the relationship between components of a sentence by separating elements from different layers of a modularly constructed sentence (see ཤེས་རབ་སྙིང་པོ་ note 22).

The sentence here consists of five discrete components: ⓐ a quotation from the root text followed by a referential locative (Wilson, case 7.6; 654–655), ⓑ a series of connected verbal phrases with the last marked in the third case (followed by a ནི་—the subject of this note), ⓒ one sentence connected by the connective particle ཞིང་ to ⓓ a second sentence also marked in the third case, and ⓔ the final verb:

> ⓐ སྡུག་བསྔལ་ཐམས་ཅད་རབ་ཏུ་ཞི་བར་བྱེད་པའི་སྔགས་སུ་ཤེས་པར་བྱ་སྟེ་ཞེས་བྱ་བ་ལ་ ⓑ ཤེས་རབ་ཀྱི་ཕ་རོལ་ཏུ་ཕྱིན་པ་འཆང་། ཀློག །ཁ་ཏོན་བྱེད་པ་དང་། ཚུལ་བཞིན་དུ་ཡིད་ལ་བྱེད་ཅིང་། གཞན་ལ་འཆད་པས་ནི་ ⓒ མིག་ནད་ལ་སོགས་པ་ནད་ཐམས་ཅད་མེད་པར་འགྱུར་ཞིང་། ⓓ ཕྱོགས་བཅུའི་སངས་རྒྱས་དང་། ལྷ་ཀླུ་ལ་སོགས་པས་སྐྱོབ་པས་ ⓔ སྐྱོབ་པར་བྱེད།

The purpose of the particle ནི་ at the end of ⓑ is to separate the first set of verbal phrases—as a reason clause—from the next sentence, ⓒ, and to emphasize that ⓑ is not a reason clause that attaches to the verb in statement in ⓒ but rather attaches as a reason clause to the verb in statement ⓓ. Thus, it emphasizes that there is not a direct causal connection between "upholding the perfection of wisdom," etc., and "all diseases ... [being] eliminated" but rather between those activities and being protected "by the buddhas of the ten directions," etc. This sentence can be contrasted grammatically with the one that immediately follows.

WHAT TO REMEMBER

The particle ནི་ performs the critical function of disambiguating the relationship between components of a sentence by separating elements from different layers of a modularly constructed sentence. The particle ནི་ may follow any syntactic element in a sentence but, while setting it apart from what immediately follows, does not change the declension of the word or phrase before it.

The Negation of Verbal Collocations and the Verb ཟ་

37

Page 70, Line 14

The verb ཟ་ is one of the most polysemous of the Tibetan verbs, with several distinct meanings and numerous verbal collocations. Verbal collocations, or phrasal verbs, are characterized by having a meaning that is either different from the individual words that comprise it, or having a connotation that is in excess of the sum of those words. The phrase encountered here is a nominalized form of the verbal collocation ཐེ་ཚོམ་ཟ་ "to have doubts" (lit. "to feed on the doubt"); when nominalized, it means "having doubts" or "one who has doubts."

A critical point of grammar raised by this phrase is the issue of negation with regard to verbal collocations. As can be seen, the negation particles མི་/མ་ are inserted within the collocation immediately before the root verb and hence ཐེ་ཚོམ་མི་ཟ་ means "to not have doubt."

WHAT TO REMEMBER

Verbal collocations are negated by the insertion of a negation particle—མི་ (with the present and future tenses) or མ་ (with the past and imperative tenses)—within the collocation itself, immediately before the root verb.

Translation of Jñānamitra's *Explanation of the Heart Sūtra*

In Sanskrit: *Ārya prajñā-paramitā-hṛdaya-vyakhya*
In Tibetan: *'Phags pa shes rab kyi pha rol tu phyin pa'i snying po'i rnam par bshad pa*

Homage to the Bhagavatī, the Perfection of Wisdom!

Regarding the statement "The Bhagavatī, the Heart of the Perfection of Wisdom," for the purpose of expressing the name [lit. defining characteristic] of the sūtra, it says, "The Bhagavatī, the Heart of the Perfection of Wisdom." Because if the name were not designated at the very outset, what sūtra it was would be uncertain, hence the name is stated. However, it is not merely limited to the designation of a name. Since, moreover, there is nothing that all the aphoristic statements of this *Heart of the Perfection of Wisdom* do not include here, [it] is called "the sūtra of sūtras."

With regard to that [title], *Bhaga* means conquering (√*bhañj*) demons (*māra*). Hence since [these demons], such as the *māra* of the aggregates, are not found when sought with this meaning of the perfection of wisdom, and because no *māras* abide [there], "conquering" [is said]. "Endowed [with]" (-*vant*) [means] endowed with the six fortunes [lordship, qualities, fame, glory, wisdom, and effort]. That is, since all the good qualities of knowledge arise from the influence of the perfection of wisdom, it is endowed [with them]. Transcendant (-*vāt*) [also] means the unlocated nirvāṇa. Because all minds, intellects, and consciousnesses are overturned by this meaning of the perfection of wisdom, and hence, since it is free from all karmic predispositions, it has passed beyond. With regard to [the feminine ending] –*i*, all the buddhas of the three times arise from practicing the meaning of the perfection of wisdom. Because they are produced by the meaning of the perfection of wisdom, and therefore the perfection of wisdom comes to be the mother of all the buddhas, [the feminine ending] –*i*/*ma* [is used]. Regarding "wisdom," since one knows [reality] just as it is by means of the three aspects of wisdom—hearing, thinking, and meditating—it is called "wisdom." Regarding "perfection," because wisdom does not perceive any phenomena whatsoever, it has passed beyond signs, the two extremes, and birth and death, and because of that, it is said to be perfect. Regarding "Heart," in all of the supreme and profound things in the *Perfection of Wisdom in 100,000 Lines* and others, there is not anything not contained in this small sūtra. Therefore, it is the called "the heart." Regarding "Homage to the Bhagavatī, the Perfection of Wisdom," it is said in the *Perfection of Wisdom in 100,000 Lines* that when one pays homage to the perfection of wisdom, it is like paying homage to all the buddhas of the three times; it is paying homage for the purpose of worship and the accumulation of merit.

Now, to the text. With regard to this perfection of wisdom, the meaning from beginning to end is clearly explained in seven parts. Moreover, if you ask what, [they are] the setting, the entry into wisdom, the defining characteristic of emptiness, the sphere of wisdom, the qualities of wisdom, the fruition of wisdom, and the dhāraṇī of wisdom. Regarding that, the setting is from "Thus have I heard" to "dwelling together." The entry into wisdom is up to "saw the five aggregates also as empty of own nature." The defining characteristic of emptiness is up to "also no attainment, and also no non-attainment." The sphere of wisdom is up through "there not being [any] attainment, they abide in and practice the perfection of wisdom." The good qualities of wisdom is through "they have gone to nirvāṇa." The fruition of wisdom is up through "they have directly and perfectly awakened to enlightenment." The dhāraṇī of wisdom is the concluding mantra and [everything] above.

[The Setting]

Now, [I] will explain the meaning of the setting. Regarding the statement "Thus have I heard," all the sets of Mahāyāna sūtras were heard by the Ārya, Mañjuśrī, and since [he] compiled [them], "I heard" is said. With regard to that, "thus" (*evaṃ; 'di skad*) is the very expression of just what is enumerated in the *Heart of Wisdom*. The statement "I heard" [means I] heard at the feet of the Transcendent Victor. What was spoken from [his] glorious throat was heard directly by the ear sense faculty. The statement "at one time" does not apply (*mi bya*) to [some] explanation of the *Heart of Wisdom* at another time but rather applies (*bya*) to the time of the explaining on just this occasion to this entourage in Rājagṛha by the Transcendent Victor.

Regarding the statement "the Transcendent Victor," [one might ask,] "Who is the teacher with regard to that?" "In what place?" "Who was the entourage?" "[They] having gathered [there], what is the meaning?" In that case, the teacher is the Buddha, the Transcendent Victor. The place is Vulture Peak in Rājagṛha. The entourage is a great assembly of monks and a great assembly of bodhisattvas. If you ask, "[They] having gathered [there], what was the purpose?" then this *Heart of the Perfection of Wisdom* was taught. With regard to that, the special explanation of the word is like what was said above. "Vulture Peak in Rājagṛha" is famous because of the good qualities of King Bimbisāra. The city of that region was designated as a general name [of the region].

"Vulture Peak" [is stated] since that region [of Rājagṛha] is very extensive. Because many birds gather at the peak, "Vulture Peak" is designated as its name. "A great assembly of monks" [means those] of great power and many in number. Regarding "a great assembly of bodhisattvas," all [of them] had directly penetrated the marvelous meaning of the perfection of wisdom, and furthermore, [there were] many bodhisattvas who had entered into the perfection of wisdom. "Were staying together" [means] the Bhagavān was surrounded by many entourages; that is, they were dwelling [with him]. [All of] this above [is] the setting.

[The Entry into Wisdom]

Now, [I] will explain [this section of the root text] in terms of the meaning of the entry into wisdom. At that time, the Bhagavān was absorbed in a samādhi on the enumeration of all phenomena called "perception of the profound." With regard to that, the Bhagavān, because of having a mind of loving compassion for all sentient beings and those in the entourage, and [wishing] to influence them, entered into absorption [into that samādhi]. "Enumeration of all phenomena called 'perception of the profound'" [means] because [the Buddha] understands and teaches by means of this Dharma text that all phenomena have passed beyond all observation and the extremes, it says, "perception of the profound." "Entered into absorption in that samādhi" [means] sitting in meditative equipoise on that very profundity.

With regard to where it says "Also at that time, the Bodhisattva, the Mahāsattva, the Ārya, Avalokiteśvara, looked at the profound practice of the perfection of wisdom and saw those very five aggregates also as empty of their own nature," "also at that time" [means] at the time of the entourage having assembled and [the Buddha] having entered into absorption.

[Everything] up to where it says that Avalokiteśvara "saw [the aggregates] as empty of their own nature" [means] that the Ārya, Avalokiteśvara, because of his mind of loving-kindness for that entourage and all sentient beings, conceived of the perfection of wisdom as utterly profound, and thought, "Those five aggregates as well are empty of an own nature that is not observed, [and] there is nothing whatsoever being other than emptiness." Regarding "the five aggregates," the form aggregate is like a ball of foam, feeling is like a water bubble, discrimination is like a mirage, compositional factors are like a plantain tree, consciousness is like an illusion. Regarding "being empty of own nature," those five aggregates are empty of the defining characteristics of each of their own natures. Hence, because they are beyond all extremes and without defining characteristics, they are just empty.

Regarding the statement "Then, the Venerable Śāriputra, through the power of the Buddha, said this to the Bodhisattva, the Mahāsattva, the Ārya, Avalokiteśvara," Śāriputra, who is the foremost in wisdom among the great śrāvakas, through the influence of the Tathāgata, asked [a question of] the Superior, Avalokiteśvara. As for the statement "How should a son of good family train, one who wishes to engage in the practice of the profound perfection of wisdom," a "son of good family" is [one who is] born from the Great Vehicle (Mahāyāna) scriptures and hence has become a child of the Tathāgata. "One who" [means] whosoever is suitable to enter the Great Vehicle. "The practice of the profound perfection of wisdom" [means] engaging—inexpressibly—[with] the profound reality of all phenomena by means of the practices of the perfection of wisdom. "How should that one who wishes to practice, train" [is] asking the question, "How should one who wishes to practice the meaning of the perfection of wisdom know [it] solely just as it is, that is, [how] should [they] train?"

"Thus he spoke, and the Bodhisattva, the Mahāsattva, the Ārya, Avalokiteśvara said this to the Venerable Śāriputra" is proclaiming [the introduction to] the answer to his question. "O Śāriputra, a son of good family or daughter of good family, whosoever wishes to engage in the practice of the profound perfection of wisdom should analyze in this way" [means] "one who wishes to practice with respect to the perfection of wisdom should analyze in accordance with the meaning of the explanation below."

"Those five aggregates also are to be purely and thoroughly seen as empty of their own nature" [means] those five aggregates [are] just empty of their own characteristics, and hence, since they are without defining characteristics, they are not produced in former times, do not abide in the present, and will not disintegrate in the future. Hence, because at all times they are not produced, do not abide, and do not cease, since their unlocated nature cannot be expressed, they are just empty. "See" [means] to see [things] in accordance with reality, just as they are, and they are not to be seen in any other way. The preceding is the entry into wisdom.

[The Defining Characteristics of Emptiness]

Now, [I] will explain [this section of the root text] in terms of the meaning of the defining characteristics of emptiness, that is, regarding the statements "form is empty; emptiness, as well, is form." Regarding that, the statement "is form" [means] that due to misunderstanding the nature of emptiness, [those with] a mind that is mistaken perceive and conceive "is form," or conventionally designate [it] by means of words. Regarding the statement "is empty," since the nature of form is emptiness, and since in earlier times also, there were no defining characteristics, there is nothing to be objectified. In the present and the future also, there are no defining characteristics. Hence, since there is nothing to be objectified, all extremes and all things do not abide. Because of [this], it is called "emptiness." Regarding the statement "emptiness is also form," even though emptiness [has] a nature that lacks objectification, [it] is designated conventionally [by the phrase] "is form," and because that does not abide separately [from it], emptiness is also form.

"Emptiness is not other than form; form is also not other than emptiness" [means] whatsoever is form, that very [thing] is inexpressible emptiness. Hence, having abandoned "forms," since emptiness is not found when sought, "emptiness is not other than form" is said. With regard to just that—whatsoever is the inexpressible emptiness—because that which is conventionally designated with the word "form" does not exist separately and is not found [when sought], "form is also not other than emptiness" is said. Regarding "similarly, feelings, discrimination, compositional factors, and consciousness are empty," in accordance with just how it was explained concerning form, so [one should] view the remaining aggregates, as well, as like that. Regarding "O Śāriputra, similarly, all phenomena are empty," saying "Śāriputra" [means] "Listen well, without being distracted"; [it is] a word in the vocative.

Similarly, all phenomena being empty [means that] just as how it was explained with regard to the five aggregates, moreover, you should know all [mundane and] transcendent phenomena—from the six sense-spheres up to omniscience—also as emptiness. "No defining characteristics" [means that] just as space is without defining characteristics, [so, too] are there no defining characteristics of the afflictions, [and] no defining characteristics of purification, as well. "No production, no cessation" [is said since] production in the present would [mean something] subsequently coming into existence out of prior nonexistence. Cessation [means something] would subsequently go into nonexistence from having previously existed. [Hence,] regarding emptiness, because it does not exist as [something that can be] objectified, it is not produced previously; since it is not produced, it does not subsequently cease.

Regarding "no defilement and no freedom from defilement," defilement [means] consciousnesses acting as subject and object. Since emptiness transcends [dualistic] consciousness, there is no defilement. Regarding no freedom from defilement, since defilement does not exist, freedom from from [it] also does not exist. Regarding "no diminishment and no fulfillment," diminishment [means] sentient beings; fulfillment [means] buddhas. Regarding "there are no," since even when sentient beings and buddhas are sought they are not found, there is no diminishment and no fulfillment.

Regarding "therefore, emptiness is not form," form is [that which has] the defining characteristic of being that which disintegrates, and since emptiness lacks defining characteristics, emptiness is not form [is said]. [Regarding] "no feeling," similarly feeling [is that which has] the defining characteristic of experiencing. [Regarding] "is not discrimination," discrimination [is that which has] the defining characteristic of apprehending. [Regarding] "no compositional factors," compositional factors [are that which has] the defining characteristic of composing. [Regarding] "no consciousness," consciousness [is that which has] the defining characteristic of apprehending particulars individually. Because emptiness does not exist as [something that can be] objectified, [it] is not consciousness. [Regarding] "is not these," the five aggregates [are that which have] the defining characteristic of being contaminated. [Hence,] emptiness is not the five aggregates.

"No eye" [is stated]. Regarding that, eye is [that which has] the defining characteristic of seeing. Because emptiness is without defining characteristics, it is not the eye. "No ear" [is stated]. Similarly the ear is [that which has] the defining characteristic of hearing. "No nose" [is stated]. The nose is [that which has] the defining characteristic of smelling. "No tongue" [is stated]. The tongue is [that which has] the defining characteristic of experiencing tastes. "No body" [is stated]. The body is [that which has] the defining characteristic of touching. "No mind" [is stated]. The mind is [that which has] the nature of differentiating particulars, and because emptiness lacks defining characteristics, it is not the mind. Thus, the six sense faculties are [those that have] the defining characteristics of apprehending, and because emptiness is without defining characteristics, it is not the six sense faculties.

"No form" [is stated]. Form is [that which has] the defining characteristics of color and shape, and because emptiness is without defining characteristics, it is not form. "No sound" [is stated]. Similarly sound [is that which has] the defining characteristic of being either pleasant or unpleasant. "No smell" [is stated]. Smell is [that which has] the defining characteristic of being smelled. "No taste" [is stated]. Taste is [that which has] the defining characteristic of having flavor. "No tactile object" [is stated]. A tactile object is [that which has] the defining characteristic of being rough or smooth to the touch. "No phenomena" [is stated]. A phenomenon is [that which has] the defining characteristic of having the aspect of a particular, and because emptiness is without defining characteristics, it is not phenomena. Thus, objects have the defining characteristic of conditions that cause objectification, but since emptiness is without defining characteristics, it is not objects.

"From 'it is not the eye constituent' up to 'it is not the mental constituent and is not the mental consciousness constituent'" [is stated]. Thus, the eighteen constituents are [those which have] the defining characteristic of poison, but since emptiness is without defining characteristics, it is not [any of] the eighteen constituents. "From 'it is not ignorance' [up to] 'it is not aging and death,' and from 'it is not the exhaustion of ignorance' up to 'it is not the exhaustion of aging and death'" [is stated]. The twelve [links of] dependent arising from ignorance to aging and death are [those which have] the defining characteristic of upholding saṃsāra, but because emptiness is without defining characteristics, it is not ignorance up to and including aging and death. From the exhaustion of ignorance up to and including the exhaustion of aging and death are [those which have] the defining characteristic of purification, but because emptiness is without defining characteristics, it is not the cessation of ignorance up to and including the cessation of aging and death.

"It is not suffering, origin, cessation, or even the path" [is stated]. Suffering [is that which has] the defining characteristic of affliction. Origin [is that which has] the defining characteristic of appropriation. Cessation [is that which has] the defining characteristic of pacification, and path is [that which has] the defining characteristic of knowledge, but because emptiness is without defining characteristics, emptiness is not [any of] the four [noble] truths.

"It is not exalted wisdom" [is stated]. Exalted wisdom is [that which has] the defining characteristic of directly perceiving all phenomena, but because emptiness is without defining characteristics, it is not exalted wisdom. "It is not attainment; it is also not nonattainment" [is stated]. Attainment is unsurpassed, perfect, complete enlightenment. Nonattainment [is] the nonattainment of the unsurpassed by sentient beings. Regarding the phrase "is not," the defining characteristic of emptiness is even lacking unsurpassed enlightenment. Since it also lacks sentient beings, it is also not attainment and is also not nonattainment. Since these [are its] enumerations, all phenomena [are] the emptiness of own nature, because it is taught that "emptiness is like that." The preceding is the defining characteristic of emptiness.

[The Sphere of Activity of Wisdom]

Now [I] will explain [this section of the root text] in terms of the meaning of the sphere of activity of wisdom. With regard to the statement "O Śāriputra, just so, bodhisattvas being without attainment, [they] abide in and practice the perfection of wisdom," because the thought "[I] have entered what has not been entered [before]" arises, then when one has merely this sphere of the perfection of wisdom, it is explained as a sign of practicing with regard to emptiness. "Just so" is said because all phenomena are emptiness. Regarding "bodhisattvas, being without attainment, abide in and practice the perfection of wisdom," bodhisattvas who have entered the Great Vehicle (*Mahāyāna*) know that there is no attainment whatsoever—from the five aggregates to omniscience—and, without seeing even the merest particle of any phenomenon, will practice in reference to the perfection of wisdom.

All phenomena are empty and hence are nonabiding natures, and furthermore, because [they] have become enveloped in confusion, with minds that are mistaken, that do not know, and that do not understand [phenomena to be] like that, [sentient beings] cycle and wander in the ocean of mundane existence. [If you ask,] "What is the nature of that mistaken mind?" [then I respond,] when it is analyzed by the three types of exalted wisdom, since the mind does not exist as [something that can be] objectified, the afflictions also are not seen, [their] being purified also is not seen, [and everything] from the five aggregates up to omniscience also is not seen. Emptiness, the lack of defining characteristics, no production, no cessation, and so forth, also are not seen. Even wisdom itself is completely and utterly unseen; that absence of seeing anything whatsoever is seeing the very nature of the mind. Just so, seeing the nature of the mind is to see enlightenment. Whoever sees enlightenment sees the Buddha by means of reality (*dharmatā*). That one who sees the Buddha by means of reality is completely and perfectly awakened into unsurpassed enlightenment itself.

On this occasion, a doubter speaks. If [he] asks, "Since you have just explained [emptiness] as the mere nonexistence of anything whatsoever, do [you] not fall into the view of nihilism of the non-Buddhists or into the pacific cessation of the śrāvakas?" [we] say in response: [it] is not like that; because [in our system, one] accomplishes the aims of sentient beings in a nonobjectifying manner and dedicates [that resulting merit] for [the attainment of] unsurpassed enlightenment, and engages in the practice of the six perfections and so forth in a nonobjectifying manner, in just that way [it] does not become a flaw. The preceding is the sphere of activity of wisdom.

[The Good Qualities of Wisdom]

Now, [I] will explain [this section of the root text] in terms of the good qualities of wisdom. Regarding [the statement] "Since the mind is without fear, there are no obstructions, and having completely transcended beyond mistakenness, one proceeds to nirvāṇa," since throughout [the processes of] hearing, thinking, and meditating upon the meaning of the emptiness of the Perfection of Wisdom [sūtras], [one] is not afraid, then because [this] overcomes the mind, mentality, consciousness, and the karmic predispositions, "there are no defilements in the mind" is said.

Having thoroughly passed beyond the sphere of activity of those who behave like children—the heretics—the śrāvakas, and the pratyekabuddhas, one exhausts all the afflictive obstructions and the obstructions to omniscience, and hence [one] goes to the great nirvāṇa. This and above are the good qualities of wisdom.

[The Fruition of Wisdom]

Now, [I] will explain [this section of the root text] in terms of the meaning of the fruition of wisdom. Regarding the statement "All the buddhas who have thoroughly passed beyond [saṃsāra] in the three times, also having dwelt in the perfection of wisdom, have directly awakened to unsurpassed perfect complete buddhahood," all the buddhas who have passed from the mundane worldly realm in the ten directions and in the three times [to full enlightenment] also have upheld this profound perfection of wisdom, have read it, recited it daily, meditated upon it, and taught it to others, and by practicing the perfection of wisdom, have directly awakened to unsurpassed enlightenment. All the buddhas of the three times, moreover, are produced by the perfection of wisdom [and] since they arise from the perfection of wisdom, the perfection of wisdom serves as the mother of all buddhas. This preceding [explanation] is the fruition of wisdom.

[The Dhāraṇī of Wisdom]

Now, [I] will explain [this section of the root text] in terms of the meaning of the magical incantation (*dhāraṇī*) of wisdom. Regarding the statement "Therefore, the mantra of the perfection of wisdom is true, and hence, unmistaken," [beginning with the word] "therefore," because [this] is [referring to] what was said above, "therefore" is said. Regarding the statement "the mantra of the perfection of wisdom is true, and hence, unmistaken," the practicing of the meaning of the perfection of wisdom as knowledge is called "mantra." Because all the phenomena of the transient world as well serve as the Great Vehicle [leading] to unsurpassed enlightenment, and [because] oneself and others will also awaken into unsurpassed enlightenment, it says "true, and hence, unmistaken." Regarding the statement "the mantra of great knowledge," since the mantra that is knowledge of the meaning of the perfection of wisdom teaches all desire, hatred, ignorance, and the sufferings of saṃsāra as lacking an own nature—that is, [as] inexpressible—the perfection of wisdom is the mantra of great knowledge. Regarding the statement "the unsurpassed mantra," because the perfection of wisdom serves to establish one in unsurpassed enlightenment, it is the unsurpassed mantra. Regarding the statement "the mantra that is unequaled and equal," since the perfection of wisdom is not equal to the practices of worldly beings, śrāvakas, or pratyekabuddhas, and [since] it makes [one's consciousness] equal to the exalted wisdom-consciousness of all the buddhas, therefore it is the mantra that is unequaled and equal. Regarding the statement "[It] should be known as the mantra that completely pacifies all suffering," by upholding the perfection of wisdom, reading it, reciting it daily, accordingly taking it to mind, and explaining it to others, [one] is protected by the buddhas of the ten directions, by gods, by nāgas, and so forth, and all diseases, such as diseases of the eye etc., will be eliminated, hence [this mantra] bestows protection.

Since, by practicing the perfection of wisdom, bad transmigrations and the entire ocean of saṃsāra are overcome, [it is] the mantra that completely pacifies all suffering. With regard to [the statement] "The mantra of the perfection of wisdom is stated: TADYATHĀ GATE GATE PĀRAGATE PĀRASAṂGATE BODHI SVĀHĀ," since this mantra of the perfection of wisdom naturally establishes the combined meaning of all supreme profundities, it is said to be a mantra of blessing.

Regarding the statement "O Śāriputra, a bodhisattva mahāsattva should practice the profound perfection of wisdom in that way," since all the buddhas of the three times also awaken [to enlightenment] through the practice of the perfection of wisdom, bodhisattvas who have entered the Mahāyāna also should practice the perfection of wisdom. Regarding the statement "Then the Bhagavān arose from that samādhi," by the power of the Bhagavān having entered into samādhi on the profound, Śāriputra asked his question, and hence Avalokiteśvara having explained [the answer], [the Bhagavān] completed his purpose and rose from that samādhi. Regarding the statement "[The Buddha,] having bestowed his benediction on the Bodhisattva, the Mahāsattva, the Ārya,

Avalokiteśvara, said, 'Well done! Well done!'" the statement of the meaning of the *Heart of the Perfection of Wisdom* is concordant with the sayings of all the buddhas. Hence, because it is unmistaken, he praised it [with] "Well done." Regarding the statement "O son of good family, it is like that; O son of good family, it is like that. One should engage in the profound perfection of wisdom just as you have taught," since that which Avalokiteśvara declared is concordant with the pronouncements of all the buddhas, "it is like that" [is said]. Bodhisattvas who have entered the Mahāyāna, moreover, should practice the perfection of wisdom just as it was taught by the noble Avalokiteśvara. Regarding the statement "even the tathāgatas will rejoice," if the tathāgatas are caused to rejoice at the explanation [given] by Avalokiteśvara, what need is there [to mention] others who have no doubt? Regarding the statement "The Bhagavān being pleased, and having spoken thus," by that pronouncement of the perfection of wisdom, everyone in the entourage, moreover, having understood the meaning of the perfection of wisdom, then because there were no obstructions to the Mahāyāna, [the Buddha] was pleased and spoke thus.

The Venerable Śāriputra, the Bodhisattva Avalokiteśvara, and everyone in the entourage together with the gods, humans, demigods, and gandharvas took great joy in what was said by the Bhagavān.

The commentary on the *Bhagavatī, the Heart of the Perfection of Wisdom* composed by the master Jñānamitra is complete.

The Sūtra Called "The Wise and the Foolish"

While the sūtras contained in the various Buddhist canons for the most part recount the philosophical and religious teachings of the Buddha, the scriptures that appear to have been most appealing to the general populace were the *jataka* tales, or narrative accounts of the previous lives of the Buddha. One collection of these stories, *The Sūtra called "The Wise and the Foolish,"* gained popularity, first along the "Silk Road,"[1] then in China, and later in Tibet and Mongolia.

Of all the stories contained within *The Sūtra called "The Wise and the Foolish,"* the story of Prince Mahāsattva giving his body to feed a hungry tigress has been one of the most popular and most prominently depicted in Buddhist art and literature[2] over the centuries. Although *The Sūtra called "The Wise and the Foolish"* was translated from Chinese into Tibetan much later than the bulk of the canon, it still preserves many of the stylistic features of a Buddhist sūtra. In addition to the formulaic opening, the setting of the story is provided before the main narrative. Like the *Heart Sūtra*, in which a question is posed and an answer received, in the story of "The Hungry Tigress," the question that lies at the center of the narrative is prompted not by philosophical inquiry but rather in response to an event in the community. In this regard, the structure of such sūtras follows a basic pattern:

- the setting of the narrative
- a provocative event
- a historical narrative recounting events in previous lives
- a summation, connecting the events in previous lives with the recent event in the narrative present

In addition to presenting the student with a new genre of literature, this text presents many of the same type of challenges encountered already, including proper names and allusions to standard Buddhist categories.

---

[1] The various chapters of the text are attested in paintings in the Mogao Caves.

[2] The story appears in many texts, including the *Jātakamālā* and *Suvarṇaprabhāsottama-sūtra*.

༄༅། །མཛངས་བླུན་ཞེས་བྱ་བའི་མདོ་ལས། སེམས་ཅན་ཆེན་པོས་སྟག་མོ་ལ་ལུས་བྱིན་པའི་ལེའུ།

༄༅། །རྒྱ་གར་སྐད་དུ། དམ་མཱུ་ཀོ་ནཱ་མ་སཱུ་ཏྲ།
བོད་སྐད་དུ། མཛངས་བླུན་ཞེས་བྱ་བའི་མདོ།

དཀོན་མཆོག་གསུམ་ལ་ཕྱག་འཚལ་ལོ།

སེམས་ཅན་ཆེན་པོས་སྟག་མོ་ལ་ལུས་བྱིན་པའི་ལེའུའོ།

འདི་སྐད་བདག་གིས་ཐོས་པ་དུས་གཅིག་ན། བཅོམ་ལྡན་འདས་མཉན་དུ་ཡོད་པ་ན་རྒྱལ་བུ་རྒྱལ་བྱེད་ཀྱི་ཚལ་མགོན་མེད་ཟས་སྦྱིན་གྱི་ཀུན་དགའ་ར་བ་ན་བཞུགས་སོ། །དེའི་ཚེ་བཅོམ་ལྡན་འདས་བསོད་སྙོམས་ཀྱི་དུས་ལ་བབ་ནས་ཤམ་ཐབས་དང་ཆོས་གོས་བགོས་ཏེ་ལྷུང་བཟེད་བསྣམས་ནས་ཀུན་དགའ་བོ་དང་བསོད་སྙོམས་ལ་གཤེགས་སོ། །

དེའི་ཚེ་གྲོང་ཁྱེར་དེ་ན་རྒན་མོ་ཞིག་ལ་བུ་དག་དུ་ཀུ་བ་གཉིས་ཤིག་ཡོད་དེ།[1] ནོར་བདག་གིས་ཟིན་ནས་ཞལ་ཆེ་བའི་མདུན་དུ་ཁྲིད་དེ། ཁྲིམས་དང་སྦྱར་ནས་[2] གསད་པ་ལ་ཐུག་ནས་[3] རིགས་ངན་གྱིས་བཀྲི་སྟེ་བསོད་པའི་གནས་སུ་ཁྲིད་པ་ལས།[4] བཅོམ་ལྡན་འདས་རྒྱང་མ་ནས་གཤེགས་པ་རྒན་མོ་མ་སྨད་གསུམ་[5] གྱིས་མཐོང་ནས་སངས་རྒྱས་གཤེགས་པའི་ཕྱོགས་སུ་ཕྱག་འཚལ་ཏེ། ལྷའི་ནང་ན་གཙོ་བོ་[6] ཐུགས་བརྩེ་བར་དགོངས་ཏེ་བདག་གི་བུ་དགུམ་པ་ལ་ཐུག་པ་འདིའི་སྐྱབས་མཛད་དུ་གསོལ་ཞེས་སྨྲས་པ། བཅོམ་ལྡན་འདས་ཀྱིས་གསན་ནས་དེ་བཞིན་གཤེགས་པའི་ཐུགས་རྗེ་ཆེན་པོས་དེ་དག་ལ་ཐུགས་བརྩེ་བར་དགོངས་ཏེ། དེ་དག་གི་སྲོག་བསྐྱབ་པའི་སླད་དུ་བཅོམ་ལྡན་འདས་ཀྱིས་ཀུན་དགའ་བོ་ལ་བཀའ་སྩལ་ཏེ། རྒྱལ་པོ་ལ་གསོལ་བ་འདེབས་སུ་བཏང་བ་དང་། རྒྱལ་པོས་ཀྱང་བཅོམ་ལྡན་འདས་ཀྱི་བཀའ་བཞིན་དེ་དག་བཏང་ངོ་། །

དེ་དག་སྲོག་བསྐྱབ་པའི་སླད་དུ་བཅོམ་ལྡན་འདས་ཀྱི་བཀའ་དྲིན་དྲན་ཞིང་རབ་ཏུ་དགའ་བ་སྐྱེས་ནས་བཅོམ་ལྡན་འདས་གང་ན་བ་དེར་སོང་སྟེ་ཕྱིན་པ་དང་། ཞབས་ལ་སྤྱི་བོས་ཕྱག་འཚལ་ནས་ཐལ་མོ་སྦྱར་ཏེ་བཅོམ་

ལྡན་འདས་ལ་འདི་སྐད་ཅེས་གསོལ་ཏོ། །བཅོམ་ལྡན་འདས་ཀྱི་བཀའ་དྲིན་ཆེན་པོས་བདག་ཅག་གི་ཚེ་སྲོག་ལྷག་མ་ཙམ་ཞིག་ལུས་པར་གྱུར་ན། ལྷའི་གཙོ་བོ་ཐུགས་བརྩེ་བར་དགོངས་ཏེ། བདག་ཅག་ཆོས་ལ་རབ་ཏུ་འབྱུང་བར་ཅི་གནང་ཞེས་གསོལ་པ་དང་། བཅོམ་ལྡན་འདས་ཀྱིས་ལེགས་པར་འོངས་སོ་ཞེས་བཀའ་སྩལ་པས། སྐྲ་དང་ཁ་སྤུ་རང་བྱི་སྟེ་གོས་ཀྱང་ངུར་སྨྲིག་ཏུ་གྱུར་ཏོ། །དེ་དག་ཤིན་ཏུ་དང་བའི་སེམས་བརྟན་པར་གྱུར་ནས་བཅོམ་ལྡན་འདས་ཀྱིས་ཅི་རིགས་པའི་ཆོས་བསྟན་པས་རྡུལ་དང་དྲི་མ་ཟད་དེ་དགྲ་བཅོམ་པར་གྱུར་ཏོ། །དེའི་མ་རྒན་མོ་ཡང་ཆོས་ཐོས་པས་ལན་ཅིག་ཕྱིར་མི་ལྡོག་པ་ཐོབ་པར་གྱུར་ཏོ། །

དེའི་ཚེ་ཀུན་དགའ་བོས་དེ་ལྟ་བུའི་དངོས་པོ་ངོ་མཚར་ཆེ་བ་དག་མཐོང་ནས་དེ་བཞིན་གཤེགས་པ་ནི་ཡོན་ཏན་དེ་སྙེད་ཅིག་མངའོ་ཞེས་བསྔགས་དེ། ཡང་འདི་སྙམ་དུ་རྒན་མོ་མ་སྨད་གསུམ་པོ་འདིས་སྔོན་ལེགས་པ་ཅི་ཞིག་བགྱིས་ན།[7] བཅོམ་ལྡན་འདས་དང་ཕྲད་དེ། ཉེས་པ་ཆེན་པོ་ལས་ཀྱང་ཐར་ལ། མྱ་ངན་ལས་འདས་པའི་བདེ་བ་ཐོབ་ནས་ལུས་གཅིག་གིས་ཕན་པ་དང་། བདེ་བའི་དོན་ཐོབ་པ་ལེགས་སོ་སྙམ་དུ་བསམས་པ་དང་། བཅོམ་ལྡན་འདས་ཀྱིས་མཁྱེན་ནས་ཀུན་དགའ་བོ་ལ་འདི་སྐད་ཅེས་བཀའ་སྩལ་ཏོ། །མ་སྨད་གསུམ་པོ་འདི་ནི་ངས་ད་ལྟར་འདི་འབའ་ཞིག་གི་དུས་སུ་གསོས་པར་མ་ཟད་ཀྱི། སྔོན་འདས་པའི་དུས་ན་ཡང་ངའི་བཀའ་དྲིན་གྱིས་གསོས་སོ། །

ཀུན་དགའ་བོས་གསོལ་པ།[8] བཅོམ་ལྡན་འདས་སྔོན་འདས་པའི་དུས་ན་ཡང་མ་སྨད་གསུམ་པོ་འདི་ཇི་ལྟར་གསོས་པ་བཅོམ་ལྡན་འདས་ཀྱིས་བསྟན་དུ་གསོལ། བཅོམ་ལྡན་འདས་ཀྱིས་ཀུན་དགའ་བོ་ལ་བཀའ་སྩལ་པ།

སྔོན་འདས་པའི་བསྐལ་པ་གྲངས་མེད་པའི་སྔ་རོལ་ན་ཛམྦུ་གླིང་[9] འདི་ན་རྒྱལ་པོ་ཤིང་རྟ་ཆེན་པོ་ཞེས་བྱ་བ་ཞིག་ཡོད་དེ། རྒྱལ་ཕྲན་ལྔ་སྟོང་སྟེང་ལ་དབང་བྱེད་དོ། །རྒྱལ་པོ་དེ་ཡང་སྲས་གསུམ་མངའ་སྟེ། རབ་ནི་སྒྲ་ཆེན་པོ་ཞེས་བྱའོ། །འབྲིང་ནི་ལྷ་ཆེན་པོ་ཞེས་བྱའོ། །ཐ་ཆུངས་ནི་སེམས་ཅན་ཆེན་པོ་ཞེས་བྱ་སྟེ། སྲས་ཐ་ཆུངས་དེ་ཆུང་ངུ་ནས་བྱམས་པ་དང་སྙིང་རྗེ་དང་ལྡན་ཏེ། ཐམས་ཅད་ལ་བུ་གཅིག་པ་དང་འདྲའོ། །

དེའི་ཚེ་རྒྱལ་པོ་དེ་བློན་པོ་དང་བཅས། བཙུན་མོ་དང་སྲས་སུ་བཅས་ཏེ་ཕྱི་རོལ་དུ་འཆག་ཅིང་། རོང་བ་ལས་ཙུང་ཟད་ཅིག་ངལ་བསོ་བའི་བར་དུ་སྲས་གསུམ་པོ་ཚལ་གྱི་ནང་དུ་རོང་རོང་བ་ལས། སྟག་མོ་གཅིག་བུ་བྱུང་ནས་ཞག་དུ་མ་ལོན་པར་བཀྲེས་སྐོམ་པས་ཉེན་ཏེ། ཕྱིར་ཡང་བུ་ཟ་ལ་ཐུག་པ་ཞིག་[10] མཐོང་ནས་རྒྱལ་བུ་ཐ་ཆུངས་དེས་ཕུ་བོ་གཉིས་ལ་སྨྲས་པ། སྟག་མོ་འདི་ནི་ཤིན་ཏུ་སྡུག་བསྔལ་གྱིས་གཟིར་ཏེ་ཉམས་ཆུང་ལ། རིད་པས་ཤི་ལ་ཐུག་པ་འདི་

བྲུ་བྲུང་མ་ཐག་པ་ཡང་ཟློས་སུ་འོང་ངོ།[11] །ཞེས་སྨྲས་པ་དང་། ཕུ་བོ་གཉིས་ཀྱིས་ཁྱོད་ཟེར་བ་བདེན་ནོ་ཞེས་སྨྲས་སོ།

ནུ་བོས་ཡང་ཕུ་བོ་གཉིས་ལ་སྨྲས་པ། སྟག་མོ་འདི་ཟས་སུ་ཅི་ཟ་ཞེས་དྲིས་ན། ཕུ་བོ་གཉིས་ཀྱིས་བསད་མ་ཐག་པའི་ཤ་རློན་དང་། ཁྲག་དྲོན་གྱིས་དེའི་ཡིད་ཆེམ་པར་འགྱུར་རོ། །ཞེས་སྨྲས་སོ། །ཡང་སྨྲས་པ། གང་སུ་ཡང་རུང་སྟེ་དེ་ལྟ་བུའི་དངོས་པོས་འདིའི་སྲོག་སྐྱབས་དེ། མི་ཉེས་པར་བྱེད་ནུས་པ་ཡོད་དམ། ཕུ་བོ་གཉིས་ཀྱིས་སྨྲས་པ། དེ་ནི། ཤིན་ཏུ་ཡང་དཀའ་བས་མེད་དོ། །

དེ་ནས་རྒྱལ་བུ་ཐ་ཆུངས་དེས་ཡིད་ལ་འདི་སྙམ་དུ་བསམས་སོ།[12] །བདག་ཡུན་རིང་པོ་ནས་འཁོར་བ་ན་འཁོར་ཞིང་ལུས་དང་སྲོག་གྲངས་མེད་པ་ཞིག་ཆུད་གསན་དེ། བར་འགའ་ནི་འདོད་ཆགས་ཀྱི་ཕྱིར། བར་འགའ་ནི་ཞེ་སྡང་གི་ཕྱིར། བར་འགའ་ནི་གཏི་མུག་གི་ཕྱིར་ལུས་བཏང་སྟེ། ཆོས་ཀྱི་ཕྱིར་བསོད་ནམས་ཀྱི་ཞིང་དང་ལན་འགའ་ཡང་མ་ཕྲད་པའི་ལུས་འདི་ཅི་རུང་སྙམ་བསམ་པ་ཐག་བཅད་ནས། གསུམ་ཆར་འགྲོགས་[13] དེ་སོང་བ་ལས་རིང་པོར་མ་ཕྱིན་པར་ཕུ་བོ་གཉིས་ལ་འདི་སྐད་ཅེས་སྨྲས་སོ། །མཆེད་གཉིས་སྔར་གཤེགས་ཤིག་[14] དང་། བདག་དོན་ཞིག་གཉེར་དེ་སྲིད་བཞིན་དུ་སླེབ་པར་མཆིའོ། །ཞེས་སྨྲས་ནས་ལམ་དེ་ཉིད་དུ་ཞུགས་ཏེ་སྟག་མོའི་ཚང་གང་ན་འདུག་པར་མྱུར་དུ་སོང་ནས་སྟག་མོའི་དྲུང་དུ་ཉལ་བ་དང་། སྟག་མོ་ཁ་ཐམས་ནས་ཟ་མ་ནུས་སོ། །དེའི་ཚེ་རྒྱལ་བུས་ཤིང་གི་ཚལ་པ་རྣོན་པོས་ལུས་ལ་ཁྲག་ཕྱུང་ནས་[15] སྟག་མོ་ལ་ལྡག་ཏུ་བཙུག་པ་[16] དང་། ཁ་ཡང་ཕྱེ་ནས་ལུས་ཀྱི་ཤ་མ་ལུས་པར་ཟོས་སོ། །

ཕུ་བོ་གཉིས་ཀྱིས་བསྡད་ནས་རིང་མོ་ཞིག་ཏུ་མ་འོངས་པས་ཕྱིར་རྗེས་བཞིན་དུ་ཚོལ་དུ་དོང་བ་ལས་སྔར་སྨྲས་པའི་ཚུལ་ལ་བརྟགས་ནས་གདོན་མི་ཟ་བར་སྟག་མོ་ལྟོགས་པ་སྐྱོད་དུ་སོང་ངོ་སྙམ་བསམས་ནས་དེར་ཕྱིན་དེ་བལྟས་པ་ན། ནུ་བོ་ཐ་ཆུངས་སྟག་གིས་ཟོས་ཏེ་ཤ་དང་ཁྲག་གིས་ཀུན་ཏུ་བསྒོས་ནས་རྩོག་རྩོག་པ་ལྟར་འདུག་པ་མཐོང་ནས་ལུས་ས་ལ་བརྡབས་ཏེ་བརྒྱལ་ལོ། །རིང་ཞིག་ལོན་པ་དང་དབུགས་ཕྱིར་ཕྱུང་ནས་ཆོ་ངེས་བཏབ་སྨྲེ་ས་ལ་འགྲོ་ཞིང་འཁམས་པར་གྱུར་ཏོ།[17] །

དེའི་ཚེ་ན་བཙུན་མོ་ཡུམ་མནལ་བའི་རྨི་ལམ་དུ་ཕུག་རོན་གསུམ་ཞིག་ཀུན་ཏུ་འཕུར་ཞིང་རྩེ་བ་ལས། ནང་གི་ཆུང་བ་གཅིག་ཁྲས་ཁྱེར་བ་སྙམ་རྨིས་མ་ཐག་ཏུ་སད་ནས་སྔངས་སྐྲག་སྟེ། རྒྱལ་པོ་ལ་བསྙད་དོ། །བདག་གིས་གཏམ་དུ་ཐོས་ན། ཕུག་རོན་ནི། བུའི་ཟླ་སྟེ། ཕུག་རོན་ནང་གི་ཆུང་ངུ་ཁྲས་ཁྱེར་བ་ལས། བདག་གི་བུ་ནང་གི་སྡུག་པ་ལ་བཀྲ་མི་ཤིས་སུ་[18] ངེས་ཀྱིས་[19] ཞེས་དེ་མ་ཐག་ཏུ་ཀུན་ཏུ་ཚོལ་བ་བཏང་བ་ལས། རིང་པོར་མ་ལོན་པར་

བུ་གཉིས་ནི་འོངས་ཀྱིས། བུ་ནང་གི་སྡུག་པ་ཅང་མ་ཉེས་སམ། ག་རེ་ཞེས་དྲིས་ན་ཕུ་བོ་གཉིས་སྐད་ཀྱིས་བརྣངས་དེ་རིང་ཞིག་ཏུ་དབུགས་ཀྱང་མ་ཕྱིན། སྨྲ་ཡང་མ་ནུས་ནས་དེའི་འོག་ཏུ་དབུགས་ཕྱིན་པ་དང་། སྡུག་གིས་ཐོས་སོ། །ཞེས་སྨྲས་སོ། །ལྷ་མོ་དེས་དེ་སྐད་ཅེས་སྨྲས་པ་ཐོས་ནས་ཁམས་ལངས་ཏེ། ས་ལ་འགྲེལ་ནས་རིང་ཞིག་ཡོན་པ་དང་། དབུགས་ཕྱིན་ཏེ། བུ་གཉིས་དང་། བཙུན་མོ་དང་། ཕོ་བྲང་སླས་སུ་བཅས་ཏེ་མྱུར་བར་རྒྱལ་བུ་གང་དུ་ཚེ་འཕོས་པའི་གནས་སུ་སོང་ངོ་། །

དེའི་ཚེ་ན་སྡུག་མོས་རྒྱལ་བུའི་ཤ་ནི་ཟད་པར་ཐོས་ནས། རུས་པ་དང་ཁྲག་འབའ་ཞིག་ས་ལ་རྟོག་རྟོག་པ་ལྟར་འདུག་པ་མཐོང་ནས་བཙུན་མོས་ནི། མགོ་ནས་བཟུང་།[20] རྒྱལ་པོས་ནི། ལག་པ་ནས་བཟུང་སྟེ་ཚེ་ངེས་བཏབ་ནས། རུས་པ་དང་དེར་ཡང་འཁམས་ནས་རིང་ཞིག་ཡོན་ཏེ་ཕྱིར་སངས་སོ། །

རྒྱལ་བུ་སེམས་ཅན་ཆེན་པོ་དེ་དེར་ཚེ་འཕོས་ནས་དགའ་ལྡན་ལྷའི་གནས་སུ་སྐྱེས་སོ། །དེ་ཅིའི་ཕྱིར་ཅི་སྤྱད་པས་འདིར་སྐྱེས་སྙམ་བསམས་ཏེ། ལྷའི་མིག་གིས་རྒྱུད་ལྔ་ཀུན་ཏུ་བལྟས་ན་བདག་ཚེ་འཕོས་པའི་རུས་བུ་ཚལ་ན་འདུག་པ་ལ་ཕ་མས་བསྐོར་ཏེ། ཤིན་ཏུ་ཡིད་ལ་གཅགས་པས་མྱ་ངན་གྱི་ཟུག་རྔུས་སྡུག་བསྔལ་ཞིང་ཚེ་ངེས་འདེབས་པ་མཐོང་ནས་ལྷས་བསམས་པ། བདག་གི་ཕ་མ་འདི་ལྟར་མི་དགའ་བའི་རྐྱེན་གྱིས་གལ་ཏེ་ན་ལུས་དང་སྲོག་གི་བར་ཆད་དུ་འགྱུར་གྱི།[21] དེ་ལ་སྤྲོ་བ་བསྐྱེད་ཅིང་གདམས་བྱར་འགྲོ་སྙམ་བསམས་ནས། ནམ་མཁའ་ལས་བབས་ཏེ་སྟེང་གི་ནམ་མཁའ་ལས་ཚིག་སྙན་པ་རྣམ་པ་སྣ་ཚོགས་ཀྱིས་ཕ་མ་གཉིས་སྤྲོ་བ་བསྐྱེད་དོ།[22] །ཕ་མ་གཉིས་ཀྱིས་ནམ་མཁར་བལྟས་ནས། ལྷ་ཁྱོད་སུ་ཞིག་བདག་ལ་སྨྲོས་ཤིག་ཅེས་སྨྲས་པ་དང་། ལྷས་སྨྲས་པ། བདག་ནི། རྒྱལ་བུ་སེམས་ཅན་ཆེན་པོ་ཞེས་བྱ་བ་ཡིན་ཏེ། བདག་གིས་ལུས་སྟག་མོ་ལྟོགས་པ་ལ་བྱིན་ནས་དགའ་ལྡན་གྱི་ལྷའི་གནས་སུ་སྐྱེས་སོ། །

རྒྱལ་པོ་ཆེན་པོ། འདི་ལྟར་མཁྱེན་པར་མཛོད་ཅིག[23] །ཇི་ཙམ་དུ་སྲིད་པ་དང་བཅས་པའི་ཆོས་ནི། མཐར་འཇིག་པར་འོང་། སྐྱེ་བ་ཡོད་ན་ངེས་པར་འཇིག་གོ །སྡིག་པ་བྱས་ན་སེམས་ཅན་དམྱལ་བར་ལྟུང་གི །དགེ་བ་བྱས་ན་མཐོ་རིས་སུ་སྐྱེ་སྟེ། སྐྱེ་བ་དང་འཇིག་པ་ནི་ཀུན་ལ་སྲིད་ན། ཅིའི་སླད་དུ་བདག་འབའ་ཞིག་གི་ཕྱིར། མྱ་ངན་གྱི་རྒྱ་མཚོར་ལྟུང་བ་མ་ཚོར། དགེ་བའི་ཕྱོགས་ལ་བརྩོན་འགྲུས་མཛོད་ཅིག[24] །

དེའི་ཕ་མས་སྨྲས་པ། ཁྱོད་ནི། སྙིང་རྗེ་ཆེན་པོས་སྟག་མོ་སྐྱོང་དེ། ཐམས་ཅད་ལ་སྙིང་བརྩེ་བ་ཡིན་ན། བདག་ཅག་བཏང་སྟེ་ཚེའི་དུས་བྱས་པས། ངེད་ཁྱོད་དྲན་པའི་ཕྱིར་ཤ་ཡང་དུམ་བུར་བཅད་པ་ཙམ་དུ་སྡུག་བསྔལ་

གྱིས་གདུངས་ན། སྙིང་རྗེ་ཆེན་པོ་སྐྱོད་པ་ཁྱོད་འདི་ལྟར་བྱ་བར་རིགས་སམ།[25] དེ་ནས་ཡང་ལྷ་དེས་ཚིག་སྙན་པ་རྣམ་པ་སྣ་ཚོགས་ཀྱི་སྒྲོ་ནས་བཤགས་ཏེ། སྤྲོ་བ་བསྐྱེད་པས་དེའི་ཕ་མ་ཡང་སྤྲོ་བ་ཅུང་ཟད་སྐྱེས་ནས་རིན་པོ་ཆེ་སྣ་བདུན་གྱི་སྒྲོམ་བྱས་ཏེ། རུས་བུ་དེའི་ནང་དུ་བཅུག་སྟེ་སྤྲས་པའི་སྟེང་དུ་མཆོད་རྟེན་བྱས་སོ། །ལྷ་ཡང་ཕྱིར་གནས་སུ་སོང་ངོ་། །རྒྱལ་པོ་དང་འཁོར་མང་པོ་རྣམས་ཀྱང་ཕྱིར་ཕོ་བྲང་དུ་འོངས་སོ། །

བཅོམ་ལྡན་འདས་ཀྱིས་ཀུན་དགའ་བོ་ལ་བཀའ་སྩལ་པ། ཁྱོད་ཀྱི་ཡིད་ལ་ཅི་སྙམ། དེའི་ཚེ་དེའི་དུས་ན་རྒྱལ་པོ་ཤིང་རྟ་ཆེན་པོ་དེ་སུ་ཡིན་སྙམ་དུ་སེམས། དེ་ནི་ད་ལྟར་ངའི་ཡབ་རྒྱལ་པོ་ཟས་གཙང་མ་ཡིན་ནོ། །དེའི་ཚེ་དེའི་དུས་ན་རྒྱལ་པོ་དེའི་བཙུན་མོ་དེ་ནི། ཡུམ་སྒྱུ་མ་ལྷ་མཛེས་ཡིན་ནོ། །དེའི་དུས་ན་སྲས་རབ་སྒྲ་ཆེན་པོ་ནི། བྱམས་པ་ཡིན་ནོ། །སྲས་འབྲིང་པོ་ལྷ་ཆེན་པོ་ནི། བ་སུ་མི་ཏྲ་ཡིན་ནོ། །དེའི་ཚེ་དེའི་དུས་ན་རྒྱལ་བུ་ཐ་ཆུངས་སེམས་ཅན་ཆེན་པོ་ནི། གཞན་དུ་མ་སེམས་ཤིག[26] །ད་ལྟར་ང་ཡིན་ནོ། །དེའི་དུས་ན་སྟག་ཕྲུག་ནི། མི་འདི་གཉིས་ཡིན་ཏེ། ངས་སྔོན་ཡང་ཡུན་རིང་པོ་ནས་བགེགས་ལས་ཐར་པར་བྱས་[27] ཏེ་སྡིག་བསྐྱབས་ནས་བདེ་བར་བྱས་སོ། །ད་མངོན་པར་སངས་རྒྱས་ནས་ཀྱང་བགེགས་ལས་ཐར་པར་མཛད་ནས་འཁོར་བའི་སྡུག་བསྔལ་ཆེན་པོ་ལས་ཡོངས་སུ་བྲལ་ལོ། །

དེའི་ཚེ་ན་ཀུན་དགའ་བོ་དང་། འཁོར་མང་པོ་ཐམས་ཅད་བཅོམ་ལྡན་འདས་ཀྱིས་གསུངས་པ་ལ་ཡི་རངས་ཏེ་མངོན་པར་བསྟོད་དོ། །

སེམས་ཅན་ཆེན་པོས་སྟག་མོ་ལ་ལུས་བྱིན་པའི་ལེའུ་སྟེ་གཉིས་པའོ།། །།

མཛངས་བླུན་ཞེས་བྱ་བའི་མདོ་སྡེ་རྫོགས་སོ།། །།རྒྱ་ནག་ལས་འགྱུར་བར་སྣང་ངོ་། །

Annotations to *The Sūtra Called "The Wise and the Foolish"*

Translation Hint ①

Page 108, Line 14

This sentence contains another instance of modular construction (see ཤེས་རབ་སྙིང་པོ་ note 22) with a noun phrase—consisting of a nominalized sentence (བྲ་རྡག་དུ་ཀུ་བ་), a number (གཉིས་), and an indefinite article (ཤིག་)—serving as the complement of a Class VIII verb of possession.

Idiomatic Expressions ②

Page 108, Line 15

As in English, Tibetan contains its own idiomatic expressions. Simply stated, such expressions are sentences or phrases that convey a meaning beyond the meaning of their individual parts. The vast majority of these that are encountered in classical Tibetan texts are the results of translating complex ideas from Sanskrit into Tibetan. In this running series of short sentences (see ཤེར་སྙིང་རྣམ་བཤད་ note 15), there are two such expressions: the verbal collocation ཁྲིམས་དང་སྦྱར་ ("to be judged"), and in the previous sentence, ཞལ་ཆེ་བ་ (the slightly amusing rendering of the Sanskrit word **vivāda*, or "magistrate").

WHAT TO REMEMBER

Idiomatic expressions are sentences or phrases that convey a meaning beyond the meaning of their individual parts. Their comprehension typically requires culture-specific knowledge. Some dictionaries (such as Das, 1902) treat these as lexical items.

③ Semimodal Expressions with Passive Participles

Page 108, Line 15

Although several auxiliary verb constructions have been seen already (see ཤེས་རབ་སྙིང་པོ་ note 11, ཤེར་སྙིང་རྣམ་བཤད་ notes 21 and 22), this passage introduces a new class of verbal postpositions: semimodal expressions. Like auxiliary verbs ("modal auxiliaries"—verbs that express a mood or tense in conjunction with a main verb), semimodal expressions are postpositional particles and phrases that likewise alter the mood or tense of a main verb although do not affect the grammar of the larger sentence—as in this example—in which the verb phrase is further modified by a gerund marker (ནས་). Hence, while བསད་ནས་ would mean "having been killed," གསད་པ་ལ་ཐུག་ནས་ means "having been about to be killed."

Another unique feature of semimodal expressions is the form in which the main verb occurs. While auxiliary verbs take their main verbs as infinitives (*verb* + པར་, etc.), semimodal expressions do not and instead take their main verbs in one of two ways. Since the active and passive voice of a verb is conveyed through the verb class and/or type and order of their accompanying nouns, and because semimodal expressions often take a bare verb, the voice must be represented in a different manner. The active voice is indicated by a bare verb (see མདོ་མཛངས་བླུན་ note 10, below), while the passive voice is indicated by the use of a passive participle (see ཤེས་རབ་སྙིང་པོ་ note 13) as seen here.

WHAT TO REMEMBER

Auxiliary verb constructions take their main verbs as infinitives. There is a class of verbal postpositions known as semimodal expressions that modify the mood of their main verb but do so without altering the grammar of the larger sentence. Some such semimodal expressions are:

(ལ་)ཐུག་ "about to do/be done ..." (ལ་)ཁད་ "about to be X"

④ The Alternate Gerund Marker ལས་

Page 108, Line 16

The fifth case/"ablative" marker ནས་ is used as a syntactic particle in Tibetan in a manner similar to the gerund conjugation in Sanskrit: to indicate an action performed by the same subject/agent of the main verb, but temporally prior to the main activity. A far less commonly seen construction is the similar deployment of the other fifth-case/"ablative" marker, ལས་, as a syntactic particle also indicating a gerund. Unlike the use of ནས་ as a gerund marker, the use of ལས་ is typically found only in "Old Tibetan" (pre-tenth century) writings and translations and in literature that attempts to mimic it for the purpose of conveying a sense of antiquity and hence authority (an example of such intentional use of anachronistic expressions in English is the contemporary use of the archaic second person singular pronoun *thou*). In addition, the use of ལས་ as a gerund marker carries a very specific connotation, that of thematic disjunction—that is, its use indicates that what follows is somehow unexpected or different in some aspect from the preceding activity. It can be translated as "although having been ..."

WHAT TO REMEMBER

When not functioning as as a case-marking particle, the syntactic particle ལས་ also functions as a gerund marker but conveys the sense that what follows is somehow distinct or unexpected in relation to the preceding activity.

Tibetan Numbers: Cumulative vs. Adjectival

Page 108, Line 16

Tibetan numerals function adjectivally much as in any other language. Since Tibetan is a postpositional language, as adjectives, numerals follow what they modify, such as in the expression འཕགས་པའི་བདེན་པ་བཞི་ ("the four truths for āryas," or "four noble truths"). A second, related use of postpositional numerals is to indicate a category of items (see དེབ་ཐེར་དམར་པོ་ note 2), while a third use is yet another linguistic feature inherited from Sanskrit—the use of a numeral to indicate the cumulative count of a group or list of items. Consequently, the passage here, རྒན་མོ་མ་སྨད་གསུམ་, should not be read as "the old woman—the mother—and her three sons" but rather as "the old woman—the mother—and her sons, [all] three [of them]." The use of such quantifying numerals is quite common and should be expected.

WHAT TO REMEMBER

Tibetan postpositional numerals follow what they modify. When functioning as adjectives, they are translated as expected; when functioning as cumulative indicators of the quantity of a group or list, they must be translated appositionally.

6 The Vocative in Supplications

Page 108, Line 17

Although the vocative has already been seen in the *Heart Sūtra* in simple polite dialogue, it also occurs in supplications, most often as a superlative epithet. Here, rather than addressing the Buddha by his title or using another synonym (such as Sugata or Tathāgata), the supplicants address him as ལྷ་ནང་ན་གཙོ་བོ་ ("Foremost among the gods").

WHAT TO REMEMBER

Supplications often open with a superlative epithet in the vocative case.

7 Conditional Marker ན་

Page 109, Line 9

The Tibetan particle ན་ most commonly occurs either as a case-marking particle (one of the seven ལ་ particles) or syntactically as an interrogative verbal suffix usually translated as "if" or "when." It is important to remember, however, that in this last usage the particle ན་ is not a word having the meaning "if" or "when." Rather, it is merely performing a syntactic function, marking a conditional circumstance. In such cases it is labeled a conditional marker. An understanding of this point is crucial to being able to decipher this sentence, since in this instance neither "if" nor "when" are appropriate renderings of the construction. Rather, the particular conditional interrogative is explicitly supplied: ཅི་ཞིག་ ("what").

WHAT TO REMEMBER

When not functioning as a case-marking particle, the Tibetan particle ན་ functions as a conditional marker that indicates a hypothetical, temporally contingent, or interrogative condition. More often than not, when it occurs as a verbal suffix, it can be rendered as "if" or "when"; sometimes, an interrogative pronoun is explicitly provided, in which case the particle ན་ remains untranslated.

Translation Hint

8

Page 109, Line 13

The basic principle of verb final constructions holds true, even when marking verbatim dialogue. In formal literature, such dialogue is often introduced by a prefatory statement. Such has already been seen in the *Heart Sūtra* (see ཤེས་རབ་སྙིང་པོ་ notes 9 and 21)—with the verb སྨྲ་ ("to say")—and here several other examples can be seen, with the verbs གསོལ་ ("to petition" or "to request") and བཀའ་སྩལ་ (high honorific "to speak"), all likewise in their participial form (སྨྲས་པ་, གསོལ་བ་, etc.).

Translation Hint

9

Page 109, Line 16

This paragraph contains five other instances of Sanskrit proper names. The first is a mixture of transliteration (ཛམྦུ་) and translation (གླིང་ = *dvīpa*), while the last four (ཤིང་རྟ་ཆེན་པོ་, སྒྲ་ཆེན་པོ་, ལྷ་ཆེན་པོ་, and སེམས་ཅན་ཆེན་པོ་) are all purely syllable-by-syllable translations. See ཤེས་རབ་སྙིང་པོ་ notes 2 and 5.

Semimodal Expressions in the Active Voice

10

Page 109, Line 22

As noted above (མདོ་མཛངས་བླུན་ note 3), auxiliary verb constructions take their main verbs as absolute infinitives (*verb* + པར་, etc.), while semimodal expressions do not. The passive construction, using a passive participle (*verb* + པ་) plus ལ་ཐུག་ to indicate "about to be done," has been seen already. Here is an instance of an active construction, in which the active voice is indicated by the use of a bare verb. Seen here, the expression conveying the preparative mode, ཟ་ལ་ཐུག་—meaning "about to eat"— is nominalized (ཟ་ལ་ཐུག་པ་; "being about to eat") and followed by an indefinite article (ཞིག་) to indicate that it should be read as a personal pronoun ("one who is about to eat"). The same holds true for accompanying definite articles (as seen below with ཤི་ལ་ཐུག་པ་འདི་ "this one who is about to die").

WHAT TO REMEMBER

Semimodal expressions take their main verb—when conveying the active voice—as a bare verb as opposed to a passive participle.

11

Simple Infinitives: Purposives

Page 110, Line 1

"Simple infinitives," when appearing with other verbs, function as subordinate phrases sometimes with their own objects. For example, the sentence encountered here can be broken up into distinct units:

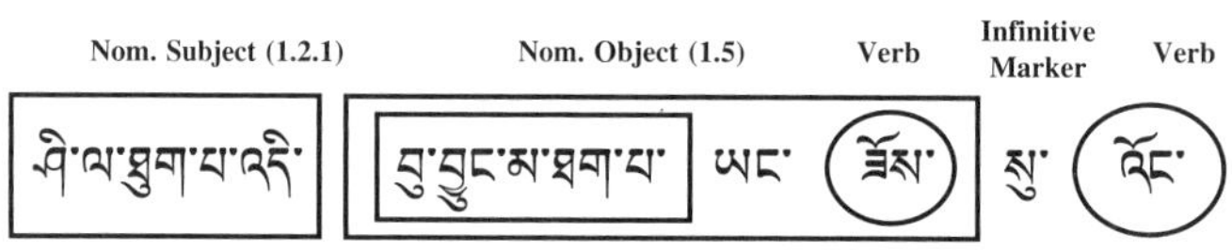

Verbs and verb-terminated phrases, when marked as simple infinitives, function in one of a number of roles: as indirect statements (including indirect speech and reporting inner thoughts), as activities externally caused or otherwise removed from the action of the main verb, and as indicating a purpose. Here is an instance of the latter—that is, marking the scope of the future activity (as indicated by the periphrastic future verb, འོང་) in terms of its purpose (e.g., "going *for the purpose of* eating ..."). See also མདོ་མཛངས་བློན་ note 18.

WHAT TO REMEMBER

One function simple infinitives can fulfill is to mark the purpose of the activity. Such usage can be seen with motion verbs such as འོང་, འཇུག་, འདོང་, and so on.

The Tibetan འདི་སྙམ་དུ 12

Page 110, Line 6

Recall that the phrase སྙམ་[པ་] was seen to function as the closing quotation marker for thoughts and dreams (see ཤེར་སྙིང་རྣམ་བཤད་ note 28), analogous to the closing quotation markers ཅེས་, ཞེས་, etc. Recall also that the closing quotation marker was used with the word འདི་སྐད་ (*evaṃ*; "thus") to mark the lead-in to a quotation that follows (see ཤེས་རབ་སྙིང་པོ་ note 9). The phrase འདི་སྙམ་དུ་ functions in precisely the same manner to indicate the lead-in to thought, as in "That youngest prince thought thus in his mind: ..." (རྒྱལ་བུ་ཐ་ཆུངས་དེས་ཡིད་ལ་འདི་སྙམ་དུ་བསམས་སོ།). Just as spoken quotations also are closed with a closing quote marker and verb of speech, so too the closing thought marker, སྙམ་བསམས་, marks its conclusion.

> WHAT TO REMEMBER
>
> The phrase འདི་སྙམ་དུ་—together with a cognitive verb, such as སེམས་—should be taken as a demonstrative pronoun indicating that a quotation of thought follows.

Translation Hint 13

Page 110, Line 9

Tibetan, as an unsegmented language, has the potential for ambiguity. Here, although གསུམ་ཚ་ could be taken as "three parts" (see བར་དོ་འཕྲང་སྒྲོལ་ note 4) marked by a case-marking particle together with the verb འགྲོགས་ ("to meet"), the correct parse of the sentence is to take གསུམ་ as the nominative subject of the phrasal verb ཚར་འགྲོགས་ ("to gather together [as a group]").

Auxiliary Verbs: The Precative Construction 14

Page 110, Line 10

Wilson (668) identifies the three imperative-marking syntactic particles as ཅིག་, ཞིག་, and ཤིག་. While other constructions are used in forming the simple imperative as a command (see མདོ་མཛངས་བླུན་ note 26 and ལམ་གཙོ་རྣམ་གསུམ་ note 11), when following the imperative form of the verb, these particles form what might be called an "aspirational imperative," known technically as the "precative." The precative shares the same features as the imperative—such as marking the recepient of the speech in the vocative—and is the mood used predominantly for prayers but also (as here) for formal/polite/aspirational requests.

WHAT TO REMEMBER

The precative construction (with the verbal postpositional ཤིག་, etc.) is used to indicate the mood used for blessings and prayer but also polite requests.

15

Translation Divergences

Page 110, Line 13

A translation divergence is a phenomenon that occurs when a sentence in one language translates into a sentence in a second language in a very different manner—either with different grammatical structures or similarly shaped grammatical structures but with different basic categories. Divergences arise independent of the translation method and are artifacts of the two languages in relation to each other. Here, such a translation divergence between Tibetan and English occurs with the verb ཕྱུང་ (present འབྱིན་; "to take out," "to throw out," etc.). Whereas in English the original location of something that is being removed is marked in the ablative case (e.g., "blood *from* his body"), in Tibetan such a thing is marked in the objective case (Wilson, case 2.1 "Place of Activity").

WHAT TO REMEMBER

A translation divergence occurs when a sentence in one language translates in a different grammatical manner. Some sentences containing the verb འབྱིན་ ("to take out"), for example, give rise to translation divergences in certain circumstances.

16

Auxiliary Verbs: Nonreflexive Causative

Page 110, Line 13

While the auxiliary verb བྱེད་ is used to form the causative construction with Class II, III, and IV verbs and the reflexive causative with Class V and VI verbs (see ཤེས་རབ་སྙིང་པོ་ note 19), the auxiliary verbs འཇུག་/བཅུག་/གཞུགས་/ཆུག་, however, are used to form the nonreflexive causative with Class V and VI verbs and take their verbs in the simple infinitive (see མདོ་མཛངས་བླུན་ notes 11 and 18, and in particular, བར་དོ་འཕྲང་སྒྲོལ་ note 1).

WHAT TO REMEMBER

The auxiliary verbs འཇུག་/བཅུག་/གཞུགས་/ཆུག་ are used to form the nonreflexive causative with Classs V and VI verbs and take their verbs in the simple infinitive.

Auxiliary Verbs: Imperfective

17

Page 110, Line 19

The auxiliary construction used to indicate an action that was ongoing in the past and is continuing, repeated, or habitual is called the "imperfective." It is easily confused with the subjunctive (see ཤེར་སྙིང་རྣམ་བཤད་ note 22) since their manner of construction is identical. Like the subjunctive, the imperfective is constructed in the form of *verb* + པར་གྱུར་, likewise utilizing the past-tense form of the weak auxiliary verb (Wilson, 620) འགྱུར་ (གྱུར་).

WHAT TO REMEMBER

The auxiliary construction *verb* + པར་གྱུར་, in addition to forming the subjunctive, is also used to indicate the imperfective—that is, to indicate an action that was ongoing in the past and is continuing (and possibly in the present), repeated, or habitual.

Simple Infinitives: Indirect Statements

18

Page 110, Line 23

Indirect speech is a grammatical construction in which the meaning of an event is conveyed descriptively. There are three distinct types of indirect statements: (1) reporting what something says without using the exact words (e.g., "the text says that ..."), (2) conveying the meaning of an event rather than relating the event directly (e.g., "it is the construction of X" vs. "X was constructed"), and (3) reporting inner thoughts. Some indirect statements use the simple infinitive (*verb* + a ལ་ particle), and this third type—reporting inner thought—that occurs here (བདག་གི་བུ་ནང་གི་སྡུག་པ་ལ་བཀྲུ་མི་ཤེས་སུ་) is one such example, in this case, reporting the thoughts of the queen.

WHAT TO REMEMBER

Indirect statements that report inner thoughts (but not opinions) do so using the simple infinitive.

⑲ Non-case Usage of the Particle ཀྱིས་ as a Verbal Emphatic

Page 110, Line 23

The suffix particle ཀྱིས་ at the end of this sentence is not functioning as a third-case marker but rather is functioning as a non-case syntactic particle similar to a semimodal expression. When occuring after a verb or sentence, this non-case usage of ཀྱིས་ indicates an emphatic statement.

WHAT TO REMEMBER

The use of ཀྱིས་ following a sentence or verb indicates an emphatic statement.

⑳ Translation Hint

Page 111, Line 7

This is another example of a translation divergence (see མདོ་མཛངས་བླུན་ note 15, above), where the fifth-case marker ནས་ is marking an "instrumental originative" (Wilson, case 5.2). Hence, the sentence , together with the lack of an object, implies a reflexive reading: "The queen held [herself] by [her] head" or simply "The queen held [her] head." The same construction is repeated for the king in the sentence that follows.

Verbal Collocations and Modifiability 21

Page 111, Line 13

Preceding another example of the syntactic continuative (see ཤེར་སྙིང་རྣམ་བཤད་ note 2), the phrase ལུས་དང་སྲོག་གི་བར་ཆད་ illustrates a unique feature of some Tibetan verbal collocations: modifiability. Some collocations take a modifier marked by the sixth ("connective") case as this one does and can be thought of as instances of translation divergences (see མདོ་མཛངས་བླུན་ note 15, above). The phrasal verb encountered here ''' (ཀྱི་) བར་ཆད་ ("to be severed," or "to be cut-short"; lit. "to cut the middle of ...") is one such example. As with others, it could also be thought of as a translation divergence.

WHAT TO REMEMBER

Some verbal collocations take a modifier marked by the sixth ("connective") case and can be considered a type of translation divergence.

Translation Hint 22

Page 111, Line 14

The Class V verb བསྐྱེད་ takes the nominalized sentence ཕ་མ་གཉིས་སྐྱོ་ as its object.

Auxiliary Verbs: Exhortative (Honorific) 23

Page 111, Line 18

Like the exhortative construction previously seen (see ཤེར་སྙིང་རྣམ་བཤད་ note 21), the construction seen here, *verb* + པར་མཛོད་ཅིག, is used to convey the honorific form of the exhortative mood ("[you] really should do X"). It combines the imperative form of the strong honorific auxiliary verb (Wilson, 619) མཛད་ (མཛོད་) and the imperative marker ཅིག.

Translation Hint 24

Page 111, Line 21

Note here that the verb མཛོད་ is the main verb of the sentence and is not functioning as an auxiliary (as in མདོ་མཛངས་བླུན་ note 23, immediately above), and hence the particle ཅིག་ marks the precative mood (see མདོ་མཛངས་བླུན་ note 14, above).

25

Translation Hint

Page 112, Line 1

Although a phrase explicitly ending the quotation is expected here, the end of the quote can be inferred from context.

26

Auxiliary Verbs: Imperative

Page 112, Line 10

Although the particles ཅིག་, ཞིག་, and ཤིག་ appeared earlier in the formation of the precative (see མདོ་མཛངས་བླུན་ note 14, above) and exhortative moods (see མདོ་མཛངས་བླུན་ note 23), here the imperative particles form the simple imperative because they appear together with the present-tense form of the verb.

WHAT TO REMEMBER

The simple imperative mood in Tibetan is formed—without any auxiliary verbs—by the use of the imperative particles ཅིག་, ཞིག་, or ཤིག་ in combination with the present tense of the main verb.

27

Auxiliary Verbs: Past Causative

Page 112, Line 11

Recall that the generic action verb བྱེད་ (or the honorific forms, མཛད་ and བགྱིད་) with nominative verbs (Class II, III, and IV verbs) forms the causative, while with agentive verbs (Classes V and VI) it can form either the causative or the emphatic (see ཤེས་རབ་སྙིང་པོ་ note 19). The same holds true with the past-tense form of the auxiliary verb བྱས་ (or the honorific forms, མཛད་ and བགྱིས་).

WHAT TO REMEMBER

Auxiliary constructions formed with the past-tense form of the auxiliary verb བྱེད་ (བྱས་—or the honorific forms, མཛད་ and བགྱིས་) likewise form either the causative or the emphatic.

The Sūtra Called "The Wise and the Foolish"

In Sanskrit: *Damamūka-nāma-sūtra*
In Tibetan: *Mdzangs blun zhes bya ba'i mdo*
[In English: The Sūtra Called "The Wise and the Foolish"]

Homage to the Three Jewels!

The Chapter in Which Mahāsattva Gives His Body to the Tigress

Thus have I heard at one time: the Bhagavān was staying in the Jetavana grove of Anāthapiṇḍika in Śrāvastī. Then, the time of [going to seek] alms having arrived, the Bhagavān put on his lower robe and religious robes, and carrying his begging bowl, went [to beg] for alms with Ānanda.

At that time, an old woman in that city had a pair of sons who were constantly stealing. A rich man having caught them, [he] led them before the magistrate. Then, having been judged [and] having been sentenced, and having been about to be killed, they were led away by an outcaste. Although having been led to the place of execution, the old mother and her two sons having seen the Bhagavān passing by at a distance, paid homage in the direction of the Buddha's passing. The [old woman] said, "O Foremost Among the Gods, think compassionately [toward us]. [I] beg [you] to act [as] a refuge for my sons who are about to be killed." This having been heard by the Bhagavān, [he] thought compassionately toward them, out of the great compassion of a tathāgata. Then, for the sake of protecting the lives of these boys, the Bhagavān spoke to Ānanda. Whereupon, he sent (*btang*) [Ānanda] to petition the king, and the king gave them up (*btang*) in accordance with the words of the Bhagavān.

Being mindful of these kind words [spoken by] the Bhagavān for the sake of protecting their lives, and great joy having been born [in them], they went to that place where the Bhagavān was. Then, having come and paid homage with their heads at his feet, they folded their hands and supplicated the Bhagavān in these words: "Because of the exceedingly kind (*drin chen pos*) words of the Bhagavān, now that what remains of our lives has been left [to us], O Foremost Among the Gods, think compassionately [toward us]—may we be permitted to be ordained into the Dharma?" Thus [they] petitioned. [And] by the Bhagavān saying "Welcome," their hair and beards fell away naturally and [their] clothes changed to saffron [ones]. [Then] they—[their] exceptionally clear minds having been stabilized, and by being taught whatsoever teachings [were appropriate] by the Bhagavān, their passions (**rajas; rdul*) and stains being removed—became arhats (*arhat; sgra bcom*). The mother of those [boys]—the old woman—as well, by hearing the teachings, attained the irreversible state of a once returner (*sakṛdāgāmin; lan gcig phyir mi ldog pa*).

Then Ānanda, having seen such very amazing events (*dngos po*), declared, "Just how many good qualities does the Bhagavān possess!" In addition to this, he thought, "What former good deeds could this old woman and her two sons have done, such that [now they] have been able to meet with the Bhagavān, and even more so, be liberated from their great faults (**doṣa, nyes pa*)? Having attained the bliss of nirvāṇa, their utilization of one lifetime and achievement of such a blissful end (*bde ba'i don*) is good." Thus he thought, and the Bhagavān, knowing this, spoke thus to Ānanda: "Regarding this old woman and her two sons, this is not the only such occasion in which I have sustained [them] in this manner. In times long since passed did I also nourish them."

Ānanda asked, "O Bhagavān, I beg the Bhagavān to teach how it was that in times long since passed, you sustained this old woman and her two sons." The Bhagavān said to Ānanda:

Before, in countless eons long since passed, in this [world of] Jambudvīpa, there lived a king called Mahāratha; [he] had sovereignty over as many as five thousand lesser kings. This king had three sons. The eldest was called Mahārāva, the middle [son] was called Mahādeva, and the youngest was called Mahāsattva. From childhood, the youngest son possessed kindness and compassion, such that all [sentient beings] were like his only child.

On one occasion, that king, together with his ministers, queen, and sons, went out [of the palace grounds] for a walk, and having journeyed [for a while], while [the royal party] rested for a little while, the three sons went for a walk in the forest. Having gone a little way, [there was] a tigress [who]—without a day having yet passed (*zhag du ma lon par*) after giving birth (lit. "a child having appeared")—was weakened with hunger and thirst. Furthermore, having seen [her] about to eat [her] offspring, the youngest prince said to his two brothers, "This tigress is tormented by great suffering, and hence has little strength. Since [she] is weak, this [tigress] who is about to die is going to eat even those to whom she has just given birth." Thus he spoke, and the two brothers responded, "What you say is true."

The younger brother again spoke to his two brothers, but when [he] asked, "What food does this tigress eat?" the two brothers replied, "Her mind will only be satisfied by warm blood and fresh meat that has just been killed." Again [the young prince asked,] "Who, by an action such as this, could protect the lives of these [cubs]? Is there one capable of acting in such a faultless manner?" The two brothers responded, "Since this is so very difficult, there is no one!"

Then, that young prince in his mind thought thus: "For a long time have I migrated through cyclic existence; a countless number of bodies and lives have I wasted. Sometimes because of desire, sometimes because of hatred, sometimes because of ignorance I have thrown away my body. How is it possible that this body has never met, on even one occasion, with a field of merit for the sake of the Dharma!" Thus he thought, and [just after] having come to that conclusion, the three brothers gathered together as a group. Having left [the tigress], but without having gone far, [the young prince] spoke thus to his two brothers: "O [my] two brothers, please go back. I must take care of one thing, so it is necessary [for me] to return later." Having said this, he went down that very same path, and having gone quickly to the place where the tigress was dwelling, lay down near the tigress, [but even though] having seized [him] in her jaws, the tigress was unable to eat him. Then, the prince, having drawn blood from his body with a sharp piece of wood, enticed the tigress to lick [him], and having also opened her mouth, she ate the flesh of his body without leaving any remaining.

The two brothers having waited, since he did not return after a long time (*ring mo zhig du*), subsequently (*rjes bzhin du*) having gone to find [their younger brother], but having thought about the manner in which he had spoken earlier, and having thought "Without a doubt, he has gone to feed the starving tigress," [they] went there. But when [they] looked, the tigress had eaten their youngest brother, and [the ground] was completely stained with [his] flesh and blood. Having seen the place [with his remains] in such a disorganized state (*rtsog rtsog pa*), [their] bodies fell to the ground and [they] fainted. After some time had passed and they regained their breath (lit. "breath-drawn out-again") they lamented (lit. "to offer lamentation"), and then [they] lay on the ground and were swooning.

At the [same] time, in a dream of the sleeping queen-mother, three pigeons having been flying and playing, the youngest among them was carried away by a hawk; having awakened immediately after this dream, [the queen] was terrified and afraid, and so related [this] to the king. "I have heard in a proverb that a pigeon [represents] the life-force (*bla*) of a child. A hawk having carried away the youngest of these pigeons, I am certain that the dearest of my sons has met with misfortune." Immediately after this was said, [they] dispatched a search party.

Before a long time had passed, however, the two princes arrived. But when asked, "Is the dearest of my boys unharmed, or what?" the two princes choked on their words, and for a long time even [their] breath would not come and they were unable to speak. Eventually (*de'i 'og du*), they recovered (*dbugs phyin*) and said, "He was eaten by a tiger." [The queen,] Devī, having heard what they had thus said, [every] part of [her] body (*khams*) froze, and having fallen to the ground, a long time passed until [eventually she] recovered (*dbugs phyin*). Then, the two boys and the queen, together with the [king and] palace retinue, quickly went to the place where the prince died.

At that time, the tigress having completely eaten the prince's flesh, only blood and bones remained as if [they had been] scattered (*rtsog rtsog pa ltar*) on the ground. Having seen [that], the queen held her head, while the king held his hands, and having lamented there and for a time, [the queen] swooned, and after a while had passed, she recovered again.

[Meanwhile,] the prince Mahāsattva, [his] life having passed away in that [place], was reborn in the Tuṣita heaven. [He] thought, "By doing what and for what reason have I been born here?" and when he thoroughly examined the five realms with his divine eyesight, [he saw] the boyish bones of his life that had passed in a place in the woods surrounded by his father and mother. Because [they] were despondent, [they] were suffering from the pain of their sorrow, and [he] saw their lamentation. Then the god thought, "If, the condition of my father and mother being unhappy in this way, will give rise to the cutting-short of [their] health and life, then I will go to comfort (lit. "generate happiness") [them] and will speak [with them]." Having thought [this], he descended from the heavens, and the various words they heard coming from the heavens above made both [his] father and mother happy. Both the father and mother, having looked up to the sky, said, "Please tell us, O god, who are you?" The god replied, "I was called 'Prince Mahāsattva,' and from having given my body to the starving tigress, I was reborn in the Tuṣita heaven.

"O great king (**mahāraja*), [you] really should understand [things] in this way: Phenomena associated with this worldly existence—in even the slightest way whatsoever—come to disintegrate in the end. If something has production, then it definitely disintegrates.

"If one has engaged in ethical transgressions, then one will fall into [the existence of] a hell-being; if one has engaged in virtuous actions, then one will be reborn in high states [of existence].

"Hence, when production and disintegration exist for all [things], for what reason is [this lamentation] on account of me alone? I did not experience (*tshor*) falling into the ocean of suffering; [rather,] I hope I made efforts toward virtue!"

[Then] his father and mother said, "By your great compassion you fed the tigress. If you are someone who has sympathy for all, treat us [likewise]. For, since your life ended, because [when I] remember you, I am tormented with suffering just as if [my] flesh as well were being cut into pieces. When [this is the case], are your deeds of great compassion really suitable as something that should be done in this manner?" Then, by way of various sorts of pleasant words, that god put [the issue] to rest. Since [he] generated happiness, and even a little happiness having been born in his father and mother, thus, they made a chest out of the seven precious substances. [They] placed his boyish bones in it, and built a stūpa on top of where it was buried. The god thus went back to his abode, and the king and his many attendants also returned to the palace.

The Bhagavān said to Ānanda, "What do you think? At that time and in that life, who do you think King Mahāratha was? He was my father during the present, King Śuddhodana. At that time and in that life, the queen of that king was the beautiful Queen Māyādevī. At that time, the elder brother Mahārāva was Maitreya [who will become the fifth Buddha of this eon]. The middle brother Mahādeva was Vasumitra [who will become the sixth

Buddha of this eon]. At that time and in that life, the youngest prince, Mahāsattva—do not think it was someone else—now, [it] is me. At that time, the tiger cubs were these two people. Even a long time before this, I acted to free them from obstacles, and having saved their lives, have made them happy. Now, having become manifestly enlightened, and moreover having been freed from obstacles, [they] are thoroughly liberated from the great sufferings of saṃsāra.

Then Ānanda and all the many members of the entourage rejoiced and praised the word of the Bhagavān.

[This is] the chapter in which Mahāsattva gives his body to the tigress; [it is chapter] two.

The Sūtra Called "The Wise and the Foolish" is finished. It appears to be from China.

Tsongkhapa's *Three Principal Aspects of the Path*

The life story (*rnam thar*) of Tsongkhapa details that on numerous occasions he received teachings from the Bodhisattva Mañjuśrī, including these instructions on the three principal aspects of the path, as a result of his meditative efforts. Thus, Tsongkhapa's *Three Principal Aspects of the Path* (*Lam gyi gtso bo rnam gsum*) points concisely at the three elements deemed central to the Buddhist path to enlightenment: the intention to definitely leave cyclic existence ("renunciation"); the generation of compassion and the altruistic aspiration for enlightenment (the "mind of enlightenment," or *bodhicitta*); and the generation of the only state of mind capable of resulting in liberation from cyclic existence and complete enlightenment (a wisdom consciousness that realizes the ultimate mode of subsistence of phenomena, "emptiness"), a prerequisite of which is the development of a correct intellectual understanding of this state of mind.

The text throughout is brief in its presentation, touching on numerous subjects that receive more extensive treatment in Tsongkhapa's other works, such as the eight leisures and ten fortunes, the sevenfold precepts for the generation of the mind of enlightenment, dependent arising and the identification of the object to be negated in the meditation on selflessness, and the procedures for correctly engendering the states of mind that lead to its direct, nonconceptual realization.

The text likewise introduces students to yet another new and very common genre of literature: poetic verse. This literary form, like so many others, was also inherited by the Tibetans from classical Indian literary culture. In the milieu of educated literary society, a hallmark of one's erudition and literary refinement was the ability to represent any topic in well-formed poetic verse. Although a number of poetic meters that codified patterns of vowel length, syllable stress, and semantic qualities were used in Indian culture, the Tibetan language only allowed for variation in the number of syllables, and hence Tibetan verse is typified merely by syllable count. Nonetheless, Tibetan culture preserved many of the other formal features of poetic composition.

In unbounded original compositions such as this—as opposed to commentaries tied to an earlier, authoritative text—the voice of the author is unsurprisingly often far more present. Such is true from the very start in verse works, in which—like a commentary—a number of typical features can be found, such as the author's promise of composition, a statement of the intended audience, humilific caveats, a statement of the content to be found in the work, and so forth.

On a grammatical level, the challenges in reading this text stem primarily from the fact that it is written in verse. The most prominent of these is the abbreviation of words, the omission of explicit grammar markers, and in some instances, the omission of redundant nouns and phrases. This text, written as a letter from Tsongkhapa to one of his students, the Lord of Tshakho, is a concise and straightforward introduction not only to the subject matter but also to the genre of verse compositions as well. In this regard, there have been several published translations and commentaries on Tsongkhapa's *Three Principal Aspects of the Path* which can be referred to for additional insight into the text.[1]

An alternate version of this same text in འབྲུ་ཚ་ script is provided in appendix 4.

[1] See, for example, Sopa and Hopkins 1990, which presents the text together with the commentary by the Fourth Paṇchen Lama.

༄༅། །ལམ་གྱི་གཙོ་བོ་རྣམ་གསུམ།[1]

རྗེ་བཙུན་བླ་མ་རྣམས་ལ་ཕྱག་འཚལ་ལོ།

རྒྱལ་བའི་གསུང་རབ་ཀུན་གྱི་སྙིང་པོའི་དོན། །རྒྱལ་སྲས་དམ་པ་རྣམས་ཀྱིས་བསྔགས་པའི་ལམ། །
སྐལ་ལྡན་ཐར་འདོད་རྣམས་[2]ཀྱི་འཇུག་ངོགས་དེ།[3] །ཇི་ལྟར་ནུས་བཞིན་བདག་གིས་བཤད་པར་བྱ།[4] ༎ ༡ ༎

གང་དག་[5]སྲིད་པའི་བདེ་ལ་མ་ཆགས་ཤིང་། །དལ་འབྱོར་དོན་ཡོད་བྱ་ཕྱིར་བརྩོན་པ་ཡིས། །
རྒྱལ་བ་དགྱེས་པའི་ལམ་ལ་ཡིད་རྟོན་པའི།[6] །སྐལ་ལྡན་དེ་དག་དང་བའི་ཡིད་ཀྱིས་ཉོན། ༎ ༢ ༎

ནམ་དག་ངེས་འབྱུང་མེད་པར་སྲིད་མཚོ་ཡི། །བདེ་འབྲས་དོན་གཉེར་ཞི་བའི་ཐབས་མེད་ལ། །
སྲིད་ལ་བརྐམ་པ་ཡིས་ཀྱང་ལུས་ཅན་རྣམས། །ཀུན་ནས་འཆིང་ཕྱིར་ཐོག་མར་ངེས་འབྱུང་བཙལ།[7] ༎ ༣ ༎

དལ་འབྱོར་རྙེད་དཀའ་ཚེ་ལ་ལོང་མེད་པ།[8] །ཡིད་ལ་གོམས་པས་ཚེ་འདིའི་སྣང་ཞེན་ལྡོག །
ལས་འབྲས་མི་བསླུ་འཁོར་བའི་སྡུག་བསྔལ་རྣམས། །ཡང་ཡང་བསམས་ན་ཕྱི་མའི་སྣང་ཞེན་ལྡོག ༎ ༤ ༎

དེ་ལྟར་གོམས་པས་འཁོར་བའི་ཕུན་ཚོགས་ལ། །ཡིད་སྨོན་སྐད་ཅིག་ཙམ་ཡང་མི་སྐྱེ་ཞིང་། །
ཉིན་མཚན་ཀུན་ཏུ་ཐར་པ་དོན་གཉེར་བློ། །བྱུང་ན་དེ་ཚེ་ངེས་འབྱུང་སྐྱེས་པ་ལགས།[9] ༎ ༥ ༎

ངེས་འབྱུང་དེ་ཡང་རྣམ་དག་སེམས་བསྐྱེད་ཀྱིས། །ཟིན་པ་མེད་ན་བླ་མེད་བྱང་ཆུབ་ཀྱི། །
ཕུན་ཚོགས་བདེ་བའི་རྒྱུ་རུ་མི་འགྱུར་བས། །བློ་ལྡན་རྣམས་ཀྱིས་བྱང་ཆུབ་སེམས་མཆོག་བསྐྱེད། ༎ ༦ ༎

[10]ཤུགས་དྲག་ཆུ་བོ་བཞི་ཡི་རྒྱུན་གྱིས་ཁྱེར། །བཟློག་དཀའ་ལས་ཀྱི་འཆིང་བ་དམ་པོས་བསྡམས། །
བདག་འཛིན་ལྕགས་ཀྱི་དྲ་བའི་སྦུབས་སུ་ཚུད། །མ་རིག་མུན་པའི་སྨག་ཆེན་ཀུན་ནས་འཐིབས། ༎ ༧ ༎

མུ་མེད་སྲིད་པར་སྐྱེ་ཞིང་སྐྱེ་བ་རུ། །སྡུག་བསྔལ་གསུམ་གྱིས་རྒྱུན་ཆད་མེད་པར་མནར། །
གནས་སྐབས་འདི་འདྲར་གྱུར་པའི་མ་རྣམས་ཀྱི། །ངང་ཚུལ་བསམས་ནས་སེམས་མཆོག་བསྐྱེད་པར་མཛོད།[11] ༎ ༨ ༎

གནས་ལུགས་རྟོགས་པའི་ཤེས་རབ་མི་ལྡན་ན། །ངེས་འབྱུང་བྱང་ཆུབ་སེམས་ལ་གོམས་བྱས་ཀྱང་། །
སྲིད་པའི་རྩ་བ་བཅད་པར་མི་ནུས་པས། །དེ་ཕྱིར་རྟེན་འབྲེལ་རྟོགས་པའི་ཐབས་ལ་འབད། ༎ ༩ ༎

གང་ཞིག་[12]འཁོར་འདས་ཆོས་རྣམས་ཐམས་ཅད་ཀྱི། །རྒྱུ་འབྲས་ནམ་ཡང་བསླུ་བ་མེད་མཐོང་ཞིང་། །
དམིགས་པའི་གཏད་སོ་གང་ཡིན་ཀུན་ཞིག་པ། །དེ་ནི་སངས་རྒྱས་དགྱེས་པའི་[13]ལམ་ལ་ཞུགས། ༎ ༡༠ ༎

སྣང་བ་རྟེན་འབྲེལ་བསླུ་བ་མེད་པ་དང་། །སྟོང་པ་ཁས་ལེན་བྲལ་བའི་གོ་བ་[14]གཉིས། །
ཇི་སྲིད་སོ་སོར་སྣང་བ་དེ་སྲིད་དུ།[15] །ད་དུང་ཐུབ་པའི་དགོངས་པ་རྟོགས་པ་མེད། ༎ ༡༡ ༎
ནམ་ཞིག་རིས་འཇོག་མེད་པར་ཅིག་ཅར་དུ། །རྟེན་འབྲེལ་མི་སླུར་མཐོང་བ་ཙམ་ཉིད་ནས། །
ངེས་ཤེས་ཡུལ་གྱི་འཛིན་སྟངས་[16]ཀུན་འཇིག་ན། །དེ་ཚེ་ལྟ་བའི་དཔྱད་པ་རྫོགས་པ་ལགས། ༎ ༡༢ ༎
གཞན་ཡང་སྣང་བས་ཡོད་མཐའ་སེལ་བ་དང་། །སྟོང་པས་མེད་མཐའ་སེལ་ཞིང་སྟོང་པ་ཉིད། །
རྒྱུ་དང་འབྲས་བུར་འཆར་བའི་ཚུལ་ཤེས་ན། །མཐར་འཛིན་ལྟ་བས་འཕྲོག་པར་མི་འགྱུར་རོ། ༎ ༡༣ ༎
དེ་ལྟར་ལམ་གྱི་གཙོ་བོ་རྣམ་གསུམ་གྱི། །གནད་རྣམས་རང་གིས་ཇི་བཞིན་རྟོགས་པའི་ཚེ། །
དབེན་པ་བསྟེན་ཏེ་བརྩོན་འགྲུས་སྟོབས་བསྐྱེད་ནས། །གདན་གྱི་འདུན་མ་མྱུར་དུ་སྒྲུབས་ཤིག་བུ།[17] ༎ ༡༤ ༎

ཞེས་པ་འདི་ནི་མང་དུ་ཐོས་པའི་དགེ་སློང་བློ་བཟང་གྲགས་པའི་དཔལ་གྱིས་ཚ་ཁོ་དཔོན་པོ་ངག་དབང་གྲགས་པ་ལ་གདམས་པའོ།། ༎

Annotations to Tsongkhapa's *Three Principal Aspects of the Path*

Reading Verse (General Features) ①

Page 133 & 603, Line 1

In previous texts we have seen increasingly complex grammatical constructions dictated by formulaic commentarial constructions and artifacts of translation. Complexity in Tibetan texts can also arise from aesthetic concerns, such as conforming to a poetic style, the most common of which is verse composed of a fixed number of syllables.

In the composition of verse, a number of poetic techniques occur. Because of space limitations, syllables will often be omitted, sometimes from words, but more often from case-marking and syntactic particles such that poetic compositions often lack explicit grammar. Authors will compensate for this in a variety of manners. One way is to rely on the phrasing of Tibetan verse in lines of two-syllable pairs (1-2, 1-2, 1-2, 1 or 1-2, 1-2, 1-2-3, etc.[1]) to indicate word or phrase boundaries. Another technique is to use parallel sentence structures, in which the same basic syntax pattern will be repeated with slight variations to indicate the underlying sentence structure. Both of these features are used in this text.

WHAT TO REMEMBER

In verse works, syllable pairs (1-2, 1-2, 1-2, 1 or 1-2, 1-2, 1-2-3, etc.) are used to indicate word and phrase boundaries, while parallel grammar (i.e., repetitious sentence structures) is used to indicate the underlying sentence structure.

---

[1] See Vekerdi 1952, 221–233. See also, Thupten Jinpa and Elsner 2000, 13*ff.*

2

Translation Hint

Page 133 & 603, Line 5

The first part of this line is an example of omitted explicit grammar. The pluralizing lexical particle རྣམས་ alerts the reader to the fact that the immediately preceding syllable, འདོད་ ("to desire"), is not functioning as a verb but rather is a verbal participle functioning as a noun (see ཤེས་རབ་སྙིང་པོ་ note 13)—indicating either an activity (འདོད་པ་; "desiring") or a substantive (འདོད་པ་; "one who desires"). Keeping in mind the modular nature of Tibetan sentence construction (see ཤེས་རབ་སྙིང་པོ་ note 22) and the fact that འདོད་ is a Class V verb, it should be easy to infer that the phrase སྐལ་ལྡན་ཐར་འདོད་རྣམས་ is an abbreviated form of the substantive, སྐལ་ལྡན་གྱིས་ཐར་པ་འདོད་པ་རྣམས་, with the extra syllables and explicit grammar omitted to fit into a seven-syllable line of verse.

3

Translation Hint

Page 133 & 603, Line 5

Each of the first three lines of this first verse ends with a noun, noun phrase, or pronoun without a case-marking particle (i.e., in the nominative). Given that the final verb in the fourth line is the Class V verb བཤད་ ("to explain"), it is highly likely that the first three lines constitute the nominative object (Wilson, case 1.4.1) of the verb. Given that the title of the work refers to three things as well, one can infer that this verse constitutes the author's declaration of the contents of the work.

4

Auxiliary Verbs: First Person Emphatic Future

Page 133 & 603, Line 5

In the very first text encountered here (see ཤེས་རབ་སྙིང་པོ་ note 11), the construction *verb* + པར་བྱ་ was introduced as one way of conveying the optative mood ("[something] should be done" or "[you] should do X"). Here, however, the same construction can be seen not as an optative indicator but rather as an emphatic future ("I will do X"). Although context is the ultimate arbiter of the identity of the construction as being an optative or future, one strong indicator of the future construction is the presence of the first-person pronoun བདག་ ("I"), as is found here, indicating the author's voice. As noted above, the fact that this is the opening verse of the work lends strong contextual evidence that if the expression is not one of homage, then it is likely the author's promise of composition, which here incorporates his humilific declaration as well as his declaration of the contents of the work.

WHAT TO REMEMBER

Auxiliary verb constructions that form the emphatic future and the optative with the *verb* + པར་བྱ་ construction are ambiguous and must be determined from context.

Translation Hint ⑤

Page 133 & 603, Line 6

This verse utilizes a relative-correlative pronoun pair (see ཤེས་རབ་སྙིང་པོ་ note 10): གང་དག་...དེ་དག་... ("whosoever ... those ..."). Consequently, each verb in the sentence must take either the relative pronoun or the correlative pronoun as its subject/agent, and this determines the structure of the sentence as a whole.

-འི་ Case Marker as Syntactic Particle ⑥

Page 133 & 603, Line 7

The suffix particle –འི་ at the end of this line of verse is not a sixth-case marker but rather is functioning as a non-case syntactic particle to mark continuation. Although noted previously (see ཤེར་སྙིང་རྣམ་བཤད་ note 11), this point is worth reiterating. More commonly used as a sixth-case clause connective marker, when such particles occur after a verb or sentence, these non-case usages of the sixth case indicate a simple continuation between the sentence that precedes it and the sentence that follows.

WHAT TO REMEMBER

Non-case syntactic particles applied to verbs and sentences are used to qualify a statement or segué to a related idea. The most common of these non-case syntactic particles seen in Tibetan literature are the ལ་ ("although ...," "but ...," etc.), used to segué from one sentence to another that qualifies it, and ནས་ ("having [done] ..."), used to mark the end of a gerund clause. Seen somewhat less frequently is the non-case use of the sixth-case particles ཀྱི་, -འི་, etc., which are used to segué to a related statement, and which can often be translated as "and ...," "but ...," etc.

7 Verb Tense in Classical Tibetan: A Discussion

Page 133 & 603, Line 9

In the sentence here, the final verb, བཙལ་, is in either the past or future tense, and given the context of the statement, likely the latter. Since both the optative (see ཤེས་རབ་སྙིང་པོ་ note 11) and deontic constructions (see གཞིའི་སྐུ་གསུམ་སྒྲོན་མེ་ note 8) take the future tense of the verb, one could hypothesize that an auxiliary verb has been omitted for metrical reasons and translate the verbal phrase as "[one should] seek ..." (བཙལ་བར་བྱ་; optative). Alternatively, assuming an omitted deontic auxiliary verb, as later commentators do, one could translate this as "[it is necessary to] seek ..." (བཙལ་དགོས་). It is possible, however, to take another approach to the final verb in this passage—taking the verb without modification (as the Fifth Dalai Lama does in his commentary) and translate it as "[those fortunate ones who desire liberation] seek ..."—but understanding how and why involves a more detailed exploration of the Tibetan verb tense system.

The issue of verb tense is typically not discussed at length in presentations of Tibetan grammar, and the four tenses (past, present, future, and imperative) are often presented at face value. This is not entirely accurate. As an introduction by way of comparison, the English language uses what is called an "absolute tense" system, meaning that the tense of the verb used in an English sentence is determined in relation to the time of its utterance by the speaker. There are other languages, however, (such as Japanese), that use what is called a "relative tense" system, meaning that the choice of verb tense is conditioned by something that *may be other* than the time of utterance (such as the *relative* relationship of the verb to the tense of the verbal activity of the larger local context). It has been argued in reference to so-called Old Tibetan (ca. seventh to ninth century C.E.) that in the early centuries of Tibetan literature, the Tibetan language might have employed a relative tense system. Assuming this to be true for the sake of argument, there is reason to believe that even if so, at some point prior to the eighteenth century, this aspect of the Tibetan language was lost.

As possible evidence of this, the Fifth Dalai Lama's (ca. 1650) acceptance of the future-tense verb བཙལ་ as a valid reading might be because he does not feel the need to posit an omitted auxiliary verb. This would be because the act of "seeking" takes place in the future *relative* to the current state of the subjects of the sentence, who have *not yet sought* renunciation (and more importantly, relative to the present tense of the other verbs, མེད་ and འཆིང་).

In contrast, later commentators, such as Losang Gyeltsen Sengge (*blo bzang rgyal mtshan seng ge*, ca. 1800), feel the need to assert བཙལ་ as part of an auxiliary construction since by the nineteenth century the use of a relative future tense may have no longer accorded with the tense system as it was then being used and understood. In brief, sometime during the seventeenth to eighteenth centuries, it is possible that classical literary Tibetan underwent a shift—from a relative tense system to an absolute tense system—and this could explain the differences between pre-eighteenth century compositions and post-seventeenth century compositions, as well as between pre-eighteenth century canonical texts (such as the Nartang recension) and post-seventeenth century *revised* canonical texts (such as the Derge recension). Possible relative tense usage of verbs can be seen in pre-eighteenth century Tibetan literature, although more research is needed to conclusively prove this hypothesis. Nonetheless, the theory should be kept in mind when reading.

WHAT TO REMEMBER

In "relative tense" contexts, the tense of a verb is conditioned by the *relative* relationship of that verb to the tense of the verbal activity of the larger local context, while in "absolute tense" contexts, the choice of verb tense is conditioned by the time of its utterance by the speaker/author. Consequently, when reading a Tibetan text, careful attention must be paid to its era of composition (or revision). Such historical considerations provide a clue as to whether the tense system might need to be read as "relative" (pre-eighteenth century) or "absolute" (post-seventeenth century).

8

Descriptive Verbs

Page 133 & 603, Line 10

This first line of verse demonstrates the level of compression possible within poetic compositions, where this single line contains two sentences: དལ་འབྱོར་རྙེད་དཀའ། and ཚེ་ལ་ལོང་མེད།. In addition, the first sentence contains its own abbreviation: དལ་འབྱོར་ being an abbreviation of དལ་བ་དང་འབྱོར་བ། ("the [eight] leisures and [ten] fortunes").

More significantly, this first sentence is a good introduction to the category of descriptive verbs. In brief, concepts represented by predicate adjectives (typically, an adjective combined with the verb "to be") are represented in Tibetan by descriptive verbs (typically, Class II verbs). Here the verb དཀའ་ conveys the idea "to be difficult." Other such verbs will be seen in later readings, such as ཆེ་ ("to be difficult"), སྙི་ ("to be soft"), and others.

WHAT TO REMEMBER

Descriptive verbs predicate qualities to a subject (concepts represented by predicate adjectives in English) and are typically Class II verbs.

9

The Verb ལགས་ and Indirect Statements Conveying Meaning

Page 133 & 603, Line 13

We have seen the use of verbal participles in lieu of finite verbs (see ཤེས་རབ་སྙིང་པོ་ note 13) as well as other representations of indirect constructions. Of the three types of indirect constructions discussed—paraphrasing, conveying the meaning of an event, and reporting inner thoughts (see མདོ་མཛངས་བླུན་ note 18)—this is an instance of the second type: conveying the meaning of an event.

Previously, verbal participles and nominalized sentences appeared in modularly constructed sentences (see ཤེས་རབ་སྙིང་པོ་ note 22). In other instances, when participles appeared as subjects or objects of verbs, they were treated as simple verbal nouns. Here, a verbal participle reappears in a very specific construction. What is seen here is a common construction with the verb ལགས་—ལགས་ being an inceptive form of the verb ཡིན་ meaning "to be [henceforth]"—in which a participle or nominalized sentence serves as the predicate of an unstated subject. Such a construction can thus be translated into English as "[This] is ..." or "[It] is ..." It is important to note that this is different from a noun phrase such as ངེས་འབྱུང་གི་སྐྱེས་པ་ ("the generation of renunciation")—that is, in an indirect construction there is no subject of the Class I verb—anaphoric or otherwise—only (syntactically) a predicate, and the internal grammar of the predicate retains the syntax of a nominalized sentence (e.g., ངེས་འབྱུང་སྐྱེས་པ་ vs. ངེས་འབྱུང་གི་སྐྱེས་པ་).

WHAT TO REMEMBER

An indirect statement that conveys the meaning of an event obliquely or descriptively rather than relating the event directly does so with a nominalized sentence and a simple verb of predication (such as ཡིན་, ལགས་, etc.). It can be translated as "[This] is ..." or "[It] is ..."

Translation Hint (10)

Page 133 & 603, Line 16

The next two verses form a complete thought. While the first four lines (i.e., the first verse) are each sentences, they do not have an explicit subject, and the same holds true for the two sentences contained in the first two lines of the second verse. It is only the third line of the second verse that reveals the function of these prior sentences as establishing the context for the last two lines. Consequently, the first six "sentences" form the first part of a run-on sentence that only concludes with the final two lines. .

Auxiliary Verbs: Honorific Imperative (11)

Page 133 & 603, Line 19

The honorific-imperative construction expresses a polite command and is typically formed by the combination of the main verb in the future tense with the imperative form of the strong honorific generic action verb མཛད་ (i.e., མཛོད་). Since the statement is in verse (with restrictions on the number of syllables), it is possible that the exhortative mood (see མདོ་མཛངས་བླུན་ note 23) is intended (as some commentators have taken it).

WHAT TO REMEMBER

The honorific-imperative construction expresses a polite command and is formed by the combination of the main verb in the future tense with the imperative form of the strong honorific generic action verb མཛད་ (i.e., མཛོད་).

(12)

Translation Hint

Page 133 & 603, Line 22

The construction གང་ཞིག་…དེ་… ("whosoever … they …") is another instance of a relative-correlative pronoun pair (see ཤེས་རབ་སྙིང་པོ་ note 10).

(13)

Translation Hint

Page 133 & 603, Line 23

Since the verb དགྱེས་ ("to be pleased") is a Class II verb, the sixth-case particle attached to it must necessarily be a clause connective to a complement (Wilson, case 6.6.4).

(14)

Translation Hint

Page 134 & 604, Line 1

The construction …འི་རྟོགས་པ་ ("the understanding of …") should be understood to distribute to the preceding phrase as well.

(15)

Translation Hint

Page 134 & 604, Line 2

The construction ཇི་སྲིད་……དེ་སྲིད་དུ་ ("as long as … for just that long …") is another instance of a relative-correlative pair (see ཤེས་རབ་སྙིང་པོ་ note 10). In this instance, however, the opening phrase has been moved to the middle of the sentence due to the constraints of the verse structure.

Ubiquitous Technical Terms of Buddhist Epistemology

Page 134 & 604, Line 4

The technical terms that occur at this point in the text, ངེས་ཤེས་ ("ascertaining consciousness") and ཡུལ་གྱི་འཛིན་སྟངས་ ("mode of apprehension of [an] object[s]"), come from the field of Buddhist epistemology—that is, the intellectual tradition of Dignāga (fl. ca. 500 C.E.) and Dharmakīrti (fl. ca. 600 C.E.). It is no exaggeration to say that the religious history of first millennium (C.E.) India is really the history of religious debates between Buddhist and post-Vedic philosophers. The principal opponents of Nāgārjuna (fl. ca. 200 C.E.) appear to have been members of the Sāṃkhya school, and although proponents of Nyāya philosophy ("Naiyāyikas") were known by Nāgārjuna, he only addresses their positions in a dismissive manner in a brief pair of texts (the *Vaidalya-sūtra* and *-prakāraṇa*). Rather, it is not until the middle of the millennium that Buddhist philosophers offer a detailed refutation of the specifics of Naiyāyika assertions. It could be argued that the Madhyamaka dialectic is intended as a highly refined critique of Buddhist philosophical positions from within the tradition itself, and hence its comprehension is more challenging to those not already versed in Buddhist philosophy; that is, it presumes a basic understanding and level of agreement on certain categories of knowledge.

The tradition of philosophical inquiry instituted by Dignāga and refined, in particular, by Dharmakīrti specifically addressed the notions of the Nyāya school as well as offered a detailed framework for interreligious debate and logical assertion. So successful was Dharmakīrti's formulation of epistemology and his critique of the Nyāya tradition that it was not until after the destruction of the Buddhist universities of north India by Muslim armies in the early thirteenth century that a "new" Nyāya tradition ("Navya-nyāya") was able to reassert itself, although in the absence of any intellectual competition it offered little more than a rehash of previously refuted theories.

Of particular significance to Tibetan literature, however, is the fact that it was during the height of this Buddhist intellectual dominance of India and, in particular, the prevalence of Dharmakīrtian epistemology in the eighth to twelfth centuries that the Buddhist intellectual and educational systems migrated to Tibet. It is therefore no surprise that the prerequisites of proper training in logic and the foundational vocabulary of Dharmakīrtian epistemology came to undergird much of Tibetan writing and can be found in nearly all genres and domains of Tibetan literature.

This is one of the reasons that a traditional education in Buddhist philosophy begins with a primer in Dharmakīrtian logic and reasoning. Two such texts are provided in the "Intermediate" section of this *Reader* (Purbujok's *Introductory Path of Reasoning* and Jampel Sampel's *Presentation of Awarenesses and Knowers*), and while these and related texts would ideally be studied first, given the challenges of the subject matter and their idiosyncratic grammatical structures, exposure to this literature has been intentionally delayed. Suffice it to say that in addition to learning basic vocabulary and grammatical structures, gaining mastery in Tibetan translation involves a degree of acculturation in the Tibetan and Buddhist worldview, and a large part of that worldview is Dharmakīrtian epistemology and its vocabulary.

WHAT TO REMEMBER

Nearly all of Tibetan literature has been impacted in one way or another by the epistemological tradition, and familiarity with its vocabulary is a necessity.

17

Translation Hint

Page 134 & 604, Line 8

The imperative form of a verb followed by ཅིག་, ཞིག་, or ཤིག་ forming the precative construction has already been seen (see མདོ་མཛངས་བླུན་ note 14). The trailing vocative, བུ་, however, is a unique occurrence dictated less by the narrative than by the requirements of verse phrasing (see ལམ་གཙོ་རྣམ་གསུམ་ note 1).

Translation of Tsongkhapa's *Three Principal Aspects of the Path*

[I] pay homage to the foremost lamas!

I will explain, in accordance with whatever abilities [I have],
The port of entry for those fortunate ones desiring liberation,
The path that is praised by the holy Conqueror's children,
And the meaning of the essence of all the scriptures of the Conqueror. // 1 //

Whosoever is not attached to the pleasures of existence,
And because of striving to make leisure and fortune meaningful
Places their confidence in the path, by means of which the conquerors
are pleased,
Those fortunate ones, listen with a clear mind! // 2 //

Without utterly pure renunciation, there is no method
For pacifying the seeking of pleasant effects in the ocean of existence; hence
Because thirst for existence, moreover, thoroughly binds
The embodied, [those fortunate ones who desire liberation] initially seek
renunciation. // 3 //

Leisure and fortune are difficult to find and life lacks extension;
Through familiarizing the mind [with this], the emphasis on the appearances of
this life is reversed.
When one thinks, again and again, about the inevitability of the [karmic] effects [of
one's] actions
And the sufferings of cyclic existence, then the emphasis on the appearances of
future lives is reversed. // 4 //

When, by meditating like that, one does not generate even for one moment
Longing for the marvels of cyclic existence, and
There arises, at all [times], day and night, an awareness that seeks
Liberation, then at that time, [this] is the generation of renunciation. // 5 //

Since, if that renunciation is not also conjoined with
Pure bodhicitta, it will not serve as the cause of
The marvelous bliss of highest enlightenment,
The intelligent ones generate the supreme bodhicitta. // 6 //

Carried by the current of the four fierce and powerful rivers,
Bound by means of tight bonds of karmic actions difficult to oppose,
Having entered into the confines of the iron net of grasping at a self,
Covered with the great darkeness of dark ignorance, [and] // 7 //

Born limitlessly in the mundane world, and in their births
Tortured uninterruptedly by the three sufferings—
Having contemplated the condition of [our] mothers
Who have come to be in a state such as this, generate the supreme bodhicitta! // 8 //

If one does not have the wisdom that realizes the mode of subsistence,
Then, although one has cultivated renunciation and bodhicitta,
Since [one] is not able to cut the root of mundane existence,
For that purpose, strive at the method of realizing dependent arising! // 9 //

Whosoever sees the effects of the causes of all phenomena of
Cyclic existence and nirvāṇa as completely inevitable,
And thoroughly destroys the mode of apprehension of objects,
They enter the path with regard to which the Buddha is pleased. // 10 //

As long as the two—the understanding of appearances [being] the inevitability of
dependent arising, and
[The understanding of] emptiness [being] free from assertions [of intrinsic
existence]—
Appear separately, for just so long
There will still be no realization of the intention of [Śākya]muni [Buddha]. // 11 //

At the time when, from just seeing the inevitability of dependent arising [and
emptiness]
As simultaneous [and] without alternating,
An ascertaining consciousness thoroughly destroys the mode of apprehension of
objects,
Then at that time, the analysis of the view [of emptiness] is complete. // 12 //

Furthermore, appearances exclude the extreme of existence,
And emptiness excludes the extreme of nonexistence.
When [one] knows the manner in which emptiness dawns as cause and effect,
Then [one] will not be captivated by views [that] grasp at an extreme. // 13 //

Thus, at the time when you yourself have realized—just as they are—
The essentials of the three principal aspects of the path,
Resort to solitude, and having generated the power of effort,
Quickly accomplish your final aim, my son. // 14 //

This is advice given to the Lord of Tshakho, Ngawang Drakpa, by the widely studied monk Losang Drakpa.

PAṆCHEN SÖNAM DRAKPA'S *NEW RED ANNALS* (SELECTIONS)

The final selection in this introductory section is an exercise in reading historical literature. It is a basic principle of responsible scholarship that research into any subject should attempt to take into account all relevant contextual information. While the ideal of pure philosophical exposition and debate is certainly a goal that is aspired for in the Buddhist tradition, it is rare for any individual to be immune from the political contingencies of their day. Consequently, when engaged in any aspect of Tibetan research, knowledge of historical and political context and the ability to accurately read such documents is a necessary skill to develop.

The text presented here—a selection from the *New Red Annals* (*Deb ther dmar po gsar ma*) by Paṇchen Sönam Drakpa (*paṇ chen bsod nams grags pa*, 1478–1554)—is a historical work written by a well-educated author renowned for his clarity of prose. A luminary of the Tibetan world, Paṇchen Sönam Drakpa served as the Fifteenth Regent of Ganden and hence, the head of the Gelukpa lineage; he was the tutor to the Third Dalai Lama, and also holds the distinction of having served as the abbot of each of the three major monasteries of the Lhasa Valley: Ganden, Drepung, and Sera. As a polymath, Paṇchen Sönam Drakpa wrote on a wide range of topics, and his collected works on the core subjects of Buddhist philosophy currently serve as the primary textbooks for the Loseling College of Drepung Monastic University.

The subject of the selection presented here is the period of the Tibetan Empire (ca. 620–842 C.E.), which marked the first unification of the Tibetan Plateau under a single king and the establishment of political relationships between Tibet as a sovereign nation-state and her neighbors China and Nepal.[1] The text covers the major events in Tibetan imperial history, including the establishment of a central government in the Lhasa Valley capable of negotiating international treaties, the introduction of Buddhism to Tibet, internal religious disputes, repeated external wars (with China), political successions, and the culminating event of the disintegration of the Tibetan imperium.

In terms of textual features, the selection introduces the genre of native-authored unrestricted narrative. In this text, the student encounters new sets of vocabulary, including Tibetan political titles and proper names, foreign words (both Sanskrit and Chinese) rendered into Tibetan, as well as Tibetan contractions and scribal abbreviations. In addition, this text demonstrates the style of historical narrative writing, in which it is necessary to keep track of the sequence of events in order to properly follow what is being said, as numerous passages presume the subjects and topics of previous statements. Moreover, this text demonstrates various techniques of textual annotation, including the insertion of qualifying statements as both footnote markers and diminished script size.

On a grammatical level, the challenges in reading this text are predominantly in terms of vocabulary and extrapolating the connotations of apparently simple statements. In addition, while most statements are fairly straightforward, there are a few passages that are more complicated, illustrating the levels of grammatical complexity that are possible when the modular nature of Tibetan noun-phrases is deployed for its full effect.

---

[1] For more information on this time period, see Beckwith 1993 and the somewhat more difficult-to-find book by Erik Haarh, *The Yar-luṅ Dynasty*, 1969.

༄༅། །རྒྱལ་རབས་འཕྲུལ་གྱི་ལྡེ་མིག་གམ་དེབ་ཐེར་དམར་པོའི་དེབ་གསར་མ་ཞེས་བྱ་བ་བཞུགས་སོ། །[1]

བཅོམ་ལྡན་འདས་དེ་བཞིན་གཤེགས་པ་དགྲ་བཅོམ་པ་ཡང་དག་པར་རྫོགས་པའི་སངས་རྒྱས་ཁྲིམས་གཉིས་[2]ཀྱི་བདག་པོ་ལ་ཕྱག་འཚལ་ལོ། །

མཁྱེན་གཉིས་གསེར་གྱི་འཁོར་ལོ་ཡིས། །འཇིག་རྟེན་གསུམ་ལ་དབང་བསྒྱུར་ཞིང་། །
ཕས་རྒོལ་བདུད་བཞི་ལས་རྒྱལ་བ། །ཀུན་མཁྱེན་ཆོས་ཀྱི་རྒྱལ་པོར་འདུད། །

ལོ་རྒྱུས་ནོར་བུའི་དཀོར་མཛོད་ཉིད། །ལེགས་པར་ཕྱེ་ནས་ལུགས་གཉིས་ཀྱི། །
ལོ་རྒྱུས་སྨྲ་འདོད་མཐའ་དག་ལ། །རྒྱལ་རབས་འཕྲུལ་གྱི་ལྡེ་མིག་བྱིན། །

དེ་ལ་འདིར་ས་ཆེན་པོ་སྐྱོང་བའི་རྒྱལ་རབས་མདོ་ཙམ་བརྗོད་ན་ལྔ་སྟེ། རྒྱ་གར་གྱི་རྒྱལ་རབས། ཤམ་བྷ་ལའི་རྒྱལ་རབས། བོད་ཀྱི་རྒྱལ་རབས། རྒྱ་ནག་དང་ཧོར་གྱི་རྒྱལ་རབས། བོད་དུ་རྒྱ་ཧོར་གྱི་ལུང་བྱུང་ཚུལ་ལོ། །

༄༅། །གསུམ་པ་བོད་ཀྱི་རྒྱལ་རབས་བཤད་པ་ནི། དེ་ཡང་བོད་ཀྱི་མི་རྣམས་ཐོག་མར་ཆགས་ཚུལ་ལ་སྤྲེའུ་དང་། བྲག་སྲིན་མོ་གཉིས་འདུས་པ་ལས་ཆགས་པའི་གནམ་མཆིས་ཤིང་། ཡང་སྟོད་ལྡན་གྱི་ཐོག་མ་རྒྱལ་པོ་སྐྱབས་སེང་གི་བུ་ལྷས་ཀོ་ར་བ་དཔུང་ཚོགས་བཅོམ་པའི་ཚེ། རྟ་པ་དེ་ཞེས་བྱ་བའི་རྒྱལ་པོ་དཔུང་ཚོགས་དང་བཅས་པ་བྱུད་མེད་ཀྱི་ཆས་སུ་བྱས་དེ་བྲོས་ནས་རི་ཁ་བ་ཅན་གྱི་ནང་དུ་ཞུགས་པའི་རིགས་ལས་ཆད་པ་སོགས་དུ་མ་ཞིག་སྣང་བ་དང་། ལུང་རྣམ་འབྱེད་དང་དུས་ཀྱི་འཁོར་ལོ་སོགས་སུ་འང་བོད་ཅེས་མང་དུ་འབྱུང་བས་ངོ་བོ་བདག་ཅག་གི་སྟོན་པ་བྱོན་པའི་དུས་ལས་ཡུལ་དང་མི་གཉིས་ཀ་ཆེས་སྔ་བར་ཆགས་པ་ཞིག་ཏུ་སྣང་།卐

…

卐རྒྱ་གར་དང་དུས་མཉམ་དུ་ཆགས་པར་བྱས་ནའང་འགལ་བ་མེད།

རྒྱལ་པོ་སྟག་རི་གཉན་གཟིགས་ཞེས་གྲགས།[3] དེའི་སྲས་གནམ་རི་སྲོང་བཙན་དེ། འདིའི་དུས་སུ་བྱུང་ནས་ཚ་རྙེད་ཅིང་། རྒྱ་ནས་རྩིས་དང་སྨན་སོགས་བྱུང་། འདིའི་སྲས་སྲོང་བཙན་སྒམ་པོ་སྟེ། འདི་ནི་སངས་རྒྱས་མྱ་ངན་ལས་འདས་ནས་ལོ་སྟོང་བཞི་བརྒྱ་ཞི་དགུ་འདས་པའི་མེ་མོ་གླང་གི་ལོ་[4]ཡར་སྟ་སྦྲ་སྟོད་ཚལ་དུ་ཕོ་བྲང་བྱམས་པ་མི་འགྱུར་གླིང་ཞེས་བྱ་བར་སྐུ་འཁྲུངས།

དགུང་ལོ་བཅུ་གསུམ་པ་ལ་ཡབ་འདས་ནས་རྒྱལ་སར་བྱོན། བཞུགས་གནས་ཕོ་བྲང་ནི་དམར་པོ་རིར་མཛད། རྒྱལ་པོ་འདི་ལ་སྤྱིར་བློན་པོ་བསམ་གྱིས་མི་ཁྱབ་ཀྱང་། མཆོག་ཏུ་གྱུར་པ་འཕྲུལ་གྱི་སྣ་ཆེན་རིན་བཟང་། ཡར་ཀླུངས་པ།[5] ཐོན་མི་སཾ་བྷོ་ཊ། མགར་སྟོང་བཙན། སྟོད་ལུང་རཾ་པ་བ། འབྲི་སེ་རུ་གོང་སྟོན། འབྲི་གུང་པ། ཉང་ཁྲི་བཟང་རྣམས་ཡིན། ཉང་སེར་བ།

ཐོན་མི་རྒྱ་གར་དུ་རྫངས་པར་བྲམ་ཟེ་ལི་བྱིན་དང་། པཎྜིཏ་ལྷ་རིག་པའི་སེངྒེ་ལ་ཡི་གེ་དང་སྒྲ་བཅས་བསླབ། བོད་དུ་བྱོན་དེ་རྒྱ་ཡིག་ལྔ་བཅུ་བོད་ཡིག་སུམ་ཅུར་གདན་ལ་ཕབ། རྒྱལ་པོ་ལ་ཡི་གེ་ཕུལ་ཞིང་བློན་པོ་རྣམས་ལའང་བསླབ། མདོ་སྡེ་དཀོན་མཆོག་གི་སྤྲིན་བསྒྱུར་བ་དང་། ཐོན་མི་མདོ་རྗེའི་སྒྲ་མདོ་ལ་སོགས་པ་བརྩམས་པ་མང་དུ་མཛད་པས། བོད་ལ་བཀའ་དྲིན་ཤིན་ཏུ་ཆེ། ཉིད་ཀྱི་ཞལ་ནས་ཀྱང་།

ཡུལ་མཐའ་ཁོབ་བོད་ཀྱི་རྒྱལ་ཁམས་འདིར།
མི་མཁས་པ་སླེབ་པའི་ཐྲ་མ་ཡིན།
ང་མུན་པ་སེལ་བའི་སྒྲོན་མེ་ཡིན།
རྗེ་རྒྱལ་པོ་ཉི་ཟླའི་ཚུལ་དུ་བཞུགས།

གྲོགས་བློན་པོའི་ཁྲོད་ན་ང་ཙམ་མེད།
བོད་ཁ་བ་ཅན་པའི་མི་རྣམས་ལ།
ང་ཐོན་མི་དྲིན་དུ་མི་ཆེའམ།[6]

གསུང་སྟེ་ཐུགས་མད་དོ། །

རྒྱལ་པོས་དགུང་ལོ་བཅུ་དྲུག་བཞེས་པ་ན་བློན་པོ་རྣམས་མངགས་སྟེ། བལ་པོའི་རྒྱལ་པོ་འོད་ཟེར་གོ་ཆའི་སྲས་མོ་ཁྲི་བཙུན་བཙུན་མོར་བཀུག་པ། སྐལ་རྫོངས་སུ། ཇོ་བོ་མི་སྐྱོད་རྡོ་རྗེ། བྱམས་པ་ཆོས་འཁོར། ཙནྡ་[7] སྒྲོལ་མ། བཻཌཱུརྱའི་ལྷུང་བཟེད་རྣམས་བྱུང་སྟེ། བོད་དུ་སངྒྱས་[8]ཀྱི་བསྟན་པ་འབྱུང་བའི་རྟེན་འབྲེལ་གྱི་མགོ་ཚུགས་པར་སྣང་།

དགུང་ལོ་བཅོ་བརྒྱད་བཞེས་པ་ན། མགར་ལ་སོགས་པའི་བློན་པོ་རྟ་པ་བརྒྱ་ཐམ་པ་མངགས་ཏེ། རྒྱ་ནག་གི་རྒྱལ་པོ་སེངྒེ་བཙན་པོའི་སྲས་མོ་ལྷ་ཅིག་ཨུན་ཤིང་ཀོང་ཇོ་[9] སློང་དུ་བཏང་བ། ཕོ་བྲང་ཟེམ་ཤིང་དུ་སླེབ་པའི་ཚེ། རྒྱལ་པོས་བསྐུར་བའི་སྐྱེས་རྣམས་ཕུལ་ཏེ། ལྷ་ཅིག་གནང་དགོས་པའི་རྒྱུ་མཚན་ཞུས་པ་ན། རྒྱ་ནག་རྒྱལ་པོ་བློན་འབངས་དང་བཅས་པ་ཤིན་ཏུ་མ་དགྱེས་ནའང་། ཅུང་ཟད་རྫུས་ནས། ཁྱེད་བོད་ཀྱི་རྒྱལ་པོ་ལ་དགེ་བ་བཅུའི་ཁྲིམས་འཆའ་བ་དང་། གཙུག་ལག་ཁང་རྩིགས་པ་དང་། འདོད་ཡོན་ལྔ་ལ་ལོངས་སྤྱོད་ནུས་པ་ཡོད་དམ། ཡོད་ན་བུ་མོ་སྟེར་བས་དྲིས་ཤོག་ཟེར།[10]

དེ་ལ་མགར་གྱིས་འཕྲིན་རེ་སྐྱེལ་བར་རྒྱ་ནས་བོད་དུ་ཕྱིན་ན་ལྷ་གཅིག་ཡོན་པའི་དུས་མི་འོང་། དེའི་ལན་དུ་ཤོག་དྲིལ་གསུམ་པོ་འདི་རྒྱལ་པོས་བསྐུར་བ་ཡིན་ཞེས་རིམ་གྱིས་ཕུལ་བའི་ནང་ན། ན་ཚིག་གསུམ་པོ་ལྷག་དང་བཅས་པ་འགྲུབ། དེ་ལྟར་བྱས་ཀྱང་བུ་མོ་མི་སྟེར་ན་ངས་སྤྲུལ་པའི་དམག་ཁྲི་ཕྲག་ལྔ་[11]བཏང་སྟེ། ཁྱོད་བསད། ལྷ་ཅིག་འཁྱེར ཡུལ་ཁམས་ཐམས་ཅད་བཅོམ་ལ། བཞག་གི་གསུང་པ་སོགས་གཟིགས་པས། རྒྱལ་པོ་ཤིན་ཏུ་སྐྲག་ནའང་མི་སྐྲག་པ་ལྟར་བཅོས་ནས། ཁྱོད་བོད་ཀྱི་རྒྱལ་པོ་དེ་ཁ་ཆོན་ཤིན་ཏུ་ཆེ་བ་གཅིག་འདུག་ཟེར།

རྒྱུན་འདི་ལས་ཞིང་བློན་པོ་མགར་གྱིས་རིག་པ་རྣོ་བའི་རྩལ་བདུན་བརྒྱད་ཙམ་བསྟན་པ་ཐུགས་སུ་མ་ཤོང་ནས་སྲས་མོ་ལྷ་ཅིག་སྐལ་རྫོངས་སུ་ཇོ་བོ་ཤཱཀྱ་མུ་ནེ་དང་བཅས་པ་ཐུགས་ལ་འཕྲེང་བཞིན་དུ་བྱིན། ཡབ་རྒྱལ་པོས་སྐྱེལ་མ་མཛད་པ།

ལྷ་ཅིག་ཇོ་བོ་རིན་པོ་ཆེ་དང་བཅས་པ་དམར་པོ་རིར་རྒྱལ་པོའི་དྲུང་དུ་ཕྱག་ཕེབས། སྐྱིད་པའི་དགའ་སྟོན་བསམ་གྱིས་མི་ཁྱབ་པ་མཛད་དེ། མཆོག་ཏུ་འཚོས་པ་ཡིན་ནོ། །རྒྱལ་པོས་ཆོས་ཀྱི་བདག་པོ་མཛད་ནས། སྤྱན་རས་གཟིགས་ཡི་གེ་དྲུག་མ་དང་། འཕགས་པ་ག་ཤིན་ཧེ་ག་ཤེད་སོགས་ཀྱི་ཆོས་སྣ་མང་གསུང་ཞིང་སྒྲོམ་བུ་འཇུགས་པ་དང་། ཁྲ་འབྲུག་ལ་སོགས་ཀྱི་གཙུག་ལག་ཁང་བཞེངས་པར་མཛད། བཙུན་མོ་གཉིས་ཀྱིས་ཀྱང་འཕྲུལ་སྣང་དང་ར་མོ་ཆེའི་གཙུག་ལག་ཁང་བཞེངས་ཏེ་ཇོ་བོ་རྣམ་གཉིས་སོ་སོར་བཞུགས། མདོར་ན་རྒྱལ་པོ་ཉིད་ཇོ་བོ་ཐུགས་རྗེ་ཆེན་པོ་དང་། བཙུན་མོ་གཉིས་ལྷ་མོ་གཉིས་ཀྱི་སྤྲུལ་པ་ཡིན་པར་ཐག་ཆོད་ཅིང་། བློན་པོ་ཐལ་ཆེར་ཡང་སྤྲུལ་པར་གྲགས་པ།

དེའི་ཚེ་བཙུན་མོ་གཉིས་ལ་ནི་སྲས་མེད། བཙུན་མོ་གཞན་གཉིས་རིམ་གྱིས་ཁབ་ཏུ་བཞེས་པ་ལ་འང་སྲས་མ་བྱུང་། རྗེས་སུ་སྟོད་ལུང་ནས་མོང་བཟའ་ཁྲི་ལྕམ་ཞེས་བྱ་བ་ལ་སྲས་མང་སྲོང་མང་བཙན་འཁྲུངས། དགུང་ལོ་བཅུ་གསུམ་པ་ལ་རྒྱལ་སར་བྱོན། རྒྱལ་སྲིད་ལོ་ལྔ་བཟུང་སྟེ་བཅོ་བརྒྱད་པ་ལ་འདས། དེ་ལ་སྲས་གུང་སྲོང་གུང་བཙན་འཁྲུངས་ལ། ནར་མ་སོན་པས། སྔར་ཡབ་རྒྱལ་པོས་སྲིད་སྐྱོང་དགོས་པ་བྱུང་། བརྒྱད་ཅུ་རྩ་གཉིས་པ་ས་ཕྲིའི་ལོ་ལ་བཙུན་མོ་གཉིས་དང་ལྷན་ཅིག་ཏུ་ཇོ་བོ་བཅུ་གཅིག་ཞལ་གྱི་ཐུགས་ཁར་ཐིམ།

དེ་ནས་དཔོན་སྲས་གུང་སྲོང་གུང་བཙན་དགུང་ལོ་བཅུ་གསུམ་པ་ལ་རྒྱལ་སར་བཏོན་པ། ལྷ་སར་མེས་ཀྱི་མཆོད་པ་འཛུགས་པ་སོགས་དཀོན་མཆོག་གསུམ་ལ་གུས་པར་མཛད། རྒྱལ་སྲིད་ལོ་བཅོ་ལྔ་བཟུང་སྟེ་ཉེར་བདུན་པ་ལ་གཙང་གི་ས་ཆར་འདས། རྒྱལ་པོ་འདིའི་དུས་སུ་རྒྱ་དམག་བོད་དུ་བྱུང་སྟེ་དམར་པོ་རི་མེ་ལ་སྲེག ཇོ་བོ་ཤཱཀྱ་མུ་ནི་འཕྲུལ་སྣང་དུ་སྦས་པས་མ་རྙེད་ཀྱང་། ཇོ་བོ་མི་སྐྱོད་རྡོ་རྗེ་ཟླ་གྲོ་གཅིག་གི་སར་ཁྱེར་ཞེས་རྒྱའི་དེབ་ཐེར་ལས་འབྱུང་། སྔར་བློན་པོ་མགར་གྱིས་བོད་དམག་འབུམ་ཚོ་ཁྲིད་དེ་རྒྱ་ཡི་ཡུལ་ཁམས་བཅོམས། མགར་རང་ཡང་དམག་དེར་འདས་ཞེས་གྲགས།

དེའི་ཚེ་སྲོང་བཙན་སྒམ་པོ་འདས་ནས་ལོ་བརྒྱད་ཅུ་ལོན། སྲས་དགུང་ལོ་བཅུ་གསུམ་པ་ལ་རྒྱལ་སར་བྱོན། བློན་པོ་མ་ཞང་ཁྲོམ་པ་སྐྱེས་དང་། བློན་པོ་སྟག་ར་ཀླུ་གོང་སོགས་ཆོས་ལ་མི་དགའ་བ་རྣམས་དབང་ཆེས་པས་ཇོ་བོ་རིན་པོ་ཆེ་དང་པོར་བྱེ་ཐིམ་དུ་སྦས། དེ་ལ་ངན་པའི་ལྟས་འགའ་བྱུང་བས་བཏོན་ཏེ་རྒྱ་གར་དུ་སྐྱེལ་བར་བཏང་བ། མང་ཡུལ་སྐྱིད་གྲོང་དུ་སླེབ་པ་ན་ལམ་ལ་མ་མཐར་ཞེས་སྐད་བཏགས་ནས་དེར་བཞུགས་སུ་གསོལ།

རྒྱལ་པོ་སྐུ་ནར་སོན་པ་ན་ཆོས་བློན་འགོས་ཁྲི་བཟང་དང་། ཞང་ཉམ་བཟང་སོགས་དང་གྲོས་བཏོན་ནས་ཆོས་བྱ་བར་གླེངས་པའི་ཚེ། བློན་ཉམ་བཟང་ན་རེ། བློན་པོ་གཞན་གཉིས་དབང་བཙན་པས་མི་འགྲུབ་ཟེར། འགོས་ན་རེ་འགྲུབ་པའི་ཐབས་ཡོད་ཀྱི། ཁོ་བོའི་རྟིང་གིས་གནོན་མཛོད་ཅིག་ཟེར། དེ་ཁ་བཞིན་གཡོ་སྒྱུའི་འཕྲུལ་གྱིས་བློན་པོ་མ་ཞང་གསོན་པོར་དུར་དུ་བཅུག སྟག་ར་བྱང་ཕྱོགས་ལ་བཅུག

ཐོག་མར་ཇོ་བོ་མང་ཡུལ་ནས་སྤྱན་དྲངས་ཏེ་ལྷ་སར་བཞུགས། སྦ་གསལ་སྣང་མངགས་ཏེ། སློབ་དཔོན་ཞི་བ་འཚོ་སྤྱན་དྲངས་པས། བོད་ལ་ལྷ་སར་ཕེབས་ཤིང་། རྗེས་ནས་སྟོད་ལུང་པ་བསམ་ཡས་སུ་ཕེབ་པ། བཙན་པོས་གུས་པའི་ཕྱག་དང་བསུ་བར་མཛད། མཁན་པོས་དགེ་བ་བཅུ་དང་རྟེན་འབྲེལ་བཅུ་གཉིས་ལས་བརྩམས་པའི་ཆོས་

མང་དུ་གསུང་པས་བོད་ཀྱི་ལྷ་སྲིན་རྣམས་མ་དགའ་སྟེ། དམར་པོ་རི་ལ་ཐོག་རྡེག་པ་དང་། འཕང་ཐང་ཡར་ལུང་ཆུས་འཁྱེར་བ་སོགས་ཆེ་འཕྲུལ་སྣ་ཚོགས་བསྟན་པ་ཉིད་མཁན་པོས་དགོངས་ནས། རེ་ཞིག་བལ་པོར་བྱོན། སློབ་དཔོན་པདྨ་སཾ་བྷ་ཝ་སྤྱན་འདྲེན་པའི་ཞལ་བཀོད་མཛད་པ་བཞིན་སྤྱན་དྲངས་ཏེ། བོད་ཀྱི་ལྷ་ཀླུ་ཐཾས་ཅད་དམ་ལ་བཏགས། མཁན་པོའང་སླར་སྤྱར་དྲངས་ནས་རྒྱལ་པོ་དགུང་ལོ་ཉི་ཤུ་རྩ་གཉིས་པ་ས་མོ་ཡོས་ཀྱི་ལོ་ལ། དཔལ་བསམ་ཡས་མི་འགྱུར་ལྷུན་གྱིས་གྲུབ་པའི་གཙུག་ལག་ཁང་གི་རྨང་བཏིང་སྟེ། ལྕགས་མོ་ཡོས་ལ་རྫོགས་པར་གྲུབ། རབ་གནས་གཙོ་བོར་མཁན་པོ་བྱང་ཆུབ་སེམས་དཔའ་དང་། སློབ་དཔོན་པདྨས་མཛད། ཤིང་མོ་ལུག་ལ་མཁན་པོའི་དྲུང་དུ་སད་མི་མི་བདུན་སོགས་རབ་ཏུ་བྱུང་།

གཞན་ཡང་དད་པ་ཅན་དང་ཤེས་རབ་ཅན་མང་པོ་རབ་ཏུ་བྱུང་བ་ལ་བཀོད་ཅིང་། སྤྱིར་ཁམས་ཡན་ཆད[12] དུ་ཆོས་ཀྱི་གྲྭ་བཅུ་གཉིས་ཙམ་དང་། ཡེར་པ་དང་མཆིམས་ཕུར་སྒྲོམ་གྲྭ་འཛུགས་པ་དང་། ལོ་པཎ་རྣམས་ཀྱིས་སྔགས་མཚན་ཉིད་ཀྱི་ཆོས་ཕལ་མོ་ཆེ་བསྒྱུར་ཞིང་འཆད་ཉན་གྱིས་གདན་ལ་འབེབས་པའི་ཞབས་ཏོག་བསྒྲུབ་པ་སྟེ། སངས་རྒྱས་ཀྱི་བསྟན་པ་རིན་པོ་ཆེའི་སྲོལ་བཏོད་པར་མཛད།

དེ་ནས་མཁན་པོས་བོད་འདིར་མུ་སྟེགས་པ་མི་འབྱུང་ཡང་། རྒྱལ་བའི་བསྟན་པ་ཁ་གཉིས་སུ་བགྱི་དེ་རྩོད་པར་འགྱུར་བས། དེའི་ཚེ་རྒྱ་གར་ནས་ཀ་མ་ལ་ཤཱི་ལ་སྤྱན་དྲངས་ལ། རྩོད་པ་བྱེད་དུ་ཆུག་ཅིག་ཅེས་པའི་ཞལ་ཆེམས་གསུངས་ནས་མྱ་ངན་ལས་འདས། དགུང་ལོ་སྟོང་ལ་གཅིག་ཆད།[13]

འཚམས་ཤིག་ནས་ལུང་བསྟན་ལྟར་རྒྱ་ནག་ནས་ཧྭ་ཤང་བྱུང་སྟེ། ལུས་ངག་གི་ཆོས་སྤྱོད་མི་དགོས་པ་དང་། བྱ་བར་མེད་ཀྱི་ངང་ལ་གནས་པས་འཚང་རྒྱ་ཞེས་བསྒྲགས་ནས་བོད་ཕལ་ཆེར་ཆད་ལྟ་ལ་སྦྱར་བ་ན། ཡེ་ཤེས་དབང་པོས་རྒྱལ་པོ་ལ་མཁན་པོའི་ལུང་བསྟན་ཡོད་ཚུལ་ཞུས་པས་བསྐུལ་སོས་ཏེ། ཀ་མ་ལ་ཤཱི་ལ་སྤྱན་འདྲེན་པའི་པོ་ཉ་བཏང་བར་ཧྭ་ཤང་གིས་གོ་ནས། བསམ་གཏན་ཉལ་བའི་འཁོར་ལོ། །བསམ་གཏན་གྱི་ལོན་དང་ཡང་ལོན་གཉིས། མདོ་སྡེ་བརྒྱད་ཅུ་ཁུངས་ལ་སོགས་པའི་བསྡུས་བརྩམས།

དེ་ནས་ཀ་མ་ལ་ཤཱི་ལ་བྱོན་པ་དང་། རྒྱལ་པོ་གུང་ལ་བཞུགས་ནས་ཧྭ་ཤང་དང་རྩོད་པས་ཕམ་པར་མཛད། ཧྭ་ཤང་རྒྱ་ཡུལ་དུ་རྫངས་ཤིང་། དཔེ་དེ་རྣམས་གཏེར་དུ་སྦས་ཞེས་གྲགས། ཀ་མ་ལ་ཤཱི་ལའི་ལུགས་དང་ཧྭ་ཤང་གི་ལུགས་གཉིས་ལ་རིམ་པ་བཞིན་རྒྱ་སྐད་དུ་ཙེན་མིན་པ་དང་ཏོན་མིན་པ[14] ཟེར་སྟེ། བོད་སྐད་དུ་རིམ་གྱིས་པ་དང་ཅིག་ཆར་བའི་མིང་ངོ་།

བསམ་ཡས་ཀྱི་རྒྱལ་བློན་འདི་དག་གི་དུས་སུ་ཡང་རྒྱ་དང་དབོན་ཞང་མ་མཐུན་ནས་དམག་འཁྲིན་རིམ་འགའ་བྱུས་ཤིང་། ལན་གཅིག་དམག་དཔོན་ལྷ་བཟང་ཀླུ་དཔལ་གྱིས་བོད་དམག་འབུམ་ཚོ་གཉིས་ཁྲིད་དེ། ཤིང་ཁྲུན་དང་། ཅིའུ་མཁར་དང་། སྨན་རྩེའི་ཡུལ་རྣམས་བཅོམ་ཞེས་རྒྱའི་དེབ་ཐེར་ཆེན་མོ་ལས་འབྱུང་།

རྒྱལ་པོ་ཁྲི་སྲོང་ལྡེ་བཙན་ལ་སྲས་མུ་ནེ་བཙན་པོ། མུ་ཏིག་བཙན་པོ། ཁྲི་ལྡེ་སྲོང་བཙན་དང་གསུམ། སྲས་ཆེ་བ་ལ་རྒྱལ་སྲིད་གཏད་དེ། རྒྱལ་པོ་རང་ཉིད་ཟུར་མཁར་གྱི་ཕོ་བྲང་གཞུག་མ་མཁར་དུ་བཞུགས་ནས་རེ་དགུ་པ་མེ་སྟག་ལ་འདས། ལོ་བདུན་དང་ཟླ་བ་དགུ་སྲིད་བཟུང་བར་བཤད་དེ། རྒྱལ་པོ་འདིས་བོད་ལ་ཕྱོག་ཕྱུག་ལན་གསུམ་དུ་སྙོམས་པར་གསུངས་ངོ། འདིས་ཡབ་མེས་ཀྱི་སྲོལ་བཞིན་བསྟན་པ་ལ་གུས་པར་མཛད་ཅིང་། བསམ་ཡས་སུ་སྡེ་སྣོད་གསུམ་གྱི་མཆོད་པ་བཙུགས་ཀྱི། མདོ་སྡེ་མཆོད་པ་ནི་དེང་སང་ཡང་མ་ནུབ། དགུང་ལོ་ཉེར་གསུམ་པ་ལ་ཡུམ་ཚེ་སྤོང་གཟའ་གསོལ་ངན་ཞུས་ཏེ་འདས།

དེ་ནས་སྲས་འཁྲིང་པོ་མུ་ཏིག་བཙན་པོ་ལ་རྒྱལ་སྲིད་གཏད་པར་འོས་ཀྱང་སྣ་ནམ་པས་ཏ་བསྐྱིགས་ནས་བཀྲོངས། ཆུང་བ་ཁྲི་ལྡེ་སྲོང་བཙན་སྐུ་ནར་མ་སོན་པ་ལ། རྒྱལ་སར་བཏོན་ན། སད་ན་ལེགས་འཛིང་ཡོན་ཞེས་གྲགས།

རྒྱལ་ཁམས་ལ་དབང་བསྒྱུར་ཏེ་དགེ་བཅུའི་ཁྲིམས་བཅས་ཤིང་། ཡབ་མེས་ཀྱིས་བཞེངས་པའི་གཙུག་ལག་ཁང་རྣམས་ལ་མཆོད་པ་རྒྱ་ཆེན་པོ་འབུལ་བ་དང་། ལོ་པཎ་མང་པོས་སྔོན་མེད་པའི་མདོ་དང་སྒྲ་བསྒྱུར་བའི་ཞབས་ཏོག་མཛད། དཀར་ཆུང་གི་གཙུག་ལག་ཁང་ཡང་བཞེངས་པར་གྲགས།[15] རྒྱལ་པོ་འདི་དང་མུ་ནེ་བཙན་པོའི་དུས་སུ་ཡང་རྒྱ་དང་དམག་འཁྲིན་རིམ་འགའ་བྱུང་ངོ།

རྒྱལ་པོ་དེ་ལ་སྲས་གཙང་མ། དར་མ། རལ་པ་ཅན། ལྷ་རྗེ། ལྷུན་གྲུབ་དང་ལྔ་ཡོད། གཙང་མ་རབ་ཏུ་བྱུང་། ལྷ་རྗེ་དང་ལྷུན་གྲུབ་གཉིས་ཆུང་ངུ་ལ་འདས། དར་མ་རྒྱན་ཡང་ཆོས་ལ་མི་དགའ་བས་ཁྲི་རལ་པ་ཅན་དགུང་ལོ་བཅུ་གཉིས་པ་ལ་རྒྱལ་སར་བཏོན། ལོ་འདི་ཁྲི་སྲོང་ལྡེ་བཙན་འདས་ནས་ལོ་སོ་གཉིས་ལོན་པའི་མེ་བྱ་དེ་ཡིན། བཙུན་མོ་དཔལ་གྱི་ངང་ཚུལ་ཁབ་ཏུ་བཞེས་ཤིང་། བྲན་ཁ་དཔལ་ཡོན་གྱིས་བློན་པོ་བྱས་ཏེ། རྒྱལ་ཁམས་ལ་དབང་བསྒྱུར། པཎྜི་ཏ་ཛི་ན་མི་ཏྲ་དང་ཤི་ལེནྡྲ་བོ་དྷི། དཱ་ན་ཤཱི་ལ་སོགས་སྤྱན་དྲངས། ལོ་ཙཱ་བ་ཀ་བ་ཅོག་ཞང་གསུམ་[16]གྱིས་ཆོས་བསྒྱུར། དགེ་འདུན་གྱི་སྡེ་མང་པོ་བཙུགས་ནས་སྒོམ་གྲྭ་བཤད་གྲྭ་འདུལ་གྲྭ་རྣམས་དར་བར་མཛད།

འདིའི་དུས་སུ་ཡང་རྒྱ་དང་དབོན་ཞང་མ་མཐུན་ནས་བོད་དམག་ཁྲི་ཚོ་མང་པོ་དྲངས་ཏེ། རྒྱའི་ཡུལ་མཁར་

རྣམས་བཅོམ་སོད་ལ།[17] བོད་ཀྱི་མཆོད་གནས་རྣམས་ཀྱིས་བར་བྱས་ནས་དབོན་ཞང་སོ་སོ་ནས་དབུ་སྐྱུང་མཛད་ཀྱི། ཆད་སོལ་གྱི་ཡི་གེ་ལྷ་སའི་རྡོ་རིང་ལ་ཡོད། རྒྱ་དང་བོད་ས་འཚམས་འཐང་ཡོད།

དེ་ལྟར་རྒྱལ་པོ་ཆོས་ལ་ཞེན་དུ་དགྱེས་པ་སྡིག་བློན་རྣམས་ཀྱིས་མ་ཐེག་ནས་ཆོས་ཁྲིམས་བཤིག་པར་གྲོས་བསྡུར་ན་རྒྱལ་པོ་མ་བཀྲོངས་ན་ཆོས་ཁྲིམས་འཇིག་མི་ཐུབ་པ་ལ་ཁ་འཆམ། ལ་ལ་ན་རེ་རྒྱལ་པོ་བཀྲོངས་ཀྱང་ལྷ་སྲས་གཙང་མ་དང་། བློན་པོ་ཆེན་པོ་གཉིས་ཆོས་ལ་དགའ་ཆེས་བས་འཇིག་མི་ཐུབ་ཟེར།

ཐོག་མར་ལྷ་སྲས་སྤྲ་གྲོ་མོན་ལ་བཙུག །ཆོས་བློན་ཆེན་པོ་བཙུན་མོ་དང་ལྷན་ཅིག་ཏུ་འདུས་སོ་ཞེས་ཕྲ་མ་བྱས་ནས་ཉེས་མེད་ཀྱང་བཀྲོངས་ཤིང་། བཙུན་མོའང་དེའི་མོད་ལ་ཤི་བས། དེ་རྗེས་རྒྱལ་པོ་དགུང་ལོ་སོ་དྲུག་པ་ལྕགས་བྱིའི་ལོ་ལ་སྦྲས་སྟག་སྣ་ཅན་དང་། ཅོ་རོ་ལྷ་ལོང་གཉིས་ཀྱིས་ཞལ་ལྟག་པར་བསྐོར་ནས་བཀྲོངས།

དེ་ནས་འབྲུང་སྟེ་བོད་ཁམས་ཀྱི་བསོད་ནམས་ནི་སྣུམ་ཟད་པའི་མར་མེ་བཞིན་ཟད། དགེ་བ་བཅུའི་རྒྱལ་ཁྲིམས་ནི་སོག་རུལ་གྱི་ཕོན་ཐག་བཞིན་ཞིག ནག་ཕྱོགས་ཀྱི་སྤྱོད་པ་ནི། ཡུལ་ངན་གྱི་རླུང་འཚུབ་བཞིན་ལངས་ནས་ལོ་པཎ་དང་མཆོད་གནས་རྣམས་ལ་ཞབས་ཏོག་མེད་པར་སོ་སོའི་ཡུལ་ལ་བཞུགས་པར་གྱུར་ཏོ།

ལྕགས་བྱ་འདི་ལ་སྡིག་བློན་རྣམས་ཀྱི་འདོད་པ་བཞིན་གཅེན་ཁྲི་དར་མ་ཨུ་དུམ་བཙན་ལོ་སོ་དགུ་པ་རྒྱལ་སར་བཏོན་ནས་ལོ་ལྔ་སྲིད་བཟུང་། དེ་ནས་བཙན་པོའི་ཐུགས་ལ་གདོན་གསོལ་ཏེ། ཐབས་དུ་མའི་སྒོ་ནས་བསྟན་པའི་རྩ་བ་སོ་སོ་ཐར་པའི་རྟེན་རབ་དུ་བྱུང་བའི་རྟགས་ཙམ་ཡང་མེད་པར་བྱས་ཏེ་སངས་རྒྱས་ཀྱི་བསྟན་པ་རིན་པོ་ཆེ་སྨད་ནས་བསྣུབས་སྟེ། སྐྱེ་འགྲོ་རྣམས་ཀྱིས་བཙན་པོ་ལ་གླང་ཞེས་དུད་འགྲོའི་མིང་ནས་འབོད་པ་སྟེ་འོས་པ་ཉིད་དོ།[18] །མཁན་པོ་དང་ཁྲི་སྲོང་ལྡེ་བཙན་མཆོད་ཡོན་གྱི་ཞིང་ལུག་ལ་རབ་བྱུང་གི་བསྟན་པ་བཙུགས་པ་ནས། བསྟན་པ་བསྣུབས་པའི་ལྕགས་བྱ་འདི་ཡན་ལ་ལོ་བརྒྱད་ཅུ་རྩ་བདུན་ཐལ། དུས་དེར་ཡང་ཇོ་བོ་རྣམ་གཉིས་རང་རང་གི་ཁྲིའི་འོག་ཏུ་སྦྲ་དགོས་པ་མ་གཏོགས་པར་ལྷ་ས་དང་བསམ་ཡས་ལ་སོགས་པའི་ལྷ་ཁང་ཆེ་བ་རྣམས་འཇིག་མ་ཐུབ།

དུས་དེར་ལྷ་ལུང་དཔལ་གྱི་རྡོ་རྗེ་ཡེར་པར་བཞུགས་པ། རྒྱལ་པོ་སྡིག་ཅན་གྱི་གཏམ་གསན་པས་སྙིང་རྗེ་ཁྲེད་པར་ཅན་འཁྲུངས་ཤིང་། ཆས་བསྒྱུར་ནས་ལྷ་སར་བྱོན་ཏེ། རྒྱལ་པོའི་དཔྲལ་བར་ལྕགས་མདའ་བསྣུན་ནས་བཀྲོངས། བྱང་ཆུབ་སེམས་དཔའ་དཔའ་བོ་སྟོབས་ལྡན་གྱི་མཛད་པ་སྟེ། དེད་དཔོན་སྙིང་རྗེ་ཆེན་པོས་མི་ནག་མདུང་ཐུང་ཅན་བསད་པ་བཞིན་ནོ། མཛད་པ་ཁམ་ཆེས་པའི་དོན་གྱིས་བཞུགས་མ་ནུས་པར་མདོ་ཁམས་སུ་བྱོན་པ་སྟང་།

འདི་ཡང་རྒྱལ་པོའི་བཀའ་ཆེམས་ལས།

དེ་ནས་བདུད་ཀྱི་སྤྲུལ་པ་སྟེ། [19] རྒྱལ་པོ་དུད་འགྲོའི་མིང་ཅན་འབྱུང་།
དེ་ཡི་ཐུགས་ལ་གདོན་གསོལ་ནས། །ལྷ་ཁང་དཀྱིལ་ཞིང་དམ་ཆོས་བསྣུབ། །

སྡེ་སྣོད་འཛིན་པའི་སྲོག་ཀྱང་གཅོད། ཆོས་མཛད་ཐམས་ཅད་གསོད་ཅིང་འཇོམས།
གླེགས་བམ་ཐམས་ཅད་མེ་ལ་བསྲེག །བླ་མ་སློབ་དཔོན་བྲན་དུ་བཀོལ། །

རབ་བྱུང་བཙུན་པ་ཆོས་དང་འབྲལ། །དགེ་འདུན་རྣམས་ལ་ཤན་པ་འཚོལ།
སངས་རྒྱས་ན་བཟའ་ཆུ་ལ་སྐྱུར། །རྟེན་གསུམ་མཆོད་ཆ་རྡོ་ཡིས་བརྡུང་། །

ཆོས་ཀྱི་མིང་ཀྱང་མེད་པར་བྱེད། །དེ་ནས་ཡེར་པའི་བྲག་ཁུང་ན།
ཕྱག་ན་རྡོ་རྗེའི་སྤྲུལ་པ་སྟེ། །དཔལ་ཞེས་བྱ་བའི་དགེ་སློང་གིས། །

སྡིག་ཅན་རྒྱལ་པོ་སྒྲོལ་བར་འགྱུར། [20] །དེ་ནས་ལོ་བསྐོར་འགའ་ཡི་བར།
སངས་རྒྱས་བསྟན་པ་མེད་པར་འགྱུར། །ཨོ་མ་སེམས་ཅན་སྙིང་རེ་རྗེ། །

ཞེས་ལུང་བསྟན།

དེའི་ཚེ་བཙུན་མོ་ཆུང་བའི་ལྟོ་བར་གདུང་རྒྱུད་ཀྱི་སྲས་གཅིག་ཆགས་ཡོད་པ་ལ། [21] བཙུན་མོ་ཆེ་བས་ཀྱང་སྲས་ལྟོ་བར་ཡོད་ཅེས་རྫུན་བྱས་ཤིང་། ཆུང་བ་ལ་གདུང་རྒྱུད་འཁྲུངས་པའི་ཚེ་སྤྲང་མོའི་བུ་ཆུང་སྐྱེས་མ་ཁད་གཅིག་ཤ་ལ་ཙར་ནས་ང་ལས་སྐྱེས་པ་ཡིན་ཟེར་བ་ན་བློན་པོ་རྣམས་ཀྱིས་ཡུམ་གསུང་བ་བཞིན་བརྟན་དུ་བཙུག་པས། མངའ་བདག་ཡུམ་བརྟན་ཞེས་གྲགས།

གདུང་རྒྱུད་ལ་ཆེན་མས་གནོད་དོགས་ནས་ཉིན་མཚན་དུ་ཉི་འོད་དང་མར་མེའི་འོད་ཀྱིས་བསྲུངས་པས་འོད་བསྲུངས་ཞེས་གྲགས། དེ་ནས་འོད་བསྲུངས་དང་། ཡུམ་བརྟན་གཉིས་སྲིད་ལ་མ་འཆམ་པར་སྔ་མས་གཡོན་རུ་དང་། ཕྱི་མས་དབུ་རུ་བཟུང་ནས་འཁྲུག་པ་བྱས། འོད་བསྲུངས་ཀྱི་འོག་ནས་བོད་སྤྱི་ལ་དབང་བའི་རྒྱལ་པོ་མེད་པས་ཆོས་ལུགས་རྣམ་པར་བཞིག་གོ །

Annotations to Paṇchen Sönam Drakpa's *New Red Annals*

Reading Historical Materials (General Features) ①

Page 151, Line 2

Historical materials as a genre tend to be very discursive, often interspersing poetry within prose and interjecting comments (in the first-person voice) within the normal flow of the narrative (i.e., third-person voice). In addition, historical materials tend to contain a plethora of proper names which, depending on the subject matter, can be indigenous Tibetan names, translated Sanskrit names, or the abbreviated names of texts and authors with which the readership is presumed to have familiarity. Consequently, as with most texts from different cultures and eras, a certain level of background knowledge is required to properly understand a text and its referents.

WHAT TO REMEMBER

When reading a text in a new domain, it is necessary to have a basic understanding of the context, topics, and personages involved.

Enumerated Phenomena ②

Page 151, Line 4

A consequence of the precise analysis of both phenomena and states of mind in Buddhist philosophy is a proliferation of enumerated lists. Numerous lists of things occur in Buddhist sūtras, and the entire category of "Manifest Knowledge" (*Abhidharma*) can be considered the first manifestation of this tradition of enumeration. In Tibet, an entire genre of literature developed to attempt to lend coherence and easy reference to such lists. Overlapping in organizational structure with early dictionaries such as the *Mahāvyutpatti*, distinct works addressing lists eventually began to be produced, known generically as "enumerated phenomena" (*chos kyi rnam grangs*), with that phrase often occurring in the title.

In some instances, the presence of a numeral in a text merely indicates the sum total of items listed (see མདོ་མཛངས་བླུན་ note 5). Here, however, we have an instance of an enumerated category, in this case, the ཁྲིམས་གཉིས་ ("two [systems of] ethics"), most likely referring to the monastic codes (*vinaya*) and bodhisattva vows.

WHAT TO REMEMBER

Familiarity with the reference of enumerated categories of phenomena comes with subject knowledge mastery, although reference works do exist (see bibliography).

3

Recognizing Proper Names

Page 152, Line 1

The occurrence of proper names in Tibetan narrative is not always obvious, but some indicators do exist. Here, for example, titles and descriptors precede the proper names given, such as "king" (རྒྱལ་པོ་), "his son" (དེའི་སྲས་), "minister" (བློན་པོ་), and so on. In addition, verbs of attribution such as གྲགས་ ("to be known (as)") and ཟེར་ ("to be called") can also signal that a proper name is being stated.

WHAT TO REMEMBER

Proper names in Tibetan are often preceded by a title and/or accompanied by a verb of attibution such as གྲགས་ ("to be known (as)") and ཟེར་ ("to be called").

4

Tibetan Dates and Calendrical System

Page 152, Line 3

Until the eleventh century, dates for Tibetan years were rendered in a twelve animal year system along with a regnal year. Beginning in the early eleventh century, a system of five elements in (redundant) pairs of male and female signs was introduced and permuted with the twelve animal signs to yield a sexagenary system that was retroactively applied to earlier eras. While names were assigned to each sixty-year cycle to distinguish one from another, the lack of such distinguishing information has led to some ambiguity in the dates of imperial-era historical events. Here, for example, the date མེ་མོ་གླང་གི་ལོ་ or "Female Fire Ox Year," can only be resolved to a Western date in reference to contextual information. Since it is known that the Tibetan Empire—commencing with the reign of Songtsen Gampo—roughly overlapped with the Chinese T'ang dynasty (ca. 618–907 C.E.), then the only "Fire Ox Year" occurring roughly at the start of that era would be in 617 C.E. Since later in the text it is stated that the Tibetan king was 82 years old at the time of his death in the ས་ཁྱིའི་ལོ་ ("Earth Dog Year"), and since Tibetan children are considered to be one year old at the time of birth, then this also agrees with the "Earth Dog Year" occurring eighty-one years later in 698 C.E.

WHAT TO REMEMBER

Tibetan calendrical dates are given in the sexagenary cycle specified by the permutation of twelve animals (mouse, ox, tiger, rabbit, dragon, snake, horse, sheep, monkey, bird, dog, and pig) with pairs of five elements (earth, iron, water, wood, and fire):

Fire Mouse (མེ་བྱི་)	616 C.E.
Fire Ox (མེ་གླང་)	617 C.E.
Earth Tiger (ས་སྟག་)	618 C.E.
Earth Rabbit (ས་ཡོས་)	619 C.E.
Iron Dragon (ལྕགས་འབྲུག)	620 C.E.
etc.	

Annotations and Script Size

5

Page 152, Line 7

As noted in the introduction to this book, there are a number of ways in which authors (or editors) can annotate a text. In addition to the use of various sigla (卐, etc.) and interlinear glosses in alternate scripts, variation in script size is another common way of indicating an annotation to a text. Here, the author (or possibly his editor) has used such an approach to provide explanatory information about the identity of persons being listed. In contemporary reproductions of this text, editors have adopted Euro-American punctuation to further demarcate such passages. When translating them, therefore, it is appropriate to treat them in the same manner as one would English parenthetical information.

WHAT TO REMEMBER

Textual annotations—whether indicated by sigla, alternate scripts, or reduced script size—function similarly to their English counterparts.

6 The Use of Sanskrit Letters as Tibetan Shorthand

Page 152, Line 21

As noted in the introduction to this book, over the centuries, Tibetan woodblock carvers developed certain forms of shorthand notation (*bsdu yig*) to expedite carving. One form of shorthand notation is the use of the Tibetan rendering of the retroflex *ḍa* (ཌ་) to indicate a -གས་ suffix—that is, rendering for example, ལ་སོགས་ as ལ་སོཌ་. Another Sanskrit derivative notation, the *anusvāra*, is occasionally used when space limitations arise. An instance of this would be to render the number three, གསུམ་, as གསུཾ་. In this case, the Sanskrit *anusvāra* (◌ཾ) is used to render the terminal syllable ནམ་ as ནཾ་, indicating a rhetorical question.

WHAT TO REMEMBER

Certain forms of shorthand notation (*bsdu yig*) were developed to expedite the carving of woodblocks and can be seen in many texts. The two most common ones are the use of the retroflex *ḍa* (ཌ་) to indicate a -གས་ suffix and the *anusvāra* (◌ཾ) to replace the suffix letter མ་.

Sanskrit Words in Tibetan Script

7

Page 153, Line 2

While nearly all Sanskrit words have an equivalent in Tibetan, occasionally an author will prefer to use an original Sanskrit word. This can be for the sake of explaining the etymology of a Sanskrit original, to avoid potential ambiguity that might arise through the use of the equivalent Tibetan term, or simply because the Sanskrit word is more commonly known or part of a proper name. Since the author is referring to a very specific statue brought from Nepal, he uses its given name, ཙནྡྲ་གྲོལ་མ་, rendering the Sanskrit word in standard fashion (see ཤེས་རབ་སྙིང་པོ་ note 2).

WHAT TO REMEMBER

Sanskrit words occasionally appear in Tibetan texts in transliteration, either in the context of an etymological explanation to avoid ambiguity or as part of a proper name.

Tibetan Contractions

8

Page 153, Line 3

Beyond the forms of shorthand notation (*bsdu yig*) used to expedite carving (see དེབ་ཐེར་དམར་པོ་ note 6, above), other instances of this phenomenon can be more accurately described as contractions. Such occurrences might be the result of a lazy scribe or an indication of a semiliterate author—a native Tibetan scholar once laughingly described such letter combinations as "the way one's mother writes her grocery list on the kitchen wall"—while others have simply become accepted contractions in modern literature (particularly in Bhutan). In any event, deciphering such irregular letter combinations requires a solid command of Tibetan vocabulary, as many replicate phonetic renderings of Tibetan words and phrases, but not always. Here, the "syllable" སངྶ་ is a contraction of སངས་རྒྱས་ ("buddha") and can be discerned phonetically; other instances, however, can be more inscrutable, such as ཐཾད་ (for ཐམས་ཅད་), or འཁོཽར་ (for འཁོར་ལོ་), etc.

WHAT TO REMEMBER

In addition to shorthand notation (see དེབ་ཐེར་དམར་པོ་ note 6, above), Tibetan texts also use contractions. Some of these can be reconstituted through their phonetic rendering, while others require reference materials (see bibliography).

9 Chinese Words in Tibetan

Page 153, Line 5

Unlike Sanskrit words transliterated into Tibetan, which maintain a close one-for-one phonetic rendering, the representation of Chinese words in Tibetan script is far more imprecise given the radical differences between the languages and dialectical variations in the pronunciation of Chinese characters. Here, for example, the name of the Chinese princess, rendered in modern English documents as "Wencheng Gongshu" (文成公主), is given here as ཝུན་ཤིང་ཀོང་ཇོ་ ("un shing kong jo"). Similarly, in the passage that follows, the name of the Chinese palace at the T'ang-era capital of Chang'an, "Jianzhang" (建章宫), is given as ཟིམ་ཤིང་ ("sim shing"). Consequently, just as knowledge of Sanskrit is critical at times for the correct understanding of Buddhist philosophical texts, knowledge of Chinese can prove equally necessary when reading Tibetan historical and biographical materials involving Tibetan-Chinese relations.

WHAT TO REMEMBER

Although Tibetan phonetic renderings of Chinese words offer an approximation of Chinese words, their identification usually requires knowledge of Chinese since such words tend to be proper names not typically included in most dictionaries.

10 Translation Hint: Nested Sentences

Page 153, Line 9

The fact that Tibetan is a modular language (see ཤེས་རབ་སྙིང་པོ་ note 22) cannot be stressed enough. This passage demonstrates levels to which modular components (sentences and noun phrases) can be nested inside each other in order to form a complex sentence.

In order to understand the manner in which this sentence is composed, it is best to represent the structural boundaries of each element. Thus, the basic sentence reads:

Gerund Marker: [ཅུང་ཟད་རྫུས་ནས།] ཁྱེད་ བོད་ཀྱི་རྒྱལ་པོ་ལ་ དགེ་བ་བཅུའི་ཁྲིམས་འཆའ་བ་དང་། གཙུག་ལག་ཁང་རྩིགས་པ་དང་། འདོད་ཡོན་ལྔ་ལ་ལོངས་སྤྱོད་ནུས་པ་ཡོད་དམ། ཡོད་ན་ བུ་མོ་སྦྱེར་བས་ ཞུས་ཤོག་ Final Verb: (ཟེར།)

"Having been slightly deceptive, ... [he] said." The next set of elements are the contents of the statement introduced by the outermost parts:

ཅུང་ཟད་རྫུས་ནས། case 8: [ཁྱེད་] case 4.1: [བོད་ཀྱི་རྒྱལ་པོ་ལ་] case 1.4.1: [དགེ་བ་བཅུའི་ཁྲིམས་འཆའ་བ་དང་། གཙུག་ལག་ཁང་རྩིགས་པ་དང་། འདོད་ཡོན་ལྔ་ལ་ལོངས་སྤྱོད་ནུས་པ་ཡོད་དམ།] case 3.3: [ཡོད་ན་བུ་མོ་སྦྱེར་བས་] Verb Phrase: (ཞུས་ཤོག་) ཟེར།

The statement thus contains five components: a term of address, an indirect object, an object, a reason clause, and a terminal verb phrase. Since the terminal verb phrase is a precative construction (see མདོ་མཛངས་བླུན་ note 14)—that is, a formal or polite request formed with the imperative tense of the verb ཞུ་ ("to ask")—the recipient being addressed is in the vocative. Since the very first word is a personal pronoun (ཁྱེད་, honorific for "you") apparently in the vocative, the recipient is understood (i.e., the Tibetan minister being spoken to). This is followed by an indirect object and a series of three sentence-questions that serve as the grammatical object of the verb ཞུས་. The final remaining component of the sentence is a reason clause which is composed of a short complex sentence itself: an introductory conditional clause (ཡོད་ན་) and its consequent, བུ་མོ་སྦྱེར་.

Tibetan Numerals: Set Multipliers

11

Page 153, Line 12

There are a number of ways of representing numerals in Tibetan. Two ways—representing simple adjectival or cumulative values—have already been seen (see མདོ་མཛངས་

སྦུན་ note 5). Here, the particle ཕྲག་ is introduced, which conveys the idea of "set(s) of." Hence, the phrase ཁྲི་ཕྲག་ལྔ་ would be translated as "five sets of ten thousand," or "fifty thousand."

WHAT TO REMEMBER

The particle ཕྲག་ serves as a postpositional adjective that conveys the idea of "set(s) of" and which is further modified by the numeral that follows it.

12 The Postpositional Phrase ཡན་ཆད་

Page 155, Line 8

The phrase ཡན་ཆད་ typically occurs with items in a list and conveys the sense of "from that point onward." When it occurs in a geographic setting, however, it conveys a comparable sense, although "onward" refers to the direction upward from that point, and so the phrase ཁམས་ཡན་ཆད་དུ་ would be translated as "in Kham and points above." Its complementary term is མན་ཆད་, meaning "... and below."

WHAT TO REMEMBER

The phrase ཡན་ཆད་ means "[that item] and onward" or in a geographic context, "[that place] and points above."

13 Translation Hint: Numeric Expressions

Page 155, Line 14

As with expressions of time, in which the number of minutes may be stated in addition to the hour or subtracted from the next hour, general numeric expressions can be similarly formed. Hence, here, with the use of the verb ཆད་ ("to subtract"), the phrase སྟོང་ལ་གཅིག་ཆད། would mean "one thousand minus one."

Translation Hint: Chinese Words in Tibetan

14

Page 155, Line 22

In this paragraph and the next, a number of Chinese words occur in Tibetan phoneticization, and as such, are not likely to be found in most dictionaries. The two given in this sentence are self-explanatory, as the author provides them simply as the Chinese equivalents of "Gradualist approach" (漸門) and "Subitist approach" (頓門). Likewise, in the following paragraph, a number of geographic names and terms occur. They are:

ཤིང་ཁུན་	:	Liangzhou (涼州)
ཅིའུ་མཁར་	:	prefectural capitals (州城)
སྨན་རྩེའི་ཡུལ་	:	areas of [southern Chinese] barbarians (蠻子)

The Verb གྲགས་ Marking Evidentiality

15

Page 156, Line 15

དེབ་ཐེར་དམར་པོ

The verb གྲགས་ ("to be renowned [as]," "to be reputed [to be]") is used here to indicate disputed information—that is, to indicate something about the reliability of the evidence for the statement. In this case, the point of contention is the construction of the Small White Temple (*dkar chung gi gtsug lag khang*), which some had attributed to one of the wives of Songtsen Gampo (*srong btsan sgam po*), an attribution that the author of this text rejects. Instead, Paṇchen Sönam Drakpa appears to be cautiously following the writings of another historian, Pawo Tsukla Trengwa (*dpa' bo gtsug lag phreng ba*), as well as the old history of the Tibetan Empire, *The Affirmation of Ba* (*Sba bzhed*), both of which attribute the temple's construction to the Tibetan king Tridé Songtsen (*khri lde srong btsan*), a.k.a. Senalek Jingyön (*sad na legs 'jing yon*).

WHAT TO REMEMBER

The verb གྲགས་ ("to be renowned [as]," "to be reputed [to be]") is also used to indicate disputed information. When functioning in this manner, the verb takes another sentence or clause as its object. As such, it can represent uncertainty regarding the evidence for the claim as well as the author's uncertainty regarding the validity of the claim. This modality of uncertainty is known as the epistemic mood.

16 Translation Hint: Abbreviated Lists of Names

Page 156, Line 21

A very common practice in Tibetan writing is the abbreviation of names—both of individuals and of groups. Here is precisely such an example where the names of the three most prominant imperial-era translators—Kawa Peltsek (*ka ba dpal brtsegs*), Jokro Lügyeltsen (*cog ro klu'i rgyal mtshan*), and Shang Yeshedé (*zhang ye shes sde*)—are abbreviated as simply "the three—Ka, Jok, and Shang" (*ka cog zhang gsum*).

17 Auxiliary Verbs: The Concessive Verb མོད་

Page 157, Line 1

The verb མོད་ has two distinct but related meanings. When མོད་ occurs as a stand-alone verb, it functions as a Class II verb of existence while conveying a degree of qualification to the assertion. The verb མོད་ can also appear as an auxiliary verb, as it does here. In such instances, མོད་ (or མོད་ཀྱང་, for extra emphasis) serves to link the preceding sentence with the one that follows, while at the same time conveying the idea that the second sentence is a qualification of the assertion(s) of the first sentence.

WHAT TO REMEMBER

The auxiliary verb མོད་ links two sentences and conveys the idea that the second sentence qualifies the assertion(s) of the first.

18 The Syllable ཉིད་ as Emphatic Verbal Suffix

Page 157, Line 16

The particle ཉིད་ serves two main functions: (1) It serves as the Tibetan equivalent of Sanskrit suffixes such as *-tā*/*-tva*, used to create abstract identity nouns (such as "emptiness"/*śūnyatā*/*stong pa nyid* from "empty"/*śūnya*/*stong pa*), or *-ka*/*-aka*/*-ika*, used to create adjectives of appurtenance (such as "forest-dwelling" or "being of the forest"/*āraṇyaka*/*dgon pa nyid* from "forest"/*āraṇya*/*dgon pa*); and (2) it serves as a restrictive suffix syllable meaning "just" or "itself" (as in *de nyid*, "just that" or "that itself"). In such instances, the

ཉིད་ particle is suffixed to a noun phrase (a pronoun, a verbal noun, a noun-adjective pair, etc.). There is another use, however, in which this particle can be applied to a verb in its participle form (see ཤེས་རབ་སྙིང་པོ་ note 13). In such instances, it acts like a postpositional emphatic adverb ("really" or "really just"); alternately, it could be thought of as a restrictive suffix syllable applied to a nominalized sentence in an indirect construction (see ལས་གཙོ་རྣམ་གསུམ་ note 9) with an omitted verb of predication, although in practice the former is a more elegant interpretation. Hence, the terminal verb phrase here, འོས་པ་ཉིད་དོ།, can be interpreted and translated as: "... [and this] was really quite appropriate."

WHAT TO REMEMBER

When the particle ཉིད་ occurs after a participial verb at the end of a sentence, it acts like a postpositional emphatic adverb ("really," "really just," "really quite," etc.).

The Syllable སྟེ་ as an Appositional Marker

19

Page 158, Line 2

Like the use of the particle གྱི་ to mark apposition between phrases (see ཤེར་སྙིང་རྣམ་བཤད་ note 35), the rhetorical continuative marker སྟེ་ can function in the same way. Although more commonly seen in commentarial texts, the differences between the uses of སྟེ་ can be subtle. When functioning as a rhetorical continuative, the particle སྟེ་ conveys the idea that the sentence that follows is somehow a consequence of the first sentence ("<sentence_1> hence, <sentence_2>"); when functioning appositionally—as it does here—the particle སྟེ་ conveys the idea that what follows is a restatement of the first sentence ("<sentence_1> that is / in other words, <sentence_2>").

WHAT TO REMEMBER

The particle སྟེ་, when functioning appositionally, conveys the idea that what follows is a restatement of the first sentence ("<sentence_1> that is / in other words, <sentence_2>").

(20) Auxiliary Verbs: The Perfective Construction

Page 158, Line 10

The verb འགྱུར་ ("to become"), when used as an auxiliary verb, can connote the emphatic future, but in this context it is indicating the perfective aspect. In general, the perfective is used to indicate the verbal activity as a whole or in the abstract and hence is used for prophecies. It is contrasted with the imperfective construction (see མདོ་མཛངས་བླུན་ note 17), which is used for continuing, repeated, or habitual activities.

WHAT TO REMEMBER

The verb འགྱུར་ ("to become"), when used as an auxiliary verb, connotes verbal activity in the abstract (the "perfective").

(21) Indirect Constructions with ཡོད་

Page 158, Line 13

While indirect constructions have been seen with Class I verbs (ཡིན་, ལགས་, etc.)—see ལས་གཙོ་རྣམ་གསུམ་ note 9—here is an instance of the same type of grammatical construction using the Class II verb ཡོད་. Just as such constructions with Class I verbs are typically translated as "it is the case that ...," so too, with Class II verbs, one can translate the specific sentence as "there is/was ..."

WHAT TO REMEMBER

An indirect statement is one that conveys the meaning of an event obliquely or descriptively rather than relating the event directly. When formed with a Class II verb, it does so with a nominalized sentence and with a verb of existence (such as ཡོད་, etc.). It can be translated as "there is ..." or "there was ..."

PAṆCHEN SÖNAM DRAKPA'S *NEW RED ANNALS*

Homage to the Bhagavān, the Tathāgata, the Arhat, the Perfectly Complete Buddha, the Lord of the Two [Systems of] Ethics [—monastic codes and bodhisattva vows]!

I pay homage to the omniscient Dharma King,
[Who] attained sovereignty over the triple world system
With the golden wheel of the two [kinds of] knowledge, and
Was victorious over the false teachers and four māras!

Having opened well this treasury of jewels
Of history, I offer up this magical key
To the royal lineages to all who wish
To proclaim the history of the two systems [of religion and government].

Regarding that, here, if one were to briefly set forth the royal lineages of those who have protected this great land, there would be five: the royal history of India, the royal history of Shambhala, the royal history of Tibet, the royal histories of China and Mongolia, [and] the manner of arisal of the Chinese and Mongolian scriptures.

Third, regarding the explanation of the royal history of Tibet: Furthermore, as for the manner in which the Tibetan people initially came about, there is the story that [they] came from the union of a monkey and a rock ogress, and yet also, [it is said that] at the beginning of the degenerate era (*kaliyuga*), at the time when the five sons of King Pāṇḍu conquered the army of the Kauravas, the king named Rūpati together with his army dressed [themselves] in the clothes of women, and having fled, from the families of those who came to the mountainous Land of Snows, there appeared many descendants and so forth. And, since in the [vinaya] chapter on scripture, Kālacakra, and so forth, the word "Tibet" occurs frequently, it appears that both the country and the people arose prior(*) to the time of arrival of the teacher of our [true] nature.

(*) If [you say that Tibet] came about at the same time as India, that is also not contradictory.

The king was known as Takri Nyenzik. His son was Namri Songtsen. At that time, salt was found in the north, and astrology, medicine, and so forth, came from China. His son was Songtsen Gampo. He was born in the latter half of the Female Fire Ox year—which was one thousand four hundred forty-nine years after the nirvāṇa of the Buddha—in upper Dratsul in the palace called "Realm of Unchanging Love" (*byams pa mi 'gyur gling*).

At the age of thirteen, his father having died, [he] came to the throne. His residential palace was built on Red Mountain. In general, although this king [had] innumerable ministers, those who were supreme were Trülgyi Nachen Ringsang ([also known as] Yarlungpa), Thonmi Saṃbhota, Gar Tongtsen ([also known as] Drishungpa), and Nyentrisang ([also known as] Driserwa).

Thonmi Saṃbhota being sent to India, he studied the alphabet and grammar with the Brahmin *Ghaṇṭadatta and Paṇḍita *Devavitsiṃha. He came back to Tibet and revised the fifty Indian letters, [turning them] into the thirty Tibetan letters. He presented the alphabet to the king and taught it as well to the ministers. He translated the set of sūtras, "The Cloud of Jewels," and since he wrote many compositions such as *Thonmi's "River Breeze" Grammatical Treatise* and others, [his] kindness to Tibet was very great. Indeed, from his very [own] mouth [he proclaimed]:

> Here, in the Kingdom of Tibet, a barbarian land,
> Prior to [my] arrival, [all] people were not educated.
> I am the lamp that dispels darkness, [although]
> [My] lord, the king, abides like the sun and the moon.
>
> Among the ministers, my friends, there is none like me.
> To the people of Tibet, the Land of Snows,
> Am I, Thonmi, not very kind?

[Thus he] spoke, and [what he] thought was true.

When the king reached sixteen years of age, [he] sent [his] ministers as an envoy, requesting as a queen, Bhirkuti, the daughter of Aṃśuvarman. As a dowry, came [a statue of] the Jowo Buddha Akṣobhyavajra, the cycle of [five] teachings of Maitreya, a sandalwood [statue of] Tāra, and a begging bowl [made] of lapis lazuli (*vaiḍūrya*). This appears to be the beginning of the conditioned arising (*rten 'brel*) of the teachings of the Buddha in Tibet.

When the king reached eighteen years of age, [he] sent [his] minister Gar (*mgar*) and others [and] one hundred horsemen as an envoy to seek Princess Wencheng Gongshu, the daughter of the Chinese king. When [they] arrived at the Jianzhang palace [in Chang'an], [they] offered the gifts that were sent by the king, but when [they] offered the reasons why it was necessary to grant the princess, the Chinese king and his attending ministers were greatly displeased. Nonetheless, being slightly deceptive, [the Chinese king] said, "You, [minister,] ask the Tibetan king: does [he] possess the ten virtuous ethics? and construct temples? and does [he] have the ability to enjoy the five sensory pleasures? Because if [he] has [them], then [I] will bestow my daughter [upon him]."

About that, [minister] Gar [thought that] if [he] were to go from China to Tibet to deliver each letter, the time of obtaining the princess would never come, so in reply to that [he] said, "These three scrolls of paper are what was sent by the king" [and] within [the scrolls] that were offered in sequence, the three conditions and more were established. Even though this is the case (*de ltar byas kyang*), if the girl is not given, I will send [an army of] fifty thousand magically-created soldiers, [and they] will kill you, steal the princess, and conquer the entire country. From seeing what was said in the presentation, even though the king was very afraid, having acted like [he] was not afraid, [he] said, "You, [minister,] that Tibetan king [of yours] is [someone] who talks very big."

But working along these lines, and [the king] having not been able to comprehend the demonstration of some seven or eight maneuvers of sharp reasoning by the minister Gar, [the king] handed over his daughter, the princess, along with [a statue of] the Lord Śākyamuni, in accordance with [his] fondness [for her]. Her father, the king, arranged for an escort.

Then, the princess together with the precious Jowo [statue] arrived before the king at the Red Hill. [The king] threw an unbelievably good party; it was supremely fitting [for the occasion]. [Then,] the king, having made himself a lord of the Dharma, recited many various Dharmas, such as the six-syllable [mantra] of Avalokiteśvara, Ārya Yamāntaka, and so forth, and [he] established meditation centers and temples such as Trendruk, and so forth. The two queens, as well, established the temples of Trülnang and Ramoche, and [there] the two forms of the Lord [Buddha] resided. In brief, it is certain that this very king [was an emanation of] the Lord of Great Compassion [Avaloḳiteśvara], and the two queens were emanations of the two goddeses [Tāra and Śrī Devī (*dpal ldan lha mo*)], and most of the ministers, as well, were renowned as emanations.

At that time, the two queens had no sons. Although by and by [he] married two other queens, no sons came. Subsequently, to Mongza Trijam from Tölung, a son, Mangsong Mangtsen, was born. At the age of thirteen, he ascended to the throne. [He] held the kingdom for five years, and in his eighteenth year, died. Although a son, Gungsong Gungtsen, was born, since he had not reached a suitable age, once more it became necessary [for Songtsen Gampo] to govern. [Finally,] at the age of eighty-two, in the Earth Dog Year, together with his two queens, [he] faded away in the presence of the Eleven-faced Lord.

Then, at the age of thirteen, the grandson Gungsong Gungtsen was elevated to the throne. Initiating the worship of ancestors in Lhasa and so forth, he showed respect to the Three Jewels. He held the government for fifteen years, and at the age of twenty-seven, died in the area of Tsang. During the time of this king, a Chinese army came into Tibet and set the Red Hill on fire. Since the Jowo Śākyamuni [statue] was hidden in the Trülnang, [they] did not find [it], although it is said in the Chinese Annals that "[they] carried the Jowo Akṣobhyavajra [statue] to a place one half day's journey [away]." Again, the minister Gar led a Tibetan army of hundreds of thousands and plundered the Chinese territories. It is said that Gar himself also died in that conflict.

At that time, eighty years had passed from the time of the death of Songtsen Gampo. The son, in his thirteenth year, ascended to the throne. But since those who disliked the Dharma, such as the ministers Manshang Trompakye, Takra Lugoṇg, etc., were very powerful, [they] initially buried the precious Jowo [statue] in a sand dune. Then, since some bad omens occurred, [they] dug [it] up, and sent it to be transported to India. [But] when they reached Mangyul in Kyidrong, [the porters] having declared "[we] will not finish the trip," [the local people] offered to let it stay there.

When the king came of age, having consulted with the Dharma ministers, Gö Trisang, Zhang Nyamsang, and others, at the time of discussing how to enact the Dharma, the minister Nyamsang said, "because of the power of the two other ministers, it cannot be accomplished." Gö said, "There is a way of accomplishing [it], and [I] will crush [them] with my heel." Just exactly like that, through ingenious deceit and trickery, the minister Mazhang was put into a tomb alive, [and] Takra was sent to the north.

First, the Jowo [Buddha statue] was invited back from Mangyul and then installed in Lhasa. Then, Ba Salnang was sent as an envoy to invite the master Śantarakṣita; first [he] came to Lhasa, and then he arrived at Samye in Tölung and was provided escort with respectful homage by the king. Because the abbot taught in many ways the Dharma beginning with the ten virtues and the twelve [links of] dependent arising, the gods and demons of Tibet were not happy. The abbot having thought about the implications of various magical omens, such as lightning striking the Red Hill, and the topsoil being carried away by the waters of the Yarlung [River], and so forth, temporarily [he] went to Nepal. In accordance with the instructions given to invite Padmasaṃbhava, [he] was invited, and [he] bound all the gods and nāgas to vows. The abbot, also, having been invited back again in the Female Earth Rabbit Year when the king was twenty-two years old, the foundation of the Migyur Lhungyi Drupa Temple at glorious Samye was laid down, and it was finished in the Female Iron Rabbit [Year]. The consecration was performed primarily by the Abbot-bodhisattva and Padmasambhava. In the Female Wood Sheep [Year], in front of the Abbot, the seven men—the "tested men"—and others, were ordained.

Moreover, it is stated that many [people] endowed with faith and endowed with wisdom were ordained. In general, in [the area of] Kham and points above, about twelve religious centers [were established], and in Yerpa and Chimpu, hermitages were established. And, translators and paṇḍitas translated predominantly Dharma (i.e., Buddhist) [treatises] on mantra and logical reasoning, and thus the respectful practice of ratifying [terminology] through explaining and teaching was established. Thus, [they] instituted the system of the precious teachings of the Buddha.

Then, the abbot [said], "Although there are no heretics here in Tibet, the teachings of the Conqueror will divide into two factions, and since there will be disputes, at that time, invite Kamalaśīla from India and enter into debate!" Having spoken his last words, [the abbot] entered into nirvāṇa. He was 999 years old.

Accordingly, just like the prophecy, Hāshang came from China, and having proclaimed that it is not necessary to practice the Dharma of body and speech, and that by abiding in a state of nonactivity, [this is] "enlightenment," in many parts of Tibet [they] fixed upon the nihilistic view. And when [that happened], Yeshé Wangpo reminded the king that [he] had forgotten, by informing [him] of the manner in which there existed the prophecy of the abbot. Hāshang having understood that messengers had been sent to invite Kamalaśīla, [he] composed the treatises *The Wheel of Latent Concentration*, both *The Attaining Concentration* and *Further Attainment [of Concentration]*, the *Original Eighty Sets of Sūtras*, and so forth.

Then, Kamalaśīla arrived. And with the king sitting in the middle, by debating with Hāshang, [he] defeated [him]. Hāshang was sent back to the country of China, and it is said that those books were hidden in a storage place. The two systems of Kamalaśīla and Hāshang, respectively, are called in Chinese Tsenminpa (漸門) and Tonminpa (頓門), and in Tibetan [by] the names of "Gradualist" and "Subitist".

At the time of the king and his ministers at Samye, again China and the son-in-law were in discord and [things] were done that occasionally led to war. One time, the general Lhasang Lupel led a Tibetan army of two hundred thousand, and the Great Chinese Annals[1] record that "the [area] of Liangzhou (涼州), prefectural capitals (州城), and areas of [southern Chinese] barbarians (蠻子) were conquered."

King Trisong Detsen [had] three sons—Muné Tsenpo, Mutik Tsenpo, and Tridé Songtsen. [He] entrusted the kingdom to the eldest. The king, himself, having taken up residence in the natural fortress (*gnyug ma mkhar*), the palace in Zur-khar, died at the age of sixty-nine in the Fire Tiger [Year]. It is said that having held the kingdom for seven years and nine months, this king commanded three times that the hungry and the rich be equaled. This [king], in accordance with the system of his forefathers, paid respect to the teachings, and at Samye [he] instituted the worship of the Tripiṭaka and the worship of the sets of Sūtra, which even nowadays has not declined. [When he reached] the age of twenty-three, [his] mother, Lady Tsepang, offered [him] poisonous food, and [he] died.

Then, it was appropriate for the middle son, Mutik Tsenpo, to take the government, although [his] horse having been rattled by [one of the ministers] Nanampa [Dorje Dujom], he was killed. The youngest, Tridé Songtsen, had not reached a suitable age, but when he ascended to the throne, [he] became known as Senalek Jingyön.

---

1 This would seem to be a reference to the *Chinese Annals* (*Rgya'i yig tshang*; a.k.a. *Rgya'i deb ther zu thu chen*) translated into Tibetan by Ugyang Ju and Guśrī Rinchen Drakpa.

Having sovereignty over the kingdom, he instituted the law of the ten virtues, made extensive offerings to the temples that were founded by his ancestors, and provided devout patronage for many translators and paṇḍitas for the translating of the grammatical treatises and sūtras that previously did not exist. He is also reputed to have founded the Small White Temple (*dkar chung gi gtsug lag khang*). During the time of this king and Mune Tsenpo, again, occasions leading to war with China arose.

This king had five sons: Tsangma, Darma, Ralpajen, Lhaje, and Lhundrup. Tsangma was ordained. Lhaje and Lhundrup both died as youths. Although Darma was the oldest, since he did not like the Dharma [Buddhism], Ralpajen ascended to the throne at the age of twelve. This year was the Fire Bird [Year] that came thirty-two years after the passing of Trisong Detsen. He married the queen, Palgyi Ngangtsul. Dranka Palyön performed ministerial [duties]. He invited the paṇḍitas Jinamitra, Śilendrabodhi, Dānaśīla, and others. The three translators Ka[wa Peltsek], Jok[ro Lügyeltsen], and Shang [Yeshedé] translated the Dharma. Having founded many groups of the Saṅgha, he expanded the meditation centers, study centers, and monastic training centers.

At that time, again, China and the son-in-law were in discord and many ten thousands of Tibetan soldiers were led, and although many Chinese territories and fortresses were conquered, Tibetan monks having intervened, the nephew [and emperor] mutually swore oaths on their lives, and the text of the written agreement exists on a stone pillar in Lhasa; [it] also has the boundaries of China and Tibet.

Just so, the king's exceptional fondness for the Dharma having been intolerable to the evil ministers, when [they] conspired to destroy the religious laws, if the king is not killed, they concluded, the destruction of the religious laws could not be accomplished. Some said, although [we may] assassinate the king, since Prince Tsangma and the two great ministers have great fondness for the Dharma, its destruction will not be accomplished.

First, the prince was sent to Patro [in the district of] Mön [near Bhutan]. Then, having spread the rumor that the Buddhist Chief Minister had had sexual intercourse with the queen, although faultless, [he] was killed; and the queen as well, immediately after that, committed suicide. After that, in the Iron Bird Year when the king was thirty-six years old, both Bey Taknajen and Joro Lhalong killed [him] by strangling [him].

Then, [after those events] had occurred, the good merit of the realm of Tibet was finished like a butter lamp that had consumed [its] oil. The royal law of the ten virtues disintegrated, like a leather strap [tied] around a bundle of rotten straw. Evil practices having arisen like a whirlwind in badlands, without there being any respectful service to the translators, paṇḍitas, and monks, [they] remained in their individual countries.

In that Iron Bird Year, in accordance with the desires of the evil ministers, the elder brother Prince Darma Ūdumtsen in his thirty-ninth year, having ascended to the throne, [he] held the government for five years. Then, a demon took up residence in the heart of the king. By way of many methods, [he] destroyed even the merest sign of ordination—[which is] the foundation of liberation and the root of the teachings—and hence the precious teachings of the Buddha were eradicated at the very root. Hence, all living beings called the king "ox" after the name of the animal, and it was most suitable. From the establishment of the ordination teachings in the Wood Sheep [Year] of the patron-priest relationship between the abbot [Śāntarakṣita] and [the king] Trisong Detsen, down to this Iron Bird year of the abolishment of the teachings, eighty-seven years elapsed. Also at that time, except for the two Lord [Buddha statues] needing to be hidden under each of their thrones, [they] were not able to destroy the great temples, such as [those at] Lhasa and Samye, and so forth.

At that time, Lhalung Pelgyi Dorje was dwelling in [Dra] Yerpa. Because of hearing the story of [this] evil king, special compassion was born [in him], and having changed his clothes, he came to Lhasa. Having shot an iron arrow at his forehead, [he] assassinated [him]. [This was] the deed of a bodhisttva and powerful hero. [It was] like when the captain, out of great compassion, killed the criminal who had a spear. Being unable to remain [in Lhasa] because of the significance of such an extraordinary deed (*mdzad pa kham ches pa*), he appears to have gone to eastern Tibet.

This, also, [appears] in the *Last Testament of the King*:

Then, there will arise an emanation of Māra, that is,
A king having the name of an animal.
An evil spirit having taken up residence in his heart,
The temples will fall down and the hold of the Dharma will be abolished.

The lives of those who hold the collections of teachings will be cut off;
All who practice the Dharma will be killed and oppressed.
All the books will be burnt in fire.
Gurus and masters will be treated as slaves.

The fully ordained will be separated from the Dharma,
Butchers will be mistaken for members of the Saṅgha.
The clothes of the Buddha [statues] will be thrown in the river.
The three kinds of shrine objects and ritual offering implements will be
beaten with rocks.

Even the name of the Dharma will be eliminated.
Then, in a cave in Yerpa,
An emanation of Vajrapāṇi,
A monk named "Pel"

Will liberate the evil king.
During some cycles of years
There will be no teachings of the Buddha.
Alas! [I] have compassion for sentient beings!

Thus it was prophesied.

At that time, there was produced a child who would be the heir in the belly of the younger queen, but the older queen, however, told the lie "[I] have a child in my belly." And, at the time when the heir was born to the younger [queen], [the older queen] having moved close to the body of a just-born small boy of a beggar-woman, when [she] said, "[He] is born from me," since the ministers were made to rely on what the queen-mother had said, [he] was called "Ngadak Yumten" ("the-lord['s-son]-relying-on-the-queen['s-assertion]").

As for the heir, since [he] was protected by the light of the sun and butter lamps day and night from possible harm by the elder queen, [he] was called "Ösung" ("guarded [by] light"). Then, Ösung and Yumten both being in disagreement over the government, the former seized the district of Yo and the latter the district of U, and [they] created conflict. After Ösung, since there was no sovereign king over all of Tibet, the religious system disappeared.

Purbujok's "Introductory Path of Reasoning" (selection from *The Collected Topics on Valid Cognition*)

Religious education throughout the world takes various forms in different cultures. Some cultures adopt an experiential approach toward education wherein a novitiate is guided through physical activities and events designed to evoke a specific emotionally charged experience. Other traditions rely predominantly on myths and stories that convey a specific lesson and overall cultural values. While elements of these pedagogical devices are present within Buddhism, in the Tibetan Buddhist educational system pioneered at Sangpu (*gsang phu*) Monastery in the eleventh century, preference was given to logical reasoning and epistemological analysis as the primary instructional approach. This is a feature that distinguishes it from other religious educational systems and is reflected in the very first texts encountered by a student entering a monastic college.

The subject of Buddhist epistemology is rooted in the thought of the Buddha Śākyamuni, though he gave no explicit discourse on the subject. Instead, the canonical foundations of Tibetan epistemology were laid by the sixth-century scholar-yogi Dignāga and his seventh-century commentator Dharmakīrti. Coincident with their foundational texts being translated into Tibetan, two main lineages of interpretation formed. The first was initiated by the twelfth-century scholar Chaba Chögyi Sengé (*phya pa chos kyi seng ge*, 1109–1169) of the Kadampa sect (*bka' gdams pa*), while the second stems from the thirteenth-century Sakya (*sa skya*) scholar Sakya Paṇḍita Kunga Gyeltsen (*sa skya paṇḍi ta kun dga' rgyal mtshan*, 1182–1251). The lineage of interpretation of *The Collected Topics* stems from the first of these. While both of these interpretational lineages are grounded in Indian commentarial traditions, the subject of the differences between the two are beyond the scope of this introduction. Georges Dreyfus presents a brilliantly framed and detailed analysis of the comparative positions of these two authors and their intellectual successors; his book[1] is highly recommended.

The text presented here,[2] a selection from Purbujok's longer work entitled *The Collected Topics on Valid Cognition*, which is the first text encountered by a young student in one of the main monastic universities, is a precise introduction to logical reasoning and basic epistemology. Although individual monastic colleges vary in their educational systems, up to four years[3] can be spent studying a primer like *The Collected Topics*—this one being composed of three sections: the introductory, middling, and greater paths of reasoning. Only the first chapter of the first of these texts is presented here.

The text, Purbujok's *Introductory Path of Reasoning* is—like some of the other texts presented here—from the literary genre of "yík-cha" (*yig cha*), or "monastic textbooks." Works from this genre have been put to various usages both historically and in contemporary settings. Members of all traditions both religious and otherwise fill the spectrum of attitudes from the most conservative and dogmatic to the most liberal and self-critical concerning their own instructional apparatus. Leaving aside the partisan rivalry often associated with college textbooks, much utility is to be found in them. Being concise presentations of very complicated philosophical issues, the works that comprise the entire textbook series have traditionally been required to be memorized by students. This inculcation of the entire content of these texts has the obvious advantage of providing one with both broad and systematic knowledge of the subjects of a Buddhist education. The danger in such knowledge, however, lies in mistaking it for the be-all and end-all of discourse on a given subject ... a culminating presentation of preestablished truths. This narrow perspective can be found among some teachers, but it is not the view of the majority of scholars, Tibetan or otherwise.

The more "open" approach to textbook literature has been described by Georges Dreyfus as Socratic or dialectically critical.[4] Within the domain of this latter approach, the primary function of textbooks is still seen to be education within a particular system of thought. However, the worldview expressed in these texts is taken as foundational—that is, as a stable basis for the exploration of other ideas and self-criticism, urging a student to develop their own understanding of the interrelationship between ideas presented. One man who took this position further than any other before him was the so-called renegade monk Gendün Chöpel (*dge 'dun chos phel*, 1905–1951). Flourishing in the early half of the twentieth century, he gained a reputation for being confrontational and unorthodox in his philosophy. As an example of this, it is said that when he sat for his defense to obtain the degree of Geshe, he adopted views contradictory to those of his own college textbooks and yet still prevailed in the debates. Such levels of achievement can only be gained, however, once one is intimately familiar with a system and all of its strengths and weaknesses. The genre of textbook literature is designed to generate precisely this sort of familiarity.

The section of the text presented here follows a basic sequence as follows:

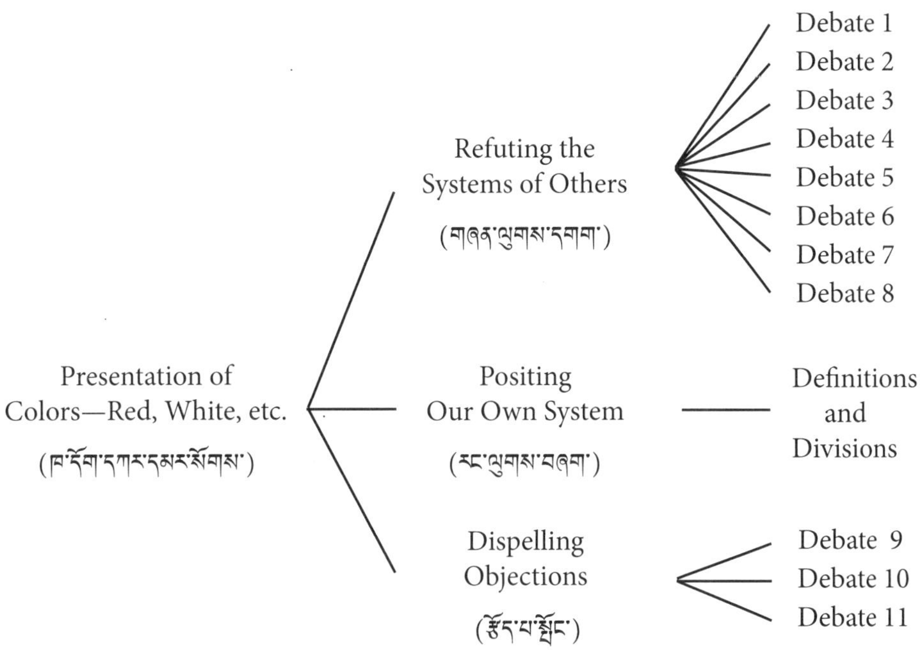

In this section, the first debate is on the interrelation between the category of color and the color red. A hypothetical opponent mistakenly asserts that these two classes of phenomena are equivalent. The textbook author then proceeds to cite absurd counter-examples designed to demonstrate the error in the assertion.

This structure is repeated with slight variations for the categories of color and white (Debate 2), the categories of color and yellow (Debate 3), the categories of color and blue (Debate 4), and so on.[5] Having refuted these mistaken assertions, the author presents the definitions of these various terms in the "Positing Our Own System" section. This chapter of the text then concludes with a final defense, or "Dispelling Objections" to these definitions, in a debate format similar to that of the first section.

[1] Dreyfus 1997.

[2] The text selection from this genre presented here is that by the Thirteenth Dalai Lama's tutor, Purbujok Jampa Gyatso (*phur bu lcog byams pa rgya mtsho*, 1825–1901). His text, "The Introductory Path of

Reasoning," is taken from his set of treatises entitled *The Presentation of Collected Topics Revealing the Meaning of the Texts on Valid Cognition, The Magical Key to the Path of Reasoning* used by the Je (*byes*) College of Sera Monastic University and the Jangtse (*byang rtse*) College of Ganden Monastic University, as well as the Dalai Lama's own monastery, Namgyal (*rnam rgyal*) College.

[3] Elizabeth Napper notes that the Gomang (*sgo mang*) College of Drepung Monastic University devotes four years to the texts, while the Loseling (*blo gsal ling*) College spends only one year on them. Lati Rinbochay and Napper 1980, 161n5.

[4] Dreyfus 1987.

[5] Perdue provides analyses of these and the other debates in his book. Perdue 1992.

[1]༄༅། །ཚད་མའི་གཞུང་དོན་འབྱེད་པའི་བསྡུས་གྲྭའི་རྣམ་བཞག་རིགས་ལམ་འཕྲུལ་གྱི་ལྡེ་མིག་ཅེས་བྱ་བ་ལས་རིགས་ལམ་ཆུང་ངུའི་རྣམ་པར་བཤད་པ་བཞུགས་སོ། །[2]

བླ་མ་དང་མགོན་པོ་འཇམ་དཔལ་དབྱངས་ལ་ཕྱག་འཚལ་ལོ།

ཡང་དག་དོན་གཟིགས་སྟོན་པ་ཚད་མ་དེས། །
ཞིགས་གསུངས་རིགས་ལམ་ཚད་མས་གསལ་མཛད་པའི། །
བདག་ཉིད་ཆེན་པོ་ཕྱོགས་གླང་ཆོས་གྲགས་སོགས། །
སྟོན་འགྲོན་འཕགས་བོད་མཁས་གྲུབ་རྣམས་ལ་འདུད།[3]

འདིར་རིགས་པའི་ལམ་གྱི་སློ་འབྱེད་བསྡུས་གྲྭའི་རྣམ་བཞག་བཤད་པ་ལ། རིགས་ལམ་ཆུང་ངུའི་རྣམ་བཞག་བཤད་པ། རིགས་ལམ་འབྲིང་གི་རྣམ་བཞག་བཤད་པ། རིགས་ལམ་ཆེན་པོའི་རྣམ་བཞག་བཤད་པ་དང་གསུམ།[4]

དང་པོ་རིགས་ལམ་ཆུང་ངུའི་ནང་ཚན་ཁ་དོག་དཀར་དམར་སོགས་ཀྱི་རྣམ་བཞག་བཤད་པ་ལ། དགག་བཞག་སྤོང་གསུམ་ལས། དང་པོ་ནི།[5]

ཁ་ཅིག་ན་རེ། ཁ་དོག་ཡིན་ན་དམར་པོ་ཡིན་པས་ཁྱབ་ཟེར་ན།[6] ཆོས་དུང་དཀར་པོའི་ཁ་དོག་ཆོས་ཅན། དམར་པོ་ཡིན་པར་ཐལ། ཁ་དོག་ཡིན་པའི་ཕྱིར།[7] ཁྱབ་པ་ཁས།[8] མ་གྲུབ་ན། ཆོས་དུང་དཀར་པོའི་ཁ་དོག་ཆོས་ཅན། ཁ་དོག་ཡིན་པར་ཐལ། དཀར་པོ་ཡིན་པའི་ཕྱིར། མ་གྲུབ་ན། ཆོས་དུང་དཀར་པོའི་ཁ་དོག་ཆོས་ཅན། དཀར་པོ་ཡིན་པར་ཐལ། ཆོས་དུང་དཀར་པོའི་ཁ་དོག་དང་གཅིག་ཡིན་པའི་ཕྱིར།[9] རྩ་བར་འདོད་ན། ཆོས་དུང་དཀར་པོའི་ཁ་དོག་ཆོས་ཅན། དམར་པོ་མ་ཡིན་པར་ཐལ། དཀར་པོ་ཡིན་པའི་ཕྱིར། མ་ཁྱབ་ན་ཁྱབ་པ་ཡོད་པར་ཐལ། དཀར་པོ་དང་དམར་པོ་གཉིས་ཀྱི་གཞི་མཐུན་མེད་པའི་ཕྱིར་ཏེ། དེ་གཉིས་འགལ་བ་ཡིན་པའི་ཕྱིར།

ཁ་ཅིག་ན་རེ། ཁ་དོག་ཡིན་ན་དཀར་པོ་ཡིན་པས་ཁྱབ་ཟེར་ན། སངས་རྒྱས་ཆེ་དཔག་མེད་ཀྱི་ཁ་དོག་ཆོས་ཅན། དཀར་པོ་ཡིན་པར་ཐལ། ཁ་དོག་ཡིན་པའི་ཕྱིར། ཁྱབ་པ་ཁས། མ་གྲུབ་ན། སངས་རྒྱས་ཆེ་དཔག་མེད་ཀྱི་ཁ་དོག་ཆོས་ཅན། ཁ་དོག་ཡིན་པར་ཐལ། མདོག་ཏུ་སྣང་བ་ཡིན་པའི་ཕྱིར། མ་ཁྱབ་ན། དེ་ལ་ཁྱབ་པ་ཡོད་པར་ཐལ། མདོག་ཏུ་སྣང་བ་ཁ་དོག་གི་མཚན་ཉིད་ཡིན་པའི་ཕྱིར།[10] རྩ་བར་འདོད་ན། སངས་རྒྱས་ཆེ་དཔག་མེད་ཀྱི་ཁ་དོག་ཆོས་ཅན། དཀར་པོ་མ་ཡིན་པར་ཐལ། དམར་པོ་ཡིན་པའི་ཕྱིར། མ་གྲུབ་ན། སངས་རྒྱས་ཆེ་དཔག་མེད་ཀྱི་ཁ་དོག་ཆོས་ཅན། དམར་པོ་ཡིན་པར་ཐལ། སངས་རྒྱས་ཆེ་དཔག་མེད་ཀྱི་ཁ་དོག་གི་ལྡོག་པ་[11]ཡིན་པའི་ཕྱིར། མ་གྲུབ་ན། སངས་རྒྱས་ཆེ་དཔག་མེད་ཀྱི་ཁ་དོག་ཆོས་ཅན། ཁྱོད་[12]ཁྱོད་ཀྱི་ལྡོག་པ་ཡིན་པར་ཐལ། ཁྱོད་གཞི་གྲུབ་པའི་ཕྱིར།[11]

ཁ་ཅིག་ན་རེ། ཁ་དོག་ཡིན་ན། སེར་པོ་ཡིན་པས་ཁྱབ་ཟེར་ན། ཨིནྡྲ་ནི་ལའི་ཁ་དོག་ཆོས་ཅན། དེར་ཐལ། དེའི་ཕྱིར།[13] ཁྱབ་པ་ཁས། མ་གྲུབ་ན། དེ་ཆོས་ཅན། དེར་ཐལ། རྩ་བའི་ཁ་དོག་ཡིན་པའི་ཕྱིར།[14] མ་གྲུབ་ན། དེ་ཆོས་ཅན། དེར་ཐལ། སྔོ་སེར་དཀར་དམར་བཞི་པོ་གང་རུང་ཡིན་པའི་ཕྱིར། རྩ་བར་འདོད་ན། དེ་ཆོས་ཅན། སེར་པོ་མ་ཡིན་པར་ཐལ། སྔོན་པོ་ཡིན་པའི་ཕྱིར། ཁྱབ་དེ། སྔོ་སེར་གཉིས་འགལ་བ་ཡིན་པའི་ཕྱིར།

ཁ་ཅིག་ན་རེ། ཁ་དོག་ཡིན་ན། སྔོན་པོ་ཡིན་པས་ཁྱབ་ཟེར་ན། གསེར་བཙོ་མའི་ཁ་དོག་ཆོས་ཅན། དེར་ཐལ། དེའི་ཕྱིར། ཁྱབ་པ་ཁས། མ་གྲུབ་ན། དེ་ཆོས་ཅན། དེར་ཐལ། ཁ་དོག་གི་བྱེ་བྲག་ཡིན་པའི་ཕྱིར། རྩ་བར་འདོད་ན། དེ་ཆོས་ཅན། སྔོན་པོ་མ་ཡིན་པར་ཐལ། སེར་པོ་ཡིན་པའི་ཕྱིར། མ་གྲུབ་ན། དེ་ཆོས་ཅན། དེར་ཐལ། གསེར་བཙོ་མའི་ཁ་དོག་ཡིན་པའི་ཕྱིར། མ་གྲུབ་ན། གསེར་བཙོ་མའི་ཁ་དོག་གསེར་བཙོ་མའི་ཁ་དོག་ཡིན་པར་ཐལ། གསེར་བཙོ་མའི་ཁ་དོག་ཡོད་པའི་ཕྱིར།

ཁ་ཅིག་ན་རེ། ཁ་དོག་ཡིན་ན། རྩ་བའི་ཁ་དོག་ཡིན་པས་ཁྱབ་ཟེར་ན། དོན་ཡོད་གྲུབ་པ་ལྗང་ཁུའི་ཁ་དོག་ཆོས་ཅན། དེར་ཐལ། དེའི་ཕྱིར། མ་གྲུབ་ན། དེ་ཆོས་ཅན། དེར་ཐལ། ཆོས་ཅན་དེ་ཡིན་པའི་ཕྱིར། རྩ་བར་འདོད་ན། དེ་ཆོས་ཅན། རྩ་བའི་ཁ་དོག་མ་ཡིན་པར་ཐལ། ཡན་ལག་གི་ཁ་དོག་ཡིན་པའི་ཕྱིར། དེར་ཐལ། སྔོ་སེར་གཉིས་ཀྱི་ཡན་ལག་གི་ཁ་དོག་ཡིན་པའི་ཕྱིར། དེར་ཐལ། ལྗང་ཁུ་ཡིན་པའི་ཕྱིར་ཏེ།[15] སྔོ་སེར་འདྲེས་པའི་ཁ་དོག་ཡིན་པའི་ཕྱིར། ཁྱབ་སྟེ། སྔོ་སེར་འདྲེས་པ་ལས་ལྗང་ཁུ། དམར་སེར་འདྲེས་པ་ལས་ལི་ཁྲི། དམར་སྔོན་འདྲེས་པ་ལས་ནག་པོར་འཇོག་པའི་ཕྱིར།[16][17]

ཁ་ཅིག་ན་རེ། ཡན་ལག་གི་ཁ་དོག་ཡིན་ན། ཡན་ལག་གི་ཁ་དོག་བརྒྱད་པོ་གང་རུང་ཡིན་པས་ཁྱབ་

ཟེར་ན། འཛམ་དབུགས་དམར་སེར་གྱི་ཁ་དོག་ཆོས་ཅན། ཡན་ལག་གི་ཁ་དོག་བརྒྱད་པོ་གང་རུང་ཡིན་པར་ཐལ། ཡན་ལག་གི་ཁ་དོག་ཡིན་པའི་ཕྱིར། ཁྱབ་པ་ཁས། མ་གྲུབ་ན། འཛམ་དབུགས་དམར་སེར་གྱི་ཁ་དོག་ཆོས་ཅན། ཡན་ལག་གི་ཁ་དོག་ཡིན་པར་ཐལ། དམར་སེར་གཉིས་ཀྱི་ཡན་ལག་གི་ཁ་དོག་ཡིན་པའི་ཕྱིར། རྩ་བར་འདོད་ན། འཛམ་དབུགས་དམར་སེར་གྱི་ཁ་དོག་ཆོས་ཅན། ཡན་ལག་གི་ཁ་དོག་བརྒྱད་པོ་གང་རུང་མ་ཡིན་པར་ཐལ། སྤྲིན་དང་དུ་བ། རྡུལ་དང་ཁུག་སྣའི་ཁ་དོག་བཞི་པོ་གང་རུང་མ་ཡིན་པ་གང་ཞིག[18] །སྣང་བ་དང་མུན་པ། གྲིབ་མ་དང་ཉི་མའི་འོད་ཟེར་གྱི་ཁ་དོག་བཞི་པོ་གང་རུང་ཡང་མ་ཡིན་པའི་ཕྱིར། རྟགས་རེ་རེ་ནས་གྲུབ་སྟེ། འཛམ་དབུགས་དམར་སེར་གྱི་ཁ་དོག་དང་གཅིག་ཡིན་པའི་ཕྱིར།

ཁ་ཅིག་ན་རེ། གཟུགས་ཡིན་ན། དབྱིབས་ཀྱི་གཟུགས་ཡིན་པས་ཁྱབ་ཟེར་ན། ཁ་དོག་གི་གཟུགས་ཆོས་ཅན། དེར་ཐལ། དེའི་ཕྱིར། ཁྱབ་པ་ཁས། མ་གྲུབ་ན། དེ་ཆོས་ཅན། དེར་ཐལ། བེམ་པོ་ཡིན་པའི་ཕྱིར། མ་གྲུབ་ན། དེ་ཆོས་ཅན། དེར་ཐལ། རྡུལ་དུ་གྲུབ་པ་ཡིན་པའི་ཕྱིར། རྩ་བར་འདོད་ན། དེ་ཆོས་ཅན། དབྱིབས་ཀྱི་གཟུགས་མ་ཡིན་པར་ཐལ། ཁ་དོག་གི་གཟུགས་དང་གཅིག་ཡིན་པའི་ཕྱིར། མ་གྲུབ་ན། དེ་ཆོས་ཅན། ཁྱོད་ཁྱོད་དང་གཅིག་ཡིན་པར་ཐལ། ཁྱོད་ཡོད་པ་ཡིན་པའི་ཕྱིར།

ཁ་ཅིག་ན་རེ། གཟུགས་ཡིན་ན། ཁ་དོག་གི་གཟུགས་ཡིན་པས་ཁྱབ་ཟེར་ན། ལྷམ་པོའི་གཟུགས་ཆོས་ཅན། དེར་ཐལ། དེའི་ཕྱིར། ཁྱབ་པ་ཁས། མ་གྲུབ་ན། དེ་ཆོས་ཅན། དེར་ཐལ། གཟུགས་ཀྱི་སྐྱེ་མཆེད་ཡིན་པའི་ཕྱིར། མ་གྲུབ་ན། དེ་ཆོས་ཅན། དེར་ཐལ། མིག་ཤེས་ཀྱི་བཟུང་བྱ་ཡིན་པའི་ཕྱིར།[19] རྩ་བར་འདོད་ན། དེ་ཆོས་ཅན། ཁ་དོག་གི་གཟུགས་མ་ཡིན་པར་ཐལ། ཁ་དོག་མ་ཡིན་པའི་ཕྱིར། ཁྱབ་སྟེ། ཁ་དོག་གི་གཟུགས་དང་། ཁ་དོག་དོན་གཅིག །དབྱིབས་ཀྱི་གཟུགས་དང་། དབྱིབས་གཉིས་དོན་གཅིག་ཡིན་པའི་ཕྱིར།

རང་གི་ལུགས་ལ། གཟུགས་ཀྱི་མཚན་ཉིད་ཡོད་དེ། གཟུགས་རུང་དེ་དེ་ཡིན་པའི་ཕྱིར། གཟུགས་དང་བེམ་པོ་གཉིས་དོན་གཅིག[20] །གཟུགས་ལ་དབྱེ་ན། གཟུགས་ཀྱི་སྐྱེ་མཆེད་དང་། སྒྲའི་སྐྱེ་མཆེད་དང་། དྲིའི་སྐྱེ་མཆེད་དང་། རོའི་སྐྱེ་མཆེད་དང་། རེག་བྱའི་སྐྱེ་མཆེད་དང་ལྔ་ཡོད། གཟུགས་ཀྱི་སྐྱེ་མཆེད་ཀྱི་མཚན་ཉིད་ཡོད་དེ། མིག་ཤེས་ཀྱི་བཟུང་བྱ་དེ་དེ་ཡིན་པའི་ཕྱིར། གཟུགས་ཀྱི་སྐྱེ་མཆེད་ལ་དབྱེ་ན་གཉིས་ཡོད་དེ། དབྱིབས་དང་ཁ་དོག་གཉིས་ཡོད་པའི་ཕྱིར། དབྱིབས་ཀྱི་མཚན་ཉིད་ཡོད་དེ། དབྱིབས་སུ་བསྟན་དུ་རུང་བ་དེ་[21] དེ་

ཡིན་པའི་ཕྱིར། དེ་ལ་དབྱེ་ན་བརྒྱད་ཡོད་དེ། རིང་བ་དང་ཐུང་བ། མཐོ་བ་དང་དམའ་བ། ལྷམ་པ་དང་ཟླུམ་པོ། ཕྱ་ལེ་བ་དང་ཕྱ་ལེ་བ་མ་ཡིན་པའི་གཟུགས་དང་བཅས་པ་བརྒྱད་ཡོད་པའི་ཕྱིར། ལྷམ་པ་ནི་གྲུ་བཞི། ཟླུམ་པོ་ནི་གོར་མོའམ་ཧྲིལ་པོ། ཕྱ་ལེ་བ་ནི་ངོས་མཉམ་པའི་དབྱིབས་ལྟ་བུ་ལ་བྱེད་རིགས་པའི་ཕྱིར།[22] མདོག་ཏུ་བསྟན་དུ་རུང་བ། ཁ་དོག་གི་མཚན་ཉིད།[23] ཁ་དོག་ལ་དབྱེ་ན་གཉིས་ཡོད་དེ། རྩ་བའི་ཁ་དོག་དང་། ཡན་ལག་གི་ཁ་དོག་གཉིས་ཡོད་པའི་ཕྱིར། རྩ་བའི་ཁ་དོག་ལ་དབྱེ་ན་བཞི་ཡོད་དེ། སྔོ་སེར་དཀར་དམར་བཞི་ཡོད་པའི་ཕྱིར། ཡན་ལག་གི་ཁ་དོག་ལ་དབྱེ་ན་བརྒྱད་ཡོད་དེ། དེར་གྱུར་པའི་སྤྲིན་དང་དུ་བ། རྡུལ་དང་ཁུག་སྣ། སྣང་བ་དང་མུན་པ། གྲིབ་མ་དང་ཉི་མའི་འོད་ཟེར་གྱི་ཁ་དོག་དང་བརྒྱད་ཡོད་པའི་ཕྱིར། སྒྲའི་སྐྱེ་མཆེད་ཀྱི་མཚན་ཉིད་ཡོད་དེ། རྣ་ཤེས་ཀྱི་ཉན་བྱ་དེ་དེ་ཡིན་པའི་ཕྱིར། སྒྲ་ལ་དབྱེ་ན་གཉིས་ཡོད་དེ། ཟིན་པའི་འབྱུང་བ་ལས་གྱུར་པའི་སྒྲ་དང་། མ་ཟིན་པའི་འབྱུང་བ་ལས་གྱུར་པའི་སྒྲ་གཉིས་ཡོད་པའི་ཕྱིར།[24] དྲིའི་སྐྱེ་མཆེད་ཀྱི་མཚན་ཉིད་ཡོད་དེ། སྣ་ཤེས་ཀྱི་མྱོང་བྱ་དེ་དེ་ཡིན་པའི་ཕྱིར། དྲི་ལ་དབྱེ་ན་གཉིས་ཡོད་དེ། ལྷན་སྐྱེས་ཀྱི་དྲི་དང་སྦྱོར་བྱུང་གི་དྲི་གཉིས་ཡོད་པའི་ཕྱིར། རོའི་སྐྱེ་མཆེད་ཀྱི་མཚན་ཉིད་ཡོད་དེ། ལྕེ་ཤེས་ཀྱི་མྱོང་བྱ་དེ་དེ་ཡིན་པའི་ཕྱིར། རོ་ལ་དབྱེ་ན་དྲུག་ཡོད་དེ། མངར་བ་དང་སྐྱུར་བ། ཁ་བ་དང་བསྐ་བ། ཚ་བ་དང་ལན་ཚ་བ་སྟེ་དྲུག་ཡོད་པའི་ཕྱིར། རེག་བྱའི་སྐྱེ་མཆེད་ཀྱི་མཚན་ཉིད་ཡོད་དེ། ལུས་ཤེས་ཀྱི་མྱོང་བྱ་དེ་དེ་ཡིན་པའི་ཕྱིར། རེག་བྱ་ལ་དབྱེ་ན་གཉིས་ཡོད་དེ། འབྱུང་བར་གྱུར་པའི་རེག་བྱ་དང་། འབྱུང་འགྱུར་གྱི་རེག་བྱ་གཉིས་ཡོད་པའི་ཕྱིར།[25] འབྱུང་བར་གྱུར་པའི་རེག་བྱ་ལ་དབྱེ་ན་བཞི་ཡོད་དེ། ས་ཆུ་མེ་རླུང་བཞི་པོ་དེ་དེ་ཡིན་པའི་ཕྱིར། སའི་མཚན་ཉིད་ཡོད་དེ། སྲ་ཞིང་འཐས་པ་དེ་དེ་ཡིན་པའི་ཕྱིར། ཆུའི་མཚན་ཉིད་ཡོད་དེ། རླན་ཞིང་གཤེར་བ་དེ་དེ་ཡིན་པའི་ཕྱིར། མེའི་མཚན་ཉིད་ཡོད་དེ། ཚ་ཞིང་སྲེག་པ་དེ་དེ་ཡིན་པའི་ཕྱིར། རླུང་གི་མཚན་ཉིད་ཡོད་དེ། ཡང་ཞིང་གཡོ་བ་དེ་དེ་ཡིན་པའི་ཕྱིར། འབྱུང་འགྱུར་གྱི་རེག་བྱ་ལ་དབྱེ་ན་བདུན་ཡོད་དེ། དེར་གྱུར་པའི་འཇམ་པ་དང་རྩུབ་པ། ལྕི་བ་དང་ཡང་བ། གྲང་བ་དང་བཀྲེས་པ། སྐོམ་པ་དང་བདུན་པོ་དེ་དེ་ཡིན་པའི་ཕྱིར།

རྩོད་པ་སྤོང་བ་ལ། ཁ་ཅིག་ན་རེ། ཆོས་དུང་དཀར་པོ་ཆོས་ཅན། ཁ་དོག་ཡིན་པར་ཐལ། དཀར་པོ་ཡིན་པའི་ཕྱིར། མ་གྲུབ་ན། དེ་ཆོས་ཅན། དེར་ཐལ། ཆོས་དུང་དཀར་པོ་ཡིན་པའི་ཕྱིར་ན། འགལ་ཁྱབ་ལ་འབུད།[26] འོ་ན་ཁྱེད་རང་ལ། རྟ་དཀར་པོ་ཆོས་ཅན། དཀར་པོ་ཡིན་པར་ཐལ། རྟ་དཀར་པོ་ཡིན་པའི་ཕྱིར། ཁྱབ་པ་འཁྲིག འདོད་མི་ནུས་ཏེ། བེམ་པོ་མ་ཡིན་པའི་ཕྱིར་ཏེ། གང་ཟག་ཡིན་པའི་ཕྱིར་ཏེ། རྟ་ཡིན་པའི་ཕྱིར། གཞན་ཡང་། ཆོས་དུང་དཀར་པོ་ཆོས་

ཅན། ཁ་དོག་ཡིན་པར་ཐལ། དཀར་པོ་ཡིན་པའི་ཕྱིར། རྟགས་ཁས། འདོད་ན། དེ་ཆོས་ཅན། ཁ་དོག་མ་ཡིན་པར་ཐལ། འབྱུང་འགྱུར་མ་ཡིན་པའི་ཕྱིར། དེར་ཐལ། འབྱུང་བ་ཡིན་པའི་ཕྱིར་ཏེ། ཆོས་དུང་ཡིན་པའི་ཕྱིར།

ཡང་ཁོ་ན་རེ། རླུང་ཆོས་ཅན། འབྱུང་འགྱུར་ཡིན་པར་ཐལ། འབྱུང་འགྱུར་གྱི་རེག་བྱ་བདུན་པོ་གང་རུང་ཡིན་པའི་ཕྱིར། མ་གྲུབ་ན། རླུང་ཆོས་ཅན། འབྱུང་འགྱུར་གྱི་རེག་བྱ་བདུན་པོ་གང་རུང་ཡིན་པར་ཐལ། ཡང་བའི་རེག་བྱ་ཡིན་པའི་ཕྱིར། དེར་ཐལ། ཡང་བ་དང་རེག་བྱ་གཉིས་ཀ་ཡིན་པའི་ཕྱིར་ཟེར་ན་མ་ཁྱབ། དེ་བཞིན་དུ་ས་ཆུ་མེ་ལ་ཡང་རིགས་འགྲེའོ།

ཁོ་ན་རེ། ཤེས་བྱ་ཆོས་ཅན། དབྱིབས་ཡིན་པར་ཐལ། ཕྲ་ལི་བ་དང་ཕྲ་ལི་བ་མ་ཡིན་པ་གཉིས་པོ་གང་རུང་ཡིན་པའི་ཕྱིར་ན་མ་ཁྱབ། མ་གྲུབ་ན། ཤེས་བྱ་ཆོས་ཅན། ཕྲ་ལི་བ་དང་ཕྲ་ལི་བ་མ་ཡིན་པ་གཉིས་པོ་གང་རུང་ཡིན་པར་ཐལ། ཕྲ་ལི་བ་མ་ཡིན་པ་ཡིན་པའི་ཕྱིར། མ་གྲུབ་ན། ཤེས་བྱ་ཆོས་ཅན། ཕྲ་ལི་བ་མ་ཡིན་པ་ཡིན་པར་ཐལ། ཕྲ་ལི་བ་མ་ཡིན་པའི་ཕྱིར། རྩ་བར་འདོད་ན། ཤེས་བྱ་ཆོས་ཅན། དབྱིབས་མ་ཡིན་པར་ཐལ། རྟག་པ་ཡིན་པའི་ཕྱིར་རོ།

Annotations to Purbujok's "Introductory Path of Reasoning" (selection from *The Collected Topics on Valid Cognition*)

① Reading Monastic Textbooks (General Features)

Page 185, Line 1

Depending upon the type of educational institution—commentarial school (*bshad grwa*) or debate school (*rtsod grwa*)—monastic textbooks tend to take one or more basic forms: "commentarial" (*bshad pa*), "general meaning" (*spyi don*), or "presentation" (*rnam bzhag*) texts; "decisive analyses" (*mtha' dpyod*); and "debate manuals" (a specific form of *yig cha*). The text presented here is an example of the latter. While the basic structure has been discussed in the introduction to this text, an important point to remember is that the purpose is to provide a standard set of well-defined terminology that allows for consistency of reference within more refined philosophical exegeses.

WHAT TO REMEMBER

Monastic textbooks provide a standard set of well-defined terminology that is meant not just to be studied but actually to be memorized in order to facilitate rapid comprehension of more refined and advanced philosophical exegeses.

② Text Titles

Page 185, Line 2

Text titles in Tibetan can be complex. Unlike text titles in English, Tibetan text titles are grammatically complete sentences terminated by the Class II verb བཞུགས་. Although simple noun phrase titles do exist, more often than not Tibetan text titles contain multiple appositional phrases composed of ornate poetic imagery. The full title of the *Introductory Path of Reasoning* is one such example. Since the text is part of a larger work, *The Collected Topics*, the title reflects this through the use of the fifth-case (originative) particle ལས་ (case 5.3):

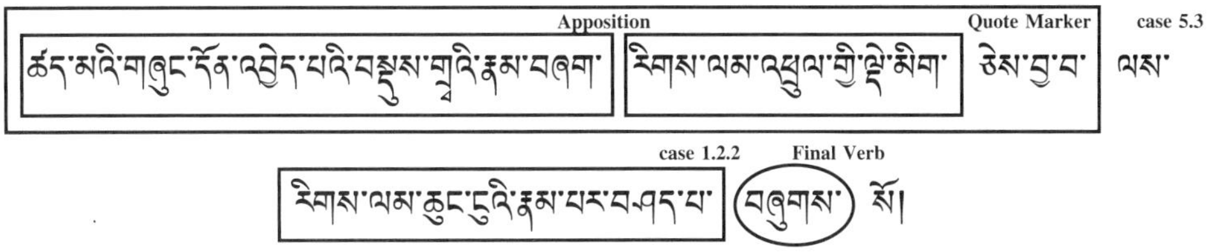

Each of these phrases can be further analyzed into its component parts. While the first is made up of two appositional noun phrases followed by a quotation marker (ཅེས་བྱ་བ་), the second is a single noun phrase. Taken literally, this sentence/text title could be translated as: "[Here,] from within 'The Presentation of Collected Topics That Reveals the Meaning of the Texts on Valid Cognition, the Magical Key to the Path of Reasoning' resides the explanation of the smaller path of reasoning." A more polished translation would be:

> The Introductory Path of Reasoning—from *The Presentation of Collected Topics Revealing the Meaning of the Texts on Valid Cognition, the Magical Key to the Path of Reasoning*

WHAT TO REMEMBER

Text titles are grammatically complete sentences formed with the verb བཞུགས་ (often left untranslated), employing the quotation marker ཞེས་བྱ་བ་, with often one or more poetic expressions applied appositively.

Initial Verse of Expression of Worship

3

Page 185, Line 9

One of the most discouraging aspects of Tibetan literature for a novice reader is the fact that often one of the most grammatically difficult passages of a text occurs in its opening lines. This is certainly the case with this text (consequently, it is sometimes useful to wait until one has read the rest of the text before attempting to read such sentences). In brief, however, this sentence is identical in basic structure to the preceding one. It is an homage, though unlike the previous sentence, it is in verse, has a complex object, and is built off a verb synonymous with ཕྱག་འཚལ་, the Class VI verb འདུད་. In this sentence there is only one object and it is marked with a second-case particle:

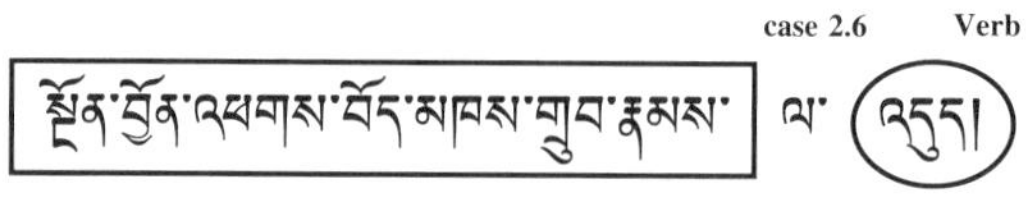

What remains—the first three lines of the stanza—is in apposition to that object. A clue to this fact is the presence of the generalizing lexical particle སོགས་ (short for ལ་སོགས་པ་), which marks a list and which often stands in apposition to what follows.

Immediately preceding the particle སོགས་ are two proper names, Dignāga (ཕྱོགས་གླང་) and Dharmakīrti (ཆོས་གྲགས་), with an appositional epithet "great beings" (བདག་ཉིད་ཆེན་པོ་). This is preceded by a sixth-case clause connective linking it to the preceding lines. Although the verb གསལ་ is a Class II verb meaning "to be clear," when it appears in a causative construction (here with the honorific auxiliary verb མཛད་; see ཤེས་རབ་སྙིང་པོ་ note 19), the verb phrase functions as a Class V verb, "to cause to be clear" or "to clarify," and hence takes an agent or instrument and a nominative object. Since the clause is connected to a list of proper names—agents (see ཤེས་རབ་སྙིང་པོ་ note 17)—the word occurring in the third case, ཚད་མ་, must be an instrument:

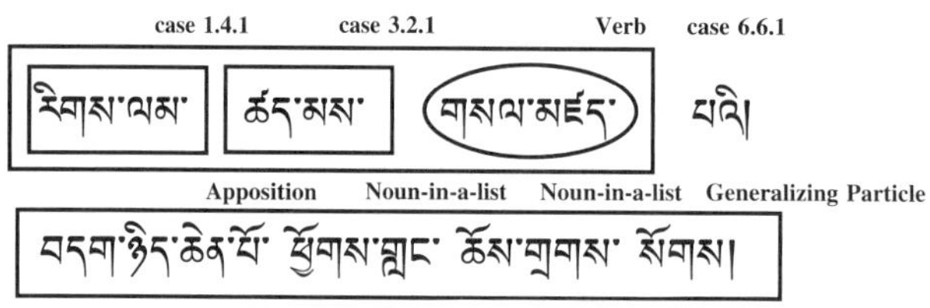

What precedes the phrase རིགས་ལམ་ is a verb, the Class V verb གསུངས་. There are two possible grammatical interpretations that one can make at this point. Either the verb གསུངས་ marks the end of a previous complete sentence, or since the passage is an homage and hence everything in this verse is part of one complete sentence, there is omitted grammar linking the verb with what follows—that is, an omitted sixth-case clause connective. The verb གསུངས་ is preceded by the Sanskritic adverb ལེགས་, while the end of the first line of verse clearly contains an agentive phrase composed of a noun (སྟོན་པ་), followed by an adjective (ཚད་མ་), followed by a pronoun (དེ་).

Again, however, we can see that this noun phrase སྟོན་པ་ཚད་མ་དེ་ is in turn also preceded by a verb, the Class V verb གཟིགས་, and again the same two grammatical possibilities exist. Here, too, there is an omitted sixth-case clause connective. Taking this phrase together with its nominative object, ཡང་དག་དོན་, and combining it with the rest of the sentence yields the complete grammar of the verse:

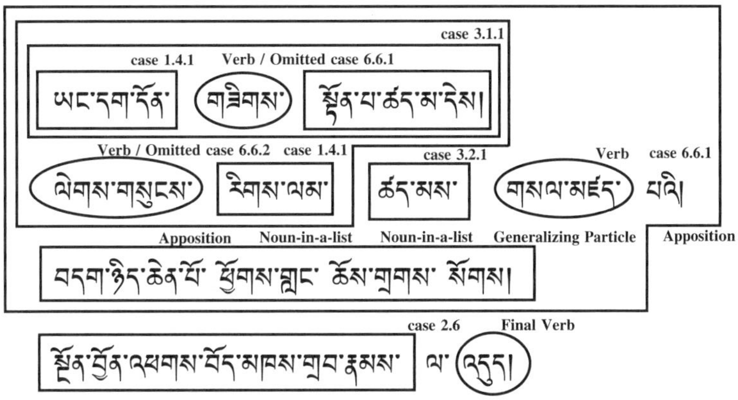

which can be translated as:

Homage to the former scholars and adepts [of the countries of]
the āryas (i.e., India) and Tibet,
The great beings Dignāga, Dharmakīrti, and others
Who clarified with valid cognition the path of reasoning well spoken
By that Valid Teacher (i.e, the Buddha) [who] saw the pure meaning [of
reality].

WHAT TO REMEMBER

When reading the opening passage of a text, watch for common verbs of homage, offering, and praise, such as ཕྱག་འཚལ་, འདུད་, འབུལ་, མཆོད་, etc., preceded by a ལ་ and often occurring at the end of multiples of four lines of fixed-length verse.

④ Omitted Verbs of Existence: ཡོད་

Page 185, Line 13

Most texts begin with one or more introductory statements of one sort or another. Such statements may be formulaic and extensive (depending on the genre of literature) or concise and straightforward. The sentence encountered here is the latter type. While this sentence could be analyzed as a variation of the topical outline format (see the next note), it can also be viewed as a separate sentence especially given the pronoun འདི་ with which the sentence begins. What is immediately noticeable is that there does not appear to be a terminal verb to the sentence. Since this sentence is grammatically and thematically distinct from what follows, it is useful to think of the sentence as having an omitted (or "implicit") verb of existence, ཡོད་. That is,

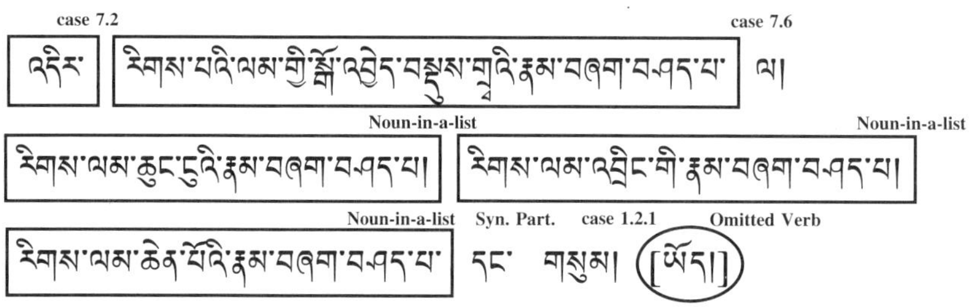

Here, with this sentence, the author expands on the textual division explicit in the title, explaining that the text which follows is only the first of three parts. Grammatically speaking, the name of the larger work is marked with a seventh-case ལ་ particle, while the three major divisions of the text are spelled out as nouns in a list. This series of phrases also displays the use of punctuation to mark grammatical divisions. Here, rather than repeatedly using the syntactic particle དང་ to link the three separate divisions of the text, they are simply punctuated by the phrase delimiter ། (*shad*) with only the last member of the list followed by a single དང་ linking the list to a cardinal number indicating the number of elements in the list.

WHAT TO REMEMBER

In certain instances where the author believes the context to be grammatically unambiguous, basic verbs of existence (ཡོད་), identity (ཡིན་), and (occasionally) action

(བྱེད་) may be omitted. Although sometimes an ornamental terminator (such as གོ་, ངོ་, དོ་, ནོ་, etc.) will be appended to a final noun to indicate the termination of a sentence, often only contextual grammatical clues and the flow of the narrative alert one to the presence of an omitted or implied verb.

Topical Outlines (ས་བཅད་)

5

Page 185, Line 16

Topical outlines are a common structure employed in complex texts. When encountering a topical outline, it is helpful to make careful note of the names and numbers of the section divisions since the topical outlines for many texts can quickly become quite complex. Here, the outline begins with the main topic marked with a seventh-case ལ་ particle, with the three major divisions of the text spelled out as nouns in a list, followed by the announcement of the start of the first division:

Apposition — **case 7.6**

[དང་པོ་ རིགས་ལམ་ཆུང་ངུའི་ནང་ཚན་ཁ་དོག་དཀར་དམར་སོགས་ཀྱི་རྣམ་བཞག་བཤད་པ་] ལ།

Nouns-in-a-list — **Apposition** — **case 5.3** — **case 1.5**

[དགག་ བཞག་ སྤོང་] [གསུམ་] ལས། [དང་པོ་] ནི།

There are a number of things to note about topical outlines in general and this one in particular. First, there is a basic pattern to topical outlines of <*ordinal numeral*> + <*topic heading*> + <*seventh-case particle*> followed by a list of subdivisions in the form of <*list*> + <*cardinal numeral*> + <*fifth-case particle*> + <*ordinal number*> + ནི་ particle. This basic pattern is repeated every time a new division is announced. When a subsequent item in a list is encountered (particularly one that has no further subdivisions), only the first half of this pattern occurs (<*ordinal number*> + <*topic heading*> + <*seventh-case particle*>), although occasionally only the section name or ordinal number followed by a seventh-case particle will be given (the author assuming that the reader has been paying attention to the progression of the text).

This instance of a topical outline, however, is slightly different from the norm in that the author does not preannounce a topical outline for the text as a whole (see སྤྱི་

མཐའ་ note 5), but rather, as the text states, for the divisions of *each* section (ནང་ཚན་). In addition, the three divisions given, དགག་བཞག་སྤོང་, are abbreviations for གཞན་ལུགས་དགག, རང་ལུགས་བཞག, and རྩོད་པ་སྤོང་།. For example, when the second division listed above is encountered, it is given simply as: རང་གི་ལུགས་ལ། omitting any overlapping vocabulary or indication of its sequence in the numerical progression.

What to Remember

Topical outlines may commence in a verbose manner, but often quickly become abbreviated to phrases like གཉིས་པ་ལ། with the division title having been specified much earlier in the text. Consequently, noting the names and number of divisions when they are first encountered is highly recommended.

6 The Opening of a Debate

Page 185, Line 18

Although the basic sentence structure employed in a debate is a "consequence" (see the next note), the start of a debate opens with the statement of the point being debated, often phrased in the form of a rhetorical question, "If someone says ..." (ཁ་ཅིག་ན་རེ། ·····ཟེར་ན།). Such is precisely the case here, where the opening statement of the first debate in the "Colors" section of the text, a conditional clause, begins with the formulaic agent ཁ་ཅིག་ "someone" followed by the syntactic particle ན་རེ་, which marks an agent, and ends with the conditional syntactic particle ན་ that follows the Class V verb ཟེར་ "to say." What remains in between these components is the statement (a complete sentence) attributed to the hypothetical opponent in the debate.

This statement, like the structure of debate, is highly formulaic as well. Here, it is the statement of a pervasion—that is, the statement of a relationship between the property of a subject (in this case, "color" ཁ་དོག་) and a class of objects that are similar in nature (in this case, "being red" དམར་པོ་ཡིན་པ་). The grammar of the sentence is thus:

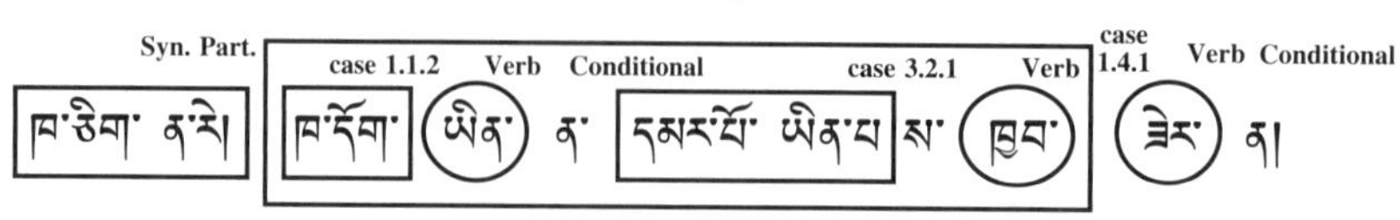

and the clause can therefore be translated as "If someone says, 'If [something] is a color, [it] is pervaded by being red,' then [we reply] ..." and the debate commences.

WHAT TO REMEMBER

A debate opens with a rhetorical question in the form of a conditional clause (ཁ་ཅིག་ན་རེ་···ཟེར་ན།). It is often also a way of signifying a change of subject.

The Structure of a Consequence (ཐལ་འགྱུར་)

Page 185, Line 19

The first step in reading a passage in Tibetan is identifying the sentence boundaries. In general, a sentence is terminated by a verb. However, in certain genres of literature, this principle is often violated. This is the case with the genre of debate manuals that form the primers in the traditional Tibetan education system in the large monastic universities. Along with a syllogism (see རིགས་ལམ་ note 16, below), a consequence (*thal 'gyur; prasaṅga*) is one of the most common constructions to be found in philosophical Buddhist texts, irrespective of topic or genre of literature.

A consequence is composed of three parts: a subject, a predicate, and a reason. These three components are easily identified by ཆོས་ཅན་ marking the subject, the presence of the Class III verb ཐལ་ following the predicate, and ཕྱིར་ marking the reason clause. The subject and the predicate serve as the thesis (*dam bca'; pratijñā*) and grammatically they form a single sentence, while the reason clause can be made up of one or more sentences. In the passage that occurs here, a simple reason (that is, a reason made up of a single sentence) is given and the entire passage can be understood grammatically as follows:

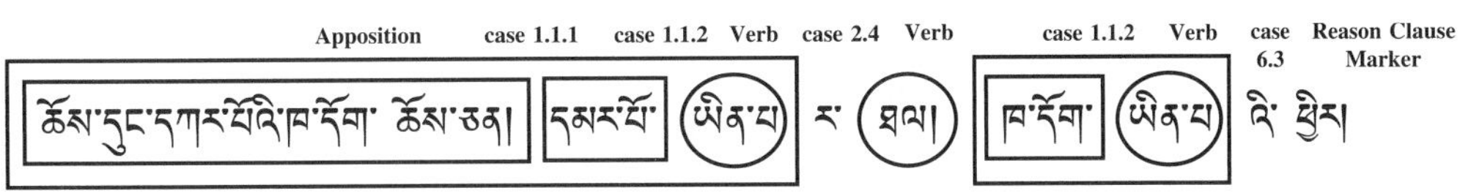

Here, the thesis occurs as the complement of the verb ཐལ་. The translation of the sentence thus reads: "It follows that the subject, the color of a white conch shell, is red, because of [being] a color."

WHAT TO REMEMBER

A consequence is one of a limited number of grammatical constructions that does not end with a verb but rather ends with the marker of a reason clause. It takes the form: **A**...ཆོས་ཅན། **B**...ཐལ། **C**...ཕྱིར། ("It follows that the subject, A, is B because of C.").

⑧ Formulaic Expression: ཁྱབ་པ་ཁས།

Page 185, Line 19

The phrase ཁྱབ་པ་ཁས། is a formulaic expression that occurs in logical debate meaning "[You] asserted the pervasion." It is an abbreviation of the full sentence: ཁྱབ་པ་ཁས་བླངས་པ་རེད།, where ཁས་ (literally, "by [one's] mouth") is the first half of the verbal collocation (see མདོ་མཛངས་བླུན་ note 21) ཁས་ལེན་ (where the verb ལེན་ means "to take (up)"), and hence means "to assert."

WHAT TO REMEMBER

Many disciplines and fields of knowledge have technical terminology and formulaic expressions. They are idiosyncratic and must simply be memorized. ཁྱབ་པ་ཁས། is one such example, meaning "[You] asserted the pervasion."

⑨ The Syntactic Particle དང་

Page 185, Line 21

The reason clause of this consequence introduces the expression དང་གཅིག. Although དང་ is often thought of as the Tibetan equivalent of the English conjunction "and," its use here—and subsequently with constructions like དང་ཐ་དད་ and དང་བཅས་པ་—demonstrates its actual identity as a syntactic particle. Wilson (674) describes the use of the syntactic particle དང་ in this context as functioning in a similar manner to its use with Class IV verbs. Rather than marking the qualifier of a verb (as it does in those instances), here the particle དང་ functions as a marker (a *post*position) used to indicate the adjective in question. Hence, ཁ་དོག་དང་གཅིག is read not as "color *and* one," but rather as "one *with* color," and similarly ཁ་དོག་དང་ཐ་དད། is read not as "color *and* different," but rather as "different *from* color."

WHAT TO REMEMBER

Tibetan particles can convey different meanings depending on their usage in different contexts. Just as the English preposition "in" usually implies containment or location but takes on a different sense in the phrase "in addition," so too the Tibetan particle དང་ often conveys the meaning "and" but can also mean "from," "to," or "with," depending on context.

Anaphora in Consequences: མ་ཁྱབ་ and དེ་

⑩

Page 186, Line 4

Here, the simple pronoun དེ་ is being used in lieu of an explicit statement of the components of the argument. The hypothetical defender having given the reply of མ་ཁྱབ། ("There is no pervasion"), the challenger states the pervasion as the predicate of the consequence དེ་ལ་ཁྱབ་པ་ཡོད་པར་ཐལ། ("It follows that there is pervasion with respect to that"). Since the response of "no pervasion" was given in reply to the statement སངས་རྒྱས་ཚེ་དཔག་མེད་ཀྱི་ཁ་དོག་ཆོས་ཅན། ཁ་དོག་ཡིན་པར་ཐལ། མདོག་ཏུ་རུང་བ་ཡིན་པའི་ཕྱིར། ("It follows that the subject, the color of the Buddha Amitāyus, is a color because of being suitable as a hue"), the student is expected to know that the pervasion being referred to is that of the predicate by the reason—that is, མ་ཁྱབ་ན། དེ་ལ་ཁྱབ་པ་ཡོད་པར་ཐལ། should be understood as meaning: [མདོག་ཏུ་རུང་བ་ཡིན་ན། ཁ་དོག་ཡིན་པས་] མ་ཁྱབ་ན། [ཁ་དོག་] ལ་ [མདོག་ཏུ་རུང་བ་ཡིན་པས་] ཁྱབ་པ་ཡོད་པར་ཐལ། མདོག་ཏུ་རུང་བ་ཁ་དོག་གི་མཚན་ཉིད་ཡིན་པའི་ཕྱིར།—"If [you say] 'There is no pervasion [that if something is suitable as a hue, then it is a color],' then [we respond,] 'It follows that there is pervasion with respect to [color, by being suitable as a hue] because suitable as a hue is the definition of color."

WHAT TO REMEMBER

There is an internal logic to the structure of a consequence that the two parties in a debate are expected to understand. Given a consequence of the form:

A ཆོས་ཅན། **B** ཡིན་པར་ཐལ། **C** ཡིན་པའི་ཕྱིར།

the pervasion of **C** by **B** is assumed to be understood. If the defender in the debate challenges the truth of the pervasion by saying མ་ཁྱབ།, that is,

C ཡིན་ན། **B** ཡིན་པས་མ་ཁྱབ།

then that pervasion forms the predicate of the next consequence, forcing the challenger to provide a new reason:

B ལ། **C** ཡིན་པས་ཁྱབ་པར་ཐལ། **D** ཡིན་པའི་ཕྱིར།

and so on in the debate until the defender gives a different reply.

11

Translation Hint: Established Bases & Conceptual Isolates

Page 186, Lines 6 and 7

The technical terms གཞི་གྲུབ་ and ལྡོག་པ་ do not receive full treatment until chapters two and three of Purbujok's text; nonetheless they are used here and elsewhere in the text without explanation. Although a complete explanation of the categories of established bases (*āśraya-siddhi*) and conceptual isolates (*vyāvṛtti*, *vyatireka*) is beyond the scope of a textual annotation, in brief, they can be understood as follows.

Established Bases

A general mark of Buddhist philosophical systems is that they assert a doctrine of selflessness (*anātmatā; bdag med pa nyid*) even if variously defined. Consequently, in constructing an ontology, the most encompassing category that can be posited is "the selfless," or "that which lacks a self." This category can be subdivided into the existent (*sat; yod pa*) and the nonexistent (*asat; med pa*). For obvious reasons, it is easy to understand that nonexistents lack a self, but equally so, such a realization is trivial in nature. Rather, it is the realization that what is thought to have a self—those things that exist—actually lacks a self that is considered a soteriologically significant realization. In other words, to realize that something lacks a self, that selflessness must be realized in reference to a valid basis. Hence, the category of established bases refers to precisely such objects: those *bases* of selflessness that have been validly *established* as existent.

Conceptual Isolates

The category of conceptual isolates is related to the idea of established bases but is somewhat more complex. As with established bases, conceptual isolates are also posited in reference to selflessness.

The Buddhist idea of selflessness is often presented in reference to the post-Vedic ("Hindu") notion of a self (Skt. *ātman*). Similar in nature to Plato's unchanging world of ideal forms (although possessing the changeable qualities of sentience, etc.), the notion of a self was considered seriously flawed by Buddhist philosophers. Based on the idea that observable phenomena are instances of universal ideals, this theory of reality suffers from what is called a proliferation of universals. That is, if a world of permanent and unchanging ideal forms is posited as existing, it very quickly becomes difficult to limit their number, since every commonly shared property soon becomes a candidate for a permanently existing universal that can be instantiated by particular individual entities. The formulation of a Buddhist-compatible explanation of commonly shared features among observable phenomena—without making recourse to universal ideas (a form of a self)—was taken up by Dignāga (ca. 480–540 C.E.) and Dharmakīrti (ca. 600 C.E.).

In keeping with the idea of selflessness, Dignāga and Dharmakīrti argued that only individual particular (*viśeṣa; bye brag*) phenomena were real, and that presumed universals (*sāmānya; spyi*) were not. Their explanation of the apparent existence of shared properties between these particulars was made in reference to the idea of double negation or exclusion (*apoha; sel ba*). Simply stated, the presumed existence of apparently shared properties is false; no such shared properties, in fact, exist. Rather, the appearance to the mind of properties shared between particulars can be attributed to the natural functioning of the mind, which artificially constructs categories in order to group things together, and does so by excluding (*sel*) items that seem different from each conceptual category.

Thus, since every individual thing is unique, it is isolated from all other similar and dissimilar things. As Perdue (1992, 416) observed, "It is the nature of any phenomenon that merely by its existence it is a negation of what is not it. A phenomenon exists in contradistinction to what is not it, for it alone is one with itself." The implications of this are that (1) a phenomenon is only one with itself, (2) it is not different from itself, and (3) it is isolated from all that is not one with it. On this basis, the philosophical tradition posits the category of isolates (*vyāvṛtti, vyatireka; ldog pa*)—that "factor that is a negation of not-being-something [and which exists] in addition to that thing" (*khyod gyi steng tu khyod ma yin pa'i dgag pa'i cha*)—a category that includes the thing itself, its definition, its generality, etc. The significance of this is that when an object is validly perceived, it does so together with all of its uncommon characteristics, whereas isolates, which are permanent, appear to thought consciousnesses in a general way and that appearance is imputed by the thought consciousness. Hence, although an established base is its own isolate, the two remain distinct.

Despite the complicated nature of these two terms, their use in this debate is less about their philosophical implications than about their logical value in formulating a tautological argument that the defender has no choice but to accept. Since it is a premise of the entire philosophical system that if something is an established base, it is necessarily its own isolate, because each is one with itself and only itself, the introduction of an isolate into the debate places the focus on just that phenomenon itself that is one with itself, forming an irrefutable assertion.

More is said about established bases and isolates in subsequent chapters of Purbujok's text. For a detailed discussion of these topics, however, refer to Perdue (1992), Dreyfus (1997), and Siderits et al. (2011).

12 Anaphora in Consequences: ཁྱོད་

Page 186, Line 7

Here, the relative pronoun ཁྱོད་ is introduced. Used in debate texts as a marker referring back to the logical subject of a statement, ཁྱོད་ can be translated variously as "that," "it," or "its own." The use of the pronoun ཁྱོད་, however, is not random and is entailed by a very specific aspect of both logical debate and the Tibetan language.

In general, the Tibetan language is indeterminate in the quantification of nouns. For example, the word བུམ་པ་ ("pot") can be taken to mean "*a* pot," "*the* pot," or "*pots,*" depending on context; similarly the word མི་རྟག་པ་ may mean "impermanence" or "that which is impermanent." In the formulation of a syllogism or a consequence, the quantification of a subject as either a general category ("all pots") or a particular ("a pot") is not always given. For example, in the consequence སྒྲ་ཆོས་ཅན། མི་རྟག་པ་ཡིན་པར་ཐལ། བྱས་པ་ཡིན་པའི་ཕྱིར། ("The subject, sound, is an impermanent [phenomenon] because of being a product"), it is true that the subject, sound, can be generalized to mean "all sounds"; however, such is not always the case (as in the present example), and technically all subjects are to be understood as only singular phenomena.

The consequence given here—སངས་རྒྱས་ཚེ་དཔག་མེད་ཀྱི་ཁ་དོག་ཆོས་ཅན། ཁྱོད་ཁྱོད་ཀྱི་ལྡོག་པ་ཡིན་པར་ཐལ། ཁྱོད་གཞི་གྲུབ་པའི་ཕྱིར།—is an instance where the subject (the Buddha Amitāyus) cannot be generalized, and so in order to state a logical argument in a generalized (i.e., valid) form, the pronoun ཁྱོད་ is used instead. Therefore, although སངས་རྒྱས་ཚེ་དཔག་མེད་ཀྱི་ཁ་དོག་ཆོས་ཅན། is the logical subject of the debate, grammatically speaking it can only be the *topic* of the debate, while ཁྱོད་ is the grammatical subject of the verb ཡིན་ and ཁྱོད་ཀྱི་ལྡོག་པ་, its predicate:

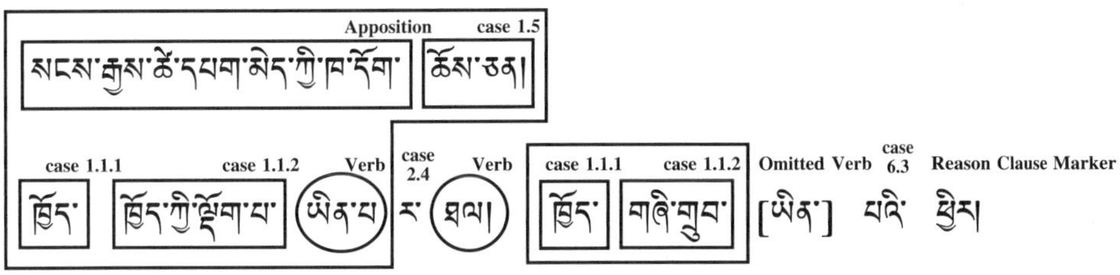

Hence, the consequence would be translated as: "It follows with respect to the subject, the color of the Buddha Amitāyus, that it is its own isolate because it is an established base." (This point is discussed at length in Perdue 1992, 85–88 and 228–230.)

WHAT TO REMEMBER

The pronoun ཁྱོད་ is used for a generalized subject of a debate in which the initial subject put forth cannot be taken as a category of objects.

13

Anaphora in Consequences: Restatement with དེ་

Page 186, Line 9

Starting with this third debate, the text begins using the simple pronoun དེ་ for the subject, predicate, and reason—where appropriate—presuming that the student is now familiar with the structure of a consequence and the procedure of debate.

In this debate, the opening statement of a pervasion gives the position of a hypothetical opponent: ཁ་དོག་ཡིན་ན། སེར་པོ་ཡིན་པས་ཁྱབ།. The challenger responds by stating a counterexample, ཨིནྡྲ་ནི་ལའི་ཁ་དོག་ཆོས་ཅན།—"the subject, the color of a sapphire," using the Sanskrit name for sapphire, *indranīla* (ཨིནྡྲ་ནི་ལ་—for a discussion of the Tibetan procedure of transliterating Sanskrit words, see ཤེས་རབ་སྙིང་པོ་ note 2). This is then followed by a restatement of the terms of the original pervasion as part of the challenger's presentation of the absurd consequence of the opponent's position. Since no new information is given, this is stated simply as: དེར་ཐལ། དེའི་ཕྱིར།—which the reader/audience is assumed to understand as སེར་པོ་ཡིན་པར་ཐལ། ཁ་དོག་ཡིན་པའི་ཕྱིར།.

WHAT TO REMEMBER

The relative pronoun དེ་ is used for the terms of a debate considered understood.

14

Anaphora in Consequences: རྟགས་མ་གྲུབ་ and དེ་

Page 186, Line 9

As with the previous consequence, this sentence uses the simple pronoun དེ་ for the understood components, here, the subject and predicate. Since the response given by the hypothetical defender is "[the reason] is not established" ([རྟགས་] མ་གྲུབ།), the structure of the challenger's response is predetermined. Since the defender calls into question the validity of the reason in relation to the subject, the subject and reason given in the first consequence become the subject and predicate to be proven in the new consequence. Hence, དེ་ཆོས་ཅན། དེར་ཐལ། should be understood as meaning ཨིནྡྲ་ནི་ལའི་ཁ་དོག་ཆོས་ཅན། ཁ་དོག་ཡིན་པར་ཐལ།, with the new reason རྩ་བའི་ཁ་དོག་ཡིན་པའི་ཕྱིར།.

WHAT TO REMEMBER

There is an internal logic to the structure of a consequence that the two parties in a debate are expected to understand. Given a consequence of the form:

A ཆོས་ཅན། **B** ཡིན་པར་ཐལ། **C** ཡིན་པའི་ཕྱིར།

where C justifies A being predicated as B. If the defender in the debate challenges the truth of this by saying རྟགས་མ་གྲུབ།, that is,

A C ཡིན་པ་རྟགས་མ་གྲུབ།

then that pair of statements forms the subject and predicate of the next consequence, forcing the challenger to provide a new reason:

A ཆོས་ཅན། **C** ཡིན་པར་ཐལ། **D** ཡིན་པའི་ཕྱིར།

and so on in the debate until the defender gives a different reply.

The Rhetorical Syntactic Particles ཏེ་, དེ་, and སྟེ་ 15

Page 186, Line 20

This reason clause demonstrates the use of the syntactic particle ཏེ་ within a rhetorical context. Used in a more broad manner than their formal function in a syllogism (see རིགས་ལམ་ note 16), but not completely unrestricted, these particles imply the simple continuation of a narrative in a rhetorical sense. Here, it announces the coming of a second reason explaining the first.

WHAT TO REMEMBER

The rhetorical syntactic particles ཏེ་, དེ་, and སྟེ་ are used to convey the continuation of a thought or narrative. They can often be translated in a simple manner indicating that continuation (i.e., "and hence, ...") or in a manner similar to a gerund phrase (i.e., "having done ...").

16

The Structure of a Syllogism

Page 186, Line 22

This sentence is a syllogism (*prayoga; sbyor ba*), the other most common construction to be found in philosophical Buddhist texts. Just as with a consequence (see རིགས་ལམ་ note 7), as a complete sentence a syllogism likewise does not end with a verb but rather with a reason clause. A syllogism takes the form of a statement predicating a property to a subject ("such-and-such is something ...") followed by a rhetorical syntactic particle (ཏེ་, དེ་, or སྟེ་ depending on euphony rules), followed by a reason clause ("... because of a certain resean.") marked by the syntactic particle ཕྱིར་. In the instance given here, there is an abbreviated initial statement (ཁྱབ་སྟེ།) and a complex reason clause, but the basic structure of the syllogism remains the same.

WHAT TO REMEMBER

A syllogism is a grammatical construction in the form of ...སྟེ། ...ཕྱིར།; that is, it is composed of a statement predicating a property to a subject followed by a rhetorical syntactic particle (ཏེ་, དེ་, or སྟེ་) followed by a reason clause marked by the syntactic particle ཕྱིར་.

17

Distributed Verbs in a Parallel Construction

Page 186, Line 22

The reason clause in this syllogism is made up of several sentences in sequence, albeit with several omitted words. Because the basic structure of each sentence is identical, the author has utilized the parallel nature of the grammar for brevity. Rather than repeating the same verbal construction for each sentence, he has provided a grammatically complete sentence only for the last portion of the reason clause. Hence, when the text states སྔོ་སེར་འདྲེས་པ་ལས་ལྗང་ཁུ། དམར་སེར་འདྲེས་པ་ལས་ལི་ཁྲི། དམར་སྔོན་འདྲེས་པ་ལས་ནག་པོར་འཇོག་པའི་ཕྱིར།, it should be understood that the Class V verb འཇོག་ distributes to the two previous (otherwise grammatically incomplete) "sentences" along with a second-case particle marking the complement in the sentence:

སྔོ་སེར་འདྲེས་པ་ལས་ལྗང་ཁུ [ར་འཇོག་པ་དང་]།

དམར་སེར་འདྲེས་པ་ལས་ལི་ཁྲི [ར་འཇོག་པ་དང་]།

དམར་སྔོན་འདྲེས་པ་ལས་ནག་པོར་འཇོག་པའི་ཕྱིར།

where the grammar of the final sentence:

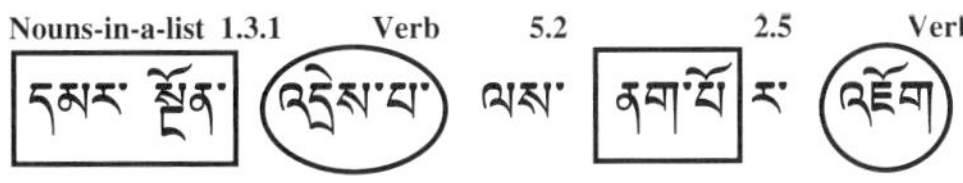

should be understood as applying to all three sentences. Thus, the syllogism can be translated as: "[Being a secondary color] is pervaded [by not being a primary color], because from a mixture of blue and yellow [the result is posited as] green, [and] from a mixture of red and yellow [the result is posited as] orange, [and] from a mixture of red and blue [the result] is posited as black."

WHAT TO REMEMBER

Within a grammatically constrained environment (such as a syllogism or the lines of a verse) parallel grammatical constructions can be exploited to eliminate repetitious elements in sequential sentences. Omitted elements are often verbs but occasionally can be other components such as complements, as well.

The Expression གང་ཞིག 18

Page 187, Line 5

The Tibetan expression གང་ཞིག can serve different functions depending on the context in which it occurs. In general, it functions as an indefinite pronoun meaning "whichever," "whatsoever," or "whomever" (much like གང་རུང་ "whichever is suitable" occurring later in the text). In the context of debate rhetoric, however, it often signifies the first part of a reason—as it does here—and hence the construction …གང་ཞིག …ཕྱིར། can be loosely translated as "because ..., and because ..."

WHAT TO REMEMBER

The expression གང་ཞིག་ when occurring in a debate marks the first part of a reason in a reason clause; otherwise, it functions as an indefinite pronoun.

19

Translation Hint

Page 187, Line 15

Recall (ཤེར་སྙིང་རྣམ་བཤད་ note 24) that a gerundive (or future passive participle) is formed by nominalizing the optative/emphatic future construction—*verb* + པར་བྱ་ (see ཤེས་རབ་སྙིང་པོ་ note 11)—producing a *verb* + པར་བྱ་བ་ construction. Here, the reason clause of this consequence contains a gerundive in its abbreviated form, བཟུང་བྱ་ (as with other object nouns, formed from the past-tense form of the verb—see ཤེར་སྙིང་རྣམ་བཤད་ note 12—in this case, འཛིན་, "to hold" or "to grasp"). Hence, it can be translated literally as "that which is to be held" but is more commonly translated simply as "object of apprehension." Here, the phrase མིག་ཤེས་ཀྱི་བཟུང་བྱ་ can be translated as "object of apprehension of an eye consciousness." This construction is frequently used, giving rise to numerous commonly occurring gerundive noun phrases such as ཤེས་བྱ་ "object of knowledge," ཤལ་བྱ་ "object of comprehension," སྤང་བྱ་ "object of abandonment," etc.

20

Explicit Subject Marking with Omitted Verbs

Page 187, Line 20

In this section of the text, "Positing Our Own System" (*rang lugs gzhag*), almost all the statements are simple declarative sentences, syllogisms, or the two in combination. Here, the passage གཟུགས་དང་བེམ་པོ་གཉིས་དོན་གཅིག is an example of a simple declarative sentence. Because there is no ambiguity concerning its import, the final verb of predication, ཡིན་, has been omitted and the two noun phrases ("form and matter, the two" and "equivalent") are stated simply with the predication being implied.

A few lines down in the text, a similar series of statements occurs as the second half of a two-part reason to the syllogism that begins དེ་ལ་དབྱེ་ན་བརྒྱད་ཡོད་དེ། spelling out the divisions (དབྱེ་བ་) of "shape" (དབྱིབས་). The second half of the reason clause utilizes a similar series of simple declarative sentences omitting the verb ཡིན་. Here, however, because the grammar of these phrases could be misinterpreted as a list, the subject and predicate are delimited by the use of the syntactic particle ནི་ demarcating the subject, as in ལྷམ་པ་ནི་གྲུབ་བཞི། ("a square [is that which has] four corners"), etc.

> WHAT TO REMEMBER
>
> Simple statements of predication ("A is B") often occur as self-contained phrases of two items with the subject marked off by ནི་ and the verb ཡིན་ omitted.

Verbs that take Sentences as their Complements: རུང་ 21

Page 187, Line 23

The verb རུང་ has occurred several times in this text and previous ones in which something has been described as "suitable as" something else. Here, however, the verb རུང་ is being used differently. The verb རུང་ is one of several verbs in Tibetan that can take a second verb or sentence as its complement. Here, བསྟན་ is not the noun "teaching" but rather the future form of the Class V verb སྟོན་ ("to teach" or "to indicate") with its own complement, དབྱིབས་. Hence, the entire sentence can be translated—when nominalized with a pronoun, as it is here—as "[that which is] suitable to be indicated as a shape." This use of རུང་ is common in many definitions.

> WHAT TO REMEMBER
>
> Several verbs in Tibetan often take a second verb or sentence as their object. The verb རུང་ is one such verb; some others are དཀའ་, རིགས་, etc.

Sentences in a List 22

Page 188, Line 3

This sentence is a complex syllogism that spells out the divisions (དབྱེ་བ་) of "shape"

(དབྱིབས་). While the thesis and first reason clause are fairly standard for a syllogism (the reason clause listing eight items—the last two identified through the use of the summation postpositional phrase ···དང་བཅས་པ་ "together with ..."; see རིགས་ལམ་ note 9), the second reason clause is grammatically different. In this second reason clause (as with the one discussed above, see རིགས་ལམ་ note 17), Purbujok has provided a list of sentences which augment the reason given in the preceding clause. These sentences (as mentioned in the previous note), however, are instances of simple predication ("A is B") and omit their final verb, ཡིན་. Thus, the clause can be thought of as:

> ལྷམ་པ་ནི་གྲུ་བཞི་ [ཡིན་པ་དང་།]
> ཟླུམ་པོ་ནི་གོར་མོའམ་ཧྲིལ་པོ་ [ཡིན་པ་དང་།]
> ཕྲ་ལེ་བ་ནི་ངོས་མཉམ་པའི་དབྱིབས་ [ཡིན་པ་] ལྟ་བུ་ལ་བྱེད་རིགས་པའི་ཕྱིར།

Concluded by the explicit Class III verb རིགས་, "to be suitable," and the verbal expression ལྟ་བུ་ལ་བྱེད་, "to give as an example," the entire passage can be translated as "... and because [it] is suitable to give as examples a square [being that which has] four corners, a round [shape being that which is] circular or spherical, [and] a level [shape being] the shape of an even surface."

WHAT TO REMEMBER

As with parallel constructions (རིགས་ལམ་ note 17), in a grammatically constrained environment simple statements of predication ("A is B") can occur as items in a list.

23 Statement of a Philosophical Definition

Page 188, Line 4

As with the sentences noted above (see རིགས་ལམ་ note 20), the passage encountered here, མདོག་དུ་བསྟན་དུ་རུང་བ། ཁ་དོག་གི་མཚན་ཉིད།, is in essence a simple declarative statement. Because Buddhist literature on the whole deals with precise concepts in the theory and practice of religious reflection, the vast majority of words encountered in these texts are technical terms with very specific meanings. Consequently, a common feature of Tibetan Buddhist texts is the high frequency of definitions (and debates over the definitions) of technical terminology.

This sentence is simple in structure with the subject and predicate clearly marked as two delimited phrases. The predicate, ཁ་དོག་གི་མཚན་ཉིད།, is a simple phrase ("the definition of color"). The subject is slightly more complex and is a nominalized sentence (see ཤེས་རབ་སྙིང་པོ་ note 22) based on the verb རུང་ (see རིགས་ལམ་ note 21). For now, it is sufficient to understand that the phrase can be rendered as "that which is suitable (རུང་བ་) to be indicated (བསྟན་) as a hue (མདོག་)."

> WHAT TO REMEMBER
>
> Whenever the word མཚན་ཉིད་ occurs at the end of a phrase—even without an ornamental terminator (e.g., མཚན་ཉིད་དོ།)—it is reasonable to expect མཚན་ཉིད་ to form the end of a simple statement of predication ("A [is] the definition of B").

Contextually Implied Anaphora 24

Page 188, Line 9

Although the instances of anaphora discussed in the context of consequences (see རིགས་ལམ་ notes 10, 12, 13, and 14) all occurred with explicit pronouns, here is an instance in a syllogism where not even a pronoun is provided and yet a referent is contextually implied. Here the syllogism reads:

སྒྲ་ལ་དབྱེ་ན་གཉིས་ཡོད་དེ།
ཟིན་པའི་འབྱུང་བ་ལས་གྱུར་པའི་སྒྲ་དང་།
མ་ཟིན་པའི་འབྱུང་བ་ལས་གྱུར་པའི་སྒྲ་གཉིས་ཡོད་པའི་ཕྱིར།

As can be seen from the two reason clauses of the syllogism, the Class IV verb ཟིན་ ("to be conjoined [with]") is missing its qualifier—that is, the answer to the question "conjoined with what?" Although one would like to see these read དེ་དང་ཟིན་པ་ ("conjoined with that") and དེ་དང་མ་ཟིན་པ་ ("not conjoined with that"), the problem is that the precise referent of such a pronoun was not previously stated. The previous syllogism:

སྒྲའི་སྐྱེ་མཆེད་ཀྱི་མཚན་ཉིད་ཡོད་དེ། རྣ་ཤེས་ཀྱི་ཉན་བྱ་དེ་དེ་ཡིན་པའི་ཕྱིར།

posits the definition of "sound sense-sphere" (སྒྲའི་སྐྱེ་མཆེད་) in reference to an "ear consciousness" (རྣ་ཤེས་); that is, the phenomena that impinge on one's auditory senses are described in reference to that sense power and its associated moments of consciousness. The syllogism under examination here, however, discusses the sounds (སྒྲ་) themselves in reference to their originating elements (འབྱུང་བ་), not their perception. Consequently, reference to an "ear consciousness" would make no sense in this context. By analogy (or "context"), however, one can discern that all of these definitions are in reference to some form of consciousness and on that basis infer that the qualifier of the verb ཟིན་ is, in fact, "consciousness" (ཤེས་པ་).

Such omissions are common in the philosophical literature with the expectation that the omitted referents will be discerned through context or familiarity with the oral commentarial tradition.

WHAT TO REMEMBER

Not all instances of anaphora are indicated with explicit pronouns. Instead, the referent of omitted sentence elements is occasionally only contextually implied.

25 འགྱུར་ / གྱུར་ as Verbs and Verbal Nouns

Page 188, Line 14

This sentence is a standard syllogism but has some subtle grammar in its reason clause. The reason clause cites the two divisions of "tangible objects" (རེག་བྱ་): འབྱུང་བར་གྱུར་པའི་རེག་བྱ་དང་། འབྱུང་འགྱུར་གྱི་རེག་བྱ།. The difference between these two hinges on the use of the verb འགྱུར་.

In the first phrase, གྱུར་ (the past tense of the Class III verb འགྱུར་) is employed as a verb (meaning "to be," "to come," "to become," or "to serve (as)"). This function is indicated by the presence of a clause-connective construction (Wilson, case 6.6.1) following it:

The phrase consequently can be translated as "a tangible object that is an element" (see Wilson, 483–484).

The second phrase, however, is employing འགྱུར་ not as a verb (as indicated by the connective particle ཀྱི་—not used with verbs) but rather as a nominalized verb (a verbal noun). As a Class III verb, འགྱུར་ has a range of meanings (as noted above), but as a noun འགྱུར་ conveys the meaning of "that which comes." Hence, the phrase འབྱུང་འགྱུར་ should be understood as འབྱུང་བ་ལས་འགྱུར་པ་ "that which comes from the elements" (*bhautika* in Sanskrit). (There are specific protocols for the formation of nouns from verbs—particularly with regard to the tense of the verb; these are discussed in ཤེར་སྙིང་རྣམ་བཤད་ note 12 and རིགས་ལམ་ note 19)

The entire syllogism, therefore, can be translated as "When tangible objects are divided, there are two, because there are the two: tangible objects that are the elements and tangible objects arisen [from] the elements." Although འབྱུང་འགྱུར་ is a sufficiently significant technical term (coming out of Abhidharma, or "Manifest Knowledge," studies) that better Tibetan dictionaries would contain it as an entry, learning etymologies of technical terms can be useful when encountering less commonly seen terms.

WHAT TO REMEMBER

Nearly every domain and genre of Tibetan literature—religious or otherwise—contains idiosyncratic sentence structures and technical terminology. Until one is fully versed in the vocabulary of a particular subject and style of a genre of literature, one needs to be especially careful when encountering verbs and verbal derivatives, paying particular attention to case markers for clues to their use.

26

Nested Conditional Sentences

Page 188, Line 21

Here, at the start of the རྩོད་པ་སྤོང་བ་ "Dispelling Objections [to Our Own System]" section of the text, Purbujok deviates slightly from the standard debate format since his role as the textbook author is now that of defender rather than challenger. Here he opens this first debate by considering a challenger both making a claim and giving their own preemptive reply to a response.

As with all Tibetan sentences, the strategy for deciphering this sentence is the same: reading from the beginning of the sentence, first locate the terminal verb and work inward. From the occurrence of ཁ་ཅིག་ན་རེ། at the inception of the sentence, we know (རིགས་ལམ་ note 6) to expect a basic ཁ་ཅིག་ན་རེ། ...ཟེར་ན། construction, followed by a response—either a consequence, a syllogism, or a simple statement ending in a terminal verb. Although the verb ཟེར་ is omitted, such a construction is indeed seen:

ཁ་ཅིག་ན་རེ། | ཆོས་དང་དཀར་པོ་ཆོས་ཅན། ཁ་དོག་ཡིན་པར་ཐལ། དཀར་པོ་ཡིན་པའི་ཕྱིར། མ་གྲུབ་ན། དེ་ཆོས་ཅན། དེར་ཐལ། ཆོས་དང་དཀར་པོ་ཡིན་པའི་ཕྱིར་ | [ཟེར་] ན།

འགལ་ཁྱབ་ལ་འཕུད།

From this perspective, the nested pair of consequences with a conditional can be seen for what they are: the statement of the hypothetical challenger as a series of consequences, occurring in the expected form (see རིགས་ལམ་ notes 7 and 14).

Having cited this hypothetical challenge, Purbujok then gives his reply. Although the expression འགལ་ཁྱབ་ is a technical term meaning "opposite pervasion," here it is more appropriate to translate it literally in terms of its etymology by recognizing ཁྱབ་ as a Class V verb and འགལ་ as its nominative object (Wilson, case 1.4.1). Hence, Purbujok's response can be translated as "[This] is thrown out as an opposite pervasion," or more felicitously as "[This argument] is dismissed, for [it] entails the opposite [of what you think it does]."

WHAT TO REMEMBER

When encountering multiple conditional phrases, first locate the end of the entire sentence as a whole by identifying its terminal verb, and only then begin analyzing what remains.

"The Presentation of the Introductory Path of Reasoning" From [the Treatise] *Revealing the Meaning of the Texts on Valid Cognition, Magical Key to the Path of Reasoning*

I bow down to the lamas and to the Protector Mañjuśrī!

Homage to the former scholars and adepts [of the countries] of āryas and Tibet,
The great beings Dignāga, Dharmakīrti, and so forth
Who clarified with valid cognition the path of reasoning which was well spoken
By the Valid Teacher [who] saw the meaning of reality.

Here with respect to explaining *The Presentation of Collected Topics* opening the door to the path of reasoning, [there are] three [divisions]: the explanation of the "Presentation of the Introductory Path of Reasoning," the explanation of the "Presentation of the Middling Path of Reasoning," and the explanation of the "Presentation of the Greater Path of Reasoning."

With regard to the first—"The Explanation of the Presentation of the Colors, Red, White, and so forth" section of "the Introductory Path of Reasoning,"—from among [its] three [sections,] "Refuting [the System of Others]," "Positing [Our Own System]," and "Dispelling [Objections to Our System]," the first [section is]:

[Section One: Refuting the Systems of Others]

[***Debate 1, First Mistaken View***]

If someone says, "Whatever is a color is necessarily red," then [we respond,] "It [absurdly] follows that the subject, the color of a white religious conch, is red because of being a color; you asserted the pervasion."

If he says, "The reason is not established," then [we respond,] "It follows that the subject, the color of a white religious conch, is a color because of being white."

If he says, "The reason is not established," then [we respond,] "It follows that the subject, the color of a white religious conch, is white because of being one with the color of a white religious conch."

If he accepts the basic consequence, then [we respond,] "It follows that the subject, the color of a white religious conch, is not red because of being white."

If he says, "There is no pervasion," then [we respond,] "It follows that there is pervasion, because a common locus of the two, white and red, does not exist; because those two are mutually exclusive."

[*Debate 2, Second Mistaken View*]

If someone says, "Whatever is a color is necessarily white," then [we respond,] "It [absurdly] follows that the subject, the color of the Buddha Amitāyus, is white because of being a color; you asserted the pervasion."

If he says, "The reason is not established," then [we respond,] "It follows that the subject, the color of the Buddha Amitāyus, is a color because of being suitable as a hue."

If he says, "There is no pervasion," then [we respond,] "It follows that there is pervasion, because suitable as a hue is the definition of color."

If he accepts the basic consequence, then [we respond,] "It follows that the subject, the color of the Buddha Amitāyus, is not white because of being red."

If he says, "The reason is not established," then [we respond,] "It follows that the subject, the color of the Buddha Amitāyus, is red because of being the isolate of the color of the Buddha Amitāyus."

If he says, "The reason is not established," then [we respond,] "It follows with respect to the subject, the color of the Buddha Amitāyus, that it is its own isolate because it is an established base."

[*Debate 3, Third Mistaken View*]

If someone says, "Whatever is a color is necessarily yellow," then [we respond,] "It [absurdly] follows that the subject, the color of a sapphire, is [yellow] because of [being a color]; you asserted the pervasion."

If he says, "The reason is not established," then [we respond,] "It follows that the subject, that [color of a sapphire], is that [i.e., a color] because of being a primary color."

If he says, "The reason is not established," then [we respond,] "It follows that the subject, [the color of a sapphire], is [a primary color] because of being one of the four—blue, yellow, white, and red."

If he accepts the basic consequence, then [we respond,] "It follows that the subject, [the color of a sapphire,] is not yellow because of being blue." [If he says, "There is no pervasion," then we respond,] "There is pervasion, because the two, blue and yellow, are mutually exclusive."

[*Debate 4, Fourth Mistaken View*]

If someone says, "Whatever is a color is necessarily blue," then [we respond,] "It [absurdly] follows that the subject, the color of refined gold, is [blue] because of [being a color]; you asserted the pervasion."

If he says, "The reason is not established," then [we respond,] "It follows that the subject, that [color of refined gold], is that [i.e., a color] because of being an instance of color."

If he accepts the basic consequence, then [we respond,] "It follows that the subject, [the color of refined gold,] is not blue because of being yellow."

If he says, "The reason is not established," then [we respond,] "It follows that the subject, [the color of refined gold,] is yellow because of being the color of refined gold."

If he says, "The reason is not established," then [we respond,] "It follows that the color of refined gold is the color of refined gold because the color of refined gold exists."

[*Debate 5, Fifth Mistaken View*]

If someone says, "Whatever is a color is necessarily a primary color," then [we respond,] "It [absurdly] follows that the subject, the color of green Amoghasiddhi, is [a primary color] because of [being a color; you asserted the pervasion]."

If he says, "The reason is not established," then [we respond,] "It follows that the subject, [the color of green Amoghasiddhi,] is [a color] because of being that subject."

If he accepts the basic consequence, then [we respond,] "It follows that the subject, [the color of green Amoghasiddhi,] is not a primary color because of being a secondary color. It follows that [the color of green Amoghasiddhi is a secondary color] because of being the secondary color composed of the two, blue and yellow."

[If he says, "There is no pervasion," then we respond,] "It follows that the subject, [the color of green Amoghasiddhi, is the secondary color composed of the two, blue and yellow] because of being green, and hence, because of being the color which is a mixture of blue and yellow.

"There is pervasion, because a mixture of blue and yellow is posited as green, a mixture of red and yellow is posited as orange, and a mixture of red and blue is posited as black."

[***Debate 6, Sixth Mistaken View***]

If someone says, "Whatever is a secondary color is necessarily one of the eight secondary colors," then [we respond,] "It [absurdly] follows that the subject, the color of orange Mañjughoṣa, is one of the eight secondary colors because of being a secondary color; you asserted the pervasion."

If he says, "The reason is not established," then [we respond,] "It follows that the subject, the color of orange Mañjughoṣa, is a secondary color because of being a secondary color composed of the two, red and yellow."

If he accepts the basic consequence, then [we respond,] "It follows that the subject, [the color of orange Mañjughoṣa,] is not any of the eight secondary colors, because of not being any of the four colors—cloud, smoke, dust, and mist; and also not being any of the four colors—illumination, darkness, shadow, and sunlight."

"The reasons are established individually because of being one with the color of orange Mañjughoṣa."

[***Debate 7, Seventh Mistaken View***]

[If someone says, "Whatever is a form is necessarily a shape-form," then we respond,] "It [absurdly] follows that the subject, a color-form, is that [i.e., a shape-form] because of that [i.e., being a form]; you asserted the pervasion."

If he says, “The reason is not established,” then [we respond,] “It follows that the subject, [a color-form,] is [a form] because of being matter.”

If he says, “The reason is not established,” then [we respond,] “It follows that the subject, [a color-form,] is [matter] because of being atomically established.”

If he accepts the basic consequence, then [we respond,] “It follows that the subject, [a color-form,] is not a shape-form because of being one with a color-form.”

If he says, “The reason is not established,” then [we respond,] “It follows with respect to the subject, [a color-form,] that it is one with itself because it is an existent.”

[*Debate 8, Eighth Mistaken View*]

If someone says, “Whatever is a form is necessarily a color-form,” then [we respond,] “It [absurdly] follows that the subject, a round form, is [a color-form] because of [being a form]; you asserted the pervasion.”

If he says, “The reason is not established,” then [we respond,] “It follows that the subject, [a round form,] is [a form] because of being a form sense-sphere.”

If he says, “The reason is not established,” then [we respond,] “It follows that the subject, [a round form,] is [a form sense-sphere] because of being an object apprehended by an eye consciousness.”

If he accepts the basic consequence, then [we respond,] “It follows that the subject, [a round form,] is not a color-form because of not being a color. [It follows that] there is pervasion because color-form and color [are mutually inclusive], and the two—shape-form and shape—are mutually inclusive.”

[Section Two: Positing] Our Own System

There is a definition of form because that which is suitable as a form is the definition of a form. The two, form and matter, are mutually inclusive. If forms are divided, there are five: form sense-spheres, sound sense-spheres, odor sense-spheres, taste sense-spheres, and tangible-object sense-spheres.

There is a definition of a form sense-sphere because an object apprehended by an eye consciousness is the definition of a form sense-sphere. If form sense-spheres are divided, there are two because there are the two, shapes and colors.

There is a definition of a shape because that which is suitable to be shown as a shape is the definition of a shape. When [shapes] are divided there are eight, because there are eight all together—long, short, high, low, square, round, level, and nonlevel forms and because [it] is suitable to give as examples a square [being that which has] four corners, a round [shape being that which is] circular or spherical, [and] a level [shape being] the shape of an even surface.

The definition of a color is that which is suitable to be indicated as a hue. If colors are divided, there are two because there are the two, primary colors and secondary colors. If primary colors are divided, there are four because there are the four—blue, yellow, white, and red. If secondary colors are divided, there are eight because there are the eight consisting of the colors of cloud, smoke, dust, mist, illumination, darkness, shadow, and sunlight, which are secondary colors.

There is a definition of a sound sense-sphere because an object heard by an ear consciousness is the definition of a sound sense-sphere. If sounds are divided, there are two because there are the two, sounds caused by elements conjoined [with consciousness] and sounds caused by elements not conjoined [with consciousness].

There is a definition of an odor sense-sphere because an object experienced by a nose consciousness is the definition of an odor sense-sphere. If odors are divided, there are two because there are the two, natural odors and manufactured odors.

There is a definition of a taste sense-sphere because an object experienced by a tongue consciousness is the definition of a taste sense-sphere. If tastes are divided, there are six because there are the six—sweet, sour, bitter, astringent, pungent, and salty.

There is a definition of a tangible-object sense-sphere because an object experienced by a body consciousness is the definition of a tangible-object sense-sphere. If tangible objects are divided, there are two because there are the two, tangible objects that are elements and tangible objects arisen from the elements. If tangible objects that are elements are divided, there are four because the four—earth, water, fire, and wind—are tangible objects that are elements. There is a definition of earth because hard and obstructive is the definition of earth. There is a definition of water because wet and moistening is the definition of water. There is a definition of fire because hot and burning is the definition of fire. There is a definition of wind, because it is "that which is light and moving." If tangible objects arisen from the elements are divided, there are seven because there are the seven consisting of smoothness, roughness, heaviness, lightness, cold, hunger, and thirst, which are tangible objects arisen from the elements.

[Section Three:] Dispelling Objections
[*Debate 9, First Objection*]

Someone might say, "It follows that the subject, a white religious conch, is a color because of being white."

If [another] says that [the reason that a white religious conch is white] is not established, [the hypothetical challenger will respond,] "It follows that the subject [a white religious conch] is [white] because of being a white religious conch."

[To this the Sūtra School defender responds,] "The opposite [of what you assert] is entailed (*'bud*) [by your reason—i.e., whatever is a white religious conch is necessarily not white]; hence [your argument] is excluded [from serious consideration]."

Then [the Sūtra School proponent would become the challenger and fling these consequences] at him: "It [absurdly] follows that the subject, a white horse, is white because of being a white horse. The pervasion is comparable."

"You cannot assert [the consequence that a white horse is white] because of [the subject's] not being matter; because of being a person; because of being a horse."

Furthermore, [there is this fault with the hypothetical opponent's position:] "It [absurdly] follows that the subject, a white religious conch, is a color because of being white. You asserted the reason [that a white religious conch is white]."

If he accepts [that a white religious conch is a color, the Sūtra School challenger responds,] "It follows that the subject [a white religious conch] is not a color because of not being arisen from the elements."

"It follows that [a white religious conch is not arisen from the elements] because of being an element; because of being a white religious conch."

[*Debate 10, Second Objection*]

Also someone [a hypothetical challenger] might say, "It follows that the subject, wind, is arisen from the elements because of being one of the seven tangible objects arisen from the elements."

If [another] says that the reason [that wind is one of the seven tangible objects arisen from the elements] is not established, [the hypothetical challenger will respond,] "It follows that the subject, wind, is one of the seven tangible objects arisen from the elements because of being the tangible-object lightness."

"It follows that [wind is the tangible-object lightness] because of being both a tangible object and light."

[To this the Sūtra School defender responds,] "There is no pervasion [i.e., even though it is true that wind is both a tangible object and light, it is not the case that whatever is both a tangible object and light is necessarily the tangible-object lightness]." Similarly, extend this reasoning also to earth, water, and fire.

[*Debate 11, Third Objection*]

Also someone [a hypothetical challenger] might say, "It follows that the subject, object of knowledge, is a shape because of being any one of the two, level or nonlevel."

[To this the Sūtra School defender responds,] "There is no pervasion [i.e., even though it is true that object of knowledge is any one of the two, level or nonlevel, it is not the case that whatever is one of the two, level or nonlevel, is necessarily a shape]."

Or, if someone were to say that [the reason of the basic consequence, i.e., that object of knowledge is one of the two, level or nonlevel] is not established, [then the Sūtra School proponent would become the challenger and respond to him,] "It follows that the subject, object of knowledge, is any one of the two, level or nonlevel, because of being nonlevel."

If he says that [the reason that object of knowledge is nonlevel] is not established, [then the Sūtra School challenger responds,] "It follows that the subject, object of knowledge, is nonlevel because of not being level."

If someone were to accept the basic consequence [that object of knowledge is a shape, the Sūtra School challenger would respond to him,] "It follows that the subject, object of knowledge, is not a shape because of being a permanent phenomenon."

Jampel Sampel's *Presentation of Awarenesses and Knowers*

The topic of "Awarenesses and Knowers" within the subject of epistemology likewise has its roots in the writings of Dignāga and Dharmakīrti with some elements from the writings of the fourth-century scholar-yogi Asaṅga.[1] As with the other subjects covered in *The Collected Topics*,[2] there are two main lineages of interpretation of "Awarenesses and Knowers" following, likewise, Chaba Chögyi Sengé (*phywa pa chos kyi seng ge*, 1109–1169) and Sakya Paṇḍita Kunga Gyeltsen (*sa skya paṇḍi ta kun dga' rgyal mtshan*, 1182–1251). The lineage of interpretation presented here also follows Chaba.

The "Awarenesses and Knowers" subjects are of principle importance in that they serve as the crux of a major dispute between Chaba and Sakya Paṇḍita. In particular, Sakya Paṇḍita took issue with Chaba's presentation of a sevenfold typology of mental states: direct perception, inferential cognition, subsequent cognition, correct assumption, consciousnesses to which an object appears but is not ascertained, doubt, and mistaken cognition. Sakya Paṇḍita's primary contention was that Chaba's typology lacked textual support in the writings of Dharmakīrti. Although not a major failing in itself, the issue points to a more fundamental split between the two authors concerning the actual operation of perception: the distinction between the bare perception of the sensible qualities of common sense-objects, and the more reified view of the direct perception of the objects themselves. Sakya Paṇḍita, holding to a close textual reading of Dharmakīrti and following the commentary of Devendrabuddhi, held the former view, while Chaba, apparently following the commentaries of Dharmottara and Mokṣākaragupta on the different types of objects of perception, asserted the latter.[3] The view held by the followers of Chaba manifests most clearly in the distinction made between valid direct perception and invalid subsequent perceptual cognitions.

Traditionally, the topics covered in the text presented here serve as the course of study in the main monastic universities for one year. This text by Jampel Sampel (*'jam dpal bsam 'phel*, d.1975), the *Presentation of Awarenesses and Knowers* is also from the textbook genre. Structurally, this work differs slightly from the preceding text in that there are no debates, only an "Our Own System" (*rang lugs*) style presentation of the subject matter.

Jampel Sampel's text, the *Presentation of Awarenesses and Knowers*, covers the basic topics of Chaba's sevenfold typology of mental states and provides an alternate classification of these mental states in terms of: status (valid vs. invalid), type (conceptual vs. nonconceptual), and other qualities. A full outline of the text is provided below.

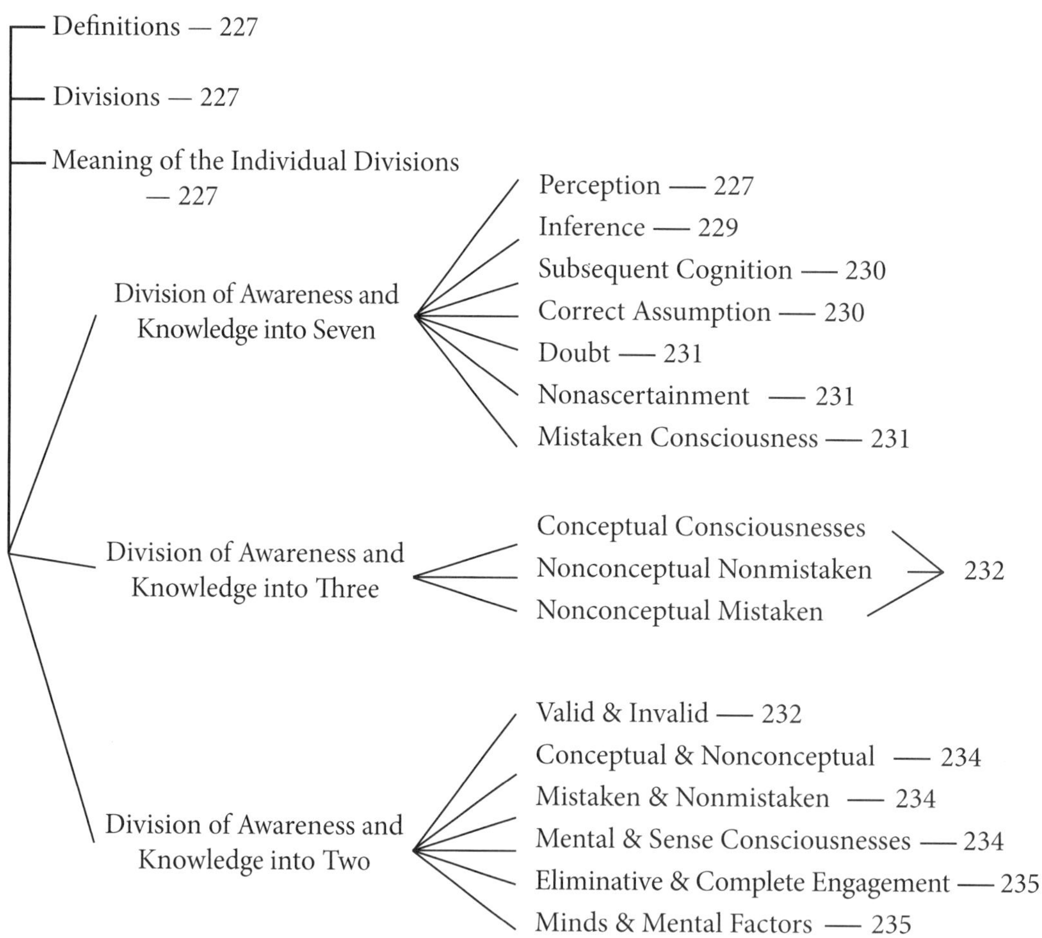

1 Lati Rinbochay and E. Napper 1980, 12.

2 Although published separately by some authors, presentations of "Awarenesses and Knowers" are often included within "Collected Topics" treatises within the "Greater Path of Reasoning" section as is Purbujok's presentation.

3 Georges Dreyfus (1997) explores many of the points of contention between these two lineages. The issue of types of objects and mental states are dealt with in particular in chapters 10, 22, and 23. See also: Klein 1986 and 1991, and Perdue 1992, 411–79.

༄༅། །བློ་རིག་གི་རྣམ་བཞག་ཉེར་མཁོ་ཀུན་འདུས་བློ་གསལ་མིག་འབྱེད་ཅེས་བྱ་བ་བཞུགས་སོ། །[1]

བློ་གཉེར་འཇམ་དཔལ་དབྱངས་ཉིད་བློས་པའི་གར།
བློ་བཟང་གྲགས་པའི་དཔལ་ལ་ཕྱག་འཚལ་ནས།
བློ་རིག་རྣམ་བཞག་ཉེར་མཁོ་ཀུན་འདུས་པ།
བློ་དམན་རིག་པའི་སྣང་བ་རྒྱས་ཕྱིར་སྤེལ།

དེ་ལ་འདིར་བློ་རིག་གི་རྣམ་བཞག་བཤད་པ་ལ་གསུམ། མཚན་ཉིད། དབྱེ་བ། དབྱེ་བ་སོ་སོའི་དོན་བཤད་པའོ།

དང་པོ་ནི། རིག་པ་བློའི་མཚན་ཉིད། གསལ་ཞིང་རིག་པ་ཤེས་པའི་མཚན་ཉིད། བློ་དང་རིག་པ་ཤེས་པ་གསུམ་དོན་གཅིག

གཉིས་པ་དབྱེ་བ་ལ་གསུམ། བློ་རིག་བདུན་དུ་དབྱེ་བ། བློ་རིག་གསུམ་དུ་དབྱེ་བ། བློ་རིག་གཉིས་སུ་དབྱེ་བའོ། དང་པོ་ཡོད་དེ། མངོན་སུམ། རྗེས་དཔག བཅད་ཤེས། ཡིད་དཔྱོད། སྣང་ལ་མ་ངེས། ཐེ་ཚོམ། ལོག་ཤེས་དང་བདུན་ཡོད་པའི་ཕྱིར།

གསུམ་པ་དབྱེ་བ་སོ་སོའི་དོན་ལ་བདུན།

དང་པོ་མངོན་སུམ་བཤད་པ་ལ་མཚན་ཉིད་དང་། དབྱེ་བ་གཉིས། རྟོག་པ་དང་བྲལ་ཞིང་མ་འཁྲུལ་བའི་རིག་པ་མངོན་སུམ་གྱི་མཚན་ཉིད། རྟོག་པ་དང་བྲལ་ཞིང་མ་འཁྲུལ་བའི་གསར་དུ་མི་སླུ་བའི་རིག་པ་མངོན་སུམ་གྱི་ཚད་མའི་མཚན་ཉིད། དེ་ལ་དབྱེ་ན། དབང་མངོན། ཡིད་མངོན། རང་རིག་མངོན་སུམ། རྣལ་འབྱོར་མངོན་སུམ་དང་བཞི།

རང་གི་ཐུན་མོང་མ་ཡིན་པའི་བདག་རྐྱེན་དབང་པོ་གཟུགས་ཅན་པ་[2] ལས་སྐྱེས་པའི་རྟོག་པ་དང་བྲལ་ཞིང་མ་འཁྲུལ་པའི་རིག་པ་དབང་མངོན་གྱི་མཚན་ཉིད། དབྱེ་ན། གཟུགས་འཛིན་དབང་མངོན། སྒྲ་འཛིན་དབང་མངོན། དྲི་འཛིན་དབང་མངོན། རོ་འཛིན་དབང་མངོན། རེག་བྱ་འཛིན་པའི་དབང་མངོན་དང་ལྔ།

རང་གི་ཐུན་མོང་མ་ཡིན་པའི་བདག་རྐྱེན་མིག་དབང་དང་། དམིགས་རྐྱེན་གཟུགས་ལ་བརྟེན་ནས་སྐྱེས་པའི་རྟོག་པ་དང་བྲལ་ཞིང་མ་འཁྲུལ་བའི་རིག་པ། གཟུགས་འཛིན་དབང་མངོན་གྱི་མཚན་ཉིད། དེས་འོག་མ་རྣམས་ལ་རིགས་འགྲེ།

རང་གི་ཐུན་མོང་མ་ཡིན་པའི་བདག་རྐྱེན་ཡིད་དབང་ལས་བྱུང་བའི་རྟོག་པ་དང་བྲལ་ཞིང་མ་འཁྲུལ་བའི་རིག་པ། ཡིད་མངོན་གྱི་མཚན་ཉིད། དེ་ལ་དབྱེ་ན། སྐབས་འདིར་བསྟན་གྱི་ཡིད་མངོན་དང་། དེ་མ་ཡིན་པའི་ཡིད་མངོན་གཉིས། རང་གི་ཐུན་མོང་མ་ཡིན་པའི་བདག་རྐྱེན་ཡིད་དབང་ལས་བྱུང་བའི་སྐབས་འདིར་བསྟན་གྱི་རྟོག་བྲལ་མ་འཁྲུལ་བའི་གཞན་རིག་དང་པོའི་མཚན་ཉིད། དཔེར་ན། གཟུགས་འཛིན་ཡིད་མངོན་ནས་རེག་བྱ་འཛིན་པའི་ཡིད་མངོན་གྱི་བར་ལྟ།[3]

སྐབས་འདིར་བསྟན་གྱི་ཡིད་མངོན་སྐྱེ་ཚུལ་ལ། སྤྱིལ་མར་སྐྱེ་བ། འཁྲིས་གསུམ་པར་སྐྱེ་བ། རྒྱུན་མཐའ་ཁོ་ནར་སྐྱེ་བ་དང་འདོད་ཚུལ་གསུམ་ལས།[4] དང་པོའི་ཚུལ་ནི། གཟུགས་འཛིན་དབང་མངོན་སྐད་ཅིག་དང་པོ་སྐྱེ། དེའི་རྗེས་སུ་གཟུགས་འཛིན་ཡིད་མངོན་སྐད་ཅིག་དང་པོ་སྐྱེས། དེའི་རྗེས་སུ་གཟུགས་འཛིན་དབང་མངོན་སྐད་ཅིག་གཉིས་པ་སྐྱེ་བ་སོགས་[5]དབང་མངོན་སྐད་ཅིག་རེ་རེའི་བར་[6]ཡིད་མངོན་སྐད་ཅིག་རེ་སྐྱེ་བར་འདོད།

གཉིས་པའི་ཚུལ་ནི་གཟུགས་འཛིན་དབང་མངོན་སྐད་ཅིག་གཉིས་པ་དང་། གཟུགས་འཛིན་ཡིད་མངོན་སྐད་ཅིག་དང་པོ། དེ་གཉིས་ཉམས་སུ་མྱོང་བའི་རང་རིག་མངོན་སུམ་དང་གསུམ་དུས་མཉམས་དུ་སྐྱེ་བར་འདོད་པ་སྟེ། མདོར་ན་ཁ་ཕྱིར་ལྟས་ཀྱི་འཁྲིས་གཉིས་དང་ཁ་ནང་ལྟས་ཀྱི་འཁྲིས་གཅིག་ཅིག་ཆར་དུ་སྐྱེས་བར་འདོད།

གསུམ་པའི་ཚུལ་ནི། རྗེ་ཡབ་སྲས་ཀྱི་དགོངས་པ། གཟུགས་འཛིན་དབང་མངོན་སྐད་ཅིག་ཐ་མའི་མཇུག་ཐོགས་ཁོ་ནར་གཟུགས་འཛིན་ཡིད་མངོན་སྐྱེ་བར་བཞེད། དེ་ཡང་ཚུར་མཐོང་གི་རྒྱུད་ལ་ནི་གཟུགས་འཛིན་ཡིད་མངོན་དུས་མཐའི་སྐད་ཅིག་མ་རེ་རེ་ལས་མི་སྐྱེས་བར་འདོད་དགོས་པར་ཡིག་ཆར་གསལ་ལོ།[7] སྐབས་འདིར་བསྟན་ཞེས་པ། གཟུགས་ཤེས་པ་ནི་རྣམ་གཉིས་ཏེ། མིག་དང་ཡིད་ལ་བརྟེན་པའོ། ཞེས་པའི་སྐབས་ལ་གོ་དགོས་སོ།

གཉིས་པ་ནི་གཞན་སེམས་ཤེས་པའི་མངོན་ཤེས་ལྟ་བུའོ།

འཛིན་རྣམ་རང་རིག་གི་མཚན་ཉིད། རྟོག་པ་དང་བྲལ་ཞིང་མ་འཁྲུལ་བའི་འཛིན་རྣམ་རང་རིག་མངོན་སུམ་གྱི་མཚན་ཉིད། དབྱེ་བ། དེར་གྱུར་པའི་ཚད་མ། བཅད་ཤེས། སྣང་ལ་མ་ངེས་དང་གསུམ།

རང་གི་ཐུན་མོང་མ་ཡིན་པའི་བདག་རྐྱེན་དུ་གྱུར་པའི་ཞི་ལྷག་ཟུང་འབྲེལ་གྱི་ཏིང་ངེ་འཛིན་ལས་སྐྱེས་པའི་

རྟོག་བྲལ་མ་འཁྲུལ་བའི་འཕགས་རྒྱུད་ཀྱི་མཁྱེན་པ་རྣལ་འབྱོར་མངོན་སུམ་གྱི་མཚན་ཉིད། དབྱེ་ན། ཉན་ཐོས། རང་རྒྱལ། ཐེག་ཆེན་གྱི་དེ་གསུམ་ཡོད། རང་རིག་མངོན་སུམ་དང་། རྣལ་འབྱོར་མངོན་སུམ་ལ་ཡིད་མངོན་ཡིན་དགོས་པར་གསུངས།

མཚན་ཉིད་དེ་རྣམས་མདོ་སྡེ་པའི་དབང་དུ་བྱས་[8]ཀྱི་[9]སེམས་ཙམ་པ་དང་། རྣལ་འབྱོར་སྤྱོད་པའི་དབུ་མ་པ་རྣམས་ཀྱིས། རྟོག་པ་དང་བྲལ་ཞིང་བག་ཆགས་བརྟན་བྱུང་གི་རིག་པ་ཞེས་སྦྱར་རོ།

ཞར་བྱུང་མངོན་སུམ་ལྟར་སྣང་གི་རྣམ་བཞག་ཙུང་ཟད་བཤད་པ་ལ།

འཁྲུལ་དང་ཀུན་རྫོབ་ཤེས་པ་དང་།

རྗེས་དཔག་རྗེས་སུ་དཔག་ལས་བྱུང་།

དྲན་དང་མངོན་འདོད་ཅེས་བྱ་བ།

མངོན་སུམ་ལྟར་སྣང་རབ་རིབ་བཅས།

ཅེས་གསུངས་པ་ལྟར། རྟོག་པ་མངོན་སུམ་ལྟར་སྣང་དྲུག་རྟོག་མེད་མངོན་སུམ་ལྟར་སྣང་གཅིག་དང་བདུན་དུ་འདོད།

རྣམ་འགྲེལ་རྩ་བས་དེ་དག་བཞིར་བསྡུ་ནས་བཤད་དོ།[10] འདི་དག་ཞིབ་ཏུ་ཤེས་པར་འདོད་ན་རྡ་སྦྱོར་བློ་རིག་དང་ཞིའུ་གསུམ་པའི་དགོངས་པ་རབ་གསལ་སོགས་ལ་ལྟ་བར་བྱའོ།།

རང་གི་རྟེན་རྟགས་ཡང་དག་ལ་བརྟེན་ནས་རང་གི་ཞལ་བྱ་ལྐོག་གྱུར་ལ་མི་སླུ་བའི་ཞེན་རིག་རྗེས་དཔག་གི་མཚན་ཉིད།

རང་གི་རྟེན་རྟགས་ཡང་དག་ལ་བརྟེན་ནས་རང་གི་ཞལ་བྱ་ལྐོག་གྱུར་ལ་གསར་དུ་མི་སླུ་བའི་རིག་པ། རྗེས་སུ་དཔག་པའི་ཚད་མའི་མཚན་ཉིད། རྗེས་དཔག་ལ་ཚད་མས་མ་ཁྱབ་པར་གསུངས། དེ་ལ་དབྱེ་ན། །ཡིད་ཆེས་རྗེས་དཔག །གྲགས་པའི་རྗེས་དཔག དངོས་སྟོབས་རྗེས་དཔག་དང་གསུམ།

རང་གི་རྟེན་ཡིད་ཆེས་ཀྱི་རྟགས་ཡང་དག་ལ་བརྟེན་ནས་རང་གི་ཞལ་བྱ་ཤིན་ལྐོག་གྱུར་ལ་མི་སླུ་བའི་ཞེན་རིག་དང་པོའི་མཚན་ཉིད། མཚན་གཞི་ནི། སྦྱིན་པས་ལོངས་སྤྱོད་ཁྲིམས་ཀྱིས་བདེ། ཞེས་པའི་ལུང་རང་གི་བསྟན་བྱའི་དོན་ལ་མི་སླུ་བར་རྟོགས་པའི་རྗེས་དཔག་ལྟ་བུ།

རང་གི་རྟེན་གྲགས་རྟགས་ཡང་དག་ལ་བརྟེན་ནས་རང་གི་ཞལ་བྱ་སྒྲ་བྱུང་གྲགས་པ་ལ་མི་སླུ་བའི་ཞེན་རིག གཉིས་པའི་མཚན་ཉིད། མཚན་གཞི། རི་བོང་ཅན་ལ་ཟླ་བ་ཞེས་པའི་སྒྲས་བརྗོད་རུང་དུ་རྟོགས་པའི་རྗེས་དཔག་ལྟ་བུ།

རང་གི་རྟེན་དངོས་སྟོབས་ཀྱི་རྟགས་ཡང་དག་ལ་བརྟེན་ནས་རང་གི་གཞལ་བྱ་ཅུང་ཟད་ལྐོག་གྱུར་ལ་མི་སླུ་བའི་ཞེན་རིག་གསུམ་པའི་མཚན་ཉིད། མཚན་གཞི། སྒྲ་མི་རྟག་རྟོགས་ཀྱི་རྗེས་དཔག་ལྟ་བུའོ།

རང་འདྲེན་བྱེད་ཀྱི་ཚད་མ་སྔ་མས་[11] རྟོགས་ཟིན་རྟོགས་པའི་ཚད་མིན་གྱི་རིག་པ་བཅད་ཤེས་ཀྱི་མཚན་ཉིད།[12] དེ་ལ་དབྱེ་ན། མངོན་སུམ་བཅད་ཤེས་དང་རྟོག་པ་བཅད་ཤེས་གཉིས། དང་པོ་ལ་དབང་མངོན་བཅད་ཤེས། ཡིད་མངོན་བཅད་ཤེས། རང་རིག་བཅད་ཤེས། རྣལ་འབྱོར་མངོན་སུམ་བཅད་ཤེས་དང་བཞི། གཉིས་པ་ལ་མངོན་སུམ་གྱིས་དྲངས་པའི་རྟོག་པ་བཅད་ཤེས་དང་། རྗེས་དཔག་གིས་དྲངས་པའི་རྟོག་པ་བཅད་ཤེས་གཉིས། མཚན་གཞི། སྔོ་འཛིན་མངོན་སུམ་གྱི་རྗེས་སུ་སྐྱེས་པའི་སྔོན་པོ་ངེས་པའི་ངེས་ཤེས་ལྟ་བུ་དང་པོ་དང་། སྒྲ་མི་རྟོག་རྟོགས་ཀྱི་རྗེས་དཔག་སྐད་ཅིག་གཉིས་པ་ལྟ་བུ་གཉིས་པ་ཡིན་པའི་ཕྱིར་ཏེ། འཐད་ལྡན་ལས།[13]

མངོན་སུམ་དང་རྗེས་སུ་དཔག་པའི་དང་པོ་སྐད་ཅིག་མ་གཉིས་ནི་ཚད་མ་ཡིན་ལ་[14] དེ་དག་གི་རྒྱུན་
དུ་གྱུར་པའི་གྲུབ་པ་དང་བདེ་བ་ཐ་མི་དད་པ་ཕྱི་མ་རྣམས་ནི་ཚད་མ་ཡིན་པ་སྤྱངས་པའོ།[15]

ཞེས་གསུངས་པའི་ཕྱིར། སྐབས་འདིའི་གྲུབ་བདེ་གཅིག་པ་འབྲས་བུ་གཅིག་པ་ལ་བྱེད་གསུངས།

རང་གི་འཇུག་ཡུལ་གྱི་གཙོ་བོར་གྱུར་པའི་ཆོས་ལ་མཐའ་གཅིག་ཏུ་ཞེན་ཀྱང་བཅད་དོན་མ་ཐོབ་པའི་རིག་པ་ཡིད་དཔྱོད་ཀྱི་མཚན་ཉིད། དེ་ལ་དབྱེ་ན། རྒྱུ་མཚན་མེད་པའི་ཡིད་དཔྱོད། རྒྱུ་མཚན་མ་ངེས་པའི་ཡིད་དཔྱོད། རྒྱུ་མཚན་ལྟར་སྣང་ལ་བརྟེན་པའི་ཡིད་དཔྱོད་དང་གསུམ། མཚན་གཞི་ནི། རྒྱུ་མཚན་གང་ཡང་མེད་པར་སྒྲ་མི་རྟག་སྙམ་པའི་བློ་ལྟ་བུ་དང་པོ་དང་། སྒྲ་བྱས་པ་དང་།[16] བྱས་ན་མི་རྟག་པས་ཁྱབ་པ་མ་ངེས་པར་བྱས་པའི་རྟགས་ལས་སྒྲ་མི་རྟག་སྙམ་པའི་བློ་ལྟ་བུ་གཉིས་པ་དང་། གཞལ་བྱའི་རྟགས་ལས་སྒྲ་མི་རྟག་སྙམ་པའི་བློ་ལྟ་བུ་གསུམ་པ་ཡིན་པའི་ཕྱིར།

དེ་ལྟར་ཡང་། རིག་གཏེར་ལས།

ཡིད་དཔྱོད་རྟགས་ལ་བརྟེན་མི་ལྟོས།
དམ་བཅའ་ཙམ་ཡིན་ཐེ་ཚོམ་འགྱུར།
རྟགས་ལ་བརྟེན་ན་ཡང་དག་གམ།
ལྟར་སྣང་གསུམ་ལས་འདའ་བ་མེད།[17]

ཅེས་གསུངས། ཡང་ན། སྣོང་བ་དང་རྟེན་རྟགས་ཡང་དག་གང་ལ་ཡང་མ་བརྟེན་པར་རང་གི་འཇུག་ཡུལ་ལ་མ་འཁྲུལ་བའི་མཐའ་གཅིག་འཛིན་གྱི་བཅད་དོན་མ་ཐོབ་པའི་ཞེན་རིག དེའི་མཚན་ཉིད་དུ་འཛོག འདིའི་སྣོང་བ་ལ་སྒོམ་བྱུང་གི་སྣོང་བ་དང་། རང་རིག་གི་སྣོང་བ་དང་། དོན་སྤྱི་དང་མ་འདྲེས་པའི་གསལ་སྣོང་གསུམ་དུ་ཡོད་པའི་དེ་གང་ལ་ཡང་མ་བརྟེན་པར་བྱ་དགོངས་པས། དེ་ལྟར་ན་བློ་ཡིན་ན་བློ་རིག་བདུན་པོ་གང་རུང་ཡིན་པས་མ་ཁྱབ་པར་སེམས་ཏེ། མི་སྡུག་པའི་ཏིང་ངེ་འཛིན་དང་། སློབ་པའི་རྒྱུད་ཀྱི་སྙིང་རྗེ་ཆེན་པོ་སོགས་ཐབས་ཀྱི་རྟོགས་རིགས་སུ་གནས་པ་རྣམས། གཞན་རྣམས་མིན་པ་གོ་སླ་ལ། སྒོམ་བྱུང་གི་སྣོང་བ་ལ་ལྟོས་པས་ཡིད་དཔྱོད་དུ་མི་རིགས། འཁྲུལ་རྒྱུས་མ་སླད་པས་ལོག་ཤེས་སུ་མི་རིགས་པའི་ཕྱིར་སྙམ་སྟེ་སྤྱད་པར་བྱའོ།

རང་སྟོབས་ཀྱིས་མཐའ་གཉིས་སུ་དོགས་པའི་རིག་པ་ཐེ་ཚོམ་གྱི་མཚན་ཉིད། དེ་ལ་དབྱེ་ན། དོན་འགྱུར་གྱི་ཐེ་ཚོམ། དོན་མི་འགྱུར་གྱི་ཐེ་ཚོམ། ཆ་མཉམ་པའི་ཐེ་ཚོམ་དང་གསུམ། མཚན་གཞི་ནི། སྒྲ་ཕལ་ཆེར་མི་རྟག་གམ་སྙམ་པའི་ཡིད་གཉིས་ལྟ་བུ་དང་པོ་དང་། སྒྲ་ཕལ་ཆེར་རྟག་ལས་ཆེ་སྙམ་པའི་ཡིད་གཉིས་ལྟ་བུ་གཉིས་པ་དང་། སྒྲ་རྟག་གམ་མི་རྟག་སྙམ་པའི་སོམ་ཉི་ལྟ་བུ་གསུམ་པ་ཡིན་པའི་ཕྱིར།

རང་གི་འཇུག་ཡུལ་དུ་གྱུར་པའི་རང་མཚན་གསལ་བར་སྣང་ཡང་དེ་ལ་ངེས་པ་འདྲེན་མི་ནུས་པའི་རིག་པ། སྣང་ལ་མ་ངེས་པའི་བློའི་མཚན་ཉིད།[18] དེ་ལ་དབྱེ་ན། དེར་གྱུར་པའི་དབང་མངོན། ཡིད་མངོན། རང་རིག་དང་གསུམ། དེར་གྱུར་པའི་རྣལ་འབྱོར་མངོན་སུམ་མེད་དེ། རྣལ་འབྱོར་མངོན་སུམ་ཡིན་ན་རང་ཡུལ་རྟོགས་པས་ཁྱབ་པའི་ཕྱིར་ཏེ། རྣམ་འགྲེལ་ལས།

བློ་གྲོས་ཆེན་པོས་མཐོང་ཉིད་ལས།[19]

རྣམ་པ་ཐམས་ཅད་ངེས་པར་བྱེད།[20]

ཅེས་གསུངས་པའི་ཕྱིར།

མཚན་གཞི་ཡང་། ཁ་བོས་སྔོན་པོ་མཐོང་ངམ་མ་མཐོང་སྙམ་དུ་ཐེ་ཚོམ་འདྲེན་པར་བྱེད་པའི་སྔོ་འཛིན་དབང་མངོན་ལྟ་བུ་དང་པོ་དང་། སོ་སྐྱེའི་རྒྱུད་ཀྱི་གཟུགས་འཛིན་ཡིད་མངོན་ལྟ་བུ་གཉིས་པ་དང་། རྒྱང་འཕེན་པའི་རྒྱུད་ཀྱི་རྗེས་དཔག་ཚད་མར་ཉམས་སུ་སྣོང་པའི་རང་རིག་ལྟ་བུ་གསུམ་པ་ཡིན་པའི་ཕྱིར་རོ།

རང་གི་འཇུག་ཡུལ་ལ་འཁྲུལ་བའི་རིག་པ་ལོག་ཤེས་ཀྱི་མཚན་ཉིད། དེ་ལ་དབྱེ་ན། རྟོག་པ་ལོག་ཤེས་དང་། རྟོག་མེད་ལོག་ཤེས་གཉིས།

མཚན་གཞི་ནི། རི་བོང་རྭ་འཛིན་རྟོག་པ་དང་། གང་ཟག་གི་བདག་འཛིན་ལྟ་བུ་དང་པོ་དང་། གཉིས་པ་ལ་དབང་ཤེས་སུ་གྱུར་པའི་དེ་དང་། ཡིད་ཤེས་སུ་གྱུར་པའི་དེ་གཉིས་ལས་ཟླ་བ་གཉིས་སྣང་གི་དབང་ཤེས་དང་གངས་རི་སྔོན་པོར་སྣང་བའི་དབང་ཤེས་ལྟ་བུ་དང་པོ་དང་། སྔོན་པོ་གསལ་བར་སྣང་བའི་རྨི་ལམ་གྱི་ཤེས་པ་ལྟ་བུ་གཉིས་པ་ཡིན་པའི་ཕྱིར།

གཉིས་པ་བློ་རིག་གསུམ་དུ་དབྱེ་བ་ཡོད་དེ། དོན་སྤྱི་བཟུང་ཡུལ་དུ་བྱེད་པའི་རྟོག་པ། རང་མཚན་བཟུང་ཡུལ་དུ་བྱེད་པའི་རྟོག་མེད་མ་འཁྲུལ་བའི་ཤེས་པ། མེད་པ་གསལ་སྣང་ཅན་བཟུང་ཡུལ་དུ་བྱེད་པའི་རྟོག་མེད་འཁྲུལ་ཤེས་དང་གསུམ་ཡོད་པའི་ཕྱིར། དང་པོ་དང་རྟོག་པ་གཉིས་དོན་གཅིག གཉིས་པ་དང་མངོན་སུམ་གཉིས་དོན་གཅིག གསུམ་པ་དང་རྟོག་མེད་ལོག་ཤེས་གཉིས་དོན་གཅིག

གསུམ་པ་བློ་རིག་གཉིས་སུ་དབྱེ་བ་ཡོད་དེ། ཚད་མ་དང་། ཚད་མིན་གྱི་ཤེས་པ་གཉིས་སུ་དབྱེ་བ། རྟོག་པ་དང་། རྟོག་མེད་ཀྱི་ཤེས་པ་གཉིས་སུ་དབྱེ་བ། འཁྲུལ་ཤེས་དང་། མ་འཁྲུལ་བའི་ཤེས་པ་གཉིས་སུ་དབྱེ་བ། ཡིད་ཤེས་དང་། དབང་ཤེས་གཉིས་སུ་དབྱེ་བ། སེལ་འཇུག་གི་བློ་དང་། སྒྲུབ་འཇུག་གི་བློ་གཉིས་སུ་དབྱེ་བ། སེམས་དང་། སེམས་བྱུང་གཉིས་སུ་དབྱེ་བ་རྣམས་སུ་ཡོད་པའི་ཕྱིར།

དེ་རྣམས་སོ་སོའི་དོན་ཡང་། གསར་དུ་མི་སླུ་བའི་རིག་པ་ཚད་མའི་མཚན་ཉིད། དབྱེ་ན། མངོན་སུམ་གྱི་ཚད་མ་དང་། རྗེས་སུ་དཔག་པའི་ཚད་མ་གཉིས། ཚད་མ་ལ་དེ་གཉིས་སུ་གྲངས་ངེས་པ་ཡང་ཡིན་ཏེ། དེ་གཉིས་ལས་མང་ན་མི་དགོས་ཤིང་ཉུང་ན་མི་འདུ་བའི་ཕྱིར། འོན་ཀྱང་འདིའི་གྲངས་ངེས་ལོག་རྟོག་སེལ་བའི་གྲངས་ངེས་ཡིན་གྱི་ཕུང་སུམ་སེལ་བའི་གྲངས་ངེས་ནི་མ་ཡིན་ཏེ།[21] ཚད་མ་ཡིན་ན་དེ་གཉིས་གང་རུང་ཡིན་པས་མ་ཁྱབ་པའི་ཕྱིར་ཏེ། སྤྱིར་ཚད་མ་དེ་དེ་གཉིས་གང་རུང་དུ་འཇོག་དཀའ་བའི་ཕྱིར།

[22]དང་པོ་གྲུབ་སྟེ། སྤྱིར་ཚད་མའི་གྲངས་ལ་རྒྱང་འཕེན་པས་མངོན་སུམ་གཅིག་པུར་འདོད་པ་ནས། ཙ་རི་ཀ་པས་བཅུ་གཅིག་ཏུ་འདོད་པའི་བར་གཞན་སྡེ་རྣམས་ཀྱིས་གྲངས་ལ་ལོག་པར་རྟོག་པ་དུ་མ་ཞིག་འབྱུང་བ་དེ་དགག་པའི་ཕྱིར་དུ་རིགས་པའི་དབང་ཕྱུག་གིས། གཞལ་བྱ་གཉིས་ཕྱིར་ཚད་མ་གཉིས་ཞེས་སོགས་དངོས་སྟོབས་ཀྱི་རིགས་པའི་སྒྲོ་དུ་མ་ནས་དེ་དག་ལེགས་པར་བཀག་ནས་ཚད་མ་ལ་དེ་གཉིས་སུ་གྲངས་ངེས་པར་སྒྲུབ་པའི་ཕྱིར་རོ།[22]

ཡང་ཚད་མ་ལ་དབྱེ་ན། རང་ལས་ངེས་ཀྱི་ཚད་མ་དང་། གཞན་ལས་ངེས་ཀྱི་ཚད་མ་གཉིས། རང་གི་གཞལ་བྱའི་བདག་ཉིད། མཐར་ཐུག་ཡུལ་སྟེང་དུ་གནས་པ་མེད་པར་རང་ཉིད་མི་འབྱུང་བ་ལ་ངེས་པ་རང་སྟོབས་ཀྱིས་

འདྲེན་ནུས་པའི་གསར་དུ་མི་སླུ་བའི་རིག་པ་རང་ལས་ངེས་ཀྱི་ཚད་མའི་མཚན་ཉིད། དེ་འདྲེན་མི་ནུས་པར་ཕྱིས་འབྱུང་ཐ་སྙད་པའི་ཚད་མ་གཞན་ལ་བརྟེན་དགོས་པའི་གསར་དུ་མི་སླུ་བའི་རིག་པ་གཞན་ལས་ངེས་ཀྱི་ཚད་མའི་མཚན་ཉིད།

དང་པོ་ལ་དབྱེ་ན། དོན་གོམས་པ་ཅན་གྱི་དབང་མངོན་གྱི་ཚད་མ། དོན་བྱེད་སྣང་ཅན་གྱི་དབང་མངོན་གྱི་ཚད་མ། རང་རིག་མངོན་སུམ་གྱི་ཚད་མ། རྣལ་འབྱོར་མངོན་སུམ་གྱི་ཚད་མ། རྗེས་སུ་དཔག་པའི་ཚད་མ་དང་ལྔ།

མཚན་གཞི། བུའི་རྒྱུད་ཀྱི་ཕའི་གཟུགས་འཛིན་པའི་དབང་མངོན་ལྟ་བུ་དང་པོ། མེས་བཙོ་སྲེག་གི་དོན་བྱེད་ནུས་པར་འཛལ་བའི་མེ་འཛིན་དབང་མངོན་ལྟ་བུ་གཉིས་པ། ཚད་མ་ཉམས་སུ་མྱོང་བའི་རང་རིག་མངོན་སུམ་ལྟ་བུ་གསུམ་པ། གང་ཟག་གི་བདག་མེད་མངོན་སུམ་དུ་རྟོགས་པའི་ཡེ་ཤེས་ལྟ་བུ་བཞི་པ། སྒྲ་མི་རྟག་རྟོགས་ཀྱི་རྗེས་དཔག་ལྟ་བུ་ལྔ་པ་ཡིན་པའི་ཕྱིར། དེ་ལྟར་ཡང་། རིག་གཏེར་ལས།

དོན་རིག་གཉིས་དང་རང་རིག་གཉིས།

རྗེས་སུ་དཔག་རྣམས་རང་ལས་ངེས།

ཞེས་པའི་དགོངས་པའོ།

གཉིས་པ་གཞན་ལས་ངེས་ཀྱི་ཚད་མ་ལ་སྒྲ་བརྗོད་རིགས་ཀྱི་སྒོ་ནས་དབྱེ་ན། སྣང་བ་རང་ལས་ངེས་ཤིང་བདེན་པ་གཞན་ལས་ངེས་པ། སྤྱིར་རང་ལས་ངེས་ཤིང་ཁྱད་པར་གཞན་ལས་ངེས་པ། སྣང་བ་ཉིད་ཀྱང་གཞན་ལས་ངེས་པ་དང་གསུམ།

མཚན་གཞི་ནི། དོན་ལ་མེའི་ཁ་དོག་ཡིན་ཞིང་རྟོག་པས་མེའི་ཁ་དོག་ཡིན་མིན་ཐེ་ཚོམ་ཟ་དུས་ཀྱི་[23] རྒྱུད་རིང་པོའི་ཁ་དོག་དམར་ལམ་པ་འཛིན་པའི་དབང་མངོན་ལྟ་བུ་དང་པོ་དང་། དོན་ལ་ཤ་པ་ཡིན་ཞིང་རྟོག་པས་ཤ་པ་ཡིན་མིན་ཐེ་ཚོམ་ཟ་དུས་ཀྱི་རྒྱུད་རིང་པོའི་ཤིང་འཛིན་དབང་མངོན་ལྟ་བུ་གཉིས་པ་དང་། ཁ་པོས་སྔོན་པོ་མཐོང་ངམ་མ་མཐོང་སྙམ་པའི་ཐེ་ཚོམ་འདྲེན་པར་བྱེད་པའི་སྔོ་འཛིན་དབང་མངོན་ལྟ་བུ་གསུམ་པ་ཡིན།

དེ་ཡང་དང་པོ་གཉིས་དངོས་དང་། ཐ་མ་བཏགས་པ་བར་འཇོག ཡང་དེ་ལ་སྒྲ་བརྗོད་རིགས་ཀྱི་སྒོ་ནས་དབྱེ་ན། མངོན་སུམ་དང་པོ་བ། ཡིད་མ་གཏད། འཁྲུལ་རྒྱུ་ཅན་དང་གསུམ་ཡང་ཡོད་དེ། རིག་གཏེར་ལས།

དང་པོ་བ་དང་ཡིད་མ་གདད།
འཁྲུལ་རྒྱུ་ཅན་རྣམས་གཞན་ལས་ངེས།

ཞེས་གསུངས་པའི་ཕྱིར།

དེ་རྣམས་ཀྱི་མཚན་གཞི་ཡང་ཡོད་དེ། སྔར་ཨུཏྤལ་མཐོང་མ་སོང་བའི་སྐྱེས་བུའི་རྒྱུད་ཀྱི་ཨུཏྤལའི་ཁ་དོག་འཛིན་པའི་དབང་མངོན་ལྟ་བུ་དང་པོ་དང་། ཡིད་གཟུགས་མཛེས་ལ་ལྷག་པར་ཆགས་དུས་ཀྱི་སྐྱེས་བུའི་རྒྱུད་ཀྱི་སྒྲ་འཛིན་དབང་མངོན་ལྟ་བུ་གཉིས་པ་དང་། སྨིག་རྒྱུ་ལ་ཆུ་འཛིན་གྱི་སྒྲོ་འདོགས་དངོས་སུ་སྐྱེས་པའི་སྨིག་རྒྱུའི་ཁ་དོག་འཛིན་པའི་དབང་མངོན་ལྟ་བུ་གསུམ་པ་ཡིན་པའི་ཕྱིར།

གསར་དུ་མི་སླུ་བ་མ་ཡིན་པའི་རིག་པ་ཚད་མིན་གྱི་ཤེས་པའི་མཚན་ཉིད། དབྱེ་ན་བཅད་ཤེས་སོགས་བློ་རིག་ཕྱི་མ་ལྔའོ།

སྒྲ་དོན་འདྲེས་རུང་དུ་འཛིན་པའི་ཞེན་རིག་རྟོག་པའི་མཚན་ཉིད། དེ་དང་སེལ་འཇུག་གི་བློ་གཉིས་དོན་གཅིག མཚན་གཞི། རྗེས་དཔག ཡིད་དཔྱོད། ཐེ་ཚོམ་གསུམ་དང་། བཅད་ཤེས་ལོག་ཤེས་གཉིས་ཀྱི་ཕྱོགས་གཅིག་རྣམས་འཇོག

སྒྲ་དོན་འདྲེས་རུང་དུ་འཛིན་པའི་ཞེན་རིག་དང་བྲལ་བའི་རིག་པ་རྟོག་མེད་ཀྱི་ཤེས་པའི་མཚན་ཉིད། དེ་དང་སྒྲུབ་འཇུག་གི་བློ་གཉིས་དོན་གཅིག མཚན་གཞི། མངོན་སུམ། སྣང་ལ་མ་ངེས་པའི་བློ་གཉིས་དང་། བཅད་ཤེས་ལོག་ཤེས་གཉིས་ཀྱི་ཕྱོགས་གཅིག་རྣམས་འཇོག

རང་གི་སྣང་ཡུལ་ལ་འཁྲུལ་བའི་རིག་པ་འཁྲུལ་ཤེས་ཀྱི་མཚན་ཉིད། མཚན་གཞི། ལོག་ཤེས་དང་རྟོག་པ་ཐམས་ཅད་དོ།

རང་གི་སྣང་ཡུལ་ལ་མ་འཁྲུལ་བའི་རིག་པ་མ་འཁྲུལ་བའི་ཤེས་པའི་མཚན་ཉིད། དེ་དང་མངོན་སུམ་གཉིས་དོན་གཅིག དེ་ཡང་མདོ་སྡེ་པའི་དབང་དུ་བྱས་ཀྱི་རྣམ་རིག་པའི་ལུགས་ལ་དེ་ལྟར་མིན་ཏེ། མངོན་སུམ་ལ་འཁྲུལ་མ་འཁྲུལ་གྱི་ཆ་གཉིས་སུ་འདོད་པའི་ཕྱིར།

རང་གི་ཐུན་མོང་མ་ཡིན་པའི་བདག་རྐྱེན་ཡིད་དབང་ལ་བརྟེན་ནས་སྐྱེས་པའི་རིག་པ་ཡིད་ཤེས་ཀྱི་མཚན་ཉིད། [24]ཡིད་དང་། ཡིད་ཤེས་ལ་མུ་བཞི། དང་པོ་ཡིན་ལ་ཕྱི་མ་མིན་པ། མིག་གི་རྣམ་ཤེས་ལྟ་བུ། ཕྱི་མ་ཡིན་ལ།

དང་པོ་མིན་པ། ཡིད་ཤེས་འཁོར་གྱི་སེམས་བྱུང་ཐམས་ཅད། གཉིས་ཀ་ཡིན་པ། ཡིད་ཀྱི་རྣམ་པར་ཤེས་པ། གཉིས་ཀ་མིན་པ་དབང་ཤེས་འཁོར་གྱི་སེམས་བྱུང་ཐམས་ཅད་དོ།

དེ་བཞིན་དུ། བུམ་འཛིན་རྟོག་པ་དང་། བུམ་པ་རྟོགས་པའི་རྟོག་པ་ལ་མུ་བཞི། ཆོས་དེ་ལ་མངོན་སུམ་དང་། ཆོས་དེ་ལ་མངོན་སུམ་ཚད་མ་གཉིས་ལ་མུ་བཞི། ཆོས་དེ་ལ་རྗེས་དཔག་ཚད་མ་དང་། ཆོས་དེ་ལ་རྟོག་པ་གཉིས་ལ་མུ་བཞི། དེའི་རྟགས་ལས་རྟོགས་པ་དང་། དེའི་རྟགས་ཀྱིས་རྟོགས་པ་ལ་ཁྱད་པར་ཡོད་ཅིང་། ཡུལ་དེ་མངོན་སུམ་གྱིས་རྟོགས་པ་དང་། མངོན་སུམ་དུ་རྟོགས་པ་ལ་ཁྱད་པར་ཡོད་ཚུལ་རྣམས་ཁྱད་པར་ཕྱེ་ནས་ཤེས་དགོས་ཏེ།[25] པཎ་ཆེན་ཉིད་ཀྱིས་བརྡའ་ཆད་འདི་རྣམས་ལ་གཅེས་པར་ཟུངས་ཤིག[26] ཅེས་གསུངས་པའི་ཕྱིར།

རང་གི་ཐུན་མོང་མ་ཡིན་པའི་བདག་རྐྱེན་དབང་པོ་གཟུགས་ཅན་པ་ལ་བརྟེན་ནས་སྐྱེས་པའི་རིག་པ་དབང་ཤེས་ཀྱི་མཚན་ཉིད། དབྱེ་ན། མིག་ཤེས། རྣ་ཤེས། སྣ་ཤེས། ལྕེ་ཤེས། ལུས་ཤེས་དང་ལྔ།

རང་ཡུལ་ལ་བརྡ་དབང་གིས་འཇུག་པའི་རིག་པ་སེལ་འཇུག་གི་བློའི་མཚན་ཉིད། དེ་དང་རྟོག་པ་གཉིས་དོན་གཅིག རང་ཡུལ་ལ་དངོས་དབང་གིས་འཇུག་པའི་རིག་པ་སྒྲུབ་འཇུག་གི་བློའི་མཚན་ཉིད། དེ་དང་རྟོག་མེད་ཀྱི་ཤེས་པ་གཉིས་དོན་གཅིག

རང་གི་འཁོར་དུ་བྱུང་བའི་སེམས་བྱུང་དང་མཚུངས་པར་ལྡན་པ་སེམས་ཀྱི་མཚན་ཉིད། སེམས་དང་། ཡིད་དང་། རྣམ་ཤེས་གསུམ་དོན་གཅིག རང་འཁོར་དུ་ལྡན་པའི་སེམས་དང་མཚུངས་པར་ལྡན་པ་སེམས་བྱུང་གི་མཚན་ཉིད། མཚུངས་པར་ལྡན་ཚུལ་ཡོད་དེ། དཔེར་ན་མིག་གི་རྣམ་ཤེས་དང་། དེའི་འཁོར་གྱི་ཚོར་བ་གཉིས་ལྟ་བུ། དམིགས་པ་གཅིག་པས་དམིགས་པ་མཚུངས། འཛིན་སྟངས་གཅིག་པས་རྣམ་པ་མཚུངས། དུས་གཅིག་པས་དུས་མཚུངས། ཐུན་མོང་མ་ཡིན་པའི་བདག་རྐྱེན་གཅིག་པས་རྟེན་མཚུངས། མིག་གི་རྣམ་ཤེས་རྫས་རེ་རེའི་འཁོར་དུ་ཚོར་བ་ཡང་རྫས་རེ་རེ་ཁོ་ན་འབྱུང་བས་རྫས་མཚུངས་པ་སྟེ་མཚུངས་ལྡན་རྣམ་པ་ལྔ་མཚུངས་ཡིན་ནོ།

མཚན་ཉིད་དེ་དག་ཀྱང་གོ་བ་གཙོ་བོར་བྱས་ཀྱི་ཚིག་སྐྱོན་གཅོད་པ་གཙོ་བོར་བྱེད་ན་མཚན་ཉིད་གང་ལ་རང་སྒྲ་ཐོག་མར་ཡོད་ཚེ་[27] མཚོན་བྱ་ལ་ཡང་རང་ཉིད་དེ་ཡིན་པའི་ཞེས་སྦྱར་དགོས་སོ།

སེམས་བྱུང་ལ་དབྱེ་ན་ང་ཚན་དྲུག་ཡོད་དེ།

ཀུན་འགྲོ་ལྔ་དང་ཡུལ་ངེས་ལྔ། དགེ་བ་བཅུ་གཅིག་རྩ་ཉོན་དྲུག
ཉེ་ཉོན་ཉི་ཤུ་གཞན་འགྱུར་བཞི། སེམས་བྱུང་ང་གཅིག་འདི་དག་གོ[28]

ཚོར་བ་འདུ་ཤེས་སེམས་པ་དང་། ཡིད་ལ་བྱེད་དང་རེག་པ་ལྔ།
གཙོ་སེམས་ཀུན་གྱི་འཁོར་དུ་ནི། འགྲོ་ཕྱིར་ཀུན་འགྲོ་ཞེས་བྱའོ།

འདུན་པ་མོས་པ་དྲན་པ་དང་། ཏིང་འཛིན་ཤེས་རབ་ལྔ་པོ་ཡུལ།
བྱེ་བྲག་པ་ལ་འཇུག་ངེས་ཕྱིར། ཡུལ་ངེས་ཞེས་པར་བཤད་པ་ཡིན།

དད་དང་ངོ་ཚ་ཤེས་ཁྲེལ་ཡོད། འདོད་ཆགས་དང་ནི་ཞེ་སྡང་དང་།
གཏི་མུག་མེད་པའི་དགེ་རྩ་གསུམ། བརྩོན་འགྲུས་ཤིན་སྦྱངས་བག་ཡོད་དང་།
བཏང་སྙོམས་རྣམ་པར་མི་འཚེ་རྣམས། གཉེན་པོ་ངོ་བོ་མཚུངས་ལྡན་སོགས།
ཅི་རིགས་སྒྲི་ནས་དགེ་བའོ།

འདོད་ཆགས་ཁོང་ཁྲོ་ང་རྒྱལ་དང་། མ་རིག་ཐེ་ཚོམ་ལྟ་བ་དྲུག
འདི་གསུམ་ཉོན་མོངས་ཅན་ཞེས་སྦྱར། རྩ་ཉོན་ཡིན་དེ་སེམས་རྒྱུད་ནི།
ཉོན་མོངས་བྱེད་པའི་གཙོ་བོའོ།

འཁྲོ་བ་འཁོན་འཛིན་འཆབ་དང་འཚིག ཕྲག་དོག་སེར་སྣ་སྒྱུ་དང་གཡོ།
རྒྱགས་དང་རྣམ་འཚེ་ངོ་ཚ་མེད། ཁྲེལ་མེད་རྨུགས་རྒོད་མ་དད་པ།
ལེ་ལོ་བག་མེད་བརྗེད་ངེས་དང་། ཤེས་བཞིན་མ་ཡིན་རྣམ་གཡེང་བཅས།
ཉེ་ཤུ་རྩ་ཉོན་འཕེལ་སྐྱེ་དང་། ཉེ་ཕྱིར་ཉེ་བའི་ཉོན་མོངས་སོ།[29]

གཉིད་འགྱོད་རྟོག་དཔྱོད་གཞན་འགྱུར་དེ། ཀུན་སློང་མཚུངས་ལྡན་ཅི་རིགས་ཀྱིས།
དགེ་དང་མི་དགེ་ལུང་མ་བསྟན། གཞན་དང་གཞན་དུ་འགྱུར་བའོ།

དེ་དག་སོ་སོའི་ངོ་བོ་དང་། བྱེད་ལས་རྣམ་གྲངས་ཁྱད་པར་སོགས།
བློ་ལྡན་རྣམས་ཀྱིས་ཤེས་འདོད་ན། ཞིབ་ཏུ་མངོན་པའི་གཞུང་ལས་ཤེས།

ཉེས་ཚོགས་མཆིས་ན་མཁས་ལ་བཤད།
དགེ་ན་བདག་འདྲའི་བློ་དམན་གྱི།
སྨོངས་པ་སེལ་བར་བྱེད་པའི་མཐུས།
རྒྱལ་བསྟན་ཡུན་དུ་གནས་གྱུར་ཅིག[30]

ཅེས་བློ་རིག་གི་རྣམ་བཞག་ཉེར་མཁོ་ཀུན་འདུས་འདི་འདྲ་ཞིག་བློ་གླིང་དཔེ་མཛོད་པ་སྟ་ཐྱི་ཀུན་གྱིས་ཡང་ཡང་བསྐུལ་བ་ལ་བརྟེན། ནྭ་སྟོད་བློ་རིག་ལ་གཞི་མ་བྱས། པཎ་ཆེན་གྱི་ཡིག་ཆར་གསལ་བ་རྣམས་ཇི་བཞིན་དུ་འཁོད། དེར་མི་གསལ་བ་མཚན་ཉིད་འགའ་ཞིག་བསྣུར་འོས་རྣམས་བློ་རིག་སྡོམ་དང་ཡོངས་འཛིན་བློ་རིག་གཉིས་དང་ཅི་རིགས་སུ་མཐུན་པར་སྦྱར་བ་འདི་ནི། བློ་གླིང་སློབ་དཔོན་ཁྲི་ཐོག་པ་རྒྱལ་རོང་དགེ་བཤེས་སྐྱོར་དཔོན་འཇམ་དཔལ་བསམ་འཕེལ་ནས་གཙུག་ཁང་གི་ཡང་ཐོག་ཏུ་སྦྱར་བ་འདི་ལ་ཞུས་དག་པ་བཤེས་གཉེན་ཡོངས་ཀྱི་བློ་མཐུན་དུ་བགྱིད་པ་དགེ་ལེགས་འཕེལ། །

① Reading Monastic Textbooks: Presentations

Page 227, Line 2

As noted in the previous text (see རིགས་ལམ་ note 1), one form of monastic textbook is the simple "presentation" (*rnam bzhag*) text. The selection presented here is an example of such a textbook. While debate manuals provide both positions to be refuted and presentations of accepted philosophical assertions (རང་ལུགས་, or "our own system"), presentation-style texts tend to present simply accepted philosophical assertions with the occasional observation concerning the assertions of others or points of contention. As with debate manuals, however, these presentation texts nonetheless likewise provide a standard set of well-defined terminology whose familiarity is presumed in more advanced treatises.

WHAT TO REMEMBER

Presentation-style textbooks provide a standard set of well-defined terminology focusing primarily on presenting accepted philosophical assertions with only occasional mention of the assertions of others or points of contention.

② Translation Hint

Page 227, Line 21

In the series of philosophical definitions provided in this text, a common pattern is followed in which category terms (such as བདག་རྐྱེན་, "own empowering condition") are given their contextual meaning by appositionally specifying a specific term (such as དབང་པོ་གཟུགས་ཅན་པ་, "a physical sense-power," in this instance). This pattern—often with a gerund phrase (…ལ་རྟེན་ནས་, "having relied upon …")—is repeated throughout the text.

The …ནས་…བར་དུ་ ("From ... Up To ...") Construction

③

Page 228, Line 8

Recall that the …ནས་…བར་(དུ་) construction is used to indicate a list of items (assumed to be known by the reader) by providing only the first and last elements of the list (see ཤེས་རབ་སྙིང་པོ་ note 15). Here is a slightly different occurrence of that same construction, but one that is followed by a quantifying number. Since this text is written in a "རང་ལུགས་"-style presentation, simple predication and assertions are the dominant sentence structures. Consequently, there is a tendency to omit the verbs of predication (ཡིན་) and simple existence (ཡོད་), and such is the case with this sentence as well. With the བར་དུ་ abbreviated simply as བར་, the sentence beginning with དབྱེ་ན། reads: "When divided [there are] five, from mental direct perceptions apprehending forms to mental direct perceptions apprehending tangible objects."

WHAT TO REMEMBER

The …ནས་…བར་དུ་ construction is a simple way to indicate a list of items by providing only the first and last elements of the list.

Segués and Run-on Sentences

④

Page 228, Line 10

Previously, run-on sentences were encountered as they were constructed with verbal participles (see ཤེར་སྙིང་རྣམ་བཤད་ note 15). Here, however, a different sort of run-on sentence is encountered in which the end of one sentence has a sixth-case marker serving as a segué appended to it, forcing the final phrase to serve double duty as both the end of the previous sentence and the start of the next one. This is a fairly common literary technique. Hence, for example, the block of text encountered here—སྤྲིལ་མར་སྐྱེ་བ། འཕྲོས་གསུམ་བར་སྐྱེ་བ། རྒྱུན་མཐའ་ཁོ་ནར་སྐྱེ་བ་དང་འདོད་ཚུལ་གསུམ་ལས། དང་པོའི་ཚུལ་ནི།—should be read as:

> སྤྲིལ་མར་སྐྱེ་བ། འཕྲོས་གསུམ་བར་སྐྱེ་བ། རྒྱུན་མཐའ་ཁོ་ནར་སྐྱེ་བ་དང་འདོད་ཚུལ་གསུམ་[ཡོད།]
> [གསུམ་ལས་]དང་པོའི་ཚུལ་ནི། …

WHAT TO REMEMBER

An alternate form of the run-on sentence is one in which the end of one sentence has a segué appended to it, forcing the final phrase to serve double duty as both the end of the previous sentence and the start of the next one.

5 Lists and the Particle སོགས་

Page 228, Line 12

The generalizing lexical particle སོགས་ (see Wilson, 662, and ཤེར་སྙིང་རྣམ་བཤད་ note 6), which typically indicates the continuation of a series or list, here indicates the continuation of an alternating series of statements. Consequently, in addition to terminating the explicit listing of sentences, it serves to indicate the continuation of the larger sentence encompassing them.

WHAT TO REMEMBER

Certain lexical particles apply only to nouns or only to verbs and sentences, while some can apply to either. The generalizing lexical particle (ལ་)སོགས་ is an example of one that can apply to both.

6 Translation Hint

Page 228, Line 12

Although the construction ་་་ནས་་་་བར་(དུ་) was just seen (see བློ་རིག་ note 3), the occurrence of the particle བར་ here is not similar. Although it connects to what it modifies by a postpositional connective (Wilson, case 6.3), rather than meaning "up to" or "until," བར་ in this case conveys the meaning of "between" (from which the word བར་དོ་—"bardo" or "intermediate state" is derived).

Translation Hint

⑦

Page 228, Line 18

This sentence reflects the multivalence of some grammatical structures. As has been previously noted, the modular nature of Tibetan sentence formation is often exploited by some authors to construct complex sentences. Like that example (see རིག་ཕྱིར་དམར་པོ་ note 10), this sentence involves several verbs serving as objects of the verbs that follow them.

The core sentence, which reads ཚུར་མཐོང་གི་རྒྱུད་ལ་ནི་གཟུགས་འཛིན་ཡིད་མངོན་དུས་མཐའི་སྐད་ཅིག་མ་རེ་རེ་ལས་མི་སྐྱེས་, then serves as the complement of the verb འདོད་, which in turn serves as the complement of the verb དགོས་. This sentence then forms the complement of the verb གསལ་, with the noun ཡིག་ཆ་ serving as its locative object. As a result, the sentence reads: "It is clear (གསལ་) in the textbook (ཡིག་ཆར་) that it is necessary (དགོས་) to assert (འདོད་) that no more than one smallest moment of a mental perception apprehending a form is produced (སྐྱེས་) in the continuum of 'one-who-looks-nearby.'"

Verbal Collocations with བྱེད་

⑧

Page 229, Line 4

While verbal collocations can be formed with nearly every verb, those formed with the verb བྱེད་ ("to make," "to do," etc.) are relatively numerous since it is the primary delexicalised verb used for the formation of such collocations in the Tibetan language, in addition to being one of the most common auxiliary verbs. The verb phrase དབང་དུ་བྱས་ falls into the category of "open" or "modifiable" verbal collocations (see མདོ་མཛངས་བླུན་ note 21) as indicated by the sixth-case connective that precedes it; it is often translated as "to be made from the viewpoint of ..." or "to be posited through the force of ..."

WHAT TO REMEMBER

A verbal collocation (or "phrasal verb" as Wilson calls it) is a multiword verbal phrase that conveys a meaning that goes beyond the literal connotation of the individual words that compose it. When reading canonical Buddhist texts, the majority of verbal collocations to be found are those constructed with a Sanskritic adverb—that is, an adverb that mimics one of the twenty or so Sanskrit verbal prefixes (རྣམ་པར་ for *vi*-, རབ་ཏུ་ for *pra*-, etc.). Other verbal collocations violate expected behavior for a verb by being grammatically connected to their object(s) by a sixth-case particle (as with དབང་དུ་བྱེད་, བརྒྱུད་ནས་བསྐྱེད་, and others).

9

Translation Hint

Page 229, Line 4

This is another example of a non-case syntactic particle (see ཤེར་སྙིང་རྣམ་བཤད་ note 2).

10

Translation Hint: Text Titles as Agents

Page 229, Line 12

Here, རྣམ་འགྲེལ་རྩ་བ་ is both the agent of the main verb, བཤད་, and of the verb in the gerund clause, བསྡུ་. A distinctive feature of the gerund construction is that it indicates an action performed by the same agent as that of the main verb, though is temporally prior to it. Although nonsentient objects, such as texts, are seldom thought of as agents (a role reserved for the author of a text), grammatically it is quite commonly seen. The greater challenge in reading such sentences is often the identification of the text to which the brief title refers. This text is fairly easy to identify, however. In general, the various subjects of study within Buddhism were codified by one or more foundational figures. Since this text on "Awarenesses and Knowers" lies within the broader subject area of Buddhist epistemology, the works of Dignāga and Dharmakīrti are frequently cited in subsequent expository and pedagogical texts. Here, the author, Jampel Sampel, is making reference to the "root [text]" (རྩ་བ་) of Dharmakīrti's *Commentary on [Dignāga's "Compendium on] Valid Cognition"* (ཚད་མ་རྣམ་འགྲེལ་; *Pramāṇavārttika*), abbreviated simply as རྣམ་འགྲེལ་རྩ་བ་. It is seldom the case that the full title of a work will be given by an author when quoting from it. Moreover, most text titles, as previously noted (see རིགས་ལམ་ note 2), are comprised of one or more ornate poetic phrases. Such brief poetic titles often serve as the commonly cited form of a text. One such example can be seen below (see བློ་རིག་ note 13).

Verbal Adjectives vs. Clause-Connective Constructions

11

Page 230, Line 3

While verbs in clause-connective constructions (see ཤེས་རབ་སྙིང་པོ་ note 17) have been seen numerous times before, this passage introduces a different type of verbal modifier. Simply stated, the difference between a verbal adjective and a verbal clause is the difference between an abstract modifier and a specific modifier; it is the difference between "a car that goes 100 miles per hour" (verbal adjective) and "a car that is going 100 miles per hour" (verbal clause). Here we see the use of a verbal adjective འདྲེན་བྱེད་ཀྱི་ཚད་མ་ ("valid cognition that induces [something]"), which could be contrasted with a clause-connective construction: འདྲེན་བྱེད་པའི་ཚད་མ་ ("valid cognition that is inducing [something]"). The former describes an abstract quality, while the latter describes a specific circumstance.

WHAT TO REMEMBER

Verbal adjectives utilize a verb phrase to express an abstract quality that adjectivally modifies a noun. They are distinguished from clause-connective constructions in that they are formed by the finite verb form (as opposed to the participle form) and thus attach to their nouns with the particles ཀྱི་, གྱི་, གི་, etc.

The Completed Action Auxiliary Verb ཟིན་

12

Page 230, Line 4

When a definition is given in a textbook, its sentence structure follows that typical of the genre: two noun phrases with an omitted terminal linking verb. So it is here, and as expected (from context), this passage provides "the definition of subsequent cognition" (བཅད་ཤེས་ཀྱི་མཚན་ཉིད་); what precedes this phrase is a single unit.

The challenge in reading this sentence lies with the use of the word ཟིན་. The verb ཟིན་ on its own is a Class IV nominative-syntactic verb. When occurring in conjunction with a second verb, however, ཟིན་ functions as an auxiliary verb to indicate the completion of an action. Hence, རྟོགས་ཟིན་ conveys the meaning of "has been realized" or when nominalized of "that which was realized." The entire sentence རང་འདྲེན་བྱེད་ཀྱི་ཚད་མ་སྔ་མས་རྟོགས་ཟིན་ as a result, serves as the object of the verb རྟོགས་ in the clause-connective (Wilson, case 6.6.1) construction རྟོགས་པའི་ཚད་མིན་. All of this, in turn, is an adjectival modifier (as indicated by the sixth-case (Wilson, case 6.1.2) connective གྱི་, just as with the ཀྱི་ before it) of "knower" (རིག་པ་). Putting the pieces together yields:

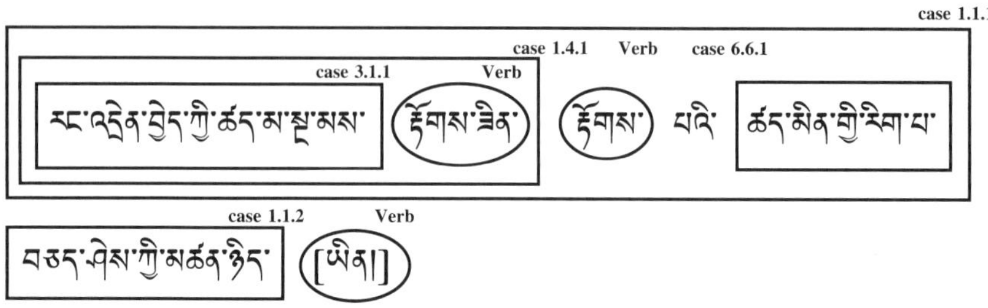

WHAT TO REMEMBER

The verb ཟིན་, when appearing with another verb, functions as an auxiliary verb indicating the completion of the action of the main verb and does not alter the syntax of the sentence.

13

Canonical Text Titles

Page 230, Line 8

As noted above (see བློ་རིག་ note 10), when text titles are cited in the body of a text (often introducing a quotation), it is rare that the full title of a work is given by an author. Rather, its abbreviated title or a poetic title will be used. Here, the title of the text being quoted—*The Correct* (འཐད་ལྡན་)—is one such example. As was previously seen (see ཤེས་རབ་སྙིང་པོ་ note 1), a canonical text begins with the statement of its title in its original language (often Sanskrit) followed by its Tibetan translation. Contemporary guides to the Tibetan Buddhist canon index these opening titles, but in the case of this text, however, this poetic title of this work does not occur in the opening of the text but rather is only found in the colophon to the text and would not normally be indexed. Authored by Dharmottara, the bibliographic title of this work is *A Commentary on [Dharmakīrti's] "Ascertainment of Valid Cognition"* (ཚད་མ་རྣམ་པར་ངེས་པའི་འགྲེལ་བཤད།; *Pramāṇa-viniścaya-ṭīkā*).

WHAT TO REMEMBER

When attempting to identify canonical texts cited in a work, there are three basic strategies: (1) relying on a teacher well versed in the subject matter, (2) consulting reference works, and (3) searching for keywords in full text. In the absence of the first resource, the latter two must be relied upon. Several electronic text initiatives aimed at providing full text searching of the canon are increasing, although in some instances these resources could also prove insufficient (see བློ་རིག་ note 15, below).

The Non-case Syntactic Particle ལ་ 14

Page 230, Line 9

As has been previously observed (see ཤེར་སྙིང་རྣམ་བཤད་ notes 2 and 18), the case-marking particle ལ་, seen here following the sentence མངོན་སུམ་དང་རྗེས་སུ་དཔག་པའི་དང་པོ་སྐད་ཅིག་མ་གཉིས་ནི་ཚད་མ་ཡིན་, is functioning not as a case marker but rather as a non-case syntactic particle (Wilson, 676–677) conveying the sense of "although" or "but"; hence the quote is comprised of two sentences.

WHAT TO REMEMBER

Non-case syntactic particles applied to verbs and sentences are used to qualify a statement or segué to a related idea. The non-case syntactic particle ལ་ ("although ...," "but ...," etc.) is often used to segué from one sentence to another that qualifies it.

Canonical Quotations 15

Page 230, Line 10

As observed in the previous note, this quote is comprised of two sentences separated by the non-case syntactic particle ལ་. The first sentence is terminated by the verb ཡིན་ with its subject explicitly marked by the first-case marker ནི་ (Wilson, case 1.1.1) and ends with the slightly awkward numeric phrase དང་པོ་སྐད་ཅིག་མ་གཉིས་ ("the two first moments").

The second sentence is somewhat more difficult and its grammar can be parsed in two different ways. In both readings of the grammar, however, the subject—marked by the ནི་ particle—is made up of two noun phrases in apposition: དེ་དག་གི་རྒྱུན་དུ་གྱུར་པའི་གྲུབ་པ་དང་བདེ་བ་ཐ་མི་དད་པ་ and ཕྱི་མ་རྣམས་. Since the previous sentence referred to the "first moments" of certain types of consciousnesses, ཕྱི་མ་ can be understood as referring to "later [moments]." While the expressions ཐ་དད་ and ཐ་མི་དད་ function like frozen verbal collocations meaning "to be different" and "to be not different," respectively, the latter—nominalized here as ཐ་མི་དད་པ་—consequently can be taken as "those that are not different." As a verb, it has as its nominative subject two verbal nouns, གྲུབ་པ་དང་བདེ་བ་ ("establishment and restful abiding"; *yogakṣema*), both modified by a clause. Thus, the subject reads: "Later [moments]—those that are not different [in terms of] establishment and restful abiding [and] which are a continuation of them."

In treating the sentence as a whole, the first approach would be to take everything up to the ཡིན་པ་ as the nominative object of the Class V verb སྤངས་. In this reading, the second sentence could be rendered as "[The assertion of] later [moments] ... being valid cognitions is abandoned," although such a reading presumes that the author (Dharmottara) is speaking in the first person. In this interpretation of the grammar, the particle ནི་ is used to demarcate the subject (being ambiguous, since it consists of two appositional noun phrases) from the predicate of the verb ཡིན་, ཚད་མ་.

Alternatively, the particle ནི་ could very easily be used to separate the subject or agent of the main verb (here, སྤངས་) from the subordinate clauses that follow. Hence, a second reading of the grammar is to take the phrase marked explicitly by the ནི་ particle as an irregular subject (Wilson, case 1.3.3; see Wilson, 630) of the Class V verb སྤངས་ and the remainder as its nominative object (Wilson, case 1.4.1). In this reading of the grammar, the second sentence would be construed as "Later [moments] ... have abandoned being valid cognitions." This would seem to be the preferred reading.

There is a larger issue with this quotation, however. The passage as quoted by Jampel Sampel does not exactly agree with its canonical source. The actual quote, as it occurs in Dharmottara's *The Correct, A Commentary on [Dharmakīrti's] "Ascertainment of Valid Cognition"* (D 4229: vol. 189, folio/line 9b.1–.2) reads:

དེ་ཉིད་ཀྱི་ཕྱིར་དང་པོའི་མངོན་སུམ་དང་རྗེས་སུ་དཔག་པའི་སྐད་ཅིག་མ་ཉིད་ཀྱིས་དོན་བྱེད་པར་ནུས་པའི་དངོས་པོའི་རྒྱུན་ངེས་པས་འཇུག་པའི་ཡུལ་དུ་བྱེད་པར་ནུས་པའི་ཕྱིར། དེའི་རྒྱུན་དུ་གྱུར་པ་གྲུབ་པ་དང་བདེ་བ་ཐ་མི་དད་པ་ཕྱི་མ་རྣམས་ཚད་མ་ཡིན་པ་སྤྲངས་པ་ཡིན་ནོ།

Though it is possible that the passage as quoted by Jampel Sampel is derived from a variant translation of Dharmottara's text or a different redaction of the *Translated Commentaries* (*bstan 'gyur*), a more likely reason for this discrepancy lies in the nature of Tibetan scholarship. In the Tibetan commentarial tradition, it is common practice to rely on the commentaries of previous generations of scholars. More likely, this passage was paraphrased by an earlier author and has served as a source for the quote by subsequent scholars.

WHAT TO REMEMBER

When encountering canonical citations, there are several issues to keep in mind. First and foremost, one must remember that a text as quoted may not be as it is preserved in the canon. In addition, although many texts in the Tibetan canon were revised and edited over the centuries in order to conform with notions of normative Tibetan grammar, many more were not. Consequently, canonical quotations can, and often do, have irregular grammatical constructions and contain archaic terminology.

Translation Hint

16

Page 230, Line 15

Here, each instance of བྱེད་པ། is a verbal noun meaning "being a product" or simply "product."

Translation Hint

17

Page 230, Line 23

As was previously seen with Tsongkhapa's text (see ལམ་གཙོ་རྣམ་གསུམ་ note 1), word, phrase, and even sentence boundaries are only implicitly indicated by syllable pairs in verse. The quotation encountered here—from the *Treasury of Reasoning* by the twelfth-century scholar Sakya Paṇḍita—utilizes precisely such metrics to convey its intended meaning. It can thus be read as:

> ཡིད་དཔྱོད་རྟགས་ལ་བརྟེན་མི་ལྟོས། དམ་བཅའ་ཙམ་ཡིན། ཐེ་ཚོམ་འགྱུར།
> རྟགས་ལ་བརྟེན་ན་ཡང་དག་གམ་ལྟར་སྣང་[ཡོད།] གསུམ་ལས་འདའ་བ་མེད།

18 Distributed Grammar—Multiple Sentences in Clauses

Page 231, Line 13

As is typical in debate manuals, here a definition is provided by giving a "sentence" that consists solely of two noun phrases in sequence without an explicit terminal linking verb (i.e., ཡིན་). The subject (the first noun phrase) displays the use of "distributed grammar"—that is, the sequential listing of multiple phrases that all attach to the final noun using the same construction (in this case, a clause connective, Wilson, case 6.6.x) but in which only the last occurrence is explicitly given. The noun phrase in question contains two clauses separated by the syntactic particle ཡང་ (Wilson, 674–675), both of which relate to the final noun phrase. The noun phrase can be seen as the two clauses—རང་གི་འཇུག་ཡུལ་དུ་གྱུར་པའི་རང་མཚན་གསལ་བར་སྣང་ and དེ་ལ་ངེས་པ་འདྲེན་མི་ནུས་—while the second noun phrase, རིག་པ་, stands in relation to both of them. Notice that the noun རིག་པ་ relates to the first clause as its complement (Wilson, case 6.6.4) and to the second clause as its explicit subject (Wilson, case 6.6.1), and hence while both stand in a clausal relationship to the noun, they need not be of the same type. Consequently, the phrase reads: "a knower to which the specifically characterized [phenomenon] that is its object of engagement clearly appears but (ཡང་) which is unable to induce ascertainment with respect to it."

It is of significance to note that this grammatical construction is not only seen in the definition but also occurs in the definiendum ("that which is being defined") as well. Here, the definiendum, སྣང་ལ་མ་ངེས་པའི་བློ་, is similarly constructed of a noun (བློ་) modified by two clauses (actually, just two verbs: སྣང་ and ངེས་) separated by a syntactic particle, the disjunctive syntactic particle ལ་ (see བློ་རིག་ note 14, above). Again, it is of significance to note that in such constructions—just as with the first half of the definition seen above—the noun to which the clause connects need not function in the same grammatical role with each verb; here, for example, བློ་ would connect to the verb སྣང་ as a qualifier but would connect to the verb ངེས་ as an agent. Hence, it reads: "an awareness to which [an object] appears but is not ascertained."

WHAT TO REMEMBER

In addition to extensive sentences, multiple verbs and connected sentences can also serve as subordinate clauses to a noun. In such cases, the conjoined sentences or verbs are not broken apart by punctuation (i.e., a "།").

The Syllable ཉིད་ as Restrictive Verbal Suffix

19

Page 231, Line 16

There are a variety of verbal suffix particles; some of these form semimodal expressions (see མདོ་མཛངས་བླུན་ notes 3 and 10), while others form a variety of different verbal nouns. The restrictive lexical particle ཉིད་ is one such verbal suffix particle. As previously seen (see དེབ་ཐེར་དམར་པོ་ note 18), the particle ཉིད་ has two main uses when applied to nouns (Wilson, 204–205): (1) it is used to create abstract nouns and adjectives from finite nouns, and (2) it is used as a restrictive suffix or emphatic ("just that very X" or "X itself"). Less commonly, it serves an emphatic function when applied to verbs. In its usage here as applied to a verb, the particle ཉིད་ places emphasis upon the verb, although in a restrictive manner, conveying the adverbial notion of "just" or "merely." Hence, the expression མཐོང་ཉིད་ does not mean "really seeing" but simply "just seeing" or "merely seeing." As a result, the particle ལས་ that terminates this phrase is not a disjunctive gerund marker (see མདོ་མཛངས་བླུན་ note 4) but simply the less commonly seen use of the ablative (fifth) case to indicate a reason (Wilson, case 5.7).

WHAT TO REMEMBER

The lexical particle ཉིད་ is often used as a restrictive or emphatic suffix as well as for the creation of abstract nouns. When applied to verbs, ཉིད་ conveys the adverbial notion of "just" or "merely," and depending on context can be translated as "just doing X" (as in མཐོང་ཉིད་ལས་… "from just seeing …") or "really just doing X" (as in བདག་གཟིར་བར་བྱེད་ཉིད་དོ། "[it is] really just harming oneself").

20

Translation Hint

Page 231, Line 17

Recall the use of the auxiliary verb བྱེད་ in translations from Sanskrit—as here with the quotation from Dharmakīrti's *Pramāṇavārttika*—to place emphasis on the active voice (see ཤེར་སྙིང་རྣམ་བཤད་ note 32). There will be more on this later (see བླ་མ་ལྔ་བཅུ་པ་ note 9).

21

Translation Hint

Page 232, Line 16

The first part of this syllogism contains two sentences separated by the non-case syntactic particle ཀྱི་ (see ཤེར་སྙིང་རྣམ་བཤད་ note 2).

22

Translation Hint

Page 232, Lines 18–21

This entire passage is a single syllogism, beginning with དང་པོ་གྲུབ་སྟེ།, and the remainder constitutes the reason clause, beginning with སྤྱིར་ཚད་མའི་གྲངས་ལ་རྒྱང་འཕེན་པས་…. The reason clause is comprised of a basic sentence with a subordinate clause which in turn has two of its own subordinate clauses. The core of the reason clause is ཚད་མ་ལ་དེ་གཉིས་སུ་གྲངས་ངེས་པར་བསྒྲུབ་པའི་ཕྱིར། ("because with respect to valid cognitions [Dharmakīrti] established that [they] are definitely enumerated as those two"). What precedes this is a gerund clause built from the verb ལེགས་པར་བཀག་, in which the agent is explicitly given, རིགས་པའི་དབང་ཕྱུག་ "the lord of reasoning" (i.e., Dharmakīrti). The basic clause is རིགས་པའི་དབང་ཕྱུག་གིས་…དེ་དག་ལེགས་པར་བཀག་ནས་… ("the lord of reasoning ... having well refuted these"), while in between these two phrases is another marked by the originative ནས་ (Wilson, case 5.1.2): གཞལ་བྱ་གཉིས་ཕྱིར་ཚད་མ་གཉིས་ཞེས་སོགས་དངོས་སྟོབས་ཀྱི་རིགས་པའི་སྒོ་དུ་མ་ནས་ ("from the many viewpoints of reasoning through the power of the fact [stating] 'Because there are two objects of comprehension, there are two valid cognitions,' and so forth"). All of this is preceded by another clause indicated by the syntactic marker ཕྱིར་དུ་ ("for the sake of ...").

A sentence in itself, this passage utilizes the …ནས་…པར་[དུ་] construction (see བློ་རིག་ note 3) as a list of nominalized sentences all in apposition with the agent of the sentence, གཞན་སྡེ་རྣམས་ཀྱིས་. This is combined with object of the verb དགག་ ("to refute") གྲངས་ལ་ལོག་པར་རྟོག་པ་དུ་མ་ཞིག་འབྱུང་བ་དེ་ ("the many erroneous conceptions which had arisen with regard to that enumeration") to form a complete sentence within the clause. Finally, the entire sentence is begun by a frozen adverbial སྤྱིར་ ("in general") and a noun phrase marked with a topical locative (Wilson, case 7.5) ཚད་མའི་གྲངས་ལ་ ("with respect to the enumeration of valid cognitions..."). Bringing all the pieces together, the final translation of the syllogism reads:

> The first [the enumeration of valid cognitions as two] is established thus. With respect to the enumeration of [types of] valid cognition in general, for the sake of refuting the many erroneous conceptions which had arisen with regard to that enumeration—from the nihilists' positing one, perception, to the followers of Caraka (*tsa ri ka pa*) positing eleven—the lord of reasoning [Dharmakīrti] refuted these well from the many viewpoints of reasoning through the power of the fact, [when he] said [in the *Commentary on 'Valid Cognition'*], "Because there are two objects of comprehension, there are two [types of] valid cognition" and so forth; [hence, Dharmakīrti] established that, with respect to valid cognitions, [there is a] definite enumeration [of them] as those two, [perception and inference].

The Word དུས་ as a Verbal Suffix

Page 233, Line 17

As a noun, the word དུས་ simply means "time." When appended to a verb, however, it functions as a temporal-clause marker meaning "when" or "at which time" (here followed by the non-case continuative particle ཀྱི་ (see ཤེར་སྙིང་རྣམ་བཤད་ note 2)). The main verb of the clause, ཟ་, is a Class V verb, whose polysemy has been discussed (see ཤེར་སྙིང་རྣམ་བཤད་ note 37). One of the meanings of this verb is "to occur" or "to have," and often, when taking ཐེ་ཚོམ་ as its object ("to have a doubt" or simply "to doubt"), it typically takes either a complement marked by a seventh-case particle (Wilson, case 7.6, as in "to have a doubt [about] ...") or a complete sentence as a thought. The latter is the case here and in the next two sentences as well, with the third sentence explicitly marking the thought with སྙམ་དུ་ (see ཤེར་སྙིང་རྣམ་བཤད་ note 28). Regarding the complement of the sentence, as previously mentioned (see ཤེར་སྙིང་རྣམ་བཤད་ note 26), an either/or construction can be formed by duplicating a verb in the negative, as is seen here with ཡིན་མིན་ ("is or is not") and in a subsequent sentence explicitly with མཐོང་ངམ་མ་མཐོང་ ("is seen or not seen"). As the third sentence in this list of three examples gives these grammatical constructions explicitly, as a whole they can be thought of as an instance of a parallel grammatical construction (see རིགས་ལམ་ note 17). This construction is repeated throughout the text.

WHAT TO REMEMBER

When the word དུས་ occurs following a verb or sentence, it functions as a temporal clause marker meaning "when" or "at which time." It is often, but not always, followed by the non-case continuative particle ཀྱི་.

24

Translation Hint

Page 234, Line 23

As with the definition that immediately precedes them, the passages beginning with ཡིད་དང་། up through གཉིས་ཀ་མིན་པ་དབང་ཤེས་འཁོར་གྱི་སེམས་བྱུང་ཐམས་ཅད་དོ། are a series of sentences with omitted linking verbs (ཡིན་) and verbs of existence (ཡོད་) and utilize ལ་ as a disjunctive syntactic particle linking the sentence pairs. Thus, they should be read as:

ཡིད་དང་། ཡིད་ཤེས་ལ་སྨུ་བཞི་ [ཡོད] །
དང་པོ་ཡིན་ལ[།] ཕྱི་མ་མིན་པ། མིག་གི་རྣམ་ཤེས་ལྟ་བུ་ [ཡིན།] །

and so forth.

25

Hierarchy of the Syntactic Particles ཅིང་/ཞིང་ and དང་

Page 235, Line 6

Understanding the grammar of this sentence hinges on recognizing the hierarchy of the syntactic particles ཅིང་ and དང་—the former connecting sentences/verbs and the latter connecting phrases. In general, this passage forms the first half of a syllogism and is composed of a base sentence, ཤེས་དགོས་, with everything that precedes that being part of a gerund clause. Within this gerund clause, there is a Class V verbal collocation, ཁྱད་པར་ཕྱེ་, its nominative object (Wilson, case 1.4.1), ཚུལ་, and two complete sentences in apposition with that object. Utilizing the technique of parallel construction, each of these sentences is terminated by the same Class II verb, ཡོད་, and is joined by the syntactic particle ཅིང་.

In both sentences, there is a verb (ཡོད་) with the same subject (ཁྱད་པར་) in the nominative (Wilson, case 1.3.1) and a pair of phrases (connected by དང་) serving as the locative complement (Wilson, case 7.6) of the verb. Diagrammatically, that is:

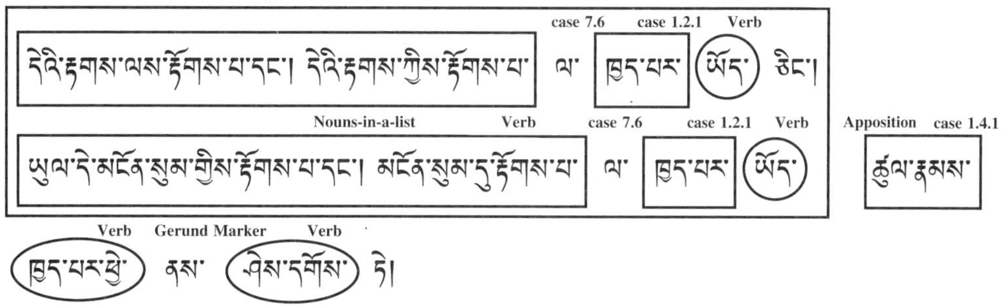

In actuality, although the sentences preceding this stand on their own syntactically, the sentences from དེ་བཞིན་དུ། onwards could be considered as being in apposition with ཚུལ་ as well.

WHAT TO REMEMBER

In general, the syntactic particle ཅིང་ is used to connect sentences (technically, verbs) while the syntactic particle དང་ is used to connect noun phrases. This hierarchy of sentences, clauses, and phrases (Wilson, 186–195) thus allows one to recognize nested parallel constructions (as in this example) and associate multiple phrases within clauses, and multiple clauses within sentences.

Translation Hint: Recognizing Requisite Grammar

26

Page 235, Line 7

The grammar of this sentence is determined by the main verb ཟུངས་, the imperative form of the Class V verb འཛིན་ ("to hold"). As previously noted (see མདོ་མཛངས་བློན་ note 14), when the imperative form of a verb is combined with the verbal suffix particle ཤིག, it forms a precative construction—the fervent expression of an aspiration. The important thing to remember about precative constructions (and imperative, and often optative and subjunctive constructions as well), however, is that they take their subject in the vocative (eighth case). Such is the case here as well. As can be seen, however, there is a problem in that there does not appear to be any noun phrase, proper or otherwise, occurring in the vocative.

Although the typical syntax for a sentence containing a Class V verb is an agent marked in the third case with an object marked in the first case, because the precative construction necessitates that the subject of the sentence be in the vocative (here, apparently, an unstated ཁྱོད་ "you"), the phrase occurring at the start of the sentence (པཎ་ཆེན་ཉིད་ཀྱིས་) cannot be the agent of the verb ཟུངས་. Similarly, given the construction གཅེས་པར་, the verb གཅེར་ ("to cherish" or "to care [for]") must be serving as the complement (Wilson, case 2.5) of the sentence. Since it is functioning as a complement and not an object, the expression གཅེས་པར་ཟུངས་ cannot mean "hold on to cherishing" (which would be གཅེས་པ་ཟུངས་) but rather must mean "hold on to [this] *as* [something] to be cherished."

A seventh-case marker, ལ་, is seen immediately preceding this construction, marking the phrase བརྡའ་ཆད་འདི་རྣམས་ ("these terms" or "this terminology"). Since གཅེས་ is both a Class V verb and is acting as a complement of ཟུངས་, this phrase cannot be associated with the verb གཅེས་. Instead, the phrase བརྡའ་ཆད་འདི་རྣམས་ must be associated with the main verb ཟུངས་ and must be the object being referred to (Wilson, case 7.6). As a result, བརྡའ་ཆད་འདི་རྣམས་ལ་གཅེས་པར་ཟུངས་ཤིག should be taken to read "With regard to these terms, hold onto [them] as something to be cherished!"

Having eliminated both verbs in this sentence—གཅེས་ and ཟུངས་—as candidates for an associated agent, the only conclusion left is that there is an omitted verb in the sentence. As previously noted (see རིགས་ལམ་ note 4), in certain instances, basic verbs of existence (ཡོད་), identity (ཡིན་), and action (བྱེད་) may be omitted. In this case, the generic action verb བྱེད་ in a clause construction has been omitted—that is, the sentence should be understood as: པཎ་ཆེན་ཉིད་ཀྱིས་[བྱེད་པའི་]བརྡའ་ཆད་འདི་རྣམས་ལ་གཅེས་པར་ཟུངས་ཤིག. In addition, since the author, Geshe Jampel Sampel, comes from the Loseling College of Drepung Monastic University, when he refers to a "Paṇchen," it should be understood as a reference to the main textbook author for the Loseling College, Paṇchen Sönam Drakpa (པཎ་ཆེན་བསོད་ནམས་གྲགས་པ་). Hence, the complete sentence can be translated literally as "With respect to these terms [that are used] by Paṇchen [Sönam Drakpa] himself, hold onto [them] as something to be cherished!" or simply as "Hold onto this terminology of Paṇchen [Sönam Drakpa] as something to be cherished!"

The Syllable ཚེ་ as a Verbal Suffix

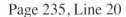

Page 235, Line 20

As previously mentioned (see ཤེར་སྙིང་རྣམ་བཤད་ note 2), the non-case syntactic particle ཀྱི་ ("but ...," "even though," "however," etc.) can be used to segué to a related, though disjunct statement. Likewise, the syntactic particle ན་ is used as a verbal suffix in a similar manner, often indicating a conditional construction ("if ..."), although occasionally it indicates a rhetorical one ("when ...") as well (see Wilson, 130, 151, and 191). Similar to the use of the word དུས་ as a verbal suffix (see བློ་རིག་ note 23), the word ཚེ་ ("time" or "lifetime") can also be used as a verbal suffix to indicate a temporal clause, meaning "when" or "at which time."

Illustrating the use of all three of these syntactic particles—as well as the terminating syntactic particle, སོ་ (see Wilson, 158–159, 184, and 665)—to separate four distinct, but connected sentences, the passage མཚན་ཉིད་དེ་དག་ཀྱང་གོ་བ་གཙོ་བོར་བྱས་ཀྱི་ཚིག་སྐྱོན་གཅོད་པ་གཙོ་བོར་བྱེད་ན་མཚན་ཉིད་གང་ལ་རང་སྒྲ་ཐོག་མར་ཡོད་ཚེ་མཚོན་བྱ་ལ་ཡང་རང་ཉིད་དེ་ཡིན་པའི་ཞེས་སྦྱར་དགོས་སོ། can be separated in reference to the syntactic particles ཀྱི་, ན་, and ཚེ་ as follows:

Sentence	Syntactic Particle & Function
མཚན་ཉིད་དེ་དག་ཀྱང་གོ་བ་གཙོ་བོར་བྱས་	ཀྱི་ disjunctive syntactic particle
ཚིག་སྐྱོན་གཅོད་པ་གཙོ་བོར་བྱེད་	ན་ conditional syntactic particle
མཚན་ཉིད་གང་ལ་རང་སྒྲ་ཐོག་མར་ཡོད་	ཚེ་ temporal clause marker
མཚོན་བྱ་ལ་ཡང་རང་ཉིད་དེ་ཡིན་པའི་ཞེས་སྦྱར་དགོས་	སོ། terminating syntactic particle

WHAT TO REMEMBER

When the word ཚེ་ occurs following a verb or sentence, it functions as a temporal clause marker meaning "when," "whenever," or "at which time."

28

Tibetan Numbers: Abbreviations

Page 236, Line 2

Recall that higher Tibetan numbers (i.e., numbers above 20) are formed through the use of multipliers (10, 100, 1000, etc.) and connecting syllables or "infixes" (see Wilson, 138–141), and there is a series of infix syllables associated with each group. For example, for numbers 30–39, the infix syllable སོ་ is used to separate the "tens" from the "digits" numbers, as in: སུམ་ཅུ་སོ་གཅིག་ (31), སུམ་ཅུ་སོ་གཉིས་ (32), སུམ་ཅུ་སོ་གསུམ་ (33), etc. The point of significance to note here, however, is that in some circumstances these numbers will be abbreviated by merely giving the infix and the digit so that, in the case of "31," it will be rendered solely as སོ་གཅིག་, leaving the refutation of an alternate interpretation ("one tooth," in this case) to context. Here, then, ང་གཅིག་ is simply the number "51."

WHAT TO REMEMBER

Higher Tibetan numbers (i.e., numbers above 20) are formed through the use of multipliers (10, 100, 1000, etc.) and connecting syllables or "infixes," and there is a series of infix syllables associated with each group. These infixes can be used in lieu of the fully spelled-out numbers. For example:

21	༢༡	ཉི་ཤུ་ཉེར་གཅིག་	or simply	ཉེར་གཅིག་
31	༣༡	སུམ་ཅུ་སོ་གཅིག་	or simply	སོ་གཅིག་
41	༤༡	བཞི་བཅུ་ཞེ་གཅིག་	or simply	ཞེ་གཅིག་
51	༥༡	ལྔ་བཅུ་ང་གཅིག་	or simply	ང་གཅིག་
61	༦༡	དྲུག་བཅུ་རེ་གཅིག་	or simply	རེ་གཅིག་
71	༧༡	བདུན་ཅུ་དོན་གཅིག་	or simply	དོན་གཅིག་
81	༨༡	བརྒྱད་ཅུ་གྱ་གཅིག་	or simply	གྱ་གཅིག་
91	༩༡	དགུ་བཅུ་གོ་གཅིག་	or simply	གོ་གཅིག་

Where such abbreviations are homonyms with other noun-adjective phrases, they are disambiguated solely by context.

Compressed Grammar in Philosophical Verse

29

Page 236, Line 22

When Buddhism came to Tibet, Tibetan culture inherited not only the content of Indian Buddhism but also many of its literary forms. One such form was the tradition of rendering philosophical statements in poetic verse. While the Sanskrit literary tradition has a wealth of various poetic forms with different meters and literary conceits, when this approach to composition was adopted by Tibetans, it took the form of fixed-length verse and compressed sentence grammar.

This passage is an example of one such rendition in which a series of philoso-phical statements are rendered in verse. Because the primary emphasis is on literary form, the content is arranged less for clarity of presentation than for literary merit. In this example, there is a main sentence of simple predication (with an omitted ཡིན་) and a complex reason clause embedded between the subject and the predicate.

The subject of the sentence is a list of twenty items (terminated by the quantifying numeral ཉེ་ཤུ་), while the predicate is their identification as "secondary afflictions" (ཉེ་བའི་ཉོན་མོངས་). Between the two phrases is a reason clause, རྩ་ཉོན་འཕེལ་སྐྱེ་དང་ཉེ་ཕྱིར་. This reason clause demonstrates nicely the sort of "compression" of grammar that authors can use in formulating poetic verse, consisting of three verbs: འཕེལ་ ("to increase"), སྐྱེ་ ("to be produced"), and ཉེ་ ("to be close" or "to be associated [with]"). Hence, the basic sentence reads: "The twenty ... are secondary afflictions, because [they] are associated [with], are produced [by], and increase [along with] the root afflictions."

WHAT TO REMEMBER

The rendition of philosophical statements in poetic verse in Tibetan takes the form of fixed-length verse and compressed sentence grammar.

The Performative Construction

30

Page 237, Line 12

Previously (see མདོ་མཛངས་བླུན་ note 14), the use of the imperative-marking particles, such as ཅིག་, ཞིག་, and ཤིག་, were seen in the formation of the "precative" or aspirational construction. Here, the *past-tense verb* + གྱུར་ཅིག་ construction is one that could be described as a "strong precative" but so much so that it functions as a performative act. Performative acts are statements that express neither true nor false conditions but rather, by their utterance, bring about the state described. Concluding homages, such as this one, often contain statements of this nature: "by having done X, let such and such be the case!" Such performative utterances bear a close resemblance to aspirational statements (hence their similarity to the precative construction) and could alternately be described as a "precative perfect"—that is, an aspirational prayer that expresses a situation that one hopes will be fulfilled in the future—although given the usual accompanying instrumental declaration ("by having done such and such, ..."), calling this construction a "performative" appears to be a more appropriate description.

WHAT TO REMEMBER

The performative construction is formed by the past-tense form of a verb suffixed with གྱུར་ཅིག་. It is an expression that, by its utterance, brings about the state described or wished for.

Translation of Jampel Sampel's *Presentation of Awarenesses and Knowers Compendium of All the Important Points Opener of the Eye of New Intelligence*

Having bowed down to the glorious Losang Drakpa
Emanation of Mañjughoṣa, himself, treasury of wisdom,
For the sake of increasing the clarity of knowledge of those with low intelligence, I am composing
This presentation of awareness and knowledge, compendium of all the important points,

With regard to that, this explanation of the presentation of awareness and knowledge has three parts: definitions, divisions, and an explanation of the meaning of each division.

First [definitions]: The definition of an awareness is a knower. The definition of a consciousness is that which is clear and knowing. The three—awareness, knower, and consciousness—[are] synonymous.

Second [divisions]: There are three divisions of awareness and knowledge: into seven, three, and two. First, the division into seven consists of [direct] perception, inference, subsequent cognition, correct assumption, [consciousnesses to which an object] appears but is not ascertained, doubting consciousnesses, and wrong consciousnesses.

Third [the meaning of the individual divisions]: the meaning of the individual divisions [has] seven [parts].

First, with respect to the explanation of perception, there are two [parts]: definitions and divisions. The definition of perception is a nonmistaken knower that is free from conceptuality. The definition of a valid perception [that is, perception that is a valid cognition] is a newly incontrovertible unmistaken knower that is free from conceptuality. When perceptions are divided, [there are] four: sense, mental, self-knowing, and yogic perceptions.

The definition of sense perception is a nonmistaken knower that is free from conceptuality and that is produced from its own uncommon empowering condition, a physical sense-power. When sense perceptions are divided, there are five: sense perceptions apprehending forms, sense perceptions apprehending sounds, sense perceptions apprehending odors, sense perceptions apprehending tastes, and sense perceptions apprehending tangible objects.

The definition of a sense perception apprehending a form is a nonmistaken knower that is free from conceptuality and that is produced in dependence upon its own uncommon empowering condition—the eye sense-power—and an observed object condition—a form. With that [as an example], extend [this] reasoning to the lower ones [i.e., the remainder of the list of sense perceptions].

The definition of mental perception is a nonmistaken knower that is free from conceptuality and that arises from its own uncommon empowering condition—a mental sense power. When that is divided, [there are] two: mental perceptions that are "indicated on this occasion" and mental perceptions that are not. The definition of the first [a mental perception indicated on this occasion] is a nonmistaken knower of [objects] other [than internal consciousnesses as] indicated on this occasion that is free from conceptuality and that arises from its own uncommon empowering condition—a mental sense power. When [mental perceptions indicated on this occasion are] divided, [there are] five, [ranging] from mental perceptions apprehending forms to mental perceptions apprehending tangible objects.

With respect to the manner [in which] mental perceptions indicated on this occasion are produced, there are three manners asserted: alternating production, production in three types, and production only at the end of a continuum; [and] from among [these], the first mode [of alternating production, asserted by Prajñākāragupta, is]: the first moment of a sense perception apprehending a form is produced; subsequently, the first moment of a mental perception apprehending the form is produced; subsequently, the second moment of a sense perception apprehending a form is produced, and so on, [thus] they assert that between each moment of sense perception, a moment of mental perception is produced.

The second mode [of production of the three types, asserted by Śaṅkarānanda] is asserted as: the three—the second moment of a sense perception apprehending a form, the first moment of a mental perception apprehending that form, and the self-knowing perception that experiences those two—are produced simultaneously. In brief, it is asserted that two types directed outward and one type directed inward are produced at one time.

The third mode [of production, only at the end of a continuum, is] the thought of the foremost father [Tsongkhapa] and his spiritual son [Gyeltsap, following Dharmottara]. It is asserted that a mental perception apprehending a form is produced only at the end of the last moment of a sense perception apprehending a form. Furthermore, it is clear in the textbook [Paṇchen Sönam Drakpa's commentary on *Dharmakīrti's Commentary on (Dignāga's) Compendium on Valid Cognition*] that it is necessary to assert that no more than one smallest moment each of a mental perception apprehending a form is produced in the continuum of one who looks ṇearby [i.e., an ordinary being]. It is necessary to understand "indicated on this occasion" as [referring to] the occasion where it is said [in sūtra]: "Consciousness of forms are of two types: those depending on the eye and the mind."

Second, [mental perceptions not indicated on this occasion] are for instance a clairvoyance which knows another's mind.

The definition of a self-knower is the apprehending aspect [of a consciousness]. The definition of a self-knowing perception is the apprehending aspect [of a consciousness] that is nonconceptual and unmistaken. When [self-knowing perceptions are] divided, there are three: valid cognitions that are those, [those that are] subsequent cognitions, and [those consciousnesses to which an object] appears but is not ascertained.

The definition of yogic perception is a nonmistaken exalted knower in the continuum of an ārya that is free from conceptuality and is produced from a samādhi ("meditative stabilization") that is the union of calm abiding and special insight and that has become its own uncommon empowering condition. When [yogic perceptions are] divided, there are three: those of śrāvakas, pratyekabuddhas, and those of the Great Vehicle (*Mahāyāna*). Self-knowing perceptions and yogic perceptions are said necessarily to be mental perceptions.

These definitions are from the viewpoint of the Sautrāntikas, although the Cittamātrins and the Yogācāra-[Svātantrika-]Mādhyamikas write "[the definition of a perception is] a nonconceptual knower arisen from stable predispositions."

Ancillarily, with respect to briefly explaining the presentation of facsimiles of perceptions, [Dignāga's *Compendium on Valid Cognition*] says:

> Mistaken [conception], conventional consciousness,
> Inferential [conception], [conception] arisen from inference,
> Memory [conception], and wishing [conception]
> [Are] facsimiles of perception along with dimness of sight.

Thus, seven facsimiles of perception are asserted with six conceptual facsimiles of perception and one nonconceptual facsimile of perception.

The root text of [Dharmakīrti's] *Commentary* [*on (Dignāga's) Compendium on Valid Cognition*] explains [these] having condensed them into four. If you wish to know about these in [more] detail, [you] should look in the Radö (*rwa stod*) *Awareness and Knowledge* and in [Paṇchen Sönam Drakpa's] *Illumination of the Thought* on the third chapter [of Dharmakīrti's *Commentary on (Dignāga's) Compendium on Valid Cognition*] and so forth.

The definition of inferential cognition is a determinative knower that, having relied on its basis, a correct sign, is incontrovertible with regard to its object of comprehension, a hidden phenomenon.

The definition of an inferential valid cognition is a [determinative] knower that, having relied on its basis, a correct sign, is newly incontrovertible with regard to its object of comprehension, a hidden phenomenon. It is said that an inferential cognition is not necessarily a valid cognition. When [inferential cognitions are] divided, [there are three]: inferential cognition through belief, inferential cognition through renown, and inferential cognition through the power of the fact.

The definition of the first [an inferential cognition through belief] is a determinative knower that, depending upon its basis, a correct sign of belief, is incontrovertible with regard to its object of comprehension, a very hidden phenomenon. An illustration [is], for instance, an inferential consciousness that realizes that the scripture that states, "From giving, resources; from ethics, a happy [migration]" is incontrovertible with respect to its indicated meaning.

The definition of the second [inferential cognition through renown] is a determinative knower that, depending upon its basis, a correct sign of renown, is incontrovertible with respect to its object of comprehension, a terminological suitability. An illustration is an inferential consciousness that realizes it is suitable to express the rabbit-possessor by the term "moon."

The definition of the third [inferential consciousness by the power of the fact] is a determinative knower that depending on its basis, a correct sign by the power of the fact, its incontrovertible with respect to its object of comprehension, a slightly hidden phenomenon. An illustration is an inferential consciousness that realizes that sound is impermanent.

The definition of a subsequent cognition is a knower that is not a valid cognition [and] that realizes what has already been realized by the earlier valid cognition inducing it. When [subsequent cognitions are] divided, [there are] two: perceptual subsequent cognitions and conceptual subsequent cognitions. With respect to the first, there are four [perceptual subsequent cognitions]: sense perception subsequent cognitions, mental perception subsequent cognitions, self-knowing subsequent cognitions, and yogic perception subsequent cognitions. With respect to the second, [there are] two: conceptual subsequent cognitions induced by perception and conceptual subsequent cognitions induced by inference. As for illustrations: the first [a conceptual subsequent cognition induced by perception] is, for instance, a determinative consciousness that ascertains blue and which is produced subsequent to a perception apprehending blue; [an illustration of] the second [a conceptual subsequent cognition induced by inference] is, for instance, the second moment of an inferential consciousness realizing the impermanence of sound. This is because it says in [Dharmottara's] *The Correct*,

> The two—the first moment of a perception and of an inferential consciousness—are valid cognitions, but later moments [which are] not different in establishment and abiding [and] that are continuations of them, have abandoned being valid cognitions.

Sameness in establishment and abiding on this occasion are said to be made with respect to sameness of effect.

The definition of a correctly assuming consciousness is a knower that does not get at [an object with respect to which superimpositions have been] eliminated, although it adheres one-pointedly to the phenomenon which is its principal object of engagement. When [correctly assuming conciousnesses are] divided, [there are] three: correctly assuming consciousnesses that lack a reason, correctly assuming consciousnesses in which the reason is not ascertained, and correctly assuming consciousnesses that depend upon a facsimile of a reason. As for illustrations, the first [a correctly assuming consciousness without ascertaining the reason] is, for instance, an awareness that thinks, "Sound is impermanent" without any reason whatsoever; the second [a correctly assuming consciousness without a reason] is, for instance, an awareness that thinks, "Sound is impermanent" based on the sign of being a product, but without having ascertained that sound is a product and that if [something] is a product [it] is necessarily impermanent; the third [a correctly assuming consciousness depending upon a facsimile of a reason] is, for instance, an awareness that thinks, "Sound is impermanent," from being the sign of an object of comprehension.

Similarly, [Sakya Paṇḍita's] *Treasury of Reasoning* says,

> [Some] correctly assuming consciousnesses are not
> contingent on depending upon a sign;
> [They] are merely assertions [and can] turn into doubt.
> [Others,] when depending on a sign, [can have] a correct
> [sign] or
> A facsimile of a sign; [thus,] there are not more than three
> [types].

Also posited as the definition of that [i.e., a correctly assuming consciousness] is: a determinative knower that, without even depending on either experience or a correct sign which is its basis, apprehends one-pointedly and is nonmistaken with respect to its object of engagement, but does not get at an object with respect to which superimpositions have been eliminated. With respect to "[without depending on] experience" in this [definition], by considering [it to mean that] it should not depend at all on anything that is [one of] the three—experience arisen from meditation, experience of self-knowing, or clear experience which is not mixed with a meaning generality—then, if [the definition of this awareness is posited] in this way, then [I] think that if [something] is an awareness, then it would not necessarily be one of the seven awarenesses. This is because a samādhi [focused] on ugliness, or great compassion in the continuum of a learner, etc.—those [awarenesses] included within the class of realizations of method—are not suitable to be correctly assuming consciousnesses since they are contingent on experience arisen from meditation, and are not suitable to be mistaken consciousnesses since they are not affected by the causes of error and it is easy to understand how they are not the others. I think this, and it should be examined.

The definition of a doubting consciousness is a knower that, by its own power, has qualms in two directions. When that [doubting consciousnesses] is divided, [there are] three: doubt tending toward the fact, doubt not tending toward the fact, and doubt [consisting] in equal parts. As for illustrations: the first [doubt tending toward the fact] is, for instance, a two [-pointed] mind that thinks, "Sound is probably impermanent." The second [doubt not tending to the fact] is, for instance, a two-pointed mind thinking, "[It] is more than [just] probable that sound is permanent." The third [doubt consisting in equal parts] is, for instance, a hesitating consciousness that thinks, "Is sound is permanent or impermanent?"

The definition of an awareness to which [an object] appears but is not ascertained is a knower to which the specifically characterized phenomenon that is its object of engagement clearly appears but that is unable to induce ascertainment with respect to it. When those are divided, [there are] three: sense perception that is that, mental perception [that is that], and self-knowing [perception that is that]. Yogic perceptions that are that [i.e., an awarenesses to which an object appears but is not ascertained] do not exist, because if [something] is a yogic perception, [it] necessarily realizes its object. This is because it says in Dharmakīrti's *Commentary [on (Dignāga's) 'Compendium on Valid Cognition'*],

> The great intelligent ones—from just seeing—
> Ascertain all aspects.

As for illustrations, moreover, the first [a sense perception to which an object appears but is not ascertained] is, for instance, a sense perception apprehending blue that induces the doubt thinking, "Did I see blue or not?" The second [a mental perception to which an object appears but is not ascertained] is, for instance, a mental perception apprehending a form in the continuum of an ordinary being. The third [a self-knower to which an object appears but is not ascertained] is, for instance, a self-knower in the continuum of a nihilist that experiences an inference as a valid cognition.

The definition of a mistaken consciousness is a knower that is mistaken with regard to its object of engagement. When that [mistaken consciousness] is divided, [there are] two: conceptual mistaken consciousnesses and nonconceptual mistaken consciousnesses.

As for illustrations, the first [a conceptual wrong consciousness] is, for instance, a conceptual consciousness apprehending the horns of a rabbit, or [for instance,] a consciousness apprehending a self of persons. As for [illustrations of] the second [nonconceptual mistaken consciousnesses], [there are] two: those that are sense consciousnesses, and those that are mental consciousnesses; [and] from among [the two nonconceptual wrong consciousnesses], the first is, for instance, a sense consciousness to which two moons appear, or [for instance,] a sense consciousness to which snow mountains appear blue. The second [nonconceptual wrong consciousnesses] is, for instance, a dream consciousness to which blue clearly appears.

Second, there is a division of awareness and knowledge into three because there are the three: conceptual consciousnesses that take a meaning generality as their apprehended object; nonconceptual, nonmistaken consciousnesses that take a specifically characterized phenomenon as their apprehended object; and nonconceptual, mistaken consciousnesses that take a clearly appearing nonexistent as their apprehended object. The two — the first [a conceptual consciousness that takes a meaning generality as its apprehended object] and conceptual consciousness—are synonymous. The two—the second [a nonconceptual, nonmistaken consciousness that takes a specifically characterized phenomenon as its apprehended object] and perception—are synonymous. The two—the third [a nonconceptual, mistaken consciousness that takes a clearly appearing nonexistent as its apprehended object] and nonconceptual wrong consciousness—are synonymous.

Third, there is a division of awareness and knowledge into two because there is the division into two of consciousnesses that are valid cognitions and nonvalid cognitions; there is the division into two of conceptual consciousnesses and nonconceptual consciousnesses; there is the division into two of mistaken consciousnesses and non-mistaken consciousnesses; there is the division into two of mental consciousnesses and sense consciousnesses; there is the division into two of eliminatively engaging awarenesses and completely engaging awarenesses, and there is the division into two of minds and mental factors.

[There are] individual meanings to these as well. The definition of a valid cognition [is] a newly incontrovertible knower. When [valid cognitions are] divided, [there are] two: perceptual valid cognitions, and inferential valid cognitions. With regard to valid cognitions, the enumeration into these two is also definitive, for if there were more than these two, they would be unnecessary, and if less, [they] would not include them all. However, this definitive enumeration is a definitive enumeration that eliminates wrong conceptions, and it is not a definitive enumeration that eliminates a third possibility, because if [something] is a valid cognition, it is not necessarily one of those two—that is, because it is difficult to posit valid cognition in general as either of those two.

The first [the enumeration of valid cognitions as two] is established thus: with respect to the enumeration of [types of] valid cognition in general, for the sake of refuting the many erroneous conceptions which had arisen with regard to that enumeration given by others—from the nihilists' positing only perception to the followers of Caraka positing eleven—the Lord of Reasoning [Dharmakīrti] refuted these well from many viewpoints of reasoning by the power of the fact, stating [in the *Commentary on (Dignāga's) Compendium on Valid Cognition*], "Because there are two objects of comprehension, there are two [types of] valid cognition" and so forth; [hence, Dharmakīrti] established a definite enumeration of [types of] valid cognition into those two [perception and inference].

Also, if valid cognitions are divided, [there are] the two: those that induce ascertainment by themselves and those in which ascertainment is induced by another. The definition of a valid cognition that induces ascertainment by itself is a newly incontrovertible knower that is able to induce through its own power an ascertainment, which it itself would not arise if its object of comprehension did not abide in relation to the final object. The definition of a valid cognition when ascertainment is induced by another is a newly incontrovertible knower that needs to rely on another conventional valid cognition [and which] arises subsequently without the ability to induce such [ascertainment itself].

When the first [valid cognition that induces ascertainment by itself] is divided, [there are] five: valid cognition that is a sense perception having a familiar object, a valid cognition that is a sense perception having the appearance of performing a function, self-knowing perceptual valid cognition, valid cognition that is a yogic perception, and inferential valid cognition.

As for illustrations: The first [a valid cognition that is a sense perception having a familiar object] is, for instance, a sense perception in the continuum of a son apprehending his father's form. The second [a valid cognition that is a sense perception having the appearance of performing a function] is, for instance, a sense perception that apprehends fire and which comprehends that fire is able to perform the function of cooking and burning. The third [a self-knowing perceptual valid cognition] is, for instance, a self-knowing perception that experiences a valid cognition. The fourth [a valid cognition that is a yogic perception] is, for instance, an exalted wisdom consciousness that directly realizes the selflessness of persons. The fifth [an inferential valid cognition] is, for instance, an inferential cognition realizing sound to be impermanent. In the same way, such [a fivefold division of valid cognitions able to induce ascertainment by themselves] is the thought of [Sakya Paṇḍita's] *Treasury of Reasoning*, which states:

> The two knowers of objects, the two self-knowers,
> And inference ascertain by themselves.

Regarding the second—valid cognitions for which ascertainment is induced by another—when [they] are terminologically divided, [there are] three: [valid cognitions that] induce ascertainment of an appearance by itself but induce ascertainment of the truth from another; [valid cognitions] that induce ascertainment with respect to a generality from itself though induce ascertainment of the particular from another; and [valid cognitions for which] even the very appearance itself is induced by another.

As for illustrations: The first [a valid cognition that induces ascertainment of an appearance by itself but induces ascertainment of the truth from another] is, for instance, a sense perception that apprehends a reddish color in the distance at the time when a conceptual consciousness has a doubt with respect to an object [wondering], "Is that or is that not the color of fire?" and [it] is the color of fire. The second [a valid cognition when ascertainment of the general is induced by itself but of the particular by another] is, for instance, a sense perception that apprehends a tree in the distance at the time when a conceptual consciousness has a doubt with respect to an object [wondering], "Is that or is that not an Aśoka tree?" and [it] is an Aśoka tree. The third [a valid cognition when ascertainment of even the mere appearance is induced by another] is, for instance, a sense perception that apprehends blue and which induces a doubting consciousness that thinks, "Did I see or not see blue?"

Furthermore, the first two [are] actual [valid cognitions] and the last is posited as an imputed one. Also, if that [valid cognitions when ascertainment is induced by another] is terminologically divided [in a different way], there are also three: initial perceptions, inattentive minds, and [those] possessing a cause of error. Because, as it says in [Sakya Paṇḍita's] *Treasury of Reasoning*,

> Initial, inattentive minds, and
> Those possessing a cause of error [are the divisions of] ascertainment
> [induced] by another.

Illustrations of these also exist. The first [an initial perception] is, for instance, a sense perception which apprehends the color of an utpala flower in the continuum of a being who has not experienced seeing an utpala flower previously. The second [an inattentive mind] is, for instance, a sense perception that apprehends a sound in the continuum of a being at a time when their mind is greatly attracted to a beautiful form. The third [a knower possessing a cause of error] is, for instance, a sense perception that apprehends the color of a mirage with respect to which, the superimposition of apprehending water with respect to [that] mirage has actually been generated.

The definition of a nonvalid consciousness is a knower that is not newly incontrovertible. When [nonvalid consciousnesses] are divided, there are the latter five [of the division of] awareness and knowledge [into seven]—subsequent cognitions, and so forth.

The definition of a conceptual consciousness is a determinative knower that apprehends a term [generality] and a meaning [generality] as suitable to be mixed. That and eliminatively engaging awareness are synonymous. With regard to illustrations: the three—[all] inferential cognitions, correctly assuming consciousnesses, and doubting consciousnesses—and a portion [i.e., some] of subsequent cognitions and wrong consciousnesses are posited [as illustrations of conceptual consciousnesses].

The definition of a nonconceptual consciousness is a knower which is free from being a determinative knower that apprehends a term [generality] and a meaning [generality] as suitable to be mixed. That and completely engaging awareness are synonymous. With regard to illustrations: the two—[all] perceptions and awarenesses to which the object appears but is not ascertained—and a portion [i.e., some] of subsequent cognitions and wrong consciousnesses are posited [as illustrations of nonconceptual consciousness].

The definition of a mistaken consciousness is a knower that is mistaken with regard to its own appearing object. Illustrations [are] all wrong consciousnesses and conceptual consciousnesses.

The definition of a nonmistaken consciousness is a knower that is not mistaken with regard to its own appearing object. That and perception are synonymous. Furthermore, [these definitions] are made from the perspective of the Sūtra School (*Sautrāntika*) but are not like [those] in the "Ideation" (*Vijñāptika*) [a.k.a. Cittamātra] system because [they] assert that perception [has] both mistaken and nonmistaken factors.

The definition of a mental consciousness is a knower that is produced in dependence on its own uncommon empowering condition, a mental sense-power. Mind and mental consciousness have four possible permutations: (1) Being the first, but not the latter, is, for instance, an eye consciousness; (2) Being the latter, but not the first, is, for instance, all the mental factors accompanying a mental consciousness; (3) Being both is, for instance, a mental consciousness; (4) Being neither is, for instance, all the mental factors accompanying a sense consciousness.

Similarly, there are four possibilities between a conceptual consciousness apprehending a pot and a conceptual consciousness that realizes a pot. Also, there are four possibilities between perception with regard to a phenomenon and perceptual valid cognition with regard to a phenomenon. There are four possibilities between inferential valid cognition with regard to a phenomenon and conceptual consciousness with regard to a phenomenon. Having distinguished these modes—[that] there is a difference between that which is realized *from* such and such a sign and that which is realized *by means of* such and such a sign, and [that] there is a difference between realizing an object *by means of* a [direct] perception and realizing [it] directly—[you] need to know [them]. Hence, it is said, "Hold onto this terminology of Paṇchen [Sönam Drakpa] as something to be cherished!"

The definition of a sense consciousness is a knower that is produced in dependence on its own uncommon empowering condition, a physical sense-power. When [sense consciousnesses are] divided, [there are] five: eye consciousness, ear consciousness, nose consciousness, tongue consciousness, and body consciousness.

The definition of a eliminatively engaging awareness is a knower that engages its object through the force of terminology. The two—that [eliminatively engaging awareness] and conceptual consciousness—are synonymous. The definition of a completely engaging awareness is a knower that engages its object through the force of the thing. The two—that [completely engaging awareness] and nonconceptual consciousness—are synonymous.

The definition of a mind is that which has concordance with the mental factors that arise as its accompaniers. The three—mind, mentality, and consciousness—are synonymous. The definition of a mental factor is that which has concordance with the mind that has it as its accompanier. A mode of having concordance exists; for example, the two—an eye consciousness and the feeling that accompanies it—for instance,

> Since the object of observation [is] the same, the object of observation is concordant;
> Since the mode of apprehension [is] the same, the aspect is concordant;
> Since [they occur at] the same time, the time is concordant;
> Since the uncommon empowering condition [is] the same, the basis is concordant; and
> Since, as the accompanier of each individual substantial entity—an eye consciousness—only each individual substantial entity—a feeling—arises as well, the substantial entity is concordant.

(1) Because [they have] the same object [of observation], [they] are similar
[with regard to] the object [of observation]
(2) Because [they have] the same mode of apprehension, [they] are similar
in aspect
(3) Because [they occur] at the same time, [they] are similar in time
(4) Because [they have] the same uncommon empowering condition,
[they] are similar in basis
(5) Because only a single substantial entity of feeling arises as the
accompanier of a single substantial entity of an eye consciousness,
[they] are similar in substantial entity.

Hence, the "five aspects of possessing concordance" are concordant.

These definitions, moreover, have been made principally [for the sake of] understanding, and if [they] are to be made principally [for the sake of] eliminating verbal faults, then when there is the word "itself" (*rang*) at the beginning in whatsoever definition (*lakṣaṇa, mtshan nyid*), it is necessary to attach [the words] "something's being that" to the definiendum (*lakṣya, mtshon bya*).

When mental factors are divided, there are six groups:

The five omnipresent [mental factors], the five object-determining [mental
factors],
The eleven virtuous [mental factors], the six root afflictions,
The twenty secondary afflictions, and the four changeable [factors]—
These are the fifty-one mental factors.

The five—feeling, discrimination,
Intention, mental engagement, and contact—
Are called "the five omnipresent [mental factors]" because [they] proceed
As the accompaniers of all principal minds.

The five—aspiration, belief,
Mindfulness, samādhi, and wisdom—

Are explained as "object-determining factors"
Because [they] are definite to engage in particular objects.

The eleven [virtuous factors—that is,] faith, modesty, embarrassment,
The three root virtues—an absence of attachment,
[Absence of] hatred, and [absence of] ignorance—
Effort, pliancy, conscientiousness,
Equanimity, and nonharmfulness—
[Are] virtues from the point of view of whichever is relevant—
[Their] entity [as] an antidote, being concordant [i.e., accompanying a virtuous mind or mental factor], and so forth.

The six [root afflictions] are desire, anger,
Pride, ignorance, doubt, and view.
[To] these [last] three attach [the adjective] "afflicted."
[All six] are root afflictions because
[They are] the principals that make the mental continuum afflicted.

Belligerence, resentment, concealment, spite,
Jealousy, miserliness, deceit, dissimulation,
Haughtiness, harmfulness, nonshame,
Nonembarrassment, lethargy, excitement, nonfaith,
Together with laziness, nonconscientiousness,
Forgetfulness, nonintrospection, and distraction—
[These] twenty are [called] secondary afflictions because [they] are close [to], are produced [by], and increase [along with] the root afflictions.

Sleep, contrition, investigation, and analysis are changeable [factors]
Because due to motivation or whatsoever associated [mental factors]
[They] change into one or another—virtuous, nonvirtuous, or neutral [types].

If the intelligent wish to understand
The functions, substantial entities, signs, distinctions, and so forth,
Of the individual natures of these,
[They can be] known in detail from the texts on *Manifest Knowledge* (*Abhidharma*).

If [any] group of faults exist, [I] confess [them all] to the wise.
If [there be] virtue [in this], then through the power of clearing away
The confusion of those with low minds like myself
May the teachings of the Conqueror long abide!

This "Presentation of Awarenesses and Knowers, A Composite of All the Important Points," [was written] based upon repeated urging by all the earlier and later Loseling librarians [for] something like this. [I] did not take as my basis the Radö *Awarenesses and Knowers*. [Rather, this] was set forth in accordance with the elucidations found in the textbooks of Paṇchen [Sönam Drakpa]. Some definitions [that were] not clear there and were suitable to change, [I] put together in accordance from [one of] the two—[Akya Yongdzin's (*a kya yongs 'dzin*)] *Summary of Awarenesses and Knowers* or the *Awarenesses and Knowers* of the Tutor (*yongs 'dzin*) [i.e., Purbujok Jampa Gyatso]. This was written by the Loseling teacher, throne-holder [i.e., abbot], and geshe of Gyelrong [regional house] and [its] recitation master, Jampel Sampel, on the top [floor] of [Gyelrong's] temple, and [it] has been made in accordance with the thoughts of the assembled editors, [my] spriritual friends. May virtue and goodness flourish!

Könchok Jikmé Wangpo's *Precious Garland: A Presentation of Tenets*

The discourses of the Buddha contain numerous, sometimes apparently contradictory teachings. One purpose of studying tenets is to gain an understanding of how certain sūtras—as a group—present a coherent picture of the Buddhist endeavor. This is the classificatory or "doxographical" function of tenets.[1] Another aspect of the study of tenet systems is as a reflection of the history of exegesis by pivotal figures of Buddhist India:

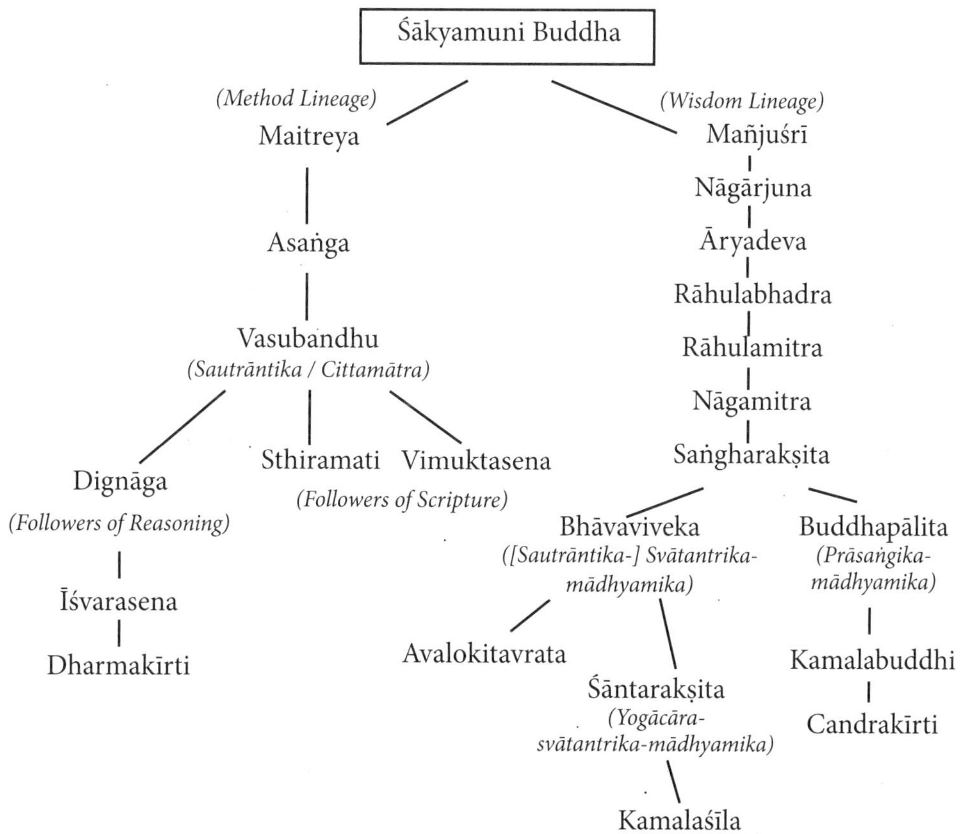

Fig. 1. Lineage of exegesis according to the tradition

Another related aspect of the study of tenets centers around its function in a meditative context: attaining a thorough understanding of the focus of one's meditative efforts. From this perspective, the presentation of tenets in this text follows an ascending hierarchy of discussion concerning the primary object to be meditated upon: the "object of negation." This hierarchy of topics (see fig. 2) reflects both a progression of philosophical systems and a progression from coarse to more refined presentations of the object of negation, culminating with what has come to be considered the highest (i.e., definitive) philosophical school, the Middle Way Consequence School (*Prasāṅgika-madhyamaka*). It is important to realize that the view presented by this highest system is taught in reference to less subtle systems. What exactly this subtle view is, is to be understood in opposition to what it is not. Hence, an understanding of the "lower" schools' assertions is necessary to properly comprehend the highest. For this reason, the study of tenets can be seen as a preliminary to the study of Madhyamaka, or "Middle Way" philosophy, proper.[2]

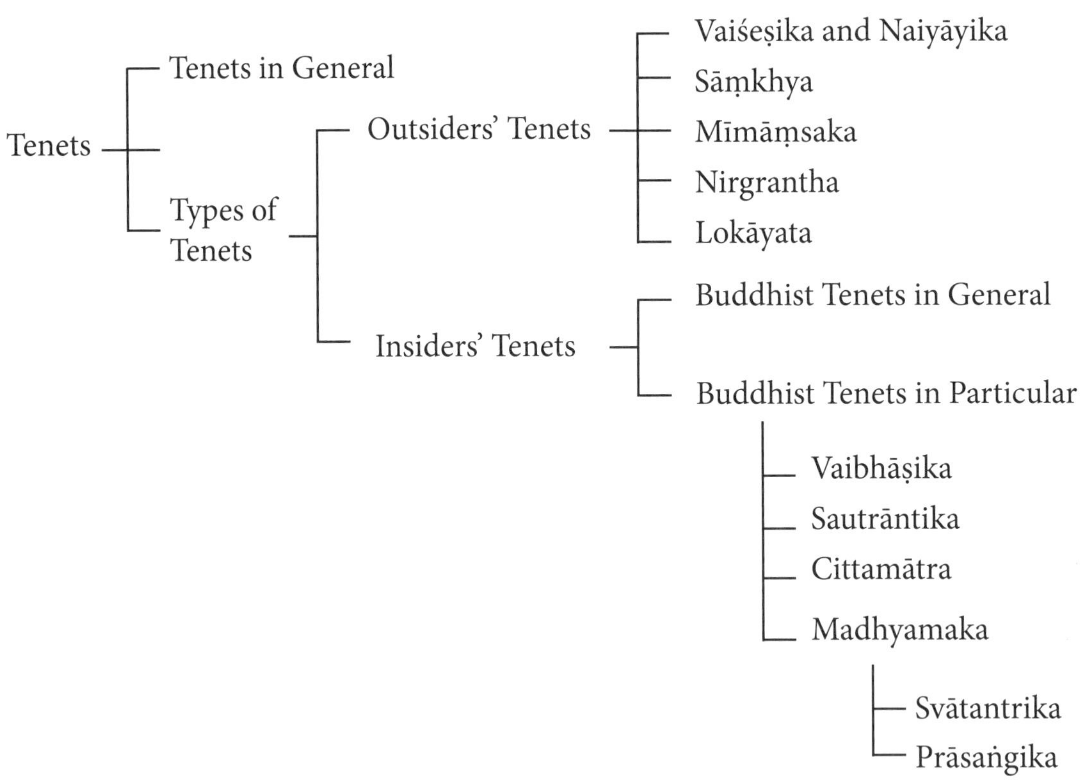

Fig. 2. Topical outline

[1] Hopkins 1996, 170–86.

[2] See Hopkins 1983, 317ff; see also, Sopa and Hopkins 1990, and Hopkins 2003.

གྲུབ་པའི་མཐའི་རྣམ་པར་བཞག་པ་རིན་པོ་ཆེའི་ཕྲེང་བ་ཞེས་བྱ་བ་བཞུགས་སོ།།

མཛད་པ་པོ། བཙུན་པ་དཀོན་མཆོག་འཇིགས་མེད་དབང་པོ།།

[1]རྨད་བྱུང་ཚོགས་གཉིས་གངས་ཀྱི་རི་བོ་སྙིང་རྗེའི་དྲོད་ཀྱིས་བཞུས་པའི་རྒྱུན།[2]
ལྷུན་གྲུབ་ཆོས་སྐུའི་འཛིན་མར་ཡོངས་འཁྱིལ་གྲུབ་མཐའ་རྣམ་བཞིའི་ཆུ་ཀླུང་འགྱེད།
འཕྲིན་ལས་རླབས་ཕྲེང་གནམ་དུ་རྐྱོང་བས་མུ་སྟེགས་བྱིས་པ་སྐྲག་བྱེད་པ།
རྒྱལ་སྲས་གདེངས་ཅན་བྱེ་བའི་འཇུག་ངོགས་ཐུབ་དབང་མ་དྲོས་མཚོ་ཆེན་རྒྱལ།[3]

རྒྱལ་བའི་རྒྱལ་ཚབ་མི་ཕམ་མགོན་པོ་དང་། རྒྱལ་བའི་མཁྱེན་རབ་གཅིག་བསྡུས་འཇམ་པའི་དབྱངས།
རྒྱལ་བས་ལུང་བསྟན་ཀླུ་སྒྲུབ་ཐོགས་མེད་ཞབས། རྒྱལ་བ་གཉིས་པ་ཡབ་སྲས་བཅས་ལ་འདུད།

གང་ཞིག་རྟོགས་ན་ཕྱི་དང་ནང་གི་བསྟན་པའི་ཁྱད་པར་ཀུན་མཐོང་ཞིང་།
རབ་འབྱམས་མཁས་པའི་མདུན་ས་དག་ཏུ་སྨྲ་བ་མཆོག་གི་བརྟུལ་ཞུགས་འཛིན།
ངོ་མཚར་གྲགས་པའི་བ་དན་དཀར་པོ་གཟུར་གནས་སྐྱེ་བོས་བསྒྲེང་བྱེད་པ།
རང་གཞན་གྲུབ་མཐའི་དེ་ཉིད་འབྱེད་ལ་མཁས་པ་སུ་ཞིག་བརྩོན་པ་འདོར།

དེ་ཕྱིར་དམ་པའི་ལེགས་བཤད་ཀུན་བསྡུས་ནས། རང་དང་སྐལ་བ་མཉམ་རྣམས་རྗེས་གཟུང་ཕྱིར།
གྲུབ་མཐའི་རྣམ་བཞག་མདོར་བསྡུས་བརྗོད་པར་བྱ། བློ་གསལ་དོན་གཉེར་ལྡན་རྣམས་གུས་བས་ཉོན།།

དེ་ཡང་ཚེ་འདིའི་སྙེད་པ་དང་། བཀུར་སྟི་དང་། ཚིགས་སུ་བཅད་པ་ལ་མི་བལྟ་ཞིང་སྙིང་ནས་གྲོལ་བ་དོན་དུ་གཉེར་བའི་གང་ཟག་གིས། བདག་མེད་པའི་ལྟ་བ་རྣམ་པར་དག་པ་ཁོང་དུ་ཆུད་པའི་ཐབས་ལ་འབད་དགོས་ཏེ། ཟབ་མོའི་ལྟ་བ་དང་བྲལ་ན་བྱམས་པ་དང་། སྙིང་རྗེ་དང་། བྱང་ཆུབ་ཀྱི་སེམས་ལ་ཇི་ཙམ་གོམས་པར་བྱས་ཀྱང་སྲིད་པ་བསྟེལ་གྱི་རྩ་བ་དྲུང་ནས་འབྱིན་པར་མི་ནུས་པའི་ཕྱིར། དེ་སྐད་དུ་ཡང་རྗེ་བཙུན་ཙོང་ཁ་པ་ཆེན་པོས།

གནས་ལུགས་རྟོགས་པའི་ཤེས་རབ་མི་ལྡན་ན། །
ངེས་འབྱུང་བྱང་ཆུབ་སེམས་ལ་གོམས་བྱས་ཀྱང་། །
སྲིད་པའི་རྩ་བ་གཅོད་པར་མི་ནུས་པས། །
དེ་ཕྱིར་རྟེན་འབྲེལ་རྟོགས་པའི་ཐབས་ལ་འབད། །

ཅེས་སོ།

དེས་ན་ལྟ་བའི་གོལ་ས་[4]སྤང་བ་དང་། བདག་མེད་ཕྲ་རགས་ཀྱི་རིམ་པ་ངེས་པར་བྱ་བའི་ཕྱིར་རང་གཞན་གྱི་གྲུབ་མཐའི་རྣམ་བཞག་མདོར་བསྡུས་ཏེ་བརྗོད་པ་ལ་གཉིས། སྤྱིར་བསྟན་པ་དང་། བྱེ་བྲག་ཏུ་བཤད་པའོ།[5]

དང་པོ་ནི། གྲུབ་མཐའ་ཞེས་པའི་ཐ་སྙད་རང་བཟོ་མ་ཡིན་ཏེ། སངས་རྒྱས་ཀྱི་ལུང་ལས་གསུངས་པའི་ཕྱིར། ཇི་སྐད་དུ། ལང་ཀར་གཤེགས་པ་ལས།

ང་ཡི་ཆོས་ཚུལ་རྣམ་གཉིས་ཏེ། །བསྟན་པ་དང་ནི་གྲུབ་མཐའ་འོ། །
བྱིས་པ་རྣམས་ལ་བསྟན་པ་བཤད། །རྣལ་འབྱོར་པ་ལ་གྲུབ་མཐའ་འོ། །

ཞེས་གསུངས་པ་ལྟར་རོ།

དེ་ཡང་གང་ཟག་ལ་དབྱེ་ན། གྲུབ་མཐས་བློ་མ་བསྒྱུར་བ་དང་། གྲུབ་མཐས་བློ་བསྒྱུར་བའོ།

དང་པོ་ནི། གཞུང་ལུགས་ལ་མ་སྦྱངས་པར་མ་བརྟགས་མ་དཔྱད་པའི་[6]བློ་ལྷན་སྐྱེས་ཀྱིས་ཚེ་འདིའི་བདེ་བ་ཙམ་དོན་དུ་གཉེར་བར་བྱེད་པའོ། གཉིས་པ་ནི། གཞུང་ལུགས་ལ་སྦྱངས་ཏེ་གཞི་ལམ་འབྲས་གསུམ་གྱི་རྣམ་བཞག་རང་གི་བློ་ངོར་གྲུབ་པའི་ཚུལ་ལུང་དང་རིགས་པའི་ལམ་ནས་སྨྲ་བར་བྱེད་པ་སྟེ།

གྲུབ་མཐའི་སྒྲ་བཤད་ཀྱང་། འགྲེལ་བཤད་ཚིག་གསལ་ལས།[7]

གྲུབ་པའི་མཐའ་སྟེ། རིགས་པ་དང་ལུང་གིས་རབ་ཏུ་བསྟན་པར་རང་གི་འདོད་པ་གྲུབ་པ་ནི།
དེ་ལས་ཕར་ཡང་འགྲོ་བ་མེད་པས་ན་མཐའ་འོ།

ཞེས་གསུངས་པ་ལྟར། ལུང་རིགས་གང་རུང་ལ་བརྟེན་ནས་ཐག་བཅད་ཅིང་གྲུབ་པའི་དམ་བཅས་པའི་དོན་དེ་ཉིད་ལས་གཞན་དུ་འདོར་མེད་པས་ན། གྲུབ་པའི་མཐའི་ཞེས་བརྗོད་པའི་ཕྱིར།

དེ་ལ་དབྱེ་ན་གཉིས། ཕྱི་རོལ་པ་དང་། ནང་པའོ། ཕྱི་པ་དང་ནང་པ་ཙམ་གྱི་ཁྱད་པར་ཡོད་དེ། སྙིང་ཐག་པ་ནས་དཀོན་མཆོག་གསུམ་ལ་སྐྱབས་སུ་འགྲོ་བའི་གང་ཟག་དེ་ནང་པ་དང་། དཀོན་མཆོག་གསུམ་ལ་བློ་མི་གཏོད་

པར་འཇིག་རྟེན་པའི་ལྷ་ལ་སྙིང་ཐག་པ་ནས་སྐྱབས་སུ་འགྲོ་བའི་གང་ཟག་དེ་ཕྱི་རོལ་པ་ཡིན་པའི་ཕྱིར།

ཕྱི་ནང་གི་གྲུབ་མཐའ་སྨྲ་བའི་ཁྱད་པར་ཡང་ཡོད་དེ། སྟོན་པ་བསྟན་པ་ལྟ་བ་གསུམ་གྱི་སྒོ་ནས་འབྱེད་པའི་ཕྱིར། དེ་ཡང་ཡིན་དེ། རང་སྡེ་རྣམས་ནི་སྟོན་པ་སྐྱོན་ཀུན་ཟད་ཅིང་ཡོན་ཏན་རྫོགས་པ་དང་། བསྟན་པ་སེམས་ཅན་ལ་འཚེ་བ་མེད་པ་དང་། ལྟ་བ་རྟག་གཅིག་རང་དབང་ཅན་གྱི་བདག་གིས་སྟོང་བར་འདོད་པའི་ཁྱད་པར་གསུམ་དང་ལྡན་ཞིང་། གཞན་སྡེ་རྣམས་ནི། དེ་ལས་བཟློག་སྟེ་སྟོན་པ་སྐྱོན་དང་བཅས་ཤིང་ཡོན་ཏན་མ་རྫོགས་པ་དང་། བསྟན་པ་སེམས་ཅན་ལ་གནོད་ཅིང་འཚེ་བ་དང་། ལྟ་བ་རྟག་གཅིག་རང་དབང་ཅན་གྱི་བདག་ཏུ་གྲུབ་པར་ཁས་ལེན་པའི་ཁྱད་པར་གསུམ་དང་ལྡན་པའི་ཕྱིར།

གཉིས་པ་བྱེ་བྲག་ཏུ་བཤད་པ་ལ། ཕྱི་རོལ་པའི་གྲུབ་མཐའི་རྣམ་བཞག་མདོར་བསྡུས་ཏེ་བཤད་པ། རང་སྡེའི་གྲུབ་མཐའི་རྣམ་བཞག་ཙུང་ཟད་ཕྱེ་སྟེ་བཤད་པའོ།

དང་པོ་ནི། གྲུབ་མཐའ་སྨྲ་བའི་ནང་ཚན་གང་ཞིག དཀོན་མཆོག་གསུམ་ལ་སྐྱབས་སུ་མི་འགྲོ་ཞིང་དེ་ལས་གཞན་པའི་སྟོན་པ་ཡོད་པར་ཁས་ལེན་པའི་གང་ཟག་དེ། ཕྱི་རོལ་པའི་གྲུབ་མཐའ་སྨྲ་བའི་མཚན་ཉིད། དེ་ལ་དབྱེ་བ་མཐའ་ཡས་ཀྱང་། བསྡུ་ན། ཁྱབ་པ་འཇུག་པ། དབང་ཕྱུག་པ། རྒྱལ་བ་པ། སེར་སྐྱ་པ། ཕུར་བུ་པ་དང་ལྔ་ལ་རྟོག་གེ་སྡེ་ལྔར་གྲགས་ཤིང་། རྩ་བའི་སྡེ་དྲུག་ཏུ་ཡང་བཤད་དེ། བྱེ་བྲག་པ་དང་། རིག་པ་ཅན་དང་། གྲངས་ཅན་པ་དང་། དཔྱོད་པ་བ་དང་། གཅེར་བུ་པ་དང་། རྒྱང་འཕེན་པ་རྣམས་སོ། དེ་རྣམས་ཀྱི་དང་པོ་ལྔ་ནི་རྟག་པར་ལྟ་བ་དང་། ཕྱི་མ་ནི་ཆད་པར་ལྟ་བ་ཡིན་ནོ།

དེ་ཡང་བྱེ་བྲག་པ་དང་རིག་པ་ཅན་པ་གཉིས་ནི་རིམ་བཞིན་དྲང་སྲོང་གཟེགས་ཟན་དང་། བྲམ་ཟེ་རྐང་མིག་གི་རྗེས་སུ་འབྲངས་པ་སྟེ། འདི་གཉིས་ལ་ནང་གསེས་ཀྱི་འདོད་པའི་ཁྱད་པར་མི་མཐུན་པ་ཙུང་ཟད་ཡོད་ཀྱང་། གྲུབ་པའི་མཐའ་སྤྱི་ལ་མི་འདྲ་བ་མེད་དོ།

དེ་ཡང་བྱེ་རིག་གཉིས[8]ཀྱིས་ཤེས་བྱ་ཐམས་ཅད་ཚིག་དོན་དྲུག་ཏུ་འདུས་པར་འདོད་ལ། ཁྲུས་དང་། དབང་བསྐུར་བ་དང་། སྨྱུང་གནས་དང་། མཆོད་སྦྱིན་དང་། སྦྱིན་སྲེག་ལ་སོགས་པ་ཐར་ལམ་དུ་ཁས་ལེན་ཞིང་། ནམ་ཞིག་བླ་མའི་མན་ངག་ལས་རྣལ་འབྱོར་བསྒོམས་ཏེ་བདག་དབང་སོགས་རྣམས་ལས་དོན་གཞན་དུ་ཤེས་ནས་དེ་ཁོ་ན་ཉིད་མཐོང་ཞིང་ཚིག་གི་དོན་དྲུག་གི་རང་བཞིན་ཁོང་དུ་ཆུད་པ་ན། བདག་ནི་ཁྱབ་པའི་རང་བཞིན་ཡིན་ཡང་བྱེད་པ་མེད་པར་ཤེས་ཏེ། ཆོས་དང་ཆོས་མ་ཡིན་པའི་ལས་གང་ཡང་གསོག་པར་མི་བྱེད། ལས་གསར་པ་མ་

བསགས་ཤིང་རྙིང་བ་ཟད་པས་སླར་རླངས་པའི་ལུས་དང་། དབང་པོ་དང་། བློ་དང་། བདེ་སྡུག འདོད་སྡང་སོགས་བདག་དང་བྲལ་ཞིང་གསར་པའི་ལུས་དང་དབང་པོ་མ་རླངས་པས། བུད་ཤིང་ཟད་པའི་མེ་བཞིན་དུ་སྐྱེ་བའི་རྒྱུན་ཆད་དེ་བདག་འབའ་ཞིག་ཏུ་གྱུར་པ་ན་ཐར་པ་ཐོབ་པ་ཡིན་ཞེས་ཟེར་རོ།

གྲངས་ཅན་པ་ནི། དྲང་སྲོང་སེར་སྐྱའི་རྗེས་སུ་འབྲངས་པ་སྟེ། ཤེས་བྱ་ཐམས་ཅད་ཉི་ཤུ་རྩ་ལྔར་གྲངས་ངེས་པ་འདོད་ལ། དེ་ཡང་བདག་དང་། གཙོ་བོ་དང་། ཆེན་པོ་དང་། ང་རྒྱལ་[9]དང་དེ་ཙམ་ལྔ་དང་། དབང་པོ་བཅུ་གཅིག་དང་། འབྱུང་བ་ལྔ་སྟེ་ཉི་ཤུ་རྩ་ལྔའོ།

དེ་ཙམ་ལྔ་ནི། གཟུགས་སྒྲ་དྲི་རོ་རེག་བྱ་ལྔའོ། དབང་པོ་བཅུ་གཅིག་ནི། བློའི་དབང་པོ་ལྔ་དང་། ལས་ཀྱི་དབང་པོ་ལྔ་དང་། ཡིད་ཀྱི་དབང་པོའོ། བློའི་དབང་པོ་ལྔ་ནི། མིག་དང་། རྣ་བ་དང་། སྣ་དང་། ལྕེ་དང་། པགས་པའི་དབང་པོ་རྣམས་སོ། ལས་ཀྱི་དབང་པོ་ལྔ་ནི། ངག་དང་། ལག་པ་དང་། རྐང་པ་དང་། རྐུབ་དང་། འདོམས་རྣམས་སོ། འབྱུང་བ་ལྔ་ནི། ས་ཆུ་མེ་རླུང་ནམ་མཁའ་རྣམས་སོ།

དེ་དག་ལས་སྐྱེ་བུ་ནི་ཤེས་པ་དང་། ལྷག་མ་ཉེར་བཞི་འདུས་བསགས་ཡིན་པས་བེམ་པོར་འདོད་ལ།[10] གཙོ་བོ་དང་། སྐྱེས་བུ་ནི་དོན་དམ་བདེན་པ་དང་། གཞན་རྣམས་ཀུན་རྫོབ་བདེན་པར་འདོད་དོ། དེ་ལ་ཡང་རྒྱུ་ཡིན་ལ་འབྲས་བུ་མ་ཡིན་པ། རྒྱུ་འབྲས་གཉིས་ཀ་ཡིན་པ། འབྲས་བུ་ཡིན་ལ་རྒྱུ་མ་ཡིན་པ། རྒྱུ་འབྲས་གཉིས་ཀ་མ་ཡིན་པའི་མུ་དང་བཞི་ཡོད་དེ།[11] དང་པོ་ནི། སྤྱི་གཙོ་བོ་དང་། གཉིས་པ་ནི། བློ་དང་། ང་རྒྱལ་དང་། དེ་ཙམ་ལྔ་སྟེ་བདུན་དང་། གསུམ་པ་ནི། ལྷག་མ་བཅུ་དྲུག་དང་། བཞི་པ་ནི། སྐྱེས་བུའོ།

དེ་ཡང་དབང་ཕྱུག་ནག་པོའི་རྒྱུད་ལས།

རྩ་བའི་རང་བཞིན་རྣམ་པར་འགྱུར་མིན་ལ།
ཆེན་པོ་སོགས་བདུན་རང་བཞིན་རྣམ་འགྱུར་ཞིང་།
བཅུ་དྲུག་པོ་ནི་རྣམ་པར་འགྱུར་བ་སྟེ།
སྐྱེས་བུ་རང་བཞིན་མ་ཡིན་རྣམ་འགྱུར་མིན།[12]

ཞེས་བཤད་པ་ལྟར་རོ།

དེ་ཡང་རྩ་བའི་རང་བཞིན་དང་། སྤྱི་དང་། གཙོ་བོ་རྣམས་དོན་གཅིག་ཡིན་ཞིང་ཁྱད་ཆོས་དྲུག་དང་ལྡན་པའི་ཤེས་བྱ་ཞིག་ལ་འདོད་དོ། སྐྱེས་བུ་དང་། བདག་དང་། ཤེས་པ་དང་། རིག་པ་རྣམས་དོན་གཅིག་མིང་གི་རྣམ་གྲངས་སོ།

ལྷག་མ་ཉེར་གསུམ་གྱི་སྐྱེ་ཚུལ་ནི། གང་གི་ཚེ་སྐྱེས་བུ་དེས་ཡུལ་ལ་ལོངས་སྤྱོད་པའི་འདོད་པ་སྐྱེས་པ་ན། རྩ་བའི་རང་བཞིན་གྱིས་སྒྲ་ལ་སོགས་པའི་རྣམ་འགྱུར་རྣམས་སྤྲུལ་པར་བྱེད་དོ། དེ་ཡང་གཙོ་བོ་ལས་ཆེན་པོ་འབྱུང་ལ། བློ་དང་ཆེན་པོ་ནི་མིང་གི་རྣམ་གྲངས་ཡིན་ཞིང་། དེ་ནི་ཕྱི་ནས་ཡུལ་དང་། ནང་ནས་སྐྱེས་བུའི་གཟུགས་བརྙན་འཆར་བའི་མེ་ལོང་ངོས་གཉིས་པ་ལྟ་བུ་ཞིག་ལ་འདོད་དེ། དེ་ལས་ང་རྒྱལ་སྐྱེས་ཤིང་། ང་རྒྱལ་ལ་དབྱེ་ན། རྣམ་པར་འགྱུར་བ་ཅན་གྱི་ང་རྒྱལ་དང་། སྙིང་སྟོབས་ཅན་གྱི་ང་རྒྱལ་དང་། མུན་པ་ཅན་གྱི་ང་རྒྱལ་དེ་གསུམ་མོ། དང་པོ་ལས་དེ་ཙམ་ལྔ་སྐྱེ་ཞིང་། དེ་ལས་འབྱུང་བ་ལྔ་སྐྱེའོ། གཉིས་པ་ལས་དབང་པོ་བཅུ་གཅིག་སྐྱེའོ། གསུམ་པ་ནི། ང་རྒྱལ་གཞན་གཉིས་ཀ་འཇུག་པར་བྱེད་པ་ཡིན་ཞེས་ཟེར་རོ།

དེ་ཡང་ལོང་བ་རྐང་ཅན་ལྟ་བུའི་རང་བཞིན་དང་། ཞ་བོ་མིག་ཅན་ལྟ་བུའི་སྐྱེ་བུ་གཉིས་གཅིག་ཏུ་འབྲེལ་ཏེ། རྣམ་འགྱུར་རྣམས་རྩ་བའི་རང་བཞིན་གྱིས་སྤྲུལ་པའི་ཚུལ་མ་ཤེས་པའི་དབང་གིས་འཁོར་བར་འཁོར་བར་འདོད་དོ། ནམ་ཞིག་བླ་མས་ཉེ་བར་བསྟན་པའི་མན་ངག་ཐོས་པ་ལ་བརྟེན་ནས་རྣམ་འགྱུར་འདི་དག་རང་བཞིན་གྱིས་སྤྲུལ་པ་ཙམ་དུ་ཟད་དོ་ཞེས་ངེས་ཤེས་ལྷག་པར་སྐྱེས་པ་ན། རིམ་གྱིས་ཡུལ་ལ་ཆགས་པ་དང་བྲལ་བར་གྱུར་བ་དེའི་ཚེ་བསམ་གཏན་ལ་བརྟེན་ནས་ལྷའི་མིག་གི་མངོན་ཤེས་བསྐྱེད་དེ། མངོན་ཤེས་ཀྱིས་གཙོ་བོ་ལ་བལྟས་པ་ན་གཙོ་བོ་དེ་གཞན་གྱི་བུད་མེད་ལྟར་ངོ་ཚ་བས་སྐྱེངས་ཏེ་རྣམ་འགྱུར་རྣམས་ཉེ་བར་བསྡུས་ཏེ། རང་བཞིན་ཡན་གར་བར་གནས་ཤིང་། དེའི་ཚེ་རྣལ་འབྱོར་པའི་བློ་ངོར་ཀུན་རྫོབ་ཀྱི་སྣང་བ་ཐམས་ཅད་ལོག་སྟེ། སྐྱེས་བུས་ཡུལ་ལ་ལོངས་སྤྱོད་པ་མེད་ཅིང་བྱེད་པ་མེད་པར་གནས་པ་དེའི་ཚེ་ཐར་པ་ཐོབ་པ་ཡིན་ནོ། ཞེས་འདོད་དོ།

དགྲོད་པ་བ་ནི། རྒྱལ་དཔོག་པའི་རྗེས་སུ་འབྲངས་པ་སྟེ། རིག་བྱེད་ལ་གང་སྣང་བ་ནི་རང་བྱུང་ཡིན་ཏེ། དེ་ནི་དེ་ཁོ་ན་ཉིད་ཡིན་ནོ་ཞེས་སྒྲོ་བཏགས་ནས་མཆོད་སྦྱིན་ལ་སོགས་པ་འབའ་ཞིག་གིས་མཐོ་རིས་ཀྱི་གོ་འཕང་ཐོབ་པར་འདོད་ལ། དེ་ནི་ངན་སོང་ལས་གྲོལ་བའི་ཐར་པ་ཙམ་དུ་ཁས་ལེན་ནོ། འོན་ཀྱང་སྡུག་བསྔལ་ཉེ་བར་ཞི་བའི་ཐར་པ་ནི་མེད་དེ། དྲི་མ་སེམས་ཀྱི་རང་བཞིན་ལ་ཞུགས་པའི་ཕྱིར་དང་། ཐམས་ཅད་མཁྱེན་པ་ཡང་མེད་དེ། ཤེས་བྱ་མཐའ་ཡས་པའི་ཕྱིར་རོ། དེ་བས་ན་བདེན་པའི་ངག་ཀྱང་མེད་དོ་ཞེས་སྨྲའོ།

གཞིར་བྱ་བ་ནི། རྒྱལ་བ་དམ་པའི་རྗེས་སུ་འབྲངས་པ་སྟེ། ཤེས་བྱ་ཐམས་ཅད་དོན་དགུར་འདུས་པར་འདོད་དེ། སྲོག་དང་། ཟག་པ་དང་། སྡོམ་པ་དང་། ངེས་པར་རྒ་བ་དང་། འཆིང་བ་དང་། ལས་དང་། སྡིག་པ་དང་། བསོད་ནམས་དང་། ཐར་པ་རྣམས་སོ།

དེ་ལ་སྲོག་ནི་བདག་ཡིན་ལ། སྐྱེས་བུ་རྣམས་ཀྱི་ལུས་ཀྱི་ཚད་ཇི་ལྟ་བ་བཞིན་དུ་ཡོད་པ། ངོ་བོ་རྟག་ལ་གནས་སྐབས་མི་རྟག་པའི་རང་བཞིན་ཅན་ཡིན་ནོ།[13] ཟག་པ་ནི། དགེ་བ་དང་མི་དགེ་བའི་ལས་རྣམས་ཡིན་ཏེ། དེའི་དབང་གིས་འཁོར་བར་ཟག་པར་བྱེད་པའི་ཕྱིར། སྡོམ་པ་ནི། ཟག་པ་འགོག་པར་བྱེད་པ་སྟེ། ལས་གསར་དུ་མི་གསོག་པའི་ཕྱིར་རོ། ངེས་པར་རྒ་བ་ནི། སྐོམ་མི་འཐུང་བ་དང་། ལུས་གདུང་བ་ལ་སོགས་པའི་དཀའ་ཐུབ་ཀྱི་སྒོ་ནས་སྔོན་བསགས་པའི་ལས་རྣམས་ཟད་པར་བྱེད་པའོ། འཆིང་བ་ནི། ལོག་པར་ལྟ་བའོ། ལས་ནི་རྣམ་པ་བཞི་སྟེ། ཕྱིས་མྱོང་བར་འགྱུར་བ་དང་། མིང་དང་། རུས་དང་། ཚེའོ། སྡིག་པ་ནི། ཆོས་མིན་པའོ། བསོད་ནམས་ནི། ཆོས་སོ།

ཐར་པ་ནི། ལུས་གཅེར་བུ་དང་། ངག་མི་སྨྲ་བ་དང་། མེ་ལྔ་བརྟེན་པ་ལ་སོགས་པའི་དཀའ་ཐུབ་ཀྱི་སྦྱོང་བ་ལ་བརྟེན་ནས་སྔར་བྱས་ཀྱི་ལས་ཐམས་ཅད་ཟད་ཅིང་། ལས་གསར་དུ་མ་བསགས་པས་འཇིག་རྟེན་ཐམས་ཅད་ཀྱི་སྟེང་ན་འདུག་པའི་གནས། འཇིག་རྟེན་འདུས་པ་ཞེས་བྱ་བ་གདུགས་དཀར་པོ་གྱེན་ལ་བསྒྲེངས་པ་ལྟ་བུ་ཞོ་འམ་ཀུ་མུ་ད་ལྟར་དཀར་བ། ཚད་དཔག་ཚད་འབུམ་ཕྲག་ཞེ་ལྔ་ཡོད་པ། སྲོག་ཡོད་པས་དངོས་ཡིན་ཅིང་། འཁོར་བ་ལས་གྲོལ་བས་དངོས་པོ་མེད་པ་ཡང་ཡིན་པ་དེར་འགྲོ་སྟེ། གནས་དེ་ལ་ནི་ཐར་པ་ཞེས་བྱའོ།

དེ་སྐད་དུ་རྒྱལ་བ་དམ་པས།

ཁ་བ་རྒྱ་སྤྲོས་མི་རྟོག་དང་།
བ་ཞོ་བ་མོ་མུ་ཏིག་མདོག
གདུགས་དཀར་བཟུང་བའི་དབྱིབས་འདྲ་བ།
ཐར་པ་ཡིན་པར་རྒྱལ་བས་བཤད།

ཅེས་འབྱུང་ངོ་།

རྒྱུད་འཕེན་པ་ནི། སྐྱེ་བ་སྔ་མ་ནས་འདིར་འོང་བ་མེད་དེ། སྐྱེ་བ་སྔ་མ་ཞེས་པ་ནི་ལུས་ཀྱང་མ་མཐོང་བའི་ཕྱིར། ལུས་བློ་ཡི་བྱུར་བ་ལས་སེམས་བློ་བྱུར་དུ་གྲུབ་པ་ཡིན་ཏེ། མར་མེ་བློ་བྱུར་དུ་གྲུབ་པ་ལས་འོད་བློ་བྱུར་དུ་གྲུབ་པ་བཞིན་ནོ། སྐྱེ་བ་འདི་ནས་ཕྱི་མར་འགྲོ་བ་ཡང་མེད་དེ། ལུས་སེམས་རྫས་གཅིག་པས་ལུས་འཇིག་པ་ན། བློ་ཡང་འཇིག་པའི་ཕྱིར། དཔེར་ན་རྡོ་འཇིག་པ་ན་རྡོའི་རི་མོ་འཇིག་པ་བཞིན་ནོ། དེས་ན་འདིས་གཞལ་བྱ་ལ་རང་མཚན[14] དང་། ཚད་མ་ལ་མངོན་སུམ་ཚད་མ་གཅིག་པུས་ཁྱབ་པར་འདོད་དེ། སྤྱི་མཚན་དང་། རྗེས་དཔག་ཚད་མ་ཁས་མི་ལེན་པའི་ཕྱིར། རྒྱུད་འཕེན་གྱི་ཁྱད་པར་འགའ་ཞིག དངོས་པོ་ཐམས་ཅད་རྒྱུ་མེད་པར་ངོ་བོ་ཉིད་ལས་བྱུང་བར་འདོད་དེ།

ཉི་ཤར་ཆུ་བོ་ཐུར་དུ་འབབ་པ་དང་།
སྲན་ཟླུམ་ཚེར་མ་གཟེངས་རིང་རྣོ་བ་དང་།
རྨ་བྱའི་མདོངས་ལ་སོགས་པའི་ཆོས་རྣམས་ཀུན།
སུས་ཀྱང་མ་བྱས་ངོ་བོ་ཉིད་ལས་བྱུང་།

ཞེས་ཟེར་རོ། སྨྲས་པ།

ལྷ་བ་ངན་པའི་མུ་ལ་སྟེགས་འཆའ་བའི།
ཕྱི་རོལ་གྲུབ་མཐའི་རང་བཞིན་མ་ལུས་པ།
ལེགས་པར་ཤེས་ཏེ་སྤོང་བར་བྱེད་པ་ནི།
ཐར་པའི་གྲོང་དུ་འཇུག་པའི་ཐེམ་སྐས་སོ།

ཞེས་བྱ་བའི་ནི་བར་སྐབས་ཀྱི་ཚིགས་སུ་བཅད་པའོ། །

གཉིས་པ་རང་སྡེའི་གྲུབ་མཐའི་རྣམ་བཞག་ཙུང་ཟད་ཕྱེ་སྟེ་བཤད་པ་ལ་གཉིས། སྤྱིར་བསྟན་པ་དང་། བྱེ་བྲག་ཏུ་བཤད་པའོ།

དང་པོ་ནི། སྟོན་པ་མཉམ་མེད་ཤཱཀྱའི་རྒྱལ་པོ་དེ་ཉིད་ཀྱིས་དང་པོར་བྱང་ཆུབ་མཆོག་ཏུ་ཐུགས་བསྐྱེད། བར་དུ་བསྐལ་པ་གྲངས་མེད་གསུམ་དུ་ཚོགས་བསགས། མཐར་རྡོ་རྗེ་གདན་གྱི་སྟེང་ལ་མངོན་པར་རྫོགས་པར་སངས་རྒྱས་ཏེ་ཡུལ་ཝཱ་རཱ་ཎ་སཱིར་ཨཱ་སི་བཟང་པོ་ལ་བདེན་པ་བཞིའི་ཆོས་ཀྱི་འཁོར་ལོ་བསྐོར།

དེ་ནས་བྱ་རྒོད་ཕུང་པོའི་རི་བོར་བཀའ་བར་མཚན་ཉིད་མེད་པའི་ཆོས་འཁོར་བསྐོར། དེ་ནས་ཡངས་པ་ཅན་ལ་སོགས་པར་ལེགས་པར་རྣམ་པར་ཕྱེ་བའི་ཆོས་ཀྱི་འཁོར་ལོ་རྒྱ་ཆེར་བསྐོར་ཏེ། མུ་སྟེགས་ཀྱི་སྟོན་པ་དྲུག་ལ་སོགས་པའི་སྨྲ་བ་ངན་པ་ཐམས་ཅད་ཟིལ་གྱིས་མནན་ནས་ཕན་བདེའི་འབྱུང་གནས་སངས་རྒྱས་ཀྱི་བསྟན་པ་རིན་པོ་ཆེ་དར་ཞིང་རྒྱས་པར་མཛད་དོ། དེའི་འོག་ཏུ་འགྲེལ་བྱེད་རྣམས་ཀྱིས་འཁོར་ལོ་གསུམ་གྱི་དགོངས་པ་སོ་སོར་བཀྲལ་བ་ལ་བརྟེན་ནས་གྲུབ་མཐའ་སྨྲ་བ་བཞི་བྱུང་སྟེ། དེ་དག་ལས་དོན་སྨྲ་སྡེ་གཉིས་ཀྱིས་འཁོར་ལོ་དང་པོ་དང་། ངོ་བོ་ཉིད་མེད་པར་སྨྲ་བས་འཁོར་ལོ་བར་པ་དང་། རྣལ་འབྱོར་སྤྱོད་པ་བ་རྣམས་ཀྱིས་འཁོར་ལོ་ཐ་མའི་རྗེས་སུ་འབྲངས་ནས་གཞི་ལམ་འབྲས་གསུམ་གྱི་རྣམ་བཞག་དམ་བཅའ་བར་བྱེད་དོ།

རང་ཅག་གི་སྟོན་པའི་རྗེས་སུ་འབྲངས་པའི་གྲུབ་མཐའ་སྨྲ་བ་ལ་བྱེ་མདོ་གཉིས་དང་དབུ་སེམས་གཉིས་ཏེ་བཞིར་གྲངས་ངེས་ཏེ། དེ་དག་ལས་ལོགས་སུ་གྱུར་པའི་གྲུབ་མཐའ་ལྔ་པ་དང་། ཐེག་པ་གསུམ་ལས་ལོགས་སུ་གྱུར་པའི་ཐེག་པ་བཞི་པ་མེད་པར་གསུངས་པའི་ཕྱིར། རྡོ་རྗེ་སྙིང་འགྲེལ་ལས།

སངས་རྒྱས་པ་ལ་བཞི་པ་དང་།
ལྔ་པ་ཐུབ་པའི་དགོངས་པ་མིན།

ཞེས་པ་ལྟར་རོ།

རང་རྒྱུད་པ་མན་ཆད་ཀྱི་རང་སྡེ་འདི་དག་ཐལ་འགྱུར་པས་གཞལ་ན་རྟག་ཆད་ཀྱི་མཐའ་གཉིས་ཀར་ལྷུང་ཡང་། རང་རང་གི་ལུགས་ལ་དབུ་མ་པར་འདོད་དེ། རྟག་ཆད་ཀྱི་མཐའ་གཉིས་དང་བྲལ་བའི་དབུས་ཁས་ལེན་པར་རློམ་པའི་ཕྱིར་རོ། དེ་ཡང་གྲུབ་མཐའ་སྨྲ་བ་བཞི་ལ་རྟག་ཆད་ཀྱི་མཐའ་སྤོང་ཚུལ་མི་འདྲ་བ་རེ་ཡོད་དེ། བྱེ་བྲག་སྨྲ་བ་རྣམས་འབྲས་བུ་སྐྱེ་བའི་ཚེ་རྒྱུ་འགག་པས་རྟག་པའི་མཐའ་སྤོང་ལ། རྒྱུའི་མཇུག་ཐོགས་སུ་འབྲས་བུ་འབྱུང་བས་ཆད་པའི་མཐའ་སྤོང་ངོ་ཞེས་ཟེར་རོ།

མདོ་སྡེ་པ་དག་འདུས་བྱས་རྣམས་རྒྱུན་མ་ཆད་པར་འཇུག་པས་ཆད་པའི་མཐའ་སྤོང་ཞིང་། སྐད་ཅིག་གིས་འཇིག་པས་རྟག་པའི་མཐའ་ལས་གྲོལ་ཞེས་འདོད་དོ། སེམས་ཙམ་པ་རྣམས་ཀུན་བཏགས་བདེན་པར་མ་གྲུབ་

པས་རྟག་པའི་མཐའ་སྤོང་ང་ལ། གཞན་དབང་བདེན་པར་གྲུབ་པས་ཆད་པའི་མཐའ་སྤོང་ངོ་ཞེས་སྨྲའོ། དབུ་མ་པ་རྣམས་ཆོས་ཐམས་ཅད་ཐ་སྙད་དུ་ཡོད་པས་ཆད་པའི་མཐའ་ལས་གྲོལ་ཞིང་། དོན་དམ་དུ་མེད་པས་རྟག་པའི་མཐའ་ལས་གྲོལ་ཞེས་བཞེད་དོ། གྲུབ་མཐའ་གོང་མ་གོང་མ་རྣམས་ཀྱིས་འོག་མ་འོག་མའི་གྲུབ་མཐའ་ཐུན་མོང་མ་ཡིན་པ་རྣམས་འགོག་པར་བྱེད་ཀྱང་། འོག་མ་འོག་མའི་ལྟ་བ་གོ་བ་དེ། གོང་མ་གོང་མའི་ལྟ་བ་གོ་བའི་ཐབས་དམ་པར་སྣང་བས། གྲུབ་མཐའ་གོང་མ་ལ་མཆོག་ཏུ་བཟུང་ནས་འོག་མ་ལ་སྨད་པར་མི་བྱའོ།།

དེས་ན། ལྟ་བ་བཀར་བཏགས་ཀྱི་ཕྱག་རྒྱ་བཞི་ཁས་ལེན་པའི་གང་ཟག་དེ། ནང་པ་སངས་རྒྱས་པའི་གྲུབ་མཐའ་སྨྲ་བའི་མཚན་ཉིད་དུ་འཇོག ཕྱག་རྒྱ་བཞི་ཡོད་དེ། འདུས་བྱས་ཐམས་ཅད་མི་རྟག་པ། ཟག་བཅས་ཐམས་ཅད་སྡུག་བསྔལ་བ། ཆོས་ཐམས་ཅད་བདག་མེད་པ། མྱ་ངན་ལས་འདས་པ་ཞི་བ་རྣམས་སོ།

གལ་ཏེ་གནས་མ་བུ་པས་གང་ཟག་གི་བདག་ཁས་བླངས་པས་ནང་པའི་གྲུབ་མཐའ་སྨྲ་བ་མ་ཡིན་པར་འགྱུར་རོ་ཞེ་ན། སྐྱོན་མེད་དེ། དེས་ཁས་བླངས་པའི་བདག་ནི་རང་རྐྱ་ཐུབ་པའི་རྫས་ཡོད་ཀྱི་བདག་ཡིན་ལ། ཕྱག་རྒྱ་བཞིའི་ནང་གི་བདག་མེད་ནི། རྟག་གཅིག་རང་དབང་ཅན་གྱིས་སྟོང་པའི་བདག་མེད་ལ་བྱེད་ཅིང་། དེ་ནི་མང་བཀུར་སྡེ་ཕྱེས་ཀྱང་ཁས་ལེན་པའི་ཕྱིར་རོ།།

གཉིས་པ་བྱེ་བྲག་ཏུ་བཤད་པ་ལ། བྱེ་བྲག་སྨྲ་བ། མདོ་སྡེ་པ། སེམས་ཙམ་པ། ངོ་བོ་ཉིད་མེད་པར་སྨྲ་བའི་གྲུབ་མཐའ་དང་བཞི།

དང་པོ་ལ། མཚན་ཉིད། དབྱེ་བ། སྒྲ་བཤད། འདོད་ཚུལ་དང་བཞི། དང་པོ་ནི། རང་རིག་མི་འདོད་ཅིང་ཕྱི་དོན་བདེན་གྲུབ་ཏུ་འདོད་པའི་ཐེག་དམན་གྱི་གྲུབ་མཐའ་སྨྲ་བའི་གང་ཟག་དེ། བྱེ་བྲག་སྨྲ་བའི་མཚན་ཉིད། གཉིས་པ་ནི། དེ་ལ་དབྱེ་ན། ཁ་ཆེ་བྱེ་བྲག་སྨྲ་བ། ཉི་འོག་པ། ཡུལ་དབུས་ཀྱི་བྱེ་བྲག་སྨྲ་བ་དང་གསུམ་ཡོད། གསུམ་པ་ནི། སློབ་དཔོན་དབྱིག་བཤེས་ཆོས་ཅན། ཁྱོད་ལ་[15]བྱེ་བྲག་སྨྲ་བ་ཞེས་བརྗོད་པའི་རྒྱུ་མཚན་ཡོད་དེ། བྱེ་བྲག་བཤད་མཛོད་ཆེན་མོའི་རྗེས་སུ་འབྲངས་ནས་གྲུབ་མཐའ་སྨྲ་བས་སམ། དུས་གསུམ་རྫས་ཀྱི་བྱེ་བྲག་ཏུ་སྨྲ་བས་ན་བྱེ་བྲག་སྨྲ་བ་ཞེས་བརྗོད་པའི་ཕྱིར། བཞི་པ་འདོད་ཚུལ་ལ། གཞིའི་འདོད་ཚུལ། ལམ་གྱི་འདོད་ཚུལ། འབྲས་བུའི་འདོད་ཚུལ་ལོ། དང་པོ་ལ་གཉིས། ཡུལ་གྱི་འདོད་ཚུལ། ཡུལ་ཅན་གྱི་འདོད་ཚུལ་ལོ།

དང་པོ་ནི། ལུགས་འདིས་ཤེས་བྱ་ཐམས་ཅད་གཞི་ལྔར་འདུས་པར་འདོད་དེ། སྣང་བ་གཟུགས་ཀྱི་གཞི། གཙོ་བོ་སེམས་ཀྱི་གཞི། འཁོར་སེམས་བྱུང་གི་གཞི། ལྡན་པ་མ་ཡིན་པའི་འདུ་བྱེད་ཀྱི་གཞི། འདུས་མ་བྱས་ཀྱི་

གཞི་རྣམས་སོ། གཞི་ལྔ་པོ་དེ་དག་ཀྱང་དངོས་པོར་འདོད་དེ། དོན་བྱེད་ནུས་པ་དངོས་པོའི་མཚན་ཉིད། ཡོད་པ། ཞེས་བྱ། དངོས་པོ་རྣམས་དོན་གཅིག འདུས་མ་བྱས་ཀྱི་ཆོས་རྣམས་རྟག་པའི་དངོས་པོ་དང་། གཟུགས་ཤེས་ལྡན་མིན་འདུ་བྱེད་གསུམ་མི་རྟག་པའི་དངོས་པོར་འདོད་དོ། དངོས་པོ་ལ་རྫས་གྲུབ་ཀྱིས་ཁྱབ་ཀྱང་རྫས་ཡོད་ཀྱིས་མ་ཁྱབ་སྟེ། དོན་དམ་བདེན་པ་དང་། རྫས་ཡོད་དོན་གཅིག ཀུན་རྫོབ་བདེན་པ་དང་། བཏགས་ཡོད་དོན་གཅིག་ཏུ་འདོད་པའི་ཕྱིར། དེ་ལ་དབྱེ་ན། བདེན་པ་གཉིས་སུ་དབྱེ་བ་དང་། ཟག་བཅས་ཟག་མེད་གཉིས་སུ་དབྱེ་བ་དང་། འཕྲོས་དོན་གཞན་བསྟན་པའོ།

དང་པོ་ནི། བཅོམ་པའམ་བློས་ཆ་ཤས་སོ་སོར་བསལ་བ་ན་རང་འཛིན་གྱི་བློ་འདོར་རུང་བའི་[16]ཆོས་སུ་དམིགས་པ་དེ། ཀུན་རྫོབ་བདེན་པའི་མཚན་ཉིད། མཚན་གཞི་ནི། རྫ་བུམ་དང་ཕྲེང་བ་ལྟ་བུ་ཡིན་ཏེ། རྫ་བུམ་ཐོ་བས་བཅོམ་པ་ན་རྫ་བུམ་དུ་འཛིན་པའི་བློ་འདོར་བའི་ཕྱིར་དང་། ཕྲེང་བའི་རྡོག་པོ་སོ་སོར་བསལ་བ་ན་ཕྲེང་བར་འཛིན་པའི་བློ་འདོར་བའི་ཕྱིར། བཅོམ་པའམ་བློས་ཆ་ཤས་སོ་སོར་བསལ་བ་ན་རང་འཛིན་གྱི་བློ་འདོར་དུ་མི་རུང་བའི་ཆོས་སུ་དམིགས་པ་དེ། དོན་དམ་བདེན་པའི་མཚན་ཉིད། མཚན་གཞི་ནི། རྡུལ་ཕྲན་ཕྱོགས་ཀྱི་ཆ་མེད་དང་། ཤེས་པ་སྐད་ཅིག་ཆ་མེད་དང་། འདུས་མ་བྱས་ཀྱི་ནམ་མཁའ་ལྟ་བུ་ཡིན་ཏེ། མཛོད་ལས།

གང་ལ་བཅོམ་དང་བློ་ཡིས་གཞན། བསལ་ན་དེ་བློ་མི་འཇུག་པ།
བུམ་ཆུ་བཞིན་དུ་ཀུན་རྫོབ་ཏུ། ཡོད་དེ་དོན་དམ་ཡོད་གཞན་ནོ།

ཞེས་གསུངས་པའི་ཕྱིར། དེས་ན་ཀུན་རྫོབ་བདེན་པ་རྣམས་དོན་དམ་དུ་མ་གྲུབ་ཀྱང་བདེན་གྲུབ་ཏུ་འདོད་དེ། ལུགས་འདིས་དངོས་པོ་ལ་བདེན་གྲུབ་ཀྱིས་ཁྱབ་པ་ཁས་ལེན་པའི་ཕྱིར།

གཉིས་པ་ནི། དམིགས་པ་དང་མཚུངས་ལྡན་གང་རུང་གི་སྒོ་ནས་ཟག་པ་རྒྱས་སུ་རུང་བའི་ཆོས་དེ། ཟག་བཅས་ཀྱི་མཚན་ཉིད། མཚན་གཞི་ནི། ཕུང་པོ་ལྔ་ལྟ་བུའོ། དམིགས་པ་དང་མཚུངས་ལྡན་གང་རུང་གི་སྒོ་ནས་ཟག་པ་རྒྱས་སུ་མི་རུང་བའི་ཆོས་དེ། ཟག་མེད་ཀྱི་མཚན་ཉིད། མཚན་གཞི་ནི། ལམ་བདེན་དང་། འདུས་མ་བྱས་ལྟ་བུ་ཡིན་ཏེ། མཛོད་ལས། ལམ་མ་གཏོགས་པའི་འདུས་བྱས་རྣམས། ཟག་བཅས། ཞེས་དང་། ཟག་མེད་ལམ་གྱི་བདེན་པ་དང་། འདུས་མ་བྱས་རྣམ་གསུམ་ཡང་སྟེ། ཞེས་གསུངས་པའི་ཕྱིར།

ཟག་བཅས་ལ་སྤང་བྱས་ཁྱབ་སྟེ། ཚོགས་སྦྱོར་གཉིས་སྤང་བྱ་ཡིན་པའི་ཕྱིར། མཐོང་ལམ་ནི་ཟག་མེད་ཁོ་ན་དང་། སྒོམ་ལམ་དང་མི་སློབ་ལམ་གཉིས་པོ་རེ་རེ་ལ་ཟག་བཅས་དང་། ཟག་མེད་ཀྱི་ལམ་གཉིས་གཉིས་ཡོད་དོ། འཕགས་ལམ་ཡིན་ན་ཟག་མེད་ཡིན་པས་ཁྱབ་ཀྱང་། འཕགས་རྒྱུད་ཀྱི་ལམ་ལ་ཟག་མེད་ཡིན་པས་མ་ཁྱབ་སྟེ། སྒོམ་ལམ་པའི་རྒྱུད་ཀྱི་ཞི་རགས་རྣམ་ཅན་དུ་གྱུར་བའི་ལམ་དེ་ཟག་བཅས་ཡིན་པའི་ཕྱིར།

གསུམ་པ་འཕྲོས་དོན་གཞན་བསྟན་པ་ནི། དུས་གསུམ་རྫས་སུ་འདོད་དེ། བྱམ་པ་བྱུམ་པའི་འདས་པའི་དུས་སུ་ཡང་ཡོད། བྱུམ་པ་བྱུམ་པའི་མ་འོངས་པའི་དུས་སུ་ཡང་ཡོད་པར་འདོད་པའི་ཕྱིར།

དགག་སྒྲུབ་གཉིས་ཁས་ལེན་ཀྱང་། མེད་དགག་ནི་ཁས་མི་ལེན་ཏེ། དགག་པ་ཡིན་ན་མ་ཡིན་དགག་ཡིན་པས་ཁྱབ་པར་འདོད་པའི་ཕྱིར།

ཁ་ཆེ་བྱེ་བྲག་སྨྲ་བ་རྣམས་མདོ་སྡེ་པ་དང་མཐུན་པར[17]ལས་འབྲས་ཀྱི་འབྲེལ་པའི་རྟེན་དུ་རྣམ་ཤེས་ཀྱི་རྒྱུན་ཁས་ལེན་ཅིང་། དེ་མ་གཏོགས་པའི་བྱེ་བྲག་སྨྲ་བ་རྣམས་ལས་འབྲས་ཀྱི་འབྲེལ་པའི་རྟེན་དུ་ཐོབ་པ་དང་། བུ་ལོན་གྱི་དཔང་རྒྱ་དང་འདྲ་བའི་ཆུད་མི་ཟ་བ་ཞེས་པ་ལྡན་མིན་འདུ་བྱེད་དུ་གྱུར་པ་ཞིག་ཁས་ལེན་ལ། ཐལ་འགྱུར་པ་དང་། འདི་གཉིས་ཀའི་ལུགས་ལ་ལུས་ངག་གི་ལས་གཟུགས་ཅན་དུ་འདོད་དོ། འདུས་བྱས་ལ་མི་རྟག་པས་ཁྱབ་ཀྱང་། སྐད་ཅིག་རེ་རེ་ནས་འཇིག་པས་མ་ཁྱབ་སྟེ། སྐྱེས་ཟིན་པའི་འོག་ཏུ[18]གནས་པའི་བྱ་བ་དང་། དེའི་འོག་ཏུ་འཇིག་པའི་བྱ་བ་འཇུག་པར་འདོད་པའི་ཕྱིར།

གཉིས་པ་ཡུལ་ཅན་གྱི་འདོད་ཚུལ་ལ། གང་ཟག ཤེས་པ། རྗོད་བྱེད་ཀྱི་སྒྲ་དང་གསུམ། དང་པོ་ནི། གདགས་གཞི་ཕུང་པོ་ལྔའི་ཚོགས་ཙམ་གང་ཟག་གི་མཚན་གཞི། མང་པོས་བཀུར་བ་ཁ་ཅིག་གིས། ཕུང་པོ་ལྔ་ཆར་གང་ཟག་གི་མཚན་གཞི་དང་། སྲུང་བ་པས། སེམས་གཅིག་པུ་གང་ཟག་གི་མཚན་གཞིར་འདོད་དོ།

གཉིས་པ་ལ་ཚད་མ་དང་། ཚད་མིན་གྱི་ཤེས་པ་གཉིས་ལས། དང་པོ་ལ། མངོན་སུམ་གྱི་ཚད་མ་དང་། རྗེས་སུ་དཔག་པའི་ཚད་མ་གཉིས་ཡོད། དང་པོ་ལ། དབང་པོའི་མངོན་སུམ། ཡིད་ཀྱི་མངོན་སུམ། རྣལ་འབྱོར་མངོན་སུམ་དང་གསུམ་ཡོད་ཀྱང་། རང་རིག་མངོན་སུམ་ཁས་མི་ལེན་ནོ། དབང་པོའི་མངོན་སུམ་གྱི་ཚད་མ་ལ་ཤེས་པས་མ་ཁྱབ་སྟེ། མིག་དབང་གཟུགས་ཅན་པ་དེ་ཡིན་པོ། ལྟ་བ། ཚད་མ་གསུམ་ཀའི་གཞི་མཐུན་ཡིན་པའི་ཕྱིར། དབང་པོའི་ཤེས་པས་ཡུལ་རྣམ་མེད་རྗེན་ཆེར་དུ་གཞལ་ཞིང་། རྟེན་བཅས་ཀྱི་མིག་གི་དབང་པོ་གཟུགས་ཅན་པས་ཀྱང་གཟུགས་མཐོང་བར་འདོད་དེ། གལ་ཏེ་རྣམ་ཤེས་ཁོ་ནས་མཐོང་ན་རྩིག་པ་ལ་སོགས་པས[19]བར་དུ་ཆོད་

པའི་གཟུགས་ཀྱང་མཐོང་བར་འགྱུར་[20]རོ་ཞེས་ཟེར་ཞིང་། སེམས་དང་སེམས་བྱུང་གཉིས་རྫས་ཐ་དད་དུ་འདོད་དོ།

གསུམ་པ་ནི། སྤྱིར་སྒྲ་ཙམ་ལ་དབྱེ་ན། ཟིན་པའི་སྒྲ་དང་། མ་ཟིན་པའི་སྒྲ་གཉིས་ཡོད། དང་པོ་ནི། སྐྱེས་བུའི་ངག་ཏུ་གྱུར་པའི་སྒྲ་ལྟ་བུ། གཉིས་པ་ནི། ཆུ་སྒྲ་ལྟ་བུ། ཟིན་མ་ཟིན་རེ་རེ་ལ་ཡང་། སེམས་ཅན་དུ་སྟོན་མི་སྟོན་གཉིས་གཉིས་[21]ཡོད། སེམས་ཅན་དུ་སྟོན་པའི་སྒྲ་དང་། ངག་གི་རྣམ་པར་རིག་བྱེད་ཀྱི་སྒྲ་དང་། རྗོད་བྱེད་ཀྱི་སྒྲ་གསུམ་དོན་གཅིག སེམས་ཅན་དུ་མི་སྟོན་པའི་སྒྲ་དང་། ངག་གི་རྣམ་པར་རིག་བྱེད་མ་ཡིན་པའི་སྒྲ་དང་། རྗོད་བྱེད་ཀྱི་སྒྲ་མ་ཡིན་པའི་སྒྲ་གསུམ་དོན་གཅིག   བཀའ་དང་བསྟན་བཅོས་གཉིས་ཀྱང་མིང་ཚིག་ཡི་གེ་འདུས་པའི་བདག་ཉིད་སྒྲ་སྤྱི་ལྡན་མིན་འདུ་བྱེད་ཁས་ལེན་པས། ལུགས་འདི་ལ་བེམ་པོ་དང་ལྡན་མིན་འདུ་བྱེད་མི་འགལ་ལམ་[22]སྙམ་མོ།

གཉིས་པ་ལམ་གྱི་རྣམ་བཞག་བཤད་པ་ལ། ལམ་གྱི་དམིགས་པ། ལམ་གྱི་སྤང་བྱ། ལམ་གྱི་རང་བཞིན་བཤད་པའོ། དང་པོ་ནི། བདེན་བཞིའི་ཁྱད་ཆོས་མི་རྟག་སོགས་བཅུ་དྲུག་ཡིན་ལ། བདག་མེད་ཕྲ་མོ་དང་གང་ཟག་གི་བདག་མེད་ཕྲ་མོ་དོན་གཅིག་ཏུ་འདོད་ཅིང་། གང་ཟག་རང་རྐྱ་ཐུབ་པའི་རྫས་ཡོད་ཀྱིས་སྟོང་པ་གང་ཟག་གི་བདག་མེད་ཕྲ་མོར་ཁས་ལེན་ནོ། སྡེ་པ་བཅོ་བརྒྱད་ཀྱི་ནང་ནས་མང་བཀུར་སྡེ་ལྟས་རང་རྐྱ་ཐུབ་པའི་རྫས་ཡོད་ཀྱིས་སྟོང་པ་གང་ཟག་གི་བདག་མེད་ཕྲ་མོར་མི་འདོད་དེ། དེས་རང་རྐྱ་ཐུབ་པའི་རྫས་ཡོད་ཀྱི་བདག་ཡོད་པར་ཁས་ལེན་པའི་ཕྱིར། ཆོས་ཀྱི་བདག་མེད་ཕྲ་རགས་ཀྱི་རྣམ་བཞག་ཁས་མི་ལེན་དེ། གཞི་གྲུབ་[23]ན་ཆོས་བདག་ཡིན་པས་ཁྱབ་པ་ཁས་ལེན་པའི་ཕྱིར།

གཉིས་པ་ལམ་གྱི་སྤང་བྱ་ལ། ཉོན་མོངས་ཅན་དང་། ཉོན་མོངས་ཅན་མ་ཡིན་པའི་མི་ཤེས་པ་གཉིས་ལས། དང་པོས་ནི་གཙོ་བོར་ཐར་པ་འཐོབ་པ་ལ་བར་དུ་གཅོད་པ་སྟེ། མཚན་གཞི་ནི། གང་ཟག་གི་བདག་འཛིན་དང་། དེའི་དབང་གིས་བྱུང་བའི་དུག་གསུམ་ས་བོན་དང་བཅས་པ་ལྟ་བུའོ། གཉིས་པས་ནི་ཐམས་ཅད་མཁྱེན་པ་འཐོབ་པ་ལ་གཙོ་བོར་བར་དུ་གཅོད་པ་སྟེ། མཚན་གཞི་ནི། དེ་བཞིན་གཤེགས་པའི་ཆོས་ཟབ་ཅིང་ཕྲ་བ་མི་ཤེས་པའི་ཉོན་མོངས་ཅན་མ་ཡིན་པའི་སྒྲིབ་པ་སོགས་མི་ཤེས་པའི་རྒྱུ་བཞི་ལྟ་བུའོ། སྒྲིབ་པ་ལ་དེ་གཉིས་ལས་ཤེས་སྒྲིབ་ཅེས་པའི་ཐ་སྙད་ཁས་མི་ལེན་ནོ།

གསུམ་པ་ལམ་གྱི་རང་བཞིན་ནི། དེ་ཡང་ཐེག་པ་གསུམ་གྱི་ལམ་ལ། ཚོགས་ལམ། སྦྱོར་ལམ། མཐོང་ལམ། སྒོམ་ལམ། མི་སློབ་ལམ་སྟེ་ལམ་ལྔའི་རྣམ་བཞག་ཁས་ལེན་ཀྱང་ས་བཅུའི་ཡེ་ཤེས་མི་འདོད་དོ། ཞེས་

བཟོད་སྐད་ཅིག་མ་བཅུ་དྲུག་གི་སྐད་ཅིག་མ་དང་པོ་བཅོ་ལྔ་[24]ནི་མཐོང་ལམ་དང་། བཅུ་དྲུག་པ་ལམ་རྗེས་ཤེས་སྒོམ་ལམ་ཡིན་ལ། ར་ཟམ་པར་འགྲོ་བ་ལྷར་རིམ་ཅན་ཁོ་ནར་སྐྱེ་བར་འདོད་དོ། ལམ་བདེན་ལ་ཤེས་པས་མ་ཁྱབ་སྟེ། ཟག་མེད་ཀྱི་ཕུང་པོ་ལྔ་ལམ་བདེན་དུ་འདོད་པའི་ཕྱིར།

གསུམ་པ་འབྲས་བུའི་རྣམ་བཞག་ནི། ཉན་ཐོས་ཀྱི་རིགས་ཅན་རྣམས་ཀྱིས་མི་རྟག་སོགས་བཅུ་དྲུག་ལ་ཚེ་གསུམ་ལ་སོགས་པའི་བར་དུ་[25]གོམས་པར་བྱས་ནས་མཐར་ཉན་ཐོས་ཀྱི་སྒོམ་ལམ་རྡོ་རྗེ་ལྟ་བུའི་ཏིང་ངེ་འཛིན་ལ་བརྟེན་ནས། ཉོན་མོངས་ཅན་གྱི་སྒྲིབ་པ་ཐོབ་པ་ཆད་པའི་ཚུལ་གྱིས་སྤངས་ཏེ་དགྲ་བཅོམ་པའི་འབྲས་བུ་མངོན་དུ་བྱེད་དོ།

བསེ་རུ་ལྟ་བུའི་རང་རྒྱལ་རྣམས་ཀྱིས་གང་ཟག་རང་རྐྱ་ཐུབ་པའི་རྫས་ཡོད་ཀྱིས་སྟོང་བར་རྟོགས་པའི་ལྟ་བ་དེ་བསྐལ་ཆེན་བརྒྱ་ལ་སོགས་པའི་བསོད་ནམས་ཀྱི་ཚོགས་དང་སྦྲེལ་ཏེ་ཚོགས་ལམ་ཆེན་པོ་མན་ཆད་དུ་ཉམས་སུ་བླངས་ནས་སྦྱོར་ལམ་དྲོད་ནས་མི་སློབ་ལམ་གྱི་བར་སྟན་ཐོག་གཅིག་ལ་མངོན་དུ་བྱེད་དོ། དམན་པའི་དགྲ་བཅོམ་པ་ཡང་རང་གི་སྤངས་རྟོགས་ལས་ཉམས་ནས་རྒྱུན་ཞུགས་སུ་འགྱུར་བ་སྲིད་པས་ཉམས་པའི་ཆོས་ཅན་སོགས་ཁས་ལེན་ནོ། ཉན་ཐོས་ལ་དགེ་འདུན་ཉི་ཤུ་དང་། ཞུགས་གནས་བརྒྱད་ཀྱི་རྣམ་བཞག་བརྗེ་ཡང་ཅིག་ཆར་བ་ཁས་མི་ལེན་ལ། ཞུགས་གནས་བརྒྱད་པོ་གང་རུང་ལ་འཕགས་པས་ཁྱབ་པར་འདོད་དོ།

བྱང་སེམས་རྣམས་ཀྱིས་ཚོགས་ལམ་གྱི་གནས་སྐབས་སུ་བསྐལ་ཆེན་གྲངས་མེད་གསུམ་གྱི་ཚོགས་རྫོགས་པར་བྱེད་ཅིང་། དེ་ནས་བསྐལ་པ་བརྒྱར་མཚན་བཟང་གི་རྒྱུ་བསྒྲུབས་ཏེ་སྲིད་པ་ཐ་མའི་ཚེ་བྱང་ཆུབ་ཀྱི་ཤིང་དྲུང་དུ་སྲོད་ལ་ལྷའི་བུའི་བདུད་བཏུལ། གུང་ལ་མཉམ་པར་བཞག་པའི་ཚེ། སྦྱོར་ལམ། མཐོང་ལམ། སྒོམ་ལམ་གསུམ་མངོན་དུ་བྱས་ནས། ཐོ་རངས་སྐྱ་རེང་ཤར་བ་ཙམ་ན་མི་སློབ་ལམ་མངོན་དུ་བྱེད་དོ། དེས་ན་སྲོད་ལ་བདུད་བཏུལ་བ་ཡན་ཆད་སོ་སྐྱེའི་གནས་སྐབས་དང་། བྱང་སེམས་ཀྱི་སྦྱོར་མཐོང་སྒོམ་གསུམ་ལ་མཉམ་བཞག་ཁོ་ནས་ཁྱབ་པར་འདོད་ཅིང་། མཛད་པ་བཅུ་གཉིས་ཀྱི་དང་པོ་དགུ་བྱང་སེམས་དང་། ཕྱི་མ་གསུམ་སངས་རྒྱས་ཀྱི་མཛད་པར་ཁས་ལེན་ནོ། ཆོས་འཁོར་ལ་མཐོང་ལམ་གྱིས་ཁྱབ་པ་དང་། ལུང་གི་ཆོས་འཁོར་ལ་བདེན་བཞིའི་ཆོས་འཁོར་གྱིས་ཁྱབ་པར་འདོད་དོ། མངོན་པ་སྡེ་བདུན་པོ་སངས་རྒྱས་ཀྱིས་གསུངས་པའི་བཀར་ཁས་ལེན་ཅིང་། བཀའ་ལ་སྒྲ་ཇི་བཞིན་པས་ཁྱབ་བོ། ཆོས་ཀྱི་ཕུང་པོ་བརྒྱད་ཁྲི་ལས། བརྒྱད་ཁྲི་བཞི་སྟོང་གི་རྣམ་བཞག་ཁས་མི་ལེན་ཏེ། མཛོད་ལས།

ཆོས་ཀྱི་ཕུང་པོ་བརྒྱད་ཁྲི་དག   གང་རྣམས་ཐུབ་པས་གསུངས་དེ་དག
ཅེས་གསུངས་པའི་ཕྱིར།

བྱང་སེམས་སྲིད་པ་ཐ་མ་པས་བྱང་ཆུབ་མངོན་དུ་བྱེད་པའི་གནས་ནི་འདོད་ཁམས་ཁོ་ནར་ངེས་པས། འོག་མིན་སྟུག་པོ་བཀོད་པ་དང་།   ལོངས་སྐུའི་རྣམ་བཞག་ཁས་མི་ལེན་ལ།   དེར་མ་ཟད་རྣམ་མཁྱེན་ཡང་མི་འདོད་དོ། ཐེག་པ་གསུམ་གྱི་དགྲ་བཅོམ་ལ་ལྷག་བཅས་པས་ཁྱབ་སྟེ།   ལྷག་མེད་དུ་མྱ་ངན་ལས་འདས་པའི་ཚེ་མར་མེ་ཤི་བ་ལྟར་རིག་པ་རྒྱུན་ཆད་པར་འདོད་པའི་ཕྱིར། དེས་ན་མཐར་ཐུག་ཐེག་པ་གསུམ་དུ་གྲུབ་པར་ཡང་ཁས་ལེན་ནོ།

ཁ་ཅིག   སྟོན་པ་མྱ་ངན་ལས་འདས་པའི་ཚེ་གདུལ་བྱ་འགའ་ཞིག་གི་ངོར་གཟུགས་སྐུའི་བཀོད་པ་བསྟུས་པ་ཙམ་ཡིན་གྱི། དོན་ལ་མྱ་ངན་ལས་འདས་པ་མེད་ཅེས་སྨྲ་བ་ནི་ཉ་དང་ཉུང་མ་བསྲེས་པའོ།

སངས་རྒྱས་འཕགས་པས་སྡུག་ཀུན་མ་ལུས་པར་སྤངས་ཀྱང་།   དེའི་རྒྱུད་ལ་སྡུག་བདེན་ཡོད་པ་མི་འགལ་ཏེ།   སྡུག་བདེན་ལ་དམིགས་པའི་ཉོན་མོངས་མ་ལུས་པར་སྤངས་པ་ན་སྡུག་བདེན་སྤངས་པར་འཇོག་པའི་ཕྱིར། གཟུགས་ཀྱི་སྐུ་ནི་སྔར་བྱང་སེམས་སྦྱོར་ལམ་པའི་ལུས་རྟེན་དང་ཚེ་གཅིག་གིས་[26]བསྡུས་པའི་ཕྱིར་སངས་རྒྱས་དཀོན་མཆོག་མིན་ཡང་སངས་རྒྱས་སུ་ཁས་ལེན་ལ། སངས་རྒྱས་དཀོན་མཆོག་ནི་དེའི་ཐུགས་རྒྱུད་ཀྱི་ཟད་མི་སྐྱེའི་ཡེ་ཤེས་ལ་འདོད་དོ།   དེ་བཞིན་དུ་སློབ་པ་འཕགས་པ་རྣམས་ཟག་བཅས་ཡིན་པས་དགེ་འདུན་དཀོན་མཆོག་མིན་ཡང་དགེ་འདུན་ཡིན་ལ།   དགེ་འདུན་དཀོན་མཆོག་ནི་དེའི་ཐུགས་རྒྱུད་ཀྱི་ལམ་བདེན་ལ་འདོད་དོ།   ཆོས་དཀོན་མཆོག་ཀྱང་བཞག་ཏུ་ཡོད་དེ།   སངས་རྒྱས་དང་ཉན་རང་གཉིས་ཀའི་རྒྱུད་ཀྱི་མྱང་འདས་དང་འགོག་བདེན་དེ་དེ་ཡིན་པའི་ཕྱིར། སྨྲས་པ།

བདག་བློའི་རྣམ་དཔྱོད་གསེར་གྱི་བུམ་པ་ཡིས། །
བྱེ་སྨྲའི་གཞུང་ལུགས་རོལ་མཚོ་ནས་བླངས་པ། །
ལེགས་བཤད་བདུད་རྩི་གསར་པའི་དགའ་སྟོན་ལ། །
བློ་གསལ་གཞོན་ནུའི་ཚོགས་རྣམས་རོལ་པར་མཛོད།[27] །

ཅེས་བྱ་བ་ནི་བར་སྐབས་ཀྱི་ཚིགས་སུ་བཅད་པའོ།།

གཉིས་པ་མདོ་སྡེ་པའི་གྲུབ་མཐའ་རྣམ་བཞག་བཤད་པ་ལ། མཚན་ཉིད། དབྱེ་བ། སྒྲ་བཤད། འདོད་ཚུལ་དང་བཞི། དང་པོ་ནི། རང་རིག་དང་ཕྱི་དོན་གཉིས་ཀ་བདེན་ཞེན་གྱིས་[28] ཁས་ལེན་པའི་ཐེག་དམན་གྱི་གྲུབ་མཐའ་སྨྲ་བའི་གང་ཟག་དེ་མདོ་སྡེ་པའི་མཚན་ཉིད། མདོ་སྡེ་པ་དང་དཔེ་སྟོན་པ་གཉིས་དོན་གཅིག གཉིས་པ་ནི། དེ་ལ་དབྱེ་ན། ལུང་གི་རྗེས་འབྲང་གི་མདོ་སྡེ་པ་དང་། རིགས་པའི་རྗེས་འབྲང་གི་མདོ་སྡེ་པ་གཉིས། དང་པོ་ནི། མངོན་པ་མཛོད་ཀྱི་རྗེས་འབྲང་གི་མདོ་སྡེ་པ་ལྟ་བུ། གཉིས་པ་ནི། ཚད་མ་སྡེ་བདུན་གྱི་རྗེས་འབྲང་གི་མདོ་སྡེ་པ་ལྟ་བུའོ། གསུམ་པ་སྒྲ་བཤད་ནི། མདོ་སྡེ་པ་དང་དཔེ་སྟོན་པ་ཞེས་བརྗོད་པའི་རྒྱུ་མཚན་ཡོད་དེ། བྱེ་བྲག་ཏུ་བཤད་པའི་རྗེས་སུ་མི་འབྲང་བར་གཙོ་བོར་བཅོམ་ལྡན་འདས་ཀྱི་མདོ་ལ་བརྟེན་ནས་གྲུབ་མཐའ་སྨྲ་བས་ན་མདོ་སྡེ་པ་དང་། ཆོས་ཐམས་ཅད་དཔེའི་སྒོ་ནས་སྟོན་པས་ན་དཔེ་སྟོན་པ་ཞེས་མཇོད་པའི་ཕྱིར།

བཞི་པ་འདོད་ཚུལ་ལ། གཞིའི་འདོད་ཚུལ། ལམ་གྱི་འདོད་ཚུལ། འབྲས་བུའི་འདོད་ཚུལ་དང་གསུམ། དང་པོ་ལ། ཡུལ་དང་། ཡུལ་ཅན་གྱི་འདོད་ཚུལ་གཉིས། དང་པོ་ནི། བློས་རིག་པར་བྱ་བ་ཡུལ་གྱི་མཚན་ཉིད། བློའི་ཡུལ་དུ་བྱ་རུང་བ་ཤེས་བྱའི་མཚན་ཉིད། ཡུལ་དང་། ཡོད་པ། ཤེས་བྱ། གཞི་གྲུབ་རྣམས་དོན་གཅིག དེ་ལ་དབྱེ་ན། བདེན་པ་གཉིས་སུ་དབྱེ་བ། རང་སྤྱི་གཉིས་སུ་དབྱེ་བ། དགག་སྒྲུབ་གཉིས་སུ་དབྱེ་བ། མངོན་ལྐོག་གཉིས་སུ་དབྱེ་བ། དུས་གསུམ་དུ་དབྱེ་བ། གཅིག་དང་ཐ་དད་གཉིས་སུ་དབྱེ་བའོ།

དང་པོ་ནི། སྒྲ་དང་རྟོག་པས་བཏགས་པ་ལ་མ་ལྟོས་པར་རང་གི་སྡོད་ལུགས་ཀྱི་ངོས་ནས་རིགས་པས་དཔྱད་བཟོད་དུ་གྲུབ་པའི་ཆོས་དེ་དོན་དམ་བདེན་པའི་མཚན་ཉིད། དངོས་པོ་དང་། དོན་དམ་བདེན་པ་དང་། རང་མཚན་དང་། མི་རྟག་པ་དང་། འདུས་བྱས་དང་། བདེན་གྲུབ་རྣམས་དོན་གཅིག རྟོག་པས་བཏགས་པ་ཙམ་དུ་གྲུབ་པའི་ཆོས་དེ་ཀུན་རྫོབ་བདེན་པའི་མཚན་ཉིད། དངོས་མེད་ཀྱི་ཆོས་དང་། ཀུན་རྫོབ་བདེན་པ་དང་། སྤྱི་མཚན་དང་། རྟག་པ་དང་། འདུས་མ་བྱས་ཀྱི་ཆོས་དང་། བརྫུན་པར་གྲུབ་པ་རྣམས་དོན་གཅིག བདེན་གཉིས་ཀྱི་སྒྲ་བཤད་ཡོད་དེ། འདུས་མ་བྱས་ཀྱི་ནམ་མཁའ་ཆོས་ཅན། ཀུན་རྫོབ་བདེན་པ་ཞེས་བྱ་སྟེ། བློ་ཀུན་རྫོབ་པའི་ངོར་བདེན་པའི་ཕྱིར་རོ། འདིའི་ཀུན་རྫོབ་པ་ནི་རྟོག་པ་སྟེ། རང་མཚན་མངོན་སུམ་དུ་མཐོང་བ་ལ་སྒྲིབ་པས་ན་ཀུན་རྫོབ་པ་ཞེས་བྱའོ། འདི་ཡང་སྒྲ་བཤད་ཙམ་ཡིན་གྱི། བློ་ཀུན་རྫོབ་པ་རྟོག་པའི་ངོར་བདེན་པ་ཡིན་ན། ཀུན་རྫོབ་བདེན་པ་ཡིན་པས་ཁྱབ་པ་མེད་དེ། དོན་དམ་བདེན་པའི་མཚན་གཞི་བུམ་པ་ལྟ་བུ་ཡང་། བློ་ཀུན་རྫོབ་པ་རྟོག་པའི་ངོར་བདེན་པའི་ཕྱིར། གང་ཟག་གི་བདག་དང་སྒྲ་རྟག་པ་ལྟ་བུ་བློ་ཀུན་རྫོབ་པ་རྟོག་པའི་ངོར་བདེན་པ་ཡིན་ཡང་། ཐ་

སྙད་དུ་ཡང་མ་གྲུབ་པའི་ཕྱིར། བུམ་པ་ཆོས་ཅན། དོན་དམ་བདེན་པ་ཞེས་བྱ་སྟེ། བློ་དོན་དམ་པའི་ངོར་བདེན་པའི་ཕྱིར། འདིའི་བློ་དོན་དམ་པ་ནི། སྣང་ཡུལ་ལ་མ་འཁྲུལ་པའི་ཤེས་པ་ལ་བྱའོ། བདེན་གཉིས་ཀྱི་འཇོག་ཚུལ་འདི་རིགས་པའི་རྗེས་འབྲང་གི་མདོ་སྡེ་པའི་ལུགས་ཡིན་ལ། ལུང་གི་རྗེས་འབྲང་གི་མདོ་སྡེ་པས། བདེན་གཉིས་ཀྱི་རྣམ་བཞག་བྱེ་སྨྲ་དང་མཐུན་པར་ཁས་ལེན་ནོ།

གཉིས་པ་ནི། དོན་དམ་པར་དོན་བྱེད་ནུས་པའི་ཆོས་དེ། རང་མཚན་གྱི་མཚན་ཉིད། མཚན་གཞི་ནི། བུམ་པ་ལྟ་བུ། དོན་དམ་པར་དོན་བྱེད་མི་ནུས་པའི་ཆོས་དེ། སྤྱི་མཚན་གྱི་མཚན་ཉིད། མཚན་གཞི་ནི། འདུས་མ་བྱས་ཀྱི་ནམ་མཁའ་ལྟ་བུ། སྤྱི་དང་བྱེ་བྲག གཅིག་དང་ཐ་དད། འགལ་བ་དང་འབྲེལ་བ་ལ་སོགས་པ་སྒྲོ་བཏགས་པའི་ཆོས་རྣམས་སྤྱི་མཚན་ཡིན་མོད་ཀྱང་། དེ་དག་ཡིན་ན་སྤྱི་མཚན་ཡིན་མི་དགོས་པའི་ཁྱད་པར་ཕྱེད་དགོས་སོ།།

གསུམ་པ་ནི། དགག་བྱ་དངོས་སུ་བཅད་པའི་ཚུལ་གྱིས་རྟོགས་པར་བྱ་བ་དགག་པའི་མཚན་ཉིད། དེ་དང་གཞན་སེལ་དོན་གཅིག དབྱེ་ན། མེད་དགག་དང་། མ་ཡིན་དགག་གཉིས། རང་དངོས་སུ་རྟོགས་པའི་བློས་རང་གི་དགག་བྱ་དེ་བཅད་ཙམ་དུ་རྟོགས་པར་བྱ་བ་མེད་དགག་གི་མཚན་ཉིད། དཔེར་ན། བྲམ་ཟེས་ཆང་མི་བཏུང་བ་ལྟ་བུའོ། རང་དངོས་སུ་རྟོགས་པའི་བློས་རང་གི་དགག་བྱ་བཀག་ཤུལ་དུ་ཆོས་གཞན་མ་ཡིན་དགག་དང་། སྒྲུབ་པ་གང་རུང་འཕེན་པ་[29] དེ་མ་ཡིན་དགག་གི་མཚན་ཉིད། དཔེར་ན། ལྷས་སྦྱིན་ཚོན་པོས་ཉིན་པར་ཟས་མི་ཟ་བ་ལྟ་བུའོ། རང་དངོས་སུ་རྟོགས་པའི་བློས་རང་གི་དགག་བྱ་དངོས་སུ་བཅད་ནས་རྟོགས་པར་བྱ་བ་མ་ཡིན་པའི་ཆོས་དེ་སྒྲུབ་པའི་མཚན་ཉིད། དཔེར་ན། བུམ་པ་ལྟ་བུའོ།

བཞི་པ་ནི། མངོན་སུམ་གྱི་ཚད་མས་དངོས་སུ་རྟོགས་པར་བྱ་བ་མངོན་གྱུར་གྱི་མཚན་ཉིད། དེ་དང་དངོས་པོ་དོན་གཅིག རྗེས་སུ་དཔག་པའི་ཚད་མས་དངོས་སུ་རྟོགས་པར་བྱ་བ་ལྐོག་གྱུར་གྱི་མཚན་ཉིད། དེ་དང་ཤེས་བྱ་དོན་གཅིག

ལྔ་པ་ནི། དངོས་པོ་གཞན་ཞིག་རང་གྲུབ་དུས་ཀྱི་སྐད་ཅིག་གཉིས་པར་ཞིག་པའི་ཆ་དེ་འདས་པའི་མཚན་ཉིད།[30] དངོས་པོ་གཞན་ཞིག་སྐྱེ་བའི་རྒྱུ་ཡོད་ཀྱང་རྐྱེན་མ་ཚང་བའི་དབང་གིས་ཡུལ་དུས་འགའ་ཞིག་ཏུ་མ་སྐྱེས་པའི་ཆ་དེ་མ་འོངས་པའི་མཚན་ཉིད། སྐྱེས་ལ་མ་འགགས་པ་[31] ད་ལྟར་བའི་མཚན་ཉིད། འདས་པ་དང་མ་འོངས་པ་གཉིས་རྟག་པ་ཡིན་ལ། ད་ལྟར་བ་དང་དངོས་པོ་དོན་གཅིག་ཏུ་འདོད་དོ། དངོས་པོ་དེའི་འདས་པ། དངོས་པོ་དེའི་ཕྱི་ལོགས་སུ་གྲུབ་ཅིང་། དངོས་པོ་དེའི་མ་འོངས་པ། དངོས་པོ་དེའི་སྔ་ལོགས་སུ་གྲུབ་པའི་ཁྱད་པར་རྣམས་ཀྱང་ཤེས་པར་བྱའོ།

དྲུག་པ་ནི། སོ་སོ་བ་མ་ཡིན་པའི་ཆོས་དེ་གཅིག་གི་མཚན་ཉིད། དཔེར་ན། བུམ་པ་ལྟ་བུའོ། སོ་སོ་བའི་ཆོས་དེ་ཐ་དད་ཀྱི་མཚན་ཉིད། དཔེར་ན། ཀ་བུམ་གཉིས་ལྟ་བུའོ། ངོ་བོ་ཐ་དད་ལ་ལྡོག་པ་[32]ཐ་དད་ཀྱིས་ཁྱབ་ཀྱང་། ལྡོག་པ་ཐ་དད་ལ་ངོ་བོ་ཐ་དད་ཀྱིས་མ་ཁྱབ་སྟེ། བྱས་པ་དང་། མི་རྟག་པ་གཉིས་ངོ་བོ་གཅིག་ཡིན་ཀྱང་། ལྡོག་པ་ཐ་དད་ཡིན་པའི་ཕྱིར། གཞན་ཡང་རྡུལ་ཕྲན་ཕྱོགས་ཀྱི་ཆ་མེད་དང་། ཤེས་པ་སྐད་ཅིག་ཆ་མེད་ཁས་ལེན་པ་སོགས་བྱེ་བྲག་སྨྲ་བ་དང་མཐུན་ཀྱང་། ཐམས་ཅད་དུ་འདྲ་བ་ནི་མ་ཡིན་དེ། བྱེ་སྨྲས་ཡོད་པར་འདོད་ཕྱིན་[33]རྫས་གྲུབ་ཏུ་འདོད་ལ། མདོ་སྡེ་པས་དེ་ལྟར་མི་འདོད་པའི་ཕྱིར། རྣམ་པར་རིག་བྱེད་མ་ཡིན་པའི་གཟུགས་ཀྱང་། བྱེ་སྨྲ་དང་ཐལ་འགྱུར་པ་གཉིས་ཀས་གཟུགས་མཚན་ཉིད་པར་ཁས་ལེན་ལ།[34] མདོ་སེམས་རང་རྒྱུད་པ་གསུམ་གྱིས་གཟུགས་མཚན་ཉིད་པ་མ་ཡིན་པར་འདོད་པའི་ཕྱིར། དེར་མ་ཟད་བྱེ་བྲག་སྨྲ་བས་རྒྱུ་འབྲས་དུས་མཉམ་པར་འདོད་ལ། མདོ་སྡེ་པ་ཡན་ཆད་ཀྱིས་དེ་ལྟར་མི་འདོད་པའི་ཕྱིར།

གཉིས་པ་ཡུལ་ཅན་གྱི་འདོད་ཚུལ་ལ། གང་ཟག ཤེས་པ། རྗོད་བྱེད་ཀྱི་སྒྲ་དང་གསུམ། དང་པོ་ནི། ལུང་གི་རྗེས་འབྲངས་ཕུང་པོའི་རྒྱུན་གང་ཟག་གི་མཚན་གཞི་དང་། རིགས་པའི་རྗེས་འབྲངས་རྣམས་ཡིད་ཀྱི་རྣམ་ཤེས་གང་ཟག་གི་མཚན་གཞིར་འདོད་དོ། གཉིས་པ་ལ། ཚད་མ་དང་། ཚད་མིན་གྱི་བློ་གཉིས། ཚད་མ་ལ་མངོན་སུམ་གྱི་ཚད་མ་དང་། རྗེས་སུ་དཔག་པའི་ཚད་མ་གཉིས། མངོན་སུམ་གྱི་ཚད་མ་ལ། དབང་པོའི་མངོན་སུམ། ཡིད་ཀྱི་མངོན་སུམ། རང་རིག་མངོན་སུམ། རྣལ་འབྱོར་མངོན་སུམ་གྱི་ཚད་མ་དང་བཞི་ཡོད་དོ། དབང་པོ་གཟུགས་ཅན་པ་ཚད་མར་མི་རུང་སྟེ། གསལ་རིག་གིས་སྟོང་ཞིང་རང་གི་ཡུལ་གཞལ་མི་ཐུབ་པའི་ཕྱིར། ཚད་མིན་གྱི་བློ་ལ། བཅད་ཤེས། ལོག་ཤེས། ཐེ་ཚོམ། ཡིད་དཔྱོད། སྣང་ལ་མ་ངེས་པའི་བློ་དང་ལྔའོ། དེ་དག་ལས་མངོན་སུམ་དང་། སྣང་ལ་མ་ངེས་པའི་བློ་གཉིས་ལ་རྟོག་བྲལ་མ་འཁྲུལ་བས་ཁྱབ་ཅིང་། རྗེས་དཔག ཡིད་དཔྱོད། ཐེ་ཚོམ་གསུམ་ནི་རྟོག་པ་ཁོ་ན་ཡིན་ནོ། ཞེས་པས་ཡུལ་འཛལ་བའི་ཚེ་རྣམ་བཅས་སུ་རྟོགས་ཤིང་། སེམས་སེམས་བྱུང་རྫས་གཅིག་ཏུ་འདོད་དོ། གསུམ་པ་ནི། རང་གི་བརྗོད་བྱའི་དོན་གོ་བར་བྱེད་པའི་མཉན་བྱ་དེ། རྗོད་བྱེད་ཀྱི་སྒྲའི་མཚན་ཉིད། དེ་ལ་བརྗོད་བྱའི་སྒོ་ནས་དབྱེ་ན། རིགས་བརྗོད་ཀྱི་སྒྲ་དང་། ཚོགས་བརྗོད་ཀྱི་སྒྲ་གཉིས། དང་པོ་ནི། གཟུགས་ཞེས་བརྗོད་པའི་སྒྲ་ལྟ་བུའོ། གཉིས་པ་ནི། བུམ་པ་ཞེས་བརྗོད་པའི་སྒྲ་ལྟ་བུའོ། ཡང་དེ་ལ་བརྗོད་ཚུལ་གྱི་སྒོ་ནས་དབྱེ་ན། ཆོས་བརྗོད་ཀྱི་སྒྲ་དང་། ཆོས་ཅན་བརྗོད་པའི་སྒྲ་གཉིས། དང་པོ་ནི། སྒྲའི་མི་རྟག་པ་ཞེས་བརྗོད་པའི་སྒྲ་ལྟ་བུའོ། གཉིས་པ་ནི། སྒྲ་མི་རྟག་པ་ཞེས་བརྗོད་པའི་སྒྲ་ལྟ་བུའོ།

གཉིས་པ་ལམ་གྱི་འདོད་ཚུལ་ལ་གསུམ་ལས། ལམ་གྱི་དམིགས་པ་ནི། བདེན་གཞིའི་རྣམ་པ་མི་རྟག་སོགས་བཅུ་དྲུག་པོ་འདི་ཉིད་ཡིན་ལ། བདག་མེད་ཕྲ་མོ་དང་། གང་ཟག་གི་བདག་མེད་ཕྲ་མོ་དོན་གཅིག་ཏུ་འདོད་ཅིང་། གང་ཟག་རྟག་གཅིག་རང་དབང་ཅན་གྱི་བདག་གིས་སྟོང་པ་[35]གང་ཟག་གི་བདག་མེད་རགས་པ་དང་། གང་ཟག་རང་རྐྱ་ཐུབ་པའི་རྫས་ཡོད་ཀྱིས་སྟོང་པ་གང་ཟག་གི་བདག་མེད་ཕྲ་མོར་འདོད་དོ། ལམ་གྱི་སྤང་བྱ་ལ། གང་ཟག་གི་བདག་འཛིན་དང་། ཉོན་མོངས་ཅན་དང་། ཉོན་མོངས་ཅན་མ་ཡིན་པའི་མི་ཤེས་པ་སོགས་ཀྱི་ཐ་སྙད་ཙམ་ཞིག་མ་གཏོགས།[36] ཆོས་ཀྱི་བདག་མེད་འཛིན་དང་། ཤེས་སྒྲིབ་སོགས་ཁས་མི་ལེན་པ་བྱེ་སྨྲ་དང་འདྲའོ། ཐེག་པ་གསུམ་གྱི་ལམ་ལ་ལམ་ལྔའི་རྣམ་བཞག་བྱེད་ཅིང་། ཤེས་བཟོད་སྐད་ཅིག་མ་བཅུ་དྲུག་པོ་མཐོང་ལམ་དུ་འདོད་ལ། མངོན་སུམ་གྱི་སྣང་ཡུལ་ལ་རང་མཚན་ཞིག་དགོས་པས། གང་ཟག་གི་བདག་མེད་ཕྲ་མོ་ཉན་ཐོས་མཐོང་ལམ་བར་ཆད་མེད་ལམ་གྱི་འཛིན་སྟངས་ཀྱི་ཡུལ་དུ་མི་འདོད་དེ། དེས་གང་ཟག་གི་བདག་གིས་དབེན་པའི་འདུ་བྱེད་དངོས་སུ་གཞལ་བའི་ཤུགས་ལ་གང་ཟག་གི་བདག་མེད་ཕྲ་མོ་རྟོགས་པར་འདོད་པའི་ཕྱིར།

གསུམ་པ་འབྲས་བུའི་འདོད་ཚུལ་ནི། དགྲ་བཅོམ་པ་སྤངས་རྟོགས་ལས་ཉམས་པ་མི་སྲིད་པ་དང་། སངས་རྒྱས་ཀྱི་གཟུགས་ཕུང་སངས་རྒྱས་སུ་ཁས་ལེན་པ་མ་གཏོགས། ཐེག་པ་གསུམ་གྱི་འབྲས་བུ་མངོན་དུ་བྱེད་ཚུལ་སོགས་བྱེ་སྨྲ་དང་མཚུངས་སོ། བྱེ་མདོ་གཉིས་ཀྱིས་ཐེག་ཆེན་གྱི་སྡེ་སྣོད་བཀར་ཁས་མི་ལེན་ཀྱང་ཕྱི་རབས་པ་རྣམས་ལ་བཀར་ཁས་ལེན་པ་ཡོད་པར་བཤད་དོ། སྨྲས་པ།

རིགས་པའི་གཞུང་ལ་ལེགས་པར་སྦྱངས་པའི་མཐུས།
རིགས་པའི་རྗེས་འབྲང་དཔེ་སྟོན་སྡེ་པ་ཡི།
རིགས་པའི་གསང་ཚིག་ཇི་བཞིན་བརྗོད་པ་འདི།
རིགས་པ་སྨྲ་བ་རྣམས་ཀྱིས་དགའ་སྟོན་མཛོད།

ཅེས་བྱ་བ་ནི་བར་སྐབས་ཀྱི་ཚིགས་སུ་བཅད་པའོ།།

གསུམ་པ་སེམས་ཙམ་པའི་གྲུབ་མཐའི་རྣམ་བཞག་བཤད་པ་ལ། མཚན་ཉིད། དབྱེ་བ། སྒྲ་བཤད། འདོད་ཚུལ་དང་བཞི། དང་པོ་ནི། ཕྱི་དོན་ཁས་མི་ལེན་ཞིང་གཞན་དབང་བདེན་གྲུབ་ཏུ་འདོད་པའི་ནང་པའི་གྲུབ་

མཐའ་སྨྲ་བའི་གང་ཟག་དེ་སེམས་ཙམ་པའི་མཚན་ཉིད་དོ། གཉིས་པ་ནི། དེ་ལ་དབྱེ་ན། སེམས་ཙམ་རྣམ་བདེན་པ་དང་། རྣམ་བརྫུན་པ་གཉིས། འདི་གཉིས་ཀྱི་ཁྱད་པར་ཡོད་དེ། སྔོན་འཛིན་མིག་ཤེས་ལ་སྔོན་པོ་སྔོན་པོར་སྣང་བ་དེ་རྣམ་བདེན་བརྫུན་གྱིས་རྩོད་གཞིའི་རྣམ་པ་ཡིན་ལ། རྣམ་བདེན་པས་སྔོན་འཛིན་མིག་ཤེས་ལ་སྔོན་པོ་སྔོན་པོར་སྣང་བ་ལྟར་གྲུབ་པར་ཁས་ལེན། རྣམ་བརྫུན་པས་སྔོན་འཛིན་མིག་ཤེས་ལ་སྔོན་པོ་སྔོན་པོར་སྣང་བ་ལྟར་མ་གྲུབ་པར་ཁས་ལེན་པའི་ཕྱིར། དེར་ཐལ། རྣམ་བདེན་བརྫུན་གཉིས་ཀས་སྔོན་འཛིན་མིག་ཤེས་ལ་སྔོན་པོ་སྔོན་པོར་སྣང་བ་དང་། སྔོན་པོ་རགས་པར་སྣང་བ་དང་། སྔོན་པོ་ཕྱི་རོལ་དོན་དུ་སྣང་བར་འདོད་པར་འདྲ་ཡང་། རྣམ་བདེན་པས་སྔོན་འཛིན་མིག་ཤེས་ལ་སྔོན་པོ་ཕྱི་རོལ་དོན་དུ་སྣང་བ་ལ་མ་རིག་པས་བསླད་པ་ཞུགས་ལ། སྔོན་པོ་སྔོན་པོར་སྣང་བ་དང་། སྔོན་པོ་རགས་པར་སྣང་བ་ལ་མ་རིག་པས་བསླད་པ་མ་ཞུགས་པར་འདོད། རྣམ་བརྫུན་པས་སྔོན་པོ་ཕྱི་རོལ་དོན་དུ་སྣང་བ་ཙམ་དུ་མ་ཟད། སྔོན་པོ་སྔོན་པོར་སྣང་བ་དང་། སྔོན་པོ་རགས་པར་སྣང་བ་ལ་ཡང་མ་རིག་པས་བསླད་པ་ཞུགས་པར་འདོད་པའི་ཕྱིར། དེས་ན་སེམས་ཙམ་པ་གང་ཞིག དབང་ཤེས་ལ་རགས་པར་སྣང་བ་སྣང་བ་ལྟར་དུ་གྲུབ་པར་འདོད་པ་དེ་སེམས་ཙམ་རྣམ་བདེན་པའི་མཚན་ཉིད། སེམས་ཙམ་པ་གང་ཞིག དབང་ཤེས་ལ་རགས་པར་སྣང་བ་སྣང་བ་ལྟར་དུ་མ་གྲུབ་པར་འདོད་པ་དེ་སེམས་ཙམ་རྣམ་བརྫུན་པའི་མཚན་ཉིད།

རྣམ་བདེན་པ་ལ་དབྱེ་ན། གཟུང་འཛིན་གྲངས་མཉམ་པ། སྒོ་ང་ཕྱེད་ཚལ་པ། སྣ་ཚོགས་གཉིས་མེད་པ་དང་གསུམ་ཡོད། འདི་གསུམ་གྱི་ཁྱད་པར་ལ་མཁས་པ་རྣམས་བཞེད་པ་མི་མཐུན་ཏེ། གུང་རུ་རྒྱལ་མཚན་བཟང་པོའི་དབུ་མའི་སྟོང་ཐུན་ལས། ཁྲ་མ་ལེབ་ཀྱི་གཞོག་སྟེང་གི་ཁྲ་བོ་འཛིན་པའི་མིག་ཤེས་ཀྱིས་ཁྲ་བོ་འཛིན་པའི་ཚེ། ཡུལ་གྱི་ངོས་ནས་སྔོ་སེར་སོགས་མི་འདྲ་བ་རེ་རེའི་རྣམ་པ་གཏད་ཅིང་། ཡུལ་ཅན་གྱི་ངོས་ནས་ཀྱང་སྔོ་སེར་སོགས་མི་འདྲ་བ་རེ་རེའི་རྣམ་པ་རྣམ་བདེན་དུ་སྐྱེ་བར་འདོད་པས་ན་གཟུང་འཛིན་གྲངས་མཉམ་པ་དང་། དེ་ལྟར་འཛིན་པའི་ཚེ་ཡུལ་གྱི་ངོས་ནས་སྔོ་སེར་སོགས་མི་འདྲ་བ་རེ་རེའི་རྣམ་པ་གཏད་ཅིང་། ཡུལ་ཅན་གྱི་ངོས་ནས་སྔོ་སེར་སོགས་མི་འདྲ་བ་རེ་རེའི་རྣམ་པ་རྣམ་མེད་དུ་སྐྱེ་བར་འདོད་པས་ན་སྒོ་ང་ཕྱེད་ཚལ་པ་དང་། དེ་ལྟར་འཛིན་པའི་ཚེ་ཡུལ་གྱི་ངོས་ནས་སྔོ་སེར་སོགས་མི་འདྲ་བ་རེ་རེའི་རྣམ་པ་མ་གཏད་ཅིང་ཁྲ་ཙམ་གྱི་རྣམ་པ་གཏད། ཡུལ་ཅན་གྱི་ངོས་ནས་སྔོ་སེར་སོགས་མི་འདྲ་བ་རེ་རེའི་རྣམ་པ་རྣམ་མེད་དུ་མ་སྐྱེས་པར་ཁྲ་ཙམ་གྱི་རྣམ་པ་རྣམ་མེད་དུ་སྐྱེས་པར་འདོད་པས་ན་སྣ་ཚོགས་གཉིས་མེད་པ་ཞེས་བཤད།

དྭང་ཆེན་ལེགས་པ་བཟང་པོ་དང་། པཎ་ཆེན་བསོད་ནམས་གྲགས་པ་སོགས་ཀྱིས་[37] ཁྲ་འཛིན་དབང་ཤེས་ལ་སྣང་བའི་སྔོ་སེར་གཉིས་རྫས་ཐ་དད་ཡིན་པ་གཞིན་དུ་ཁྲ་འཛིན་མིག་ཤེས་ཀྱི་སྟེང་ན་མིག་ཤེས་རྫས་ཐ་དད་པ་དུ་མ་

ཡོད་པར་ཁས་ལེན་པས་ན་གཟུང་འཛིན་གྲངས་མཉམ་པ་དང་། སྔོན་པོ་དང་སྔོན་འཛིན་མིག་ཤེས་གཉིས་སྤྱིར་ཤེས་པའི་བདག་ཉིད་ཡིན་ཀྱང་དེ་གཉིས་རྫས་ཐ་དད་དུ་ཁས་ལེན་པས་ན་སྒོང་ཕྱེད་ཚལ་པ་དང་། ཁྲ་བོའི་སྟེང་གི་སྔོ་སེར་གཉིས་རྫས་གཅིག་ཡིན་པ་བཞིན་དུ་ཁྲ་འཛིན་མིག་ཤེས་ཀྱི་སྟེང་གི་སྔོ་སེར་འཛིན་པའི་དབང་ཤེས་གཉིས་རྫས་གཅིག་ཏུ་འདོད་པས་ན་སྣ་ཚོགས་གཉིས་མེད་པ་ཞེས་བཤད།

གྲུབ་མཐའ་ཆེན་མོ་ལས། ཁྲ་འཛིན་མིག་ཤེས་ཀྱིས་ཁྲ་བོ་ལ་བལྟས་པའི་ཚེ། ཁྲ་བོའི་སྟེང་གི་སྔོ་སེར་སོགས་ཀྱི་གྲངས་དང་མཉམ་པའི་རྣམ་ཤེས་རིགས་མཐུན་ཅིག་ཆར་དུ་སྐྱེ་བར་འདོད་པས་ན་གཟུང་འཛིན་གྲངས་མཉམ་པ་དང་། སྔོན་པོ་དང་སྔོན་འཛིན་མིག་ཤེས་གཉིས་གྲུབ་དུས་ལ་ལྟོས་ནས་[38] སྔ་ཕྱི་པ་ཡིན་ཀྱང་། དམིགས་དུས་ལ་ལྟོས་ནས་རྫས་གཅིག་ཏུ་ཁས་ལེན་པས་ན་སྒོང་ཕྱེད་ཚལ་པ་དང་། ཁྲ་འཛིན་མིག་ཤེས་ཀྱིས་རང་ཡུལ་ལ་བལྟས་པའི་ཚེ། ཡུལ་གྱི་སྟེང་གི་སྔོ་སེར་སོགས་ཀྱི་གྲངས་དང་མཉམ་པའི་རྣམ་ཤེས་རིགས་མཐུན་ཅིག་ཆར་དུ་མི་སྐྱེ་བར་ཁྲ་འཛིན་མིག་ཤེས་གཅིག་པུ་དེ་ཁྲ་བོའི་སྟེང་གི་སྔོ་སེར་སོགས་འཛིན་པའི་དབང་ཤེས་ཡིན་པར་ཁས་ལེན་པས་ན་སྣ་ཚོགས་གཉིས་མེད་པ་ཞེས་བཤད་པས་ལུགས་དེ་གསུམ་གྱི་ནང་ནས་གང་བདེ་བ་གཟུང་བར་བྱའོ། གཟུང་འཛིན་གྲངས་མཉམ་པ་ལ་རྣམ་ཤེས་ཚོགས་བརྒྱད་འདོད་པ་དང་། རྣམ་ཤེས་ཚོགས་དྲུག་འདོད་པ་གཉིས། སྣ་ཚོགས་གཉིས་མེད་པ་ལ་རྣམ་ཤེས་ཚོགས་དྲུག་སྨྲ་བ་དང་། རྣམ་ཤེས་གཅིག་པུར་སྨྲ་བ་གཉིས་ཡོད་པར་བཤད་དོ།

རྣམ་བརྫུན་པ་ལ་དབྱེ་ན། དྲི་བཅས་དང་། དྲི་མེད་རྣམ་བརྫུན་པ་གཉིས་ཡོད། སེམས་ཀྱི་ངོ་བོ་མ་རིག་པའི་བག་ཆགས་ཀྱི་དྲི་མས་བསླད་པར་འདོད་པས་ན་དྲི་བཅས་པ་དང་། སེམས་ཀྱི་ངོ་བོ་མ་རིག་པའི་བག་ཆགས་ཀྱི་དྲི་མས་ཙུང་ཟད་ཀྱང་མ་བསླད་པར་འདོད་པས་ན་དྲི་མེད་པ་ཞེས་ཟེར། ཡང་ན་སངས་རྒྱས་ཀྱི་ས་ན་མ་རིག་པ་མེད་ཀྱང་འཁྲུལ་པའི་སྣང་བ་ཡོད་པར་འདོད་པས་ན་དྲི་བཅས་པ་དང་། སངས་རྒྱས་ཀྱི་ས་ན་མ་རིག་པ་མེད་པས། འཁྲུལ་སྣང་ཡང་མེད་པར་འདོད་པས་དྲི་མེད་པ་ཞེས་ཟེར།

ཡང་སེམས་ཙམ་པ་ལ་དབྱེ་ན། ལུང་གི་རྗེས་འབྲང་དང་། རིགས་པའི་རྗེས་འབྲང་གཉིས། དང་པོ་ནི། ས་སྡེ་ལྔའི་རྗེས་འབྲང་དང་། གཉིས་པ་ནི། ཚད་མ་སྡེ་བདུན་གྱི་རྗེས་འབྲང་རྣམས་སོ།

གསུམ་པ་སྒྲ་བཤད་ནི། ཅིའི་ཕྱིར་སེམས་ཙམ་པ་ཞེས་བྱ་ཞེ་ན། ཆོས་ཐམས་ཅད་སེམས་ཀྱི་བདག་ཉིད་ཙམ་དུ་སྨྲ་བས་ན་སེམས་ཙམ་པའམ་རྣམ་རིག་པ་དང་། རྣལ་འབྱོར་པའི་གཞིའི་སྒོ་ནས་ལམ་གྱི་སྤྱོད་པ་ཉམས་ལེན་གཙན་ལ་འབེབས་པས་རྣལ་འབྱོར་སྤྱོད་པ་བ་ཞེས་ཀྱང་བྱའོ།

བཞི་པ་འདོད་ཚུལ་ལ། གཞི་ལམ་འབྲས་བུ་གསུམ་ལས། དང་པོ་ལ་ཡུལ་དང་ཡུལ་ཅན་གཉིས། དང་པོ་ནི། ཤེས་བྱ་ཐམས་ཅད་མཚན་ཉིད་གསུམ་དུ་འདུས་པར་འདོད་དེ། འདུས་བྱས་ཐམས་ཅད་གཞན་དབང་། ཆོས་ཉིད་ཐམས་ཅད་ཡོངས་གྲུབ། དེ་ལས་གཞན་པ་རྣམས་ཀུན་བཏགས་སུ་འདོད་པའི་ཕྱིར། དེ་གསུམ་པོ་རང་ངོས་ནས་གྲུབ་པ་དང་། རང་བཞིན་གྱིས་གྲུབ་པར་འདོད་ཀྱང་། བདེན་པར་གྲུབ་མ་གྲུབ་ཀྱི་ཁྱད་པར་ཡོད་དེ། ཀུན་བཏགས་བདེན་མེད་དང་། གཞན་དབང་ཡོངས་གྲུབ་གཉིས་བདེན་གྲུབ་ཏུ་འདོད་པའི་ཕྱིར།

དོན་དམ་པར་མ་གྲུབ་ཀྱང་རྟོག་པའི་ངོ་བོར་གྲུབ་པ་ནི། ཀུན་བཏགས་ཀྱི་མཚན་ཉིད། དེ་ལ་དབྱེ་ན། རྣམ་གྲངས་པའི་ཀུན་བཏགས་དང་། མཚན་ཉིད་ཡོངས་སུ་ཆད་པའི་ཀུན་བཏགས་གཉིས། དང་པོ་ནི། ཤེས་བྱ་ལྟ་བུའོ། གཉིས་པ་ནི། བདག་གཉིས་ལྟ་བུའོ།

རྒྱུ་རྐྱེན་གཞན་གྱི་དབང་ལ་བརྟེན་ནས་བྱུང་ཞིང་ཡོངས་གྲུབ་ཀྱི་རྟེན་དུ་གྱུར་པ་སྟེ། གཞན་དབང་གི་མཚན་ཉིད། དེ་ལ་དབྱེ་ན། དག་པའི་གཞན་དབང་དང་། མ་དག་པའི་གཞན་དབང་གཉིས། དང་པོ་ནི། འཕགས་པའི་རྗེས་ཐོབ་ཡེ་ཤེས་དང་། སངས་རྒྱས་ཀྱི་མཚན་དཔེ་ལྟ་བུའོ། གཉིས་པ་ནི། ཟག་བཅས་ཉེར་ལེན་གྱི་ཕུང་པོ་ལྟ་བུའོ།

བདག་གཉིས་གང་རུང་གིས་སྟོང་པའི་དེ་བཞིན་ཉིད་དེ། ཡོངས་གྲུབ་ཀྱི་མཚན་ཉིད། དེ་ལ་དབྱེ་ན། ཕྱིན་ཅི་མ་ལོག་པའི་ཡོངས་གྲུབ་དང་། འགྱུར་མེད་ཡོངས་གྲུབ་གཉིས། དང་པོ་ནི། འཕགས་པའི་མཉམ་བཞག་ཡེ་ཤེས་ལྟ་བུའོ། གཉིས་པ་ནི། ཆོས་ཉིད་ལྟ་བུའོ། ཕྱིན་ཅི་མ་ལོག་པའི་ཡོངས་གྲུབ་ཡོངས་གྲུབ་ཀྱི་དབྱེ་བར་བཀོད་ཀྱང་། ཡོངས་གྲུབ་མ་ཡིན་ཏེ། གང་ལ་དམིགས་ན་སྒྲིབ་པ་ཟད་པར་འགྱུར་བའི་རྣམ་དག་ལམ་གྱི་དམིགས་པ་མཐར་ཐུག་མ་ཡིན་པའི་ཕྱིར། ཡང་ཤེས་བྱ་ལ་དབྱེ་ན། ཀུན་རྫོབ་བདེན་པ་དང་། དོན་དམ་བདེན་པ་གཉིས། ཐ་སྙད་དཔྱོད་བྱེད་ཀྱི་རིགས་ཤེས་ཀྱི་ཚད་མས་རྙེད་པའི་དོན་དེ་ཀུན་རྫོབ་བདེན་པའི་མཚན་ཉིད། བརྫུན་པ་དང་། ཀུན་རྫོབ་བདེན་པ། ཐ་སྙད་བདེན་པ་རྣམས་དོན་གཅིག དོན་དམ་དཔྱོད་བྱེད་ཀྱི་རིགས་ཤེས་ཀྱི་ཚད་མས་རྙེད་པའི་དོན་དེ་དོན་དམ་བདེན་པའི་མཚན་ཉིད། སྟོང་ཉིད། ཆོས་དབྱིངས། ཡོངས་གྲུབ། དོན་དམ་བདེན་པ། ཡང་དག་མཐའ། དེ་བཞིན་ཉིད་རྣམས་དོན་གཅིག་ཏུ་འདོད་དོ། དོན་དམ་བདེན་པ་ཡིན་ན་རང་གི་མཚན་ཉིད་ཀྱིས་གྲུབ་པས་ཁྱབ་ཀྱང་། ཀུན་རྫོབ་བདེན་པ་ཡིན་ན་རང་གི་མཚན་ཉིད་ཀྱིས་གྲུབ་པས་མ་ཁྱབ་སྟེ། གཞན་དབང་རང་གི་མཚན་ཉིད་ཀྱིས་གྲུབ་ཀྱང་། ཀུན་བཏགས་ཀྱི་ཆོས་རྣམས་རང་གི་མཚན་ཉིད་ཀྱིས་མ་གྲུབ་པའི་ཕྱིར། བརྫུན་པ་ཡིན་ན་བརྫུན་པར་གྲུབ་མི་དགོས་དེ། གཞན་དབང་དེ་བརྫུན་པ་ཡིན་ཀྱང་བརྫུན་པར་མ་གྲུབ་པའི་ཕྱིར།

དུས་གསུམ་དང་། མེད་དགག་གི་འཇོག་ཚུལ་མདོ་སེམས་རང་རྒྱུད་པ་གསུམ་མཐུན་ནོ། གཟུགས་སོགས་དོན་ལྡོག་པོ་དེ་ཕྱི་རོལ་དོན་དུ་མ་གྲུབ་སྟེ། ཀུན་གཞིའི་རྣམ་ཤེས་ཀྱི་སྟེང་དུ་ཐུན་མོང་དང་ཐུན་མོང་མ་ཡིན་པའི་ལས་ཀྱིས་བག་ཆགས་བཞག་པའི་མཐུས་ནང་ཤེས་པའི་རྫས་ཀྱི་སྟེང་ནས་སྐྱེས་པ་ཡིན་པའི་ཕྱིར། རྣམ་བདེན་པ་ལྟར་ན། གཟུགས་སོགས་དོན་ལྡོག་པོ་དེ་ཕྱི་རོལ་གྱི་དོན་མ་ཡིན་ཀྱང་རགས་པར་གྲུབ་པར་ཁས་ལེན། རྣམ་བརྫུན་པས་དེ་ལྟར་ན་ཕྱི་རོལ་དོན་དུ་གྲུབ་དགོས་པས་རགས་པར་མ་གྲུབ་པར་ཁས་ལེན་ནོ།

གཉིས་པ་ཡུལ་ཅན་གྱི་འདོད་ཚུལ་ནི། ལུང་གི་རྗེས་འབྲང་རྣམས་ཀྱིས་རྣམ་ཤེས་ཚོགས་བརྒྱད་འདོད་པས་ཡིད་ཀྱི་རྣམ་པར་ཤེས་པ་དང་། ཀུན་གཞིའི་རྣམ་ཤེས་གང་ཟག་ཏུ་ཁས་ལེན་ཞིང་། རིགས་པའི་རྗེས་འབྲང་གིས་ཡིད་ཀྱི་རྣམ་པར་ཤེས་པ་གང་ཟག་གི་མཚན་གཞིར་འདོད་དོ། དེ་ལ་ཀུན་གཞིའི་རྣམ་ཤེས་ནི་ནང་གི་བག་ཆགས་ལ་དམིགས་ཤིང་རྣམ་པ་རིས་སུ་མ་ཆད་པ། ངོ་བོ་མ་བསྒྲིབས་ལུང་མ་བསྟན། གྲོགས་སེམས་བྱུང་ཀུན་འགྲོ་ལྔ་ཁོ་ན་དང་མཚུངས་པར་ལྡན་པའི་གཙོ་བོ་ཡིད་ཀྱི་རྣམ་པར་རིག་པ་བརྟན་པས་རབ་ཏུ་ཕྱེ་བ་ཞིག་ལ་འདོད་དོ། དེ་ཡང་བསྒྲིབས་མ་བསྒྲིབས་གཉིས་ལས་བསྒྲིབས་ལུང་མ་བསྟན་མ་ཡིན། དགེ་རྩ་ཆད་པའི་རྒྱུད་ལ་ཡང་ཡོད་པས་དགེ་བ་མ་ཡིན། ཁམས་གོང་ན་ཡོད་པས་མི་དགེ་བའང་མ་ཡིན་ནོ།

ཉོན་ཡིད་ནི། དམིགས་པ་ཀུན་གཞི་ལ་དམིགས་ནས་རྣམ་པ་ངར་སེམས་པའི་རྣམ་པ་ཅན།[39] ངོ་བོ་བསྒྲིབས་ལུང་མ་བསྟན་ཞིག་ལ་འདོད་དེ། འཇུག་ཤེས་དྲུག་གི་འཇོག་ཚུལ་སྤྱི་དང་མཐུན་ནོ། ཚད་མ་ལ་མངོན་རྗེས་གཉིས་དང་། མངོན་སུམ་བཞིའི་རྣམ་བཞག་ཁས་ལེན་ཞིང་། རང་རིག་མངོན་སུམ་དང་། རྣལ་འབྱོར་མངོན་སུམ་གཉིས་ལ་མ་འཁྲུལ་པའི་ཤེས་པས་ཁྱབ། རྣམ་བདེན་པས་ཚུར་མཐོང་གི་རྒྱུད་ཀྱི་སྔོན་འཛིན་མིག་ཤེས་དེ་མ་འཁྲུལ་བའི་ཤེས་པར་འདོད་ལ། རྣམ་བརྫུན་པ་ལྟར་ན་ཚུར་མཐོང་གི་རྒྱུད་ཀྱི་དབང་པོའི་མངོན་སུམ་ལ་འཁྲུལ་ཤེས་ཀྱིས་ཁྱབ། དེའི་རྒྱུད་ཀྱི་ཡིད་ཀྱི་མངོན་སུམ་ལ་འཁྲུལ་མ་འཁྲུལ་གྱི་ཆ་གཉིས་ཡོད་པར་འདོད་དོ།

གཉིས་པ་ལམ་གྱི་རྣམ་བཞག་ལ་གསུམ་ལས། དང་པོ་ལམ་གྱི་དམིགས་པ་ནི། བདེན་བཞིའི་ཁྱད་ཆོས་མི་རྟག་སོགས་བཅུ་དྲུག་དང་། གང་ཟག་རྟག་གཅིག་རང་དབང་ཅན་གྱིས་གྲུབ་པས་སྟོང་པ་གང་ཟག་གི་བདག་མེད་རགས་པ་དང་། གང་ཟག་རང་རྐྱ་ཐུབ་པའི་རྫས་ཡོད་ཀྱིས་སྟོང་པ་གང་ཟག་གི་བདག་མེད་ཕྲ་མོ་ཡིན་ལ། གཟུགས་དང་གཟུགས་འཛིན་ཚད་མ་རྫས་གཞན་གྱིས་སྟོང་པ་དང་། གཟུགས་གཟུགས་འཛིན་རྟོག་པའི་ཞེན་གཞིར་རང་གི་མཚན་ཉིད་ཀྱིས་གྲུབ་པས་སྟོང་པ་གཉིས་ཆོས་ཀྱི་བདག་མེད་ཕྲ་མོར་འདོད་དོ། བདག་མེད་ཕྲ་མོ་གཉིས་ཀ་སྟོང་

ཉིད་དུ་འདོད་ཅིང་། སྟོང་ཉིད་ལ་དེ་གང་རུང་མི་དགོས་ཏེ། འགོག་བདེན་དང་ཤུང་འདས་གཉིས་ཀྱང་སྟོང་ཉིད་དུ་འདོད་པའི་ཕྱིར། འདུས་བྱས་ཀྱི་ཆོས་རྣམས་རང་འཛིན་ཚད་མ་དང་རྗེས་གཅིག་ཏུ་འདོད་ལ། འདུས་མ་བྱས་ཀྱི་ཆོས་རྣམས་རང་འཛིན་ཚད་མ་དང་ངོ་བོ་གཅིག་ཏུ་འདོད་དོ།

གཉིས་པ་ལམ་གྱི་སྤང་བྱ་ལ་ཉོན་སྒྲིབ་དང་། ཤེས་སྒྲིབ་གཉིས། དང་པོ་ནི། གང་ཟག་གི་བདག་འཛིན་ཕྲ་རགས་གཉིས་ས་བོན་དང་བཅས་པ་དང་། རྩ་ཉོན་དྲུག ཉེ་ཉོན་ཉི་ཤུ་ལྷ་བུའོ། གཉིས་པ་ནི། ཆོས་ཀྱི་བདག་འཛིན་བག་ཆགས་དང་བཅས་པ་ལྷ་བུའོ། དེ་ཡང་བྱང་སེམས་རྣམས་ཀྱིས་ཤེས་སྒྲིབ་སྤང་བྱའི་གཙོ་བོར་བྱེད་ཀྱང་། ཉོན་སྒྲིབ་སྤང་བྱའི་གཙོ་བོར་མི་བྱེད། ཐེག་དམན་སློབ་པ་རྣམས་ཀྱིས་ཉོན་སྒྲིབ་སྤང་བྱའི་གཙོ་བོར་བྱེད་ཀྱང་། ཤེས་སྒྲིབ་སྤང་བྱའི་གཙོ་བོར་མི་བྱེད་དོ།

གསུམ་པ་ལམ་གྱི་རྣམ་བཞག་ནི། ཐེག་པ་གསུམ་པོ་རེ་རེ་ལའང་ཚོགས་སྦྱོར་གཉིས། མཐོང་སྒོམ་གཉིས། མི་སློབ་ལམ་དང་ལྔའི་རྣམ་བཞག་བྱེད་ལ། ཐེག་ཆེན་ལ་དེའི་སྟེང་དུ་ས་བཅུའི་རྣམ་བཞག་ཀྱང་ཁས་ལེན་ནོ།

གསུམ་པ་འབྲས་བུ་མངོན་དུ་བྱེད་ཚུལ་ནི། ཐེག་དམན་རིགས་ངེས་རྣམས་ཀྱིས་གང་ཟག་གི་བདག་མེད་ཀྱི་དབང་དུ་བྱས་པའི་ཡོངས་གྲུབ་བསྒོམ་བྱའི་གཙོ་བོར་བྱས་ཏེ། གོམས་པ་མཐར་ཕྱིན་པ་ན་ཐེག་དམན་གྱི་སྒོམ་ལམ་རྡོ་རྗེ་ལྟ་བུའི་ཏིང་ངེ་འཛིན་ལ་བརྟེན་ནས་ཉོན་སྒྲིབ་མ་ལུས་པར་སྤངས་པ་དང་དུས་མཉམ་དུ་ཐེག་དམན་དགྲ་བཅོམ་པའི་འབྲས་བུ་མངོན་དུ་བྱེད་དོ། ཉན་རང་གཉིས་ཀྱིས་བསྒོམ་བྱའི་བདག་མེད་དང་། སྤང་བྱའི་ཉོན་མོངས་ལ་ཁྱད་པར་ཅུང་ཟད་ཀྱང་མེད་པས་ཉན་རང་གཉིས་ཀ་ལ་ཞུགས་གནས་བརྒྱད་ཀྱི་རྣམ་བཞག་འཐད་ཀྱང་། རང་རྒྱལ་ནི་འདོད་པའི་རྟེན་ཅན་དུ་ངེས་པས་དགེ་འདུན་ཉི་ཤུའི་རྣམ་བཞག་བྱར་མེད་དོ། འོན་ཀྱང་ཉན་རང་གཉིས་ལ་ཁྱད་པར་མེད་པ་མ་ཡིན་ཏེ། བསྐལ་པ་བརྒྱར་བསོད་ནམས་ཀྱི་ཚོགས་ཀྱི་གོམས་པ་བསྒྲིངས་མི་བསྒྲིངས་དང་། དེའི་དབང་གིས་འབྲས་བུ་ལའང་མཆོག་དམན་ཡོད་པར་འདོད་དོ།

ལུང་གི་རྗེས་འབྲང་རྣམས་ཀྱིས་ཐེག་དམན་དགྲ་བཅོམ་པ་ཞི་བ་བགྲོད་པ་གཅིག་པུ་བ་ཐེག་ཆེན་ལམ་དུ་འཇུག་པར་མི་འདོད་ཅིང་། བྱང་ཆུབ་ཡོངས་འགྱུར་པའི་དགྲ་བཅོམ་པ་ཐེག་ཆེན་ལམ་དུ་འཇུག་པར་འདོད་དོ། དེ་ཡང་ལྷག་བཅས་ནས་ཡིན་གྱི། ལྷག་མེད་ནས་འཇུག་པ་མ་ཡིན་ཏེ། མཐར་ཐུག་ཐེག་པ་གསུམ་དུ་གྲུབ་པར་འདོད་པའི་ཕྱིར། རིགས་པའི་རྗེས་འབྲང་རྣམས་ཀྱིས་ཐེག་དམན་དགྲ་བཅོམ་པ་ཐེག་ཆེན་ལམ་དུ་འཇུག་པར་འདོད་དེ། མཐར་ཐུག་ཐེག་པ་གཅིག་ཏུ་གྲུབ་པར་ཁས་ལེན་པའི་ཕྱིར།

ཐེག་ཆེན་རིགས་ཅན་རྣམས་ཀྱིས་ཆོས་ཀྱི་བདག་མེད་ཀྱི་དབང་དུ་བྱས་པའི་ཡོངས་གྲུབ་བསྒོམ་བྱའི་གཙོ་བོར་བྱས་ཏེ། གྲངས་མེད་གསུམ་གྱི་ཚོགས་དང་འབྲེལ་བར་ཉམས་སུ་བླངས་ནས་ས་བཅུ་ལམ་ལྔ་རིམ་གྱིས་བགྲོད་དེ་རྒྱུན་མཐའི་བར་ཆད་མེད་ལམ་གྱིས་སྒྲིབ་གཉིས་ཟད་པར་སྤངས་ཏེ། འོག་མིན་དུ་རང་དོན་སྤངས་རྟོགས་ཕུན་ཚོགས་ཆོས་ཀྱི་སྐུ་དང་། གཞན་དོན་འཕྲིན་ལས་ཕུན་ཚོགས་གཟུགས་ཀྱི་སྐུ་གཉིས་མངོན་དུ་བྱེད་དོ། ཀུན་བཏུས་ཀྱི་རྗེས་འབྲང་འགའ་ཞིག་ལྟར་ན། མིའི་རྟེན་ལ་འཚང་རྒྱ་བའང་ཡོད་པར་མངོན་ནོ། སངས་རྒྱས་བཀའ་ལ་དྲང་ངེས་ཀྱི་ཁྱད་པར་ཡང་ཁས་ལེན་ཏེ། དགོངས་འགྲེལ་ལས་བཤད་པའི་འཁོར་ལོ་དང་པོ་གཉིས་དྲང་དོན་གྱི་མདོ་དང་། འཁོར་ལོ་ཐ་མ་ངེས་དོན་གྱི་མདོར་བཞེད་པའི་ཕྱིར། དྲང་ངེས་ཀྱི་དོན་ཡང་ཡོད་དེ། དངོས་བསྟན་སྒྲ་ཇི་བཞིན་དུ་ཁས་ལེན་དུ་མི་རུང་བའི་མདོ་དེ་དྲང་དོན་གྱི་མདོ་དང་། དངོས་བསྟན་སྒྲ་ཇི་བཞིན་དུ་ཁས་ལེན་དུ་རུང་བའི་མདོ་དེ་ངེས་དོན་གྱི་མདོར་འཇོག་པའི་ཕྱིར།

མྱང་འདས་ལ་ལྷག་བཅས་ལྷག་མེད་མི་གནས་པའི་མྱང་འདས་གསུམ་དང་། སངས་རྒྱས་ཀྱི་སྐུ་ལ་ཆོས་ལོངས་སྤྲུལ་གསུམ་དང་། ཆོས་སྐུ་ལ་ངོ་བོ་ཉིད་སྐུ་དང་། ཡེ་ཤེས་ཆོས་སྐུ་གཉིས་དང་། ངོ་བོ་ཉིད་སྐུ་ལ་རང་བཞིན་རྣམ་དག་དང་། གློ་བུར་དྲི་བྲལ་གྱི་ངོ་བོ་ཉིད་སྐུ་གཉིས་དང་བཅས་ཁས་ལེན་པས་ཐེག་པ་ཆེན་པོའི་གྲུབ་མཐའ་སྨྲ་བ་ཞེས་བྱའོ། སྨྲས་པ།

རྣམ་འདྲེན་ཐུབ་པའི་གསུང་གི་རྗེས་འབྲངས་ཏེ།
རྣམ་རིག་ཙམ་དུ་སྨྲ་བའི་གྲུབ་པའི་མཐའ།
རྣམ་མང་མཁས་པའི་གསུང་བཞིན་བཀོད་པ་འདིར།
རྣམ་དཔྱོད་ལྡན་རྣམས་དགའ་བས་འཇུག་པར་རིགས།

ཞེས་བྱ་བ་ནི་བར་སྐབས་ཀྱི་ཚིགས་སུ་བཅད་པའོ།།

བཞི་པ་ངོ་བོ་ཉིད་མེད་པར་སྨྲ་བ་དབུ་མ་པའི་གྲུབ་མཐའི་རྣམ་བཞག་བཤད་པ་ལ། མཚན་ཉིད། སྒྲ་བཤད། དབྱེ་བ། ཕྱེ་བ་སོ་སོའི་དོན་བཤད་པ་དང་བཞི། དང་པོ་ནི། བདེན་གྲུབ་ཀྱི་ཆོས་རྡུལ་ཙམ་ཡང་མེད་པར་ཁས་ལེན་པའི་ནང་པའི་གྲུབ་མཐའ་སྨྲ་བའི་གང་ཟག་དེ་དབུ་མ་པའི་མཚན་ཉིད།

གཉིས་པ་སྒྲ་བཤད་ནི། ཅིའི་ཕྱིར་དབུ་མ་པ་ཞེས་བྱ་ཞེ་ན། རྟག་ཆད་ཀྱི་མཐའ་གཉིས་དང་བྲལ་བའི་དབུས་ཁས་ལེན་པས་ན་དབུ་མ་པ་དང་། ཆོས་རྣམས་ལ་བདེན་གྲུབ་ཀྱི་ངོ་བོ་ཉིད་མེད་པར་སྨྲ་བས་ན་ངོ་བོ་ཉིད་མེད་པར་སྨྲ་བ་ཞེས་བརྗོད་པའི་ཕྱིར།

གསུམ་པ་ནི། དེ་ལ་དབྱེ་ན། དབུ་མ་རང་རྒྱུད་པ་དང་། ཐལ་འགྱུར་པ་གཉིས་ཡོད། བཞི་པ་ཕྱེ་བ་སོ་སོའི་དོན་ལ། རང་རྒྱུད་པ་དང་། ཐལ་འགྱུར་བའི་ལུགས་བཤད་པ་གཉིས། དང་པོ་ལ། མཚན་ཉིད། སྒྲ་བཤད། དབྱེ་བ། གྲུབ་མཐའི་འདོད་ཚུལ་དང་བཞི། དང་པོ་ནི། རང་གི་མཚན་ཉིད་ཀྱིས་གྲུབ་པ་ཐ་སྙད་དུ་ཁས་ལེན་པའི་ངོ་བོ་ཉིད་མེད་པར་སྨྲ་བ་དེ། རང་རྒྱུད་པའི་མཚན་ཉིད། གཉིས་པ་ནི། ཅིའི་ཕྱིར་དབུ་མ་རང་རྒྱུད་པ་ཞེས་བྱ་ཞེ་ན། ཚུལ་གསུམ་[40] རང་ངོས་ནས་གྲུབ་པའི་རྟགས་ཡང་དག་ལ་བརྟེན་ནས་བདེན་དངོས་འགོག་པར་བྱེད་པས་ན་དེ་ལྟར་བརྗོད་པའི་ཕྱིར། གསུམ་པ་ནི། དེ་ལ་དབྱེ་ན། རྣལ་འབྱོར་སྤྱོད་པའི་དབུ་མ་རང་རྒྱུད་པ་དང་། མདོ་སྡེ་སྤྱོད་པའི་དབུ་མ་རང་རྒྱུད་པ་གཉིས། ཕྱི་དོན་ཁས་མི་ལེན་ཞིང་། རང་རིག་ཁས་ལེན་པའི་དབུ་མ་པ་དེ་དང་པོའི་མཚན་ཉིད། མཚན་གཞི་ནི། སློབ་དཔོན་ཞི་བ་འཚོ་ལྟ་བུ། རང་རིག་ཁས་མི་ལེན་ཞིང་། ཕྱི་དོན་རང་གི་མཚན་ཉིད་ཀྱིས་གྲུབ་པ་ཁས་ལེན་པའི་དབུ་མ་པ་དེ་གཉིས་པའི་མཚན་ཉིད། མཚན་གཞི་ནི། སློབ་དཔོན་ལེགས་ལྡན་འབྱེད་ལྟ་བུ། སྒྲ་བཤད་ཀྱང་ཡོད་དེ། གཞིའི་རྣམ་བཞག་སེམས་ཙམ་པ་དང་མཐུན་པར་ཁས་ལེན་པས་ན་རྣལ་འབྱོར་སྤྱོད་པའི་དབུ་མ་པ་དང་། མདོ་སྡེ་པ་ལྟར་རྡུལ་ཕྲ་རབ་བསགས་པའི་ཕྱི་རོལ་གྱི་དོན་ཁས་ལེན་པས་ན་མདོ་སྡེ་སྤྱོད་པའི་དབུ་མ་པ་ཞེས་བརྗོད་དོ།

རྣལ་འབྱོར་སྤྱོད་པའི་དབུ་མ་རང་རྒྱུད་པ་ལ་ཡང་རྣམ་བདེན་པ་དང་མཐུན་པའི་དབུ་མ་པ་དང་། རྣམ་བརྫུན་པ་དང་མཐུན་པའི་དབུ་མ་པ་གཉིས་ཡོད། དང་པོ་ནི། ཞི་བ་འཚོ་དང་། ཀ་མ་ལ་ཤཱི་ལ་དང་། འཕགས་པ་གྲོལ་སྡེ་ལྟ་བུའོ། གཉིས་པ་ནི། སློབ་དཔོན་སེང་གེ་བཟང་པོ་དང་། ཛེ་ཏཱ་རི་དང་། ལྭ་བ་པ་ལྟ་བུ་སྟེ། ཛེ་ཏཱ་རི་ནི་རྣམ་བརྫུན་དྲི་བཅས་པ་དང་མཐུན་ལ། ལྭ་བ་པ་ནི་རྣམ་བརྫུན་དྲི་མེད་དང་མཐུན་པར་བཤད་དོ།།

བཞི་པ་གྲུབ་མཐའི་འདོད་ཚུལ་ལ། རྣལ་འབྱོར་སྤྱོད་པའི་དབུ་མ་རང་རྒྱུད་པའི་ལུགས་དང་། མདོ་སྡེ་སྤྱོད་པའི་དབུ་མ་རང་རྒྱུད་པའི་ལུགས་བཤད་པ་གཉིས།

དང་པོ་ལ། གཞི་ལམ་འབྲས་གསུམ་ལས། དང་པོ་གཞིའི་རྣམ་བཞག་ལ་ཡུལ་དང་ཡུལ་ཅན་གཉིས་ལས། དང་པོ་ནི། གཞི་གྲུབ་ན་རང་གི་མཚན་ཉིད་ཀྱིས་གྲུབ་པས་ཁྱབ་པར་བཞེད་དེ། ཆོས་གང་ཡིན་ཀྱང་

བཏགས་དོན་བཙལ་ན་རྙེད་བར་འདོད་པའི་ཕྱིར། དེས་ན་རང་བཞིན་གྱིས་གྲུབ་པ། རང་གི་མཚན་ཉིད་ཀྱིས་གྲུབ་པ། རང་གི་སྡོད་ལུགས་ཀྱི་ངོས་ནས་གྲུབ་པ། རང་ངོས་ནས་གྲུབ་པ་རྣམས་དོན་གཅིག་ཏུ་འདོད།

ཞེས་བྱ་ལ་དབྱེ་ན། དོན་དམ་བདེན་པ་དང་། ཀུན་རྫོབ་བདེན་པ་གཉིས་ལས། རང་མངོན་སུམ་དུ་རྟོགས་པའི་མངོན་སུམ་གྱི་ཚད་མས་རང་ཉིད་གཉིས་སྣང་ནུབ་པའི་ཚུལ་གྱིས་རྟོགས་པར་བྱ་བ་དེ་དང་པོའི་མཚན་ཉིད། རང་མངོན་སུམ་དུ་རྟོགས་པའི་མངོན་སུམ་གྱི་ཚད་མས་གཉིས་སྣང་དང་བཅས་པའི་ཚུལ་གྱིས་རྟོགས་པར་བྱ་བ་དེ་གཉིས་པའི་མཚན་ཉིད། བུམ་པ་བདེན་སྟོང་ལྟ་བུ་དང་པོའི་མཚན་གཞི་དང་། བུམ་པ་ལྟ་བུ་གཉིས་པའི་མཚན་གཞི་ཡིན་ནོ། དོན་དམ་བདེན་པ་ལ་རྒྱས་པར་དབྱེ་ན། སྟོང་ཉིད་བཅུ་དྲུག་དང་། བསྡུ་ན་སྟོང་ཉིད་བཞིར་ཡོད། ཀུན་རྫོབ་བདེན་པ་ལ་དབྱེ་ན། ཡང་དག་ཀུན་རྫོབ་དང་། ལོག་པའི་ཀུན་རྫོབ་གཉིས་ལས། དང་པོ་ནི། ཆུ་ལྟ་བ་དང་། གཉིས་པ་ནི། སྨིག་རྒྱུའི་ཆུ་ལྟ་བུའོ། ལུགས་འདིས་ཤེས་པ་ཡིན་ན་ཡང་དག་ཀུན་རྫོབ་ཡིན་པས་ཁྱབ་པར་འདོད་དོ།

གཉིས་པ་ཡུལ་ཅན་ལ། ཡིད་ཀྱི་རྣམ་པར་ཤེས་པ་གང་ཟག་གི་མཚན་གཞི་དང་། ཀུན་གཞི་དང་ཉོན་ཡིད་ཁས་མི་ལེན་ཞིང་རྣམ་ཤེས་ཚོགས་དྲུག་ཏུ་འདོད་པ་རང་རྒྱུད་པ་གཉིས་ཀ་མཐུན་ནོ།[41] བློ་ལ་ཚད་མ་དང་། ཚད་མིན་གྱི་བློ་གཉིས། ཚད་མ་ལ་མངོན་སུམ་གྱི་ཚད་མ་དང་། རྗེས་སུ་དཔག་པའི་ཚད་མ་གཉིས། མངོན་སུམ་ལ་དབང་པོའི་མངོན་སུམ། ཡིད་ཀྱི་མངོན་སུམ། རང་རིག་མངོན་སུམ། རྣལ་འབྱོར་མངོན་སུམ་དང་བཞིར་ཡོད་ལ། མངོན་སུམ་ཕྱི་མ་གཉིས་ལ་མ་འཁྲུལ་བའི་ཤེས་པས་ཁྱབ་པར་ཁས་ལེན་ནོ། ཕྱི་རོལ་དོན་དུ་གྲུབ་པ་ཁས་མི་ལེན་པས་སྔོན་པོ་དང་སྔོན་འཛིན་མངོན་སུམ་གཉིས་རྫས་གཅིག་ཏུ་འདོད་དོ།

གཉིས་པ་ལམ་གྱི་རྣམ་བཞག་ལ་གསུམ་ལས། དང་པོ་ལམ་གྱི་དམིགས་པ་ནི། གང་ཟག་རྟག་གཅིག་རང་དབང་ཅན་གྱིས་སྟོང་པ་གང་ཟག་གི་བདག་མེད་རགས་པ་དང་། གང་ཟག་རང་རྐྱ་ཐུབ་པའི་རྫས་ཡོད་ཀྱིས་སྟོང་པ་གང་ཟག་གི་བདག་མེད་ཕྲ་མོ་དང་། གཟུགས་དང་གཟུགས་འཛིན་ཚད་མ་རྫས་གཞན་གྱིས་སྟོང་པ་ཆོས་ཀྱི་བདག་མེད་རགས་པ་དང་། ཆོས་ཐམས་ཅད་བདེན་གྲུབ་ཀྱིས་སྟོང་པ་ཆོས་ཀྱི་བདག་མེད་ཕྲ་མོར་བཞེད་དོ། གཉིས་པ་ལམ་གྱི་སྤང་བྱ་ནི། གང་ཟག་གི་བདག་འཛིན་ཉོན་སྒྲིབ་དང་། ཆོས་ཀྱི་བདག་འཛིན་ཤེས་སྒྲིབ་ཏུ་འདོད་ཅིང་། ཤེས་སྒྲིབ་ཡང་གཟུང་འཛིན་རྫས་གཞན་དུ་འཛིན་པ་ལྟ་བུ་ཤེས་སྒྲིབ་རགས་པ་དང་། ཕུང་སོགས་ཀྱི་ཆོས་བདེན་གྲུབ་ཏུ་འཛིན་པ་ལྟ་བུ་ཤེས་སྒྲིབ་ཕྲ་མོ་གཉིས་སུ་འདོད་དོ། གསུམ་པ་ལམ་གྱི་རང་བཞིན་ནི། ལམ་ལྔ་གསུམ་བཅོ་ལྔ་ཁས་ལེན་པར་འདྲ་ལ། ཁྱད་པར་ནི། རང་རྒྱལ་གྱི་བར་ཆད་མེད་ལམ་དང་། རྣམ་གྲོལ་ལམ་ལ་གཉིས་སྣང་གི་རྣམ་པ་ཅན་དགོས་པར་ཁས་ལེན་ནོ།

གསུམ་པ་འབྲས་བུའི་རྣམ་བཞག་ལ། རང་རྒྱལ་ནི་ཤེས་སྒྲིབ་རགས་པ་སྤང་བྱའི་གཙོ་བོར་བྱེད་པའི་ཕྱིར་ཞུགས་གནས་བརྒྱད་ཀྱི་རྣམ་བཞག་མི་བརྗེ་ཡང་། ཉན་ཐོས་ལ་གང་ཟག་ཡ་བརྒྱད[42] ཡོད་པར་བཞེད་ལ། ཉན་ཐོས་རིགས་ངེས་རྣམས་ཀྱིས་གང་ཟག་གི་བདག་མེད་རྟོགས་པའི་ལྟ་བ་བསྒོམ་བྱའི་གཙོ་བོར་བྱས་ཏེ། མཐར་སྒོམ་ལམ་རྡོ་རྗེ་ལྟ་བུའི་ཏིང་ངེ་འཛིན་ལ་བརྟེན་ནས་ཉོན་སྒྲིབ་མ་ལུས་པར་སྤངས་པ་དང་དུས་མཉམ་དུ་དགྲ་བཅོམ་པའི་འབྲས་བུ་མངོན་དུ་བྱེད་དོ། རང་རྒྱལ་རིགས་ངེས་རྣམས་ཀྱིས་གཟུང་འཛིན་གཉིས་སྟོང་གི་ལྟ་བ་བསྒོམ་བྱའི་གཙོ་བོར་བྱས་ཏེ། མཐར་སྒོམ་ལམ་རྡོ་རྗེ་ལྟ་བུའི་ཏིང་ངེ་འཛིན་ལ་བརྟེན་ནས་ཉོན་སྒྲིབ་དང་། ཤེས་སྒྲིབ་རགས་པ་མ་ལུས་པར་སྤངས་པ་དང་དུས་མཉམ་དུ་རང་རྒྱལ་དགྲ་བཅོམ་པའི་འབྲས་བུ་མངོན་དུ་བྱེད་དོ།

ཐེག་དམན་གྱི་མྱང་འདས་ལ་ལྷག་བཅས་མྱང་འདས་དང་། ལྷག་མེད་མྱང་འདས་གཉིས་ལས། དང་པོ་ནི། སྔ་མའི་ལས་ཉོན་གྱིས་འཕངས་པའི་སྡུག་བསྔལ་གྱི་ཕུང་པོའི་ལྷག་མ་དང་བཅས་པའི་མྱང་འདས་དང་། གཉིས་པ་ནི། སྡུག་བསྔལ་གྱི་ཕུང་པོ་དང་བྲལ་བའི་གནས་སྐབས་ལ་འདོད་དོ། ཉན་རང་དགྲ་བཅོམ་པ་ཡིན་ན་ཐེག་ཆེན་ལམ་དུ་འཇུག་པས་ཁྱབ་སྟེ། མཐར་ཐུག་ཐེག་པ་གཅིག་ཏུ་གྲུབ་པར་འདོད་པའི་ཕྱིར། དེས་ན་ལུགས་འདི་ལ་ཉན་རང་གཉིས་སྤང་བྱ་དང་། རྟོགས་རིགས་མི་འདྲ་བའི་དབང་གིས་ཐོབ་བྱའི་འབྲས་བུ་ལའང་མཆོག་དམན་ཡོད་དོ།

ཐེག་ཆེན་རིགས་ངེས་རྣམས་ཀྱིས་བྱང་ཆུབ་མཆོག་ཏུ་སེམས་བསྐྱེད་དེ། ཚོགས་ལམ་ཆེན་པོའི་གནས་སྐབས་སུ་ཆོས་རྒྱུན་གྱི་ཏིང་ངེ་འཛིན་ལ་བརྟེན་ནས་མཆོག་གི་སྤྲུལ་སྐུ་ལས་གདམས་ངག་དངོས་སུ་ཉན་ཅིང་། དེའི་དོན་ཉམས་སུ་བླངས་པ་ལ་བརྟེན་ནས་སྟོང་པ་ཉིད་ལ་དམིགས་པའི་སྒོམ་བྱུང་གི་ཤེས་རབ་ཐོག་མར་སྐྱེས་པའི་ཚེ་སྦྱོར་ལམ་དུ་འཕོས་པ་ཡིན་ཞིང་། དྲོད་ཀྱི་གནས་སྐབས་སུ་མཐོང་སྤང་ཀུན་ནས་ཉོན་མོངས་གཟུང་རྟོག་མངོན་གྱུར་པ་ཉམས་སྨྲོད་པར་བྱེད་ཅིང་། རྩེ་མོ་ཐོབ་པའི་ཚེ་མཐོང་སྤང་རྣམ་བྱང་གཟུང་རྟོག་མངོན་གྱུར་པ་དང་། བཟོད་པ་ཐོབ་པའི་ཚེ་མཐོང་སྤང་རྫས་འཛིན་རྟོག་པ་མངོན་གྱུར་པ་དང་། ཆོས་མཆོག་ཐོབ་པའི་ཚེ་མཐོང་སྤང་བཏགས་འཛིན་རྟོག་པ་མངོན་གྱུར་པ་རྣམས་སྨྲོད་པར་བྱེད་དོ། དྲོད་རྩེ་བཟོད་མཆོག་བཞི་ལ་རིམ་པ་བཞིན་དུ་སྣང་བ་ཐོབ་པའི་ཏིང་ངེ་འཛིན་དང་། སྣང་བ་མཆེད་པའི་ཏིང་ངེ་འཛིན་དང་། དེ་ཁོ་ན་ཉིད་ཀྱི་ཕྱོགས་གཅིག་ལ་ཞུགས་པའི་ཏིང་ངེ་འཛིན་དང་། བར་ཆད་མེད་པའི་ཏིང་ངེ་འཛིན་ཞེས་ཟེར་རོ།

དེའི་མཇུག་ཐོགས་སུ་མཐོང་ལམ་བར་ཆད་མེད་ལམ་གྱིས་ཉོན་སྒྲིབ་ཀུན་བཏགས་དང་། ཤེས་སྒྲིབ་ཀུན་བཏགས་ས་བོན་དང་བཅས་པ་སྤངས་ནས་རྣམ་གྲོལ་ལམ་དང་འགོག་པའི་བདེན་པ་གཉིས་མངོན་དུ་བྱེད་དོ། སྒོམ་

ལམ་སྐོར་དགུས་སྒོམ་སྤང་ཉོན་མོངས་བཅུ་དྲུག་གི་ས་བོན་དང་། སྒོམ་སྤང་ཤེས་སྒྲིབ་བརྒྱ་དང་བརྒྱད་ཀྱི་ས་བོན་རིམ་ཅན་དུ་སྤོང་བར་གསུངས་སོ། མཐར་རྒྱུན་མཐའི་བར་ཆད་མེད་ལམ་ལ་བརྟེན་ནས་ཉོན་མོངས་པ་དང་། ཤེས་བྱའི་སྒྲིབ་པ་ལྷན་སྐྱེས་གཉིས་ཅིག་ཅར་དུ་སྤངས་ནས་སྐད་ཅིག་གཉིས་པ་ལ་བླ་ན་མེད་པའི་བྱང་ཆུབ་ཐོབ་པར་འགྱུར་དེ་རིགས་ངེས་ཀྱིས་འབྲས་བུ་མངོན་དུ་བྱེད་ཚུལ་ལོ། ཐེག་ཆེན་གྱི་མྱང་འདས་དང་། མི་གནས་པའི་མྱང་འདས་དོན་གཅིག་ཏུ་འདོད་ཅིང་། སངས་རྒྱས་ཀྱི་སྐུ་ལ་བཞིར་གྲངས་ངེས་པར་འདོད་ལ། འཕགས་སེང་གཉིས་ཀྱང་སྐུའི་བསྟན་ཚུལ་ལ་རྩོད་ཀྱི། གྲངས་ངེས་ལ་མི་རྩོད་དོ། སངས་རྒྱས་ཀྱི་བཀའ་ལ་དྲང་དོན་གྱི་མདོ་དང་། ངེས་དོན་གྱི་མདོའི་རྣམ་བཞག་བྱེད་དེ། ཀུན་རྫོབ་བདེན་པ་དངོས་བསྟན་བསྟན་བྱའི་གཙོ་བོར་བྱས་ནས་སྟོན་པའི་མདོ་དྲང་དོན་གྱི་མདོ་དང་། དོན་དམ་བདེན་པ་དངོས་བསྟན་བསྟན་བྱའི་གཙོ་བོར་བྱས་ནས་སྟོན་པའི་མདོ་ངེས་དོན་གྱི་མདོ་ཡིན་པའི་ཕྱིར། དགོངས་འགྲེལ་ལས་བཤད་པའི་འཁོར་ལོ་དང་པོ་དྲང་དོན་དང་། བར་བ་དང་ཐ་མ་གཉིས་ལ་དྲང་ངེས་གཉིས་གཉིས་ཡོད་པར་འདོད་དོ།

གཉིས་པ་མདོ་སྡེ་སྤྱོད་པའི་དབུ་མ་རང་རྒྱུད་པའི་ལུགས་ལ། གཞི་ལམ་འབྲས་གསུམ་ལས། དང་པོ་ནི། ལུགས་འདིས་ཕྱི་དོན་འདོད་ཅིང་རང་རིག་ཁས་མི་ལེན་པ་ཙམ་མ་གཏོགས་གཞིའི་རྣམ་བཞག་ཕལ་ཆེར་སྔ་མ་དང་འདྲའོ། གཉིས་པ་ལམ་གྱི་ཁྱད་པར་ལ། ཉན་རང་རིགས་ངེས་ལ་ཆོས་ཀྱི་བདག་མེད་རྟོགས་པ་མེད་པར་བཞེད་ཅིང་། གཟུང་འཛིན་རྫས་གཞན་གྱིས་སྟོང་པར་རྟོགས་པའི་ཡེ་ཤེས་ཁས་མི་ལེན་ལ། ཕྱི་རོལ་དོན་འཛིན་གྱི་རྟོག་པ་ཡང་ཤེས་སྒྲིབ་ཏུ་མི་འདོད་དོ། གསུམ་པ་འབྲས་བུའི་རྣམ་བཞག་ལ། ཉན་རང་གཉིས་སྤང་བྱའི་སྒྲིབ་པ་དང་། རྟོགས་བྱའི་བདག་མེད་ལ་ཕྲ་རགས་མེད་པས་རྟོགས་རིགས་མི་འདྲ་བ་མེད་ཅིང་། ཞུགས་གནས་བརྒྱད་ཀྱི་རྣམ་བཞག་གཉིས་ཀ་ལ་བྱེད་དོ། ཐེག་ཆེན་རིགས་ངེས་རྣམས་ཀྱིས་སྒྲིབ་གཉིས་རིམ་ཅན་དུ་སྤོང་བར་བཞེད་དེ། ས་བརྒྱད་པ་ཐོབ་པའི་ཚེ་ཉོན་མོངས་པའི་སྒྲིབ་པ་ཟད་པར་སྤངས་པ་རྟོག་གེ་འབར་བ་ལས་བཤད་པའི་ཕྱིར། འོན་ཀྱང་ཐལ་འགྱུར་པ་ལྟར་ཉོན་སྒྲིབ་མ་ཟད་བར་དུ་ཤེས་སྒྲིབ་སྤོང་བའི་མགོ་མི་རྩོམ་པར་བཞེད་པའང་མིན་ནོ། མི་འདྲ་བའི་ཁྱད་པར་དེ་ཙམ་ཞིག་མ་གཏོགས་གཞི་ལམ་འབྲས་གསུམ་གྱི་རྣམ་བཞག་ཕལ་ཆེ་བ་[43]རྣལ་འབྱོར་སྤྱོད་པའི་དབུ་མ་རང་རྒྱུད་པ་དང་མཐུན་ནོ།

སྨྲས་པ།

རང་མཚན་ཡོད་ཀྱང་བདེན་པར་མེད་བཞེད་པའི།
རང་རྒྱུད་སྨྲ་བའི་གྲུབ་མཐའི་རྣམ་དབྱེ་ཀུན།
རང་བཟོ་སྤངས་ཏེ་ལེགས་པར་བརྗོད་པ་འདི།
རང་ཉིད་མཁས་འདོད་རྣམས་ཀྱིས་ཟུངས་ཤིག་ཀྱེ།

ཞེས་བྱ་བ་ནི་བར་སྐབས་ཀྱི་ཚིགས་སུ་བཅད་པའོ། །

གཉིས་པ་ཐལ་འགྱུར་པའི་ལུགས་བཤད་པ་ལ། མཚན་ཉིད། སྒྲ་བཤད། འདོད་ཚུལ་དང་གསུམ། དང་པོ་ནི། རང་གི་མཚན་ཉིད་ཀྱིས་གྲུབ་པ་ཐ་སྙད་ཙམ་དུ་ཡང་མི་བཞེད་པའི་ངོ་བོ་ཉིད་མེད་པར་སྨྲ་བ་དེ་ཐལ་འགྱུར་བའི་མཚན་ཉིད། མཚན་གཞི་ནི། སངས་རྒྱས་བསྐྱངས། ཟླ་གྲགས། ཞི་བ་ལྷ་ལྟ་བུའོ། གཉིས་པ་ནི། ཅིའི་ཕྱིར་ཐལ་འགྱུར་བ་ཞེས་བྱ་ཞེ་ན། ཐལ་འགྱུར་ཙམ་གྱིས་ཕྱི་རྒོལ་གྱི་རྒྱུད་ལ་བསྒྲུབ་བྱ་རྟོགས་པའི་རྗེས་དཔག་སྐྱེ་བར་འདོད་པས་ན་དེ་ལྟར་བརྗོད་པའི་ཕྱིར། གསུམ་པ་གྲུབ་མཐའི་འདོད་ཚུལ་ལ། གཞི་ལམ་འབྲས་གསུམ་ལས། དང་པོ་ནི། གཞི་གྲུབ་ན་རང་གི་མཚན་ཉིད་ཀྱིས་མ་གྲུབ་པས་ཁྱབ་པར་ཁས་ལེན་དེ། གཞི་གྲུབ་ཚད་ལ་[44]རྟོག་པས་བཏགས་ཙམ་གྱིས་ཁྱབ་པ་ཁས་ལེན་པ་གང་ཞིག དེའི་ཚིག་ཟུར་གྱི་ཙམ་སྒྲས་[45]རང་གི་མཚན་ཉིད་ཀྱིས་གྲུབ་པ་གཅོད་པར་བཞེད་པའི་ཕྱིར། གཞི་གྲུབ་དང་། ཡུལ་དང་། ཤེས་བྱ་རྣམས་དོན་གཅིག དེ་ལ་དབྱེ་ན། མངོན་ལྐོག་གཉིས་སུ་དབྱེ་བ་དང་། བདེན་པ་གཉིས་སུ་དབྱེ་བའོ།

དང་པོ་ནི། རྟགས་ལ་མ་བརྟེན་པར་མྱོང་སྟོབས་ཀྱིས་རྟོགས་ནུས་པའི་ཆོས་དེ་མངོན་གྱུར་གྱི་མཚན་ཉིད། མངོན་སུམ་དང་། མངོན་གྱུར་དང་། དབང་པོའི་ཡུལ་དང་། ལྐོག་ཏུ་མ་གྱུར་པའི་ཆོས་བཞི་དོན་གཅིག་མིང་གི་རྣམ་གྲངས་སོ། མཚན་གཞི་ནི། གཟུགས་སྒྲ་དྲི་རོ་རེག་བྱ་ལྟ་བུའོ། རྒྱུ་མཚན་ནམ་རྟགས་ལ་བརྟེན་ནས་རྟོགས་དགོས་པའི་ཆོས་དེ་ལྐོག་གྱུར་གྱི་མཚན་ཉིད། ལྐོག་གྱུར་དང་། མངོན་སུམ་མ་ཡིན་པའི་ཆོས་དང་། རྗེས་དཔག་གི་གཞལ་བྱ་རྣམས་དོན་གཅིག་མིང་གི་རྣམ་གྲངས་སོ། མཚན་གཞི་ནི། སྒྲ་མི་རྟག་པ་དང་། སྒྲ་ཆོས་གི་བདག་མེད་ལྟ་བུ་ལ་བྱེད། དེས་ན་ལུགས་འདི་ལ་མངོན་ལྐོག་གཉིས་དང་། གཞལ་བྱའི་གནས་གསུམ་འགལ་བར་བཞེད་དོ།

གཉིས་པ་ནི། ཐ་སྙད་དཔྱོད་བྱེད་ཀྱི་ཚད་མས་རྙེད་དོན་གང་ཞིག ཐ་སྙད་དཔྱོད་བྱེད་ཀྱི་ཚད་མ་རང་ཉིད་ལ་ཐ་སྙད་དཔྱོད་བྱེད་ཀྱི་ཚད་མར་སོང་བ་དེ་རང་ཉིད་ཀུན་རྫོབ་བདེན་པ་ཡིན་པའི་མཚན་ཉིད། མཚན་གཞི་ནི།

བུམ་པ་ལྟ་བུའོ། དེ་ལ་དབྱེ་ན། ཡང་དག་ཀུན་རྫོབ་དང་། ལོག་པའི་ཀུན་རྫོབ་གཉིས་མི་འབྱེད་དེ། ཡང་དག་ཀུན་རྫོབ་མེད་པའི་ཕྱིར། ཀུན་རྫོབ་ཡིན་ན་ཡང་དག་མ་ཡིན་དགོས་པའི་ཕྱིར། དེ་ཡིན་ན་ལོག་པ་ཡིན་དགོས་པའི་ཕྱིར། འོན་ཀྱང་ཀུན་རྫོབ་ལ་འཇིག་རྟེན་རང་དགའ་བའི་ཤེས་ངོ་ལ་ལྟོས་ཏེ་ཡང་ལོག་གཉིས་སུ་འབྱེད་དེ། གཟུགས་དེ་འཇིག་རྟེན་ཤེས་ངོ་ལ་ལྟོས་ཏེ་ཡང་དག་དང་། མེ་ལོང་ནང་གི་བྱད་བཞིན་གྱི་གཟུགས་བརྙན་དེ་འཇིག་རྟེན་ཤེས་ངོ་ལ་ལྟོས་ཏེ་ལོག་པ་ཡིན་པའི་ཕྱིར། འཇིག་རྟེན་ཤེས་ངོ་ལ་ལྟོས་ཏེ་ཡང་དག་ཡིན་ན་ཡོད་པས་མ་ཁྱབ་སྟེ། གཟུགས་བདེན་གྲུབ་དེ་དེ་ཡིན་པའི་ཕྱིར།

མཐར་ཐུག་དཔྱོད་བྱེད་ཀྱི་ཚད་མས་རྙེད་དོན་གང་ཞིག མཐར་ཐུག་དཔྱོད་བྱེད་ཀྱི་ཚད་མ་རང་ཉིད་ལ་མཐར་ཐུག་དཔྱོད་བྱེད་ཀྱི་ཚད་མར་སྣང་བ་དེ་རང་ཉིད་དོན་དམ་བདེན་པ་ཡིན་པའི་མཚན་ཉིད། མཚན་གཞི་ནི། བུམ་པ་རང་བཞིན་གྱིས་མེད་པ་ལྟ་བུའོ། དབྱེ་བ་སྔར་དང་འདྲ། གཞན་ཡང་འདས་མ་འོངས་ཞིག་པ་རྣམས་དངོས་པོར་འདོད་ཅིང་། ཕྱི་རོལ་གྱི་དོན་ཡང་ཁས་ལེན་ཏེ། གཟུང་འཛིན་ངོ་བོ་ཐ་དད་དུ་གྲུབ་པར་བཞེད་པའི་ཕྱིར།

ཡུལ་ཅན་གྱི་འདོད་ཚུལ་ནི། རང་གི་གདགས་གཞི་ཕུང་པོ་ལྔའམ་བཞི་ལ་བརྟེན་ནས་བཏགས་པའི་ང་ཙམ་དེ་གང་ཟག་གི་མཚན་གཞིར་འདོད་ཅིང་། གང་ཟག་ལ་ལྡན་མིན་འདུ་བྱེད་ཀྱིས་ཁྱབ། བློ་ལ་ཚད་མ་དང་། ཚད་མིན་གྱི་བློ་གཉིས་ཡོད། ཚད་མ་ལ་མངོན་སུམ་གྱི་ཚད་མ་དང་། རྗེས་སུ་དཔག་པའི་ཚད་མ་གཉིས། མངོན་སུམ་གྱི་ཚད་མ་ལ་དབང་པོའི་མངོན་སུམ་གྱི་ཚད་མ། ཡིད་ཀྱི་མངོན་སུམ་གྱི་ཚད་མ། རྣལ་འབྱོར་མངོན་སུམ་གྱི་ཚད་མ་དང་གསུམ་ཡོད། རང་རིག་མངོན་སུམ་མི་འདོད་ཅིང་། སེམས་ཅན་གྱི་རྒྱུད་ཀྱི་དབང་ཤེས་ལ་འཁྲུལ་ཤེས་ཀྱིས་ཁྱབ།

རྣལ་འབྱོར་མངོན་སུམ་ལ་འཁྲུལ་མ་འཁྲུལ་གཉིས་ཡོད་དེ། མཉམ་བཞག་ཟག་མེད་ཀྱི་ངོ་བོར་གྱུར་པའི་རྣལ་འབྱོར་མངོན་སུམ་དེ་མ་འཁྲུལ་བ་དང་། ཚུར་མཐོང་གི་རྒྱུད་ཀྱི་ཕྲ་བའི་མི་རྟག་པ་མངོན་སུམ་དུ་རྟོགས་པའི་རྣལ་འབྱོར་མངོན་སུམ་དེ་འཁྲུལ་ཤེས་ཡིན་པའི་ཕྱིར། ཕྱི་མ་དེར་ཐལ། སོ་སྐྱེའི་རྒྱུད་ཀྱི་ཤེས་པ་ཡིན་པའི་ཕྱིར། བཅད་ཤེས་ཡིན་ན་མངོན་སུམ་གྱི་ཚད་མ་ཡིན་པས་ཁྱབ་སྟེ། སྒྲ་མི་རྟག་པར་རྟོགས་པའི་རྗེས་དཔག་སྐད་ཅིག་གཉིས་པ་དེ་རྟོག་པར་གྱུར་པའི་མངོན་སུམ་ཚད་མ་དང་། གཟུགས་འཛིན་དབང་པོའི་མངོན་སུམ་སྐད་ཅིག་གཉིས་པ་དེ་རྟོག་མེད་དུ་གྱུར་པའི་མངོན་སུམ་ཚད་མ་ཡིན་པའི་ཕྱིར།

རྗེས་དཔག་ལ་དབྱེ་ན། དངོས་སྟོབས་རྗེས་དཔག གྲགས་པའི་རྗེས་དཔག དཔེ་ཉེར་འཇལ་གྱི་རྗེས་དཔག ཡིད་ཆེས་རྗེས་དཔག་དང་བཞི་ཡོད། ཡུལ་དེ་ལ་འཁྲུལ་ཡང་[46]ཡུལ་དེ་རྟོགས་པ་མི་འགལ་ཏེ། སྒྲ་མི་རྟག་

རྟོགས་ཀྱི་རྗེས་དཔག་དེ་སྒྲ་མི་རྟག་པ་ལ་འཁྲུལ་ཡང་དེ་རྟོགས་པར་ཁས་ལེན་པའི་ཕྱིར། གཉིས་སྣང་ཅན་གྱི་ཤེས་པ་ཡིན་ན་རང་གི་སྣང་བ་ལ་མངོན་སུམ་གྱི་ཚད་མ་ཡིན་པས་ཁྱབ་སྟེ། སྒྲ་རྟག་འཛིན་རྟོག་པ་དེ་རང་གི་སྣང་བ་ལ་མངོན་སུམ་གྱི་ཚད་མ་ཡིན་པའི་ཕྱིར། ཤེས་པ་ཡིན་ན་རང་གི་གཞལ་བྱ་རྟོགས་པས་ཁྱབ་སྟེ། རི་བོང་རྭའི་དོན་སྤྱི། རི་བོང་རྭ་འཛིན་རྟོག་པའི་གཞལ་བྱ་དང་། སྒྲ་རྟག་པའི་དོན་སྤྱི་སྒྲ་རྟག་འཛིན་རྟོག་པའི་གཞལ་བྱ་ཡིན་པའི་ཕྱིར།

གཉིས་པ་ལམ་གྱི་རྣམ་བཞག་ལ་གསུམ་ལས། དང་པོ་ལམ་གྱི་དམིགས་པ་ནི། གང་ཟག་རང་རྐྱ་ཐུབ་པའི་རྫས་ཡོད་ཀྱིས་སྟོང་པ་གང་ཟག་གི་བདག་མེད་རགས་པ་དང་། གང་ཟག་བདེན་པས་སྟོང་པ་གང་ཟག་གི་བདག་མེད་ཕྲ་མོར་འདོད་དོ།

བདག་མེད་ཕྲ་མོ་གཉིས་སྟོང་གཞིའི་སྒོ་ནས་འབྱེད་པ་ཡིན་གྱི། དགག་བྱའི་སྒོ་ནས་མི་འབྱེད་དེ། གཞི་གང་ཟག་གི་སྟེང་དུ་དགག་བྱ་བདེན་གྲུབ་བཀག་པ་གང་ཟག་གི་བདག་མེད་ཕྲ་མོ་དང་། གཞི་ཕུང་སོགས་ཀྱི་སྟེང་དུ་དགག་བྱ་བདེན་གྲུབ་བཀག་པ་ཆོས་ཀྱི་བདག་མེད་ཕྲ་མོ་ཡིན་པའི་ཕྱིར། གང་ཟག་གི་བདག་མེད་ཕྲ་མོ་དང་། ཆོས་ཀྱི་བདག་མེད་ཕྲ་མོ་གཉིས་ལ་ཕྲ་རགས་མེད་ཅིང་གནས་ལུགས་མཐར་ཐུག་ཏུ་འདོད་དོ།

གཉིས་པ་ལམ་གྱི་སྤང་བྱ་ནི། བདག་འཛིན་ཕྲ་རགས་ས་བོན་དང་བཅས་པ་དང་། དེའི་དབང་གིས་བྱུང་བའི་དུག་གསུམ་ས་བོན་དང་བཅས་པ་ཉོན་སྒྲིབ་ཏུ་འདོད་དེ། བདེན་འཛིན་ཉོན་སྒྲིབ་ཏུ་འདོད་པའི་ཕྱིར། བདེན་འཛིན་གྱི་བག་ཆགས་དང་། དེའི་དབང་གིས་བྱུང་བའི་གཉིས་སྣང་འཁྲུལ་བའི་ཆ་དང་། བདེན་གཉིས་ངོ་བོ་ཐ་དད་དུ་འཛིན་པའི་དྲི་མ་རྣམས་ཤེས་སྒྲིབ་ཏུ་འདོད་དོ།

གསུམ་པ་ལམ་གྱི་རང་བཞིན་ནི། ཐེག་པ་གསུམ་པོ་རེ་རེ་ལའང་ལམ་ལྔ་ལྔའི་རྣམ་བཞག་དང་། ཐེག་ཆེན་ལ་ས་བཅུའི་རྣམ་བཞག་ཀྱང་མདོ་སྡེ་པ་བཅུ་པ་ལ་བརྟེན་ནས་བྱེད་དོ། ཐེག་པ་གསུམ་ལ་ཤེས་རབ་ཀྱི་རྟོགས་རིགས་མི་འདྲ་བ་མེད་དེ། འཕགས་པ་ལ་ཆོས་ཀྱི་བདག་མེད་མངོན་སུམ་དུ་རྟོགས་པས་ཁྱབ་པ་ཁས་ལེན་པའི་ཕྱིར།

གསུམ་པ་འབྲས་བུ་མངོན་དུ་བྱེད་ཚུལ་ནི། ཐེག་དམན་རིགས་ངེས་རྣམས་ཀྱིས་བདག་མེད་པའི་ལྟ་བ་རིགས་པ་མདོར་བསྡུས་ཙམ་གྱིས་བསྒོམས་པ་ལ་བརྟེན་ནས། མཐར་ཐེག་དམན་གྱི་སྒོམ་ལམ་རྡོ་རྗེ་ལྟ་བུའི་ཏིང་ངེ་འཛིན་གྱིས་བདེན་འཛིན་ས་བོན་དང་བཅས་པ་སྤངས་པ་དང་དུས་མཉམ་དུ་རང་གི་བྱང་ཆུབ་མངོན་དུ་བྱེད་དོ། དབུ་མ་རང་རྒྱུད་པ་མན་ཆད་ཀྱིས་ལྷག་མེད་མྱང་འདས་ཐོབ་པ་ལ་དེའི་སྔོན་དུ་ལྷག་བཅས་མྱང་འདས་འཐོབ་དགོས་པར་འདོད་ཀྱང་། ལུགས་འདི་ལ་ལྷག་བཅས་ཀྱི་སྔོན་དུ་ལྷག་མེད་མྱང་འདས་འཐོབ་དགོས་པར་འདོད་དོ། ཉན་རང་གཉིས་ལ་ཞུགས་

གནས་ཀྱི་རྣམ་བཞག་ཁས་ལེན་ཞིང༌། ཞུགས་གནས་བརྒྱད་པོ་གང་རུང་ལ་འཕགས་པས་ཁྱབ་པར་ཁས་ལེན་ནོ།

ཐེག་ཆེན་གྱི་བྱང་ཆུབ་མངོན་དུ་བྱེད་ཚུལ་ནི། བྱང་སེམས་རྣམས་ཀྱིས་བདག་མེད་པའི་ལྟ་བ་རིགས་པའི་རྣམ་གྲངས་མཐའ་ཡས་པའི་སྒོ་ནས་གྲུས་པར་བསྒོམས་ཏེ་སྒྲིབ་པ་སྤོང་བར་བྱེད་ལ། དེ་ཡང་ཉོན་སྒྲིབ་ཟད་པར་མ་སྤངས་པར་ཤེས་སྒྲིབ་སྤོང་བའི་མགོ་མི་རྩོམ་ལ། ཤེས་སྒྲིབ་སྤོང་བའི་མགོ་ས་བརྒྱད་པ་ནས་རྩོམ་པ་ཡིན་ཞིང༌། དམན་ལམ་སྔོན་དུ་མ་སོང་བའི་བྱང་སེམས་རྣམས་ཀྱིས་ས་བརྒྱད་པ་ཐོབ་པ་ན་ཉོན་སྒྲིབ་ཟད་པར་སྤངས་ཏེ། མཐར་རྒྱུན་མཐའི་བར་ཆད་མེད་ལམ་ལ་བརྟེན་ནས་ཤེས་སྒྲིབ་མ་ལུས་པར་སྤངས་པ་དང་དུས་མཉམ་དུ་སྐུ་བཞིའི་གོ་འཕང་མངོན་དུ་བྱེད་དོ། མྱང་འདས་དང་འགོག་བདེན་ལ་དོན་དམ་བདེན་པས་ཁྱབ་པར་འདོད་དོ།

དགོངས་འགྲེལ་ལས་བཤད་པའི་འཁོར་ལོ་གསུམ་གྱི་དང་པོ་དང༌། ཐ་མ་ལ་དྲང་དོན་གྱི་མདོས་ཁྱབ་སྟེ། དེ་ལ་སྟོང་ཉིད་དངོས་སུ་སྟོན་པའི་མདོ་མེད་པའི་ཕྱིར། དེའི་བར་པ་ལ་ངེས་དོན་གྱི་མདོས་ཁྱབ་པར་བཞེད་དེ། ཤེས་རབ་སྙིང་པོ་ངེས་དོན་གྱི་མདོ་ཡིན་པའི་ཕྱིར།

ཐལ་འགྱུར་པ་རྣམས་ཀྱི་ཁྱད་ཆོས་ཀྱི་གཙོ་བོ་ནི། བརྟེན་ནས་བཏགས་པའི་གཏན་ཚིགས་ལ་བརྟེན་ནས་ཕྱི་ནང་གི་ཆོས་རྣམས་ལ་རང་གི་མཚན་ཉིད་ཀྱིས་གྲུབ་པ་མ་ལུས་པར་ཁེགས་ཀྱང༌། ཐ་སྙད་དུ་མིང་ཀུང་བཏགས་ཡོད་ཙམ་ལ་བཅིང་གྲོལ་དང༌། རྒྱུ་འབྲས་དང༌། གཞལ་བྱ་འཇལ་བྱེད་ལ་སོགས་པ་གཞན་ངོར་སྐྱེལ་མི་དགོས་པར་རང་ལུགས་ལ་བསྐྱོན་མེད་དུ་འཇོག་ཤེས་པ་དེ་ཉིད་ཡིན་ནོ། དེང་སང་འགའ་ཞིག་ལྟ་བ་མཐོན་པོར་རློམ་ཏེ་སྣང་ཕྱོགས་ཀྱི་ཆོས་རྣམས་འཁྲུལ་སྣང་ཙམ་ཡིན་ཞེས་མོ་གཤམ་གྱི་བུ་ལྟར་གཏན་མེད་དུ་བཟུང་ནས་ཅི་ཡང་ཡིད་ལ་མི་བྱེད་པ་ཉམས་ལེན་གྱི་མཆོག་ཏུ་འཛིན་པ་རྣམས་ལ་ཐལ་འགྱུར་པའི་དྲི་ཙམ་ཡང་མི་བྲོའོ།

དེས་ན་སྲིད་པའི་ཕུན་ཚོགས་མཐའ་དག་མེ་འབར་བའི་ཀྲུབས་ལྟར་མཐོང་ནས་གྲོལ་བ་དོན་དུ་གཉེར་བ་དག་གིས་ཆོས་ལྟར་བཅོས་པའི་ལྟ་བ་ངན་པ་མ་ལུས་པ་སྤངས་ཏེ་གྲུབ་མཐའ་ཐམས་ཅད་ཀྱི་ཡང་རྩེ་དབུ་མ་ཐལ་འགྱུར་བའི་རིང་ལུགས་ལ་མཆོག་ཏུ་གུས་པར་བྱའོ།

སྨྲས་པ།

གཞུང་ལུགས་གསེར་གྱི་འཛིན་མར་ཡོངས་འཁྲིལ་ཚིག་དོན་གཏིང་མཐའ་དཔག་པར་དཀའ།
བློ་དམན་བྱིས་པའི་སྙིང་ལ་འཇིགས་སྐྱེར་སྣ་ཚོགས་རིགས་པའི་རླབས་ཕྲེང་གཡོ།

རྣམ་མང་ལྟ་བའི་ཆུ་ཀླུང་སྟོང་འགྲེད་བློ་གསལ་གཉིས་སྐྱེས་རོལ་བའི་གནས།
ཕྱི་ནང་གཞུང་ལུགས་ཆུ་གཏེར་ཆེན་པོའི་དེ་ཉིད་མ་ལུས་སུ་ཡིས་དཔོག

འོན་ཀུན་སྐྱེ་བས་ཐོབ་པའི་གྲུ་རྫིངས་ནི། །སྦྱོར་བྱུང་མཐུན་པའི་རླུང་གིས་ཉེར་བསྐུལ་ཏེ།
གྲུབ་མཐའ་རྒྱ་མཚོའི་དབུས་སུ་སོན་པ་ལས། །ལེགས་བཤད་ནོར་བུའི་འཕྲེང་བ་དེང་འདིར་རྙེད།

གང་དག་མཁས་མཆོག་བྱེ་བའི་མདུན་ས་རུ། །ལེགས་བཤད་གཏམ་གྱི་དགའ་སྟོན་སྤེལ་འདོད་ན།
རང་གཞན་གྲུབ་མཐའི་སྙིང་པོ་མདོར་བསྡུས་འདི། །བློ་གསལ་གཞོན་ནུའི་ཚོགས་ཀྱིས་བསྟེན་བྱ་ཡིན།

དེང་དུས་མཁས་རློམ་སྐྱེ་བོ་སྤྱི་བརྟོལ་ཅན། །རྒྱ་ཆེན་གཞུང་ལ་ཡུན་རིང་མ་སྦྱངས་པར།
རྙེད་བཀུར་བསྡུ་ཕྱིར་རྩོམ་པའི་ཟློས་གར་གྱིས། །ངལ་བ་ལྷུར་ལེན་གང་དེ་ཨོ་མ་མཚར།

རྣམ་དཔྱོད་མཁའ་ལས་ལེགས་བཤད་འོད་སྟོང་ཅན། །ཤར་བས་ཉེས་བཤད་ཀུན་དུ་ཟུམ་བྱེད་ཀྱང་།
རྣམ་དག་གཞུང་ལུགས་འདབ་བརྒྱའི་ཚལ་ཆེན་པོ། །ངོ་མཚར་དོན་གྱི་འཛུམ་དཀར་ཅི་ཡང་རྒོད།

རྒྱ་བོད་མཁས་པའི་གཞུང་གི་བཅུད་བསྡུས་ནས། །རབ་འབྱམས་གྲུབ་མཐའ་གསལ་བྱེད་བཀོད་འདི་ཡང་།
འགྲན་སེམས་ཕྲག་དོག་དབང་གིས་མ་ལགས་ཏེ། །རང་དང་སྐལ་མཉམ་བློ་གྲོས་འཕེལ་ཕྱིར་ཡིན།

ཚུལ་འདིར་འབད་པ་ལས་བྱུང་ལེགས་སྤྱད་ནི། །ཟླ་བའི་འོད་ཀྱང་ཟིལ་གྱིས་གནོན་པ་དེས།
འགྲོ་ཀུན་ལྟ་ངན་གཙོང་རོང་ལས་བསྒྲལ་ཏེ། །ཡང་དག་ལམ་གྱིས་རྟག་ཏུ་དབུགས་འབྱིན་ཤོག

ཅེས་ཕྱི་ནང་གི་གྲུབ་མཐའི་རྣམ་བཞག་མདོར་བསྡུས་པ་རིན་པོ་ཆེའི་འཕྲེང་བ་ཞེས་བྱ་བ་འདི་ནི་དད་བརྩོན་རྣམ་དཔྱོད་དང་ལྡན་པ་ཀུ་ཤྲི་ངག་དབང་སྐལ་བཟང་དང་། དགེ་སློང་ངག་དབང་བཟང་པོ་གཉིས་ཀྱིས་བསྐུལ་ངོར། བརྩོན་པ་

དཀོན་མཆོག་འཇིགས་མེད་དབང་པོས་ཆུ་སྤྲུལ་ཆུ་སྟོད་ཟླ་བའི་ཡར་ཚེ་ལ་སྦྱར་བའི་[47] ཡི་གེ་པ་ནི་རྟ་མགྲིན་ཚེ་རིང་ངོ་། སརྦ་མངྒ་ལཾ།།

Reading Original Compositions (General Features)

Page 277, Line 4

In original compositions—particularly with narrative expositions—there are a number of formulaic components that occur at the start of the text. Among these features are: an opening homage to the Buddha and/or foundational individuals in the transmission lineage of the subject area; a "promise of composition" in which the author sets forth his motivation for writing the work; an exhortation to the audience to listen attentively to what he has to say; and so on. The first three of these have been seen already in previous texts (such as Tsongkhapa's *Three Principal Aspects of the Path*—although not explicitly identified as such), and they are also seen here in the opening four verses of the text: homage to the Buddha, homage to the lineage, promise of composition, and exhortation to the audience/readership. Depending on how closely the work is linked to a previous composition, other factors may occur as well (see the "Introduction" to Jñānamitra's *Explanation*, 59–60). In addition, because such components are often rendered in verse, the grammar can be terse, relying on structural elements to convey the full meaning (see ལམ་གཙོ་རྣམ་གསུམ་ note 1 and བློ་རིག་ note 17).

WHAT TO REMEMBER

In original compositions there are a number of formulaic components that occur at the start of the text, such as an opening homage to the Buddha and/or foundational lineage figures, the "promise of composition," an exhortation to the audience, and so on. When occurring in verse—as they often do—those grammatical considerations can also come into play.

②

Poetic Metaphor

Page 277, Line 4

This opening verse of homage is a good example of poetic metaphor in verse composition. In this passage, the Buddha is compared to the Kailash region in the Himalayan Mountains. In each line of the verse, different attributes of the Buddha are analogized to different aspects of mountainous terrain and their characteristics and functions, that is:

snow mountain	two accumulations of merit and wisdom
warmth	compassion
earth	truth body (*dharmakāya*)
rivers	different systems of tenets
waves on the water	enlightened activities emanating throughout space
Lake Manasarovar	the Buddha
nāgas	bodhisattvas ("children of the Muni")

Such metaphors are common and can be progressive and extended to great lengths.

WHAT TO REMEMBER

Poetic metaphors are common in verse homages. With each pair of words or phrases often stated in apposition, they can be deciphered by reading the sentence in two ways reflecting each half of the metaphor.

③

Translation Hint

Page 277, Line 7

While this final verb (རྒྱལ་) could be translated in the precative—that is, as reflecting an aspirational prayer ("⌊may you⌋ be victorious")—since it occurs in an opening homage, it is more likely an explicit praise (i.e., a declarative statement with a vocative).

The Particle ས་ Following Verbs

Page 278, Line 6

In the first text encountered, the application of particles to a verb to produce verbal nouns and participles was seen (see ཤེས་རབ་སྙིང་པོ་ note 13). Here, we see a different sort of particle, the simple syllable ས་, functioning in a similar manner. Rather than forming the participial form of the verb, the addition of the particle ས་ turns a verb into a specific kind of noun, a "spatial noun." As implied by its literal meaning ("ground"), the addition of ས་ to a verb means something like the "basis" or "foundation" (i.e., the "ground") for engaging in that activity. Thus, if the verb འཁྲུལ་ means "to go astray" or "to be mistaken," then འཁྲུལ་ས་ means the "foundation for going astray" or "basis for being mistaken."

WHAT TO REMEMBER

The application of the particle ས་ to a verb forms a noun conveying the idea of the "basis" or "foundation" for engaging in that activity.

Topical Outlines (ས་བཅད་)

Page 278, Line 7

As previously noted (see རིགས་ལམ་ note 5), one of the most common grammatical constructions found in all of Tibetan literature is the "topical outline" (ས་བཅད་). A topical outline typically begins with the main topic marked by a seventh-case ལ་ particle followed by the number of divisions of that topic and a list of their names. Occasionally, such an introductory statement is framed as a conditional sentence ("if the topic of X is divided, ..."). Here, the referred topic, a number, and a list is provided:

	case 7.6	APP	Omitted Verb
བརྗོད་པ་	ལ་	གཉིས།	སྤྱིར་བསྟན་པ་དང་། བྱེ་བྲག་ཏུ་བཤད་པའོ།

The final verb ཡོད་ is omitted but implied.

There are a number of things to note about topical outlines. Following the first statement of the outline at its broadest level (as with this example, above), subsequent statements follow a basic pattern in which the number of the item in the list is given—with or without restatement of the name of the division—and its subdivisions, if any, often, but not always, are introduced with an explicit statement of the number of subdivisions. Where there are no subdivisions and the reader is assumed to be aware of the context of the narrative, simple numbers are given (དང་པོ་ནི།, གཉིས་པ་ནི།, etc.). Variations on this basic pattern will be seen in texts outside the genre of monastic textbooks as well.

In this text, the author is kind to the reader. For example, when the second division statement appears (285, line 13), the text reads: གཉིས་པ་བྱེ་བྲག་ཏུ་བཤད་པ་ལ།, repeating the name of the division.

WHAT TO REMEMBER

Topical outlines commence in an explicit manner, but they quickly become abbreviated, relying on the memory of the student with regard to the section of the text. Consequently, noting the names and the number of divisions when they are first encountered is imperative.

6 Multiple Verbs in a Clause Construction

Page 278, Line 14

While the distribution of a single verb across multiple sentences has been seen (see རིགས་ལམ་ note 17), this sentence demonstrates the application of two verbs to a single sentence and specifically, in this case, within a clause construction. The main verb of the sentence is the verbal collocation དོན་དུ་གཉེར་ ("to seek"), while the agent of the sentence—བློ་ལྷན་སྐྱེས་ ("innate awareness")—is modified by a clause (Wilson, case 6.6.1). Unlike a standard clause-connective construction (see ཤེས་རབ་སྙིང་པོ་ note 17), this construction deploys two verbs in sequence: བརྟགས་ and དཔྱད་. Both of these verbs are negated, and together with the locative-absolute construction (see ཞེར་སྙིང་རྣམ་བཤད་ note 9) that precedes it, the noun phrase and its clause can be translated as "an innate awareness that, without having been trained in scriptural systems, does not investigate [and] does not analyze."

WHAT TO REMEMBER

When an author wishes to apply two or more verbs to the same subject or object, the verbs can simply be listed sequentially. This approach can be used in standard sentence constructions as well as in clauses.

Identifying Text Titles and Citations

7

Page 278, Line 17

As noted previously (see ཤེར་སྙིང་རྣམ་བཤད་ note 7), when text titles are cited in the body of a text, it is seldom the case that the full bibliographic title of a work will be given by an author. Rather, an abbreviated, alternate, or poetic title will be used. Although the identity of many texts can be discerned from context (such as famous or standard canonical sources for a given topic), in other cases, the full reference of an introduced quotation is not obvious. Here is one such example. The text passage quoted here is introduced with the title འགྲེལ་བཤད་ཚིག་གསལ།, and since ཚིག་གསལ། is the name of a famous philosophical text (Candrakīrti's *Prasannapadā*—"Clear Words"), one might be tempted to think that this is the intended reference, but a quick search of that text would not locate the passage given. While this is not unusual—there are differences in spellings between different recensions of the canon—in this case, however, it is simply that Candrakīrti's is not the text being quoted. Rather, one must resort to a searchable catalog of the canon which precisely locates such a named text: the འགྲེལ་བཤད་ཚིག་རབ་ཏུ་གསལ་བ།—the *Clear Words, An Explanatory Commentary [on (Maitreya's) Ornament for Clear Realization]* attributed to Dharmamitra.

WHAT TO REMEMBER

In the absence of recognizable quotations or texts, the next best option for identifying quotations is using a full-text search engine to search the Tibetan canon.

8 Abbreviations of Proper Names

Page 279, Line 19

A consequence of the syllabic nature of Tibetan is the ease with which abbreviations of lists can be formed by combining words and dropping syllables. The phrase encountered here, བྱེ་རིག་, is one such example, in which the proper names བྱེ་བྲག་པ་ (Vaiśeṣika) and རིག་པ་ཅན་པ་ (Naiyāyika), previously encountered in the paragraph above, have been combined and shortened to form an abbreviation. Its potential ambiguity has then been compensated for by the quantifier གཉིས་ that follows. Several other instances of this can be seen in this text—some more obvious than others—such as:

ཕྱི་ནང་	ཕྱི་རོལ་པ་དང་ནང་པ་	outsiders and insiders
བྱེ་སྨྲ་	བྱེ་བྲག་སྨྲ་བ་	Vaibhāṣika
བྱེ་མདོ་	བྱེ་བྲག་སྨྲ་བ་དང་མདོ་སྡེ་པ་	Vaibhāṣika and Sautrāntika
དབུ་སེམས་	དབུ་མ་དང་སེམས་ཙམ་	Madhyamaka and Cittamātra
རྟག་ཆད་	རྟག་ལྟ་དང་ཆད་ལྟ་	permanence and nihilism
བྱང་སེམས་	བྱང་ཆུབ་སེམས་དཔའ་	bodhisattva
རྣམ་བདེན་བརྫུན་	རྣམ་བདེན་པ་དང་རྣམ་བརྫུན་པ་	True and False Aspectarians

WHAT TO REMEMBER

Lists of proper names are often abbreviated following their initial introduction. In such instances, typically the first syllable of each name is preserved and concatenated together. Depending on the ambiguity of the resulting compound, this may or may not be followed by a numeric quantifier.

9 Translation Hint: Contextual Meanings

Page 280, Line 5

While it is a general feature of most (if not all) languages that words can be polysemous, this is certainly true of Tibetan. When reading philosophical texts, however, an added complication comes in from the polysemous nature of Sanskrit technical terms, which can shift meaning not only from context to context but also from philosophical school to philosophical school. As a result, certain words in Sanskrit can result in identical or ambiguous renderings in Tibetan. Here, for example, the word *ahaṃkāra*—referring to the Sāṃkhya philosophical concept of an "I-principle"—is translated as ང་རྒྱལ་, which in a Buddhist context would typically render *abhimāna* ("pride"). A number of such terms occur in this text, such as:

Tibetan	General	Sāṃkhya	Buddhist
ང་རྒྱལ་	pride	I-principle	pride
རང་བཞིན་	nature	nature	own character
གཙོ་བོ་	foremost	principle	foremost
བློ་	awareness	intellect	awareness
སྤྱི་	general	general principle	generality/universal

etc. See also གཞིའི་སྐུ་གསུམ་སྒྲོན་མེ་ note 6.

Translation Hint: Buddhist Technical Terminology

Page 280, Line 11

In the hierarchy of connective syntactic particles (see བློ་རིག་ note 25), དང་ tends to connect phrases within a sentence and can do so within the context of a distributed verb (see རིགས་ལམ་ note 17). Such is also the case here. The sentence consists of a reason clause formed with the verbal participle ཡིན་པ་ marked in the third case (Wilson, case 3.3) followed by the Class V verb འདོད་ ("to assert") with its objective complement (Wilson, case 2.5), བེམ་པོ་ (hence "[it] is asserted as matter"). In the reason clause, there is what appears to be an indirect statement with the same sort of sequential verb construction seen above (see གྲུབ་མཐའ་ note 6), but this is not the case. Rather than functioning as verbs, here འདུས་ ("to gather") and བསགས་ ("to accumulate") are the nouns འདུས་པ་ ("collection") and བསགས་པ་ ("aggregation").

In the classification of physical objects coming out of the classical literature, there is a four-tiered hierarchy of matter: atoms (*paramāṇu;* རྡུལ་ཕྲན་), mere collections of atoms (*saṃghāta;* འདུས་པ་), aggregations of atoms (*saṃcita;* བསགས་པ་) which possess their own collective structure, and coarse objects (*sthūla;* རགས་པ་). Since this passage of the text is critiquing the Sāṃkhya School's presentation of reality, their twenty-five "faculties" are being redistributed into standard Buddhist categories. Hence, the passage reads: "Since, from among these, the person [is] the consciousness, and the remaining twenty-four are [mere] collections and aggregations, [those] are asserted as matter."

11 Lists and the Syntactic Particle དང་

Page 280, Line 14

The syntactic particle དང་, when used as a connective ("and"), replicates the usage of the Sanskrit connective *ca*. That is, it can be used either: (1) after each item in a list, or (2) at the end of the list. An example of the first was seen a few sentences earlier:

བློའི་དབང་པོ་ལྔ་ནི། མིག་དང་། རྣ་བ་དང་། སྣ་དང་། ལྕེ་དང་། པགས་པའི་དབང་པོ་རྣམས་སོ།
"The five mental faculties are those of the eye, ear, nose, tongue, and skin."

While this sentence demonstrates the second form (followed by a quantifying number), in instances where the divisions of a list are considered obvious, the particle དང་ will be omitted entirely, as was also previously seen:

འབྱུང་བ་ལྔ་ནི། ས་ཆུ་མེ་རླུང་ནམ་མཁའ་རྣམས་སོ།
"The five elements are earth, water, fire, wind, and space."

WHAT TO REMEMBER

The syntactic particle དང་, when used as a connective ("and"), replicates the usage of the Sanskrit connective *ca*. That is, it can be used either: (1) after each item in a list, or (2) at the end of the list.

12 Translation Hint: Non-Buddhist Text Quotations

Page 280, Line 21

This verse is a quote from the Sāṃkhya root text attributed to Īśvarakṛṣṇa, the *Sāṃkhya-kārikā*. The Sanskrit for this verse reads:

mūlaprakṛtir avikṛtir mahadādyāḥ prakṛtivikṛtayaḥ sapta /
ṣoḍaśakas tu vikāro na prakṛtir na vikṛtiḥ puruṣaḥ //

As can be seen, the two lines of Sanskrit verse are rendered (commonly) as four lines in the Tibetan. While most vocabulary is standard, some technical terms require special attention (and reference to the Sanskrit source) for proper translation. See གྲུབ་མཐའ་ note 9 (above).

Translation Hint

13

Page 282, Line 5

This sentence, like many concise definitions, utilizes abbreviated sentences as items in a list (see རིགས་ལམ་ note 22). In specifying the precise assertions of the Indian Jain or "Nirgrantha" (གཅེར་བུ་པ་; "the naked ones") tradition, the author deals one by one with the nine categories listed. Here, the first category, སྲོག་ ("life"), is addressed using a series of disjunctive syntactic particles (see བློ་རིག་ note 14) and participles (see ཤེས་རབ་སྙིང་པོ་ note 13). Consequently, the treatment of this topic consists of four "sentences":

དེ་ལ་སྲོག་ནི་བདག་ཡིན་ལ།
སྐྱེས་བུ་རྣམས་ཀྱི་ལུས་ཀྱི་ཚད་ཇི་ལྟ་བ་བཞིན་དུ་ཡོད་པ་
ངོ་བོ་རྟག་ [ཡིན་] ལ་
གནས་སྐབས་མི་རྟག་པའི་རང་བཞིན་ཅན་ཡིན་ནོ།

In the previous text, the expression (ཀྱི་)གནས་སྐབས་ ("in the context [of]") was seen on several occasions. In the fourth line here, however, གནས་སྐབས་ is being used as a simple noun meaning "condition" or "state," yielding the translation:

> Here, although life is the self, [it] exists, accordingly, as exactly the same size as a person's body. Its nature is such that, although its entity is permanent, its states are impermanent.

The use of such grammatical constuctions is reflective of Könchok Jikmé Wangpo's writing style and will be seen repeatedly throughout this text.

14 Translation Hint: Specifically and Generally Characterized Phenomena

Page 283, Line 4

The distinction between specifically characterized phenomena (རང་མཚན) and generally characterized phenomena (སྤྱི་མཚན) is a central topic in Buddhist epistemology and the subsequent presentations of Buddhist philosophy that draw on that vocabulary.

These topics are covered in depth in the sixth chapter of Purbujok's *Introductory Path of Reasoning* (available as a supplemental exercise). In brief, however, a specifically characterized phenomenon is a phenomenon that is established by way of its own character without being merely imputed by a term or conceptual consciousness. In general, a specifically characterized phenomenon is an impermanent phenomenon—something that changes moment by moment—and performs a function (*artha-kriyā* in Sanskrit). Such phenomena are typically the objects perceived by the sense faculties.

This category of phenomena is contrasted with its complement: generally characterized phenomena. Generally characterized phenomena are permanent phenomena—things that do *not* change moment by moment—and are merely imputed by a conceptual consciousness or a name. For example, the conceptual category of "non-cow" is a generally characterized phenomena. It does not perform a function, nor does it change moment by moment; it exists solely as an object of consciousness and not in terms of its own character.

Here, by saying that all objects of comprehension—that is, all things that exist—are necessarily specifically characterized phenomena, an extreme materialist philosophy is being advocated.

15 Translation Hint

Page 285, Line 18

Recall the use of anaphora with a nongeneralizable subject in a debate-style "consequence" (see རིགས་ལམ་ note 12).

16 Non-Adverbial Qualifiers

Page 286, Line 7

Recall that there are four distinct types of clause connectives (see ཤེས་རབ་སྙིང་པོ་ note 17).

This sentence demonstrates one of the more difficult ones to recognize: the clause connective to a qualifier. Because the primary verb in the clause, རུང་, is a Class III verb, and the preceding word, བློ་, is in the nominative (i.e., is the subject of the verb), the phrase བློ་འདོར་རུང་བའི་ཆོས་ is easily reconstituted as a complete sentence: བློ་ཆོས་[ལ་]འདོར་རུང་. Since the second verb, འདོར་, serves as the complement in the sentence (see རིགས་ལམ་ note 21), the word ཆོས་ must be a qualifier.

Normally, qualifiers are thought of as adverbs, that is, that they "qualify" the activity of the verb, answering the question "how?" But this is a very specific (if common) form of qualifiers. Recall that, in actuality, it is more accurate to say that a qualifier restricts the scope of application of the verb in some way (see ཤེས་རབ་སྙིང་པོ་ note 8). It is in this sense that the word ཆོས་ is a qualifier of the verb རུང་. Hence, were this reconstructed sentence to be translated into English, it would read: "an awareness is suitable to be cancelled with respect to a [certain] phenomenon." As a result of this type of analysis, the clause བློ་འདོར་རུང་བའི་ཆོས་ can now be correctly rendered: "a phenomenon with respect to which an awareness is suitable to be cancelled."

WHAT TO REMEMBER

The qualifier of a sentence need not be an adverb and only need be something that *qualifies* the activity of the verb by modifying it or restricting its scope of application.

Locative Absolute 17

Page 287, Line 9

Recall that a locative-absolute construction is a complete or partial sentence that expresses (a) a condition in which something takes place or (b) some type of accompanying circumstance (see ཤེར་སྙིང་རྣམ་བཤད་ note 9). While this construction has been seen in its common, negated form, here is an instance of a locative-absolute construction without negation. The passage still conveys "a condition or accompanying circumstance" but does so in a positive light. Hence, the passage ending with "…དང་མཐུན་པར་ can be translated as "being in accord with ..."

WHAT TO REMEMBER

A locative-absolute construction is a complete or partial sentence that expresses (a) a condition in which something takes place or (b) some type of accompanying circumstance. When formed with a verb without negation, it functions grammatically the same, although it indicates a positive condition.

18 Translation Hint

Page 287, Line 13

This passage involves an auxiliary construction with the verb ཟིན་ (see བློ་རིག་ note 12) and the postposition འོག་ཏུ་.

19 Lists and the Particle སོགས་

Page 287, Line 23

As previously noted (see ཤེར་སྙིང་རྣམ་བཤད་ note 6 and བློ་རིག་ note 5), the syntactic phrase ལ་སོགས་པ་ is used to indicate that the remainder of a list of items has been omitted, and it is typically translated as "and so forth," or simply "etc." While such an understanding is suitable for known, discrete lists of items, in the case where a general list of exemplary or illustrative items is presented, the phrase ལ་སོགས་པ་ takes on a more generic sense of "such as ..." Such is the case in its usage here, where no specific list is being referred to.

WHAT TO REMEMBER

The syntactic phrase ལ་སོགས་པ་ is used to indicate that either the remainder of a list has been omitted or that a generic list is implied, exemplified by the item explicitly listed.

Auxiliary Verbs: The Perfective Construction

20

Page 288, Line 1

As previously noted, the perfective construction is used to indicate verbal activity in the abstract sense or when referring to the activity as a whole, as in prophesies (see དེབ་ཐེར་དམར་པོ་ note 20). Here, although no prophecy is being made, the narrative is still discussing a hypothetical situation, and such verbal activity is likewise represented by a perfective construction.

WHAT TO REMEMBER

A hypothetical state, when occurring in the concluding clause of a sentence, is indicated by the perfective and formed with the future-tense auxiliary verb འགྱུར་.

Tibetan Numbers: Reduplication

21

Page 288, Line 4

The reduplication—repetition either exactly or with a slight change—of numbers in Tibetan is used to indicate distribution to a previously specified list or generic category. Here, the reduplication of the number གཉིས་ follows a phrase containing the pronoun རེ་རེ་ ("each one"), indicating the object that the distribution applies to. Hence, the entire sentence can be translated as: "Each one [of these] ... has two [divisions] each." The construction is seen again near the end of the text where ལྔ་ལྔ་ likewise correlates with a preceding རེ་རེ་ ("each") to mean "each [of the preceding list of things] has five [items] each."

WHAT TO REMEMBER

The reduplication of numbers in Tibetan is used to indicate distribution to a previously specified list or generic category. This is often, but not always, marked by the adjective རེ་རེ་ ("each").

22

Rhetorical Questions with འམ་ etc.

Page 288, Line 8

The disjunctive syntactic particles འམ་, གམ་, ངམ་, etc., are typically used to indicate alternatives, and hence they are translated as "or." When occurring at the end of a sentence, however, they indicate a rhetorical question. In keeping with this latter usage, they can be thought of as conveying the idea: "or is it?"

An additional thing to note about rhetorical questions in Tibetan is that they are framed in the negative voice. Hence, while in English a rhetorical question would be stated as "Is [something] really the case?" in Tibetan the same question would be phrased as "Is [something] not the case?" in which the negative can be thought of as merely an emphatic.

WHAT TO REMEMBER

The particles འམ་, གམ་, etc., at the end of a sentence indicate a rhetorical question, while negation in a rhetorical question is merely emphatic.

23

Translation Hint

Page 288, Line 14

See རིགས་ལམ་ note 11 for the meaning of this technical term.

24

Tibetan Numbers: Combinations of Types

Page 289, Line 1

Here the phrase བརྗོད་སྐད་ཅིག་མ་བཅུ་དྲུག་གི་སྐད་ཅིག་མ་དང་པོ་བཅོ་ལྔ་ contains both an adjectival ordinal number, དང་པོ་ ("first"), and a cardinal number, བཅོ་ལྔ་ ("fifteen"). It is important to note that word order is crucial in analyzing these compounds since སྐད་ཅིག་མ་དང་པོ་བཅོ་ལྔ་ ("the fifteen first moments" or "the first fifteen moments") would be different from སྐད་ཅིག་མ་བཅོ་ལྔ་དང་པོ་ ("the first of the fifteen moments").

WHAT TO REMEMBER

Tibetan numbers take three forms: cardinal, ordinal, and quantifying.

The number three (གསུམ་), for example, is a simple cardinal number, as in བེམ་ཤེས་ལྡན་མིན་འདུ་བྱེད་གསུམ་ ("the three—matter, consciousness, and nonassociated compositional factors"), in which the number occurs appositionally with the nouns in the list.

གསུམ་པ་, however, is an adjectival ordinal number, as in the example: རྟགས་གསུམ་པ་མ་གྲུབ་ན། ("If [he says,] the third reason is not established ...").

Finally, a third form expressing a quantity is formed using the པོ་ suffix, such as གསུམ་པོ་ in the expression ལྡོག་ཆོས་གསུམ་པོ་ ("all three isolate phenomena"). It is important to note that for གཅིག་ this yields གཅིག་པོ་ (often translated as "unique") in contrast to its irregular form in the ordinal: དང་པོ་. The suffix དག་ can also serve this function.

The Use of བར་དུ་ to Designate a Duration of Time 25

Page 289, Line 5

Previously (see ཤེས་རབ་སྙིང་པོ་ note 15 and བློ་རིག་ note 3), the བར་དུ་ construction has been used to indicate a sequence of items. Here, however, it is being used to indicate a duration of time. Consequently, ཚེ་གསུམ་ལ་སོགས་པའི་བར་དུ་ should be translated not as "up to three lifetimes, etc." but as "over the course of three lifetimes, or more."

WHAT TO REMEMBER

In addition to a range, བར་དུ་ can be used to express a duration of time.

Non-case Use of ཀྱིས་ etc., to Mark Adverbial Qualifiers 26

Page 290, Line 11

Wilson (638) mentions in passing that one of the non-case uses of third-case agentive particles is to mark adverbs. Here is one such example. The verb in this reason clause, བསྡུས་, is a Class IV verb of conjunction that takes its qualifier marked with the syntactic particle དང་, which is, indeed, seen here. What is also seen, however, is a second qualifier marked with a non-case གིས་ particle. Since the phrase being marked is a temporal one, it expresses a qualification of the activity of the verb and hence can be translated as "during X period of time" or "in X period of time."

WHAT TO REMEMBER

Certain temporal expressions and other adverbial phrases can be used to qualify a verb by deploying the third-case particles ཀྱིས་, གྱིས་, གིས་, etc., in a non-case usage. See also གྲུབ་མཐའ་ note 28.

27 The Honorific Precative Construction with མཛོད་

Page 290, Line 21

Although the precative construction, which uses one of the three imperative-marking syntactic particles (ཅིག་, ཞིག་, and ཤིག་) following the imperative form of the verb, has been previously seen (see མདོ་མཛངས་བླུན་ note 14), it can also be formed by the addition of the imperative form of the auxiliary verb མཛད་ (i.e., མཛོད་) to the past, present, or future form of any verb. The resulting verb phrase constitutes the honorific form of the precative and shares the same feature as the other form of the precative: the recipient of the speech is marked in the vocative.

WHAT TO REMEMBER

The auxiliary construction, when occurring with the verb མཛོད་, indicates the honorific form of the precative.

Translation Hint: Adverbial Qualifiers

28

Page 291, Line 2

As noted above (see གྲུབ་མཐའ་ note 26), the qualifier in a sentence can be marked with a non-case use of a third-case agentive particle (such as གྱིས་). Here is yet another example of that grammatical form, demonstrating the author's predilection for such constructions.

Just as with its use above, which indicated a temporal qualifier, here the qualifier marks a sentence fragment (a verb and its complement) and consequently indicates a more abstract temporal qualifier. This and other such phrases can thus be translated as the expression "while doing X."

Translation Hint

29

Page 292, Line 13

Recall the use of participles (see ཤེས་རབ་སྙིང་པོ་ note 13) as substantives (see ཤེར་སྙིང་རྣམ་བཤད་ note 12). Here, the verb འཕེན་ ("to imply") occurs as the participle འཕེན་པ་ ("the implied" or "that which is implied").

Translation Hint: Time

30

Page 292, Line 20

Buddhist philosophy typically does not discuss time as an abstract entity but only in relation to objects. Consequently, speaking of "the past" is meaningless, and one can only speak of "the past of an object," as is seen here.

Translation Hint

31

Page 292, Line 21

This passage follows the same pattern seen before with སྣང་ལ་མ་ངེས་ (see བློ་རིག་ notes 14 and 18): it contains a verb, a disjunctive syntactic particle (ལ་), and another verb.

Translation Hint

32

Page 293, Line 2

Recall the discussion of "isolates" (ལྡོག་པ་); see རིགས་ལམ་ note 11.

33

The Adverbial Phrase Marker ཕྱིན་ (and ཕྱིན་ཆད་)

Page 293, Line 5

Wilson (659–60) notes that adverbial phrase markers can be distinguished from postpositions in that the latter are both declinable and connect to what precedes them with a postpositional connective (Wilson, case 6.3), whereas adverbial phrase markers do not. Here the adverbial phrase marker ཕྱིན་ (also seen fully as ཕྱིན་ཆད་)—not to be confused with the past-tense form of the verb འགྲོ་—is used to indicate that the phrase that precedes it sets a condition for what follows. It can be translated as "once ..." or "...; henceforth ..."

WHAT TO REMEMBER

The adverbial phrase marker ཕྱིན་ (or ཕྱིན་ཆད་) is used to indicate that the phrase that precedes it sets a condition for what follows. It can be translated as "once ..." or "...; henceforth ..."

34

Translation Hint: Semantic Range of མཚན་ཉིད་(པ་)

Page 293, Line 7

This sentence reveals the importance of subtle points of grammar. Thus far in this text, statements providing the definition of terms have been given in the form "<*noun-phrase*> + <*term*> + "ཀྱི་མཚན་ཉིད་།." While this would appear to be the same sort of statement, it is not. The first thing to note is that the word མཚན་ཉིད་པ་ does *not* attach to what precedes it with a connective particle, thus indicating that it must be taken as an adjective ("fully characterized" or "fully qualified") rather than as a noun ("definition" or "defining characteristic").

35

The Nominalization of Verbs and Sentences

Page 294, Line 3

A key to understanding the modular nature (see ཤེས་རབ་སྙིང་པོ་ note 22) of Tibetan sentences is the nominalization of verbs, verb phrases, and complete sentences. The nominalization of verbs and sentences is a common way of forming nouns and noun phrases in philosophical discourse. Here, གང་ཟག་རྟག་གཅིག་རང་དབང་ཅན་གྱི་བདག་གིས་སྟོང་པ་ is one such example of a nominalized complete sentence that functions as a noun phrase. As a sentence, གང་ཟག་རྟག་གཅིག་རང་དབང་ཅན་གྱི་བདག་གིས་སྟོང་། has a translation that is very straightforward: a person is empty of a permanent, unitary, and independent self.

With the addition of the nominalizing particle པ་, the entire sentence is converted into a noun phrase, in this case: a person's being empty of a permanent, unitary, and independent self. A similar construction is seen in the immediately following sentence as well.

WHAT TO REMEMBER

Verbal nouns and participles are the nominalized forms of a verb and generally refer to the abstract idea of an action or state—"being something" or "the action of doing something." When verbs are nominalized with a པ་ or བ་ suffix, the resulting word can function as either a verbal noun or adjectivally as a verbal participle. For example, སྣང་ can mean "to appear," while སྣང་བ་ can function as a verbal participle meaning "appearing" (as in སྣང་བའི་ཡུལ་ "appearing object") or as a verbal noun meaning "[someone/something that] appears" or "appearance" (as in ཀུན་རྫོབ་ཀྱི་སྣང་བ་ "the appearance of conventional [phenomena]").

The Verb གཏོགས་ as Phrase Marker

36

Page 294, Line 6

In its normal usage, the verb གཏོགས་ functions like any other Class III verb. When negated, however, it sometimes functions as a frozen adverbial phrase marker. In such instances (as the one seen here), it indicates an exception to what follows. Hence, it can be translated as "except for ..."

WHAT TO REMEMBER

The verb གཏོགས་, when negated, can function as a frozen adverbial phrase marker indicating an exception to what follows; it can be translated as "except for ..."

37 Translation Hint

Page 295, Line 22

Although the previous and following opinions on the meaning of the names of the subdivisions of True Aspectarian Cittamātrins are accompanied by a text citation, here the opinion is introduced solely by the names of specific people followed by an agentive marker.

38 Idiosyncratic Constructions with the Verb ལྟོས་

Page 296, Line 7

In its normal usage, the verb ལྟོས་ functions like any other Class II verb, usually meaning "to be dependent upon" or "to be contingent upon." Although identical to a gerund construction (which would normally indicate a preceding action performed by the same subject/agent of the main verb), here, however, the construction ལྟོས་ནས་ functions as an adverbial expression that is related to its dominant meaning but renders the phrase associated with it as a qualifier of the main sentence. It can be translated as "from the perspective (of)."

WHAT TO REMEMBER

Sometimes when the verb ལྟོས་ occurs in the construction ལྟོས་ནས་, it functions as an adverbial expression that can be translated as "from the perspective (of)."

39 The Lexical Suffix ཅན་ as Frozen Verb

Page 298, Line 13

Wilson (202–204) notes that the suffix syllable ཅན་ can be used to show possession or ownership of a thing or attribute. It attaches to the end of a word to form new nouns. Like the possessive suffixes (derived from the Class IV verbs བཅས་ and ལྡན་), the suffix syllable ཅན་ can be similarly understood as the frozen form of an archaic Class VIII verb. Consequently, sentences ending with ཅན་ can be considered terminated by a Class VIII verb or by a noun phrase with an omitted ཡིན་.

> WHAT TO REMEMBER
>
> The suffix syllable ཅན་ can be understood as the frozen form of an archaic Class VIII verb and read in certain contexts as still functioning as a verb.

Translation Hint: Three Modes of a Correct Logical Sign (40)

Page 301, Line 8

The sixth and seventh selections contained in this *Reader*—the excerpt from *The Collected Topics* and the *Presentation of Awarenesses and Knowers*—are part of the general introduction to logical thinking in the Tibetan educational system. The third part—not included here—is a presentation of the topic of "Signs and Reasonings" that deals with the formal aspects of logical argumentation. Here, mention of "the three modes" (ཚུལ་གསུམ་) refers to the theory of logical reasoning laid out in the texts of this latter category and refers to the three characteristics that a "sign" (or "reason") must have to be correct.

For example, given the syllogism "the subject, sound, is impermanent because of being a product," three modes can be specified: the property of the subject (*pakṣadharma*; *phyogs chos*), a forward pervasion (*anvaya-vyāpti*; *rjes khyab*), and a reverse pervasion (*vyatireka-vyāpti*; *ldog khyab*). The property of the subject is "sound is a product." The forward pervasion is "whatever is a product is necessarily impermanent," while the reverse pervasion is "whatever is permanent is necessarily a nonproduct." For a logical "sign" (or "reason") to be correct, all three modes must be true. A full treatment of the topic of "Signs and Reasonings" can be found in Rogers (2009).

Translation Hint (41)

Page 302, Line 11

མཐུན་ is a Class IV verb whose paradigmatic grammar entails a nominative subject and a qualifier marked by a syntactic particle. Here, however, rather than one item "being in accord" (མཐུན་) with another item, the grammatical subject is a collective noun phrase ("both [subschools of] Svātantrikas") with the verb conveying a reflexive sense ("being in accord [with each other]"). There is still the question, however, of how to grammatically describe the remainder of the sentence—i.e., the phrases that precede the grammatical subject. Given the absence of any grammatical connection to the final verb, the only option would appear to be a "topical nominative" (Wilson, case 1.5), and although not explicitly marked by the particle ནི་, the resulting translation supports the syntax.

42 The Numeric Prefix ཡ་

Page 303, Line 2

As an adjective, the syllable ཡ་ means "upper" (as opposed to མ་, "lower"). As a numeric prefix, however, ཡ་ means something like "from among a set of." For example, ལྷམ་ཡ་གཅིག་ means "one of a pair of shoes." Hence, the expression encountered here, གང་ཟག་ཡ་བརྒྱད་, would mean "eight from among the sets of persons [i.e., approachers and abiders]."

WHAT TO REMEMBER

As a numeric prefix, the syllable ཡ་ means "from among a set of."

43 Translation Hint

Page 304, Line 20

The expression ཐལ་ཆེ་བ་ functions here as a free-floating frozen adverb.

44 The Adverbial Phrase Marker ཚད་ལ་

Page 305, Line 12

As a noun, ཚད་ means something like "measure" or "a certain amount" of something. By extension, the expression ཚད་ལ་ functions as a free-floating adverbial phrase marker qualifying the statements of the sentence. Hence, here, as part of a larger two-part reason clause (see རིགས་ལམ་ note 18) of a syllogism (see རིགས་ལམ་ note 16), the phrase གཞི་གྲུབ་ཚད་ལ་ ("to the extent [to which something is] an established base") restricts the scope of the reason clause.

The Use of སྒྲ་ to Indicate a Term Marked for Discussion

45

Page 305, Line 13

Previously, both the standard quote markers ཞེས་, ཅེས་, etc. (see ཤེར་སྙིང་རྣམ་བཤད་ note 5), and thought marker སྙམ་ (see ཤེར་སྙིང་རྣམ་བཤད་ note 28) have been seen. Here, a third type of quotation marker—indicating less a quotation and more a highlighted term—is seen: སྒྲ་.

In the passage encountered here, the second part of the reason clause opens with the phrase དེའི་ཚིག་ཟུར་གྱི་ཙམ་སྒྲས་, with the final word, སྒྲ་, marked in the instrumental case. The syllable pair ཙམ་སྒྲས་ could thus be literally translated as "by means of the term 'merely'" and displays the manner in which སྒྲ་ functions to mark a term (typically a single syllable or word) for discussion. Hence, the phrase preceding it is simply an adjectival modifer: "that is an indirect expression (ཚིག་ཟུར་) of that." The key to understanding the meaning of this entire passage, however, is recognizing that the anaphoric pronoun དེ་ ("that"—see རིགས་ལམ་ notes 10–14) resolves to the first half of the syllogism—the thesis—which in this case is the statement predicating a property to a subject: གཞི་གྲུབ་ན་རང་གི་མཚན་ཉིད་ཀྱིས་མ་གྲུབ་པས་ཁྱབ་པར་ཁས་ལེན་ ("[Prasāṅgikas] assert that if [something] is an established base, then [it] is necessarily not established by way of its own character").

ཡང་ as a Conjunctive and Disjunctive Particle

46

Page 306, Line 23

Wilson (673) notes that the syllable ཡང་ can be used to indicate conjunction or disjunction between nouns, pronouns, adjectives, or verbs. Here is such an instance, where the non-case use of a ལ་ (see བློ་རིག་ note 14) would be ambiguous and the use of the verbal conjunctive ཞིང་, ཅིང་, etc., would produce too forceful a break within the noun phrase since ཡུལ་དེ་ལ་འཁྲུལ་ཡང་ཡུལ་དེ་རྟོགས་པ་—"being mistaken with regard to that object, and yet realizing that object"—is the subject of the verb འགལ་.

WHAT TO REMEMBER

The syllable ཡང་ can be used to indicate conjunction or disjunction between nouns, pronouns, adjectives, or verbs where other delimiters would be inappropriate.

47

Translation Hint

Page 310, Line 1

This is another instance of a simple conjunction (see ལམ་གཙོ་རྣམ་གསུམ་ note 6 and ཤེར་སྙིང་རྣམ་བཤད་ note 11).

TRANSLATION OF KÖNCHOK JIKMÉ WANGPO'S *PRECIOUS GARLAND: A PRESENTATION OF TENETS*

The stream [that arises from] the snowy mountain of [the Buddha's] two
 marvelous collections [of merit and wisdom], being melted by the
 warmth of his compassion,
Gathering in a circle on the earth of the spontaneous truth body, sent forth
 the rivers of the four schools of tenets;
The successive waves of his enlightened activities extending into space,
 made the childlike tīrthikas feel fear.
O Chief of Subduers—the great Lake Manasarowar [that is the source of
 the great rivers of India and], the harbor of ten million nāga sons of the
 Conqueror—[you] are victorious!

Homage to the Regent of the Conqueror, the undaunted protector
 [Maitreya],
To the wisdom of the conquerors collected into one, Mañjughoṣa,
To the feet of Nāgārjuna and Asaṅga who were prophesied by the
 Conqueror,
And to the second conqueror [Tsongkhapa], and his spiritual sons [Gyel-
 tsap and Kedrup].

If anyone understands [this presentation of tenets], then [they] will see
 all the features of the outsider [i.e., non-Buddhist] and insider [i.e.,
 Buddhist] teachings,
And adhere to the mode of conduct of the best of propounders among
 countless scholars.
Being a white banner, renowned as amazing, raised by an unbiased being—
What wise person would cast aside the effort of differentiating the
 principles of our own and others' tenets?

Therefore, having condensed all the good explanations of excellent
[beings],
In order to provide for those whose lot is similar to mine,
I will set forth this condensed presentation of tenets.
Those who seek clear understanding should listen respectfully.

Moreover, persons who are not looking for poetry, respect, and material goods of this life but who seek liberation from the depths of their hearts must work at the means of understanding the correct view of selflessness. For, no matter how much you have internalized love, compassion, and the altruistic aspiration to enlightenment, if you are without the profound view [of selflessness], you are unable to remove the root of suffering.

The foremost venerable great Tsongkhapa says [in his *Three Principal Aspects of the Path*]:

If one does not have the wisdom that realizes the mode of subsistence,
Then, although one has cultivated renunciation and bodhicitta,
Since [one] is not able to cut the root of mundane existence,
For that purpose, strive at the method of realizing dependent arising!

Hence, in order to abandon any basis for a mistaken view, and to delineate the gradation of coarse and subtle selflessnesses, I will give a brief explanation of our own and others' presentations of tenets.

This explanation has two parts: a general teaching and a detailed explanation.

First [the general teaching]: the designation "tenets" is not my own fabrication because it was mentioned in Buddha's scriptures. The *Descent into Laṅka Sūtra* states:

My doctrine has two modes, advice and tenets.
To children I speak advice, and to yogis, tenets.

Furthermore, if persons are divided, there are two [types of persons]: those whose minds have not been affected by tenets and those whose minds have been affected by tenets.

The first [those whose minds have not been affected by tenets] are [those who], without having been trained in a textual system, seek only the pleasures of this life with an innate awareness that neither investigates, nor analyzes, nor studies. The second [those whose minds have been affected by tenets] have been trained in some textual system. [They] propound a way of establishing—from their own perspective—a presentation of the three: bases, paths, and fruits, [which is established through their own understanding though not necessarily true in fact] through citing scripture and reasoning.

Hence, the etymology of tenet (*grub mtha'*) [is]—as [Dharmamitra's] *Clear Words, An Explanatory Commentary [on (Maitreya's) "Ornament for Clear Realization"]* states:

> "Tenet" ("established conclusion") [signifies] one's own assertion *established* (*grub*) within being demonstrated by reasoning and scripture. Because one will not pass beyond this assertion, it is a *conclusion* (*mtha'*).

Hence, a tenet [lit. "established conclusion"] is that very meaning of a thesis which is decided upon and established in dependence upon either scripture and/or reasoning and which [from the perspective of one's own mind] will not be forsaken for something else.

When those [schools of tenets] are divided, [there are] two [types]: outsider [non-Buddhist] and insider [Buddhist schools]. There is a difference between mere outsiders and insiders because persons who go for refuge to the Three Jewels from the depths of their hearts are insiders and persons who go for refuge from the depths of their hearts to a god of the transient world without turning their minds toward the Three Jewels are outsiders.

Also, there are distinguishing features between proponents of insider and outsider tenets because [they] can be differentiated from three perspectives of teacher, teaching, and view. That is [the case,] moreover, because regarding our own [Buddhist] schools, there are the three distinguishing features of:

(1) a teacher—one who has extinguished all faults and [whose] good qualities have been completed.
(2) teachings that do not endanger any sentient being.
(3) asserting a view empty of [asserting] a self that is permanent, unitary, and independent.

and [because] the others' schools' [views] are the opposite of these, possessing the three distinguishing features of:

(1) Their teachers have faults and have not completed their good qualities.
(2) They have teachings that harm and endanger sentient beings.
(3) They assert a view establishing a permanent, unitary, independent self.

Second ["detailed explanation"]: [We] abbreviate the presentation of outsider's tenets [with this] explanation; and [we] can differentiate the presentation of our own tenets just a little [with this] explanation.

First, the internal divisions of proponents of [outsider] tenets. The definition of a proponent of outsiders' tenets is: a person who does not go for refuge to the Three Jewels and asserts that there is a [perfect] teacher other than [the Three Jewels]. If divided, there are an infinite number. In brief, however, they are renowned as five—[that is] the five [Indian] schools of philosophers: the followers of Viṣṇu [Vaiṣṇava], the followers of Īśvara (Śiva) [Aiśvara], the followers of the Jina (the "Conqueror" Mahāvīra) [Jaina], the followers of Kapila [Sāṃkhya], and the followers of Bṛhaspati [Cārvāka]. They are also set forth as the six fundamental schools [of Indian philosophy]: Vaiśeṣika, Naiyāyika, Sāṃkhya, Mīmāṃsaka, Nirgrantha [Jaina], and Lokāyata [a.k.a. Cārvāka]. The first five of these [have] views of eternalism, and the last holds a view of nihilism.

[VAIŚEṢIKA AND NAIYĀYIKA]

Moreover, the Vaiśeṣikas and the Naiyāyikas are followers of the sage Kaṇāda and the Brahmin Akṣapāda [a.k.a. Gautama], respectively. Although these two [schools] have slightly different distinguishing features in their innermost assertions, there is no difference in their general tenets.

Moreover, both the Vaiśeṣikas and the Naiyāyikas assert that all objects of knowledge are included among six categories [of existents]. [They] assert ablutions, initiations, fasting, sacrifice, burnt offerings, and so forth, as the paths to liberation. At that time, [when one] has meditatively cultivated yoga in accordance with the quintessential instructions of a guru, then [yogis] having known a self that is independent and so on as factually other (*don gzhan*) than those sense faculties etc., thereby see reality and fully understand the nature of the six categories [of existents]. [At that time, they] know the self to be an all-pervasive nature but lacking activity. [They] are not caused to accumulate any virtuous (*chos*) or nonvirtuous karma. [They] do not accumulate any new karma, and by extinguishing the old ones, the self separates from the repeatedly assumed body, sense powers, awarenesses, pleasures and pains, desires and hatreds, and so forth, and does not assume a new body with sense faculties, and thereby, like a fire that has consumed its fuel, the continuum of births is severed. When the self has [thus] been isolated [without any of its qualities—desire, hatred, pleasure, pain, and so forth—], this is said to be the attainment of liberation.

[Sāṃkhya]

The Sāṃkhyas ("Enumerators") are followers of the sage Kapila. They assert that all objects of knowledge are definitely enumerated in twenty-five [categories]. The twenty-five [categories] are the self (*puruṣa*), principal [or fundamental nature] (*prakṛti*), the great one [or intellect] (*mahat*), I-principle (*ahaṃkāra*), five [subtle objects arisen from] just that [I-principle] (*tanmātra*), eleven faculties (*indriya*), and five elements (*bhūta*).

The five [subtle objects arisen from] just that [I-principle] are [visible] forms, sounds, odors, tastes, and tangible objects. The eleven faculties are the five mental faculties, the five action faculties, and mental sense-power. The five mental faculties are those of the eye, ear, nose, tongue, and skin. The five action faculties are speech, arms, legs, anus, and genitalia. The five elements are earth, water, fire, wind, and space.

From among these twenty-five categories, the person [is asserted to be] consciousness, while the remaining twenty-four—because of being collections and aggregations [of particles]—are asserted to be matter. The person and the principal [are asserted to be] ultimate truths, and the others are asserted to be conventional truths. Furthermore, there are four possibilities [for these twenty-five categories]: that which is a cause but not an effect, that which is both a cause and an effect, that which is an effect but not a cause, and that which is neither a cause nor an effect. The first [being a cause but not an effect] is the general principle [i.e., fundamental nature]. The second [being both causes and effects] is the seven: intellect, the I-principle, and the five subtle objects. The third [being effects but not causes] are the remaining sixteen [i.e., the eleven faculties and the five elements]. The fourth [being neither a cause nor an effect] is the person. Moreover, in Īśvarakṛṣṇa's tantra [the *Sāṃkhya-kārikās*, stanza 3, it states]:

> The fundamental progenerative nature (*mūla-prakṛti*) is not something created.
> The seven—the "great one" and so forth—are progenerative natures and
> something created.
> The sixteen are something created.
> The person (*puruṣa*) is not a progenerative nature nor something created.

It is explained like that.

Furthermore, "fundamental nature," "general [principal]," and "principal" are equivalent. [The fundamental nature] is asserted to be an object of knowledge that possesses six distinguishing characteristics. Person, self, consciousness, and basic mind are equivalent and synonymous.

The mode of production of the remaining twenty-three is: at any time when the desire of the person to enjoy objects is produced, the fundamental nature causes the emanation of manifestions, such as sounds and so forth. The great one arises from the principal [i.e., the fundamental nature]. "Intellect" and "great one" are equivalent and synonymous. The intellect is asserted to be like a two-sided mirror in which appear [the reflections of] objects from the outside and the reflection of the person from the inside. From that [intellect] the I-principle is produced, and if the I-principle is divided, there are three [divisions]: the activity-dominated I-principle, the lightness-dominated I-principle, and the darkness-dominated I-principle. From the first [the activity-dominated I-principle] the five subtle objects are produced, and from these, the five elements are produced. From the second [the lightness-dominated I-principle] the eleven faculties are produced. The third [the darkness-dominated I-principle] is said to be the motivator of both of the other I-principles.

Moreover, [the Sāṃkhyas] assert that [one] mistakes the [fundamental] progenerative nature—which is like a blind man with good legs—and the person—which is like a cripple with good eyesight—to be one, and hence [one] cycles in cyclic existence through the force of that ignorance of the manner in which creations are created by the fundamental progenerative nature. When, in dependence upon hearing the quintessential instructions pointed out by a guru, one fully generates definite knowledge that these creations are no more than merely the emanations of the fundamental nature, then one gradually separates from the craving for objects. At that time, through relying on the concentrations, the clairvoyance of the divine eye is generated. The fundamental nature, when it is seen by this clairvoyant consciousness, is flushed with shame like another's wife [that is, like a mistress when seen by the wife]; it gathers its creations [and disappears]. The fundamental nature then dwells alone [separate from the self] with the result that, from the perspective of the yogi, all appearances of conventional phenomena disappear. The person then abides without enjoying objects and without action; at that time, liberation is attained. So it is asserted.

[Mīmāṃsaka]

The Mīmāṃsakas ["Analyzers" or "Ritualists"] are the followers of Jaimini. Having made the exaggeration that whatever appears in the Vedas is self-produced [because the Vedas were not made by anyone] and that that [which is expressed in the *Vedas*] is reality (*tattva*), [they] assert that only sacrifices and so forth [which are revealed in the Vedas] [lead one to] attain a state of high [rebirth in the future]. However, this [state of higher rebirth] is asserted to be merely liberation from bad transmigrations. [They assert] moreover, [that] there is no liberation that is a thorough extinguishing of suffering because defilements subsist in the nature of the mind [and, therefore, to eliminate defilements would be to eliminate the mind] and also because there is no omniscience since objects of knowledge are limitless. Hence, [the Mīmāṃsakas] also propound that there is no true speech [of a person; i.e., only the Vedas are true].

[Nirgrantha]

The Nirgranthas [Jainas] are followers of the Jina Ṛṣabha. They assert that all objects of knowledge are included in nine categories: life, contamination, restraint, wearing down, bond, action, ethical transgression, merit, and liberation.

Here, although life is the self, [it] exists, accordingly, as exactly the same size as a person's body. Its nature is such that, although its entity is permanent, its states are impermanent. Contamination is actions that are virtuous and nonvirtuous because through the force of those [actions one] is caused to fall into cyclic existence. Restraint is that which causes contaminations to cease because [on account of it] actions are not newly accumulated. Wearing down is bringing about the exhaustion of previously accumulated actions [i.e., karmic matter] by way of asceticism, such as not drinking liquids, tormenting the body, and so forth. A bond is a wrong view. Actions are of four types: [the determiners in general of] what will be experienced in a later life, of name, of lineage, and of life span. Ethical transgression is nonvirtue. Merit is virtue.

Regarding liberation: in dependence upon engaging in deeds of ascetic practices, such as going naked, not speaking, relying on the five fires [fires in front, back, on both sides, and the sun above], and so forth, all previously committed actions [i.e., karma] are consumed, and since actions are not newly accumulated, there exists a place that is at the top of all worlds, called Consummation of the Worlds, like a white umbrella held upside down, white like yogurt or a white water lily, the size of four million five hundred thousand *yojana*s, and since this place has life, it is a thing. Because it is free from cyclic existence, it is also a nonthing; it is to there [that one] goes. This place is called liberation.

As was said by the Jina Ṛṣabha:

> The Jinas explain that liberation
> Is like the shape of a white umbrella held [upside down]
> [With] the color of snow, Chinese incense, a [lily] flower,
> Cow's yogurt, frost, and pearl.

Such statements occur [in their writings].

[LOKĀYATA]

Regarding the Lokāyatas [or Cārvākas ("Hedonists")]: [they say that] one does not come to this [life] from a previous life because no one whosoever perceives a "previous life." From an adventitious body, a mind is adventitiously established, just as light is adventitiously established from the adventitious existence of a lamp. Also, one does not go to a future life from this life because, since body and mind are one substantial entity, when the body perishes, the mind also perishes. For example, when a stone is destroyed, likewise a picture on the stone is destroyed. Therefore, because of this, [they] assert that all objects of comprehension [i.e., all existents] are necessarily specifically characterized phenomena, and [they assert] that [all] valid cognitions are necessarily only direct valid cognitions because they do not accept [the existence of] generally characterized phenomena and inferential valid cognitions. Some distinctive Lokāyatas assert that all phenomena arise causelessly and from their own nature. [They] say:

> The rising of the sun, the running downward of a river,
> The roundness of a pea, the sharpness of the point of a thorn,
> The spot of a peacock [feather], and so forth—all phenomena
> Arise from their own nature, without being made by anyone whatsoever.

[Hence, I] declare:

> Understanding well—without exception—the nature
> Of outsiders' tenets, which are fords
> To the extremes of bad views, bringing about the abandonment [of those]
> [Is] the ladder that leads to the city of liberation.

[This is] a stanza between sections.

SECOND: [BUDDHIST TENETS]

If the presentation of our own sets of tenets are slightly differentiated, then with regard to their explanation there are two: a general teaching and an explanation of the particulars.

First: [General Exposition of Buddhist Tenets]

The unequaled teacher, this very King of the Śākyas, at the beginning, generated an attitude [of dedication] toward [attaining] highest enlightenment. In the middle, [he] amassed the collections [of merit and wisdom] for three countless eons. In the end, in the vicinity of Vajrāsana [Bodhgaya], he became directly and completely enlightened, and at Vārāṇasī he turned the wheel of doctrine of the four [noble truths] for the five good ascetics [who had previously practiced asceticism with him].

Then, speaking on Vulture Peak, he turned the wheel of doctrine of characterlessness. Then, at Vaiśālī etc., he extensively turned the wheel of doctrine of good differentiation. Having outshone all the inferior proponents [of tenets], such as the six teachers of the heretics, the precious teachings of the Buddha—a source of help and happiness—flourished and were disseminated widely. After that, in dependence upon the individual explanations of the thought of the three wheels by commentators, the four schools of tenets arose. From among these, the two schools that propound [truly existent external] objects [having been followers of] the first wheel, the Niḥsvabhāvavādins ("Proponents of Non-Entityness") [having been followers of] the middle wheel, and the Yogācārins ("Yogic Practitioners") having been followers of the final wheel, [all] commit to [their] presentations of the three—basis, paths, and fruits.

As for proponents of tenets who are followers of our teacher, [they] are definitively enumerated as the four—that is, the two [lower schools of] Vaibhāṣika and Sautrāntika, and the two [higher schools of] Madhyamaka and Cittamātra—because it is said that [there is no] fifth system of tenets apart from these [four] and that there is no fourth vehicle apart from the three vehicles [Śrāvaka, Pratyekabuddha, and Bodhisattva vehicles]. Just as Vajragarbha's *Commentary* [*on the Condensation of the Hevajra Tantra*] says:

> For Buddhists, [the existence of] a fourth [vehicle] and
> a fifth [school of tenets] is not [part of] the Subduer's thought.

When these [other Buddhist] schools of ours—[those] on or below [the level of] the Svātantrika School—are assessed by the Prāsaṅgika School, they are all found to fall to both extremes of permanence and annihilation, although each asserts their own system as a middle way because they consider [themselves] to assert a middle that is free from the two extremes of permanence and nihilism. Moreover, the four [groups of] proponents of tenets each have a different way of abandoning the extremes of permanence and nihilism. The Vaibhāṣikas [say that they] abandon the extreme of permanence because [they assert that] when an effect is produced, its cause ceases, and [they] say that they abandon the extreme of nihilism because [they assert that] an effect arises after the termination of a cause.

The Sautrāntikas assert that because [they] posit compounded phenomena as an uninterrupted continua [they] abandon the extreme of nihilism, and because [they posit that compounded phenomena] disintegrate from moment to moment that [they] are free from the extreme of permanence. The Cittamātrins propound that they abandon the extreme of permanence by [asserting that] imputational natures are not truly established and yet abandon the extreme of nihilism by [asserting that] other-powered natures are truly established.

The Mādhyamikas assert that they are free from the extreme of nihilism because [they assert that] all phenomena are conventionally existent and that [they] are free from the extreme of permanence because [they assert that all phenomena] are ultimately nonexistent. Although the tenets of each of the lower schools that are not held in common [with the higher schools] are refuted by each of the higher schools of tenets, since the understanding of each of the lower views appears to be an excellent method of understanding each of the higher views, having held a higher [tenet system] as superior, you should not despise the lower [tenets].

Thus, [we] posit that a person who asserts the four seals [that] designate a view as [being] the word [of the Buddha], as the definition of a proponent of Buddhist—"insider"—tenets. The four seals are that

(1) All compounded phenomena [are] impermanent,
(2) All contaminated things [are of the nature of] suffering,
(3) All phenomena [are] selfless, [and]
(4) Nirvāṇa [is] peace.

If [a hypothetical objector] says, "Since the Vatsīputrīyas [a subschool of the Vaibhāṣika School] assert a self of persons, [by this definition, they] would not be proponents of Buddhist tenets," [then we respond,] there is no fault [with our definition] because although the self that is asserted by them is a self-sufficient substantially existent self, the selflessness [asserted] within the four seals refers to the selflessness that is an emptiness of a permanent, unitary, independent self, and that [selflessness] is also asserted by the five Saṃmitīya schools [—the Vātsīputrīyas being one of those five].

SECOND: [THE EXPLANATIONS IN PARTICULAR]

Regarding the explanations in particular, there are the four tenet systems of the Vaibhāṣikas ("Proponents of the *Great Exposition* School"), the Sautrāntikas ("Sūtra School"), the Cittamātrins ("Mind-Only School"), and the Niḥsvabhāvavādins ("Proponents of Non-Entityness").

[FIRST: THE VAIBHĀṢIKAS]

The first [—the presentation of the tenets of the Vaibhāṣikas—has] four [parts]: definition, divisions, etymology, and manner of assertion [of tenets]. Regarding the first, the definition of a Vaibhāṣika is that person who propounds the tenets of the Hīnayāna ("Lesser Vehicle") who does not accept self-cognizing consciousness and who does assert external objects as being truly established. Second ["divisions"]: if they are divided, there are three: the Kaśmirī Vaibhāṣikas, the Aparāntakas, and the Magadha Vaibhāṣikas. The third ["etymology"]: Regarding the master Vasumitra, there is a reason for calling someone [like him] a Vaibhāṣika because he propounds tenets having been a follower of the *Great Ocean of Detailed Explanations* (*Mahāsagaravibhāṣa*) or [alternately,] because he propounds that the three times [i.e., objects in the past, present, and future] are particulars [or instances] of substantial entities, hence [he] is called a Vaibhāṣika. The fourth—manner of assertion [of tenets]—[has three parts]: manner of asserting the basis, manner of asserting the path, and manner of asserting the fruits. The first [has] two [parts]: the manner of asserting objects and the manner of asserting the object-possessors [i.e., subjects].

Regarding the first [assertions regarding objects], this system asserts that all objects of knowledge are included within five [categories of] basic objects (*gzhi*)—objects that are appearing forms, objects that are main minds, objects that are accompanying mental factors, objects that are compositional factors not associated [with either minds or mental factors], and uncompounded objects. These five objects, moreover, are asserted to be "things" [because] the definition of a thing [is] that which is able to perform a function. Existent, object of knowledge, and thing are mutually inclusive [categories]. Uncompounded phenomena [are asserted to be] permanent things; forms, consciousnesses, and nonassociated compositional factors are asserted to be impermanent things. [All] things are necessarily substantially established, but [they] are not necessarily substantially existent because [they] assert [that] ultimate truth and being substantially existent are mutually inclusive and [that] conventional truth and being imputedly existents are mutually inclusive. If that [topic] is divided, [there is] the division into the two truths, the division into the contaminated and the uncontaminated, and teachings on other ancillary topics.

[First: The Two Truths]

Regarding the first [the division into the two truths], the definition of a conventional truth is: that which is observed as a phenomenon with respect to which an awareness apprehending it is suitable to be cancelled when [that object] is broken up or separated by a mind into individual parts. Illustrations are, for instance, a clay pot and a rosary because, when a clay pot has been broken with a hammer, the awareness apprehending [that object] as a clay pot is cancelled, and because when [a rosary] is separated into individual beads, the awareness that apprehends [that object] as a rosary is cancelled. The definition of an ultimate truth is: that which is observed as a phenomenon with respect to which an awareness apprehending it is not suitable to be cancelled when [that object] is broken up or separated by a mind into individual parts. Illustrations are, for instance, directionally (i.e., spatially) partless particles, temporarily partless moments of consciousness, and noncompounded space because, as [Vasubandhu's] *Treasury [of Manifest Knowledge* (VI.4)] says:

That which [is such that] when broken or mentally separated
into other [parts], an awareness of it no longer operates,
Like a pot or water, conventionally
Exists; [all] others [are] ultimately existent.

Therefore, it is asserted that conventional truths are not ultimately established, although they are truly established, because this system asserts that [all] things are necessarily truly established.

[Second: The Contaminated and the Uncontaminated]

Regarding the second [the division into contaminated and uncontaminated], the definition of a contaminated object is: a phenomenon with respect to which contaminations are amenable to increase from the point of view of either [being] an object of observation or [being something] possessing concomitance [with the afflictions]. Illustrations are, for instance, the five aggregates. The definition of an uncontaminated object is: a phenomenon with respect to which contaminations are not amenable to increase from the viewpoint of either [being] an object of observation or [being something] possessing concomitance [with the afflictions]. Illustrations are, for instance, true paths and noncompounded [phenomena] because, as [Vasubandhu's] *Treasury* [*of Manifest Knowledge*] says, "all compounded phenomena, except for [true] paths, are contaminated" and "the uncontaminated [consists of] true paths and the three noncompounded [phenomena]."

All contaminated objects are necessarily objects to be abandoned because [even] the two [paths of] accumulation and preparation are to be abandoned. The path of seeing is only uncontaminated, while the path of meditation and path of no more learning each have both [instances of] contaminated and uncontaminated paths. If [something] is an ārya's path, [it] is necessarily uncontaminated, although the paths in the continuum of an ārya are not necessarily uncontaminated because a path that has aspects of [both] peacefulness [and] coarseness in the continuum of one on the path of meditation is contaminated.

[Third: Other Ancillary Topics]

Third—regarding teachings on other ancillary topics—the three times [i.e., objects in the past, present, and future] are asserted to be substantial entities because the Vaibhāṣikas assert that a pot exists even at the time of the past of a pot and that a pot exists even at the time of the future of a pot.

Although they assert that both negative [phenomena] and positive [phenomena] exist, they do not accept [the existence of] nonaffirming negatives because they assert that if [something] is a negative phenomenon, it is necessarily an affirming negative.

The Kaśmirī Vaibhāṣikas—being in accord with the Sautrāntikas—assert the continuum of consciousness as the basis upon which actions (*karma; las*) are connected with their effects, and all [other] Vaibhāṣikas except for those [i.e., the Kaśmirī Vaibhāṣikas] assert something that is a nonassociated compositional factor—said to be an "obtainer" (*prāpti; thob pa*) and "non-waster" (**avipraṇāśa, chud mi zad ba*) like a seal that guarantees a loan—as the basis upon which actions are connected with their effects. However, in the system of both Prāsaṅgika [Madhyamaka] and this one, it is asserted that actions of body and speech are endowed with form. [Hence,] although [all] compounded phenomena are necessarily impermanent, [they] do not necessarily disintegrate moment by moment because [the Vaibhāṣikas] assert that [these phenomena] engage in the activity of duration following the completion of production and in the activity of disintegration following that.

[Second: Assertions Regarding Object-Possessors (i.e., Subjects)]

The second—the manner of asserting the object-possessors [i.e., subjects]—[has] three [parts]: persons, consciousnesses, and sounds of expression. Regarding the first [i.e., persons], the mere collection of the five aggregates [that are its] basis of imputation [is] an illustration of a person. Some of the Saṃmitīyas (*mang pos bkur ba*) [assert that] all five aggregates [are] an illustration of a person, [while] the Āvantakas assert the mind alone as an illustration of a person.

Regarding the second [consciousnesses], from among the two [parts]—valid cognition and invalid consciousnesses—the first has two [parts]: perceptual valid cognition and inferential valid cognition. With regard to the first [i.e., perceptual valid cognitions], there are three [kinds]: sense perceptions, mental perceptions, and yogic perceptions; however, [they] do not assert self-cognizing perception. [They assert that] a sense perceptual valid cognition is not necessarily a consciousness because a physical eye sense is a common locus of the three—being matter [not consciousness], being a perception, and being a valid cognition. [They] assert that a sense consciousness comprehends its object nakedly, without [taking on] the aspect [of that object], and that even a physical eye sense-power which is the basis [of an eye consciousness] perceives form [because they] say that if only the consciousness sees, then even forms that are obstructed by [things] such as walls and so forth would be seen, and [they] assert a mind and its mental factors to be different substantial entities.

Regarding the third [sounds of expression], in general, when mere sounds are divided, there are two [types]: sounds [arisen from elements] conjoined [with consciousness] and sounds [arisen from elements] not conjoined [with consciousness]. The first [is], for instance, sound that could serve as the speech of a person. The second [is], for instance, the sound of water. Each of these—conjoined or not conjoined [with consciousness]—moreover, has two [divisions] each—indicating or not indicating [something] to sentient beings. The three—sound that indicates [something] to sentient beings, sound [that is] spoken revelation, and expressive sound—are mutually inclusive; the three—sound that does not indicate [something] to sentient beings, sound that is not spoken revelation, and nonexpressive sound—are mutually inclusive. Since both the word [of the Buddha] and the treatises (*śāstra*), moreover, are asserted to be entities that are collections of words, phonemes, letters, term generalities, [and] nonassociated compositional factors, [I] wonder, "In this system, are matter and nonassociated compositional factors really mutually exclusive?"

Second—an explanation of the presentation of paths—[has three parts]: explanations of the objects of observation of the paths, objects to be abandoned on the paths, and the nature of the paths. The first—[objects of observation of the paths]—are the sixteen attributes of the four truths, impermanence, and so forth, although [the Vaibhāṣikas] assert subtle selflessness and subtle selflessness of persons to be mutually inclusive and [yet] accept that a person's emptiness of being substantially existent in the sense of being self-sufficient as the subtle selflessness of persons. From among the eighteen schools [of the Vaibhāṣikas], the five Saṃmitīya schools do not assert the emptiness of being substantially existent in the sense of being self-sufficient as the subtle selflessness of persons because they assert that a substantially existent self in the sense of being self-sufficient exists. [They] do not assert a presentation of coarse and subtle selflessnesses of phenomena because they hold that if [something] is an established base, then [it] neccessarily is a self of phenomena.

With regard to the second—objects to be abandoned on the paths—from among the two [divisions], afflicted and nonafflicted ignorance, the first (i.e., afflicted ignorance) is primarily a hindrance to the attainment of liberation. Illustrations [are,] for instance, the conception of a self of persons and the three poisons that arise through the force of that together with their seeds. The second (i.e., nonafflicted ignorance) is the principal hindrance to the attainment of omniscience. Illustrations [are,] for instance, the four causes of ignorance, such as the nonafflictive obstruction that is being ignorant of the profound and subtle qualities of a tathāgata. With regard to the obstructions, from among those two [i.e., obstructions to liberation and obstructions to omniscience], [the Vaibhāṣikas] do not accept the conventional designation "obstructions to omniscience," [preferring "nonafflictive ignorance"].

With regard to the third—the nature of the paths—furthermore, although [they] assert a presentation of the five paths—the path of accumulation, the path of preparation, the path of seeing, the path of meditation, and the path of no more learning—for the three vehicles, they do not accept the exalted wisdoms of the ten [bodhisattva] grounds. They assert that the first fifteen moments of the sixteen moments of forbearance and knowledge [constitute] the path of seeing, and [they assert] that the sixteenth moment—the subsequent knowledge of the path—is [the first moment of] the path of meditation and that [these moments] are generated solely sequentially, like a goat going across a bridge. True paths are not necessarily consciousnesses because [the Vaibhāṣikas] assert the five uncontaminated aggregates as true paths.

With regard to the third—the presentation of the fruits—those with the Śrāvaka lineage, having familiarized [themselves] with the sixteen attributes [of the four noble truths], impermanence, and so forth, over the course of three lifetimes or more, in the end, having relied on the vajra-like samādhi of the śrāvaka's path of meditation, [they] abandon the afflictive obstructions by means of the method of the cessation of [their] obtaining [causes, i.e., the potentialities that cause one to have those afflictive emotions]; then [they] manifest the fruit of an arhat.

Rhinoceros-like pratyekabuddhas—having trained on the great path of accumulation and below in the view that realizes that the person is empty of substantial existence in the sense of being self-sufficient, in conjunction with [amassing] a collection of merit for one hundred great eons and so forth—then, in a single [meditative] session, [they] actualize [the stages] from the heat level of the path of preparation up to [and including] the path of no more learning. Since it is possible for Hīnayāna arhats to become stream-enterers having degenerated from their abandonments and realizations, [Vaibhāṣikas] assert [the existence of some] religious practitioners (*chos can*) and others who [can] degenerate. Regarding śrāvakas, although [the Vaibhāṣikas] enumerate a presentation of the twenty types of [members of] the Saṅgha and eight approachers and abiders, [they] do not assert simultaneity [of the abandonment of the afflictions]. Thus, [they] assert that whosoever is [one of] the eight approachers and abiders is necessarily an ārya.

Bodhisattvas complete their collections [of merit and wisdom] over three [periods of] countless great eons in the context of abiding on the path of accumulation, and from this, [they] establish the causes of the excellent marks [of a buddha] over one hundred eons, and then, in their final lifetime, subdue the demon of the devaputras at twilight in front of the bodhi tree. At midnight, when in meditative equipoise, having actualized the three—the path of preparation, path of seeing, and path of meditation—at just the break of dawn, [they] actualize the path of no more learning [and become a buddha]. Therefore, [they] assert [that] the activities of subduing the demon at twilight and [those] prior [to that were] in the context of being an ordinary being and [that] the three paths of preparation, seeing, and meditation of a bodhisattva are necessarily only meditative equipoises. Hence, [they] assert the first nine of the twelve acts [of a buddha to be deeds of] a bodhisattva, and the last three to be the deeds of a buddha. [The Vaibhāṣikas] assert that a wheel of Dharma is necessarily a path of seeing and that a verbal wheel of Dharma is necessarily a wheel of Dharma of the four [noble] truths. [They] assert that the seven sets [of treatises] of Abhidharma are words that were spoken by the Buddha and [that] those words are necessarily literal. [Other] than the eighty thousand heaps of doctrine, [they] do not assert a presentation of eighty-four thousand heaps of doctrine because, as [Vasubandhu's] *Treasury* [*of Abhidharma*] says:

The eighty thousand bundles of doctrine
Whatsoever, [are] those which were spoken by the Subduer.

The abode in which bodhisattvas in their final existence actualize enlightenment is definitely just the desire realm; therefore, [the Vaibhāṣikas] do not assert a presentation of a Heavily Adorned Akaniṣṭha [Heaven] (*akaniṣṭha-ghanavyūha*) or an enjoyment body (*sambhogakāya*), and not only that but [they] also do not assert omniscience. [All] arhats of the three vehicles necessarily [attain a nirvāṇa] with remainder because [they] assert that at the time of [attaining] nirvāṇa without remainder there is a severing of the continuum of consciousness, like the death of a flame. Hence, they assert the accomplishment of three final vehicles.

Someone arguing [that] "at the time of nirvāṇa, the Teacher [Buddha] merely withdrew a display of a physical body from the sight of certain trainees and, in actuality, did not pass from suffering" is confusing fish with turnips [i.e., two things that are long and white].

Although ārya buddhas have abandoned all sufferings without exception, it is not contradictory that true sufferings exist within their continua, because when the afflictions that take as their objects true sufferings are abandoned without exception, that is posited as the abandonment of true sufferings. As for the physical body [of a buddha] (*rupakāya*), [the Vaibhāṣikas] assert that because [it] is included in the same lifetime with the physical basis (i.e., body) of a bodhisattva previously on the path of preparation, that therefore [it] is not a Buddha Jewel (i.e., an object of refuge), although [it is] a buddha. The Buddha Jewel is asserted to be the exalted wisdom of extinction [and] nongeneration [of the obstructions] within the mental continuum of that [buddha]. Similarly, because ārya learners (i.e., those on the paths of seeing and meditation) are those who have contamination, [they] are not [part of] the Saṅgha Jewel, although they are [members of] the Saṅgha. Hence, the Saṅgha Jewel is asserted to be true paths in the mental continuum of [those ārya learners]. A Dharma Jewel also exists [as something] to be posited because the true paths and nirvāṇas within the continuum of buddhas and both śrāvakas and pratyekabuddhas are that [Dharma Jewel].

[Stanza between sections:]

With the golden vase of my mind's analysis
Taken from the ocean of the system of the Vaibhāṣikas,
May [you], o multitude of youths with clear minds, be delighted with
This festival of fresh ambrosia—[these] eloquent explanations!

[Second: The Sautrāntikas]

The second—the explanation of the presentation of the tenets of the Sautrāntikas—[has] four [parts]: definition, divisions, etymology, and manner of assertion [of tenets]. Regarding the first, the definition of a Sautrāntika [is] a person propounding Hīnayāna tenets who asserts both external objects and self-cognizing consciousness while conceiving [of them as] truely [existent]. The two [names] Sautrāntika and Dārṣṭāntika are mutually inclusive. Regarding the second [divisions], when divided, [there are] two: Sautrāntika Followers of Scripture and Sautrāntika Followers of Reasoning. The first [are], for instance, Sautrāntika Followers of Vasubandhu's *Treasury of Abhidharma*. The second [are], for instance, Sautrāntika Followers of [Dharmakīrti's] seven treatises on valid cognition. Regarding the third [etymologies], there is a reason for calling them Sautrāntikas and Dārṣṭāntikas; since they propound tenets having relied principally upon the sūtras of the Bhagavān without being followers of the [*Great*] *Detailed Exposition* (*Mahāvibhāṣā*), [they are called] Sautrāntikas, and since [they] teach all doctrines by way of examples (*dṛṣṭānta*), [they] are called Dārṣṭāntikas.

Regarding the fourth—the manner of asserting [tenets]—[there are] three [parts]: the manner of asserting the basis, the manner of asserting the path, and the manner of asserting the fruits. The first [has] two [parts]: [the manner of asserting] objects, and the manner of asserting subjects ("object-possessors"). Regarding the first, the definition of an object [is] that which is to be known by an awareness. The definition of an object of knowledge [is] that which is suitable to be an object of an awareness. Object, existent, object of knowledge, and established base are mutually inclusive. If that is divided, [then there are] the divisions into the two truths, the division into the two—specifically [characterized phenomena] and generally [characterized phenomena]—the division into the two—negative [phenomena] and positive [phenomena]—the division into the two—manifest [phenomena] and hidden [phenomena]—the division into the three times, [and] the division into the two—the one and the different.

Regarding the first [the division into the two truths], the definition of an ultimate truth [is] a phenomenon that is established as [capable] to withstand analysis through reasoning from the point of view of its own mode of subsistence without depending on imputation by terms or conceptual consciousnesses. [Functioning] thing, ultimate truth, specifically characterized [phenomenon], impermanent [thing], compounded [phenomenon], and truly established [phenomenon are] mutually inclusive. The definition of a truth-for-a-thoroughly-obscured [-awareness] (a.k.a. a "conventional truth") [is] a phenomenon that is established as merely being imputed by a conceptual consciousness. Nonfunctioning phenomenon, truth-for-a-thoroughly-obscured [-awareness], generally characterized phenomenon, permanent phenomenon, uncompounded phenomenon, and falsely established [phenomenon are] mutually inclusive. There are etymologies for the two truths. [For example,] the subject, uncompounded space, is called a truth-for-the-obscured because [it is] a truth from the perspective of a thoroughly obscured awareness. The thorough obscuration of this [refers to] a conceptual consciousness, [and it] is called thoroughly obscured since [it] is obstructed with respect to directly seeing specifically characterized [phenomena]. This, however, is merely an etymology, for if [something] is a truth from the perspective of a conceptual consciousness—that is, for an obscured awareness—[then it] is not necessarily a truth-for-an-obscured[-awareness] because a pot—an illustration of an ultimate truth—for instance, is also a truth from the perspective of a conceptual consciousness, a thoroughly obscured awareness. Although, for instance, a self of persons and "permanent sound" are truths from the perspective of a conceptual consciousness, a thoroughly obscured awareness, [they] are not established, even conventionally. The subject, a pot, is called an ultimate truth because [it] is a truth from the perspective of an ultimate awareness. The ultimate awareness of this is given as [an example of] a consciousness that is not mistaken with regard to its appearing object. This way of positing the two truths is the system of the Sautrāntika School Following Reasoning, but the Sautrāntika School Following Scripture asserts a presentation of the two truths that accords with [that of] the Vaibhāṣikas.

Regarding the second [the division into specifically and generally characterized phenomena], the definition of a specifically characterized [phenomenon is] a phenomenon that is ultimately able to perform a function. An illustration [is], for instance, a pot. The definition of a generally characterized [phenomenon is] a phenomenon that is ultimately unable to perform a function. An illustration [is], for instance, uncompounded space. Although imputed phenomena—such as generality and particular, same and different, mutually exclusive and related, etc.—are generally characterized [phenomena], [it] is necessary to distinguish the distinction that if [something] is [one of] these, then it is not necessarily a generally characterized [phenomenon].

Regarding the third [the division into negative and positive phenomena], the definition of a negative [phenomenon is] an object that is to be realized by means of the method of explicitly eliminating an object of negation. That and exclusion-of-another [are] mutually inclusive. If [this] is divided, [there are] two: nonaffirming negations and affirming negations. The definition of a nonaffirming negation [is] that which is to be realized as the mere elimination of its own object of negation by an awareness that explicitly realizes it. If [something is given] as an example, [there is,] for instance, a Brahmin's not drinking beer. The definition of an affirming negation [is] that which is implied—being either a positive [phenomenon] or the affirming negation of another phenomenon—in place of the negation of the object of negation by an awareness that explicitly realizes it. If [something is given] as an example, [there is,] for instance, fat Devadatta's not eating food during the daytime. The definition of a positive phenomenon [is] a phenomenon that is not [something] that is to be realized from the explicit elimination of its own negated element by the awareness explicitly realizing it. If [something is given] as an example, [there is,] for instance, a pot.

Regarding the fourth [the division into manifest and hidden phenomena], the definition of a manifest phenomenon [is] that which is to be explicitly realized by a perceptual valid cognition. That and [functioning] thing are mutually inclusive. The definition of a hidden phenomenon [is] that which is to be explicitly realized by an inferential valid cognition. That and object of knowledge are mutually inclusive.

Regarding the fifth [the division into the three times], the definition of the pastness [of an object is] that factor which disintegrated in the second moment after the time of its establishment—[being] something other than the [functioning] thing itself. The definition of the futureness [of an object is] that factor which has not been produced in whatsoever place [and] time through the force of the incompleteness of [its] conditions, although the cause of production—something other than the [functioning] thing itself—does exist. The definition of the present [of an object is] that which has been produced but has not ceased. Both the pastness and the futureness [of an object] are permanent [because they are mere absences and do not undergo momentary change], while present [object] and [functioning] thing are asserted to be mutually inclusive. [One] should understand, moreover, the distinctive features—that the pastness of a thing is established in reverse order after a thing and the futureness of a thing is established in reverse order prior to a thing.

Regarding the sixth [the division into one and different], the definition of [something that is] one [is] a phenomenon that is not diverse. If [something is given] as an example, [there is,] for instance, a pot. The definition of different [is] those phenomena that are diverse. An example is pillar and pot. Although different entities are necessarily different isolates, different isolates are not necessarily different entities, because although [the categories of] product and impermanent thing are the same entities (i.e., mutually inclusive), [they] are different isolates. Furthermore, although [the Sautrāntikas] are in accord with the Vaibhāṣikas—such as asserting directionally partless particles and [temporally] partless moments of consciousness—it is not that [they] are similar in all [respects], because once the Vaibhāṣikas assert [something] to be existent, [they must] assert [it] as substantially established, but the Sautrāntikas do not assert [existence to be] like that. Nonrevelatory forms, moreover, are asserted by both the Vaibhāṣikas and Prāsaṅgika [Mādhyamikas] to be fully qualified forms. However, the three—Sautrāntikas, Cittamātrins, and Svātantrika [Mādhyamikas]—assert that [they] are not fully qualified forms. Not only that, but the Vaibhāṣikas assert [some] causes and effects to be simultaneous, whereas the Sautrāntikas and higher [schools] do not assert [things] like this.

Regarding the second—assertions regarding object-possessors [i.e., subjects]—[there are] three [parts]: persons, consciousnesses, and terms of expression. Regarding the first, the [Sautrāntika] Followers of Scripture [assert] the continuum of the aggregates to be an illustration of a person, and the [Sautrāntika] Followers of Reasoning assert the mental consciousness to be an illustration of a person.

Regarding the second, [there are] two [parts]: valid cognition and nonvalid awareness. Valid cognition [has] two [types]: perceptual valid cognition and inferential valid cognition. Perceptual valid cognition has four [types]: sense perceptions, mental perceptions, self-cognizing perceptions, and yogic perceptions. A physical sense-power is not suitable as a valid cognition because [it] is empty of [the qualities of] being clear and knowing, and [it] is incapable of comprehending its object. Non-valid awareness [has] five [types]: subsequent cognition, wrong consciousness, doubt, correct assumption, and an awareness to which an object appears but is not ascertained. From among these, two—perception and awarenesses to which an object appears but is not ascertained—are necessarily free of conceptuality and unmistaken, while the three—inference, correctly assuming [consciousness], and doubt—are only conceptual consciousnesses. [They] assert that, at the time when a consciousness comprehends an object, [it] realizes [its object] in an aspectually mediated [manner] and that minds and mental factors are one substantial entity. Regarding the third [— terms of expression—] the definition of a term of expression [is] an object of hearing that causes the meaning that is its own object of expression to be understood. When [these] are divided from the perspective of [their] objects of expression, [there are] two [types]: terms that express types and terms that express collections. The first [is,] for instance, the term that expresses "form." The second [is,] for instance, the term that expresses "pot." Also, when that is divided from the perspective of [their] manner of expression, [there are] two [types]: terms that express qualities and terms that express the things qualified. The first [is,] for instance, the term that expresses "the impermanence of sound." The second [is,] for instance, the term that expresses "impermanent sound."

Regarding the second—the manner of asserting the path—from among [its] three [parts, the first], the object of observation of the path, is just these sixteen—impermanence and so forth—aspects of the four [noble] truths. [They] assert that the subtle selflessness [of phenomena] and the subtle selflessness of persons are mutually inclusive. [They also] assert that a person's being empty of a permanent, unitary, and independent self is the coarse selflessness of persons and a person's being empty of being substantially existent in the sense of being self-sufficient is the subtle selflessness of persons. As for [the second,] the object of abandonment of the path, except for some mere conventionalities—such as the concept of a self of persons, afflicted and non-afflicted ignorance, etc.—the [Sautrāntikas'] nonassertion of neither a conception of a self of phenomena, nor obstructions to omniscience, etc., is similar to [the assertions of] the Vaibhāṣikas. Regarding [the third,] the paths of the three vehicles, [they] give a presentation of the five paths and assert the sixteen moments of knowledge and forbearance as the path of seeing. However, since the appearing object of perception must be a specifically characterized phenomenon, [the Sautrāntikas] do not assert the subtle selflessness of persons as the object of the mode of apprehension by an uninterrupted path of a śrāvaka's path of seeing because they assert that the subtle selflessness of persons is realized as the implicit [aspect] of the explicit comprehension of compositional phenomena that are devoid of a self of persons.

Regarding the third [part]—the mode of assertion of the fruits [of the path]—except for [asserting that] an arhat's falling from [his] abandonments and realization is not possible and asserting the form aggregate of a buddha as a buddha, [the Sautrāntikas' assertions] are similar to [those of] the Vaibhāṣikas—such as the ways of actualizing the fruits of the three vehicles and so forth. Although both the Vaibhāṣikas and the Sautrāntikas do not accept the scriptural collections (**piṭaka; sde snod*) of the Mahāyāna as the word [of the Buddha], it is said that later members of the lineages have accepted [them] as the word [of the Buddha]. Stanza between sections:

> Through the force of having trained well in the texts of reasoning,
> Those propounding reasoning should [indulge in] this festival of delight—
> This expression, just as they are, of the secret words of reasoning
> Of the Dārṣṭāntikas Following Reasoning!

[Third: The Cittamātrins]

Third, with regard to the explanation of the presentation of the tenets of Cittamātra (i.e., "Proponents of Mind-Only") [there are] four parts: definition, divisions, etymology, and manner of asserting [tenets]. Regarding the first, the definition of a Cittamātrin is: a person who propounds [those] Buddhist tenets that assert other-powered [natures] to be truly existent and who does not assert external objects. Regarding the second, when that is divided, [there are] two [types]: True Aspectarian Cittamātrins and False Aspectarian [Cittamātrins]. There are differences between these two [groups] because (1) the appearance of a blue [patch] as blue to an eye consciousness perceiving blue is the "aspect" [that is the] basis of debate between the True and False Aspectarians, for (2) True Aspectarians assert that an appearance of blue as blue to an eye consciousness apprehending blue exists as [it] appears, [whereas] False Aspectarians assert that an appearance of blue as blue to an eye consciousness apprehending blue does not exist as [it] appears. It follows that that [is the case] because both True and False Aspectarians are similar in asserting that (1) blue appears as blue to an eye consciousness apprehending blue, (2) blue appears as a coarse object, and (3) blue appears as an external object. However, True Aspectarians assert that pollution by ignorance applies (*zhugs*) to the appearance of blue to an eye consciousness apprehending blue as an external object, but that pollution by ignorance does not apply to the appearance of blue as blue and the appearance of blue as a coarse object, [whereas] False Aspectarians assert that pollution by ignorance applies not only to an appearance of blue as an external object but also to the appearance of blue as blue and [to] the appearance of blue as a coarse object. Therefore, the definition of a True Aspectarian Cittamātrin is any Cittamātrin who asserts that the appearance [of something] as a coarse object to a sense consciousness is established as it appears. The definition of a False Aspectarian Cittamātrin is any Cittamātrin who asserts that the appearance [of something] as a gross object to a sense consciousness is not established as it appears.

When True Aspectarians are divided, there are three [types]: Proponents of an Equal Number of Subjects and Objects, Half-Eggists, and Non-Pluralists. The assertions of scholars are not in agreement with regard to the differences between these three. As it is explained in Gungru Gyeltsen Sangpo's *Distillation of the Middle Way* (*Dbu ma'i stong thun*):

> [Regarding Proponents of an Equal Number of Subjects and Objects,] because they assert that when an eye consciousness apprehending the mottled colors on the wing of a butterfly apprehends that mottle, from the side of the object, aspects of each of the different colors—blue, yellow, and so forth—are cast [to the perceiving consciousness], and from the subject's side as well, aspects

of each of the different [colors] of blue, yellow, and so forth, are produced as true aspects, hence [they are called] Proponents of an Equal Number of Subjects and Objects. [Regarding Half-Eggists,] because [they] assert that, when that is likewise apprehended, from the side of the object, aspects of each of the different colors—blue, yellow, and so forth—are cast [to the perceiving consciousness] and from the subject's side, aspects of each of the different colors—blue, yellow, and so forth—are produced in an aspectless manner, hence [they are called] Half-Eggists. [Regarding Non-Pluralists,] because [they] assert that, when that is likewise apprehended, from the side of the object, aspects of each of the different colors—blue, yellow, and so forth—are not cast [to the perceiving consciousness] but the aspect of only the mottle is cast, and from the subject's side, aspects of each of the different colors—blue, yellow, and so forth—are not produced in an aspectless manner but the aspect of only the mottle is produced in an aspectless manner, hence [they are called] Non-Pluralists.

Drungchen Lekpa Sangpo, Paṇchen Sönam Drakpa, and others explain that:

> Because they assert that just as the two [colors of] blue and yellow that appear to a sense consciousness apprehending a mottle are different substantial entities, [so too] within the eye consciousness apprehending the mottle there are many substantially different eye consciousnesses, [they are called] Proponents of an Equal Number of Subjects and Objects. Because they assert that, although in general a [patch of] blue and an eye consciousness apprehending the blue are of the entity of consciousness, those two are different substantial entities, [they are called] Half-Eggists. Because they assert that just as the two [colors of] blue and yellow within a mottle are one substantial entity, [so too] the two sense consciousnesses that apprehend the blue and the yellow within the eye consciousness apprehending the mottle are one substantial entity, [they are called] Non-Pluralists.

[Jamyang Shepa's] *Great Exposition of Tenets* explains that:

> Because [they] assert that at the time when an eye consciousness apprehending the mottle [of colors on the wing of a butterfly] looks at the mottle, similar types of consciousnesses that are equal [in number] to the number of [colors]—blue, yellow, and so forth within the mottle—are produced simultaneously, [they are called] Proponents of an Equal Number of Subjects and Objects. Because [they] assert that although both blue and an eye consciousness apprehending blue are prior and subsequent entities from the perspective of [their] time of establishment, [they] are one substantial entity from the perspective of the time of [their] observation, [they are called] Half-Eggists. Because [they] assert that at the time when an eye consciousness apprehending a mottle looks at its object, without similar types of consciousnesses that are equal [in number] to the number of [colors]—blue, yellow, and so forth within the object—being produced simultaneously, the sole eye consciousness that apprehends the mottle is the sense consciousness that apprehends blue, yellow, and so forth within the mottle, [they are called] Non-Pluralists.

Hence, from among these three systems, [one] should hold whatever is most appealing. It is explained that Proponents of an Equal Number of Subjects and Objects [have] two [types]: those who assert eight sets of consciousnesses and those who assert six sets of consciousnesses, [and that] Non-Pluralists have two [types]: proponents of six sets of consciousnesses and proponents of a single consciousness.

When False Aspectarians are divided, there are two [types]: Tainted [False Aspectarians] and Non-Tainted False Aspectarians. It is said that because [they] assert that the nature of the mind is polluted by the stain of the latencies of ignorance, [they are called] Tainted [False Aspectarians], and because [they] assert that the entity of the mind is not polluted in even the slightest by the stain of the latencies of ignorance, [they are called] Non-Tainted [False Aspectarians]. Alternately, it is said that because [they] assert that although there is no ignorance on the level of buddhahood, there are mistaken appearances, [they are called] Tainted False Aspectarians, and because [they] assert that since there is no ignorance on the level of buddhahood, mistaken appearances also do not exist, [they are called] Non-Tainted [False Aspectarians].

Furthermore, when Cittamātrins are divided, there are two [types]: Followers of Scripture and Followers of Reasoning. The first are followers of [Asaṅga's] five *Grounds* (*bhūmi*) treatises, and the second are followers of [Dharmakīrti's] seven valid cognition treatises.

Regarding the third [part]—etymologies—if [you] ask, "Why are [they] called Cittamātrins ('Proponents of Mind-Only')?" [then] because they propound all phenomena to be merely the entity of the mind, [they are called] "Proponents of Mind-Only" or "Proponents of Cognition," and because they settle the practice of the deeds of the path from the perspective of [their] basis in yoga, [they] are called Yogācārins ("Yogic Practitioners") as well.

Regarding the fourth [section]—the manner of asserting [tenets]—from among the three [parts], basis, path, and fruits, the first [has] two [parts]: [assertions regarding] objects and [assertions regarding] subjects ("object-possessors"). Regarding the first, [they] assert that all objects of knowledge are included within the three natures, because [they] assert all compounded phenomena [as] other-powered natures, all ultimate realities (i.e., emptinesses) [as] thoroughly established natures, and [anything] other that those [as] imputational natures. Although [they] assert that all three of these are established from their own side and are established by way of their own character, there is a difference [with regard to these in terms] of being truly established and not being [truly] established, because [they] assert that there are no truly [established] imputational natures, but both other-powered natures [and] thoroughly established natures [are] truly established.

The definition of an imputational nature [is] that which is not ultimately established but is established as an entity for a conceptual consciousness. When that [is] divided, [there are] two [types]: enumerated [or existent] imputational natures and imputational natures whose characteristics are utterly nonexistent [i.e., nonexistent imputational natures]. The first [is,] for instance, [the category of] object of knowledge; the second [is,] for instance, the two selves [i.e., of persons and of phenomena].

The definition of an other-powered nature is that which arises in dependence upon the power of others, that is, causes and conditions, and which serves as the basis of a thoroughly established nature. When that is divided, [there are] two [types]: pure other-powered natures and impure other-powered natures. The first [i.e., pure other-powered natures is,] for instance, an ārya's exalted wisdom of subsequent attainment and the major and minor marks of a buddha. The second [is,] for instance, the aggregates appropriated [through] contaminated [actions and afflictions].

The definition of a thoroughly established nature [is] a suchness that is an emptiness of either of the two selves [of persons or of phenomena]. When that is divided, [there are] two [types]: nonerroneous thoroughly established natures and immutable thoroughly established natures. The first [is,] for instance, an ārya's exalted wisdom of meditative equipoise. The second [is,] for instance, the ultimate reality [of phenomena]. Although nonerroneous thoroughly established natures are stated as a division of thoroughly established natures, [they actually] are not thoroughly established natures because [they] are not final objects of observation of a path of purification, which then extinguish obstructions when they are observed. Again, when objects of knowledge are divided, [there are] two [types]: conventional truths and ultimate truths. The definition of a conventional truth [is] that object that is found by [the sort of] valid cognition that is the type of consciousness that engages in the analysis of conventionalities. Falsity, conventional truth, and nominal truth are mutually inclusive. The definition of an ultimate truth [is] that object that is found by [the sort of] valid cognition that is the type of consciousness that engages in the analysis of an ultimate. Emptiness, dharmadhātu, thoroughly established nature, ultimate truth, limit of reality, and thusness are asserted to be mutually inclusive. If [something] is an ultimate truth, then it is necessarily established by way of its own character. However, if [something] is a conventional truth, then it is not necessarily established by way of its own character, because although other-powered natures are established by way of their own character, imputational phenomena are not established by way of their own character. If [something] is a falsity, it is not necessary that it is falsely established, because although other-powered natures are falsities, they are not established falsely.

The Sautrāntikas', Cittamātrins', and Svātantrikas' manner of positing the three times and nonaffirming negatives are in agreement. The five [sense] objects, such as forms and so forth, are not established as external objects because [they] are produced from within the substantial entity of an internal consciousness through the power of latent predispositions deposited by common and uncommon actions in the mind-basis-of-all. In accordance with the True Aspectarians, it is asserted that although the five [sense] objects—forms and so forth—are not external objects, [they] do exist as coarse objects.

The False Aspectarians assert that if such were the case, then since forms and so forth would have to be external objects, [the five types of sense objects] are not established as coarse objects.

Regarding the second [section], the manner of asserting subjects, since the Followers of Scripture assert eight sets of consciousnesses, [they] assert the mental consciousness and the mind-basis-of-all as the person; the Followers of Reasoning assert the mental consciousness as the illustration of a person. With regard to that, a mind-basis-of-all observes the latent predispositions, does not discriminate aspects [of its objects], [its] entity is undefiled and neutral, [and] since this main mental knower, which is associated solely with the five omnipresent mental factors that accompany [it], is stable, [it] is asserted as something that is prevalent. Moreover, from among the two [possibilities of] being defiled or nondefiled, [it] is nondefiled and neutral. Because [it] also exists in the continuum of [one whose] roots of virtue have been severed, [a mind-basis-of-all] is not virtuous; since [it] exists [for those] in the upper realms [i.e., the form and formless realms], [it] is also not nonvirtuous.

Regarding the afflicted mind (*kliṣṭamanas*), having focused on the mind-basis-of-all—[its] object of observation—[it] has the aspect of considering [the mind-basis-of-all] as a sort of "I." [They] assert that [its] entity is one of being defiled and neutral; [their] manner of presentation of the six operative consciousnesses is in agreement with the general [presentation]. With regard to valid cognition, [Cittamātrins] assert the two—perception and inference—and a presentation of four [types of] perception [sense, self-cognizing, mental, and yogic perceptual valid cognitions]. Both self-cognizing perceptions and yogic perceptions are necessarily nonmistaken consciousnesses. True Aspectarians assert that an eye consciousness apprehending blue [and being] in the continuum of one-who-sees-nearby [i.e., an ordinary being] is a nonmistaken consciousness. However, if [presented] in accordance with the False Aspectarians, [all] sense perceptions in the continuum of one-who-sees-nearby are necessarily mistaken consciousnesses. [Also, they] assert that there exist both mistaken and nonmistaken factors in mental perceptions in such a continuum.

Regarding the second [part]—the presentation of the path—from among the three [sections], the first, objects of observation of the paths, is: the sixteen distinguishing features of the four noble truths such as impermanence and so forth, the coarse selflessness of persons [being] a person's emptiness of being permanent, unitary, and independent, and the subtle selflessness of persons [being] a person's emptiness of being substantially existent in the sense of being self-sufficient. However, [Cittamātrins] assert the two—the emptiness of being separate substantial entities of a form and a valid cognition apprehending [that] form, and the emptiness of a form being established by way of its own character as the referent basis of a conceptual consciousness apprehending [that] form—as the subtle selflessnesses of phenomena. Both subtle selflessnesses are asserted as emptiness, although an emptiness is not necessarily either of those because [they] assert both true cessations and nirvāṇas as emptinesses also. [They] assert compounded phenomena to be the same substantial entity as the valid cognitions that apprehend them. Uncompounded phenomena are asserted to be the same entity as the valid cognitions that apprehend them.

Regarding the second [section]—objects of abandonment of the path—[there are] two: afflictive obstructions and obstructions to omniscience. The first [are,] for instance, the coarse or subtle conception of a self of persons together with [their] seeds, the six root afflictions, and twenty secondary afflictions. The second [—obstructions to omniscience—are,] for instance, the conception of a self of phenomena together with [their] latent predispositions. Moreover, bodhisattvas take the obstructions to omniscience as their main object of abandonment, although [they] do not take the afflictive obstructions as their main object of abandonment. Hīnayāna learners [i.e., śrāvakas and pratyekabuddhas on the paths of accumulation, preparation, seeing, and meditation] take the afflictive obstructions as their main object of abandonment, although [they] do not take the obstructions to omniscience as their main object of abandonment.

Regarding the third [section]—presentation of the path—for each of the three vehicles, moreover, a presentation of the five [paths]—the two [paths of] accumulation and preparation, the two [paths of] seeing and meditation, and the path of no more learning—is made. For Mahāyāna, [Cittamātrins] assert a presentation of ten [bodhisattva] grounds on top of this as well.

Regarding the third [part]—the manner of manifesting the fruits—those whose Hīnayāna lineage is definite take the thoroughly established nature in terms of the selflessness of persons as [their] main object of meditation. When familiarization [with this thoroughly established nature] has been completed, then having relied on the vajra-like samādhi of the Hīnayāna path of meditation, the afflictive obstructions are abandoned without exception, and simultaneously [they] actualize the fruit of a Hīnayāna arhat. Since there is not even the slightest difference with regard to the afflictions that are to be abandoned and the selflessness that is to be meditated upon by śrāvakas and pratyekabuddhas, the presentation of the eight approachers and abiders is correct with regard to both śrāvakas and pratyekabuddhas. However, as for pratyekabuddhas, since it is definite that [they] have a basis of support [only] in the desire realm, there is no presentation of the twenty [types of] saṅgha to be applied [to them]. Still, it is not the case that there are no differences at all between śrāvakas and pratyekabuddhas. It is asserted that superiority and inferiority exist as well for the fruits through the force of whether cultivation of the collection of merit is extended [i.e., by pratyekabuddhas] or not extended [i.e., by śrāvakas] over one hundred eons.

[Cittamātrin] Followers of Scripture do not assert that a Hīnayāna arhat who is solely directed to peace [ever] enters the Mahāyāna path, but [they] do assert that an arhat whose enlightenment becomes transformed [into that of a bodhisattva] does enter the Mahāyāna path. That [entry], moreover, is from [a nirvāṇa] with remainder, and it is not an entry from [a nirvāṇa] without remainder because they assert that [the vehicles] are established as three final vehicles. [Cittamātrin] Followers of Reasoning assert that [all] Hīnayāna arhats enter into the Mahāyāna because they assert that [the vehicles] are established as [only] one final vehicle.

Those endowed with the Mahāyāna lineage take as their main object of meditation the thoroughly established nature in terms of the selflessness of phenomena. Having practiced [meditation on the selflessness of phenomena] in conjunction with [amassing] the collections of merit over [a periods of] three countless eons, [they] gradually traverse the five paths and the ten grounds. By means of the uninterrupted path at the end of their continuum [as a sentient being], they exhaustively abandon the two obstructions. Thus, in the Akaniṣṭha Heaven, [they] actualize the dharmakāya ("truth body")—[being] the marvelous abandonment [of obstructions] and realization [of selflessness that is the fulfillment of] one's own aims—and the two rūpakāyas ("form bodies")—[being] the marvelous enlightened activities [that are the fulfillment of] others' aims. According to some followers of [Asaṅga's] *Compendium* [*of Manifest Knowledge*] (*Abhidharmasamuccaya*), it is evident that becoming enlightened also can exist in a human basis (i.e., body). Regarding the word of the Buddha, [Cittamātrins] also assert the distinction between definitive and interpretable scriptures because [they] assert the first two wheels [of the Dharma] as described in the [*Sūtra*] *Unraveling the Thought* (*Saṃdhinirmocana-sūtra*) to be sūtras of interpretable meaning and the final wheel to be [comprised of] sūtras of definitive meaning. There are also [other criteria for] definitive and interpretable meanings because [they] posit those sūtras whose explicit teachings are not suitable to be accepted literally [as] sūtras of interpretable meaning and those sūtras whose explicit teachings are suitable to be accepted literally as sūtras of definitive meaning.

Since [Cittamātrins] assert [that] nirvāṇa [has] three [types]: with remainder, without remainder, and nonabiding nirvāṇa; [that] bodies of the Buddha [have] three [types]: dharma-[kāya] ("truth body"), saṃbhoga-[kāya] ("enjoyment body"), and nirmāṇakāya ("emanation body"); [that] the dharmakāya [has] two [types]: svabhāvakāya ("nature body") and jñānadharmakāya ("wisdom truth body"); together with a svabhāvakāya [that has] two [types]: [a svabhāvakāya that is] naturally pure and a svabhāvakāya [that is] free of adventitious defilements, [Cittamātrins] are called proponents of Mahāyāna tenets. Stanza between sections:

> It is right for the discriminating to enter with joy
> Into this arrangement [stated] in accordance [with] the speech of a great many scholars
> Of the tenets of those propounding cognition-only; [they are]
> Those who follow the word of the Guide, the Muni ("Subduer").

[Fourth: The Niḥsvabhāvavādins or Mādhyamikas]

Fourth, with regard to the explanation of the presentation of the tenets of Niḥsvabhāva-vādins (i.e., "Proponents of Non-Entityness") or Mādhyamikas (i.e., "Proponents of the Middle Way"), [there are] four [parts]: definition, etymologies, divisions, and explanations of the meaning of the individual divisions. Regarding the first, a person who propounds [a system of] Buddhist tenets that asserts that there are no truly established phenomena, not even the merest atom [is] the definition of a Mādhyamika ["Proponent of the Middle Way"].

Regarding the second [part]: if you ask, "Why are they called Proponents of the Middle Way?" then [we respond] it is because [that], since they assert a middle that is free from the two extremes of permanence and annihilation, [they are called] "Proponents of the Middle Way," and since [they] propound that [all] phenomena lack a truly established entityness, [they] are called "Proponents of Non-Entityness."

Third, when those are divided, [there are] two: Svātantrikas ["Proponents of Autonomous [Syllogisms]"] and Prāsaṅgikas ["Proponents of Consequences"]. Fourth, as for the meaning of the individual divisions, [there are] two [sections]: the explanation of the systems of the Svātantrikas and of the Prāsaṅgikas. The first [section, the system of Svātantrika, has] four [parts]: definition, etymology, divisions, and the mode of asserting tenets. Regarding the first, the definition of a Svātantrika [Mādhyamika] is a proponent of non-entityness who asserts [phenomena] as conventionally established by way of their own character. As for the second, if you ask, "Why are they called Svātantrika-Mādhyamikas?" then [we respond that], since [they] refute truly [existent] things through having relied on a correct [logical] sign whose three modes are established from their own side [i.e., "autonomously"], [they] are called like that. Third, when that is divided, [there are] two: Yogācāra-Svātantrika-Mādhyamikas ["Yogic Practice Middle Way Autonomy [School]"], and Sautrāntika-Svātantrika-Mādhyamikas ["Middle Way Autonomy School Following Sūtra"]. A Mādhyamika who does not assert external objects and who asserts self-cognizing [awarenesses] is the definition of the first [i.e., a Yogācāra-Svātantrika-Mādhyamika]. An illustration [is], for instance, the master Śāntarakṣita [who is considered to be the founder of this subschool]. A Mādhyamika who does not assert self-cognizing [awarenesses] and who asserts that external objects [are] established by way of their own character is the definition of the second [i.e., a Sautrāntika-Svātantrika-Mādhyamika]. An illustration [is], for instance, the master Bhāvaviveka [who is considered to be the founder of this subschool and the Svātantrika School as a whole]. There are etymologies as well. Since [they] assert a presentation of the basis in accordance with the Cittamātrins, [they are called] Yogācāra-Mādhyamikas, and since [they] assert external objects that are composed of subtle particles like the Sautrāntikas [assert], [they] are called Sautrāntika-Mādhyamikas.

Yogācāra-Svātantrika-Mādhyamikas, moreover, have two [subschools]: Mādhyamikas who accord with True Aspectarians and Mādhyamikas who accord with

False Aspectarians. The first [are,] for instance, Śāntarakṣita, Kamalaśīla, and Ārya Vimuktisena. The second [are,] for instance, the master Haribhadra, Jetāri, and Kambalapāda. [Moreover,] it is explained that Jetāri accords with the Tainted False Aspectarians, and Kambalapāda accords with the Non-Tainted False Aspectarians.

Fourth, as for the manner of asserting tenets, there are two [parts]: [the explanation of] the system of Yogācāra-Svātantrika-Mādhyamikas ["Yogic Practice Middle Way Autonomy [School]"] and the explanation of the presentation of Sautrāntika-Svātantrika-Mādhyamikas ["Middle Way [Autonomy School] Following Sūtra"].

As for the first [—Yogācāra-Svātantrika-Mādhyamikas—] from among the three [sections], the basis, paths, and fruits, the first—the presentation of the basis—[has] two [parts]: objects and subjects (lit. "object-possessors"). From among [those], regarding the first, [they] assert that if [something is] an established base, then [it] is necessarily established by way of its own character because they assert that whatever is a phenomenon—although an imputed object—if it is sought, then [it] is found. Therefore, [they] assert that being intrinsically established, being established by way of its own character, being established from the point of view of its own mode of subsistence, and being established from its own side are mutually inclusive.

When objects of knowledge are divided, [there are] two—ultimate truths and conventional truths—[and] from among [these]: that object that is to be realized by a perceptual valid cognition that directly realizes it [and which does so] in a manner in which its own dualistic appearances have disappeared, is the definition of the first, [and] that object that is realized by a perceptual valid cognition that directly realizes it [and which does so] in a dualistic manner, is the definition of the second. The emptiness of true existence [of] a pot, for instance, [is] an illustration of the first [i.e., an ultimate truth], while, for instance, a pot is an illustration of the second [i.e., a conventional truth]. If ultimate truths are extensively divided, [there are] sixteen emptinesses, and if condensed, there are four [emptinesses]. If conventional truths are divided, [there are] two—real conventional truths and unreal conventional truths—[and] from among [those,] the first [is,] for instance, water, [and] the second [is,] for instance, the water of a mirage. This system asserts that if [something] is a consciousness, then [it] is necessarily a real conventional truth.

Regarding the second—[assertions regarding] subjects—[as for] asserting a mental consciousness [as] the "illustration" [i.e., "basis of designation"] of the person, and not asserting neither a mind-basis-of-all nor an afflicted mind, and in asserting the collection of consciousnesses to be six [in number], both [divisions of] the Svātantrika [Madhyamaka School—Yogācāra and Sautrāntika—] are in agreement. With regard to awarenesses, [there are] two [kinds]: valid cognitions and nonvalid awarenesses. With regard to valid cognitions, [there are] two [types]: perceptual valid cognitions and inferential valid cognitions. With regard to perception, there are four [types]: sense perception, mental perception, self-cognizing perception, and yogic perception, although [they] assert that the last two [—self-cognizing and yogic—] perceptions are necessarily unmistaken consciousnesses. Since [they] do not accept the establishment [of things] as external objects, [they] assert that the two—a blue [patch] and a perception apprehending a blue [patch]—are the same substantial entity.

With regard to the second, the presentation of the paths, from among the three [parts—objects of observation of the paths, objects abandoned by the paths, and nature of the paths—] the first, objects of observation of the path, are asserted [by the Yogācāra Svātantrikas] to be: the emptiness of being permanent, unitary, and independent of a person is the coarse selflessness of persons; the emptiness of being substantially existent in the sense of being self-sufficient of a person is the subtle selflessness of persons; the emptiness of a form and the valid cognition apprehending the form being substantially other is the coarse selflessness of phenomena; and the emptiness of true existence of all phenomena is the subtle selflessness of phenomena. Regarding the second, objects of abandonment of the path, [Yogācāra Svātantrikas] assert the conception of a self of persons [to be] the afflictive obstructions [to liberation] and the conception of a self of phenomena to be the obstructions to omniscience. [They also] assert obstructions to omniscience as [being of] two [types]: the conception of apprehending [subject] and apprehended [object] as [being] different substantial entities, for instance, as a *coarse* obstruction to omniscience, and the conception of phenomena, such as the aggregates etc., as truely established, for instance, as a *subtle* obstruction to omniscience. Regarding the third, the nature of the paths, [the Yogācāra Svātantrika School] is similar [to the other tenet systems] in asserting the fifteen—the three [sets] of five paths [for the three vehicles]. As for the difference [between the schools], [the Yogācāra Svātantrika School] asserts that an uninterrupted path and a path of release of a pratyekabuddha must have the aspect of [realizing] an emptiness of duality [of subject and object].

With regard to the third, the presentation of the fruits [of the path], because pratyekabuddhas take as their main object of abandonment the coarse obstructions to omniscience [the conception that subject and object are different entities], the presentation of the eight approachers and abiders is not applicable [to pratyekabuddhas]. However, it is asserted that there are eight from among the sets of persons [i.e., approachers and abiders] with respect to śrāvakas. Those firm in the Śrāvaka lineage take as their main object of meditative cultivation the view that realizes the selflessness of persons. Finally, having relied upon the vajra-like samādhi of their path of meditation, [they actualize] the abandonment without exception of all obstructions to liberation and simultaneously actualize the fruit of a [śrāvaka] arhat. Those firm in the Pratyekabuddha lineage take as their main object of meditative cultivation the view of apprehending [subject] and apprehended [object] being empty of duality. Finally, having relied upon the vajra-like samādhi of their path of meditation, [they actualize] the abandonment without exception of the afflictive obstructions and coarse obstructions to omniscience and simultaneously actualize the fruit of a pratyekabuddha arhat.

Lesser Vehicle nirvāṇas [are] of two [types], those with remainder and those without remainder. From among [these], the first [is asserted to be] a nirvāṇa having the remainder of miserable aggregates that were impelled by former [contaminated] actions and afflictions, and the second is asserted to be a state devoid of miserable aggregates. If [someone] is a śrāvaka or pratyekabuddha arhat, [they] will necessarily enter the Mahāyāna because [the Yogācāra-Svātantrika School] asserts [the vehicles] to be established in terms of one final vehicle. Therefore, in this system, there is also [a distinction of] inferiority and superiority with respect to the fruits that are to be attained, [posited] through the force of a difference between the objects of abandonment and the types of realization [of śrāvakas and pratyekabuddhas].

Those firm in the Mahāyāna lineage generate a mind [of altruistic aspiration] towards highest enlightenment. During the great level of the path of accumulation [from among the division of this path into small, middling, and great levels], having relied upon the samādhi of the stream of doctrine, [they] listen directly to preceptual instructions from supreme emanation bodies. Having relied upon practicing the meaning of these [instructions], when the wisdom arisen from meditation that observes emptiness is initially generated, [that] is the passing on to the path of preparation. [Then] on the occasion of the heat [level of the path of preparation], the manifest conception of thoroughly afflicted objects—that are to be abandoned on the [path of] seeing—is caused to diminish. At the time of attaining the peak [level of the path of preparation], the manifest conception of pure objects that are to be abandoned on the [path of] seeing, at the time of attaining the forbearance [level of the path of preparation], the manifest conception of a subject [that apprehends objects as] substantially [existent], and at the time of attaining the highest mundane qualities [level of the path of preparation], the manifest conception of a subject [that apprehends objects as] imputed—[all] are [respectively] caused to diminish. The four—heat, peak, forbearance, and highest mundane qualities—respectively, are called "the samādhi of achieving perception [of emptiness]," "the samādhi of the increase of the perception [of emptiness]," "the samādhi that has entered into one side of suchness," and "the uninterrupted samādhi."

Immediately after that, the artificial afflictive obstructions and the artificial obstructions to omniscience together with their seeds having been abandoned by an uninterrupted path of the path of seeing, both a path of release [of the path of seeing] and a true cessation [of the artificial obstructions] are then actualized. It is said that, by means of the nine steps of the path of meditation, the seeds of the sixteen afflictions that are to be abandoned by the path of meditation and the seeds of the one hundred eight obstructions to omniscience that are to be abandoned by the path of meditation are gradually abandoned. Finally, in dependence on the uninterrupted path at the end of the continuum [of one's existence as a sentient being], the [innate] afflictions and innate obstructions to omniscience having been simultaneously abandoned, in the next moment, unsurpassed enlightenment is attained. This is the manner in which the fruit is actualized by those who are firm in the [Bodhisattva] lineage. [They] assert that a Mahāyāna nirvāṇa and a nonabiding nirvāṇa are mutually inclusive and [they] assert that the bodies of a buddha are definitely enumerated as four. Even though both Ārya [Vimuktisena] and Haribhadra debated about the teachings regarding the bodies [of a buddha in Maitreya's *Ornament for Clear Realization*], they did not debate about the number [being limited to four: nature body, wisdom body, complete enjoyment body, and emanation body]. With respect to the word of the Buddha, a presentation of sūtras of definitive meaning and sūtras of interpretable meaning is made; this is because sūtras that teach [the Dharma] having taken the explicit teaching of conventional truths as their main object of exposition are sūtras of interpretable meaning, and sūtras that teach [the Dharma] having taken ultimate truths as their main object of exposition are sūtras of definitive meaning. With respect to the wheels [of Dharma] as explained in the *Saṃdhinirmocana-sūtra*, the first [turning of the wheel is asserted to be of] interpretable meaning; both the middle and final [turnings of the wheel of Dharma] are each asserted to have two [types], definitive and interpretable.

Regarding the second—the system of the Sautrāntika-Svātantrika Mādhyamikas—from among the three [sections]—basis, path, and fruits—the first [the basis] is: except that this system asserts external objects and does not assert self-cognizing consciousness, their presentation of the basis is mostly the same as the previous [presentation, that of the Yogācāra-Svātantrika Mādhyamikas]. Second, with respect to differences regarding the paths, [the Sautrāntika-Svātantrika Mādhyamikas] assert that those firm in the Śrāvaka and Pratyekabuddha lineages lack the realization of the selflessness of phenomena and do not assert an exalted wisdom that realizes that subject and object are empty of being different substantial entities, although [they] do not assert that a conceptual consciousness apprehending external objects to be an obstruction to omniscience. Third, regarding the presentation of the fruits, since the obstructions that are the objects of abandonment of both śrāvakas and pratyekabuddhas and the selflessness that is the object to be realized [by them] lack [any difference in terms of] coarseness or subtlety, there is no difference in their type of realization, and [Sautrāntika-Svātantrika Mādhyamikas] make a presentation of the eight approachers and abiders for both [śrāvakas and pratyekabuddhas]. They assert that those firm in the Mahāyāna lineage abandon the two obstructions serially because [Bhāvaviveka] explains in his *Blaze of Reasoning* that, at the time when the eighth ground is attained, the afflictive obstructions are exhaustively abandoned. However, [they] are not like the Prāsaṅgikas in that [the Prāsaṅgikas] assert that the start of the abandonment of the obstructions to omniscience does not commence until the obstructions to liberation have [all] been exhausted. With the exception of only these distinctive differences, the [Sautrāntika-Svātantrika Mādhyamikas'] presentation of the basis, paths, and fruits mostly accords with that of the Yogācāra-Svātantrika Mādhyamikas.

Thus, a stanza between sections:

O you—those whose wish themselves to be wise—take up
This eloquent expression, free of my own fabrication,
[With] all the distinctions of the tenets of the Proponents of Svātantrika
Who assert that although [things] exist by way of their own character, [they]
do not truly exist.

[Part Two: The Prāsaṅgika Mādhyamikas]

Second, regarding the explanation of the Prāsaṅgika system, [there are] three [parts]: definition, etymology, and mode of assertion [of tenets]. First, a proponent of non-entityness who does not assert, even merely conventionally, [that for phenomena there is] establishment by way of their own character [is] the definition of a Prāsaṅgika ["Consequentialist"]. Illustrations [are] for instance, Buddhapālita, Candrakīrti, and Śāntideva. Second, [etymology,] if you ask, "Why are they called Prāsaṅgikas ["Consequentialists"]?" then [we respond] that since [they] assert [that] an inferential consciousness that realizes what is to be proven [can] be generated in the continuum of the opponent merely by [presenting that person with an absurd] consequence [of their own position], [they] are called like that. Third, as for the mode of asserting tenets, from among the three [parts]—basis, path, and fruit—regarding the first [the basis,] [they] assert that if [something is] an established base, [it] is necessarily not established by way of its own character, because [they] assert [that] to the extent [to which something is] an established base, [it] is necessarily merely imputed by conceptuality, and because [they] assert that the word "merely"—[being] an indirect expression of that—eliminates establishment by way of own character. Established base, object, and object of knowledge are mutually inclusive. When those are divided, [there are] the divisions into the two, the manifest and the hidden and the division into the two truths.

Regarding the first, [the division into manifest and hidden phenomena,] a phenomenon that is able to be known through the force of being experienced without relying upon a [logical] sign [is] the definition of manifest phenomenon. Directly perceived [object], manifest [phenomenon], object of a sense power, and nonhidden phenomenon—[these] four [are] mutually inclusive and synonymous. Illustrations [are,] for instance, forms, sounds, smells, tastes, and tacticle objects. A phenomenon that must be known in dependence upon signs or reasonings [is] the definition of hidden phenomenon. Hidden [phenomenon], nondirectly perceived phenomenon, and object of comprehension of an inferential consciousness [are] mutually inclusive and synonymous. Illustrations are given as, for instance, the impermanence of a sound and a sound's selflessness of phenomena. Therefore, in this system, the two—manifest [phenomena] and hidden [phenomena]—[are asserted to be mutually exclusive], and the three categories of objects of comprehension [the manifest, the (slightly) hidden, and the very hidden] are [also] asserted to be mutually exclusive.

Regarding the second, [the division into the two truths,] whatsoever object [that is] found by a valid cognition that engages in the analysis of conventionalities, and with respect to which that valid cognition that engages in the analysis of conventionalities amounts to [being] a valid cognition that engages in the analysis of conventionalities—just that [is] the definition of [something's] being a conventional truth. Illustrations [are,] for instance, a pot. When [those] are divided, [they] are not divided into real conventional [truths] and unreal conventional [truths], because there are no real conventional [truths], because if [something] is a conventional [truth, it] is necessarily [something that is] not real, [and] because if it is [a conventional truth], then it is necessarily unreal. However, regarding conventional [truths], contingent upon the perspective of an ordinary worldly consciousness, [they] are divided into the two: real and unreal. [That is] because a form, contingent upon a worldly consciousness, [is] real, and a reflection of a face (*bzhin*) appearing (*byad*) in a mirror, contingent upon a worldly consciousness, is unreal. [Hence,] if [something] is real—contingent upon a worldly consciousness—[it] does not necessarily exist because truly established forms are that [i.e., only "real" contingent upon a worldly consciousness].

Whatever object [that is] found by a valid cognition that engages in final analysis, and with respect to which that valid cognition that engages in final analysis amounts to [being] a valid cognition that engages in final analysis—just that [is] the definition of [something's] being an ultimate truth. An illustration [is,] for instance, a pot's absence in terms of its own nature. The divisions are similar to the previous [divisions given in the Svātantrika section]. Furthermore, [they] assert past [phenomena], future [phenomena], and disintegration to be [functioning] things, and [they] also assert external objects because [they] assert subject and object to be established as different entities.

Regarding the mode of asserting subjects, [they] assert the mere "I" that is imputed in dependence upon four or five aggregates—its own basis of designation—to be the basis of the name "person" and [that] a person is necessarily a nonassociated compositional factor. [The category of] awareness has two [types]: valid and nonvalid awarenesses. Valid cognition [has] two [types]: perceptual valid cognitions (or "valid perception") and inferential valid cognitions (or "valid inference"). Perceptual valid cognition has three [types]: sense perceptual valid cognitions, mental perceptual valid cognitions, and yogic perceptual valid cognitions. Self-cognizing perception is not asserted, and a sense consciousnesses within the continuum of a sentient being is necessarily a mistaken consciousness.

Yogic perception has two [types]: mistaken and unmistaken, because the yogic perception that has the nature of an uncontaminated meditative equipoise [is] an unmistaken one, and the yogic perception within the continuum of an ordinary being ("of one-who-sees-nearby") that directly realizes subtle impermanence is a mistaken consciousness. It follows that the latter [one] is that ["a mistaken consciousness"] because of being a consciousness in the continuum of an ordinary being. If [something] is a subsequent cognition, then [it] is necessarily a valid perception because the second moment of an inferential consciousness that realizes that sound is impermanent is a conceptual valid perception and the second moment of a sense perception apprehending a form is a nonconceptual valid perception.

When inference is divided, there are four [types]: inference through the power of the fact, inference through renown, inference through example, and inference through correct belief. Being mistaken with respect to an object and yet realizing that object are not mutually exclusive because [Prāsaṅgikas] assert that an inferential cognition realizing that a sound is impermanent realizes that, even though [it] is mistaken with respect to impermanent sound. If [something] is a consciousness that possesses dualistic appearances, [it] is necessarily a valid perception with respect to its own appearing object because [even] a conceptual consciousness that [mistakenly] apprehends sound [as] permanent is a valid perception with respect to its own appearing object. If [something] is a consciousness [whether correct, wrong, conceptual, or nonconceptual], [it] necessarily realizes its own object of comprehension because [for example,] the object universal of the horns of a rabbit is the object of comprehension of a conceptual consciousness apprehending the horns of a rabbit and [because, for example,] the object universal of permanent sound is the object of comprehension of a conceptual consciousness apprehending permanent sound.

Second, with regard to the presentation of the path, from among the three [parts: assertions regarding objects of observation of the path, assertions regarding objects abandoned by the paths, and assertions regarding the nature of the paths], the first [is] objects of observation of the path. [With regard to this,] a person being empty of substantial existence in the sense of self-sufficiency [is asserted to be] the coarse selflessness of persons, and a person being empty of true existence is asserted to be the subtle selflessness of persons.

The two subtle selflessnesses [of persons and of phenomena] are differentiated from the perspective of the basis [upon which] emptiness [is predicated—persons and phenomena—] and are not differentiated from the perspective of the object of negation. [This is] because the negation of true establishment—the object of negation in relation to a person [as a] basis [of negation]—is the subtle selflessness of persons, and the negation of true establishment—the object of negation in relation to the aggregates etc., [as a] basis [of negation]—is the subtle selflessness of phenomena. The subtle selflessness of persons and the subtle selflessness of phenomena lack coarseness and subtlety, and [they] are asserted to be the final mode of subsistence [of persons and other phenomena].

Second, regarding objects of abandonment of the path, the coarse and subtle conceptions of a self together with their seeds and the three poisons that arise through the force of that together with their seeds are asserted to be the afflictive obstructions because [Prāsaṅgikas] assert the conception of true existence as an afflictive obstruction. The karmic predisposition to the conception of true existence, the factor of mistaken dualistic appearances that arise through the force of that, and the taint of apprehending the two truths as different entities are asserted to be the obstructions to omniscience.

Third, regarding the nature of the path, [Prāsaṅgikas] give a presentation of five paths each for each of the three vehicles and also [give] a presentation of ten grounds for the Great Vehicle, having relied on the *Sūtra on the Ten Grounds.* The three vehicles do not have different types of wisdom realizations because [they] assert that [all] āryas necessarily directly realize the selflessness of phenomena.

Third, regarding the manner of actualizing the fruit [of the path], those who are definite in the Hīnayāna lineage cultivate the view of selflessness through only brief reasonings, and in dependence on this, in the end, [they] actualize their own [Lesser Vehicle] enlightenment simultaneously with abandoning the conception of true existence together with its seeds by means of a vajra-like samādhi of the Hīnayāna path of meditation. The Svātantrika Mādhyamikas and those below assert that—with regard to the attainment of nirvāṇa without remainder—it is necessary to attain nirvāṇa with remainder [of contaminated aggregates] prior to that. However, in this system, [Prāsaṅgikas] assert that it is necessary to attain nirvāṇa without remainder [of false appearances of intrinsic existence] prior to [nirvāṇa] with remainder. [The Prāsaṅgikas] assert a presentation of [the eight] approachers and abiders for śrāvakas and pratyekabuddhas, and they assert that whosoever is [one of] the eight approachers and abiders is necessarily an ārya.

Regarding the manner in which enlightenment in the Great Vehicle is actualized, bodhisattvas extensively cultivate the view of selflessness from the perspective of limitless numbers of reasonings and hence bring about the abandonment of the obstructions. Moreover, the beginning of the abandonment of the obstructions to omniscience is not begun until the afflictive obstructions are exhaustively abandoned, for the beginning of the abandonment of the obstructions to omniscience is begun from the eighth [bodhisattva] ground [and onward]. Bodhisattvas who have not previously entered onto the Hinayāna path, when they attain the eighth [bodhisattva] ground, exhaustively abandon the afflictive obstructions. Hence, in the end, having relied upon the uninterrupted path at the end of the continuum [of being a sentient being], [they] abandon the obstructions to omniscience without exception and simultaneously manifest the state of the four [buddha] bodies. [The Prāsaṅgikas] assert that nirvāṇa and true cessations are necessarily ultimate truths.

The first and last of the three wheels that are explained in the *Sūtra Unraveling the Thought* (*Saṃdhinirmocana-sūtra*) are necessarily sūtras of interpretable meaning because among them there are no sūtras that explicitly teach emptiness. It is asserted that among the middle [turning] of these [three wheels there] are necessarily sūtras of definitive meaning because the *Heart of [the Perfection of] Wisdom [Sūtra]* is a sūtra of definitive meaning.

The main distinguishing feature of the Prāsaṅgikas is just that knowledge of (1) refuting, without exception, establishment by way of their own character with regard to internal and external phenomena based on the reason that [they] are dependently imputed, as well as (2) undeniably positing—in their own system [and] without needing to rely on another's perspective—bondage and liberation, cause and effect, object of comprehension and comprehender, and so forth, as merely existing imputedly as well as nominally [and] conventionally. Nowadays, some are conceited about high [philosophical] views. Hence, having held [phenomena] to be utterly nonexistent, like the son of a barren woman, saying "phenomena of the class [of] appearing [objects] are merely mistaken appearances," those who hold nonattention to anything whatsoever to be the supreme practice have not experienced even the merest scent of the Prāsaṅgika [School].

Therefore, having seen all the marvels of mundane existence as like a pit of blazing fire, those who seek liberation [should] abandon, without exception, [all] bad views that have been fabricated to seem like the Dharma and should value as supremely precious the tradition of the Prāsaṅgika Madhyamaka [School]—the pinnacle of all tenet [systems].

[Thus, I] declare:

[Concluding stanzas]

The depth of words and meanings gathered on the golden earth [of] the
 textual systems is difficult to fathom.
Successive waves of various reasonings move about [which] cause fear in
 the hearts of children of low intellect.
[It is] a place of sport for birds ("the twice born") of clear intellect, [and
 which] sends forth a thousand rivers of manifold views;
Who can fathom the entirety of the reality of the ocean ("the great treasury
 of waters") of the textual systems of Buddhists and non-Buddhists?

However, the boat obtained through birth,
Is impelled by a favorable wind arisen from endeavor, and
Although having arrived in the middle of the ocean of tenets,
Finds here, presently, [this] garland of jewels of eloquence.

If anyone wishes to spread the feast of eloquent discourse
Before ten million supreme scholars, then
This condensed essence of the tenets of ourselves and others
Is something to be relied upon by youthful groups with clear minds.

Nowadays, arrogant persons [who] consider themselves wise
Without having trained for a long time in the great [and] extensive texts,
By the vain display of composing [texts] for the sake of amassing honor
and gain,
Such [persons] are intent on tiring [themselves]—O, it is amazing!

By means of the sun ("the possessor of a thousand lights") of eloquent
explanations dawning in the sky of analysis
The jasmines of faulty explanations are caused to close, although
Whatsoever brilliant countenances of the marvelous meanings [of]
The great garden of the lotuses ("the hundred-petaled") of the pure
scriptural systems [become] effulgent.

Having condensed the essence of the scriptures of the scholars of India and
Tibet,
This arrangement that clarifies the countless tenets, however,
Was not [something done] through the force of competitiveness [or]
jealousy but rather
It is for the sake of furthering the intellect of those [whose] lot is equal to
my own.

In this way, that good deed [that] has arisen from effort—
Outshining even the light of the moon—
Liberates all transmigrators from the chasm of bad views; hence,
May the correct path forever provide [them] relief!

This brief presentation of insider and outsider tenets—called *A Precious Garland*—was composed by the Venerable Könchok Jikmé Wangpo during the waxing of the [sixth] month of Pūrvāṣādhā in the Water Snake [Year] (1773), in the face of requests by both the faithful, energetic, and discriminating Gushri Ngawang Kelsang and the monk Ngawang Sangpo; the scribe was Damdrin Tsering.

Sarvamaṅgalam ("May all virtues increase!")

Yangjen Gaway Lodrö's *Lamp Illuminating the Presentation of the Three Bodies that are the Bases [of Purification]*

On the simplest level, the entirety of the Buddhist endeavor centers around the intentional manipulation of states of consciousness and their deployment to religious ends. Yangjen Gaway Lodrö's text, the *Lamp Illuminating the Three Bodies that are the Bases [of Purification]*, covers the subject considered essential to any tantric practice: the various states of mind that naturally manifest at the time of death and the repurposing ("purification") of these states in service of one's religious aim. In laying out this process, Yangjen Gaway Lodrö (*dbyangs can dga' ba'i blo gros*, 1740–1827)—a student of Könchok Jikmé Wangpo (the author of the previous reading)—follows the description found in the Guhyasamāja tantric system. In that system, the three phases of death, intermediate state (*bar do*), and rebirth are analyzed in terms of both their components and roles in tantric practice. With regard to death, the text discusses the eight stages of dissolution while also presenting points of debate concerning technical terms and metaphors used in the system. In his discussion of the intermediate state, the author describes the qualities of being in that condition as well as the different scriptural sources of knowledge concerning such a state. As a segué to the section on rebirth, the different manners in which a being's existence in the intermediate state may come to an end is presented in the context of objections and answers. The section on rebirth follows a similar pattern of presenting the fundamental layout of the process of rebirth following the "death" of the intermediate-state being, discussing the development of the fetus on both the coarse and subtle physiological levels. The text concludes with a brief discussion of the manner in which the previous presentations accord with tantric practice.

In terms of a reading challenge, this text is an example of specialized literature in which a single topic of a larger system is explored in detail. The format of the text is one of a straightforward narrative, drawing upon the concepts and vocabulary introduced in the preceding text while presenting similar material in greater depth and from a synthetic perspective. It integrates numerous non-tantric sources and a wide range of standard Buddhist terminology. A translation with commentary was published in Lati Rinbochay and Hopkins (1985).

༄༅། །གཞིའི་སྐུ་གསུམ་གྱི་རྣམ་གཞག་རབ་གསལ་སྒྲོན་མེ་ཞེས་བྱ་བ་བཞུགས་སོ། །

ན་མོ་གུ་རུ་མཉྫུ་གྷོ་ཥ་ཡ།[1]

[2]སྦྱང་གཞི་སྐྱེ་ཤི་བར་དོ་ལྷུགས་ཀྱི་ཁམས། །
སྦྱོང་བྱེད་ཟབ་ལམ་རིམ་གཉིས་གསེར་འགྱུར་རྩི། །
སྦྱངས་འབྲས་རྣམ་དག་སྐུ་གསུམ་རིན་ཆེན་ལ། །
དབང་བསྒྱུར་ཟུང་འཇུག་མགོན་པོར་ཕྱག་འཚལ་ལོ། །

འདིར་བླ་མེད་ཁྲི་ལམ་གྱིས་སྙིགས་དུས་ཀྱི་ཚེ་ཐུང་གཅིག་ལ་ཁ་སྦྱོར་ཡན་ལག་བདུན་ལྡན་གྱི་ཟུང་འཇུག་གི་སྐུ་མངོན་དུ་བྱེད་པའི་ཉེ་ལམ་ཟབ་མོ་རིམ་པ་གཉིས་ཀྱི་བགྲོད་ཚུལ་ཤེས་པ་ལ། སྦྱང་གཞི་གཞིའི་སྐུ་གསུམ་གྱི་རྣམ་གཞག་ལ་གོ་བ་ཆགས་པ་ཤིན་དུ་གལ་ཆེ།

དེས་ན་ལམ་རིམ་པ་གཉིས་ཀྱི་སྦྱང་གཞི་སྐྱེ་ཤི་བར་དོ་གསུམ་གྱི་རྣམ་གཞག་བཤད་པ་ལ་གསུམ། འཆི་བའི་རིམ་པ། བར་དོ་འགྲུབ་པའི་རིམ་པ། དེས་སྐྱེ་སྲིད་དུ་སྐྱེ་བ་ལེན་པའི་ཚུལ་བཤད་པའོ།

དང་པོ་ནི། བསྐལ་པ་དང་པོའི་འཛམ་བུ་གླིང་པའི་མི་རྣམས་རྫུས་ཏེ་སྐྱེས་པ་དང་། ཚེ་ལོ་དཔག་ཏུ་མེད་པ་ཐུབ་པ། དབང་པོ་ཀུན་ཚང་བ། ལུས་རང་འོད་ཀྱིས་ཁྱབ་པ། མཚན་དཔེ་རྫོགས་མཐུན་པས་བརྒྱན་པ། ཁ་ཟས་ལ་མི་ལྟོས་པར་དགའ་བའི་ཟས་ཟ་བ། རྫུ་འཕྲུལ་གྱིས་ནམ་མཁའ་ལ་འགྲོ་ནུས་པ་སོགས་ཆོས་བདུན་ལྡན་ཤ་སྟག་ཡིན་པ་ལ། ཁམ་ཟས་ལ་སྲེད་པའི་བག་ཆགས་སད་པའི་རྐྱེན་གྱིས་ཁམ་ཟས་རགས་པ་བཟོས་པས་སྙིགས་མ་རྣམས་བསང་གཅིར་གྱུར་ཏེ་འདོན་པའི་སྒྲ་ཕོ་མོའི་དབང་པོ་སོགས་དོད་དོ།

དེར་སྔོན་གྱི་འཁྲིག་པའི་བག་ཆགས་ལྡན་པ་གཉིས་ཀྱིས་གཅིག་ལ་གཅིག་སེམས་ཆགས་ཏེ་ལོག་པར་ཞུགས་པ་ལ་བརྟེན་ནས་མངལ་དུ་སེམས་ཅན་ཆགས་ནས་རིམ་གྱིས་མངལ་སྐྱེས་སུ་གྱུར་ཅིང་། །དེ་ལ་ས་ཆུ་མེ་རླུང་རྩ་ཐིག་ལེའི་ཁམས་དྲུག་གམ། ཡང་ན་ཕ་ལས་ཐོབ་པའི་རུས་པ་རྐང་ཁུ་བ་གསུམ་དང་། མ་ལས་ཐོབ་པའི་ཤ་པགས་པ་ཁྲག་གསུམ་སྟེ་ཁམས་དྲུག་ཚང་བ་ལ་འཛམ་བུ་གླིང་པའི་མི་མངལ་སྐྱེས་ཁམས་དྲུག་ལྡན་ཟེར། སྔགས་

བླ་མེད་ཀྱི་ལམ་གྱི་ཐོག་མ་ནས་ཉམས་སུ་བླངས་ནས་སྙིགས་དུས་ཀྱི་ཚེ་ཐུང་གཅིག་ལ་འཚང་རྒྱ་བར་ངེས་པའི་གང་ཟག་ཡིན་ན། དེ་འདྲའི་འཛམ་བུ་གླིང་པའི་མི་མངལ་སྐྱེས་ཁམས་དྲུག་ལྡན་ཡིན་པས་ཁྱབ་པོ། དེའི་ལུས་ལ་རྩ་སྟོང་ཕྲག་བདུན་ཅུ་རྩ་གཉིས་རོ་རྐྱང་དབུ་མ་གསུམ་དང་བཅས་པ་ཡོད་ལ། མཐར་འཆི་བའི་ཚེ་རྩ་སྟོང་ཕྲག་བདུན་ཅུ་རྩ་གཉིས་ཀྱི་རླུང་ཐམས་ཅད་རོ་རྐྱང་གཉིས་སུ་འདུས་ཤིང་། དེ་གཉིས་ཀྱི་རླུང་ཡང་རྩ་དབུ་མ་ལ་ཐིམ།

རྩ་དབུ་མའི་སྟོད་སྨད་ཀྱི་རླུང་རྣམས་ཀྱང་མཐར་སྙིང་གའི་རྩ་འདབ་ཀྱི་ཧྲྀ་དིའི་[3]ནང་གི་ཁམས་དཀར་དམར་གའུ་ཁ་སྦྱར་གྱི་ཚུལ་དུ་ཡོད་པའི་དབུས་ན་ཤིན་ཏུ་ཕྲ་བའི་རླུང་སེམས་ངོ་བོ་གཅིག་པའི་ཆ་ཤས་སྲོག་འཛིན་གྱི་རླུང་མི་ཤིགས་པ་ལ་ཐིམ་པའི་སྒོ་ནས་འཆི་དགོས་ཏེ། ལུས་ཀྱི་ཆ་ཤས་གང་ཡང་རུང་བ་ཞིག་ན་ཤིན་ཏུ་ཕྲ་བའི་རླུང་མ་གཏོགས་པའི་རྣམ་ཤེས་ཀྱི་རྟེན་བྱེད་པའི་རླུང་ཙུང་ཟད་ཅིག་གནས་ན་འཆི་བ་མི་སྲིད་པས་སོ།[4]

དེ་ཡང་ཕུང་པོ་ལྔ། ཁམས་བཞི། སྐྱེ་མཆེད་དྲུག ། ཡུལ་ལྔ། གཞི་དུས་ཀྱི་ཡེ་ཤེས་ལྔ་སྟེ། རགས་པ་ཉེར་ལྔ་ཐིམ་པའི་སྒོ་ནས་འཆི་དགོས་ལ། ཐིམ་རིམ་ནི་དང་པོར་གཟུགས་ཕུང་གི་རིགས་ཀྱི་ཆོས་ལྔ་ནི། གཟུགས་ཀྱི་ཕུང་པོ། གཞི་དུས་ཀྱི་མེ་ལོང་ཡེ་ཤེས། སའི་ཁམས། མིག་གི་དབང་པོ། རང་རྒྱུད་ཀྱིས་བསྡུས་པའི་གཟུགས་ཏེ་ལྔ་པོ་དུས་མཉམ་དུ་ཐིམ་པར་འགྱུར་བས་[5]དེ་རྣམས་སོ་སོའི་ཐིམ་པའི་རྟགས་ནི། གཟུགས་ཕུང་ཐིམ་པའི་ཕྱི་རྟགས་སུ་ཡན་ལག་རྣམས་སྔར་ལས་ཕྲ་རུ་འགྲོ་ཞིང་། ལུས་ཉམ་ཆུང་བ་དང་། ནུས་པ་མེད་པར་འགྱུར་རོ། གཞི་དུས་ཀྱི་མེ་ལོང་ཡེ་ཤེས་ནི། མེ་ལོང་ལ་གཟུགས་བརྙན་སྣང་བ་བཞིན་དུ་ཡུལ་དུ་མ་ཅིག་ཅར་དུ་གསལ་བར་སྣང་བའི་ཤེས་པ་ཞིག་ལ་བཤད་ལ། དེ་ཐིམ་པའི་ཕྱི་རྟགས་སུ་མིག་མི་གསལ་ཞིང་རབ་རིབ་ཏུ་འགྱུར། སའི་ཁམས་ཐིམ་པའི་ཕྱི་རྟགས་སུ་ལུས་ཤས་ཆེར་སྐམ་ཞིང་ཡན་ལག་རྣམས་ལྷོད་ལྷོད་པོར་འགྲོ་བ་དང་། ལུས་ས་འོག་ཏུ་བྱིང་བ་ལྟ་བུའི་ཉམས་འབྱུང་། མིག་གི་དབང་པོ་ཐིམ་པའི་ཕྱི་རྟགས་སུ་མིག་འབྱེད་འཛུམ་མི་ནུས། རང་རྒྱུད་ཀྱིས་བསྡུས་པའི་གཟུགས་ཐིམ་པའི་ཕྱི་རྟགས་སུ་ལུས་ཀྱི་བཀྲག་མདངས་ཡལ་ཞིང་ཉམས་སྟོབས་ཟད་པར་འགྱུར་རོ། དེ་རྣམས་ཀྱི་ནང་རྟགས་སུ་སྨིག་རྒྱུ་ལྟ་བུ་ཞེས་བྱ་བ་སོས་ཀའི་དུས་སུ་བྱེ་མ་ལ་ཉི་འོད་ཕོག་པ་ན་ཆུར་སྣང་བ་ལྟ་བུ་སྔོ་མེར་པའི་སྣང་བ་འབྱུང་ངོ་།

དེའི་རྗེས་སུ་ཚོར་ཕུང་གི་རིགས་ཀྱི་ཆོས་ལྔ་དུས་མཉམ་དུ་ཐིམ་སྟེ། ཚོར་ཕུང་ཐིམ་པ་ན་ཕྱི་རྟགས་སུ་དབང་ཤེས་འཁོར་གྱི་ཚོར་བ་བདེ་སྡུག་བཏང་སྙོམས་གསུམ་ལུས་ཤེས་ཀྱིས་ཉམས་སུ་མི་མྱོང་། གཞི་དུས་ཀྱི་མཉམ་ཉིད་ཡེ་ཤེས་ནི་བདེ་སྡུག་བཏང་སྙོམས་གསུམ་ཚོར་བར་རིགས་གཅིག་ཏུ་དྲན་པའི་ཤེས་པ་ལ་བཤད་ཅིང་། དེ་ཐིམ་པའི་ཕྱི་རྟགས་སུ་ཡིད་ཤེས་འཁོར་གྱི་ཚོར་བ་བདེ་སྡུག་བཏང་སྙོམས་གསུམ་མི་དྲན། ཆུའི་ཁམས་ཐིམ་པའི་ཕྱི་རྟགས་ལ།

ཁ་ཆུ་དང་། ཏྲུལ་དང་། གཅིན་དང་། ཁྲག་དང་། ཁུ་བ་རྣམས་ཤས་ཆེར་སྐམ། རྣ་བའི་དབང་པོ་ཐིམ་པའི་ཕྱི་རྟགས་སུ་ཕྱི་ནང་གི་སྒྲ་མི་ཐོས། རང་རྒྱུད་ཀྱིས་བསྡུས་པའི་སྒྲ་ཐིམ་པའི་ཕྱི་རྟགས་སུ་རྣ་བའི་ནང་གི་ཙུར་སྒྲ་མི་འབྱུང་ངོ་། དེ་རྣམས་ཀྱི་ནང་རྟགས་སུ་དུ་བ་ལྟ་བུ་ཞེས་བྱ་བ་དུ་བ་འཁྲིགས་པའི་དཀྱིལ་ནས་དུད་ཁང་ནས་དུ་བ་འབྱུང་བ་ལྟ་བུ་སྔོ་ཡོད་ཡོད་པ་ལྟ་བུའི་སྣང་བ་འཆར་རོ།

དེའི་རྗེས་སུ་འདུ་ཤེས་ཀྱི་ཕུང་པོའི་རིགས་ཀྱི་ཆོས་ལྔ་དུས་མཉམ་དུ་ཐིམ་ལ། འདུ་ཤེས་ཀྱི་ཕུང་པོ་ཐིམ་པའི་ཕྱི་རྟགས་སུ་ཕ་མ་ལ་སོགས་པའི་ཉེ་དུ་སོགས་ཀྱི་དོན་མི་དྲན། གཞི་དུས་ཀྱི་སོར་རྟོག་ཡེ་ཤེས་ནི་ཉེ་དུ་སོགས་ཀྱི་མིང་སོ་སོར་དྲན་པའི་ཤེས་པ་ལ་བཤད་ཅིང་། དེ་ཐིམ་པའི་ཕྱི་རྟགས་སུ་ཕ་མ་ལ་སོགས་པའི་ཉེ་དུ་རྣམས་ཀྱི་མིང་མི་དྲན། མེའི་ཁམས་ཐིམ་པའི་ཕྱི་རྟགས་སུ་ལུས་ཀྱི་མེ་དྲོད་ཡལ་ནས་བཟའ་བཏུང་འཇུ་བའི་ནུས་པ་ཉམས། སྣའི་དབང་པོ་ཐིམ་པའི་ཕྱི་རྟགས་སུ་སྣ་སྒོ་ནས་རླུང་ནང་དུ་སྡུད་པ་ཞན་ཅིང་ཕྱིར་དྲག་ལ་རིང་དུ་རྒྱུ་བའི་དབུགས་བརྩེགས་མ་འབྱུང་། རང་རྒྱུད་ཀྱིས་བསྡུས་པའི་དྲི་ཐིམ་པའི་ཕྱི་རྟགས་སུ་སྣས་དྲི་ཞིམ་མི་ཞིམ་གང་ཡང་མི་ཚོར། དེ་རྣམས་ཀྱི་ནང་རྟགས་སུ་མཁའ་སྣང་ལྟ་བུ་ཞེས་ཀྱང་བྱ། སྲིན་བུ་མེ་ཁྱེར་ལྟ་བུ་ཞེས་བྱ་བ་དུད་ཁང་ནས་དུ་བ་སྔོ་ཡོད་པ་འབྱུང་བ་ལྟ་བུའི་གསེབ་ནས་མེ་སྟག་དམར་ཆིག་ཆིག་པ་ལྟ་བུ་འམ། ཡོས་རྫོས་པའི་སླ་ངའི་རྒྱབ་ཀྱི་དྲིག་པ་ལ་མེ་སྟག་དམར་ཡལ་ཡལ་འོང་བ་ལྟ་བུའི་སྣང་བ་འབྱུང་ངོ་།

དེའི་རྗེས་སུ་འདུ་བྱེད་ཀྱི་ཕུང་པོའི་རིགས་ཀྱི་ཆོས་ལྔ་དུས་མཉམ་དུ་ཐིམ་པར་འགྱུར་ཏེ། འདུ་བྱེད་ཀྱི་ཕུང་པོ་ཐིམ་པའི་ཕྱི་རྟགས་སུ་ལུས་ཀྱི་བྱ་བ་བསྐྱལ་བསྐྱོད་སོགས་མི་ནུས། གཞི་དུས་ཀྱི་བྱ་གྲུབ་ཡེ་ཤེས་ནི་འཇིག་རྟེན་པའི་ཕྱིའི་བྱ་བ་དང་དགོས་པ་སོགས་དྲན་པའི་ཤེས་པ་ལ་བཤད་ཅིང་། དེ་ཐིམ་པའི་ཕྱི་རྟགས་སུ་འཇིག་རྟེན་པའི་ཕྱིའི་བྱ་བ་དང་དགོས་པ་སོགས་གང་ཡང་མི་དྲན། རླུང་གི་ཁམས་ཐིམ་པའི་ཕྱི་རྟགས་སུ་སྲོག་འཛིན་སོགས་རླུང་བཅུ་རང་རང་གི་གནས་ནས་སྙིང་གར་འཕོ་ཞིང་དབུགས་ཕྱི་ནང་དུ་རྒྱུ་བ་ཆད། ལྕེའི་དབང་པོ་ཐིམ་པའི་ཕྱི་རྟགས་ལ་ལྕེ་སྦོམ་ཞིང་ཐུང་ལ་ལྕེའི་རྩ་བ་སྔོན་པོར་འགྱུར། རང་རྒྱུད་ཀྱིས་བསྡུས་པའི་རོ་ཐིམ་པའི་ཕྱི་རྟགས་སུ་ལྕེས་རོ་དྲུག་གང་ཡང་མི་མྱོང་། སྐབས་འདིར་ལུས་དབང་དང་རེག་བྱ་ཡང་ཐིམ་དགོས་པས་དེ་ཐིམ་པའི་ཕྱིར་རྟགས་ལ་རེག་བྱ་འཇམ་རྩུབ་གང་ཡང་མི་མྱོང་ངོ་། །དེ་རྣམས་ཀྱི་ནང་རྟགས་སུ་མར་མེ་འབར་བ་ལྟ་བུ་ཞེས་བྱ་བ་མར་མེ་ཟད་ཁར་རྩེ་མོ་ད་ལ་ལ་འགྲོ་བ་ལྟ་བུའི་སྣང་བ་འབྱུང་ངོ་།

དེ་ཡང་འབྱུང་བ་བཞི་སྔ་མ་ཕྱི་མ་ལ་ཐིམ་ཚུལ་ནི་འབྱུང་བ་སྔ་མས་རང་རང་གི་རྣམ་ཤེས་ཀྱི་རྟེན་བྱེད་པའི་ནུས་

པ་ཉམས་ནས་ཕྱི་མའི་ནུས་པ་གསལ་དུ་སོང་བ་ལ་འབྱུང་བ་སྔ་མ་ཕྱི་མ་ལ་ཐིམ་ཞེས་བཤད་པ་ཡིན་གྱི། འབྱུང་བ་སྔ་མ་ཞིག་ཕྱི་མའི་རང་བཞིན་དུ་སོང་བ་ནི་མ་ཡིན་ནོ། ས་ཆུ་ལ་ཐིམ་ཞེས་པ་ས་རླུང་གིས་རྣམ་ཤེས་ཀྱི་རྟེན་བྱེད་པའི་ནུས་པ་ཉམས་ནས་ཆུ་རླུང་གིས་རྣམ་ཤེས་ཀྱི་རྟེན་བྱེད་པའི་ནུས་པ་གསལ་དུ་སོང་བས་ན། སྔ་མའི་ནུས་པ་ཕྱི་མ་ལ་འཕོས་པ་འདྲ་བ་ཞིག་འབྱུང་བས་ས་ཆུ་ལ་ཐིམ་ཞེས་བཤད་ལ། ས་རང་དགའ་བ་ཞིག་ཆུ་རང་དགའ་བ་ཞིག་ལ་ཐིམ་པ་ནི་མ་ཡིན་ནོ། །དེས་གཞན་རྣམས་ལའང་རིགས་འགྲེའོ།

འབྱུང་བཞི་ཐིམ་རྗེས་སུ་རང་བཞིན་[6]བརྒྱད་ཅུའི་རྟོག་པའི་སེམས། སྣང་བ་དཀར་ལམ་པའི་སེམས། མཆེད་པ་དམར་ལམ་པའི་སེམས། ཉེར་ཐོབ་ནག་ལམ་པའི་སེམས། འཆི་བ་འོད་གསལ་གྱི་སེམས་དེ་[7]རྣམ་ཤེས་ཀྱི་ཕུང་པོའི་རིགས་ཀྱི་ཆོས་ལྔ་པོ་འདི་རྣམས་རིམ་ཅན་དུ་འཆར་དགོས་སོ།[8] རང་བཞིན་བརྒྱད་ཅུའི་རྟོག་པའི་སེམས་དང་། དེའི་བཞོན་པར་གྱུར་པའི་རླུང་གཉིས་སྣང་བ་དཀར་ལམ་པའི་སྤྲོ་རོལ་དུ་ཐིམ་དགོས་དེ། དེ་དང་སྣང་བའི་སེམས་གཉིས་འཛིན་སྟངས་མི་མཐུན་ཞིང་ཕྲ་རགས་ཀྱི་ཁྱད་པར་ཆེ་བས་སྣང་བ་རང་དུས་སུ་དེ་འདྲའི་རྟོག་རགས་པ་མེད་པའི་ཕྱིར། དེས་ན་རང་བཞིན་བརྒྱད་ཅུའི་ཀུན་རྟོག་བཞོན་པའི་རླུང་དང་བཅས་པ་སྣང་བ་ལ་ཐིམ་པའི་རྗོམ་པའི་ཆོ་མར་མེ་འབར་བ་ལྟ་བུའི་སྣང་བ་འབྱུང་། དེ་སྣང་བ་ལ་ཐིམ་པའི་སྣང་བ་རང་དུས་ཀྱི་རྟགས་ནི་སྟོན་གྱི་ནམ་མཁའ་གཡའ་དག་པའི་ཚེ་མཚན་མོ་ཟླ་བ་ཤར་བའི་འོད་ཀྱིས་ཁྱབ་པའི་ནམ་མཁའ་ལྟ་བུ་ཤིན་དུ་དྭངས་ཤིང་སྟོང་སང་ངེ་བ་ལ་འོད་ཀྱི་སྣང་བ་དཀར་པོའི་རྣམ་པ་ཞིག་འཆར་ལ།

དེ་ལྟར་འཆར་བའི་རྒྱུ་ནི། སྙིང་ག་ཡན་ཆད་ཀྱི་རོ་རྐྱང་གི་རླུང་ཐམས་ཅད་དབུ་མའི་ཡར་སྣ་ནས་ཞུགས་པའི་སྟོབས་ཀྱིས་སྤྱི་བོའི་རྩ་མདུད་གྲོལ་བའི་དབུས་ན་ཕ་ལས་ཐོབ་པའི་ཐིག་ལེ་དཀར་པོ་ཧཾ་ཡིག་མགོ་ཐུར་བསྟན་གྱི་རྣམ་པར་ཡོད་པ་ཆུའི་རང་བཞིན་ཅན་ཡིན་པས་ཐུར་ལ་འོངས་དེ། སྙིང་གའི་རོ་རྐྱང་གི་མདུད་པ་དྲུག་སྐོར་གྱི་སྟེང་དུ་སླེབ་པའི་བར་ལ་དེ་འདྲའི་སྣང་བ་འབྱུང་བ་ཡིན་གྱི། ཕྱི་རོལ་ནས་ཟླ་འོད་སོགས་ཀྱི་སྣང་བ་ཤར་བ་མ་ཡིན་ནོ། དེ་ལ་སྣང་བ་དང་སྟོང་པ་ཞེས་བྱའོ།

དེའི་རྗེས་སུ་སྣང་བ་དང་བཞོན་པའི་རླུང་དང་བཅས་པ་མཆེད་པ་ལ་ཐིམ་ནས་མཆེད་པའི་སེམས་ཤར་བའི་ཚེ་སྟོན་གནམ་གཡའ་དག་པ་ལ་ཉི་འོད་ཀྱིས་ཁྱབ་པ་ལྟ་བུ་སྔར་ལས་ཀྱང་ཆེས་དྭངས་པའི་སྟོང་སང་ངེ་བ་དམར་པོ་འམ་དམར་སེར་གྱི་སྣང་བ་འཆར་ལ། དེའི་རྒྱུ་ནི་སྙིང་ག་མན་ཆད་ཀྱི་རོ་རྐྱང་གི་རླུང་ཐམས་ཅད་དབུ་མའི་མར་སྣ་ནས་ཞུགས་པའི་སྟོབས་ཀྱིས་ནོར་བུའི་རྩ་འཁོར་གྱི་མདུད་པ་དང་ལྟེ་བའི་རྩ་འཁོར་གྱི་མདུད་པ་རྣམས་རིམ་གྱིས་གྲོལ་བས་ལྟེ་བའི་རྩ་

འཁོར་གྱི་དབུས་སུ་མ་ལས་ཐོབ་པའི་ཐིག་ལེ་དམར་པོ་ཨ་ཐུང་ཤད་ཀྱི་རྣམ་པར་ཡོད་པ་མེའི་རང་བཞིན་ཅན་ཡིན་པས་ཡར་འོངས་ཏེ། སྙིང་གའི་རོ་རྐྱང་གི་མདུད་པ་དྲུག་སྐོར་གྱི་འོག་ཏུ་སླེབ་པའི་བར་ལ་དེ་འདྲའི་སྣང་བ་འབྱུང་བ་ཡིན་ལ། ཕྱི་རོལ་ནས་ཉི་འོད་སོགས་ཀྱི་སྣང་བ་ཤར་བ་མ་ཡིན་ནོ། །དེ་ལ་སྣང་བ་མཆེད་པ་དང་ཤིན་ཏུ་སྟོང་པ་ཟེར་རོ།

དེའི་རྗེས་སུ་མཆེད་པ་བཞིན་པའི་རླུང་དང་བཅས་པ་ཉེར་ཐོབ་པ་ལ་ཐིམ་པའི་ཉེར་ཐོབ་ཀྱི་སྟོད་ཀྱི་ཚེ་སྟོན་གནམ་གཡའ་དག་པ་ལ་མཚམས་ཀྱི་སྨག་འཐུག་པོས་ཁྱབ་པ་ལྟ་བུ་སྟོང་སང་ནག་ལམ་པའི་སྣང་བ་འཆར་ལ། དེ་ནི་དབུ་མའི་ནང་གི་ཡས་རླུང་མས་རླུང་རྣམས་སྙིང་གའི་དབུ་མའི་ནང་དུ་འདུས་པའི་སྟོབས་ཀྱིས་སྙིང་གའི་རོ་རྐྱང་གི་མདུད་པ་དྲུག་སྐོར་གྲོལ་ཏེ། སྟེང་གི་ཐིག་ལེ་དཀར་པོ་མར་བབ། འོག་གི་ཐིག་ལེ་དམར་པོ་ཡར་འོངས་ཏེ། སྙིང་གའི་ཧྲྀ་དིའི་དབུས་ན་མི་ཤིགས་པའི་ཐིག་ལེ་དཀར་དམར་གཡུ་ཁ་སྦྱར་གྱི་ཚུལ་དུ་ཡོད་པའི་དབུས་སུ་ཆུད་ནས་ཕྲད་པའི་རྐྱེན་གྱིས་དེ་འདྲའི་སྣང་བ་བྱུང་བ་ཡིན་གྱི། ཕྱི་རོལ་ནས་མུན་པ་སོགས་ཀྱི་སྣང་བ་ཤར་བ་མ་ཡིན་ནོ། །དེ་ལ་ཉེར་ཐོབ་དང་སྟོང་པ་ཆེན་པོ་ཞེས་བྱའོ།

དེ་ཡང་ཉེར་ཐོབ་ཀྱི་སྟོད་ཡུལ་སྣང་དང་བཅས་པ་སྐྱེས་ལ། ཉེར་ཐོབ་ཀྱི་སྨད་ལ་ཡུལ་སྣང་གང་ཡང་མི་དྲན་པར་དྲན་མེད་དུ་བརྒྱལ་བ་ལྟར་ནག་འཐོམས་ཀྱིས་འགྲོ །དེ་ནས་ཤིན་ཏུ་ཕྲ་བའི་རླུང་སེམས་ལས་གློ་བུར་དུ་བྱུང་བའི་རླུང་སེམས་མཐའ་དག་འགགས་ཏེ། དང་པོ་ནས་གཞི་ལ་ཡོད་པའི་ཤིན་ཏུ་ཕྲ་བའི་རླུང་སེམས་ཀྱི་དྲན་པ་མ་གསོས་པའི་བར་[9]དེར་ཉེར་ཐོབ་ཀྱི་སྨད་དྲན་མེད་དེ་འོང་བ་ཡིན་ལ། དེའི་རྗེས་སུ་ཤིན་ཏུ་ཕྲ་བའི་རླུང་སེམས་ཀྱི་དྲན་པ་གསོས་ཏེ་འཆི་བ་འོད་གསལ་འཆར་རོ།

ཀུན་རྟོག་གཡོ་བ་དང་ཐིམ་པའི་བར་དུ་[10]འབྱུང་ཞིང་སྟོན་གནམ་གཡའ་དག་ལ་ཟླ་འོད་ཀྱིས་ཁྱབ་པ་ལྟ་བུའི་སྟོང་སང་དཀར་ལམ་པའི་སྣང་བ་འཆར་གྱི། དེ་ལས་གཞན་པའི་གཉིས་སྣང་རགས་པ་གཞན་གང་ཡང་མི་འཆར་བའི་ཡིད་ཀྱི་ཤེས་པ་ནི། སྣང་བ་དཀར་ལམ་པའི་མཚན་ཉིད་དང་། ཀུན་རྟོག་གཡོ་བ་དང་ཐིམ་པའི་བར་དུ་འབྱུང་ཞིང་སྟོན་གནམ་གཡའ་དག་པ་ལ་ཉི་འོད་ཀྱིས་ཁྱབ་པ་ལྟ་བུའི་སྟོང་སང་དམར་ལམ་པའི་སྣང་བ་འཆར་གྱི། དེ་ལས་གཞན་པའི་གཉིས་སྣང་རགས་པ་གཞན་གང་ཡང་མི་འཆར་བའི་ཡིད་ཀྱི་ཤེས་པ་ནི། སྣང་བ་མཆེད་པའི་མཚན་ཉིད། ཀུན་རྟོག་གཡོ་བ་དང་ཐིམ་པའི་བར་དུ་འབྱུང་ཞིང་སྟོན་གནམ་གཡའ་དག་པ་ལ་མཚམས་ཀྱི་སྨག་འཐུག་པོས་ཁྱབ་པ་ལྟ་བུའི་སྟོང་སང་ནག་ལམ་པའི་སྣང་བ་འཆར་གྱི། དེ་ལས་གཞན་པའི་གཉིས་སྣང་རགས་པ་གཞན་གང་ཡང་མི་འཆར་བའི་ཡིད་ཀྱི་ཤེས་པ་ནི། སྣང་བ་ཉེར་ཐོབ་ཀྱི་མཚན་ཉིད།

ཉེར་ཐོབ་འོད་གསལ་ལ་ཐིམ་ནས་འོད་གསལ་ཤར་བའི་ཚེ་ཉེར་ཐོབ་ཀྱི་སྣང་དྲན་མེད་དེ་སངས་ནས་གཉིས་སྣང་རགས་པ་ཙུང་ཟད་ཀྱང་མེད་པར་སྟོན་གྱི་ནམ་མཁའ་གཡའ་དག་པ་ལ་ཟླ་འོད་ཉི་འོད་མུན་པ་སྟེ་སྒྲིབ་བྱེད་ཀྱི་རྐྱེན་གསུམ་དང་བྲལ་བའི་ཐོ་རངས་ཀྱི་ནམ་མཁའི་རང་མདོག་ཇི་ལྟ་བ་བཞིན་སྟོང་སང་ཤིན་ཏུ་དྭངས་པའི་སྣང་བ་སྟོང་ཉིད་མངོན་སུམ་དུ་རྟོགས་པའི་མཉམ་གཞག་གི་སྣང་བ་འདྲ་བ་ཞིག་འཆར་རོ།

དེ་ལྟར་འཆར་བའི་རྐྱེན་ཡང་ཐིག་ལེ་དཀར་དམར་གཉིས་མི་ཤིགས་པའི་ཐིག་ལེ་དཀར་དམར་ལ་ཐིམ། དབུ་མའི་ནང་གི་རླུང་ཐམས་ཅད་ཀྱང་ཤིན་ཏུ་ཕྲ་བའི་སྲོག་འཛིན་གྱི་རླུང་ལ་ཐིམ་པས་དང་པོ་ནས་གཞི་ལ་ཡོད་པའི་ཤིན་ཏུ་ཕྲ་བའི་རླུང་སེམས་མངོན་དུ་གྱུར་པས་ན་དེ་འདྲའི་སྣང་བ་ཤར་བ་ཡིན་གྱི། ཕྱི་རོལ་གྱི་ནམ་མཁའི་སྟོང་སང་སྣང་བ་ནི་མ་ཡིན་ནོ། །དེ་ལ་འཆི་བ་འོད་གསལ་དང་ཐམས་ཅད་སྟོང་པ་ཞེས་བྱ་སྟེ། འཆི་བ་དངོས་དེ་ཡིན་ནོ།

དེ་ནི་གཞིའི་ཆོས་སྐུ་དང་། སྟོང་སང་དེ་ལ་གཞིའི་ངོ་བོ་ཉིད་སྐུ་དང་། དེ་ཡུལ་དུ་བྱེད་པའི་བློ་དེ་ལ་གཞིའི་རྟོགས་པ་ཡེ་ཤེས་ཆོས་ཀྱི་སྐུ་ཞེས་ཀྱང་ཟེར་རོ། དེ་ལ་ཐ་མལ་པའི་མི་རྣམས་ཞག་གསུམ་གྱི་བར་དུ་གནས་ལ། དེ་ནས་ཁམས་དཀར་དམར་གྱི་རྟགས་འོང་ངོ་། །ནད་ཀྱིས་ལུས་ཟུངས་ཟད་དྲག་པ་ལ་ཞག་ཇི་ཙམ་སོང་ཡང་ཁམས་དཀར་དམར་གྱི་རྟགས་མི་འོང་བའང་སྲིད་ལ། རྣལ་འབྱོར་པས་རྟོགས་པ་མཐོ་དམའི་དབང་གིས་འོད་གསལ་དེ་ཆོས་སྐུ་དང་བསྲེས་ནས་འཛོག་པ་ལ་ཞག་གྲངས་མང་ཉུང་ངེས་པ་མེད་པར་གསུང་།

སྣང་མཆེད་ཐོབ་གསུམ་འོད་གསལ་དང་བཅས་པའི་ཐིམ་ཚུལ་དེ་ཡང་སེམས་སྔ་མ་སྔ་མའི་ནུས་པ་འགགས་ནས་ཕྱི་མ་ཕྱི་མ་གསལ་དུ་སོང་བ་ལ་སྔ་མ་ཕྱི་མ་ལ་ཐིམ་ཞེས་བྱའི།[11] སྔ་མ་ཕྱི་མའི་རང་བཞིན་དུ་སོང་བ་ནི་མ་ཡིན་ནོ།

སྟོན་གྱི་ནམ་མཁའ་དཔེར་བཟུང་བ་ནི། དབྱར་དུས་ཀྱི་ཆར་གྱིས་སའི་རྡུལ་བར་སྣང་ལ་[12]ལྡང་བ་ལེགས་པར་མནན་པ་དང་། སྤྲིན་གྱི་སྒྲིབ་བྱེད་དང་བྲལ་བ་གཉིས་ཚོགས་ཤིན་ཏུ་དྭངས་པ་མང་དུ་འབྱུང་བ་སྟོན་གྱི་དུས་ཡིན་པས་སྟོན་གྱི་ནམ་མཁའ་དཔེར་བཟུང་བ་དང་། ནམ་མཁའ་དེ་ཐོགས་བཅས་རགས་པ་དགག་ཙམ་གྱི་སྟོང་སང་ཡིན་པ་ལྟར། སྟོང་པ་བཞི་ཡང་ཡིད་ངོར་ཀུན་རྟོག་རགས་པའི་སྣང་བ་ལོག་ནས་སྟོང་སང་གི་སྣང་བ་འཆར་བ་གཉིས་སྣང་ཚུལ་མཚུངས་པས་དཔེ་དོན་སྦྱར་བ་ཡིན་གྱི། གནས་སྐབས་དེ་ན་ནམ་མཁའ་སོགས་ཀྱི་སྣང་བ་ཤར་བ་མ་ཡིན་ནོ།

འོ་ན་སྣང་བའི་སྔ་རོལ་དུ་རང་བཞིན་བརྒྱད་ཅུ་བཞོན་པའི་རླུང་དང་བཅས་པ་ཐིམ་ཟིན་ན། སྣང་མཆེད་ཐོབ་གསུམ་གྱི་དུས་སུ་ཐིམ་རྒྱུའི་[13]རླུང་མེད་དམ་སྙམ་ན། སྤྱིར་རླུང་ལ་ཕྲ་རགས་མང་དུ་ཡོད་པའི་རགས་པ་རྣམས་ཐིམ་ཚར་[14]ཡང་ཕྲ་བ་ཡོད་དོ། །དེས་ན་རླུང་ཕྲ་བ་གཅིག་པུས་ཤེས་པའི་རྟེན་བྱེད་པའི་དུས་ནི་རླུང་སྣང་བ་ལ་ཐིམ་པ་ནས་

ཉེར་ཐོབ་འོད་གསལ་ལ་ཐིམ་པའི་བར་དུ་ཡིན་ནོ།

སྟོང་པ་བཞིའི་སྐབས་སུ་ཤེས་པ་སྔ་མ་སྔ་མ་ཡུལ་སྣང་དང་བཅས་པ་ལས་ཕྱི་མ་ཕྱི་མ་རྣམས་ཡུལ་སྣང་དང་བཅས་ཇེ་ཕྲ་ཇེ་ཕྲར[15]སོང་བའི་སྟོབས་ཀྱིས་ཡིད་ངོར་ཀུན་རྫོབ་ཀྱི་སྣང་བ་རགས་པ་ལོག་ནས་སྟོང་སང་ངེ་བ་ཞིག་ཤར་བ་ཡིན་གྱི་སྟོང་ཉིད་ཡུལ་དུ་བྱེད་པ་ནི་མ་ཡིན་ནོ། །དེས་ན་ལམ་མི་བསྒོམས་པའི་ཐ་མལ་པ་ལ་དེ་དག་གི་སྐབས་སུ་བདེན་གྲུབ་ཁོ་ན་ལས་བདེན་མེད་ཀྱི་སྣང་བ་མི་འཆར་དེ། སྐབས་འདིའི་སྟོང་པ་བཞི་པོ་སེམས་ཅན་འཆི་ཚད་ཐམས་ཅད་ལ་འཆར་བས་འཆི་བའི་སྐབས་སྟོང་ཉིད་རྟོགས་ན་འབད་མེད་དུ་གྲོལ་བར་ཐལ་བའི་ཕྱིར་རོ། །

ཐ་མལ་པ་རྣམས་ཀྱིས་འཆི་བ་འོད་གསལ་དེ་སྣང་ལ་མ་ངེས[16]པའི་ཚུལ་གྱིས་མྱོང་བ་ཡིན་གྱི། ངེས་ཤེས་དང་བཅས་དེ་མྱོང་བ་མིན་ནོ། །དེ་ནི་མའི་འོད་གསལ་ཡིན་ལ། ལམ་དུས་ཀྱི་གཉིད་དང་སད་པའི་སྐབས་སུ་བསྒོམས་སྟོབས་ཀྱིས་ཤར་བའི་འོད་གསལ་ལ་བུའི་འོད་གསལ་ཞེས་བྱ། དེ་གཉིས་འཆི་བ་འོད་གསལ་གྱི་དུས་སུ་བསྲེས་ནས་བསྒོམས་པ་ལ་འོད་གསལ་མ་བུ་འདྲེས་པ་ཞེས་ཟེར་རོ།

འོ་ན་འཆི་བ་འོད་གསལ་དེ་སྤྱིར་འོད་གསལ་མཚན་ཉིད་པ[17]ཡིན་ནམ་ཞེ་ན། རྣལ་འབྱོར་པས་འོད་གསལ་མ་བུ་བསྲེས་དེ་ལྷ་ཐོག་ཏུ་འཇོག་པ་ནི་འོད་གསལ་མཚན་ཉིད་པ་ཡིན་ཡང་། དེ་ལྟར་མ་ཡིན་པར་ཐ་མལ་པ་ལ་རང་ཤུགས་ཀྱིས་ཤར་བའི་འཆི་བ་འོད་གསལ་ནི་གཉིས་སྣང་རགས་པ་འགགས་པ་ཙམ་ལ་འོད་གསལ་ཞེས་བཏགས་པ་ཡིན་གྱི་མཚན་ཉིད་པ་ནི་མིན་ནོ། །སྤྱིར་འོད་གསལ་ལ་གཉིས་ལས། སྟོང་ཉིད་ཕྲ་མོ་ཡུལ་གྱི་འོད་གསལ་དང་། དེ་རྟོགས་པའི་ཡེ་ཤེས་ཡུལ་ཅན་གྱི་འོད་གསལ་དུ་འཇོག་གོ

འཆི་བའི་རིམ་པ་འདི་རྣམས་སྔགས་བླ་མེད་ཀྱི་བསྐྱེད་རྫོགས་གཉིས་ཀྱིས་འཆི་བ་ཆོས་སྐུར་འཁྱེར་བའི་ལམ་འཁྱེར་དང་། དཔེ་དང་དོན་གྱི་འོད་གསལ་རྣམས་ཀྱི་སྦྱང་གཞིའི་གཙོ་བོ་ཡིན་པས[18]འདི་རྣམས་ལ་གོ་བ་ལེགས་པར་ཆགས་པ་ཤིན་ཏུ་གལ་ཆེའོ།

གཉིས་པ་བར་དོ་འགྲུབ་པའི་རིམ་པ་བཤད་པ་ནི། དེ་ལྟར་འཆི་བ་འོད་གསལ་གྱི་སེམས་དེ་གཡོ་མེད་དུ་ཇི་ཙམ་གནས་པའི་མཐར། དེའི་ངང་ནས་འདར་འཕྲིག་ཙམ་གྱིས་ཅུང་ཟད་གཡོ་བ་ཞིག་འོང་ལ། དེ་བྱུང་བའི་ཚེ་འོད་གསལ་ལས་ལྡང་བར་རྩོམ་པ་ཡིན་པས་མཚམས་དེ་ནས་ཤིན་ཏུ་ཕྲ་བའི་རླུང་སེམས་དེ་སྙིང་གའི་ཁམས་དཀར་དམར་གྱི་ཐིག་ལེ་ཁ་བཤག་གི་ཕྱེ་བའི་ནང་ནས་ཕྱི་རོལ་དུ་རྒྱུངས་དེ་ཐོན་ནས་ལུས་འདི་བོར་དེ། བར་དོའི་ལུས་གྲུབ་པ་ཡིན། དེ་

དང་དུས་མཉམ་དུ་སྙིང་གཞི་ཁམས་དཀར་པོ་ཐུར་དུ་བབས་ནས་རྟགས་ཀྱི་རྩེ་དང་། དམར་པོ་གྱེན་དུ་སོང་ནས་སྤྱིང་གི་སྣ་སྒྲོ་ནས་ཕྱིར་འབྱུང་ངོ་།

དེ་ཡང་འཆི་བ་འོད་གསལ་གྱི་བཞོན་པར་གྱུར་བའི་རླུང་འོད་ཟེར་ལྔ་པ་དེས་བར་དོའི་ལུས་ཀྱི་ཉེར་ལེན་དང་སེམས་ཀྱི་ལྷན་ཅིག་བྱེད་རྐྱེན་བྱེད་ལ། འཆི་བ་འོད་གསལ་གྱི་སེམས་དེས་བར་དོའི་ལུས་ཀྱི་ལྷན་ཅིག་བྱེད་རྐྱེན་དང་སེམས་ཀྱི་ཉེར་ལེན་བྱས་པ་ལ་བརྟེན་ནས། གང་དུ་སྐྱེ་འགྱུར་གྱི་མིའི་རྣམ་པ་ཅན་གྱི་བར་དོ་རླུང་གི་ལུས་ཅན་རྣམ་སྨིན་གྱི་ཕུང་པོ་སྙིང་པ་ལས་ལོགས་སུ་ཕྱེ་བའི་ཚུལ་གྱིས་དངོས་གནས་ལ་འགྲུབ་པོ།

དེའི་ཚེ་སྣང་མཆེད་ཐོབ་གསུམ་སོགས་སྔར་བཤད་པ་ལས་གོ་རིམ་བཟློག་སྟེ་ལུགས་ལྡོག་གི་ཉེར་ཐོབ་ནག་ལམ་པ་ཤར་བ། འཆི་བ་འོད་གསལ་འགགས་པ། བར་དོ་གྲུབ་པ་རྣམས་དུས་མཉམ་ཡིན་དེ། མངོན་པ་གོང་འོག་དང་ས་སྐྱེ་སོགས་མང་པོ་ནས[19]འཆི་སྲིད་འགགས་པ་དང་བར་སྲིད་གྲུབ་པ་གཉིས་སྲང་མདའི་མཐོ་དམན་བཞིན་དུ་དུས་མཉམ་པར་གསུངས་ཤིང་། བར་སྲིད་པ་རྫུས་སྐྱེས་ཡིན་པས་དབང་པོ་དང་ཡན་ལག་ཉིང་ལག་ཐམས་ཅད་ཅིག་ཅར་དུ་གྲུབ་པའི་ཕྱིར་རོ།

བར་དོ་གྲུབ་མ་ཐག་པའི་སེམས་ནི་ལུགས་ལྡོག་གི་ཉེར་ཐོབ་ཡིན་ལ། དེ་ལས་ལུགས་ལྡོག་གི་མཆེད་པ་དང་། དེ་ལས་སྣང་བ་དང་། སྣང་བ་དེ་ལས་རང་བཞིན་བརྒྱད་ཅུའི་ཀུན་རྟོག་རྣམས་སྐྱེས་ཏེ་བར་དོ་བ་དེས་སྐྱེ་གནས་དང་ཁྲི་འཚོར་བ་སོགས་ཀྱི་ཕྱིར་དུ་མངོན་པར་རྒྱུག་པ་ཡིན་ནོ། དེ་དག་གི་ཚེའང་སྔར་བཤད་པའི་རིམ་པ་ལས་བཟློག་སྟེ་ཉེར་ཐོབ་ནས་སྨིག་རྒྱུའི་བར་གྱི་རྟགས་རྣམས་རིམ་བཞིན་འབྱུང་། ཤ་ཁྲག་རྡོས་བཅས་སོགས་འབྱུང་ལུས་རགས་པ་སྤངས་པའི་རླུང་ཙམ་ལས་གྲུབ་པའི་ཡིད་ལུས་ཞིན་དུ་ཕྲ་བའི་བར་དོ་བ་དེ་ལ། གཞིའི་ལོངས་སྐུ་དང་། དྲི་ཟ་ཞེས་བྱའོ།

འོན་དེ་འདྲའི་བར་དོ་བ་ཡོད་པའི་དཔེ་ཇི་ལྟ་བུ་ཡིན་ཞེ་ན། དཔེར་ན་རང་ཅག་རྣམས་གཉིད་དུ་འགྲོ་བ[20]ན་གཉིད་ཀྱི་སྐབས་ཀྱི་རྟགས་བཞི་དང་སྟོང་པ་བཞི་འཆི་དུས་དང་འདྲ་བ་སྐྱེམ་ཙམ་རེ་ཤར་ནས་གཉིད་ཀྱི་འོད་གསལ་འཆར་ལ། དེ་ལས་ལྡང་བར་རྩོམ་པ་ན་རྨི་ལམ་གྱི་ལུས་སུ་ལྡང་བར་རྩོམ་ཞིང་། གཉིད་ཀྱི་འོད་གསལ་ལས་ལངས་པ་ན་རྨི་ལམ་གྱི་ལུས་གྲུབ་སྟེ། རྨི་ལམ་གྱི་སྐབས་ཀྱི་བྱ་བྱེད་སྣ་ཚོགས་ཞིག་བྱེད་ཅིང་། གཉིད་སད་པར་རྩོམ་པའི་ཚེ་རྨི་ལམ་གྱི་རླུང་ལུས་དེ་མེ་ལོང་ལ་ཧ་བཏབ་པ་བཞིན་མཐའ་ནས་ཡལ་ཏེ་སྙིང་གར་འདུས་ནས་ཕུང་པོ་སྙིང་པའི་སྙིང་གཞི་ནཱ་ཌཱིའི་ནང་གི་ཞིན་དུ་ཕྲ་བའི་རླུང་སེམས་ངོ་བོ་དབྱེར་མེད་ལ་ཐིམ་ནས་གཉིད་སད་དེ། བྱ་བྱེད་སྣ་ཚོགས་ལ་འཇུག་པ་བཞིན་ནོ།

དེ་ལྟ་བུའི་བར་དོའི་ངོ་བོའི་ཁྱད་པར་ནི་དབང་པོ་ཀུན་ཚང་བ། རྫུ་སྐྱེས་ཡིན་པས་ཡན་ལག་དང་ཉིང་ལག་ཐམས་ཅད་ཅིག་ཅར་དུ་རྫོགས་པ། ཕྲ་བའི་ལུས་ཅན་ཡིན་པས་རྡོ་རྗེ་ཕ་ལམ་གྱིས་ཀྱང་གཞིག་ཏུ་མེད་པ། མའི་མངལ་ལྟ་བུའི་སྐྱེ་གནས་མ་གཏོགས་རི་རབ་སོགས་གང་ལའང་ཐོགས་པ་མེད་པ། ལས་ཀྱི་རྫུ་འཕྲུལ་གྱི་ཤུགས་ཀྱིས་སྐད་ཅིག་ལ་ཇི་ལྟར་འདོད་པ་བཞིན་འགྲོ་ནུས་ཤིང་སངས་རྒྱས་ཀྱིས་ཀྱང་དགག་པར་མི་ནུས་པའོ།

མཛོད་ལས།[21] འགྲོ་བ་གང་གི་བར་སྲིད་གྲུབ་ན་དེ་ལས་འགྲོ་བ་གཞན་དུ་མི་ལྡོག་པར་བཤད་ཀྱང་། ཀུན་བཏུས་ལས། གང་གི་བར་སྲིད་གྲུབ་ནའང་དེར་སྐྱེ་བའི་ངེས་པ་མེད་པར་འགྲོ་བ་གཞན་དུ་ལྡོག་པ་ཡོད་པར་གསུངས། འོན་ཀྱང་མངོན་པ་གོང་འོག་གཉིས་གའི་ལུགས་ལའང་བར་དོའི་རྟེན་ལ་དགྲ་བཅོམ་ཐོབ་པའི་བར་འདོད་པ་[22]ཡོད་པས་མཐའ་གཅིག་ཏུ་སྐྱེ་སྲིད་ལེན་དགོས་པས་ཁྱབ་པ་ཁས་མི་ལེན་ནོ། མིང་གི་རྣམ་གྲངས་ནི། ཡིད་ལས་བྱུང་བ་དང་། སྲིད་འཚོལ་དང་། དྲི་ཟ་དང་། སྲིད་པ་བར་མ་དང་། མངོན་པར་འགྲུབ་པའི་སྲིད་པ་ཞེས་མཛོད་ལས་བཤད་དོ།[23]

ཚེ་ཚད་ཀྱི་ཁྱད་པར་ནི་རིང་མཐའ་ཞག་བདུན་ཡིན་ཡང་སྐྱེ་བའི་རྐྱེན་ཚོགས་ན་བར་སྲིད་གྲུབ་པའི་མོད་ལ་སྐྱེ་སྲིད་དུ་ཉིང་མཚམས་སྦྱོར་བའང་ཡོད་པས་ངེས་པ་མེད། གལ་ཏེ་ཞག་བདུན་ནས་སྐྱེ་བའི་རྐྱེན་མ་ཚོགས་ན་ཞག་བདུན་གྱི་མཐར་འཆི་ཆུང་རེ་བྱས་ཏེ་ཡང་བར་དོ་དེ་ཉིད་གྲུབ་སྟེ་གནས་སོ། །དེ་ལྟར་བྱས་ཏེ་ཞག་བདུན་ཕྲག་བདུན་འདས་པ་ན་ངེས་པར་སྐྱེ་བའི་རྐྱེན་ཚོགས་ཏེ་སྐྱེ་སྲིད་ལེན་པས་ཁྱབ་པར་སའི་དགོངས་གཞིར་གསུངས་སོ།

ཞག་བདུན་གྱི་མཐར་འཆི་ཆུང་རེ་བྱེད་ཚུལ་ནི། བར་དོའི་རླུང་ལུས་དེ་མེ་ལོང་ལ་ཧ་བཏབ་པ་མཐའ་ནས་སྡུད་པ་བཞིན་སྟོད་སྨད་ནས་རིམ་གྱིས་སྙིང་གར་འདུས་ཏེ་བར་དོའི་གནས་སྐབས་ཀྱི་རང་བཞིན་བརྒྱད་ཅུའི་རྟོག་པ་བཀོན་པའི་རླུང་དང་བཅས་པ་ཐིམ་ནས། བར་དོ་འཆི་བའི་རྟགས་བཞི་དང་སྟོང་པ་བཞི་སྐྱིམ་ཙམ་རེ་སྒྱུར་བའི་ཚུལ་གྱིས་ཤར་ནས་བར་དོ་ཤི་བའི་འོད་གསལ་མངོན་དུ་བྱས། དེ་ནས་འོད་གསལ་དེའི་བཞོན་པའི་རླུང་གིས་ཉེར་ལེན་བྱས་ནས་ལུགས་ལྡོག་ཏུ་ལངས་པའི་ཉེར་ཐོབ་གྲུབ་པ་དང་དུས་མཉམ་དུ་བར་དོའི་རླུང་ལུས་སྔར་བཞིན་གྲུབ་པ་ཡིན་ནོ། །བར་དོའི་རྟེན་ལ་འཆི་ཆུང་ཇི་ཙམ་བྱས་ཀྱང་བར་སྲིད་རང་ལ་བསྡུ་ལ།

བར་དོ་བ་དེས་རང་གི་སྔ་མའི་ལུས་རྟེན་མཐོང་ཡང་ལས་ཀྱི་འབྲེལ་པ་ཆད་པའི་སྟོབས་ཀྱིས་ལུས་རྟེན་རྙིང་པ་དེ་ངའི་ལུས་ཡིན་སྙམ་པ་དང་དེ་ལ་འཇུག་འདོད་ཀྱི་བློ་མི་སྐྱེ་བར་སའི་དགོངས་གཞི་ལས་གསུངས།

ཁ་ཅིག །བར་དོའི་ཚེ་ཚད་ཞག་བདུན་དུ་གསུངས་པ་དེ་རིགས་དྲུག་རང་རང་གི་ཞག་གི་དབང་དུ་བྱས་པ་ཡིན་ཟེར་བ་མི་འཐད་དེ། དེ་ལྟར་ན་དམྱལ་བ་པ་དང་ཁམས་གོང་མའི་ལྷ་རྣམས་ཀྱི་བར་དོ་ལ་འགྲོ་བ་དེ་དང་དེའི་ཞག་

བདུན་སོགས་ཀྱི་བར་དུ་གནས་པ་ཞིག་ཡོད་དགོས་པས་ལོ་བྱེ་བ་ཕྲག་ཤིན་དུ་མང་པོའི་བར་དུ་ཡང་སྐྱེ་བའི་རྐྱེན་མི་ཚོགས་པར་བར་དོར་གནས་པ་ཞིག་ཁས་ལེན་དགོས་པས་ཐལ་ཆེ་བར་འགྱུར་བའི་ཕྱིར་རོ།

སྲིད་པར་འཕོ་ཚུལ་གྱི་ཁྱད་པར་ནི། དམྱལ་བར་སྐྱེ་ན་བཤང་ལམ་ནས་འཕོ་ལ། ཡི་དྭགས་སུ་སྐྱེ་ན་ཁ་དང་། དུད་འགྲོར་སྐྱེ་ན་དྲི་ཆུའི་ལམ་དང་། མིར་སྐྱེ་ན་མིག་དང་། འདོད་ལྷར་སྐྱེ་ན་ལྟེ་བ། གནོད་སྦྱིན་དུ་སྐྱེ་ན་སྣ། གྲུབ་པའི་ལྷ་དང་མིའམ་ཅིར་སྐྱེ་ན་རྣ་བ། གཟུགས་ཁམས་སུ་སྐྱེ་ན་སྨིན་མཚམས་ཀྱི་དབུས། གཟུགས་མེད་དུ་སྐྱེ་ན་སྤྱི་བོ་ནས་འཕོ་བར་རྒྱུད་བརྟག་པ་བརྒྱད་པ་[24]སོགས་ལས་བཤད།

འོན། ས་སྡེ་སོགས་སུ་ལུས་འདོར་བ་ན་སྙིང་ག་ནས་རྣམ་ཤེས་འཕོ་བར་བཤད་པ་དང་འགལ་ལོ་ཞེ་ན། མི་འགལ་ཏེ་ལུས་ཀྱི་ནང་དུ་རྣམ་ཤེས་འཕོ་བ་ན་ཐོག་མར་སྙིང་ག་ནས་འཕོ་བ་ཡིན་ཡང་། དེ་ནས་ལུས་ཀྱི་ཕྱི་རོལ་དུ་འཕོ་བ་ན་སྒོ་སོ་སོ་ནས་འཕོ་བར་བཤད་པ་བཞིན་ཡིན་པའི་ཕྱིར།

ཡང་མཛོད་ལས། རིམ་གྱིས་འཆི་ན་རྐང་པ་དང་། ལྟེ་བ་སྙིང་གར་ཡིད་འཆི་འཕོ།[25] ཞེས་དང་། འགྲེལ་པར་ངན་སོང་དུ་སྐྱེ་ན་རྐང་པ་དང་། མིར་སྐྱེ་ན་ལྟེ་བ་དང་། ལྷར་སྐྱེ་བ་དང་དགྲ་བཅོམ་པ་འཆི་ན་སྙིང་གར་རྣམ་ཤེས་འགག་གོ །ཞེས་གསུངས་པ་ཇི་ལྟར་ཡིན་སྙམ་ན། དེ་ནི་གནས་དེ་དག་ཏུ་ཡིད་འགག་པའི་དོན་དུ་འགྲེལ་པ་ལས་བཤད་པ་ལྟར། རྐང་པ་ལ་སོགས་པའི་གནས་དེ་དག་ཏུ་ལུས་དབང་འགགས་པའི་སྟོབས་ཀྱིས་ཡིད་ཀྱི་རྣམ་ཤེས་འགག་ཚུལ་སོ་སོ་བསྟན་པ་ཙམ་ཡིན་གྱི། གནས་དེ་དག་ནས་རྣམ་ཤེས་ཕྱི་རོལ་དུ་འཕོ་བར་སྟོན་པ་མ་ཡིན་པས་སྔར་བཤད་པ་དང་འགལ་བ་མེད་དོ།

མཐོང་ཚུལ་གྱི་ཁྱད་པར་ནི། བར་དོ་རིགས་མཐུན་དང་ལྷའི་མིག་རྣམ་པར་དག་པས་མཐོང་བར་མཛོད་ལས་བཤད། དེ་ལ་ལྷའི་མིག་སྐྱེས་སྟོབས་ཀྱིས་ཐོབ་པ་ནི་མ་དག་པ་དང་། བསྒོམས་སྟོབས་ཀྱིས་ཐོབ་པ་ནི་ལྷའི་མིག་དག་པ་ལ་འདོག་གོ །བར་དོ་གོང་མ་གོང་མས་འོག་མ་འོག་མ་མཐོང་བའི་ལུགས་ཀྱང་མཛོད་འགྲེལ་ལས་བཤད། བོང་ཚོད་ཀྱི་ཁྱད་པར་ནི། འཇམ་དབྱངས་གླིང་པའི་མིའི་བར་དོ་བྱིས་པ་ལོ་ལྔའམ་དྲུག་ལོན་པ་ལྟ་བུར་མཛོད་འགྲེལ་དུ་བཤད་ཀྱང་མཐའ་གཅིག་ཏུ་ངེས་པ་ཅན་མ་གསུངས་སོ།

རྣམ་པའི་ཁྱད་པར་ནི། ངན་འགྲོའི་བར་དོ་ཕུར་བ་ནག་པོ་བཀྲུང་བའམ་མཚན་མོ་མུན་ནག་གིས་ཁྱབ་པ་ལྟ་བུ་དང་། བདེ་འགྲོའི་བར་སྲིད་སྣམ་བུ་དཀར་པོ་བཀྲུང་བའམ་མཚན་མོ་ཟླ་འོད་ཀྱིས་ཁྱབ་པ་ལྟ་བུའི་ཉམས་འབྱུང་བར་སའི་དངོས་གཞིར་གསུངས།

ཁ་དོག་གི་ཁྱད་པར་ནི། དམྱལ་བའི་བར་དོ་སྡོང་དུམ་མེས་ཚིག་པ་ལྟ་བུ་དང་། ཡི་དྭགས་ཀྱི་བར་དོ་ཆུ་ལྟ་བུ། དུད་འགྲོའི་བར་དོ་དུ་བ་ལྟ་བུ། འདོད་པའི་ལྷ་མིའི་བར་དོ་གསེར་ལྟ་བུ། གཟུགས་ཁམས་པའི་བར་དོ་དཀར་པོ་སོགས་སུ་དགའ་བོ་མངལ་འཇུག་གི་མདོ་ལས་བཤད།

བྱད་གཟུགས་ཀྱི་ཁྱད་པར་ནི། གང་དུ་སྐྱེ་འགྱུར་གྱི་འགྲོ་བ་དེའི་སྔོན་དུས་ཀྱི་སྲིད་པའི་ཤ་ཚུགས་ཅན་ནམ་ལུས་དབྱིབས་ཅན་ཡིན་པར་མཛོད་ལས་གསུངས་ཤིང་། སྲིད་པ་བཞི་ནི། སྐྱེ་སྲིད་དུ་ཉིང་མཚམས་སྦྱོར་བའི་སྐད་ཅིག་དང་པོ་སྐྱེ་སྲིད་དང་། དེའི་སྐད་ཅིག་གཉིས་པ་ནས་འཆི་སྲིད་མ་གྲུབ་པའི་བར་གྱི་སྲིད་པ་ནི་སྔོན་དུས་ཀྱི་སྲིད་པ་དང་། འཆི་བའི་སྐད་ཅིག་ཐ་མའམ་འཆི་བ་འོད་གསལ་ཉམས་སུ་མྱོང་བའི་དུས་ཀྱི་སྲིད་པ་ནི་འཆི་སྲིད་དང་། འཆི་སྲིད་དང་སྐྱེ་སྲིད་གཉིས་ཀྱི་བར་དུ་བྱུང་བའི་སྲིད་པ་ནི་བར་སྲིད་དོ།

སྔོན་དུས་ཀྱི་སྲིད་པ་ཞེས་པའི་ཚིག་ཙམ་ལ་འཁྲུལ་ནས་བར་དོ་བ་དེ་སྐྱེ་བ་སྔ་མའི་ལུས་ཀྱི་རྣམ་པ་ཅན་དུ་འདོད་པ་དང་། ཡང་ཕྱི་མའི་ལུས་ཀྱི་དབྱིབས་ཅན་དུ་བཤད་པ་མཐོང་ནས་ཞག་ཕྱེད་དང་བཞི[26]སྐྱེ་བ་སྔ་མ་དང་། ཕྱེད་དང་བཞི་སྐྱེ་བ་ཕྱི་མའི་ལུས་ཀྱི་རྣམ་པ་ཅན་དུ་འདོད་པ་ནི་ཁུངས་རྣམ་དག་གང་ཡང་མེད་པའི་སྒྲོ་བཏགས་ཁོ་ནར་ལམ་རིམ་ཆེན་མོར་གསུངས། དེས་ན་སྔོན་དུས་ཀྱི་སྲིད་པ་ཞེས་པའི་སྔོན་ནི་ཚེ་ཕྱི་མའི་འཆི་སྲིད་ལ་ལྟོས་པའི་སྔོན་ཡིན་གྱི་བར་དོ་ལ་ལྟོས་པའི་སྔོན་དུ་འཛིན་པ་མ་ཡིན་ནོ། །མཛོད་ལས་ཀྱང་། སྔོན་དུས་སྲིད་འབྱུང་ཤ་ཚུགས་ཅན། ཞེས་པའི་འབྱུང་ཞེས་པ་ནི་མ་འོངས་པའི་ཚིག་ཡིན་གྱི་འདས་ཚིག་མ་ཡིན་པའི་ཕྱིར་རོ།

ཡང་གང་དུ་སྐྱེ་འགྱུར་གྱི་སེམས་ཅན་དེའི་རྣམ་པ་ཅན་དུ་བཤད་པ་ལ། འགའ་ཞིག་གིས་དེ་ལྟར་ན་དབང་པོ་མ་ཚང་བའི་འགྲོ་བ་དེའི་བར་དོ་བ་ཡང་དབང་པོ་མ་ཚང་བར་སྨྲ་བ་ནི་ཆེས་མི་འཐད་དེ། སྐྱེ་གནས་སུ་སྐྱེ་བའི་འོག་ཏུ་མིག་སོགས་དབང་པོ་མ་ཚང་བ་འབྱུང་གི་བར་དོ་ལ་དབང་པོ་མ་ཚང་བ་གང་ནས་ཀྱང་མ་བཤད་པའི་ཕྱིར་དང་། རང་ཉིད་གང་དུ་སྐྱེ་འགྱུར་གྱི་འགྲོ་བའི་རྣམ་པ་ཅན་དུ་བཤད་པ་ཙམ་གྱིས་ཆ་ཀུན་ནས་འདྲ་དགོས་ན་ཧ་ཅང་ཐལ་ཆེ་བར་འགྱུར་རོ།

བར་དོའི་འགྲོ་ཚུལ་གྱི་ཁྱད་པར་ནི། ལྷའི་བར་དོ་གྱེན་དང་། མིའི་བར་དོ་ཐད་ཀ་དང་། ངན་འགྲོའི་བར་དོ་སྤྱི་བོ་ཐུར་དུ་ཚུགས་ནས་འགྲོ་བར་སའི་དངོས་གཞི་ལས་གསུངས། དེ་ཡང་འདོད་གཟུགས་གཉིས་སུ་སྐྱེ་བ་ལ་བར་དོ་བསྒྲུད་དགོས་པས་ཡར་གྱི་མཚམས་མེད་ཀྱི་ལས་དང་མར་གྱི་མཚམས་མེད་གཉིས་ལ་བར་དོ་མེད་པར་འདོད་པ་མི་འཐད་པར་ལམ་རིམ་ཆེན་མོར་གསུངས་ལ། གཟུགས་མེད་དུ་སྐྱེ་བ་ལ་བར་དོ་མེད་དེ་གང་དུ་ཤི་འཕོས་པའི་གནས་དེ་

ཉིད་དུ་གཟུགས་མེད་ཀྱི་མིང་གཞིའི་ཕུང་པོ་གྲུབ་བོ། །དེས་ན་གཟུགས་མེད་ཁམས་སུ་སྐྱེ་འགྱུར་གྱི་གང་ཟག་དེས་འཆི་བ་འོད་གསལ་གྱི་ངང་ནས་གཟུགས་མེད་ཀྱི་ཏིང་ངེ་འཛིན་མངོན་དུ་བྱེད་ཀྱི་འཆི་བ་འོད་གསལ་ལས་ལུགས་ལྡོག་ཏུ་ལངས་པའི་ཉེར་ཐོབ་ཀྱི་སེམས་མི་འཆར་དེ། དེ་འདྲའི་ཉེར་ཐོབ་ཀྱི་སེམས་ནི་བར་དོའི་སེམས་ཡིན་པར་ཕྱིར་རོ། གཟུགས་མེད་ལ་འདོད་གཟུགས་གཉིས་ལས་གཞན་དུ་གནས་ཡོགས་པ་མེད་དོ།

བར་དོ་ཁྱད་པར་བ་སྐྱེ་བ་གཅིག་གིས་ཐོགས་པའི་བྱང་སེམས་དགའ་ལྡན་ནས་འཕོས་ནས་ཡུམ་གྱི་ལྷུམས་སུ་འཇུག་པའི་བོར་དོ་དེ། གཞོན་ནུ་མཚན་དཔེས་བརྒྱན་པ། འོད་ཀྱིས་གླིང་བཞི་བྱེ་བ་ཕྲག་བརྒྱ་གསལ་བར་བྱེད་པར་མཛོད་འགྲེལ་དང་རྣམ་གཞག་རིམ་པར་གསུངས་ལ། འོན་བཙུན་པ་ཆོས་ལྡན་རབ་འབྱོར་གྱིས། གླང་པོ་ཆེ་དཀར་པོ་མཆེ་བ་དྲུག་ལྡན་གྱི་རྣམ་པས་ལྷུམས་སུ་ཞུགས་པར་བཤད་པ་དང་འགལ་ལོ་ཞེ་ན། དེས་བཤད་པ་ལྟར་ཁས་ལེན་དགོས་པའང་མེད་ལ། འོན་ཀྱང་དེ་ནི་ཡུམ་གྱི་རྨི་ལམ་དང་མཐུན་པར་བསྟན་པ་ཙམ་ཡིན་གྱི། མིར་སྐྱེ་འགྱུར་གྱི་བར་དོ་དུད་འགྲོའི་རྣམ་པ་ཅན་འདོད་ན་བསྟན་བཅོས་ཚད་ལྡན་མང་པོ་དང་འགལ་བའི་ཕྱིར། དེ་ནི་ཐེག་དམན་གྱི་ལུགས་ལ་སྒྲ་ཇི་བཞིན་པ་དང་། ཐེག་ཆེན་གྱི་ལུགས་ལ་རྫུལ་བསྟན་ཙམ་དུ་ཁས་ལེན་ནོ།

བར་དོའི་རྣམ་གཞག་འདི་དག་བླ་མེད་ཀྱི་བསྐྱེད་རིམ་གྱི་བར་དོ་ལོངས་སྐུར་འཁྱེར་བའི་ལམ་འཁྱེར་དང་། དག་མ་དག་གི་སྒྱུ་ལུས་ཀྱི་སྦྱང་གཞི་ཡིན་པས་ཞིབ་ཏུ་ཤེས་པ་གལ་ཆེའོ། །

གསུམ་པ་དེས་སྐྱེ་གནས་སུ་སྐྱེ་བ་ལེན་པའི་ཚུལ་ནི། དེ་ཡང་བར་དོ་བ་དེས་མའི་མངལ་དུ་སྐྱེ་བ་ལེན་པ་ལ། གནས་གསུམ་མངོན་དུ་གྱུར་ཅིང་ཉེས་པ་གསུམ་དང་བྲལ་བ་ཞིག་དགོས་ཏེ། མ་ནད་མེད་ཅིང་ཟླ་མཚན་གྱི་ཁྲག་དང་ལྡན་པའི་སྐབས་ཡིན་པ། དྲི་ཟ་ཉེ་བར་འཁོར་ཞིང་འཇུག་འདོད་པ། ཕོ་མོ་གཉིས་ཕན་ཚུན་ཆགས་ཤིང་ཕྲད་པ་སྟེ་གནས་གསུམ་མངོན་དུ་གྱུར་པ་དང་། མའི་མངལ་གྱི་དབུས་ནས་ཀྱི་དབྱིབས་དང་འདྲ་བ་དང་། གྲོག་མོའི་རྐེད་པ་དང་། ཙ་སོང་གི་ཁ་ལྟ་བུ་དང་། རླུང་མཁྲིས་བད་ཀན་གསུམ་གྱིས་བཀག་པ་སྟེ་མངལ་གྱི་ཉེས་པ་དང་། ཕ་མ་གཉིས་གང་རུང་ལས་ཁུ་ཁྲག་མ་བྱུང་བའམ་བྱུང་ཡང་སྔ་ཕྱིར་འབབ་པ་དང་། དུས་མཉམ་དུ་བབས་ཀྱང་གང་རུང་ཞིག་རུལ་བ་སྟེ་ས་བོན་གྱི་ཉེས་པ་དང་། དྲི་ཟ་དེ་ཕོ་མོ་གཉིས་ཀྱི་བུར་སྐྱེ་བའི་ལས་མ་བསགས་པའམ། ཕོ་མོ་གཉིས་དེའི་ཕ་མར་འགྱུར་བའི་ལས་མ་བསགས་པ་ལས་ཀྱི་ཉེས་པ་སྟེ་ཉེས་པ་གསུམ་དང་བྲལ་བ་དགོས་པ་མངལ་འཇུག་གི་མདོ་ལས་གསུངས་ལ། འདུལ་བ་ལུང་ལས་གནས་དྲུག་མངོན་དུ་འགྱུར་དགོས་པར་གསུངས་པ་ཡང་དོན་འདྲའོ།

དེ་ལྟར་མངལ་དུ་སྐྱེ་བ་ལེན་པའི་མཐུན་རྐྱེན་གསུམ་ཚང་ཞིང་འགལ་རྐྱེན་གསུམ་དང་བྲལ་བའི་དྲི་ཟ་དེས། ཕ་མ་གཉིས་ཉལ་པོ་བྱེད་པ་རྨི་ལམ་བཞིན་དུ་མཐོང་སྟེ་འཁྲིག་པ་སྤྱོད་པར་འདོད་པའི་དབང་གིས་ཕོར་སྐྱེ་ན་མ་ལ་ཆགས་ཞིང་ཕ་ལ་འབྲལ་འདོད་དང༌། མོར་སྐྱེ་ན་ཕ་ལ་ཆགས་ཞིང་མ་ལ་འབྲལ་འདོད་སྐྱེ་ལ། དེ་ནས་གང་ལ་ཆགས་པ་དེ་ལ་འཁྱུད་པར་རྩོམ་པ་ན། ལས་ཀྱི་དབང་གིས་ལུས་གཞན་གང་ཡང་མི་སྣང་བར་ཕོ་མོ་གང་ཡིན་དེའི་མཚན་མ་ཙམ་སྣང་བས་ཁོང་ཁྲོ་སྐྱེས་ཏེ་ཆགས་སྡང་གཉིས་ཀྱིས་འཆི་རྐྱེན་བྱས་ནས་མངལ་དུ་འཇུག་གོ

དྲི་ཟ་དེས་ཕ་མ་ཉལ་པོ་བྱེད་པ་མེད་བཞིན་དུ་ཁུ་ཁྲག་ལ་འཁྲུལ་ནས་ཉལ་པོ་བྱེད་པར་མཐོང་བར་ས་མང་པོ་པ་ལས་གསུངས་ཤིང༌། མཛོད་འགྲེལ་དུ་ཕ་མ་ཉལ་པོ་བྱེད་པ་མཐོང་བར་ཡང་བཤད་དོ། །དེ་ཡང་ཕོ་མོ་གཉིས་སྙོམས་འཇུག་བྱས་པ་ན་དབང་པོ་གཉིས་བསྣུབས་པའི་སྟོབས་ཀྱིས་ཐུར་སེལ་གྱི་རླུང་གྱེན་དུ་གཡོས་ཏེ་སུམ་མདོའི་གཏུམ་མོ་ཕལ་པ་རྣམས་སྦྲར་བའི་དྲོད་ཀྱིས་ཐིག་ལེ་དཀར་དམར་ཞུ་བ་རྣམས་རྩ་སྟོང་ཕྲག་བདུན་ཅུ་རྩ་གཉིས་ཀྱི་སྦུབས་སྟོང་རྣམས་ནས་བབས་པས་ལུས་སེམས་བདེ་བས་ཆེམ་ཞིང་སྐབས་དེར་ཆགས་པ་དྲག་པོའི་སྐབས་སུ་བབ་པ་ན། མཇུག་ཏུ་ཁུ་བ་སྐ་བ་རེ་འབྱུང་ལ། དེའི་རྗེས་སུ་ཕ་མ་གཉིས་ཀ་ལས་ཁུ་ཁྲག་གི་ཐིག་པ་རེ་ངེས་པར་འབྱུང་བ་དེ་མའི་སྐྱེ་གནས་སུ་འདྲེས་ནས་འོ་མ་སྐོལ་བའི་སྤྲིས་མ་ཆགས་པ་ལྟར་ཡོད་པའི་དབུས་སུ་བར་དོ་ཤི་བའི་རྣམ་ཤེས་འཇུག་ལ།[27]

དེའི་ཚུལ་ནི་ཐོག་མར་བར་དོ་པའི་ཁའམ་སྤྱི་བོ་དང་མའི་སྐྱེ་གནས་ཀྱི་སྒོ་གསུམ་པོ་གང་རུང་ནས་ཞུགས། རྩ་སྟོང་ཕྲག་དོན་གཉིས[28]ཀྱི་ནང་ནས་བབས་པའི་ཐིག་ལེ་དང་འགྲོགས་ཏེ་བར་དོའི་གནས་སྐབས་ཀྱི་ཀུན་རྟོག་གཡོ་བའི་རླུང་རྣམས་ཐིམ་ནས་སྣང་མཆེད་ཐོབ་གསུམ་རིམ་བཞིན་ཤར། བར་དོ་འཆི་བའི་འོད་གསལ་རྣམས་སྔར་ལུས་རགས་པ་འདོར་བའི་སྐབས་སུ་བཤད་པ་ལས་ཡུན་ཐུང་བ་སྐྱེམ་ཙམ་རེ་མྱུར་བའི་ཚུལ་གྱིས་འཆར་ལ། དེའི་ཚེ་སྐྱིག་རྒྱུ་ནས་འོད་གསལ་གྱི་བར་གྱི་རྟགས་རྣམས་འབྱུང་ཞིང་འོད་གསལ་དེའི་རིགས་འདྲ་ཕྱི་མ་ཞིག་གིས་ཁུ་ཁྲག་འདྲེས་པའི་དབུས་སུ་ཉིང་མཚམས་སྦྱར་ནས་སྐྱེ་བ་བླངས་པ་དང་ལུགས་ལྡོག་གི་ཉེར་ཐོབ་གྲུབ་པ་དུས་མཉམ།

ཉེར་ཐོབ་ཀྱི་སེམས་སྐད་ཅིག་དང་པོ་དེ་ནི་སྐྱེ་བའི་སྲིད་པ་ཞེས་ཐ་སྙད་འདོགས་པའི་གཞི་དང༌། སྐྱེ་གནས་སུ་དང་པོར་ཉིང་མཚམས་སྦྱར་བའི་སེམས་ཡིན་ལ། དེ་ལས་ཉེར་ཐོབ་སྐད་ཅིག་གཉིས་པ་མན་དང༌། དེ་ལས་མཆེད་པ་དང༌། དེ་ལས་སྣང་བ་དང༌། སྣང་བ་ལས་རང་བཞིན་བརྒྱད་ཅུའི་ཀུན་རྟོག་རྣམས་བཞོན་པའི་རླུང་དང་བཅས་པ་སྐྱེ་ཞིང༌། སྣང་བའི་བཞོན་པའི་རླུང་ལས་རྣམ་ཤེས་ཀྱི་རྟེན་བྱེད་པའི་ནུས་པ་ཁྱད་པར་ཅན་དུ་གྱུར་པའི་རླུང་སྐྱེ། དེ་ལས་དེ་འདྲའི་ནུས་པ

ཁྱད་པར་ཅན་དུ་གྱུར་པའི་མེའི་ཁམས་དང་། དེ་ལས་དེ་འདྲའི་ནུས་པ་ཅན་གྱི་ཆུའི་ཁམས་དང་། དེ་ལས་དེ་འདྲའི་ནུས་པ་ཅན་གྱི་སའི་ཁམས་རྣམས་རིམ་གྱིས་སྐྱེའོ།

བར་དོ་སྒོ་གང་ནས་མངལ་དུ་འཇུག་པ་ནི། རྣམ་བཞག་རིམ་པར་རྣམ་སྣང་གི་སྒོ་སྤྱི་བོ་ནས་འཇུག་པར་བཤད་ལ། སྦྱོར་འབྱུང་དང་རྡོ་རྗེ་ཕྲེང་བ་གཉིས་སུ་ཕའི་ཁ་ནས་འཇུག་པར་བཤད་པས་ན། ཐོག་མར་བར་དོ་པའི་ཁའམ་སྤྱི་བོ་ནས་ཞུགས་དེ་པའི་གསང་གནས་ནས་འཐོན། མའི་པདྨར་ཞུགས་ནས་མངལ་དུ་ཁུ་ཁྲག་གི་དབུས་སུ་བར་དོ་ཤི་བའི་རྣམ་ཤེས་ཉིང་མཚམས་སྦྱོར་བ་ཡིན་ནོ། །མཛོད་འགྲེལ་ལས། མའི་སྐྱེ་གནས་ཀྱི་སྒོ་ནས་འཇུག་པར་བཤད་པས། དེ་ལྟར་ན་མའི་སྐྱེ་གནས་ཀྱི་སྒོ་དང་། ཕའི་ཁ་དང་སྤྱི་བོ་སྟེ་མངལ་དུ་འཇུག་པའི་སྒོ་གསུམ་ཡོད་པར་ཤེས་པར་བྱའོ།

འདི་ནི་མངལ་སྐྱེས་ཀྱི་མིའི་བར་སྲིད་འཇུག་པའི་དབང་དུ་བྱས་ཀྱི། སྤྱིར་ན་བར་སྲིད་ཐོགས་མེད་ཡིན་པས་འཇུག་པའི་སྒོ་ལ་བུ་ག་མི་དགོས་དེ། ལྕགས་ཀྱི་ཐོ་ལུམ་གཤགས་པའི་ནང་ནས་སྲིན་བུ་འབྱུང་བར་གྲག་གོ །ཞེས་མཛོད་འགྲེལ་ལས་བཤད་པ་དང་། ཤིན་དུ་སྲ་བའི་བྲག་དང་རྡོ་རིལ་སེར་ཁ་མེད་པའི་ནང་དུའང་སེམས་ཅན་ཡོད་པའི་ཕྱིར།

མངལ་དུ་ལུས་རིམ་གྱིས་འཕེལ་ཚུལ་ནི། མངལ་དེ་ནི་མའི་ཕོ་བའི་འོག་ལོང་གའི་སྟེང་གི་བར་དེར་ཡོད་པར་མངལ་འཇུག་ལས་བཤད་དོ། །དེ་ལ་དང་པོར་མེར་མེར་པོ་ནི། ཕྱི་འོ་མ་སྐོལ་བའི་སྤྲིས་མ་ལྟ་བུས་གཡོགས་པ་ལ་ནང་ཞིན་དུ་སླ་བའོ། །དེ་ནས་བཟུང་སྟེ་ཕུང་པོ་རགས་པ་གྲུབ་པ་ཡིན་པས་འཆི་བ་ལ་ཐུག་གི་བར་གྱི་ལུས་ཕྲ་རགས་རྣམས་འབྱུང་བ་བཞིའི་ཁམས་ལས་གྲུབ་པ་ཡིན་པས། ས་རླུང་གིས་འཛིན་པར་བྱེད། ཆུ་རླུང་གིས་སྡུད་པར་བྱེད། མེ་རླུང་གིས་མ་རུལ་ཅིང་སྨིན་པར་བྱེད།[29] རླུང་རླུང་གིས་རྒྱས་པར་བྱེད་དོ།

མེར་མེར་པོར་ཞག་བདུན་སོང་བ་ན་རླུང་གསར་པ་སྐྱེ་སྟེ་རླུང་གིས་སྨིན་པར་བྱས་པ་ལས་ལྟར་ལྟར་པོ་ནི་ཕྱི་ནང་གཉིས་ཀ་ཞོ་ལྟར་སྐྱ་ལ་ཤར་མ་གྱུར་པའོ། །དེ་ཞག་བདུན་སོང་བ་ན་དེ་ནས་ཡང་རླུང་གསར་པ་སྐྱེ་སྟེ་སྨིན་པར་བྱས་པ་ལས་གོར་གོར་པོ་ནི་ཤར་ནི་གྱུར་ལ་མནན་མི་བཟོད་པའོ། །དེ་ཞག་བདུན་སོང་བ་ན་རླུང་གསར་པས་སྨིན་པར་བྱས་པ་ལས་མཁྲང་འགྱུར་དུ་གྱུར་པ་ནི་ཤ་སྐྱ་ཞིང་མནན་བཟོད་པའོ། །དེ་ཞག་བདུན་སོང་བ་ན་ཡང་རླུང་གསར་པས་སྨིན་པར་བྱས་པ་ལས་རྐང་ལག་འགྱུས་པ་ནི་བརླ་གཉིས་དང་དཔུང་པ་གཉིས་མགོ་བོའི་མཚན་མ་སྟེ་འབུར་པོ་ལྔ་གསལ་བར་དོད་པ་སྟེ་མངལ་གྱི་གནས་སྐབས་ལྔར་རྣམ་གཞག་རིམ་པར་གསུངས་ལ། མཛོད་འགྲེལ་དང་། ལུང་གི་མངལ་འཇུག་ལས། ནུར་ནུར་པོ་དང་། མེར་མེར་པོ་དང་། ཕྱི་མ་གསུམ་སྔར་བཞིན་དུ་བཤད་ཅིང་། སའི་དངོས་གཞི་ལས་དེ་གཉིས་ལྡོག་སྟེ་བཤད་ཀྱང་མིང་འདོགས་ཀྱི་རིམ་པ་མི་འདྲ་བ་ཙམ་མ་གཏོགས་དོན་ལ་འགལ་བ་མེད་པར་གསུང་།

བདུན་ཕྲག་བཞི་པའི་ཁོངས་སུ་ཐིག་ལེ་དཀར་དམར་རྣམས་དྭངས་སྙིགས་ཕྱེ་ནས། དཀར་པོ་ལས་ནང་དུ་ཁ་བ་ཀང་རུས་པ་སྦྲི་ཕ་ལས་ཐོབ་པའི་མཛོད་གསུམ་དང་། ཐིག་ལེ་དམར་པོ་ལས་ཕྱི་རུ་ཤ་པགས་པ་ཁྲག་སྦྲི་མ་ལས་ཐོབ་པའི་མཛོད་གསུམ་འབྱུང་། རྣམ་ཤེས་ཐོག་མར་གང་དུ་ཞུགས་པའི་ཁ་ཁྲག་གི་གནས་དེ་ཕྱིས་སྙིང་གར་འགྱུར་བའི་དེར་ཤིན་དུ་ཕྲ་བའི་རླུང་སེམས་གཉིས་དང་། ཁ་ཁྲག་གི་དྭངས་མ་གཉིས་དེ་བཞི་འདུས་པའི་གོང་བུ་ཡུངས་ཀར་སྒོར་པོའི་ཚད་ཙམ་པ་དེའི་དབུས་སུ་འཕྲུམས་ནས་རྩ་དབུ་མ་དང་། གཡས་གཡོན་དུ་རྩ་རོ་རྐྱང་གཉིས་ཀྱིས་དབུ་མ་ལ་ལན་གསུམ་གྱིས་དཀྲིས་པ་ཆགས།

དེ་ནས་གྱེན་རྒྱུའི་རླུང་ཡར་སྐྱེ། ཐུར་སེལ་གྱི་རླུང་མར་སོང་བའི་སྟོབས་ཀྱིས་རོ་རྐྱང་དབུ་མ་གསུམ་ཡར་མར་དུ་གྱེས་ཏེ། མགོ་མཇུག་གཉིས་ཕྲ་ལ་དབུས་སྦོམ་པ་ཉའི་དབྱིབས་ལྟ་བུ་འབྱུང་། དེ་ནས་རིམ་གྱིས་འབུར་པོ་ལྔ་དང་། དེ་རྗེས་ཡན་ལག་ལྔ་དང་། དེའི་འོག་དུ་སྐྲ་དང་སེན་མོ་དང་བ་སྤུ་ལ་སོགས་པ་དང་དབང་པོ་གཟུགས་ཅན་པ་རྣམས་དང་། ཕོ་མོའི་མཚན་མ་དང་། ཁ་ནས་རྒྱུ་བའི་དབུགས་རླུང་དང་། བྱེད་པ་ལྕེ་ཀན་ལ་སོགས་པའི་ངག་གི་གནས་བརྒྱད། ཡིད་ཤེས་ཡུལ་ལ་གཡོ་བའི་དྲན་པ་རྟོགས་པ་རྣམས་རིམ་བཞིན་འབྱུང་བར་འགྱུར་རོ།

དེ་ལྟར་མངལ་ཆགས་ནས་བུ་ཡིན་ན་མའི་གློ་གཡས་སུ་ཁ་རྒྱབ་ངོས་སྒལ་གཞུང་ལ་ཕྱོགས་ཏེ་ཙོག་པུ་དང་། བུ་མོ་ཡིན་ན་མའི་གློ་གཡོན་དུ་ཁ་མདུན་ངོས་སུ་ཕྱོགས་ཏེ་ཙོག་པུར་གནས།

མངལ་དུ་གནས་པའི་ཡུན་ཚད་ཀྱང་དགའ་བོ་མངལ་འཇུག་གི་མདོ་ལས་ཞག་བདུན་ཕྲག་སོ་བརྒྱད་རྫོགས་ནས་བཙའ་བར་གསུངས་པས། ཞག་ཉིས་བརྒྱ་རེ་དྲུག་དང་། སའི་དངོས་གཞིར་དེའི་སྟེང་དུ་ཞག་བཞི་བསྣན་ནས་ཞག་ཉིས་བརྒྱ་བདུན་ཅུ་རྫོགས་ནས་བཙའ་བར་གསུངས། སྦྱོར་འབྱུང་ལས་ཟླ་བ་བཅུ་པ་ལ་ཕྱིར་འབྱུང་བའི་སེམས་དང་ལྡན་པར་གསུངས་ཏེ། དེ་གསུམ་ག་ཟླ་བ་རིལ་པོ་དགུ་དང་དོ་བཅུར་བྱེད་པ་ལ་མཐུན་ཏེ། མངལ་འཇུག་དང་སའི་དངོས་གཞི་ལས་གསུངས་པའི་ཞག་ནི་ཉིན་ཞག་དང་ཟླ་བ་ནི་ཚེས་ཟླའི་དབང་དུ་བྱེད་དོ།

དེ་ཡང་བདུན་ཕྲག་སོ་ལྔ་པ་ལ་ཕུང་ཁམས་སྐྱེ་མཆེད་ཡན་ལག་དང་ཉིང་ལག །སྐྲ་སེན་སོགས་ལུས་དང་། ངག་སྨྲ་བའི་གནས་ལྕེ་ཀན་དང་། ཡིད་ཤེས་ཡུལ་ལ་འཇུག་པའི་དྲན་པ་རྣམས་རྫོགས་ཏེ་བདུན་ཕྲག་སོ་དྲུག་པ་ལ་མངལ་དུ་མི་དགའ་ཞིང་ཕྱིར་འབྱུང་འདོད་སྐྱེ། སོ་བདུན་པ་ལ་མངལ་དུ་དྲི་ང་བ་དང་མི་གཙང་བའི་འདུ་ཤེས་སྐྱེ། མཐར་ཉིན་ཞག་བདུན་ཕྲག་སོ་བརྒྱད་པ་ལ་སྔོན་གྱི་ལས་ལས་སྐྱེས་པའི་ཡན་ལག་ཅེས་བྱ་བའི་རླུང་ལངས་ནས། མངལ་གྱི་སེམས་ཅན་དེའི་ལུས་མགོ་མཇུག་བསྒྱུར་ཏེ། ལག་པ་གཉིས་བཙུམ་སྟེ་མའི་རུམ་ནས་མངལ་གྱི་སྒོར་ཕྱོགས་པར་བྱེད་དོ།

དེ་ནས་ཡང་སྔོན་གྱི་ལས་ལས་སྐྱེས་པའི་ཁ་ཐུར་དུ་ལྷ་བ་ཞེས་བྱ་བའི་རླུང་ལངས་ནས། མངལ་གྱི་སེམས་ཅན་མགོ་ཐུར་དང་རྐང་པ་གྱེན་དུ་བསྟན་པ་དྲི་ཆུའི་ལམ་དུ་ཕུལ་བར་བྱེད་དེ་བདུན་ཕྲག་སོ་བརྒྱད་པའི་མཐར་ཕྱིར་ཐོན་ནས་ཐ་མལ་པའི་མིག་ལམ་དུ་གྱུར་དེ། བྱིས་པ། གཞོན་ནུ། དར་བབ། དར་ཡོལ། རྒས་པ་སྟེ་བཅོས་པའི་གནས་སྐབས་ལྔ་པོ་རིམ་གྱིས་འབྱུང་བ་ཡིན་ནོ།

དེ་ཡང་རྩ་རླུང་ཐིག་ལེ་ཆགས་ཚུལ་ནི། ཐོག་མར་སྙིང་གཞི་རོ་རྐྱང་དབུ་མ་གསུམ་དང་། ཤར་གྱི་སུམ་སྐོར་མ། ལྟེའི་འདོད་མ་སྟེ་རྩ་ལྔ་དུས་མཉམ་དུ་ཆགས། དེ་རྗེས་དབུ་མ་དང་ལྷན་ཅིག་ཏུ་གནས་པའི་བདུད་དྲལ་མ་དང་། ནུབ་ཀྱི་ཁྲིམ་མ། བྱང་གི་གདུམ་མོ་གསུམ་དུས་མཉམ་དུ་ཆགས་པ་ལ་སྙིང་གར་ཐོག་མར་ཆགས་པའི་རྩ་བརྒྱད་ཅེས་བྱའོ།

དེ་ནས་ཕྱོགས་ཀྱི་རྩ་བཞི་ལས་གཉིས་གཉིས་སུ་གྱེས་[30]དེ་མཚམས་ཀྱི་རྩ་འདབ་བཞི་དང་། སྙིང་གཞི་རྩ་འདབ་བརྒྱད་ཀྱི་རྒྱུན་གསུམ་གསུམ་དུ་གྱེས་ནས་གནས་ཉེར་བཞིའི་རྩ་ཉེར་བཞི་ཆགས། ཉེར་བཞི་པོ་རེ་རེ་ལས་གསུམ་གསུམ་དུ་གྱེས་པས་བདུན་ཅུ་རྩ་གཉིས་དང་། དེ་རེ་རེ་ལས་སྟོང་སྟོང་དུ་གྱེས་དེ་ལུས་ལ་རྩ་བདུན་ཁྲི་ཉིས་སྟོང་ཆགས་པ་ཡིན་ནོ།

རླུང་ཆགས་ཚུལ་ནི། དང་པོར་མངལ་དུ་ཉིང་མཚམས་སྦྱར་ནས་ཟླ་བ་དང་པོ་ལ་སྲོག་འཛིན་གྱི་རླུང་ཕྲ་བ་ལས་སྲོག་འཛིན་རགས་པ་སྐྱེ། དེའི་ཚེ་སེམས་ཅན་དེའི་ལུས་ཀྱི་དབྱིབས་ཉའི་རྣམ་པ་ལྟ་བུར་ཡོད། ཟླ་བ་གཉིས་པ་ལ་སྲོག་འཛིན་གྱི་རླུང་དེ་ལས་ཐུར་སེལ་སྐྱེ། དེའི་ཚེ་སེམས་ཅན་དེའི་ལུས་འབུར་པོ་ཟླ་དོང་པ་རུས་སྦལ་ལྟ་བུར་ཡོད། ཟླ་བ་གསུམ་པ་ལ་ཐུར་སེལ་ལས་མཉམ་གནས་སྐྱེ། དེའི་ཚེ་སེམས་ཅན་དེའི་ལུས་སྟོད་ཙུང་ཟད་སྦྲུར་བ་ཕག་རྒོད་ཀྱི་རྣམ་པར་ཡོད། ཟླ་བ་བཞི་པ་ལ་མཉམ་གནས་ལས་གྱེན་རྒྱུ་སྐྱེ། དེའི་ཚེ་ལུས་སྟོད་ཙུང་ཟད་རྒྱས་པ་སེང་གེའི་རྣམ་པར་ཡོད། ཟླ་བ་ལྔ་པ་ལ་གྱེན་རྒྱུ་ལས་ཁྱབ་བྱེད་སྐྱེ། དེའི་ཚེ་སེམས་ཅན་དེའི་ལུས་མིའུ་ཐུང་གི་དབྱིབས་སུ་ཡོད་པར་བཤད།

ཟླ་བ་དྲུག་པ་ལ་མིག་གི་སྒོར་རྒྱུ་བའི་རླུང་རྒྱུ་བ་ཞེས་བྱ་བ་དང་། འབྱུང་བ་ས་སྐྱེ། ཟླ་བ་བདུན་པ་ལ་རྣ་བའི་སྒོར་རྒྱུ་བའི་རླུང་རྣམ་པར་རྒྱུ་བ་དང་འབྱུང་བ་ཆུ་སྐྱེ། ཟླ་བ་བརྒྱད་པ་ལ་སྣའི་སྒོར་རྒྱུ་བའི་རླུང་ཡང་དག་པར་རྒྱུ་བ་དང་འབྱུང་བ་མེ་སྐྱེ། ཟླ་བ་དགུ་པ་ལ་ལྗེའི་སྒོར་རྒྱུ་བའི་རླུང་རབ་ཏུ་རྒྱུ་བ་དང་འབྱུང་བ་རླུང་སྐྱེ། ཟླ་བ་བཅུ་པ་ལ་ལུས་ཀྱི་སྒོར་རྒྱུ་བའི་རླུང་ངེས་པར་རྒྱུ་བ་ཞེས་བྱ་བ་དང་འབྱུང་བ་ནམ་མཁའི་ཁམས་སྐྱེ། དེའི་ཚེ་ལུས་ཀྱི་སྟོབས་སྟོང་རྣམས་

འབྱུང་ངོ་། །མངལ་དུ་ རླུང་བཅུ་ཆགས་ཀྱང་དེར་སྣ་སྒོ་ནས་འབྱུང་འཇུག་མི་བྱེད་ལ། ཕྱིར་བཙས་མ་ཐག་ཏུ་སྣ་སྒོ་ནས་འབྱུང་འཇུག་བྱེད་པར་གསུངས་སོ།

ཐིག་ལེ་ཆགས་ཚུལ་ནི། ཁམས་དཀར་དམར་གྱི་དྭངས་མ་དང་ཤིན་ཏུ་ཕྲ་བའི་རླུང་སེམས་འདུས་པའི་གོང་བུ་ཡུངས་ཀར་སྒྲིམ་པོའི་ཚད་ཙམ་པ་སྙིང་གཞི་རྡོ་རྗེའི་དབུས་ཀྱི་སྦུབས་སྟོང་ཙུང་ཟད་ཡོད་པའི་ནང་དུ་གནས་པ་དེ་ལ་མི་ཤིགས་པའི་ཐིག་ལེ་ཞེས་བྱ་ལ། དེ་ནས་ཐིག་ལེ་དཀར་པོ་དེ་ལས་ཆ་ཤས་གཅིག་སྤྱི་བོའི་རྩ་འཁོར་གྱི་ནང་དུ་སོང་སྟེ་གནས་པ་ལ་ཧཾ་ཡིག་ཅེས་བྱ། དེས་ལུས་ཀྱི་གནས་གཞན་གྱི་ཐིག་ལེ་དཀར་པོ་རྣམས་དངོས་སམ་བརྒྱུད་པའི་སྒོ་ནས་འཕེལ་བར་བྱེད། སྙིང་གཞི་ཐིག་ལེ་དམར་པོ་ལས་ཆ་ཤས་གཅིག་ལྟེ་བའི་རྩ་འཁོར་གྱི་ནང་དུ་སོང་སྟེ་གནས་པ་ལ་གཏུམ་མོ་ཞེས་བྱ་སྟེ། དེས་ལུས་ཀྱི་གནས་གཞན་རྣམས་ཀྱི་ཁམས་དམར་པོ་རྣམས་དངོས་བརྒྱུད་ཅི་རིགས་པའི་སྒོ་ནས་འཕེལ་བར་བྱེད་དོ།

རྩ་འཁོར་རེ་རེ་ན་ཐིག་ལེ་ཆ་ཤས་རེ་གནས་ཀྱང་། སྤྱི་བོའི་རྩ་འཁོར་ནི་ཁམས་དཀར་པོ་འཕེལ་བའི་གནས་ཀྱི་གཙོ་བོ་དང་། །ལྟེ་བའི་རྩ་འཁོར་ནི་ཁམས་དམར་པོ་འཕེལ་བའི་གནས་ཀྱི་གཙོ་བོ་ཡིན་ལ། སྙིང་གཞི་རྩ་འཁོར་ནི་ཁམས་དཀར་དམར་ཆ་མཉམ་དུ་འཕེལ་བའི་གནས་ཡིན་ནོ། །ཁམས་དཀར་དམར་དེ་ཡང་ནམ་དགོས་པའི་ཚེ་སྐྱེ་བ་ཡིན་གྱི་སྔོན་དུ་རྒྱ་བླུག་པ་ལྟར་ཡོད་པ་མིན་གསུངས།

སྐྱེ་གནས་སུ་ཉིང་མཚམས་སྦྱར་ནས་རགས་པའི་ལུས་སྐྱེ་བ་བླངས་པ་དེ་ལ་གཞིའི་སྤྲུལ་སྐུ་ཞེས་བྱའོ།

དེ་ལྟར་བར་དོ་བ་མངལ་དུ་ཉིང་མཚམས་སྦྱར་ནས་སྐྱེ་བ་ལེན་པའི་རྣམ་གཞག་འདི་དག་ནི། བསྐྱེད་རིམ་པའི་སྐྱེ་བ་སྤྲུལ་སྐུར་འཁྱེར་བའི་ལམ་འཁྱེར་དང་། རྫོགས་རིམ་པའི་དག་མ་དག་གི་སྒྱུ་ལུས་རྣམས་རགས་པའི་སྤྲུལ་སྐུ་འཛིན་པའམ་ཞུགས་པོ་སྙིང་པ་ལ་ཞུགས་དེ་ཐ་མལ་པའི་མིག་ལམ་དུ་གྱུར་པ་དང་རྣམ་པ་མཐུན་ཞིང་དེ་དག་གི་སྦྱང་གཞི་ཡིན་ནོ།

དེ་ཡང་བསྐྱེད་རྫོགས་གཉིས་ཀྱི་སྦྱང་གཞི་ལ་ཁྱད་པར་མེད་པས་བསྐྱེད་རིམ་ནི། གཞིའི་འཆི་བ་དང་། བར་དོ་དང་། སྐྱེ་བ་གསུམ་སྦྱང་གཞིར་བྱས་ནས་སྦྱོང་བྱེད་ལ་དེ་གསུམ་དང་རིམ་བཞིན་རྣམ་པ་མཐུན་པར་འཆི་བ་ཆོས་སྐུར་འཁྱེར་བའི་ལམ་འཁྱེར་དང་། བར་དོ་ལོངས་སྐུར་འཁྱེར་བའི་ལམ་འཁྱེར་དང་། སྐྱེ་བ་སྤྲུལ་སྐུར་འཁྱེར་བའི་ལམ་འཁྱེར་གསུམ་ཡན་ལག་དང་བཅས་པ་བསྒོམས་ཏེ་བརྒྱུད་ནས་ཐ་མལ་གྱི་འཆི་བ། བར་དོ། སྐྱེ་བ་གསུམ་སྦྱངས་ནས། དེ་གསུམ་དང་རྣམ་པ་ཇི་ལྟར་བ་བཞིན་མཐུན་པའི་སྐུ་གསུམ་མངོན་དུ་བྱེད་པ་ཡིན་ལ། རྫོགས་རིམ་ནི་གཞིའི་ཆོས་གསུམ་པོ་དེ་དང་རྣམ་པ་ཇི་ལྟར་བ་བཞིན་མཐུན་པའི་ལམ་གྱིས་དེ་གསུམ་དངོས་སུ་སྦྱོང་བྱེད་ཡིན་ནོ།

དེ་ཡང་འཆི་བ་འོད་གསལ་དང་རྣམ་པ་ཇི་ལྟ་བ་བཞིན་མཐུན་པ་ནི། ལུས་དབེན། ངག་དབེན། སེམས་དབེན། སྒྱུ་ལུས། སློབ་པའི་ཟུང་འཇུག་རྣམས་ཀྱི་གནས་སྐབས་ཀྱི་སྣང་མཆེད་ཐོབ་གསུམ་འོད་གསལ་དང་བཅས་པ་ཡིན་ལ། བར་དོ་དང་རྣམ་པ་ཇི་ལྟ་བ་བཞིན་མཐུན་པ་ནི། རིམ་པ་གསུམ་པའི་མ་དག་པའི་སྒྱུ་ལུས་དང་། སློབ་པའི་ཟུང་འཇུག་གི་དག་པའི་སྒྱུ་ལུས་ཡིན་ཞིང་། སྐྱེ་བ་དང་རྣམ་པ་ཇི་ལྟ་བ་བཞིན་མཐུན་པ་ནི། དག་མ་དག་གི་སྒྱུ་ལུས་རྣམས་ཕུང་པོ་རྙིང་པ་ལ་ཞུགས་ཏེ་ཐ་མལ་པའི་མིག་ལམ་དུ་གྱུར་པ་དེ་ཡིན་ནོ།

རྫོགས་རིམ་གྱི་ལམ་དེ་རྣམས་ཀྱིས་སྐྱེ་ཤི་བར་དོ་གསུམ་སྦྱོང་ཚུལ་དངོས་ནི། རྫོགས་རིམ་གྱི་རྣལ་འབྱོར་པས་རང་རྒྱུད་ཀྱི་ཤིན་ཏུ་ཕྲ་བའི་རླུང་སེམས་ངོ་བོ་དབྱེར་མེད་ཀྱི་ཡ་གྱལ་ཤིན་ཏུ་ཕྲ་བའི་སེམས་དེ་རིགས་འདྲ་གཅིག་ནས་གཅིག་ཏུ་བརྒྱུད་དེ་འཆི་བ་རང་དགའི་འོད་གསལ་དུ་འགྱུར་བ་དེ་ཏིང་ངེ་འཛིན་གྱི་མཐུས་བཀག་ནས། དེ་དང་རྣམ་པ་ཇི་ལྟ་བ་བཞིན་མཐུན་པའི་ལམ་དུས་སུ་དཔེ་དང་དོན་གྱི་འོད་གསལ་དང་། འབྲས་བུའི་འོད་གསལ་ཆོས་ཀྱི་སྐུར་བསྒྱུར་བ་ནི་འཆི་བ་སྦྱོང་ཚུལ་དང་། རྫོགས་རིམ་གྱི་རྣལ་འབྱོར་པས་དེ་འདྲའི་ཤིན་ཏུ་ཕྲ་བའི་རླུང་དེ་རིགས་འདྲ་གཅིག་ནས་གཅིག་ཏུ་བརྒྱུད་དེ་འཆི་བ་འོད་གསལ་རང་དགའ་བའི་གཞོན་པ་བྱས་ནས་བར་དོའི་ལུས་སུ་ལྡང་བ་དེ་ཏིང་ངེ་འཛིན་གྱི་མཐུས་བཀག་ནས། བར་དོ་དང་རྣམ་པ་ཇི་ལྟར་བ་བཞིན་མཐུན་པའི་མ་དག་པའི་སྒྱུ་ལུས་དང་། སློབ་མི་སློབ་ཀྱི་ཟུང་འཇུག་གི་དག་པའི་སྒྱུ་མའི་སྐུར་བསྒྱུར་བ་ནི་བར་དོ་སྦྱོང་ཚུལ་ཡིན་ལ།

དེ་ལྟ་བུའི་སྒྱུ་ལུས་གྲུབ་པ་ན་བར་དོ་གདན་ནས་ཁེགས་ཤིང་དེའི་མཐུས་ལས་ཉོན་གྱིས་མངལ་དུ་སྐྱེ་བ་འཛིན་པའི་སྐྱེ་བའང་ཁེགས་ནས་བར་དོ་མའི་མངལ་དུ་སྐྱེ་བ་ལེན་པ་དང་རྣམ་པ་མཐུན་པར་སྒྱུ་ལུས་ཕུང་པོ་རྙིང་པ་ལ་ཞུགས་ཏེ་ཆོས་འཆད་པ་དང་ལམ་གོང་མ་སྒྲུབ་པའི་རྩོལ་བ་བྱེད་པ་ནི་སྐྱེ་བ་སྦྱོང་ཚུལ་ཡིན་ནོ།

དེས་ན་སྐྱེ་ཤི་བར་དོ་གསུམ་དངོས་སུ་འགོག་པར་བྱེད་པའི་རྩ་བ་ནི་སྒྱུ་ལུས་ཀྱི་དངོས་རྒྱུར་གྱུར་པའི་སེམས་དབེན་མཐར་ཐུག་གི་དཔེའི་འོད་གསལ་ཉིད་ཡིན་ཏེ། དེས་འཆི་བ་དངོས་སུ་ཁེགས་པའི་སྟོབས་ཀྱིས་བར་དོ་དང་སྐྱེ་བ་རང་ཤུགས་ཀྱིས་ཁེགས་པའི་ཕྱིར་རོ། །དེ་འདྲའི་དཔེའི་འོད་གསལ་ལས་སྒྱུ་ལུས་གྲུབ་པའི་ཚེ་བར་དོ་གདན་ནས་ཁེགས་པ་ཡིན་ཏེ། བར་དོའི་ལུས་སུ་ལྡང་བའི་ཤིན་ཏུ་ཕྲ་བའི་རླུང་དེ་སྒྱུ་མའི་སྐུར་གྱུར་ཟིན་པའི་ཕྱིར། བར་དོ་གདན་ནས་ཁེགས་ན་ལས་ཉོན་གྱིས་སྐྱེ་བ་མི་ལེན་པའི་རྒྱུ་མཚན་གྱིས། སྒྱུ་ལུས་ཐོབ་ན་ཚེ་དེ་ལ་འཚང་རྒྱ་བས་ཁྱབ་བོ།

གོང་དུ་བཤད་པ་དེ་རྣམས་ཀྱི་ཤེས་བྱེད་ཀྱི་ལུང་འདྲེན་རྣམས་མངས་གིས་དོགས་ནས་མ་བྲིས་པས། རྗེ་ཡབ་སྲས་ཀྱི་ལེགས་བཤད་དང་རྗེས་འབྲང་མཁས་གྲུབ་དམ་པ་རྣམས་ཀྱི་གསུང་ལས་ཤེས་པར་བྱའོ། །

སྨྲས་པ།

ཚུལ་འདི་རྒྱལ་བ་གཉིས་པ་ཡབ་སྲས་དང་། །
རྗེས་འབྲང་མཁས་པའི་གསུང་བཞིན་བྲིས་མོད་ཀྱང་། །
དམ་པའི་དགོངས་པ་མ་ལོན་ནོངས་པའི་ཚོགས། །
ཅི་མཆིས་བླ་མ་ལྷ་དང་མཁས་ལ་བཤགས། །

འདིས་མཚོན་དགེ་བས་བདག་གཞན་འགྲོ་བ་ཀུན། །
ཟབ་ལམ་རིམ་པ་གཉིས་ཀྱི་རྣལ་འབྱོར་གྱིས། །
མ་དག་སྐྱེ་ཤི་བར་དོ་སྐུ་གསུམ་དུ། །
སྒྱུར་མཛད་ལམ་བཟང་མྱུར་དུ་མཐར་ཕྱིན་ཤོག །

ཅེས་པ་འདི་ནི་གྱི་ན་པ་དབྱངས་ཅན་དགའ་བའི་བློ་གྲོས་ཀྱིས་དམ་པའི་གསུང་ལས་བཏུས་ཏེ་རང་གི་བརྗེད་བྱང་དུ་བྲིས་པའོ།། །།

Annotations to Yangjen Gaway Lodrö's *Lamp Illuminating the Presentation of the Three Bodies that are the Bases [of Purification]*

Sanskrit Homages 1

Page 384, Line 3

While nearly all the texts encountered thus far contain opening homages (see ཤེས་རབ་སྙིང་པོ་ note 3), they have been in straightforward Tibetan. Here is an opening homage in Sanskrit rendered in Tibetan transliteration. In romanized form (see ཤེས་རབ་སྙིང་པོ་ note 2), this is: *namo guru mañjughoṣāya*. As with the use of Latin in English compositions, the use of Sanskrit by a Tibetan author is often to demonstrate their erudition. Here, the homage is easily understood with a minimal knowledge of Sanskrit: *namo* is the euphonic form of *namas* meaning "homage" or "salutation," *guru* means teacher, and *mañjughoṣāya* is the dative declension of *mañjughoṣa* (an alternate name for *mañjuśrī*). Hence, the opening homage simply states, "Homage to the teacher, Mañjughoṣa!"

WHAT TO REMEMBER

At least a minimal knowledge of Sanskrit grammar and vocabulary can be useful in working with more advanced Tibetan texts.

Translation Hint 2

Page 384, Line 5

As with the previous text, this text opens with a verse of poetic metaphor (see གྲུབ་མཐའ་ note 2), indicating the structure of the text as a whole and expanding on the meaning of the title ("the three bodies that are the bases"). As indicated in the opening line, "basis" (གཞི་) refers to the three "bodies" of birth, death, and the intermediate state (སྐྱེ་ཤི་བར་དོ་) as "bases of purification" (སྦྱང་གཞི་), while the following two lines follow the same pattern of apposition with the "agents of purification" (སྦྱོང་བྱེད་) and "fruits of purification" (སྦྱངས་འབྲས་).

3

Sanskrit Abbreviations

Page 385, Line 5

As previously noted, occasionally an author will use a Sanskrit word in transliteration despite the existence of a Tibetan translation for the same word (see དེབ་ཐེར་དམར་པོ་ note 7). Here, the word meaning "central channel" occurs twice in the same sentence, once in translation (རྩ་དབུ་མ་) and again in transliteration (དྷཱུ་ཏི་). The point to note here, however, is the manner in which the Sanskrit word, when occurring in Tibetan script (*dhū ti*), is an abbreviation of the original word, *avadhūti*. Such renderings are rather common and can be seen with proper names as well, such as with the highly influential eleventh/twelfth-century paṇḍita associated with Vikramaśīla University, Abhayākaragupta, whose name is fully rendered in Tibetan as འཇིགས་མེད་འབྱུང་གནས་སྦས་པ་ but who is commonly referred to simply as ཨ་བྷྱ་ (*a bhya*).

WHAT TO REMEMBER

Sanskrit words, when occurring in Tibetan script, are often an abbreviation of the original and must usually be discerned from context.

4

Translation Hint

Page 385, Line 8

The ending of this sentence with a phrase marked in the third case is simply an alternate formation of a reason clause and is functionally equivalent to ending it with a ཕྱིར་.

5

Run-on Sentences and Authorial Style

Page 385, Line 12

It has been previously noted that verbal participles can be used in lieu of a finite verb in the construction of run-on sentences (see ཤེར་སྙིང་རྣམ་བཤད་ note 15) and that, occasionally, separating punctuation can be omitted as well. Here, a different sort of authorial style can be seen in the production of run-on sentences. Rather than stringing together participles or omitting connecting punctuation (such as ཞིང་, etc.), the author uses third-case marked reason clauses to terminate sentences in order to link them together. The result is a sort of "stream-of-consciousness" style of composition, in which a sequence of statements are linked together in the form of "... and because of this, ..."

WHAT TO REMEMBER

An alternate form of run-on sentence can be formed by linking statements together with a series of reason clauses.

The Word རང་བཞིན་

Page 387, Line 6

In Buddhist discourse, the word རང་བཞིན་ occurs repeatedly with different meanings in different contexts—both positive and negative—often derived from different underlying Sanskrit technical terms (*svabhāva*, *svarūpa*, *prakṛti*, etc.) which themselves may be polysemous. In the very first text in this *Reader* (the *Heart Sūtra*), the term རང་བཞིན་ was translated as "own nature" and referred to an exaggerated status of existence mistakenly attributed to phenomena. This is its predominant meaning in a Buddhist philosophical context.

In the preceding text (*Precious Garland*), however, the term རང་བཞིན་ appeared in several contexts. For example, in the discussion of the non-Buddhist philosophies of the Vaiśeṣikas and the Naiyāyikas, it was asserted that by means of various ritual and ascetic practices, they come to understand "the nature" (རང་བཞིན་) of their six categories of existents. In that and similar generic contexts, རང་བཞིན་ referred to "reality" (that is, the manner in which things actually exist), and occurred in generic phrases such as "the nature of the mind" (སེམས་ཀྱི་རང་བཞིན་). In the discussion of Sāṃkhya philosophy in that same text, however, རང་བཞིན་ meant "progenerative nature" (*prakṛti*)—a quality of certain phenomena.

Here, however, the term རང་བཞིན་ is being used in its Buddhist tantric context and refers to the category of "instinctual natures" (*prakṛti*) that operate on a fundamental level of the mind but which are nonetheless conceptual (རྟོག་པ་/ཀུན་རྟོག་).

WHAT TO REMEMBER

The term རང་བཞིན་ changes meaning within both Buddhist and non-Buddhist contexts and in tantric and non-tantric texts.

7

Translation Hint

Page 387, Line 7

Here, the particle དེ་ functions as an apposition marker, as seen in other texts (see དེབ་ཐེར་དམར་པོ་ note 19).

8

Auxiliary Verbs: Deontic Construction

Page 387, Line 8

Although the verb དགོས་ by itself is a Class VII verb ("to need") with its own requisite grammar, when following another verb (rarely with པར་/བར་), it forms the deontic mood (conveying "necessity"). Another indication that དགོས་ is functioning as a modal auxiliary rather than as the primary verb is the fact that the requisite grammar of the Class III verb འཆར་ still dominates the sentence:

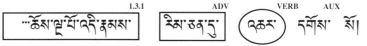

1.3.1	ADV	VERB	AUX	
…ཆོས་ལྔ་པོ་འདི་རྣམས་	རིམ་ཅན་དུ་	འཆར་	དགོས་	སོ།

"These five phenomena must dawn in stages."

If དགོས་ was the primary verb in the sentence, the grammatical subject, ཆོས་ལྔ་པོ་འདི་རྣམས་, would be marked with a ལ་ particle.

WHAT TO REMEMBER

When following another verb, the verb དགོས་ forms the deontic mood (conveying "necessity"). The requisite grammar of the sentence, however, remains determined by the main verb.

The ་་་ནས་་་བར་[དུ་] ("From ... Up To ...") Construction

9

Page 388, Line 14

Previously, the ་་་ནས་་་བར་དུ་ construction was used to indicate a sequence of items (see ཤེས་རབ་སྙིང་པོ་ note 15 and བློ་རིག་ note 3). Here, however, the ་་་ནས་་་བར་དུ་ construction is being used to indicate a "temporal sequence." A clue to this is the fact that although the sentence begins with what appears to be a numeric sequence, དང་པོ་ནས་ ("from the first"), the concluding phrase is not numeric but rather a condition phrased in the negative: ཡོད་པའི་ཤིན་ཏུ་ཕྲ་བའི་རླུང་སེམས་ཀྱི་དྲན་པ་མ་གསོ་ ("mindfulness of the very subtle wind and mind has not reactivated"). Hence, this ་་་ནས་་་བར་དུ་ construction should be understood to express the idea of "from *some point in time* ... until and so long as *some condition* is not met."

WHAT TO REMEMBER

Sequences expressed by the ནས་་་བར་དུ་ construction may be temporal—indicated by a concluding condition for fulfillment—in addition to simple lists.

The Use of བར་དུ་ to Designate an Intermediate Duration

10

Page 388, Line 16

Previously, བར་དུ་ was seen as a means of indicating a specified duration of time (see སྒྲུབ་མཐའ་ note 25). Here, another construction is seen in which བར་དུ་ is used to indicate an intermediate duration of time between two specified events—in this case, the dissolution (ཐིམ་པ་) and stirring (གཡོ་བ་) of the mind of eighty instinctual conceptual natures, or "conceptions" (ཀུན་རྟོག་).

WHAT TO REMEMBER

The བར་དུ་ construction can be used to indicate an intermediate duration of time between two specified events. With two verbs, the construction conveys the meaning of "between X and Y occurring ..."

11

Translation Hint

Page 389, Line 15

The verbal suffix -འི་ here, is another instance of a non-case continuative particle (agglutinative) seen previously (see ཤེར་སྙིང་རྣམ་བཤད་ note 11).

12

Translation Hint

Page 389, Line 16

A proper reading of this sentence hinges on a number of factors, one of which is the correct recognition of potentially ambiguous words such as སྟོན་ ("autumn"), བར་སྣང་ ("sky"), etc.

13

Future Active Participles

Page 389, Line 22

The future active participle expresses an action that is yet to be performed and is usually indicated in English by the phrase "about to," although it is often translated by the simple infinitive, "to [do] X." The future participle is built off either the present or future form of the verb and is indicated by a verbal suffix, the future participle lexical particle, རྒྱུ་. Here, precisely such a case is seen in the phrase ཐིམ་རྒྱུའི་རླུང་ ("winds that are to dissolve").

WHAT TO REMEMBER

The future active participle expresses an action that is yet to be performed or about to be performed; it is marked by རྒྱུ་ or occasionally ཁ་མ་. It can be translated simply by "to (do) X," or in the case of ཁ་མ་, by the phrase "about to (do) X."

14

Auxiliary Verbs: Completed Action Verb ཚར་

Page 389, Line 23

Although the more commonly seen completed action auxiliary verb is ཟིན་ (see བློ་རིག་ note 12), a completed action can be indicated using the auxiliary verb ཚར་ (here, followed by

ཡང་ bridging the two sentences—see གྲུབ་མཐའ་ note 46). Hence, the sentence རགས་པ་རྣམས་ཐིམ་ཚར་ཡང་ཕྲ་བ་ཡོད་དོ། can be translated as: "Even though the coarse ones have dissolved, the subtle ones still exist."

> WHAT TO REMEMBER
>
> The verb ཚར་, when appearing with another verb, functions as an auxiliary verb indicating the completion of the action of the main verb and does not alter the syntax of the sentence.

Reduplication of Adjectives 15

Page 390, Line 3

Reduplication has previously been seen with numbers (see གྲུབ་མཐའ་ note 21). Here, a similar form of reduplication is seen, although with indefinite adjectives. With numbers, reduplication was used to indicate distribution to a list. With adjectives, however, reduplication is used both to indicate distribution to a list as well as to convey a sense of cascading intensity with each application of the adjective—that is, "increasingly more X."

> WHAT TO REMEMBER
>
> Reduplication of adjectives is used to indicate distribution to a list with a sense of cascading intensity with each application of the adjective.

Translation Hint 16

Page 390, Line 7

Recall the grammar and significance of this phrase from its previous occurrence in an epistemological context (see བློ་རིག་ notes 14 and 18, and in general, ལམ་གཙོ་རྣམ་གསུམ་ note 16).

17

Translation Hint

Page 390, Line 11

Recall the grammatical cues to the translation of མཚན་ཉིད་པ་ (see གྲུབ་མཐའ་ note 34).

Translation Hint

18

Page 390, Line 17

The reason clause contains two parts with both a distributed subject (འཆི་བའི་རིམ་པ་འདི་རྣམས་) and a distributed verb (ཡིན་).

19

Major Texts Commonly Cited

Page 391, Line 9

As noted previously, text citations to canonical texts are seldom given in their full bibliographic form (see ཤེར་སྙིང་རྣམ་བཤད་ note 7 and གྲུབ་མཐའ་ note 7). While some are presented in an abbreviated manner, others are referred to only obliquely. Here, for example, the phrase མངོན་པ་གོང་འོག་དང་ས་སྡེ་ refers to textual sources for the opinion that follows. The first word, མངོན་པ་, is an abbreviation for ཆོས་མངོན་པ་, meaning "Manifest Knowledge" (*abhidharma*), while the adjectives གོང་ ("higher") and འོག་ ("lower") refer to the Mahāyāna and (so-called) Hīnayāna presentations: Asaṅga's *Compendium of Manifest Knowledge* (*Abhidharmasamuccaya*) and Vasubandhu's *Treasury of Manifest Knowledge* (*Abhidharmakośa*). The second source mentioned is similarly abbreviated, although it was previously seen in the གྲུབ་མཐའ་ text as ས་སྡེ་ལྔ་—[Asaṅga's] five *Grounds* (*Bhūmi*) treatises. The point to be understood is that just as with any other classical literature collection a certain degree of familiarity with the identities of foundational texts in each domain is presumed on the part of a reader.

WHAT TO REMEMBER

Within the corpus of Tibetan Buddhist canonical literature, certain texts are considered the purview of "common knowledge" and so typically only receive abbreviated citation.

Some of the major ones are as follows.

རྩ་བའི་ཤེས་རབ་	Nāgārjuna's *Fundamental Treatise on the Middle Way called "Wisdom"*
བཞི་བརྒྱ་	Āryadeva's *Four Hundred Stanzas*
རྟོག་གེ་འབར་བ་	Bhāvaviveka's *Blaze of Reasoning*
ཚིག་གསལ་	Candrakīrti's *Clear Words* commentary on Nāgārjuna's *"Wisdom"*
སྤྱོད་འཇུག་	Śāntideva's *Engaging in the Deeds of a Bodhisattva*
བྱམས་སྡེ་ལྔ་	Maitreya's five treatises
བྱང་ས་	Asaṅga's *Grounds of Bodhisattvas*
ས་སྡེ་	Asaṅga's five *Grounds* treatises
ཀུན་བཏུས་	Asaṅga's *Compendium of Manifest Knowledge*, or Dignāga's *Compendium of Valid Cognition*
ཚད་མ་སྡེ་བདུན་	Dharmakīrti's seven treatises on valid cognition
མཛོད་	Vasubandhu's *Treasury of Manifest Knowledge*
རྒྱན་སྣང་	Haribhadra's *Illumination* of Maitreya's *Ornament*
འདུལ་བ་	The *Foundations of Monastic Discipline*, or Guṇaprabha's *Aphorisms on Monastic Discipline*
སྒྲོན་གསལ་	Candrakīrti's *Brightening Lamp* commentary on Guhyasamāja
དྲི་མེད་འོད་	Kulika Puṇḍarīka's *Stainless Light* commentary on Kālacakra

Idiomatic Expressions

20

Page 391, Line 18

Tibetan and English share a surprising number of idiomatic expressions. The verbal phrase encountered here, གཉིད་དུ་འགྲོ་, is one such example.

WHAT TO REMEMBER

Idiomatic expressions are sentences or phrases that convey a meaning beyond the meaning of their individual parts. While some require culture-specific knowledge, others can be translated literally into English when the idiom is shared.

21 Recognizing Paraphrases

Page 392, Line 5

Although quotations and references to canonical texts have been seen already, it is important to distinguish between a proper quotation and a paraphrase. While both a quotation and a paraphrase can provide a source and a suitable verb (such as བཤད་, གསུངས་, etc.), a paraphrase will lack a closing quotation marker (such as ཅེས་, etc.; see ཤེར་སྙིང་རྣམ་བཤད་ note 5).

WHAT TO REMEMBER

Although quotations and paraphrases have elements in common, a critical difference is the presence or absence of a closing quotation marker.

22 Translation Hint

Page 392, Line 7

This is another instance of a nominalized sentence (see གྲུབ་མཐའ་ note 35) serving as the subject of a verb. As previously noted (see ཤེར་སྙིང་རྣམ་བཤད་ note 12), since the verb འདའ་ is in the present tense, the nominalized phrase would indicate the agent-noun. Hence, the phrase བར་འདའ་བ་ should be translated as "one who has passed beyond the intermediate state."

23 Locating Canonical Quotations

Page 392, Line 9

Although the author cites the source for his scriptural citation—in this case, Vasubandhu's *Treasury of Knowledge* (*Abhidharmakośa*)—the citation is not entirely correct. Since Vasubandhu's *Treasury* (like many "root" texts) is composed in verse, this passage cannot be from this text but rather must be (and is) from Vasubandhu's *Commentary* to the text. Furthermore, our author is paraphrasing slightly (or following another previous author's paraphrase) since the sentence as preserved in the canon actually reads: སྲིད་པ་ཚོལ་བ་རྣམས་གང་ཞེ་ན། ཡིད་ལས་བྱུང་དང་སྲིད་ཚོལ་དང་། དྲི་ཟ་སྲིད་པ་བར་མ་དང་། འགྲུབ་པའོ། ("If you ask, 'What are those who seek existence?' [they are] the 'mind-arisen,' 'seekers-of-existence,' 'scent-eaters,' '[those of] the intermediate state,' and '[those in] a state of establishing existence.'").

WHAT TO REMEMBER

When attempting to locate canonical quotations, one cannot assume that the author has quoted a passage accurately or completely. In such instances, the use of e-text or online search tools to locate partial phrase matches becomes invaluable.

Translation Hint 24

Page 393, Line 6

Sometimes, textual citation—such as the one given here—can be less than useful, if not actually wrong. Although the source for this information is given as the "eighth section of the tantra," there are no clues to exactly which text this might refer to. By searching the entire Kangyur, one can find three possible sources for the description given: the nineteenth chapter of the *Saṃvarodaya-tantra* (a text with 33 chapters), the eighth chapter of the *Sampuṭa-tantra* (a text in 10 chapters), and the twenty-first chapter of the *Vajraḍaka-tantra* (a text in 50 chapters). The second source would appear to be the source being referred to by the author, although the first source provides a closer match to the passage paraphrased.

Translation Hint 25

Page 393, Line 10

Occasionally, two verbs will form a collocation, but more often they will simply be another form of distributed verbs within a sentence (see ཤེས་རབ་སྙིང་པོ་ note 16).

Numerical Expressions: Half-numbers 26

Page 394, Line 10

Numerical expressions can be rather tricky in Tibetan, with numerous particles indicating different concepts. Here, the expression ཕྱེད་དང་ is one such example, which could be translated literally as "half and," although it actually conveys a different meaning. Yet another example to underscore the idea that the syllable དང་ is *not* the equivalent of the English word "and"—but rather a syntactic particle—here the syllable དང་ indicates subtraction ("minus"). Thus, the expression that occurs in the text here, ཕྱེད་དང་བཞི་, actually means "four minus a half" or "three and a half."

WHAT TO REMEMBER

When encountering numerical expressions, careful attention must be paid to the position and meaning of accompanying particles. One should remember that the expression ཕྱེད་དང་, for instance, connotes "minus a half."

27

Translation Hint

Page 396, Line 13

Occasionally, when translating, it is worthwhile to break up long sentences with complex subordinate clauses into separate sentences in English. Here is one such sentence whose literal translation—replicating the structure of the Tibetan original—would prove unneccessarily cumbersome. The base sentence is ཡོད་པའི་དབུས་སུ་…རྣམ་ཤེས་འཇུག ("the consciousness enters into the middle of something that exists") with everything else being modifying subordinate clauses. A literal translation would read something like: "The consciousness of the dying intermediate-state being enters into the middle of something that exists like the cream that forms on boiling milk from the drops of semen and blood that emerged from both the father and the mother, respectively, having been mixed in the place of birth in the mother."

28

Translation Hint

Page 396, Line 15

Here is another example of an abbreviated number (see བློ་རིག་ note 28) that could be mistakenly read as a noun-adjective phrase ("one meaning" or "one object").

Auxiliary Verbs: Causative Constructions and Negated Past-Tense Verbs

29

Page 397, Line 15

Recall that causative constructions are formed by combining the present-tense form of the main verb with the present-tense form of the generic action verb བྱེད་ (see ཤེས་རབ་སྙིང་པོ་ note 19). The sentence encountered here contains two verbs, རུལ་ and སྨིན་, both of which receive the distributed action of the auxiliary, བྱེད་. While the latter verb (སྨིན་) forms a standard causative construction, the former (རུལ་) merits further discussion. The first thing to note is that the verb in question is negated: མ་རུལ་. Although all tenses of the verb རུལ་ are the same, the presence of མ་ as its negation prefix indicates that རུལ་ is in the past tense (since མི་ is used with present and future-tense verbs). Since རུལ་ is a Class II verb conveying the passive activity "to decay," "to rot," or "to putrify," the construction མ་རུལ་བར་བྱེད་ would convey the idea of acting to prevent such ongoing passive activity or to maintain a state of nonactivity. This same sort of construction is seen in the following sentence as well with རྒྱས་པར་བྱེད་.

WHAT TO REMEMBER

A causative construction formed with a negated past-tense verb conveys the sense of maintaining a state of nonactivity or preventing the activity from transpiring.

Idiosyncratic Usage Paradigms of the Verb འགྱེས་

30

Page 399, Line 9

Although the verb འགྱེས་ functions in many contexts like a typical Class III ("nominative-objective") verb, occasionally it is seen in a sentence structure that violates the expected usage. As seen here, the pattern *originative + locative complement + verb* commonly occurs in select uses of this verb. The sentence encountered here, ཕྱོགས་ཀྱི་རྩ་བཞི་ལས་གཉིས་གཉིས་སུ་གྱེས་, is one such example. If one were to force the grammar in English, it would translate as something like: "From the four channels of the cardinal directions, [each] splits into two each." Although it is unheard of to find a subject marked in the ablative/originative, the import of the sentence is clear: "The four channels of the cardinal directions split into two each." The effective grammar of such a translation holds for similar grammatical patterns involving the verb འགྱེས་ as well and is not restricted to just this context and literary domain.

WHAT TO REMEMBER

The the verb འགྱེས་ occasionally occurs in constructions in which it is suitable to translate the sentence as if taking the subject of the verb as marked in the ablative.

Translation of Yangjen Gaway Lodrö's *Lamp Illuminating the Presentation of the Three Bodies that are the Bases [of Purification]*

Homage to the Teacher, Mañjughoṣa!

> Homage to the Lord of Union, who has mastery over
> The iron elements [of] birth, death, and the intermediate state—the bases of purification—
> The planned transformation into gold [by] the two stages of the profound path—the agents of purification—and
> The precious thoroughly pure three bodies—the fruits of purification.

Here, in order to know the mode of progression of the profound short path, by means of which is actualized the body of union endowed with the seven features of face-to-face [deities] in one short lifetime of this degenerate era through the unsurpassed path, the production of an understanding with regard to the presentation of the three basic bodies—the bases of purification—is very important.

Therefore, with regard to the explanation of the presentation of the three: birth, death, and the intermediate state—the bases of purification of the two stages of the path—[there are] three [parts]: the explanations of (1) the stages of death, (2) the stages of achieving the intermediate state, and (3) the manner in which a being takes [re]birth in the rebirth state.

As for the first [i.e., the stages of death], during the first eon [after the formation of this world system], the humans of this world were in disguise; [they] only had seven features—[spontaneous] birth, an immeasurable life span, all complete sense faculties, a body pervaded by its own light, adornment with similitudes of the major and minor marks [of a buddha], sustenance by the food of joy without eating coarse food, and magically flying in the sky. However, due to activation of predispositions established by craving for material food [in previous lives], they ate coarse sustenance, and because of this, the undigested [part of the food] turned into feces and urine. [Hence,] the male and female organs—the doors of expulsion—and so forth protruded.

Because [there were] two who possessed predispositions for copulation [established] in [lives] prior to this, [their] minds became attached to one another, and hence, in dependence on their engaging in contrary actions, sentient beings became attached to the womb and thus gradually came to be womb-born. Regarding that, the six complete constituents are [either] the six—earth, water, fire, wind, channels, and drops—or, [according to another interpretation], the six constituents are bone, marrow, and seminal fluid obtained from the father, and flesh, skin, and blood obtained from the mother, and hence womb-born humans of this world are said to have six constituents. If one is a person who is definite to become enlightened in one short lifetime of this degenerate era, through practicing from the beginning the path of unsurpassed mantra (i.e., *anuttaratantra*), [they] are necessarily a womb-born human of Jambudvīpa having the six constituents, just like this. The bodies of these [humans of this world] have seventy-two thousand channels together with the right, left, and central channels. At the end, at the time of death, all the winds of the seventy-two thousand [channels] gather in the right and left channels, and the winds in these two also dissolve into the central channel.

As for the winds in the upper and lower [parts] of the central channel, furthermore, in the end, death is necessary from the perspective of these parts of the single essence of the very subtle wind-mind—in the middle of which the white and red constituents within the central channel at the channel petals of the heart [cakra] exist in the manner of [two] face-to-face small boxes (*ga'u*)—dissolving into the indestructible life-bearing wind because, if the slightest wind that acts as a basis of consciousness—except for this very subtle wind—dwells in any part of the body, death is [otherwise] not possible.

Moreover, death necessarily [occurs] by way of the dissolution of the twenty-five gross objects—the five aggregates, the four constituents, the six sources, the five objects, and the five basic wisdoms. As for the stages of dissolution, initially, the five phenomena in the class of the aggregate of forms—that is, the aggregate of forms, the basic mirror-like wisdom, the earth constituent, the eye sense-power, and the visible forms [colors and shapes] included within one's own continuum—dissolve simultaneously. And because of this, the signs of the individual dissolutions of these [five phenomena in the class of the aggregate of forms] are, as the external sign of the dissolution of the form aggregate, the limbs [of one's body] become smaller than before, and one's body becomes weak and powerless. The basic mirror-like wisdom is explained to be an [ordinary] consciousness to which many objects appear simultaneously and clearly, just as reflections appear in a mirror. As an external sign of its dissolution, one's eye [sight] becomes unclear and clouded. As an external sign of the dissolution of the earth constituent, the body becomes very thin, the limbs loose, and an experience like the body sinking under the earth occurs. As an external sign of the dissolution of the eye sense-power, one cannot open or close the eyes. As an external sign of the dissolution of the visible forms included within one's own continuum, the luster of one's body fades and one's strength will be exhausted. The internal sign of that [dissolution of these five] is the arising of a bluish appearance called "like a mirage." It is a blue shimmering appearance like the appearance [of air] as water when sunlight strikes the sand in the summer.

After that, the five phenomena on the level of the aggregate of feelings dissolve simultaneously. When the aggregate of feelings dissolves, the external sign is that the body consciousness can no longer experience the pleasure, pain, and neutral feelings which accompany the sense consciousnesses. The basic wisdom of equality is explained to be an [ordinary] consciousness that is mindful of the three—pleasurable, painful, and neutral feelings—as of one type, [that is,] as feeling. As an external sign of the dissolution of that, one is no longer mindful of the pleasure, pain, and neutral feelings that accompany the mental consciousness. As an external sign of the dissolution of the water constituent, one's saliva, sweat, urine, blood, and seminal fluid dry greatly. As an external sign of the dissolution of the ear sense-power, one can no longer hear external or internal sounds. As an external sign of the dissolution of the sounds included within one's own continuum, the *ur* sound inside the ears no longer arises. The internal sign of the dissolution of these five is the dawning of an appearance like blue puffs of smoke, like smoke from a chimney from the middle of billowing smoke, called "like smoke."

After that, the five phenomena on the level of the aggregate of discriminations dissolve simultaneously. As an external sign of the dissolution of the aggregate of discriminations, one is no longer mindful of the affairs of relatives such as one's father and mother, etc. The basic wisdom of individual investigation is explained to be an [ordinary] consciousness that is mindful in particular of the names [purposes, and so forth] of relatives. As a sign of its dissolution, one can no longer remember the names even of one's parents. As an external sign of the dissolution of the fire constituent, the warmth of the body having diminished, the ability to eat, drink, and digest [or "digest food and drink"] is lost. As an external sign of the dissolution of the nose sense-power, the inhalation of wind [air] through the nose is weak, and whereas [the exhalation] outward is strong, the breaths which are long and protracted occur piled one on top of the other. As an external sign of the dissolution of the odors included within one's own continuum, one cannot smell any fragrant or unfragrant odors with one's nose. The internal sign of the dissolution of these five is the arising of an appearance called "like fireflies." It is the occurrence of an appearance which is like burning red sparks from within, for instance, puffs of smoke rising from a chimney, or like fading red sparks in the soot on the bottom of a frying pan [used for] parching grain.

After that, the five phenomena on the level of the aggregate of compositional factors dissolve simultaneously. As the external sign of the dissolution of this aggregate, one is unable [to perform] physical actions such as agitating [the body], moving about, etc. The basic wisdom of achieving activities is explained to be a consciousness that is mindful of external worldly activities, purposes, and so forth [of this and future lives, as well as how to achieve them]. As an external sign of its dissolution, one is not mindful of any external worldly activities, purposes, and so forth. As an external sign of the dissolution of the wind constituent, the ten winds—such as the [gross] life-bearing wind and so forth—shift from their own abodes to the heart, and the breath ceases to move in and out. As an external sign of the dissolution of the tongue sense-power, the tongue becomes thick and short, and the root of the tongue turns blue. As an external sign of the dissolution of the tastes included within one's own continuum, one can no longer experience any of the six tastes [sweet, sour, bitter, astringent, pungent, and salty]. At this point, since the body sense-power and tactile [faculty] must also dissolve, as an external sign of their dissolution, one can no longer experience any smoothness or roughness. As an internal sign of the dissolution of these [seven], there is the arising of an appearance called "like a burning butter lamp"—it is like the passing of a shooting star [or] the sputtering point of a butter-lamp [flame] when it is about to go out.

Moreover, regarding how the former four elements dissolve into the latter, the capacity of [the wind associated with] a former element [in the list of earth, water, fire, and wind] to serve as a basis of consciousness having degenerated, and the capacity of a latter one [to do so] becoming more manifest, is explained as "the dissolution of a former element into a latter one." Although, it is not a case of a former element becoming of the nature of another. Hence, saying "earth dissolves into water" [means that] the capacity of the earth-wind to act as a basis of consciousness having degenerated, since the capacity of the water-wind to act as a basis of consciousness becomes more manifest, then, since something similar to a transference of the capacity of the former to the latter occurs, it is explained as "earth dissolving into water." But it is not that ordinary earth dissolves into ordinary water. Thus, extend this reasoning to the other [dissolutions] as well.

After the four elements dissolve, these five phenomena of the class of the aggregate of consciousness—the conceptual mind of the eighty instinctual natures, the mind of vivid white luminosity, the mind of vivid red increase, the mind of vivid black near-attainment, and the mind of the clear light of death—must dawn in stages. Both the conceptual mind of the eighty instinctual natures and the wind which serves as its mount must dissolve prior to the path of radiant white luminosity because the modes of apprehension [of] both that and the mind of luminosity are discordant, and since the difference in coarseness and subtlety [between these two] is great, coarse minds such as that [of the eighty conceptions] cannot exist at the time of its [white] appearance. Therefore, at the time when the eighty instinctual natures together with the wind that is their mount begin to dissolve into the [radiant white] luminosity, an appearance like a burning butter lamp arises. Regarding the sign of the time of its own appearance—when that [mind of the eighty instinctual natures] has dissolved into [radiant white] luminosity—a white aspectual appearance of light dawns as extreme clarity and utter vacuity, like the sky pervaded by the light of the rising nighttime moon when the autumn sky is free of dust.

Regarding the conditions of such a dawning, because of having the nature of water, that which exists in the aspect of an upside-down *HAṂ* syllable—the white drop which was obtained by the father in the center of the cakra at the head which is loosened through the force of all the winds in the right and left channels above the heart having entered through the door of the upper opening of the central channel—comes downward. Until it arrives on top of the six-circled knot of the right and left channels at the heart, the radiant white luminosity arises. Thus, this is not a case of an appearance of moonlight and so forth shining from the outside. That is called "appearance" [because an appearance like moonlight dawns] and "the empty" [because of being devoid of the eighty conceptions as well as the wind that serves as their mount].

After that, the mind of [white] luminosity together with the wind that serves as its mount dissolves into the mind of increase; at the time when the mind of increase dawns, there is the appearance of a red or orange utter vacuity that is even more clear than before, like an autumn sky, free of dust, pervaded by sunlight. Regarding the conditions for that, by the knot of the cakra in the jewel [sexual organ] and the knot of the cakra at the navel gradually loosening through the force of all the winds in the right and left channels below the heart entering the central channel through its lower opening [at the base of the spine or in the sexual organ], the red drop that is obtained from the mother, which exists in the form of the single [vertical] line of a short-form "Ā" [in the Devanāgarī script] in the middle of the cakra at the navel, being of the nature of fire, comes upward. Until it arrives below the six-circled knot of the right and left channels at the heart, [a red or orange] appearance like that arises. Although, it is not a case of the illumination of sunlight and so forth shining from outside. That is called "increase of appearance" [because of being very vivid like sunlight] and "the very-empty" [because of being devoid of the mind of appearance as well as the wind that serves as its mount].

After that, the mind of increase together with the wind that serves as its mount dissolves into the mind of near-attainment; at the time of the first part of [the mind of] near-attainment, there is the appearance of a radiant black utter emptiness, like an autumn sky free of dust and pervaded by the thick darkness of the beginning of night. Through the force of the upper and lower winds within the central channel having gathered in the central channel at the heart, the six-circled knot of the right and left channels at the heart is loosened. Thereupon, the white drop that is above [in the form of an upside-down syllable *HAṂ*] descends, and the red drop that is below [in the form of a vertical line] ascends. Having entered into the middle of the white and red indestructible drops in the center of the central channel at the heart that exist in the manner of face-to-face reliquary boxes, due to the condition of their meeting, an appearance like that [the radiant appearance of near-attainment] arises. It is not a case of an appearance of darkness and so forth coming from the outside. That is called "near-attainment" [because of being near the clear light] and "the great-empty" [because of being devoid of the mind of increase as well as the wind that serves as its mount].

Moreover, the first part of the mind of near-attainment is produced accompanied by an appearing object; but, during the latter part of the mind of near-attainment, a confounding darkness comes without one being mindful of any object, as if fainting into unconsciousness. Then all the winds and minds that adventitiously arise from the very subtle wind and mind cease. So long as the mindfulness of the very subtle wind and mind—which has existed [nonmanifestly] from the beginning in the basic [ordinary state]—has not reactivated, that unconscious latter portion of the mind of near-attainment continues there, but after that, when mindfulness of the very subtle wind and mind has been revived, the clear light of death dawns.

A mental consciousness—(1) that occurs between the dissolution and stirring of the [mind of eighty instinctual] conceptions, (2) to which an appearance of radiant white vacuity dawns like an autumn sky free of defilement pervaded by moonlight, and (3) to which no other coarse dualistic appearance that is other than that appears—is the definition of a mind of radiant white luminosity. A mental consciousness—(1) that occurs between the dissolution and stirring of the [mind of eighty instinctual] conceptions, (2) to which an appearance of radiant red vacuity dawns like an autumn sky free of defilement pervaded by sunlight, and (3) to which no other coarse dualistic appearance that is other than that appears—is the definition of a mind of increasing luminosity. A mental consciousness—(1) that occurs between the dissolution and stirring of the [mind of eighty instinctual] conceptions, (2) to which an appearance of radiant black vacuity dawns like an autumn sky free of defilement pervaded by the thick darkness of the beginning of night, and (3) to which no other coarse dualistic appearance that is other than that appears—is the definition of [a mind of] luminous near-attainment.

At the time when the clear light dawns—[the mind of] near-attainment having dissolved into the clear light—and the unconscious latter part of the mind of near-attainment having been cleared away, without even the slightest coarse dualistic appearances, something dawns like the appearance of a meditative equipoise that directly realizes emptiness—an appearance of extremely clear vacuity, similar to the natural color, exactly as it is, of the sky at dawn of the autumn sky free from dust and free of the three conditions of pollution: moonlight, sunlight, and darkness.

Thus, [as for] the cause of the clear light appearance, moreover, the white and red drops dissolve [respectively] into the white and red indestructible drops [at the heart]. By means of all the winds inside the central channel dissolving into the very subtle life-bearing wind, the very subtle wind and mind that have existed in the ordinary state from the beginning [in a nonmanifest state] are made manifest, whereby such an appearance dawns. Thus, this is not a case of an appearance of vacuous sky from the outside. This is called the "clear light of death" and "the all-empty." It is actual death.

This is the basic truth body (*dharmakāya*) [so called because it is the basis of purification to be transformed into a truth body]. The vacuity is called the basic nature body (*svabhāvakāya*), and the mind that takes it as its object is called the basic realization wisdom truth body (*jñānadharmakāya*). [Most] ordinary humans remain in the clear light for three days, whereupon the signs of the white and red constituents occur. However, for those in whom the physical constituents have been severely consumed by disease, even though however many days pass, the signs of the red and white constituents do not occur and are [not] possible. Also, yogis—through the force of higher and lower realizations—having mixed that clear light with the truth body, are said [to be able to remain] in that state for an indefinite greater or lesser number of [extra] days.

The way that the minds of appearance, increase, and near-attainment together with the mind of clear light dissolve, moreover, is called "dissolution of the former into the latter" from the capacity of each former mind having ceased and each successive one becoming more manifest, but it is not that the former becomes of the nature of the latter.

As for taking the autumn sky as an example, [one] takes the autumn sky as an example since during the time of autumn there frequently occurs, and with great clarity, a composite of the two—the summer rains suppressing well [clouds of] earthen dust rising up into the sky, and [the sky] being free of the obstruction of clouds. Also, just as that sky is an utter vacuity that is the mere absence of coarse obstructions, the four empties as well are associated in terms of example and meaning since the modes of appearance of these two—having reversed the appearances of coarse conceptions to the mind [and] the dawning of the appearance of utter vacuity—are similar. Hence, it is not that appearances of the sky and so forth dawn on these occasions.

If [you] think, "Well then, if prior to the mind of luminosity, the eighty instinctual natures as well as the winds that serve as their mounts have dissolved, are there no winds that are about to dissolve at the time of the three—[the minds of] luminosity, increase, and [near-]attainment?" then in general, regarding winds, there are many—coarse and subtle—although even though the coarse [ones] have dissolved, the subtle still exist. Therefore, the time when only the subtle winds act as a basis of consciousness is from the dissolving of wind [from among the four elements] into luminosity up to the dissolving of near-attainment into the clear light.

On the occasion of the four empties, coarse conventional appearances having vanished for such a mind, through the force of the latter [minds] together with the appearance of objects having become each more subtle than the former minds and [their] appearing objects, an utter vacuity dawns, but this is not a case of taking emptiness as an object [of mind]. Because of that, for an ordinary person who has not cultivated the path, on these occasions, [other] than only [the appearance of] true establishment, appearances of non-true [existence] do not arise because, since the four empties on this occasion dawn for all dying sentient beings, then if emptiness were realized during death, there would be the [absurd] consequence that [everyone] would be effortlessly freed [from cyclic existence].

Ordinary beings experience the clear light of death in the manner of its appearing without being ascertained and do not experience [it] together with a mind of ascertainment. That [clear light of death] is the "mother" clear light, whereas that clear light which dawns through the power of meditation during sleep and the waking state while on the spiritual path is called the "son" clear light. Having mixed these two during the clear light of death, [it] is called "mixing the mother and son clear lights in meditation."

If you ask, "Well then, is the clear light of death in general a fully qualified clear light?" then although the mother and son clear lights that are mixed and then stabilized within the view [of emptiness] by a yogi are a fully qualified clear light, not being like that, the clear light of death that dawns for an ordinary being by its own accord is [a case of] imputing [the name] "clear light" to merely the stopping of coarse dualistic appearances, and [it] is not fully qualified. In general, with regard to the clear light, from among the two [types], [one can] posit (1) the clear light of the object—the subtle emptiness [of inherent existence]—and (2) the clear light of the subject—the exalted wisdom consciousness that realizes that [emptiness].

Since these stages of death [are] the adopted path that takes death as the truth body by means of the two [stages of] generation and completion of unsurpassed mantra, and [since they] are also the main bases of purification [by means] of the metaphoric and actual clear lights, the proper formulation of an understanding of these is very important.

[Part] Two: The Stages of Achieving the Intermediate State

Thus, at the end of howsoever long that mind of clear light abides in [a state of] motionlessness, with the mere fluctuation within that state, a slight movement comes about. When that occurs, since it initiates the rising from the clear light, at this point, the very subtle wind and mind leave the opened drop of the white and red constituents at the heart and pass outside, and the body is abandoned. Then, a body of the intermediate state is established. Simultaneously with that, the white constituent at the heart, having dropped downward, emerges from the tip of the [male or female] sign, while the red [constituent], having moved upward, emerges from the opening of the upper nose.

Moreover, that five-light-ray wind that serves as the mount of the clear light of death acts as the substantial cause of the body of the intermediate state and the cooperative condition of the mind. In dependence on the mind of the clear light of death having acted as the cooperative cause of the body of the intermediate state and the substantial cause of the mind, the intermediate state—being endowed with a body of wind—which has the aspect of the human being as one which is to be born, is established as something that abides in actuality, in a manner that is separate from the old aggregates of [the previous lifetime which was] a fruition [of prior actions].

At that time, the three minds of appearance, increase, and near-attainment that were explained earlier appear in reverse order. The dawning of the radiant black mind of near-attainment of the reverse process, the stoppage of the clear light of death, and the achievement of the intermediate state are simultaneous. [That is] because [passages] from many [texts]—such as the upper [Mahāyāna] and lower [Hīnayāna] *Manifest* [*Knowledge* treatises] *(Abhidharma)* and [Asaṅga's] sets of *Grounds* (*Bhūmi*) [treatises]—say that the stoppage of the death state and the achievement of the intermediate state are simultaneous, like [the movement up and down of] the higher and lower [ends] of a scale, and [because,] since a being of the intermediate state is spontaneously born, all of its major and secondary limbs are established simultaneously.

The mind that immediately follows the establishment of the intermediate state is that of near-attainment of the reverse process. From it, the mind of increase of the reverse process [is generated], and from this, appearance, and from that appearance the eighty instinctual natures are generated. That intermediate-state being rushes about for the sake of a birthplace, olfactory sensations [for nourishment,] and so forth. At these times as well, [there is] a reversal of the steps that were previously explained, and hence the signs—from the [black] near-attainment to mirage—occur in sequence. That bardo being, whose very subtle mental body that is achieved from wind alone and which has abandoned the coarse body [of the] elements together with corpulent flesh and blood and so forth, is called a "basic enjoyment body" and "gandharva."

Well then, if you ask, "What kind of example of the existence of such an intermediate-state being is there?" then [we reply,] nowadays, when going to sleep, something similar to the time of death—the four signs and the four empties on the occasion of sleep—having dawned just briefly, the clear light of sleep dawns. When we begin to rise from that, we begin to arise in a dream body, and when we arise from the clear light of sleep, a dream body is achieved. Thus we perform one of the various activities in the context of a dream. Then, at the time when we begin to awaken from sleep, that wind body of the dream fades away from the outside like breath placed on a mirror. Then, having gathered at the heart, and having dissolved into the undifferentiable entity [of] the very subtle wind and mind inside the central channel (*avadhūti*) at the heart of the old [physical] aggregates, we awaken from sleep. Then [we] accordingly engage in various activities.

Regarding the distinctive features of the entity of such an intermediate-state being, [there are five]: (1) all the sense faculties are complete; (2) since it is a spontaneously born [being], all its major and minor limbs are simultaneously completed; (3) since it is endowed with a subtle body, there is no destroying [it] even with a diamond; (4) except for birthplaces such as the mother's womb, it is not obstructed even by such things as mountains and so forth; and (5) through the force of its magical activity, in an instant it can go wherever it wants and not even a buddha is able to stop it.

In [Vasubandhu's] *Treasury* [*of Knowledge*] (*Abhidharmakośa*) it is explained that when the intermediate state of some [particular type of] transmigrator is achieved, it does not revert from that into another [type of] transmigrator. However, in [Asaṅga's] *Compendium* [*of Knowledge*] (*Abhidharmasamuccaya*) it is said that even when an intermediate state of some [type of being] has been achieved, being without any certainty of being born in that [way], there [can be] reversal into another [type of] transmigration. However, in the systems of both the lower [Hīnayāna] and upper [Mahāyāna] *Knowledge* [traditions] (*Abhidharma*), since there are those who have passed beyond the intermediate state who have attained the state of an arhat in dependence upon the intermediate state, it is not asserted that one necessarily needs to absolutely take rebirth. Synonyms are explained in [Vasubandhu's *Commentary* on his] *Treasury [of Knowledge]* as "those-arisen-from-the-mind," "seekers-of-existence," "gandharvas," "[those in] the intermediate state," and "[those in] a state of establishing existence."

Regarding the particulars of the length of life [in the intermediate state], the longest [amount of time] is seven days; however, when the causes for rebirth accumulate, since there are even [cases of] bridging the gap to the birth state immediately upon achieving the intermediate state, there is no certainty. If the conditions of birth do not accumulate after seven days, at the end of the seventh day, each [time] a small death occurs, and just that intermediate state is established [again] and [one] abides [in it]. [It is] said in [Asaṅga's] *Actuality of the Grounds (Bhūmivastu)* that [it is] done like that, and when seven sets of seven days have passed, the conditions for rebirth definitely aggregate and rebirth is necessarily taken.

Regarding the mode of each small death enacted at the end of a week, the wind body of the intermediate-state being gathers in the heart in stages from the top and the bottom, like breath on a mirror [evaporating] from the edges [inward]. The eighty instinctual natures of the intermediate state together with the wind that serves as their mount having dissolved, and the four signs and the four empties of an intermediate-state being's death having dawned just briefly [and] in a quick manner, the clear light of the death state is actualized. Then, the wind that serves as the mount of the clear light having acted as the substantial cause, simultaneously with achieving the mind of near-attainment of the reverse process, the wind body of an intermediate-state being is achieved as before. However many small deaths occur while having the life support of an intermediate-state being, [they] are included within the intermediate state [and not the death state].

From within [Asaṅga's] *Actuality of the Grounds* it is said that, even when that intermediate-state being sees its former physical body, due to the force of having severed the connection with that body, it does not generate a mind wishing to enter it nor think, "That old physical support is my body."

Someone saying [that] the statement that the life span of an intermediate-state being is seven days is made from the perspective of the days of each of the six types [of transmigrators] is not correct, because if it were like that, then since an intermediate-state being [who is to be reborn] as a hell being or as a god of the upper realms would necessarily be someone who dwells in those states for the seven days of such and such beings, and since one would have to assert that there are cases of dwelling in the intermediate state for a great many millions of years without aggregating the conditions for rebirth, it would result in a great [absurd] consequence.

Regarding the specifics of the manner of passing on to [the next] existence, it is explained in the eighth section of the [*Saṃpuṭa*] *Tantra* and so forth that if one is to be reborn as a hell being, one exits from the anus; if one is to be reborn as a hungry ghost, [one exits from] the mouth; if one is to be reborn as an animal, [one exits from] the urinary passage; if one is to be reborn as a human, [one exits from] the eye; if one is to be reborn as a god of the desire realm, [one exits from] the navel; if one is to be reborn as a *yakṣa*, [one exits] from the nose; if one is to be reborn as a god of magical accomplishment, or as a *kiṃnara*, [one exits from] the ear; if one is to be reborn in the form realm, [one exits from] the middle of the brow, and if one is to be reborn in the formless realm, [one exits from] the crown of the head.

However, if [someone] says, "[This] is contradictory with the explanation in [Asaṅga's] sets of *Grounds* [treatises] and so forth that when the body is abandoned, the consciousness exits from the heart," then there is no contradiction, because when the consciousness shifts within the body, initially [it] exists from the heart; however, from there, when it passes outside the body, it is in accordance with the explanation that it exits from these individual doors.

Also, if [someone] wonders what [it] means when, in [Vasubandhu's] *Treasury* [*of Manifest Knowledge*], it says, "When dying in stages, the mind dies and exits at the feet, navel, or heart," and, in [his] commentary, "If one is to be reborn in a bad migration, [the consciousness ceases at] the feet, if reborn as a human, [the consciousness ceases at] the navel, if reborn as a god or when an arhat dies, the consciousness ceases at the heart" then just as the commentary explains that as the meaning of the mind's ceasing at those places, these passages merely indicate different ways that the mental consciousness stops through the force of the body sense's ceasing in places such as the feet. Since it does not teach that the consciousness exits to the outside from those places, there is no contradiction with the earlier explanation.

As for the distinctive characteristics of the modes of perception, [Vasubandhu's] *Treasury* [*of Manifest Knowledge*] explains that [they] are seen by those of similar bardo type and by those with a pure divine eye (i.e., clairvoyants). Regarding that, it is posited that a divine eye that is obtained [merely] through the force of birth is impure, while [one that is] obtained through the force of meditation is a pure divine eye. [Vasubandhu's] *Commentary on the "Treasury* [*of Knowledge*]" also explains that intermediate-state beings of each higher type perceive each of the lower ones. As for its particular dimensions, although it is explained in [Vasubandhu's] *Commentary on the "Treasury* [*of Knowledge*]" that an intermediate-state being of a human of this world [is] about [the size of] a child for whom five or six [years] have elapsed, it is not said that such is one-pointedly certain.

As for the features of its aspect, [Asaṅga's] *Actuality of the Grounds* says that, to an intermediate-state being of a bad migration [animal, hungry ghost, or hell being], there appears an outstretched black flag or night pervaded by darkness; whereas, to an intermediate-state being of a happy migration [human, demigod, or god], there appears an outstretched white cloth or night pervaded by moonlight.

As for the feature of color, it is explained in the *Sūtra* [*of the Teaching*] *to Nanda on Entry into the Womb* that [the body's color in] the intermediate state of a hell being is like a log burned by fire, the intermediate state of a hungry ghost is like water, the intermediate state of an animal is like smoke, the intermediate state of a god or human of the desire realm is like gold, and the intermediate state of a god of the form realm is white, and so forth.

As for the features of its shape, [Vasubandhu's] *Treasury* [*of Knowledge*] says that an intermediate-state being has the fleshly appearance or physical shape of the prior state of that transmigrator in whatever [state] it will be reborn. There are four states:

1. The first moment of connecting to the birth state [is] the *birth state*.
2. Existence from the second moment after that [connecting to the new life] just up to the establishment of the death state [is] the *prior state*.
3. Existence during the last moment of death or at the time of experiencing the clear light of death [is] the *death state*.
4. The existence that occurs between the death state and birth state is the *intermediate state*.

Having been mistaken with regard to the mere words of the expression "prior state," [some] assert that an intermediate-state being has the physical aspect of the former life. Also, having seen the explanation that it has the physical shape of the next [life], the assertion that it has the physical aspect of the former life for three and a half days and of the next life for three and a half days is said in [Tsongkhapa's] *Great Exposition of the Stages of the Path* to be a mere fabrication that lacks any authentic source whatsoever. Hence, [the word] "prior" in the expression "prior state" is a "prior" that is contingent upon the death state of the next life; it is not something posited as a "prior" that depends on the intermediate state. The word "occur" in the statement from [Vasubandhu's] *Treasury [of Knowledge]* that says, "possessing the fleshly form of the prior state that will occur," is a word in the future tense and is not a word in the past tense.

Also, with regard to the explanation that an intermediate-state being has the aspect of that sentient being of whom it will be reborn, some say that if that is so, then the intermediate-state being of a transmigrator who [in his next life] will not have complete sense faculties also does not have complete sense faculties; this is gravely mistaken, because there being incomplete sense faculties in the intermediate state of one who will be born with incomplete sense faculties—such as eyes, etc.—after being born in a place of birth [such as a womb] is not explained in any [scripture] whatsoever, and [because] if, by the mere explanation that oneself would possess the aspects of a transmigrator who will be born as any such kind whatsoever, that they would necessarily be similar in all aspects, then that would be an extreme [absurd] consequence.

As for the features of its manner of movement, [Asaṅga's] *Actuality of the Levels* says that an intermediate-state being of a god proceeds upward; of a human, straightforward; and of a bad migration, beginning head first, downward. Moreover, since it is necessary to pass through the intermediate state for birth in both the desire and form [realms], [Tsongkhapa's] *Great Exposition of the Stages of the Path* says that the assertion that there is no intermediate state for both those [who have committed] actions of direct transition upward and [who have committed actions] of direct transition downward is not correct. However, there is no intermediate state for rebirth in a formless realm, and hence the aggregates, which are the basis of a name of a formless being [that is, the being's mind and mental factors], are achieved in just the place of death. Thus, a person who is to be reborn in a formless realm actualizes a formless samādhi from within the state of the clear light of death, and there is no dawning of the mind of near-attainment upon arising from the clear light of death in the reverse process because a mind of near-attainment such as that would be a mind of the intermediate state. Thus, the formless realm has no separate place other than the desire and form realms.

[Vasubandhu's] *Commentary on the "Treasury [of Knowledge]"* and [Nāgabodhi's] *Ordered Stages [of the Means of Achieving Guhyasamāja]* say that a special intermediate-state being—a bodhisattva who is obstructed [from obtaining enlightenment] by just one [rebirth]—[is] an intermediate-state being who, having left Tuṣita, enters into the mother's womb, [is] a youth adorned with the major and minor marks, and illuminates a billion sets of four continents with light. In that case, if you say, "[This] contradicts the explanation by Bhadanta Dharmasubhuti that [Śākyamuni Buddha] entered the womb in the form of a six-tusked white elephant," then it is not necessary to accept [things] in accordance with the explanation by him. However, [it] is merely a teaching in accordance with the mother's dream. If it were asserted that an intermediate-state being who is to be reborn as a human has the aspect of an animal, then because it would contradict many valid treatises, that is asserted to be literal in the Hīnayāna systems but is asserted as merely a [special] mode of teaching in the Mahāyāna.

As for these presentations of the intermediate state, since [one] takes up the path that is [the practice of] taking the intermediate state as an enjoyment body (*saṃbhogakāya*) in the generation stage of unsurpassed [yoga tantra], and [it] is the basis of purification of the impure and pure illusory bodies [in the stage of completion], knowing [them] in detail is important.

Part three: the manner in which one takes rebirth in the birth place. Moreover, in order for that intermediate-state being to take rebirth in a mother's womb, three [favorable] circumstances must be manifest and [it] must be free of three faults:

1. The mother must be free from disease and in a condition of still menstruating.
2. The gandharva [intermediate-state being] must be nearby and wish to enter.
3. The male and female must desire each other and meet.

[These] are the three circumstances that must manifest. Moreover:

4. The center of the mother's womb being similar to the shape of a barley seed, an ant's waist, or a camel's mouth, or being obstructed by wind, bile, or phlegm—[these are] the faults of the womb.
5. The semen and blood not arising from either the father or the mother [respectively], or arising and yet one descending earlier and [the other] later, or descending simultaneuosly although either being rotten—[these are] the faults of the seed.
6. The gandharva not having accumulated the karma of being born as the child of that father and mother, or both the father and mother not having accumulated the karma of serving as its father and mother—[these are] the faults of karma.

[These are] the three faults that it is necessary to be free from as stated in the *Sūtra on the Entry into the Womb*. This is also similar in meaning to the statement in the Vinaya scriptures that six circumstances must be manifest.

In that way, that gandharva—for whom the three concordant conditions for taking rebirth in a womb are complete and who is free from the three contradictory conditions—sees, in an illusory manner, both the father and mother lying together, and through the force of wanting to engage in copulation, if it is to be reborn as a male, [it] has desire for the mother and wishes to be separate with regard to the father; whereas, if it is to be reborn as female, [it] has desire for the father and generates the wish to be separate with regard to the mother. Then, when it begins to embrace whichsoever one [it] has desire for, through the force of karma, without any such other [parts of] the body appearing, since merely the sexual organ of whichever—the father or mother—appears, anger is generated. This desire and hatred having served as the conditions for death [of the intermediate-state being], [it] enters the womb.

It is said in the "Many Grounds" [chapter of Asaṅga's *Actuality of the Grounds*] that, in accordance with the father and mother not actually lying together [at that time], that gandharva having been mistaken about [its perception of] the semen and blood, sees [it] as lying together. [Vasubandhu's] *Commentary on the "Treasury [of Knowledge],"* however, explains that it [actually] sees the father and mother lying together. Moreover, when the father and mother have become absorbed together [in sexual intercourse], through the force of the rubbing together their two sexual organs, the downward-voiding wind shifts upward. [Then] through the red and white drops melted by heat of the ignition of the ordinary inner-heat (*gtum mo*) of the three-way intersection [of the central, right, and left channels at the solar plexus] descending within the empty insides of the seventy-two thousand channels, body and mind are satisfied by bliss, and in that context, when [it] descends during a period of strong desire, at [its] conclusion, a thick regenerative fluid arises. After that, the drops of semen and blood emerge from both the father and the mother, respectively, and are mixed in the place of birth in the mother. The consciousness of the dying intermediate-state being [then] enters into the middle of this [mixture], which is like the cream that forms on boiled milk.

With regard to how this [occurs], initially the intermediate-state being enters from any of three doors—the mouth of the father or top of [his] head, or the mother's womb. It then associates with the regenerative fluid that has descended from within the seventy-two thousand channels. The winds that move the instinctual natures during the intermediate state dissolve, whereupon the three [minds of] appearance, increase, and near-attainment dawn in stages. [These and] the clear light of the intermediate-state being's death appear in a quick manner with each merely being generated for a period shorter than those explained earlier at the point of leaving the previous coarse body. At that time, the signs from mirage to clear light occur, and a continuation of a similar type of the clear light makes—in the center of the mixed semen and blood—the connection to the new life. Having done [that], the taking of rebirth and the establishment of [the mind of] near-attainment of the reverse process are simultaneous.

That first moment of the mind of near-attainment is the basis of designating the verbal convention "birth state" and the mind of initially taking rebirth in the birthplace. From that, the second and following moments of near-attainment are produced; from that, increase; from that, appearance; from appearance, the eighty instinctual natures as well as the winds that are their mounts. From the wind that is the mount of the mind of appearance, [there comes] a wind that has a special capacity for acting as a basis of consciousness. From that, a fire constituent that has a special capacity similar to that; from that, a water constituent that has a similar capacity to that; and from that, an earth constituent that has such a capacity are generated in sequence.

With regard to the door through which an intermediate-state being enters the womb, in [Nāgabodhi's] *Ordered Presentation* [*of the Stages of the Guhyasamāja Sādhana*] (*Rnam bzhag rim pa*) it is explained that [it] enters through the top of the head, [which is] the door of Vairocana. However, since in both the *Saṃvarodaya* [*Tantra*] (*Sdom 'byung*) and the *Vajramāla* [*Tantra*] it is explained that it enters through the male's mouth, initially, the intermediate-state being enters through the male's mouth or through the top of the head and emerges from the father's secret place. Having entered the mother's lotus, the consciousness of the dying intermediate-state being connects [itself] to the middle of the semen and blood. Since [Vasubandhu's] *Commentary on the "Treasury* [*of Knowledge*]*"* explains that [it] enters through the door of the mother's womb, then just so, it should be understood that there are three doors of entry to the womb—the father's mouth, the top of the father's head, and the door to the mother's womb.

This [presentation] has been made from the perspective of [the mode of entry of] a human intermediate-state being that is womb-born. In general, however, since an intermediate-state being is unobstructed [in its movements], a hole for a door of entry is not needed because [Vasubandhu's] *Commentary on the "Treasury* [*of Knowledge*]*"* explains "it is well known that organisms are found inside a mass of iron that has been split apart," and there are sentient beings in very hard rocks and small yellow stones that have no openings.

Regarding the manner in which the body gradually develops in the womb, from the [*Sūtra of the Teaching to Nanda on*] *Entry into the Womb*, [it is] explained that the womb is in that intervening space below the mother's stomach and above the large intestine. Thus, initially, the oval-shaped [fetus] is covered on the outside by something like the cream of boiled milk, but inside it is runny. From this point it possesses [coherence], and since the coarse [physical] aggregates are established, the subtle and coarse bodies that last until death are achieved from the constituents of the four elements. Hence, the earth-wind causes holding; the water-wind causes cohesion; the fire-wind maintains nonputrefaction and causes maturation; the wind-wind causes development.

When the oval-shaped fetus has passed seven days, a new wind is produced, and from the maturation that has occurred by means of [that] wind, the "lump" becomes viscous both outside and inside, like yogurt, but has not become fleshy. When another seven days pass, then a new wind is produced, and from maturation [due to it], the oval-shaped [fetus] becomes fleshy but cannot withstand pressure. After another seven days, it has become hard due to maturation by a new wind; the flesh is now dense and can bear pressure. When this, in turn, has passed seven days, due to maturation by a new wind, legs and arms form; the five protuberances—indications of the two thighs, two shoulders and head—protrude clearly. [Nāgabodhi's] *Ordered Presentation [of the Stages of the Guhyasamāja Sādhana]* called [these] the five states in the womb. Also, [Vasubandhu's] *Commentary on the "Treasury [of Knowledge]"* and the *Entry into the Womb* scripture explain elongated, oval-shaped, and the latter three in accordance with the previous [explanation], and [Asaṅga's] *Actuality of the Levels* reverses the [first] two [as here]. Hence, although that is the explanation, it is said that, except for there being a difference in the order of the designation of names, there is no contradiction in the meaning.

During the fourth week, the white and red drops having divided into refined and unrefined portions, from the white [drops arise] the three substances obtained from the father—semen, marrow, and bone for the interior; and from the red drops arise the three substances obtained from the mother—flesh, skin, and blood for the exterior. The place in the semen and blood where the consciousness initially enters later becomes the heart, and in it [there are] the two—the very subtle wind and mind—and the two pure essences of semen and blood. Then, a ball that is a composite of [those] four [factors]—about the size of the thickness of a mustard seed—having been enveloped in the middle of that, the central channel and on the left and right—the *lalana* and *rasana* channels—wrapping around [it] three times, bind [it].

Then, through the force of the upward-moving wind being generated upward and the downward-voiding wind going downward, the three channels—the central, the *lalana*, and the *rasana*—diverge upward and downward. Both the top and bottom [of the body at this point] are thin, but the middle, being bulbous, develops like the shape of a fish. Then, gradually, the five protuberances, and after them the five limbs, and subsequently, hair, nails, body hair, etc., and the physical sense-powers, the male or female gender signs, the breath-wind that moves through the mouth, the eight sources of speech—the [sound] producer, the tongue, the palette, and so forth—and the mindfulness which is the movement of the mental consciousness to objects—a complete [set of these] arise naturally.

Having developed in the womb in that way, if [the child] is a boy, [he] is oriented toward the [mother's] backbone, facing backwards, on the mother's right side, [remaining] upright; if a girl, [she] is oriented toward the [mother's] backbone, facing foreward, on the mother's left side, [remaining] upright.

Regarding the length of time spent in the womb, since the *Sūtra of* [*the Teaching to*] *Nanda on Entry into the Womb* says that having completed thirty-eight weeks, birth occurs, [that would be] two hundred sixty-six days. In [Asaṅga's] *Actuality of the Levels*, having added four days on top of that, it is said that having completed two hundred and seventy days, birth occurs. The *Saṃvarodaya Tantra* speaks of a mind-possessor that emerges in the tenth month. All three of these are in agreement with regard to taking [the period] as nine months and some portion of a tenth. [It should be noted that] a day that is spoken of in the *Sūtra of* [*the Teaching to*] *Nanda on Entry into the Womb* and [Asaṅga's] *Actuality of the Grounds* [is made in terms of] solar days, and a month is made in terms of lunar months.

Moreover, during the thirty-fifth week, the body—that is to say, the aggregates, constituents, sources, limbs, secondary limbs, hair, nails, and so forth—speech—that is, the sources of pronunciation, tongue, and palette—and the mind—that is, mindfulness that is engagement by a consciousness with an object—are complete. Hence, in the thirty-sixth week, [the child] generates dislike for the womb and the desire to emerge [from it]. In the thirty-seventh week, [it] generates a discrimination of bad odor and filthiness in the womb. Finally, in the thirty-eighth week, a wind called "secondary" that is generated from former actions, having arisen, the body of that sentient being in the womb turns upside down. Its two arms contract, and it orients itself away from the gestational heat of the mother and toward the door of the womb.

Then, also, a wind called "looking downward" that is generated from former actions, having arisen, the sentient being in the womb—being oriented with its head down and feet up—pushes itself toward the urinary tract. Hence, at the end of the thirty-eighth week, having emerged outside, it comes into the path of ordinary vision. [This, then,] is the occurrence, in stages, of the five states of development: child, youth, pubescent, adult, and old age.

Furthermore, as for the manner of the formation of the channels, winds, and drops, initially, five channels of the heart form simultaneously—the central, right, and left channels, as well as the "threefold" (*traivṛtta*) in the east [front] and the "impassioned" (*kāminī*) in the south [right]. After that, three channels form simultaneously—the "daughter of Māra" (*māradārikā*) [rear central] channel that abides with [and behind] the central channel, the "householder" (*gehā*) in the west [back] channel, and the "inner heat" (*caṇḍikā*) in the north [left] channel. These are called the eight channels that initially form at the heart.

Then, the four channels of the cardinal directions [at the heart] split into two each; [these] four channel-petals of the intermediate directions and [their] continuation into the eight channel-petals of the heart, having split into three each, form the twenty-four channels of the twenty-four places. By each of the twenty-four splitting into three each, [there are] seventy-two, and each of these splits into a thousand each. Hence, [this is] the forming of the seventy-two thousand channels in the body.

With respect to the manner of the formation of the winds, having initially connected to the new life in the womb, in the first month, the coarse life-bearing wind is produced from the subtle life-bearing wind. At that time, the shape of the body of that sentient being is similar in aspect to a fish. In the second month, the downward-voiding [wind] is produced from the life-bearing wind. At that time, the body of that sentient being, having five protuberances projecting out, is similar to a turtle. In the third month, the [fire]-dwelling [wind] is produced from the downward-voiding [wind]. At that time, the upper body of that sentient being, being slightly bent, has the form of a wild boar. In the fourth month, the upward-moving [wind] is produced from the [fire]-dwelling [wind]. At that time, the upper body, being slightly broad, has the form of a lion. In the fifth month, the pervasive [wind] is produced from the upward-moving [wind]. At that time, the body of that sentient being is said to have the shape of a short dwarf.

In the sixth month, the [secondary] wind that moves through the door of the eyes—called "moving"—and the earth element are produced. In the seventh month, the [secondary] wind that moves through the door of the ears—[called] "the intensely moving"—and the water element are produced. In the eighth month, the [secondary] wind that moves through the door of the nose—[called] "the thoroughly moving"—and the element fire are produced. In the ninth month, the [secondary] wind that moves through the door of the tongue—[called] "the strongly moving"—and the element wind are produced. In the tenth month, the [secondary] wind that moves through the door of the body—called "definitely moving"—and the element of the space constituent are produced. At that time, the empty places in the body arise. It is said that, although the ten winds form in the womb, [coarse] inhalation and exhalation from the door of the nose does not occur, but outside [the womb], immediately after birth, [coarse] inhalation and exhalation from the door of the nose does occur.

Regarding the manner in which the drops are formed, the mass that is a composite of the pure essences of the white and red constituents [drops] and the very subtle wind and mind—being merely the size of a bulbous white mustard seed—abiding inside the slight empty place that exists in the central channel at the heart is called "the indestructible drop." Then, from that white drop, one part goes [up] into the cakra at the crown of the head and remains there; [that] is called "the letter *HAṂ*." That [either] directly or indirectly increases the white drops in other places in the body. From the red drop at the heart, one part goes [down] into the cakra at the navel and abides there; it is called "the inner heat." It directly or indirectly—as is suitable—increases the red constituent in other places in the body.

Although a portion of each drop dwells in each cakra, the cakra at the top of the head is the main source of increasing the white constituent, while the cakra at the navel is the main source of increasing the red constituent. However, the cakra at the heart is a source of increasing, in equal parts, the white and red constituents. It is said, furthermore, that whenever the white and red constituents are needed, accordingly, they are produced and thus do not exist like water poured in a vessel [i.e., of limited quantity].

This [period] from connecting to the new life in the place of conception [through to and including] assuming a coarse body is called the basic emanation body (*nirmāṇa-kāya*).

These presentations of the intermediate-state being taking rebirth [and] having bridged the gap to the womb in this way are similar in aspect to (1) the generation stage [practice, in which one] takes up the path into which [one] brings birth as an emanation body, and (2) the completion stage [practice, in which] the pure and impure illusory bodies are assumed as a coarse emanation body or [in which one] abides in the old physical aggregates and thereby comes into the path of ordinary vision; hence, [birth] is the basis of purification of these.

Moreover, since there is no difference in the bases being purified by means of the stages of generation and completion [in unsurpassed yoga tantra], as for generation stage, having taken basic death, the intermediate state, and birth as the bases of purification,

[one] cultivates, as activites of purification, the three [practices of] taking up the path into which [one] brings death—in accordance with the three [appearances: brilliant white, orange increase, and black near-attainment] and the [eighty] instinctual natures—as the dharma body, taking up the path into which [one] brings the intermediate state as the enjoyment body, and taking up the path into which [one] brings birth as the emanation body, all together with their secondary [practices]. Hence, continuously having purified the three—ordinary death, intermediate state, and birth—[this] is the actualization of the three bodies that accord in aspect, just as they are, with the three of them, while the stage of completion is that which actually purifies those [i.e., basic death, intermediate state, and rebirth] by means of a path that accords in aspect, just as they are, with the three basic phenomena.

Furthermore, those [factors in the stage of completion] that accord in aspect, just as they are, with the clear light of death are the three—[white] appearance, increase, and near-attainment—together with the clear light, [all of which] are [manifested during] the isolation of body, isolation of speech, isolation of mind, illusory body, and union of a learner. Those [factors in the stage of completion] that accord in aspect with the intermediate state are the impure illusory body of the third stage [when the above six stages are condensed to five by taking the first two as one] and the pure illusory body of a learner's union. Those [factors] that accord in aspect with birth are the abiding of the pure and impure illusory bodies in the old aggregates [the ordinary body] and come into the path of ordinary vision.

Regarding the actual manner in which the paths of the completion stage purify birth, death, and the intermediate state, a yogi of the completion stage passes from one to another similar type of very subtle mind from among the undifferentiable entity of the very subtle wind and mind in his own continuum; and [that] becomes the clear light of ordinary death. Then, having stopped [this process] through the power of a samādhi, at the time when the path is in accordance—just as it is—with the aspect of that [clear light], [the yogi transforms it into] the metaphoric and actual clear light, and [then death] transforms into the dharma body—the fruitional clear light; that is the manner in which one purifies death. [Likewise,] a yogi of the completion stage passes from one to another similar type of that very subtle wind that is similar to that [undifferentiable entity of the very subtle wind and mind in his own continuum]; having served as the mount of the ordinary clear light of death, [it] arises as the body of an intermediate-state being. Then, having stopped [this process] through the power of a samādhi, [the yogi transforms it into] the impure illusory body that accords—just as it is—with the aspect of that intermediate state and into the pure illusory body of union of a learner and non-learner; that is the manner in which one purifies the intermediate state.

But when [one] achieves such an illusory body, the intermediate state ceases forever, and through the power of that, rebirth that is the taking of birth in the womb through [contaminated] actions and afflictions having ceased as well, then an illusory body enters the old physical aggregates, being similar in aspect to an intermediate-state being taking birth in a mother's womb. Hence, making the effort of explaining the Dharma [to others] and achieving the higher paths is the manner in which one purifies birth.

Thus, the root of actually stopping the three—birth, death, and the intermediate state—is just the metaphoric clear light, [which manifests] at the completion of mind-isolation and that serves as the direct cause of an illusory body, because through the power of its actually stopping death, the intermediate state and birth stop of their own accord. When an illusory body is achieved from such a metaphoric clear light, the intermediate state is stopped forever because that very subtle wind that would arise as the body of an intermediate-state being has become an illusory body. When the intermediate state is finally stopped, [one] does not take-up rebirth by means of [contaminated] actions and afflictions, and for that reason, when [one] attains an illusory body, [one] will necessarily become fully enlightened in that [same] lifetime.

Having been concerned that the scriptural sources for what has been made known in the above explanation might be too many, [I] did not write [them] down. Hence, [they] should be known from the excellent explanations of the foremost father [Tsongkhapa], and his spiritual sons [Gyeltsap and Kedrup] and from [the writings of] the excellent scholars and adepts who follow [them].

Thus, [I] say:

Although [I] have written this procedure according to the speech
Of the second conqueror—the father—his sons, and scholarly followers,

I make a confession to the lamas, gods, and scholars for whatsoever
Collection of errors that stray from the thought of the excellent that may exist [in it here].

By means of the virtue represented by this, may all migrators—myself and others—
Quickly complete the excellent path [that] transforms
Impure birth, death, and the intermediate state into the three bodies
Through the yoga of the two stages of the profound path.

This was collected from the scriptures of the holy ones by the lazy Yangjen Gaway Lodrö and was written down as his own reminder.

The Fourth Paṇchen Lama's *Prayer for Release from the Dangerous Bardo*

The Fourth[1] Paṇchen Lama's seventeen-stanza poem is a guide to specific Buddhist techniques for overcoming fear of death and potentially utilizing the stages of dying in religious practice. In terms of content, it covers much of the same material dealt with at length in the previous text as well as material (and vocabulary) seen in Tsongkhapa's *Three Principal Aspects of the Path* (selection four in this *Reader*).

As with Tsongkhapa's *Three Principal Aspects of the Path*, this text is a condensed and versified presentation of a topic that typically receives more extensive treatment. This text, like many other works composed in verse, is intended for consumption by an audience already familiar with the subject matter. As such, these texts tend to serve the function of a memory aid—a mnemonic poem—rather than a definitive exposition. Such a text might require a commentary for full comprehension or, in this case, be a summation of a larger work.

In brief, the first seven stanzas of the Paṇchen Lama's poem offer an explanation of how to approach dying constructively. After an initial stanza about taking refuge in the Buddha, his teachings (*Dharma*), and the spiritual community (*Saṅgha*), the next two stanzas (stanzas two and three) address the importance of valuing the present lifetime as an opportunity for spiritual practice. Stanzas four and five speak to adopting a perspective that can handle both the overwhelming suffering that can accompany the time near death and the delusions that appear while dying. Stanzas six and seven prescribe how to achieve the most favorable conditions for death by remembering what to practice and by remaining joyful.

The next three stanzas (stanzas eight through ten) describe at length the appearances that occur during the first four phases of dying and how to meditate throughout them. This section draws on previous knowledge of the collapse of the physical elements that support consciousness and their corresponding experiences. These gradually open the way for three deeper, subtle minds to manifest themselves as described in the following stanza (stanza eleven). This verse lays out the structure of mind and body according to unsurpassed yoga tantra (*anuttarayoga-tantra*). Stanzas twelve and thirteen address the culminating experience of the fundamental innate mind of clear light.

The last four stanzas (stanzas fourteen through seventeen) describe the intermediate state after death and before the next life and show how to react to the often horrific events that can occur during that state. These stanzas detail how various levels of practitioners can seek to direct their ensuing rebirth.

As a reading exercise, texts such as this one offer the student the opportunity to draw on the vocabulary, knowledge, and conceptual context spelled out in a previously encountered text (in this case, the immediately preceding selection in this *Reader*) while navigating the concise syntax of verse.

---

[1] In actuality, Losang Chögyi Gyeltsen (*blo bzang chos kyi rgyal mtshan*, 1570–1662) was the first individual to hold the title "Paṇchen"—an abbreviation of the phrase "great scholar" (*paṇḍi ta chen po*)—a title bestowed upon him by the Fifth Dalai Lama as an act honoring his teacher. Later, some individuals, in an attempt to elevate the lineage to a status similar to that of the Dalai Lamas, retroactively applied the title to his reincarnation lineage since Losang Chögyi Gyeltsen had been a recognized reincarnation with three predecessors, beginning with the student of Tsongkhapa, Kedrup Gelek Pel Sangpo (*mkhas grub dge legs dpal bzang po*, 1385–1438). Consequently, some bibliographic sources will refer to Losang Chögyi Gyeltsen as the First Paṇchen Lama, while others place him fourth in the lineage. Since this latter numbering scheme has been adopted by the U.S. Library of Congress, that system is followed here.

༄༅། །བར་དོ་འཕྲང་སྒྲོལ་གྱི་གསོལ་འདེབས་འཇིགས་སྒྲོལ་གྱི་དཔའ་བོ།

ན་མོ་གུ་རུ་མཉྫུ་གྷོ་ཥ་ཡ།

དུས་གསུམ་བདེ་གཤེགས་ཆོས་དང་ཚོགས་བཅས་ལ། །
བདག་དང་མཁའ་མཉམ་འགྲོ་བ་མ་ལུས་པ། །
བྱང་ཆུབ་སྙིང་པོའི་བར་དུ་སྐྱབས་སུ་མཆི། །
འདི་ཕྱི་བར་དོའི་འཇིགས་ལས་བསྐྱལ་དུ་[1]གསོལ། ། ༡ །།

རྙེད་དཀའ་འཇིག་པར་སླ་བའི་རྟེན་བཟང་འདིར། །
ཁེ་ཉེན་སྐྱིད་སྡུག་འདམ་གའི་[2]སྐབས་ཡིན་པས། །
དོན་མེད་ཚེ་འདིའི་བྱ་བས་མི་གཡེང་བར། །
དོན་ཆེན་སྙིང་པོ་ལེན་པར་བྱིན་གྱིས་རློབས། ། ༢ །།

འདུས་པ་འབྲལ་ཞིང་བསགས་པ་མ་ལུས་འཛད། །
མཐོན་པོའི་མཐའ་རྒྱུད་སྐྱེས་པའི་ཐ་མ་འཆི།[3] །
འཆི་བར་མ་ཟད་ནམ་འཆི་ཆ་[4]མེད་པའི། །
ཡོང་མེད་རྒྱུད་ལ་སྐྱེ་བར་བྱིན་གྱིས་རློབས། ། ༣ །།

གཟུང་འཛིན་རྣམ་རྟོག་འཁྲུལ་པའི་གྲོང་ཁྱེར་དུ། །
མི་གཙང་འབྱུང་བཞི་སྒྱུ་མའི་ཕུང་པོ་དང་། །
རྣམ་ཤེས་འབྲལ་ཁའི་འཆི་རྐྱེན་སྣ་ཚོགས་པའི།[5] །
གནད་གཅོད་སྡུག་བསྔལ་ཞི་བར་ ×[6] ། ། ༤ །།

གཅེས་པར་བསྐྱངས་པའི་ལུས་ཀྱིས་དགོས་དུས་བསླུས། །
འཇིགས་རུང་གཤིན་རྗེའི་དགྲ་བོ་མངོན་དུ་གྱུར། །
དུག་གསུམ་མཚོན་གྱིས་རང་སྲོག་གཅོད་པའི་ཚེ། །
མི་དགེའི་འབྲུལ་སྣང་ཞི་བར་ × ། ། ༤ །།

སྨན་པས་བོར་ཞིང་རིམ་གྲོས་བཟློག་ཏུ་མེད། །
གཉེན་རྣམས་གསོན་དུ་རེ་བའི་རེ་ཐག་ཆད། །
རང་ཉིད་ཅི་བྱ་གཏོལ་མེད་གྱུར་པའི་ཚེ། །
བླ་མའི་གདམས་ངག་དྲན་པར་ × ། ། ༥ །།

སེར་སྣས་བསགས་པའི་ཟས་ནོར་ཤུལ་དུ་ལུས།[7] །
བརྩེ་ཞིང་གདུང་བའི་གཉེན་དང་གདན་བྲལ་བྱས། །
ཉམ་ངའི་གནས་སུ་གཅིག་པུར་འགྲོ་བའི་ཚེ། །
དགའ་སྐྱོའི་གདེངས་དང་ལྡན་པར་ × ། ། ༦ །།

ས་ཆུ་མེ་རླུང་འབྱུང་བ་རིམ་གྱིས་ཐིམ། །
ལུས་ཀྱི་སྟོབས་ཤོར་ཁ་[8]སྣ་བསྐམས་ཤིང་བརྗེས། །
དྲོད་བསྡུས་དབུགས་བརྩེགས་ངར་སྒྲ་འབྱིན་པའི་ཚེ། །
དགེ་སེམས་སྟོབས་ལྡན་སྐྱེ་བར་ × ། ། ༧ །།

འཇིགས་སྐྲག་འཁྲུལ་སྣང་སྣ་ཚོགས་ཁྱད་པར་དུ། །
སྒྲིག་རྒྱུ་དུ་བ་མཁའ་འདྲའི་སྣང་བ་ཤར། །

རང་བཞིན་བརྒྱད་ཅུའི་བསྒོན་པ་འགགས་པའི་ཚེ། །
འཆི་མེད་གནས་ལུགས་རྟོགས་པར་ × । ॥ ༩ ॥

སྣང་ཁམས་རྣམ་ཤེས་ཐིམ་པར་རྫོམ་པ་ན། །
ཕྱི་དབུགས་རྒྱུན་ཆད་གཉིས་སྣང་རགས་པ་ཐིམ། །
མར་མེ་འབར་འདྲའི་སྣང་བ་ཤར་བའི་ཚེ། །
དྲན་ཤེས་ཤུགས་དྲག་སྐྱེ་བར་ × । ॥ ༡༠ ॥

སྣང་མཆེད་ཐོབ་གསུམ་སྔ་མ་ཕྱི་མར་ཐིམ། །
ཟླ་ཉི་སྨུན་པས་ཁྱབ་འདྲའི་ཉམས་ཤར་ཚེ། །
འཁོར་འདས་སྟོང་པར་རྟོགས་པའི་རྣལ་འབྱོར་གྱིས། །
རང་ངོ་རང་གིས་ཤེས་པར་ × । ॥ ༡༡ ॥

ཉེར་ཐོབ་ཐམས་ཅད་སྟོང་པར་ཐིམ་པ་ལས། །
ཀུན་རྟོག་སྤྲོས་པ་ཀུན་ཞི་སློད་བྱེད་ཀྱི། །
རྐྱེན་བྲལ་སྟོན་གནམ་ལྟ་བུའི་ཉམས་ཤར་ཚེ། །
འོད་གསལ་མ་བུ་འཕྲོད་པར་ × । ॥ ༡༢ ॥

སྟོང་བཞིའི་དུས་སུ་གློག་གི་རྗེས་འགྲོ་བཞི། །
ཚངས་པའི་མེ་ཡིས་རི་བོང་ཅན་བཞུས་དེ།[9] །
ལྷན་སྐྱེས་བདེ་སྟོང་སྤྲུར་བའི་ཡེ་ཤེས་ལ། །
རྩེ་གཅིག་མཉམ་པར་འཇོག་པར་ × । ॥ ༡༣ ॥

དེ་ལས་ལངས་ཚེ་འཆི་བའི་འོད་གསལ་གྱི། །
རླུང་སེམས་ཙམ་ལས་མཚན་དཔེའི་དཔལ་འབར་བ། །
བར་དོ་ལོངས་སྤྱོད་རྫོགས་པའི་སྐུར་བཞེངས་ནས། །
སྤྲུ་མའི་དིང་འཛིན་རྫོགས་པར × ། ། ༡༣ །།

གལ་དེ་ལས་ཀྱིས་བར་དོ་གྲུབ་གྱུར་ན།[10]།
འཕྲུལ་དུ་བདགས་པས་སྐྱེ་འཆི་བར་དོ་ཡི། །
སྡུག་བསྔལ་བདེན་པར་མེད་པའི་ཚུལ་རྟོགས་ནས། །
འཁྲུལ་སྣང་དག་པར་འཆར་བར × ། ། ༡༤ །།

འབྱུང་བ་ལོག་པའི་སྒྲ་བཞི་འཇིགས་སྣང་གསུམ། །
མ་ངེས་རྟགས་རྣམས་སྣ་ཚོགས་ཤར་བའི་ཚེ། །
ཕྱི་ནང་གསང་བ་བསྐྱུར་བའི་རྣལ་འབྱོར་གྱིས། །
རྣམ་དག་ཞིང་དུ་སྐྱེ་བར × ། ། ༡༥ །།

མཁའ་སྤྱོད་རིག་པ་འཛིན་པའི་རྟེན་མཆོག་གམ། །
ཚངས་སྤྱོད་བསླབ་གསུམ་ལྡན་པའི་ལུས་བཟུང་སྟེ། །
རིམ་གཉིས་ལམ་གྱི་རྟོགས་པ་མཐར་ཕྱིན་ནས། །
སྐུ་གསུམ་མྱུར་དུ་ཐོབ་པར་བྱིན་གྱིས་རློབས། ། ༡༦ །།

ཅེས་བར་དོ་འཕྲང་སྒྲོལ་གྱི་གསོལ་འདེབས་འཇིགས་སྒྲོལ་གྱི་དཔའ་བོ་ཞེས་བྱ་བ་འདི་ཡང་། དོན་གཉེར་བ་འགའ་ཞིག་གིས་བསྐུལ་བའི་དོན་དུ། མདོ་རྒྱུད་དམ་པའི་མན་ངག་བཞིན་དུ་ཤཱཀྱའི་བཙུན་པ་བློ་བཟང་ཆོས་ཀྱི་རྒྱལ་མཚན་གྱིས། ཆོས་གྲྭ་ཆེན་པོ་དཔལ་ལྡན་འབྲས་སྤུངས་ཀྱི་གཟིམས་ཁང་དུ་སྦྱར་བ་འདི་ཉིད་སྟོད་མིན་དང་སྟགས་ཟླ་མེད་ཀྱི་

དབང་མ་ཐོབ་པ་རྣམས་ལ་གསང་བར་བྱ་བ་ཁོ་ན་ཡིན་ཅིང་། རང་ཉིད་ཡི་དམ་གང་ལ་བྱེད་པ་དེའི་གསོལ་འདེབས་ཀྱི་མཇུག་ཏུ་སྦྱར་བས་ཆོག[12]ཅིང་། དོན་དྲན་བཞིན་པས་ཉམས་སུ་བླངས་ན་འཆི་གཞི་གདམས་པའི་རྒྱལ་པོར་འགྱུར་རོ།། །།

Annotations to The Fourth Paṇchen Lama's *Prayer for Release from the Dangerous Bardo*

① Simple Infinitives: External Action

Page 445, Line 8

Recall the function of the "simple infinitive" (see མདོ་མཛངས་བླུན་ notes 11 and 18) to mark indirect statements, purposives, and activities externally caused or otherwise removed from the action of the main verb. While the first two have been seen already, here is an instance of the third use. This is seen commonly—as it is here—with supplications and prayers since the activity/agency of the subordinate infinitive is removed from the action of the main verb and its agent.

WHAT TO REMEMBER

Prayers, supplications, and other statements in which the activity of a subordinate phrase is caused or removed from that of the main verb use the simple infinitive.

② The Verbal Suffixes ཀ་/ཀོ་/ཁ་/ག་

Page 445, Line 11

Although འདམས་ is a verb ("to choose") and verbal suffixes have been seen in other contexts (see དེབ་ཐེར་དམར་པོ་ note 18, and see བློ་རིག་ notes 23 and 27), the expression འདམས་ག་ is a noun ("choice"). Just as with པ་, པོ་, བ་, or བོ་ in the masculine (and མ་ or མོ་ in the feminine; see ཤེར་སྙིང་རྣམ་བཤད་ note 12), the suffix syllables ཀ་, ཀོ་, ཁ་, and ག་ form the neuter nouns: mainly abstract nouns and concepts—although with numbers they serve an indicative function (e.g., གཉིས་ཀ་ "both" or "those two"). The suffix ཀ་ (and occasionally ཀོ་) follows syllables ending in ག་, ད་, བ་, and ས་; the suffix ཁ་ follows syllables ending in ན་, ར་, and ལ་;

and the suffix ག་ follows syllables ending in ང་, མ་, and འ་. Keep in mind, however, that occasionally scribes will confuse these (such is, in fact, seen in different printings of this text), and that the suffixes are also homographs with other suffixes and words (such as ཀ་, a verbal suffix meaning "about to"; ཀོ་, "leather"; ཁ་, "mouth"; ག་, "where," etc.).

WHAT TO REMEMBER

Like other nouns formed from verbs, the suffix syllables ཀ་, ཁ་, ག་, and ཀོ་ form the neuter nouns, mainly with abstract nouns and concepts.

Recognizing Scriptural References

3

Page 445, Line 16

Tibetan compositions are full of literary allusions to the Buddhist canon. Here, for example, the Paṇchen Lama echoes a famous verse from the canonical text *The Categorical Sayings* (*Udānavarga; Ched du brjod pa'i tshoms*; v. I.22), which reads:

བསགས་པ་ཀུན་གྱི་མཐའ་ཟད་ཅིང་། །	The end of all accumulation is exhaustion;
བསླང་བའི་མཐའ་ནི་འགྱེལ་བར་འགྱུར། །	The end of erecting is falling down.
ཕྲད་པའི་མཐའ་ན་བྲལ་བ་སྟེ། །	The end of meeting is separation;
གསོན་པའི་མཐའ་ནི་འཆི་བ་ནི། །	The end of living is death.

For this reason, it is advisable to read widely in the canonical scriptures.

WHAT TO REMEMBER

The Tibetan canon and commentarial treatises are highly self-referential. Just as English literature contains many famous phrases and passages familiar to all literate readers, so too similar passages exist in Tibetan. By reading more and more of the foundational literature in the Tibetan Buddhist tradition, these references will be more easily recognized when they are encountered in subsequent works.

④ Translation Hint: The Syllable ཆ་

Page 445, Line 17

The syllable ཆ་ has numerous meanings and functions. As a suffix, it can mean "part (of)," "fraction (of)," or "all together." As a noun, it can mean "pair," "even number," "portion," "moment of time," or "certainty" (this last one being the meaning intended here).

⑤ Translation Hint

Page 445, Line 22

This verse displays the multiple uses of the agglutinative sixth-case particle འི་ in the condensed grammar of a verse: the first occurrence (following the verbal phrase འབྲལ་ག་) is a clause connective to an instrument (see ཤེས་རབ་སྙིང་པོ་ note 17), while the second occurrence (following the noun སྣ་ཚོགས་) is an apposition marker (see ཤེར་སྙིང་རྣམ་བཤད་ note 35).

⑥ Repeated Passages and Scribal Abbreviations

Page 445, Line 23

Although movable-type printing technology had been pioneered in China in the eleveneth century, its use did not become widespread in Asia. Consequently, the vast majority of printing houses in Tibet relied on woodblock printing or scribal reproduction in order to produce books for distribution. Since both processes relied on manual effort, scribes devised a number of shorthand techniques for conserving effort (see introduction: Remarks on Tibetan Block-print Eccentricities).

Here, the Paṇchen Lama begins utilizing a repetitive phrase. Omitted almost entirely in some editions (as replicated here), the elided passage is indicated with the simple symbol "X."

> **WHAT TO REMEMBER**
>
> Occasionally, when repetitious phrases occur in a text, the scribe will indicate them with the symbol X, ༈, or another such indicator.

Translation Hint 7

Page 446, Line 11

Here, ལུས་ is the verb "to be left (behind)" and not the noun "body."

Translation Hint 8

Page 446, Line 17

Although ཁ་ agrees with the euphony rules for a neuter noun suffix following a syllable ending in ར་ (see བར་དོ་འཕྲང་སྒྲོལ་ note 2, above), here ཁ་ is the noun "mouth."

Tantric Metaphors and "Twilight Language" 9

Page 447, Line 20

The term "twilight language" was coined by Hara Prasad Śāstrī in the early twentieth century as a translation of the tantric mode of discourse known as *sandhyā* or *sandhābhāṣā* (more accurately translated as "ulterior language") and has since been taken as a general term to refer to the extensive set of tantric metaphors found in many root tantras, tantric "songs," and commentarial texts. Here, we encounter an example of precisely such metaphors. While most readers of tantric literature are familiar with euphemisms for the male and female sexual organs (*vajra* and *padma*—"lotus"—respectively), such "coded" or "poetic" terms exist for a wide range of tantric terminology. This vocabulary is drawn from the root tantras that intentionally encoded their discussions in symbolic terms. The passage encountered here, for example, echoes statements to be found in the *Hevajra Tantra* (v. I.i.31):

caṇḍālī jvalitā nābhau |	ལྟེ་བར་གཏུམ་མོ་འབར་བ་ཡིས། ।
dahati pañcatathāgatān |	དེ་བཞིན་གཤེགས་པ་ལྔ་བསྲེགས་ཤིང་། ।
dahati ca locanādīḥ |	སྤྱན་ལ་སོགས་པ་ཡང་བསྲེགས་ཏེ། ।
dagdhe haṃ sravate śaśī ||	བསྲེགས་པས་རི་བོང་ཅན་ཧཾ་འཛག ।

By *cāṇḍalī* blazing up at the navel,
[It] burns the five tathāgatas, and
Burns Locana and the others;
Because of burning, the *HAṂ* moon melts.

Here, the seed syllable *HAṂ* is located in the "Great Bliss" cakra (located at the crown of the head), the site of the "white drop" (*śaśī*; *ri bong can*; "the rabbit-possessor," i.e., "the moon"). Similarly, here "moon" (*candra*; *zla ba*) also refers to the "white drop" at the crown cakra (mentioned explicitly in the previous text), while the "lightning-following fire of Brahma" (*glog gi rjes 'gro ba'i tshangs pa'i me*) refers to the "winds" in the central channel (again, as described in the previous text).

WHAT TO REMEMBER

A large number of metaphors can be found in tantric "songs" and commentarial texts that serve to "encode" the specific practices and entities being discussed such that only a person with familiarity or knowledge of the practices can successfully understand the import of the text. Some of these are fairly standard, while others are contextual (for example, "moon" could mean "white drops" as here, or in another context could refer to the left channel, *lalanā*). In the absence of familiarity with the subject matter, oral or textual commentary is required to successfully decode such references.

10 **Auxiliary Verbs: The Subjunctive Construction in Protasis**

Page 448, Line 6

Recall that the subjunctive construction expresses a hypothetical situation (see ཞེར་སྙིང་རྣམ་བཤད་ note 22). As noted, it is often seen with the conditional marker ན་ ("if")—as it is here. In such sentences, the first half of a complete statement (called "protasis") expresses the lead-in idea "if [something] *were* to be ..." Typically, such lead-in sentences are followed by a concluding statement ("apodosis") in the perfective (see གྲུབ་མཐའ་ note 20). Here, however, the author concludes with an aspirational prayer.

WHAT TO REMEMBER

The subjunctive is often seen with the conditional marker ན་ ("if") as the first half of a complete statement (called "protasis"); such lead-in sentences are typically followed by a concluding statement ("apodasis") in the perfective.

Translation Divergences with the Verb ཆོག་ (11)

Page 449, Line 2

The verb ཆོག་ occurs in two basic sentence structures: as a Class II verb meaning "to be permissible" and as a Class IV verb (of containment) meaning "to be fulfilled to a sufficient degree" or simply "to suffice." The latter use (seen here) is another example of a translation divergence between Tibetan and English, where the syntax of the sentences do not align. Consequently, English translations typically render such sentences in the active voice, taking the qualifier (marked by the syntactic particles གྱིས་, etc.) as the subject. See also དངོས་གྲུབ་སྒྲུབ་ཐབས་ note 3.

WHAT TO REMEMBER

When the Class IV form of the verb ཆོག་ occurs in a text, the resulting syntax is divergent from its English equivalent. Consequently, the qualifier (marked by the syntactic particles གྱིས་, etc.) is treated as the subject in English.

Fourth Paṇchen Lama's
Prayer for Release from the Dangerous Bardo

Homage to the Teacher, Mañjughoṣa!

To the Sugatas of the three times, together with the Dharma, and
the Spiritual Community,
I and all beings as infinite [in number] as space, without exception,
Go for refuge until [we attain] the heart of enlightenment.
[I] pray [for all of us] to be released from the frights of this [life], the next, and
the intermediate state. // 1 //

Since, in this [lifetime], the good foundation [of a human body with leisure and
fortune], which is difficult to find and easily disintegrates,
Is an opportunity for a choice [between] profit and loss, happiness and suffering,
Without being distracted by the activities of this life, which are meaningless,
May we be so blessed as to take up the essence of this great objective. // 2 //

[The end of] coming together [is] separation, and [the end of] what has been
accumulated without exception [is] being depleted;
The final end of rising up is descending, and the end of birth is death.
Not only will [we] die, [but] the time of death is uncertain. Hence,
May [we] be blessed to generate in [our] continuum [the understanding that a
means to bring about] an extension [of our life] does not exist. // 3 //

In this city of mistaken conceptions of subject and object,
May [we] be blessed to pacify suffering and being killed—
The various conditions for death—which [is] the separation of consciousness
From the illusory aggregates [composed of] the four elements [arisen from the]
impure [substances from one's parents]. // 4 //

When [we] are deceived at times of need by this body, which is sustained as something to be cherished, and
The enemy—the Lord of Death—[who] is able to instill fear manifests, and
We sever our own lives with the weapon of the three poisons, at that time
May we be blessed to pacify the mistaken appearances of nonvirtue. // 5 //

When doctors forsake [us] and there is no [efficacy] in warding off [death] by special rites, and
Friends have lost all expectations, hoping [for us] to recover, and
We, ourselves, have become uncertain about what to do, at that time
May we be blessed to remember the instructions of our teacher. // 6 //

When food and wealth accumulated with miserliness are left behind,
And [we] have been separated forever from cherished and longed-for friends, and
[We] go alone to a dreadful place, at that time
May we be blessed to be possessed of the confidence of joy and enthusiasm. // 7 //

When the elements—earth, water, fire, and wind—dissolve in stages, and
Physical strength is lost, [and] the mouth and nose dry up and pucker,
Warmth withdraws, breaths are gasped, and coarse sounds emerge, at that time
May we be blessed such that a powerful mind of virtue is generated. // 8 //

When various frightful and horrible mistaken appearances, and in particular,
The appearances of mirage, smoke, and fireflies dawn, and
The mounts of the eighty instinctual natures cease, at that time
May we be blessed to realize the mode of being [that is] death's lack [of intrinsic existence]. // 9 //

When the wind constituent begins to dissolve into consciousness, and then
The continuum of external breathing ceases, and coarse dualistic appearances dissolve,
[Following which] an appearance like a burning butter lamp dawns, at that time
May we be blessed to generate strong mindfulness and introspection. // 10 //

When appearance, increase, and [near-]attainment dissolve [in the manner of]
the former into the latter, [and]
Experiences like [the sky] pervaded by moonlight, sunlight, and darkness dawn,
at that time
May we be blessed to know our own nature
Through the yoga of realizing saṃsāra and nirvāṇa to be empty. // 11 //

When near-attainment dissolves into the all-empty, and
All conceptual elaborations [have been] pacified, and an experience
Like an autumn sky free from polluting conditions dawns, at that time,
May we be blessed such that the mother and son clear lights are suitable to be
mixed. // 12 //

At the time of the four empties, the lightning-following
Fire of Brahma melts the moon, and hence
May we be blessed to set [our minds] in one-pointed [profound meditation]
In the exalted wisdom of conjoined innate bliss and emptiness. // 13 //

When [we] emerge from that, having risen up from the mere wind and mind
Of the clear light of death, in a perfect intermediate-state enjoyment body,
Blazing with the glory of the major and minor marks [of a buddha],
May we be blessed to perfect the illusion[-like] samādhi. // 14 //

If, however, due to karma, the intermediate state were to be established,
Having realized the mode of the lack of true [existence] of the sufferings
Of birth, death, and the intermediate state, because of [their] being
adventitiously imputed,
May we be blessed such that mistaken appearances dawn as pure [ones]. // 15 //

When the four sounds of the disappearance of the elements, the three frightful
appearances [of the lower rebirths], and
Various signs of an uncertain [future life] appear, at that time

Through the yoga of transforming the outer, the inner, and the secret,
May we be blessed to be born in a purified land. // 16 //

[Having] the supreme [physical] support of a sky-traveling tantric adept
(*khecara-vidyādhara*), or
Having taken the body of a celibate practitioner endowed with the three
trainings,
And having completed the realizations of the path of the two stages
[of generation and completion],
May we be blessed to quickly attain the three [buddha] bodies. // 17 //

This [poem] entitled, "Prayers for Release from the Dangerous Bardo, the Hero Releasing from Fright," moreover, was composed for the purpose of being encouraged by those who were intent [upon enlightenment] in accordance with the quintessential instructions of the holy sūtras and tantras by the Buddhist monk Losang Chögyi Gyeltsen in his residence at the glorious Drepung Monastic University; this very [composition] is only something that is a secret to those who are not [suitable] vessels and have not obtained unsurpassed mantra empowerments. By appending [this] to the end of supplication prayers to whichever of one's own tutelary deities, [it] will suffice. For if [you] practice in accordance with [this] memorandum, you will become a king of advice on the subject of death.

Chapter One of Śāntideva's *Engaging in the Deeds of a Bodhisattva*

Although the author of two other texts, *The Compendium of Learning* (*Śikṣāsamuccaya; Bslab pa kun las btus pa*) and *The Compendium of Teachings* (*Sūtrasamuccaya; Mdo kun las btus pa*), Śāntideva is most famous for his *Engaging in the Deeds* (*Spyod 'jug*). Traditional biographies record that Śāntideva expounded the text in front of a great public gathering at Nālandā much to the surprise of his fellow monks who thought him to be lazy and uneducated.

The text itself is written in verse and is comprised of ten chapters, each corresponding to a different subject: the beneficial qualities of the mind of enlightenment (*bodhicitta*), disclosure of transgressions, full engagement of the mind of enlightenment, conscientiousness, introspection, patience, effort, concentration, perfection of wisdom, and dedication of merits.

As one of the most popular texts to emerge from first millenium Buddhist India, Śāntideva's *Engaging in the Deeds of a Bodhisattva* has been the object of numerous commentaries in India and Tibet (sample pages of two different styles of commentary are shown on the following page).[1] In the absence of a commentary, however, the challenge is to discern the import of the abbreviated Tibetan grammar which, at times, can also be slightly convoluted as a result of being translated from Sanskrit.

An alternate version of this same text in འབམ་ཡིག་ script is provided in appendix 4.

[1] The two sample commentaries are the annotations of the Mongolian polymath Agwangdamba (*ngag dbang bstan pa*, 1814–1885), *Mirror of Clear Words, Annotations to [Śāntideva's] "Engaging in the Deeds of a Bodhisattva"* (*Byang chub sems dpa'i spyod pa la 'jug pa'i mchan bu tshig gsal me long*), and those of Khenpo Kunpel (*mkhan po kun dpal*, c.1862–c.1940) a.k.a. Kunsang Chödrak (*kun bzang chos grags*), *Drop of Nectar, Sacred Word of Mañjuśrī, Word Commentary to [Śāntideva's] "Engaging in the the Deeds of a Bodhisattva"* (*Byang chub sems dpa'i spyod pa la 'jug pa'i tshig 'grel 'jam dbyangs bla ma'i zhal lung bdud rtsi'i thig pa*).

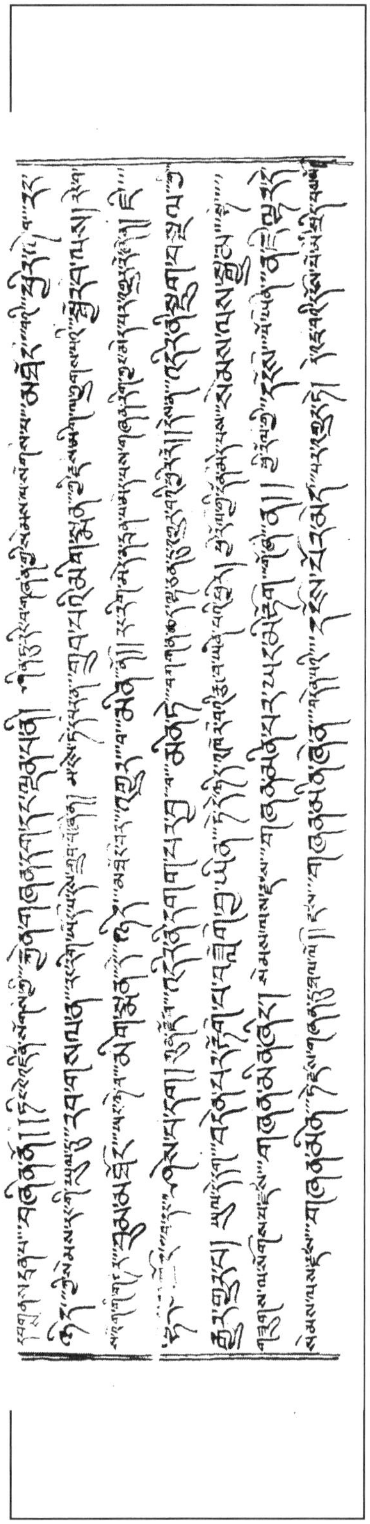

A Sample Page from Agwangdamba's "*Annotations*"

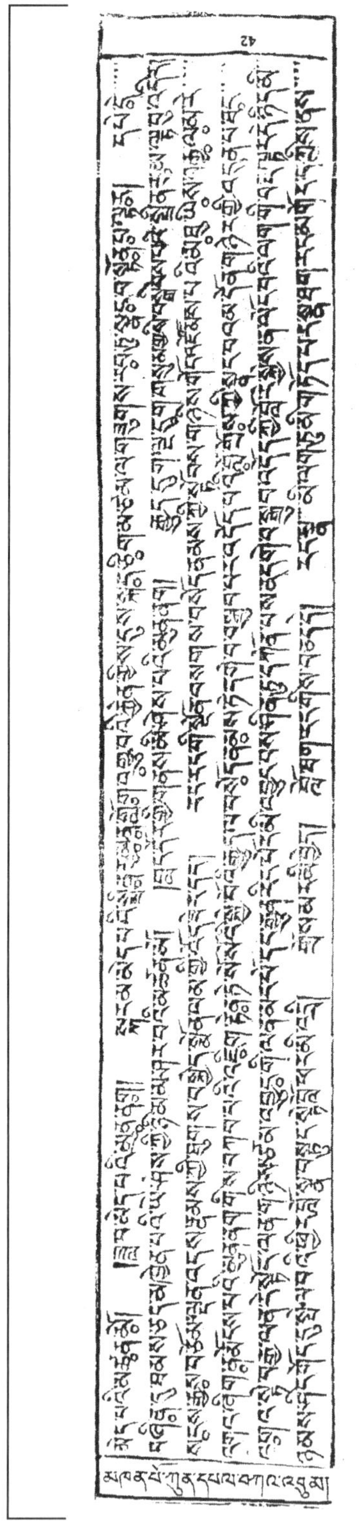

A Sample Page from Khenpo Kunpel's "*Word Commentary*"

༄༅། །བྱང་ཆུབ་སེམས་དཔའི་སྤྱོད་པ་ལ་འཇུག་པ་ལས།

ལེའུ་དང་པོ།

སངས་རྒྱས་དང་བྱང་ཆུབ་སེམས་དཔའ་ཐམས་ཅད་ལ་ཕྱག་འཚལ་ལོ།

[1]བདེ་གཤེགས་ཆོས་ཀྱི་སྐུ་མངའ་སྲས་བཅས་དང་། །ཕྱག་འོས་ཀུན་ལའང་གུས་པར་ཕྱག་འཚལ་ཏེ། །
བདེ་གཤེགས་སྲས་[2]ཀྱི་སྡོམ་ལ་འཇུག་པ་ནི། །ལུང་བཞིན་མདོར་བསྡུས་ནས་ནི་བརྗོད་པར་བྱ། ། ༡་༡ །།

སྔོན་ཆད་མ་བྱུང་བ་ཡང་འདིར་བརྗོད་མེད། །སྡེབ་སྦྱོར་མཁས་པའང་བདག་ལ་ཡོད་མིན་[3]ཏེ། །
དེ་ཕྱིར་གཞན་དོན་བསམ་པའང་བདག་ལ་མེད། །རང་གི་ཡིད་ལ་བསྒོམ་ཕྱིར་ངས་འདི་བརྩམས། ། ༡་༢ །།

དགེ་བ་བསྒོམ་ཕྱིར་བདག་གི་དད་པའི་ཤུགས། །འདི་དག་གིས་ཀྱང་རེ་ཞིག་འཕེལ་འགྱུར་ལ། །
བདག་དང་སྐལ་བ་མཉམ་པ་གཞན་གྱིས་ཀྱང་། །ཅི་སྟེ་འདི་དག་མཐོང་ན་དོན་ཡོད་འགྱུར། ། ༡་༣ །།

དལ་འབྱོར་འདི་ནི་རྙེད་པར་ཤིན་ཏུ་དཀའ། །སྐྱེས་བུའི་དོན་སྒྲུབ་ཐོབ་པར་གྱུར་པ་ལ། །
གལ་ཏེ་འདི་ལ་ཕན་པ་མ་བསྒྲུབས་ན། །ཕྱིས་འདི་ཡང་དག་འབྱོར་པར་ག་ལ་འགྱུར། ། ༡་༤ །།

ཇི་ལྟར་མཚན་མོ་མུན་ནག་སྤྲིན་རུམ་ན། །གློག་འགྱུ་སྐད་ཅིག་རབ་སྣང་སྟོན་པ་ལྟར། །
དེ་བཞིན་སངས་རྒྱས་མཐུ་ཡིས་བརྒྱ་ལམ་ན། །འཇིག་རྟེན་བསོད་ནམས་བློ་གྲོས་ཐང་འགའ་འབྱུང་། ། ༡་༥ །།

དེ་ལྟས་དགེ་བ་ཉམ་ཆུང་ཉིད་ལ་རྟག །སྡིག་པ་སྟོབས་ཆེན་ཤིན་ཏུ་མི་བཟད་པ། །
དེ་ནི་རྫོགས་པའི་བྱང་ཆུབ་སེམས་མིན་པ། །དགེ་གཞན་གང་གིས་ཟིལ་གྱིས་གནོན་པར་འགྱུར། ། ༡་༦ །།

བསྐལ་པ་དུ་མར་རབ་དགོངས་མཛད་པ་ཡི། །ཐུབ་དབང་རྣམས་ཀྱིས་འདི་ཉིད་ཕན་པར་གཟིགས། །
འདིས་ནི་ཚད་མེད་སྐྱེ་བོའི་ཚོགས་རྣམས་ཀྱིས། །བདེ་མཆོག་བདེ་བླག་ཉིད་དུ་ཐོབ་པར་བྱེད། །། ༡·༧ །།

སྲིད་པའི་སྡུག་བསྔལ་བརྒྱ་ཕྲག་གཞོམ་འདོད་ཅིང་། །སེམས་ཅན་མི་བདེ་བསལ་བར་འདོད་པ་དང་། །
བདེ་མང་བརྒྱ་ཕྲག་སྤྱོད་པར་འདོད་པས་ཀྱང་། །བྱང་ཆུབ་སེམས་ཉིད་རྟག་ཏུ་གཏང་མི་བྱ། །། ༡·༨ །།

བྱང་ཆུབ་སེམས་སྐྱེས་གྱུར་ན་སྐད་ཅིག་གིས། །འཁོར་བའི་བཙོན་རར་བསྡམས་པའི་ཉམ་ཐག་རྣམས། །
བདེ་གཤེགས་རྣམས་ཀྱི་སྲས་ཞེས་བརྗོད་བྱ་ཞིང་། །འཇིག་རྟེན་ལྷ་མིར་བཅས་པས་ཕྱག་བྱར་འགྱུར། [4] །། ༡·༩ །།

གསེར་འགྱུར་རྩི་ཡི་རྣམ་པ་མཆོག་ལྟ་བུར། །མི་གཙང་ལུས་འདི་བླངས་ནས་རྒྱལ་བའི་སྐུ། །
རིན་ཆེན་རིན་ཐང་མེད་པར་བསྒྱུར་བས་ན། །བྱང་ཆུབ་སེམས་ཞེས་བྱ་བ་རབ་བརྟན་ཟུངས། །། ༡·༡༠ །།

འགྲོ་བའི་དེད་དཔོན་གཅིག་པུ་ཚད་མེད་བློས། །ལེགས་པར་ཡོངས་སུ་བརྟགས་ན་རིན་ཆེ་བས། །
འགྲོ་བའི་གནས་དང་བྲལ་བར་འདོད་པ་རྣམས། །རིན་ཆེན་བྱང་ཆུབ་སེམས་ལེགས་བརྟན་པར་བཟུང་། [5] །། ༡·༡༡ །།

དགེ་བ་གཞན་ཀུན་ཆུ་ཤིང་[6] བཞིན་དུ་ནི། །འབྲས་བུ་བསྐྱེད་ནས་ཟད་པར་འགྱུར་བ་ཉིད། །
བྱང་ཆུབ་སེམས་ཀྱི་ལྗོན་ཤིང་རྟག་པར་ཡང་། །འབྲས་བུ་འབྱིན་པས་མི་ཟད་འཕེལ་བར་འགྱུར། །། ༡·༡༢ །།

སྡིག་པ་ཤིན་ཏུ་མི་བཟད་བྱས་ན་ཡང་། །དཔའ་ལ་བརྟེན་ནས་འཇིགས་པ་ཆེན་པོ་ལྟར། །
གང་ལ་བརྟེན་ནས་ཡུད་ཀྱིས་སྒྲོལ་འགྱུར་བ། །དེ་ལ་བག་ཅན་རྣམས་ཀྱིས་ཅིས་མི་བསྟེན། །། ༡·༡༣ །།

དེས་ནི་དུས་མཐའི་མེ་བཞིན་སྡིག་ཆེན་རྣམས། །སྐད་ཅིག་གཅིག་གིས་ངེས་པར་སྲེག་པར་བྱེད། །
དེ་ཡི་ཕན་ཡོན་དཔག་ཏུ་མེད་པ་དག །བྱམས་མགོན་བློ་དང་ལྡན་པས་ནོར་བཟང་བཤད། [7] །། ༡·༡༤ །།

བྱང་ཆུབ་སེམས་དེ་མདོར་བསྡུས་ན། །རྣམ་པ་གཉིས་སུ་ཤེས་བྱ་སྟེ། །
བྱང་ཆུབ་སྨོན་པའི་སེམས་དང་ནི། །བྱང་ཆུབ་འཇུག་པ་ཉིད་ཡིན་ནོ། ༎ ༡.༡༥ ༎

འགྲོ་བར་འདོད་དང་འགྲོ་བ་ཡི། །བྱེ་བྲག་ཇི་ལྟར་ཤེས་པ་ལྟར། །
དེ་བཞིན་མཁས་པས་འདི་གཉིས་ཀྱི། །བྱེ་བྲག་རིམ་བཞིན་ཤེས་པར་བྱ། ༎ ༡.༡༦ ༎

བྱང་ཆུབ་སྨོན་པའི་སེམས་ལས་ནི། །འཁོར་ཚེ་འབྲས་བུ་ཆེ་འབྱུང་ཡང་། །
ཇི་ལྟར་འཇུག་པའི་སེམས་བཞིན་དུ། །བསོད་ནམས་རྒྱུན་ཆགས་འབྱུང་བ་མིན། ༎ ༡.༡༧ ༎

གང་ནས་བཟུང་སྟེ་སེམས་ཅན་ཁམས། །མཐའ་ཡས་རབ་ཏུ་དགྲོལ་བའི་ཕྱིར། །
མི་ལྡོག་པ་ཡི་སེམས་ཀྱིས་སུ།[8] །སེམས་དེ་ཡང་དག་བླངས་གྱུར་པ། ༎ ༡.༡༨ ༎

དེང་ནས་བཟུང་སྟེ་གཉིད་ལོག་གམ། །བག་མེད་གྱུར་ཀྱང་བསོད་ནམས་ཤུགས། །
རྒྱུན་མི་འཆད་པར་དུ་མ་ཞིག །ནམ་མཁའ་མཉམ་པ་རབ་ཏུ་འབྱུང་། ༎ ༡.༡༩ ༎

འདི་ནི་འཐད་པ་དང་བཅས་པར། །ལག་བཟངས་ཀྱིས་ནི་ཞུས་པ་ལས། །
དམན་མོས་སེམས་ཅན་དོན་གྱི་ཕྱིར། །དེ་བཞིན་གཤེགས་པ་ཉིད་ཀྱིས་གསུངས། ༎ ༡.༢༠ ༎

སེམས་ཅན་རྣམས་ཀྱི་ཀླད་ནད་ཙམ། །བསལ་ལོ་སྙམ་དུ་བསམས་ན་ཡང་། །
ཕན་འདོགས་བསམ་པ་དང་ལྡན་དེ། །བསོད་ནམས་དཔག་མེད་ལྡན་གྱུར་ན། ༎ ༡.༢༡ ༎

སེམས་ཅན་རེ་རེའི་མི་བདེ་བ། །དཔག་ཏུ་མེད་པ་བསལ་འདོད་ཅིང་། །
རེ་རེའང་ཡོན་ཏན་དཔག་མེད་དུ། །བསྒྲུབ་པར་འདོད་པ་སྨོས་ཅི་དགོས། ༎ ༡.༢༢ ༎

ཕའམ་ཡང་ན་མ་ཡང་རུང་། །སུ་ལ་འདི་འདྲའི་ཕན་སེམས་ཡོད། །
ལྷ་དང་དྲང་སྲོང་རྣམས་ཀྱང་རུང་། །ཚངས་པ་ལ་ཡང་འདི་ཡོད་དམ། ༎ ༧་༢༣ ༎

སེམས་ཅན་དེ་དག་ཉིད་ལ་སྔོན། །རང་གི་དོན་དུ་འདི་འདྲའི་སེམས། །
རྨི་ལམ་དུ་ཡང་མ་རྨིས་ན། །གཞན་གྱི་དོན་དུ་ག་ལ་སྐྱེ། ༎ ༧་༢༤ ༎

གཞན་དག་རང་གི་དོན་དུ་ཡང་། །མི་འབྱུང་སེམས་ཅན་དོན་སེམས་གང་།[9] །
སེམས་ཀྱི་རིན་ཆེན་ཁྱད་པར་འདི། །སྔ་ན་མེད་པའི་རྨད་ཅིག་འབྱུངས། ༎ ༧་༢༥ ༎

འགྲོ་བ་ཀུན་གྱི་དགའ་བའི་རྒྱུ། །སེམས་ཅན་སྡུག་བསྔལ་རྩིར་གྱུར་པ། །
རིན་ཆེན་སེམས་ཀྱི་བསོད་ནམས་གང་། །དེ་ལ་ཇི་ལྟར་གཞལ་གྱིས་ལང་། ༎ ༧་༢༦ ༎

ཕན་པར་བསམས་པ་ཙམ་གྱིས་ཀྱང་། །སངས་རྒྱས་མཆོད་ལས་ཁྱད་འཕགས་ན། །
སེམས་ཅན་མ་ལུས་ཐམས་ཅད་ཀྱི། །བདེ་དོན་བརྩོན་པ་སྨོས་ཅི་དགོས། ༎ ༧་༢༧ ༎

སྡུག་བསྔལ་འདོར་འདོད་སེམས་ཡོད་ཀྱང་། །སྡུག་བསྔལ་ཉིད་ལ་མངོན་པར་རྒྱུག །
བདེ་བ་འདོད་ཀྱང་གཏི་མུག་པས། །རང་གི་བདེ་བ་དགྲ་ལྟར་འཇོམས། ༎ ༧་༢༨ ༎

གང་ཞིག་བདེ་བས་ཕོངས་པ་དང་། །སྡུག་བསྔལ་མང་ལྡན་དེ་དག་ལ། །
བདེ་བ་ཀུན་གྱིས་ཚིམ་པ་དང་། །སྡུག་བསྔལ་ཐམས་ཅད་གཅོད་བྱེད་ཅིང་། ༎ ༧་༢༩ ༎

གཏི་མུག་ཀྱང་ནི་སེལ་བྱེད་པ། །དེ་དང་དགེ་མཚུངས་ག་ལ་ཡོད། །
དེ་འདྲའི་བཤེས་ཀྱང་ག་ལ་ཡོད། །བསོད་ནམས་དེ་འདྲའང་ག་ལ་ཡོད། ༎ ༧་༣༠ ༎

ཕན་བཏགས་ལན་ལྡོན་གང་ཡིན་པ། །དེ་ཡང་རེ་ཞིག་བསྔགས་འོས་ན། །
མ་བཅོལ་ལེགས་པར་བྱེད་པ་ཡི། །བྱང་ཆུབ་སེམས་དཔའ་སྨོས་ཅི་དགོས། །། ༡་༣༡ །།

འགྲོ་བ་ཉུང་ཟད་ནར་མའི་ཟས་སྦྱོར་བ། །སྐད་ཅིག་ཟས་ཙམ་སྦྱིན་པར་བྱེད་པ་དང་། །
བརྙས་བཅས་ཉིན་ཕྱེད་འགྲངས་པར་བྱེད་པ་ཡང་། །དགེ་བ་བྱེད་པ་ཡིན་ཞེས་སྐྱེ་བོས་བཀུར། །། ༡་༣༢ །།

སེམས་ཅན་གྲངས་མཐའ་ཡས་ལ་དུས་རིང་དུ། །བདེ་བར་གཤེགས་ཀྱི་བདེ་བ་བླ་ན་མེད། །
ཡིད་ལ་བསམ་པ་མཐའ་དག་རྫོགས་བྱེད་པ། །རྟག་ཏུ་སྦྱིན་པ་ལྟ་ཞིག་སྨོས་ཅི་དགོས། །། ༡་༣༣ །།

གང་ཞིག་དེ་འདྲའི་རྒྱལ་སྲས་སྦྱིན་བདག་ལ། །གལ་ཏེ་ངན་སེམས་སྐྱེད་པར་བྱེད་པ་དེ། །
ངན་སེམས་བསྐྱེད་པའི་གྲངས་བཞིན་བསྐལ་པར་ནི། །དམྱལ་བར་གནས་པར་འགྱུར་ཞེས་ཐུབ་པས་གསུངས། །། ༡་༣༤ །།

འོན་ཏེ་གང་ཞིག་ཡིད་རབ་དང་བྱེད་ན།[10] །དེ་ཡི་འབྲས་བུ་དེ་བས་ལྷག་པར་འཕེལ། །
རྒྱལ་སྲས་རྣམས་ལ་དོ་གལ་ཆེན་པོས་ཀྱང་། །སྡིག་པ་མི་འབྱུང་དགེ་བ་ངང་གིས་འཕེལ། །། ༡་༣༥ །།

གང་ལ་སེམས་ཀྱི་དམ་པ་རིན་ཆེན་དེ། །སྐྱེས་པ་དེ་ཡི་སྐུ་ལ་ཕྱག་འཚལ་ཞིང་། །
གང་ལ་གནོད་པ་བྱས་ཀྱང་བདེ་འབྲེལ་བ། །བདེ་བའི་འབྱུང་གནས་དེ་ལ་སྐྱབས་སུ་མཆི། །། ༡་༣༦ །།

བྱང་ཆུབ་སེམས་དཔའི་སྤྱོད་པ་ལ་འཇུག་པ་ལས། བྱང་ཆུབ་སེམས་ཀྱི་ཕན་ཡོན་བཤད་པ་ཞེས་བྱ་བ་སྟེ་ལེའུ་དང་པོའོ།། །།

Annotations to Chapter One of Śāntideva's *Engaging in the Deeds of a Bodhisattva*

1

High Classical Philosophical Verse

Pages 463 & 605, Line 6

As previously noted, the tradition of poetic verse was a well-established form in classical Indian literary culture. Because concise and poetic expression was a valued trait in such compositions, replicating the density of thought in translation remained a challenge to the Tibetan translators. Some chose to expand their translations beyond four lines, while others utilized abbreviated words and sentences to adhere to the four-line restriction.

Consequently, when reading canonical works in verse, one must be more flexible in terms of expectations of precise wording and syntax to be encountered.

WHAT TO REMEMBER

Philosophical works written in verse, particularly when translated from Sanskrit, often contain abbreviated words in compact syntax.

2

Translating Gendered Pronouns

Pages 463 & 605, Line 7

It is important to keep in mind when reading Buddhist literature that the vast majority of authors were men whose audience was predominantly male. Consequently, masculine pronouns tend to dominate when the audience is explicitly addressed. Taking this into account, there are contexts in which it is acceptable to generalize statements into gender-neutral forms but also others in which it is not. For example, in the first text encountered in this *Reader*, there is a passage in which one of the two primary interlocutors, Śāriputra, inquires about the proper practices of a "son of good family" (རིགས་ཀྱི་བུ་). The response given by Avalokiteśvara answers Śāriputra but also clarifies the scope of his response as applying to both "a son of good family or daughter of good family" (རིགས་ཀྱི་བུའམ་རིགས་ཀྱི་བུ་མོ་), pointing out a fault in reasoning on the part of Śāriputra. In such a (hopefully, obvious) case, it would be wrong to generalize "son" to "child."

Similarly, in text passages that deal with the theoretical stages of progress of bodhisattvas, the use of gender-inclusive pronouns such as "they" or "he [or she]" is appropriate, but only contextually. The texts themselves state that from the eighth bodhisattva "ground" onward, bodhisattvas take rebirth only in male form. Consequently, when translating passages in this context, masculine-only pronouns are required in order to accurately convey what is being said by the text irrespective of any philosophical objections the translator might have about the underlying philosophy of the text.

WHAT TO REMEMBER

The translation of masculine pronouns into gender-neutral or gender-inclusive pronouns can only take place within an awareness of the source context and theoretical implications of gender choice.

Indirect Statements with ཡིན་ and མིན་ and Evidentiality

3

Pages 463 & 605, Line 9

Recall that one of the uses of indirect statements is to report inner thoughts (see ལམ་གཙོ་རྣམ་གསུམ་ note 9). Here, the Tibetan translators have subtly used an indirect construction, *verb* + ཡིན་/མིན་ (here, ཡོད་མིན་ instead of མེད་), to convey Śāntideva's opinion of himself.

This issue—indirect statements—points to a larger topic in Tibetan grammar: evidentiality. Evidentiality refers to modes of speaking that convey the speaker's own assessment of the evidence for the statement they make. Evidentials—most commonly seen in spoken Tibetan—are auxiliary verbs whose use conveys different levels of reliability to the statements being made. The most simple example (again, in colloquial Tibetan) is the verbal འདུག་, which implies first-hand knowledge or at least a high degree of certainty as opposed to the verbal phrase ཡོད་རེད་, which implies that the speaker does *not* have first-hand knowledge of what is being asserted (or that what is being asserted is something that is just commonly known or believed). The verb རེད་ by itself has no evidential dimension and merely reports ostensibly objective factual knowledge.

WHAT TO REMEMBER

Indirect expressions can be used to indicate inner thoughts or personal opinion, while the larger category of evidentially qualified statements can express the speaker's own assessment of the evidence for the statement made. Indirect statements are fairly common, while evidentially qualified statements tend to occur only in spoken Tibetan.

4 The Perfective Construction in Apodosis

Pages 464 & 606, Line 8

As previously noted (see བར་དོ་འཕྲང་སྒྲོལ་ note 10), when a hypothetical statement occurs, it is often in a conditional construction as the introductory clause of a sentence (known as the "protasis"). Such is then typically followed by a concluding statement (known as the "apodosis") deploying the auxiliary verb འགྱུར་ to form the perfective construction, which is used to indicate such hypothetical activity as a whole or in an abstract sense (see མདོ་མཛངས་བླུན་ note 17 and གྲུབ་མཐའ་ note 20).

WHAT TO REMEMBER

A two-part hypothetical statement and its consequence ("if [something] were ..., then [something else] would ...") takes the first half (protasis) in the subjunctive (formed with གྱུར་) and the second half (apodosis) in the perfective (formed with འགྱུར་).

The Tibetan Translations and Sanskrit Originals ⑤

Pages 464 & 606, Line 14

While there is much truth to the statement that the Tibetan canon represents a highly faithful set of translations of Indian Sanskrit originals, there is also a certain amount of falsity to that statement since it masks much of the subtlety of the Tibetans' contributions to the canon. There are places where the Tibetan translation of a text renders visible subtle aspects of a text that are not explicitly present in the original. For example, in the passage examined above (see སྤྱོད་འཇུག་ note 3), the verbal construction ཡོད་མིན་ was used to convey a subtle dimension of the narrative, whereas in the Sanskrit original *na ... mamāsti* simply meant "I do not have."

Similarly, here, two phrases occur at the end of this verse and the previous one—རབ་བརྟན་ཟུངས་ and ལེགས་བརྟན་པར་བཟུང་—both of which translate the same underlying Sanskrit, *sudṛḍhaṃ gṛhṇata*, a phrase that simply means "hold firmly." In the first instance, the Tibetan translators chose to render the statement as an imperative, while in the second instance, a more standard, etymological translation (*su-* = ལེགས་; *dṛḍha* = བརྟན་; *gṛhṇata* = བཟུང་) was implemented. In such instances, one can see that while the Tibetan translators were faithful to the wording of a text, they also did not shy away from making subtle changes to its rendering in order to convey the larger implications of a statement in context.

WHAT TO REMEMBER

Although Tibetan translations often possess a high degree of fidelity to their Sanskrit originals, there can be a variance in subtle phrasing not found in the source texts. Thus, it should not be presumed that they exactly reflect no longer extant originals.

Proper Nouns: Indian Flora and Fauna ⑥

Pages 464 & 606, Line 16

One of the most challenging types of vocabulary that one may encounter in a text—more so than proper names—are words in the categories of flora and fauna. Indian literature is fond of forming similes with various animals and plants; here, ཆུ་ཤིང་ ("a plantain tree") is one such example. Being hollow, a plantain tree is a common type of plant utilized by authors in analogies requiring something lacking substance or an inner essence. More difficult are the lists of various types of flowers and birds adorning "pure lands" and other idyllic places (such as can be seen in the tenth chapter of Śāntideva's text). When encountered, Sanskrit equivalents or other such reference materials are required to fully identify them.

WHAT TO REMEMBER

Buddhist literature abounds with proper nouns representing the wealth of flora and fauna found in the Indian subcontinent. When encountered, Sanskrit equivalents or other such reference materials are required to fully identify them.

7 Translation Hint

Pages 464 & 606, Line 23

This is a reference to the story of the encounter between the bodhisattva Maitreya and the young pilgrim, Sudhana, as told in the *Flower Ornament Sūtra* (*Avataṃsaka-sūtra*) and referred to in Śāntideva's *Compendium of Learning*. Many of the references in Śāntideva's *Engaging in the Deeds of a Bodhisattva* can be found in this other composition.

8 Filler Syllables in Verse

Pages 465 & 607, Line 11

Since Tibetan verse is written in an odd number of syllables, occasionally an author will need to fill in a line of verse with an extra syllable. Often the syllable ནི་ will serve this purpose, but where the use of such a syllable would be inappropriate, a syllable such as སྣུ་ will suffice.

WHAT TO REMEMBER

Since Tibetan verse is written in an odd number of syllables, occasionally an author will need to fill in a line of verse with an extra syllable; they are typically grammatically irrelevant and obvious.

Translation Hint (9)

Pages 466 & 608, Line 7

The key to translating this verse is recognizing that the phrases marked by ཀང་ and འདི་ are a relative-correlative pair. See ཤེས་རབ་སྙིང་པོ་ note 10.

Translation Hint (10)

Pages 467 & 609, Line 13

Here, དང་ is the verb "to be clear," and རབ་དང་ is an abbreviation for རབ་ཏུ་དང་བ་ ("sincere") functioning as an adjective; the main verb is བྱེད་.

Translation of Chapter One of Śāntideva's *Engaging in the Deeds of a Bodhisattva*

Homage to all buddhas and bodhisattvas!

I respectfully pay homage to the sugatas who are endowed with the dharmakāya,
Together with their sons, as well as to all who are worthy of veneration.
Having condensed, in accordance with scripture, engaging in
The vows of a child of the Sugata, I shall proclaim [them]. // I.1 //

There is nothing being said here that has not also occurred in previous explanations.
I do not have, moreover, any skill in composition;
Because of this, I do not have, either, any thought of others' benefit.
[Hence,] I have composed this in order to cultivate [it] in my own mind. // I.2 //

Because of cultivating virtue, the force of my faith
May temporarily increase as well through these [words], and yet
Others who are equal in fortune to myself, as well,
Perhaps when [they] see these [words], it may be meaningful [for them]. // I.3 //

This [life of] leisure and fortune is very difficult to find.
Although [it] would bring about attainment of a person's goals,
If I do not accomplish [anything of any] benefit in this [lifetime],
How will [I] encounter these again in future [lifetimes]? // I.4 //

Just as a flash of lightning, for an instant, reveals brilliantly illuminated [things],
On a dark night under heavy clouds, just
Like that, through the power of the Buddha, occasionally,
Thoughts of [engaging in] merit in the world, for a few moments, occur. // I.5 //

Just so, virtue is constantly in a weakened state, [and]
The great power of unethical behavior is extremely difficult to resist.
Thus, by what other virtue—something that is not the perfect
Mind of enlightenment—will it be overcome? // I.6 //

The powerful sages, who have contemplated for many eons,
Have seen just this [mind of enlightenment] as beneficial;
By means of this, limitless masses of beings
Are caused to easily attain supreme bliss. // I.7 //

Those who wish to overcome the hundreds of sorrows of mundane existence,
Those who wish to clear away the unhappiness of sentient beings,
As well as those who wish to partake in hundreds of forms of happiness,
Should never forsake this mind of enlightenment. // I.8 //

When the mind of enlightenment has been generated, in that very instant,
The destitute, who are bound in the prison of saṃsāra,
Will be called "children of the Sugata" and
Will come to be venerated by the world together with its gods and humans. // I.9 //

[Being] just like an excellent type of gold-making elixir,
Since, having taken up this unclean body, [it] transforms [that]
Into the priceless jewel of a conqueror's body,
Hold firmly onto the "mind of enlightenment"! // I.10 //

Since [it] was [found to be] of great value when well and thoroughly examined
By the immeasurable mind of the Sole Guide of Transmigrators,
Those who wish to be free from the abodes of transmigrators
Hold on firmly to [this] precious jewel—the mind of enlightenment. // I.11 //

All other virtues, [being] like a plantain tree,
Having produced fruit, [they] will simply cease to exist;

The tree of the mind of enlightenment, being eternal, however,
Does not cease to exist through bearing fruit, but increases. // I.12 //

Even if I have committed utterly unbearable ethical transgressions,
Just like having relied upon a hero [at times of] great fear,
Having relied on that [mind of enlightenment], [one] is instantaneously liberated;
Thus, why do the conscientious not resort to [this]? // I.13 //

This [mind of enlightenment], just like the fire at the end of an eon,
In a single instant, incinerates [all of one's] great ethical transgressions;
All the immeasurable good qualities of this
Were explained by the wise protector Maitreya to Sudhana. // I.14 //

If [one were] to summarize that mind of enlightenment,
[It] is to be known as of two types;
[They] are the mind that aspires to enlightenment
And the one that is actually engaged towards enlightenment. // I.15 //

Just as with knowing just what is the distinction
Between wishing to go and [actually] going,
Similarly, the wise should understand in sequence
The distinction between these two. // I.16 //

From the mind that aspires to awaken,
Great results occur [even] when in saṃsāra. However,
Merit does not continuously arise
Similar to the mind that engages in whichever manner. // I.17 //

From whatever [point in time] having seized [that mind], that is, for the sake of
Thoroughly liberating limitless realms of sentient beings,
Were [one] to have completely taken up that mind
With an irreversible intention, [then] ... // I.18 //

Having seized [that mind] from that time hence, even were [one] asleep
Or even unconcerned, a manifold [and]
Uninterrupted force of merit
Equal to the sky will come forth. // I.19 //

This, together with correct reasonings,
In the *Questions of Subāhu* [*Sūtra*]
Was spoken of by the Tathāgata
For the sake of sentient beings inclined toward the Lesser [Vehicle]. // I.20 //

Even if one thinks, "I will clear away
[Even] the slightest headaches of sentient beings,"
It is [a thought that is] endowed with a beneficial intention. Hence,
If [that] has come to be endowed with limitless merit, // I.21 //

Then what need is there to mention wishing
To dispel the limitless misery
Of each sentient being and wishing
Each, as well, to realize limitless good qualities? // I.22 //

If even a father or a mother is also not capable [of this],
Who [then] has a benevolent intention such as this?
Are even the gods and sages capable [of this]?
Does even Brahmā have this? // I.23 //

As for just these sentient beings, if previously
[They] have not dreamed even in a dream
Of an aspiration such as this for their own sake,
How would it ever be generated for the sake of others? // I.24 //

That aspiration, for the purpose [of benefiting] sentient beings, [that] does not arise
[In] others, even for their own sake,

Just this special jewel of the mind—
A marvel that previously did not exist—is [what is] born. // I.25 //

The cause of happiness of all transmigrators
Serves as a remedy [for] the sufferings of sentient beings.
Whatsoever merits of this precious mind [there may be],
As for those, how would they be comprehensible? // I.26 //

If the mere intention to benefit [others], moreover,
Far exceeds [the merit of] venerating the buddhas,
Then what need is there to mention striving for the purpose of the happiness
Of all sentient beings without exception? // I.27 //

Although [they] have a mind that wishes eliminate suffering,
They run toward that very suffering.
Although [they] desire happiness, out of delusion
[They] destroy their own happiness, like [it was] an enemy. // I.28 //

Whosoever is bereft of happiness and
Is possessed of many sorrows, to them
[This mind] brings about satisfaction with all joys, and
The severance of all suffering, and ... // I.29 //

Causes confusion to be cleared away as well.
Where is there a virtue that is equal to that?
Where is there a friend, moreover, who is like that?
Where is there a merit even like that? // I.30 //

If whosoever repays help
Is worthy of praise for some time, then
What need is there to speak of a bodhisattva
Who does good without being asked? // I.31 //

[One who] consistently [gives] plain food to a few transmigrators,
[Or] who gives the merest [amount of] food even once, and
Which satisfies them for only half a day, and [who does so] with scorn,
People honor, saying "[He] engages in virtue." // I.32 //

What need is there to mention just such a one who constantly gives
For a long time, to limitless sentient beings,
The unsurpassed bliss of the sugatas
Completely accomplishing all their aspirations? // I.33 //

The Sage has said, "Whosoever, if [they] generate
Harmful thoughts toward a benefactor—
A child of the Victor such as this—[they] will remain in a hell
For eons similar in number to the harmful thoughts generated." // I.34 //

Yet, if someone generates a sincere mind,
Its fruits will increase to surpass that.
Even [if] something of great import [is brought] against the children of the Victor,
Negative [karma] will not arise, [and instead] virtue naturally increases. // I.35 //

I pay homage to the esteemed body of anyone whosever
In whom that precious holy mind has been generated, and
I go for refuge to that source of bliss,
To anyone [to whom] harm has been done and yet [they] remain happy. // I.36 //

From the *Engaging in the Deeds of a Bodhisattva*, [this completes] chapter one, called "Explaining the Benefits of the Mind of Enlightenment."

Aśvaghoṣa's *Fifty Verses on the Guru*

In preparation for the study and practice of tantra, emphasis is repeatedly placed upon the necessity of proper reliance upon a "guru" or spiritual teacher. An often misunderstood concept, guru devotion in a Buddhist context has been frequently (and mistakenly) characterized as indistinguishable from the "devotional attitude" (*bhakti*) found in the various other religions. Although in many religions simple devotion is considered to be a sufficient path to liberation, such is not the case in Buddhism; moreover, in Buddhist tantric traditions, while guru devotion is considered necessary, it is not sufficient.

Guru devotion is an essential aspect of the tantric path for the simple reason that the presence and guidance of a knowledgeable and skilled teacher is considered indispensable for a student engaged in tantric practices, which are often characterized as rapid, powerful, and at times, dangerous. Hence, the identification and selection of a teacher worthy of one's trust and respect is considered to be of the utmost importance prior to committing to such a relationship on the part of the student. Similarly, the investigation of the qualities and suitability of a potential student is equally important on the part of a teacher. As Tsongkhapa points out:

> The instructor investigates whether the person to be instructed is a suitable receptacle or not. The person to be instructed investigates whether the instructor has the qualifications or not. In this way they make a mutual investigation of whether a relationship is right or not. Were one not to make such an investigation, and were one to establish a guru-disciple relationship with anyone at all, the pledges of the guru would degenerate because of having revealed the secrets to an unsuitable vessel, and the disciple's pledges would degenerate because of the inability to honor the commitments undertaken.[1]

This idea that the guru-disciple relationship is mutually binding in terms of conduct holds true not just in the realm of tantric teachings, however. In Tsongkhapa's *Great Exposition of the Stages of the Path to Enlightenment,* for example, reliance upon a teacher is presented as an important aspect of religious instruction and practice even within the exoteric, sūtric path. Addressing the maintenance of ethical conduct on the part of a teacher, Tsongkhapa states,

> If you have not accomplished virtue yourself, when you say to others, "You have to engage in this; you have to reject that," they will say, "Why do you tell others, 'Accomplish this aim,' when you do not accomplish it yourself? You still need someone else to correct you," and will not listen to what they have to practice.[2]

Consequently, just as a burden of responsibility lies with the student to adequately evaluate a potential teacher, an equal burden of responsibility lies with a would-be teacher to live up to the standards of knowledge and conduct of an instructor of the religious path. The devotion of a disciple to a guru does not absolve either from adhering to proper codes of conduct. These criteria and expectations of both guru and disciple form the subject of Aśvaghoṣa's text.

In terms of reading challenges, the text displays both terse syntax and idiosyncracies from Sanskrit that reflect alternate uses of auxiliary constructions and vocabulary specific to the Indian cosmos.

---

[1] Sparham 1999, 39.

[2] Lamrim Translation Committee 2004, 2:319.

༄༅། བླ་མ་ལྔ་བཅུ་པ།

༄༅།།རྒྱ་གར་སྐད་དུ། གུ་རུ་པཉྩ་ཤཱཾ་ཤི་ཀ །
བོད་སྐད་དུ། བླ་མ་ལྔ་བཅུ་པ།

བཅོམ་ལྡན་འདས་རྡོ་རྗེ་སེམས་དཔའ་ལ་ཕྱག་འཚལ་ལོ།

དཔལ་ལྡན་རྡོ་རྗེ་སེམས་དཔའི་གནས་ཐོབ་རྒྱུར་གྱུར་པ། །
བླ་མའི་ཞབས་ཀྱི་པདྨ་རྗེ་བཞིན་བཏུད་བྱས་ཏེ། །
དེ་བསྟེན་པ་ནི་དྲི་མེད་རྒྱུད་མང་ལས་གསུངས་པ། །
མདོར་བསྡུས་བཤད་པ་འདི་ནི་གུས་པས་ཉན་པར་གྱིས།[1] ༎ ༡ ༎

དབང་བསྐུར་མཆོག་ཐོབ་རྡོ་རྗེ་ཡི། །སློབ་དཔོན་ལ་ནི་དེ་བཞིན་གཤེགས། །
ཕྱོགས་བཅུའི་འཇིག་རྟེན་ཁམས་བཞུགས་པས།[2] །དུས་གསུམ་དུ་ནི་མངོན་ཕྱག་འཚལ། ༎ ༢ ༎

མཆོག་ཏུ་དད་པས་དུས་གསུམ་དུ། །དཀྱིལ་འཁོར་མི་རྟོག་བཅས་ཐལ་མོས། །
སྟོན་པ་བླ་མ་བསྙེན་བཀུར་ཞིང་། །ཞབས་ལ་སྤྱི་བོས་ཕྱག་བྱའོ།[3] ༎ ༣ ༎

ཁྱིམ་པའམ་ནི་གསར་བུ་ལ། །འཇིག་རྟེན་སྨོད་པ་སྤང་བའི་ཕྱིར། །
དམ་ཆོས་ལ་སོགས་མདུན་བཞག་སྟེ། །བརྟུལ་ཞུགས་འཛིན་པས་བློས་ཕྱག་བྱ། ༎ ༤ ༎

གདན་བསྟབ་པ་དང་ལྡང་བ་དང་། །དོན་གྱི་བྱ་བ་སོགས་བསྙེན་བཀུར། །
བརྟུལ་ཞུགས་ཅན་གྱིས་ཀུན་བྱ་སྟེ། །ཕྱག་བྱ་དམ་པ་མིན་ལས་སྤང་། ༎ ༥ ༎

བླ་མ་དང་ནི་སློབ་མ་དག །མཚུངས་པར་དམ་ཚིག་ཉམས་འགྱུར་བས།[4] །
དཔའ་བོས་དང་པོར་སློབ་དཔོན་དང་། །སློབ་མའི་འབྲེལ་པ་བརྟག་པར་བྱ། ༎ ༦ ༎

བློ་ལྡན་སློབ་མས་བླ་མར་ནི། །སྙིང་རྗེ་མེད་ཅིང་ཁྲོ་ལ་གདུག །
ཁེངས་ཤིང་ཆགས་ལ་མ་བསྡམས་དང་། །སྨྲིམས་དང་བཅས་པར་མི་བྱའོ། ༎ ༧ ༎

བརྟན་ཞིང་དུལ་ལ་བློ་གྲོས་ལྡན། །བཟོད་ལྡན་དྲང་ལ་གཡོ་སྒྱུ་མེད། །
སྔགས་དང་རྒྱུད་ཀྱི་སྦྱོར་བ་ཤེས། །སྙིང་བརྩེར་ལྡན་ཞིང་བསྟན་བཅོས་མཁས། ༎ ༨ ༎

དེ་ཉིད་བཅུ་ནི་ཡོངས་སུ་ཤེས། །དཀྱིལ་འཁོར་འདྲི་བའི་ལས་ལ་མཁས། །
སྔགས་བཤད་པ་ཡི་སྦྱོར་བ་ཤེས། །རབ་ཏུ་ཞི་ཞིང་དབང་པོ་དུལ། ༎ ༩ ༎

དེ་འདྲའི་མགོན་ལ་བསམས་བྱས་ནས། །སློབ་མར་གྱུར་ནས་བརྙས་ན་ནི། །
སངས་རྒྱས་ཐམས་ཅད་བརྙས་པས་ན། །དེས་ནི་རྟག་ཏུ་སྡུག་བསྔལ་འཐོབ། ༎ ༡༠ ༎

སློབ་དཔོན་ལ་ནི་སྨོད་པ་དེ། །ཡམས་དང་འཚེ་བའི་ནད་རྣམས་དང་། །
གདོན་དང་རིམས་དང་དུག་རྣམས་ཀྱིས།[5] །སྨོངས་ཆེན་དེ་ནི་འཆི་བར་འགྱུར། ༎ ༡༡ ༎

རྒྱལ་པོ་མེ་དང་སྦྲུལ་གདུག་དང་། །ཆུ་དང་མཁའ་འགྲོ་ཆུན་པོ་དང་། །
གདོན་དང་ལོག་འདྲེན་རྣམས་ཀྱིས་ཀྱང་།[6] །བསད་ནས་སེམས་ཅན་དམྱལ་བར་འགྲོ། ༎ ༡༢ ༎

ནམ་ཡང་སློབ་དཔོན་དག་གི་ནི། །ཀུན་ཏུ་སེམས་དཀྲུགས་མི་བྱ་སྟེ། །
གལ་ཏེ་རྨོངས་པས་བྱས་གྱུར་ན།[7] །དམྱལ་བར་ངེས་པར་འཚེད་པར་འགྱུར། ༎ ༡༣ ༎

མནར་མེད་ལ་སོགས་འཇིགས་རུང་བའི། །དམྱལ་བ་བསྟན་པ་གང་ཡིན་པ། །
སློབ་དཔོན་ལ་ནི་སྨོད་པ་རྣམས། །དེར་ནི་གནས་པར་ཡང་དག་བཤད། ། ༢༣ །།

དེ་བས་འབད་པ་ཐམས་ཅད་ཀྱིས། །རྡོ་རྗེ་སློབ་དཔོན་བློ་གྲོས་ཆེ། །
དགེ་བ་རབ་ཏུ་མི་སྨྲོམས་པ། །ནམ་ཡང་སྨད་པར་མི་བྱའོ། ། ༢༤ །།

བླ་མ་ལ་ནི་གུས་བཅས་ཡོན། །རྗེས་སུ་མཐུན་པར་སྦྱིན་པར་བྱ། །
དེས་ནི་རིམས་སོགས་གནོད་པ་རྣམས། །ཕྱིར་ཞིང་[8] འབྱུང་བར་མི་འགྱུར་རོ། ། ༢༥ །།

རང་གི་དམ་ཚིག་སློབ་དཔོན་ནི། །སྦྱིན་མིན་བུ་དང་ཆུང་མ་དང་། །
རང་སྲོག་གིས་ཀྱང་བསྙེན་བྱ་ན། །ཡོངས་སྤྱོད་གཡོ་བ་སྨོས་ཅི་དགོས། ། ༢༦ །།

གང་ཕྱིར་བསྐལ་པ་བྱེ་བ་ནི། །གྲངས་མེད་པར་ཡང་རྙེད་དཀའ་བའི། །
སངས་རྒྱས་ཉིད་ཀྱང་བརྩོན་ལྡན་ལ། །ཚེ་འདི་ཉིད་ལ་སྟེར་བར་བྱེད།[9] ། ༢༧ །།

རྟག་ཏུ་རང་གི་དམ་ཚིག་བསྲུང་། །རྟག་ཏུ་དེ་བཞིན་གཤེགས་པ་མཆོད། །
རྟག་ཏུ་བླ་མ་ལ་ཡང་འབུལ། །འདི་ནི་སངས་རྒྱས་ཀུན་དང་འདྲ། ། ༢༨ །།

མི་ཟད་དེ་ནི་འདོད་པ་ཡིས། །ཅུང་ཟད་ཡིད་འོང་གང་དང་གང་། །
ཞིན་ཏུ་ཁྱད་པར་གྱུར་པ་ཉིད། །དེ་དང་དེ་ནི་བླ་མར་སྦྱིན། ། ༣༠ །།

དེ་བྱིན་སངས་རྒྱས་ཐམས་ཅད་ལ། །རྟག་ཏུ་བྱིན་པ་ཉིད་དུ་འགྱུར། །
དེ་བྱིན་བསོད་ནམས་ཚོགས་ཡིན་ཏེ། །ཚོགས་ལས་དངོས་གྲུབ་མཆོག་ཏུ་འགྱུར། ། ༣༡ །།

དེ་བས་སློབ་མ་སྙིང་རྗེ་གཏོང་། །ཚུལ་ཁྲིམས་བཟོད་པའི་ཡོན་ཏན་ལྡན། །
སློབ་དཔོན་དང་ནི་རྡོ་རྗེ་འཛིན། །ཐ་དད་པར་ནི་མི་བརྟག་གོ། ༎ ༢༢ ༎

མཆོད་རྟེན་བཤིག་འདྲའི་སྡིག་འཇིགས་པས། །ཁྲིབ་མའང་བགོམ་པར་མི་བྱ་ན། །
ལྷམ་དང་སྟན་དང་བཞོན་པ་སོགས། །བགོམ་མི་བྱ་བ་སྨོས་ཅི་དགོས། ༎ ༢༣ ༎

བློ་གྲོས་ཆེན་པོ་དགའ་སེམས་ཀྱིས། །བླ་མའི་བཀའ་ནི་འབད་དེ་མཉན། །
རིགས་པ་ཡིས་ནི་མི་ནུས་པ། །མི་ནུས་དེ་ལ་ཚིག་གིས་སྦྲུང་། ༎ ༢༤ ༎

བླ་མ་ལས་ནི་དངོས་གྲུབ་དང་། །མཐོ་རིས་དང་ནི་བདེ་བ་འཕྲོབ། །
དེ་བས་འབད་པ་ཐམས་ཅད་ཀྱིས། །བླ་མའི་བཀའ་ལས་འདའ་མི་བྱ། ༎ ༢༥ ༎

བླ་མའི་རྫས་ནི་སྲོག་ཇི་བཞིན། །བླ་མའི་སྡུག་པའང་བླ་མ་བཞིན། །
དེ་ཡི་འཁོར་ནི་གཉེན་བཞིན་དུ། །མཉམ་པར་བཞག་པས་རྟག་ཏུ་བསམས། ༎ ༢༦ ༎

མལ་སྟན་འདུག་དང་སྔོན་འགྲོ་དང་། །གཙུག་ཏོར་དག་དང་བཅས་པ་དང་། །
སྟན་ལ་རྐང་འཇོག་རྐེད་པར་ནི། །ལག་གཞག་མཆེ་བར་མི་བྱའོ། ⑩ ༎ ༢༧ ༎

བླ་མ་དག་ནི་ལངས་པ་ན། །ཉལ་དང་འདུག་པར་མི་བྱའོ། །
རྟག་ཏུ་དེ་ཡི་བྱ་བ་ལ། །ལྡང་མཁས་ཕུན་སུམ་ཚོགས་པར་བྱ། ༎ ༢༨ ༎

མཆིལ་མ་ལ་སོགས་འདོར་བ་དང་། །སྟན་ལ་རྐང་འཇོག་རྐྱོང་བ་དང་། །
འཆག་དང་རྩོད་པར་སྨྲ་བ་དག །བླ་མའི་མདུན་དུ་མི་བྱའོ། ༎ ༢༩ ༎

ཡན་ལག་མཉེ་དང་གར་དག་དང་། །གླུ་དང་རོལ་མོ་མི་བྱ་ཞིང་། །
གདམས་གྱི་སྦྱོར་བ་མང་པོ་རྣམས། །ཐོས་པའི་ཉེ་འཁོར་དུ་མི་བྱ། ॥ ༣༠ ॥

བཏུད་དེ་སྟན་ལས་ལྡང་བ་དང་། །གུས་པ་ཡིས་ནི་འདུག་པར་བྱ། །
མཚན་ཆུ་འཇིགས་བཅས་ལམ་དུ་ནི། །བསྐོ་བ་ཐོབ་ན་མདུན་འགྲོ་བྱ། ॥ ༣༡ ॥

སློབ་དཔོན་གྱིས་ནི་མཐོང་མདུན་དུ། །ཁྲི་དང་ལྡན་པས་ལུས་གཙུ་དང་། །
ཀ་བ་ལ་སོགས་བརྟེན་མི་བྱ། །སོར་མོའི་ཚིགས་ནི་དྲང་མི་བྱ། ॥ ༣༢ ॥

རྐང་པ་བཀྲུ་དང་ལུས་བཀྲུ་དང་། །དྲིལ་དང་མཉེ་བ་ལ་སོགས་པ། །
ཕྱག་ནི་སྔོན་དུ་འགྲོ་བས་བྱ། །དེ་བཞིན་མཐར་ནི་ཅི་བདེར་བྱ། ॥ ༣༣ ॥

དེ་ཡི་མཚན་སྨོས་བརྗོད་ན་ནི། །མིང་མཐར་ཞལ་སྔར་[11]ལྡན་པས་བྱ། །
གཞན་དག་གུས་པར་བྱ་བའི་ཕྱིར། །ཁྱད་པར་གྱི་ནི་ཚིག་ཀྱང་བརྗོད། ॥ ༣༤ ॥

བླ་མ་ལ་ནི་བཀའ་སྩལ་ཏུ། །བཀའ་བཞིན་བགྱིད་ཅེས་བརྗོད་བྱས་ལ། །
ཐལ་མོ་སྦྱར་ཞིང་མ་ཡེངས་པས། །བླ་མས་བསྐོ་བ་མཉན་པར་བྱ། ॥ ༣༥ ॥

དགོད་དང་ལུད་པ་ལ་སོགས་པ། །ལག་པས་ཁ་ནི་དགབ་པར་བྱ། །
བྱ་བ་ཟིན་ནས་འཛམ་པ་ཡི། །ཚིག་དག་གིས་ནི་གདས་པར་བྱ། ॥ ༣༦ ॥

མདུན་དུ་དུལ་བར་འདུག་པ་དང་། །གོས་སོགས་ཚུལ་བཞིན་བསྡམས་པ་དང་། །
པུས་བཙུགས་ཐལ་མོ་སྦྱར་བ་ཡིས། །མཉན་སོགས་འདོད་ལ་གསོལ་གསུམ་གདབ། ॥ ༣༧ ॥

བསྙེན་བཀུར་སྤྱོད་པ་ཐམས་ཅད་ལ། །ཡིད་ནི་ང་རྒྱལ་མེད་པར་བྱ། །
ངོ་ཚ་འཛེམས་ཤིང་བསྔམས་པ་ཡིས། །བག་མ་གསར་པའི་ཚུལ་གནས་བྱ། ༎ ༣༨ ༎

སྒེག་པ་ལ་སོགས་བྱ་བ་ཀུན། །སློན་པའི་མདུན་དུ་སྤང་བར་བྱ། །
གཞན་ཡང་དེ་འདྲའི་བྱ་བ་ནི། །རང་གིས་བརྟགས་ལ་དོར་བར་བྱ། ༎ ༣༩ ༎

རབ་གནས་དཀྱིལ་འཁོར་སྦྱིན་སྲེག་དང་། །སློབ་མ་སྡུད་དང་འཆད་པ་རྣམས། །
ཡུལ་དེར་བླ་མ་གནས་པ་ན། །རྗེས་མ་གནང་བར་[12]མི་བྱའོ། ༎ ༤༠ ༎

སྦྱིན་དབྱེ་སོགས་ལས་ཅི་ཐོབ་པ། །དེ་ཀུན་བླ་མ་རྣམས་ལ་དབུལ། །
དེ་ཡིས་བསྔབས་པ་བླངས་ནས་ནི། །གཞན་དག་ལ་ནི་ཅི་བདེར་བྱ། ༎ ༤༡ ༎

བླ་མའི་སློབ་མ་སློབ་མར་མིན། །སློབ་མའང་བླ་མའི་མདུན་དུ་མིན། །
བསྙེན་བཀུར་དག་དང་ལྡང་བ་དང་། །ཕྱག་སོགས་བྱེད་པ་བཟློག་པར་བྱ། ༎ ༤༢ ༎

སློབ་དཔོན་ལ་ནི་གང་འབུལ་དང་། །བླ་མས་ཀྱང་ནི་གང་སྩོལ་པ། །
དེ་ལ་བདུད་དེ་ལག་གཉིས་ཀྱིས། །བླ་དང་ལྡན་པས་བླང་བར་བྱ། ༎ ༤༣ ༎

དྲན་པ་བརྗེད་མེད་གྱུར་པ་དང་། །རང་གི་ཀུན་སྤྱོད་ལ་བརྩོན་པས། །
སྤྱན་གྱི་རང་སྤྱོད་ལས་འདས་པ། །དགའ་བས་ཕན་ཚུན་བཟློག་པར་བྱ། ༎ ༤༤ ༎

ན་བས་བླ་མའི་བྱ་བ་ལ། །བདུད་དེ་རྗེས་མ་གནང་བར་ཡང་། །
བཀག་པ་རྣམས་ནི་སྤྱད་བྱས་ཀྱང་། །དགེ་སེམས་ལྡན་ལ་སྡིག་མི་འགྱུར། ༎ ༤༥ ༎

འདིར་མང་སྨྲ་བ་ཅི་ཞིག་དགོས། །བླ་མ་དགྱེས་བྱེད་གང་ཡིན་བྱ། །
མི་མཉེས་བྱེད་ཀུན་སྤང་བར་ནི། །དེ་དང་དེ་ལ་འབད་དེ་སྤྱད། ༎ ༤༦ ༎

དངོས་གྲུབ་སློབ་དཔོན་རྗེས་འབྲང་ཞེས། །རྡོ་རྗེ་འཛིན་པ་ཉིད་གསུང་བས། །
ཤེས་ནས་དངོས་པོ་ཐམས་ཅད་ཀྱིས། །བླ་མ་ཡོངས་སུ་མཉེས་པར་བྱ། ༎ ༤༧ ༎

བསམ་པ་དག་པའི་སློབ་མ་ནི། །དཀོན་མཆོག་གསུམ་ལ་སྐྱབས་སོང་ལ། །
བླ་མའི་རྗེས་སུ་འཇུག་པ་ནི། །ཁ་ཏོན་བྱ་བར་སྦྱིན་པར་བྱ། ༎ ༤༨ ༎

དེ་ནས་སྔགས་སོགས་སྦྱིན་པ་ཡིས། །དམ་ཆོས་སྣོད་དུ་བྱས་ནས་སུ། །
རྩ་བའི་ལྟུང་བ་བཅུ་བཞི་ནི། བཀླག་དང་འཛིན་པ་ཉིད་དུ་བྱ།[13] ༎ ༤༩ ༎

དེ་ལྟར་བླ་མའི་རྗེས་འཇུག་སློབ་མ་ནི། །མ་ལུས་ཕན་བསྐྱེད་སྐྱོན་མེད་འདི་བྱས་པའི། །
དགེ་བ་མཐའ་ཡས་བདག་གིས་ཅི་བསགས་པ། །དེས་ནི་འགྲོ་ཀུན་མྱུར་དུ་རྒྱལ་གྱུར་ཅིག ༎ ༥༠ ༎

བླ་མ་ལྔ་བཅུ་པ་སློབ་དཔོན་ཆེན་པོ་རྟ་དབྱངས་ཀྱིས་མཛད་པ་རྫོགས་སོ། རྒྱ་གར་གྱི་མཁན་པོ་པདྨཱ་ཀ་ར་ཝརྨ་དང་།
ཞུ་ཆེན་གྱི་ལོ་ཙཱ་བ་དགེ་སློང་རིན་ཆེན་བཟང་པོས་བསྒྱུར་ཅིང་ཞུས་ཏེ་གཏན་ལ་ཕབ་པའོ།

Annotations to Aśvaghoṣa's *Fifty Verses on the Guru*

① Auxiliary Verbs: Honorific Imperative

Page 483, Line 11

Recall that the auxiliary construction *verb* + པར་གྱིས་ཤིག was used to convey an exhortative mood ("[you] really should do X"; see ཤེར་སྙིང་རྣམ་བཤད་ note 21). Here, the construction *verb* + པར་གྱིས་ forms the honorific imperative.

WHAT TO REMEMBER

The use of the auxiliary verb construction *verb* + པར་གྱིས་ conveys the honorific imperative mood.

② Translation Hint

Page 483, Line 14

The sentence དེ་བཞིན་གཤེགས་ཕྱོགས་བཅུའི་འཇིག་རྟེན་ཁམས་[ལ་]བཞུགས། ("a tathāgata dwells in the worldly realm of the ten directions") is here nominalized (recall ཤེས་རབ་སྙིང་པོ་ note 22) and serves as the agent of the main sentence (with the Class V verb མངོན་ཕྱག་འཚལ།).

③ Verbal Collocations with བྱེད་

Page 483, Line 17

As noted previously, verbal collocations formed with the verb བྱེད་ ("to make," "to do," etc.) are relatively numerous (see བློ་རིག་ note 8). A unique feature of these collocations, however, is the manner in which they can simultaneously convey their primary meaning as well as their a modal meaning without undergoing alteration. Here is one such example.

Since the optative mood is formed by the *future-tense verb* + བར་བྱ་ (see ཤེས་རབ་སྙིང་པོ་ note 11) construction, the optative form of the verb ཕྱག་བྱེད་ would be expected to be ཕྱག་བྱ་བར་བྱ་ but such is not the case. In general, collocations in བྱེད་ double as their own causative, optative, etc., auxiliaries.

WHAT TO REMEMBER

The optative constructions (and similar constructions) of verbal collocations in བྱེད་ double as their own causative, optative, etc., auxiliaries.

Sanskrit Middle Voice (*ātmanepada*) in Translation

4

Page 484, Line 1

This passage underscores the necessity of a minimal working knowledge of Sanskrit for the proper understanding of classical Tibetan. Sanskrit verbs, when conjugated, typically take one of two types of endings referred to as active-voice (*parasmaipada*) terminations and middle-voice (*ātmanepada*) terminations. Typically, Sanskrit verbs take one or the other termination, while some can take either.

The point of interest here is that in some Tibetan translations from Sanskrit, the original "termination" is explicitly indicated through the use of auxiliary verbs. Previously (see ཤེར་སྙིང་རྣམ་བཤད་ note 31), the auxiliary construction *verb* + བར་འགྱུར་ was described as a way to place emphasis on the passive voice (with a possible reflexive dimension) and was an alternate use to its more common usage in the formation of the explicit future or in the perfective construction (see དེབ་ཐེར་དམར་པོ་ note 20).

More accurately, while the use of this construction can be loosely described as placing emphasis on the passive voice in the action of the verb, what is actually being indicated is the middle-voice termination of the original Sanskrit verb with its full range of implications—primarily, the verbal activity being reflexive. That is, the activity of the verb applies to the subject, "one's self" (the *ātma* in *ātmanepada*), but it also acts as an indicator of improper actvity, etc. Hence, in general, this use of འགྱུར་ as an auxiliary verb can be described as forming a reflexive construction.

WHAT TO REMEMBER

In Tibetan translations of Sanskrit works, when the source verb occurs with a "middle-voice" termination, it is represented in Tibetan with the auxiliary construction *verb* + པར་འགྱུར་ and can convey the reflexivity of the verbal activity.

⑤ Instruments with Nominative Verbs

Page 484, Line 17

In this sentence we see a phrase marked with a third-case particle occurring with a nominative verb (the Class III verb འཆི་, "to die") in the reflexive construction just described (see བླ་མ་ལྔ་བཅུ་པ་ note 4). Since Class III verbs do not take agents marked in the third case, the phrase would have to be either a reason clause or (more likely) an instrument.

This sentence thus points to the difference between the grammar of a sentence and the *requisite* grammar of a sentence. Recall that the basis of Wilson's presentation of Tibetan grammar is the concept of requisite syntax—the idea that verbs can be classified by their distinctive accompanying sentence components. Consequently, it is not that a reason clause or an instrument marked in the third case can only occur with Class V and VI verbs but rather that only Class V and VI verbs *require* the third case to mark their agents.

WHAT TO REMEMBER

Both instruments and reasons marked in the third case can accompany nominative verbs; only third-case-marked agents do not.

⑥ References to the Indian Cultural Pantheon

Page 484, Line 20

As with references to various flora and fauna (see སྤྱོད་འཇུག་ note 6), Buddhist texts can contain references to the larger pantheon of Indian culture, from literary allusions to various classes of beings presumed to exist in the larger culture. Here, for example, several classes of beings are mentioned in this verse and the previous one. While simply translating the names of these is usually sufficient in most cases, understanding their identity and significance requires deeper knowledge of classical Indian culture.

WHAT TO REMEMBER

The Indian cultural pantheon is rich in its enumeration of various classes of physical and semiphysical beings. Some of these are:

ཀླུ་	*Nāgas*: A class of semiphysical beings said to typically inhabit bodies of water; they are depicted with a human head/torso (with a snake's tongue and tail) and the hood of a cobra, and they are able to masquerade as humans
མཁའ་འགྲོ་	*Ḍākas*: Male counterparts to the *ḍākinīs*; also called *Viras* (དཔའ་བོ་)
མཁའ་འགྲོ་མ་	*Ḍākinīs*: Cannibalistic female demons; in the tantras, they (*vajraḍākinīs*) are sources of tantric instructions
གྲུལ་བུམ་	*Kumbhāṇḍas*: A type of nature spirit with a human body and animal head
ཆུ་སྲིན་	*Makaras*: A type of sea monster depicted with the body of a fish and the head of an elephant
གདོན་	*Vighnas*: Obstructive spirits
གནོད་སྦྱིན་	*Yakṣas*: Nature spirits who dwell in and around trees
འབྱུང་པོ་	*Bhūtas*: Harmful elemental spirits who are known to obstruct rainfall
མ་མོ་	*Mātṛkās*: "Mothers"—a class of female spirits who are hostile and known to carry disease sacks; they are typically depicted as ugly emaciated women with matted hair and withered breasts
སྨྱོ་བྱེད་	*Unmādakas*: A class of demons that cause madness
ཤ་ཟ་	*Piśācas*: Ogre-like "flesh-eaters"
རོ་ལངས་	*Vetālas*: Zombies or reanimated corpses
ལོག་འདྲེན་	*Vināyakas*: A group of four goblin-like troublesome demons
སྲིན་པོ་	*Rākṣasās*: A class of beings with prominant fangs and magical powers (flight, physical transformation, etc.) who like to feast on human flesh
སྲུལ་པོ་	*Pūtanas*: A class of female demons that afflict children

7 Auxiliary Verbs: Subjunctive Causative

Page 484, Line 23

Recall that the past-tense form of the auxiliary verb བྱེད་ (བྱས་—or the honorific forms, མཛད་ and བགྱིས་) can form the causative or the emphatic (see མདོ་མཛངས་བླུན་ note 27). Auxiliary verbs can be combined—as can be seen here—to convey more complex sentiments, such as the formation of a subjunctive-causative, expressing a hypothetical situation as the first half of a complete statement (see བར་དོ་འཕྲང་སྒྲོལ་ note 10) with the phrase [དཀྲུགས་] བྱས་པར་གྱུར་ ("were [you] to have [upset him]...").

WHAT TO REMEMBER

The use of the auxiliary construction that forms the subjunctive can take a past-tense causative auxiliary verb to form the subjunctive-causative construction.

8 Translation Hint

Page 485, Line 8

Recall that the syntactic particle ཞིང་ is used to connect verbs or sentences (see བློ་རིག་ note 25). Here, however, since ཕྱིར་ is not a verb, the implication is that the final verb distributes to both phrases. In the latter part, འགྱུར་ functions as an auxiliary verb modifying the verb འབྱུང་, while in the first part འགྱུར་ serves as the main verb with the adverb ཕྱིར་.

9 Sanskrit Active Voice (*parasmaipada*) in Translation

Page 485, Line 14

As observed above (see བླ་མ་ལྔ་བཅུ་པ་ note 4), the verbal conjugation forms ("terminations") of Sanskrit verbs can be explicitly indicated in Tibetan translation. It was noted in passing (see ཤེར་སྙིང་རྣམ་བཤད་ note 32 and བློ་རིག་ note 20) that the auxiliary verb བྱེད་ can be used to emphasize the active voice. More accurately, however, just as འགྱུར་ is used to explicitly indicate the middle-voice (*ātmanepada*) terminations in works translated from Sanskrit, so too the auxiliary verb བྱེད་ is used to indicate the active-voice (*parasmaipada*) termination rather than a causative construction (see ཤེས་རབ་སྙིང་པོ་ note 19).

Hence, when used in this manner, the construction can indicate the full range of implications of the active-voice termination of the original Sanskrit verb, such as the agency of the verb functioning for the benefit of an "other" (the *para-* in *parasmaipada*) rather than for the benefit of the actual agent—a reflexive activity, as indicated by a middle-voice termination. However, there are a number of variations (or exceptions) to this general rule. As with the original Sanskrit, when a pronoun explicitly indicating the reflexivity of a verbal activity occurs, or if the verbal activity is inherently reflexive ("to eat", etc.), the *verb* + པར་བྱེད་ construction can be used (particularly in a causative sense).

WHAT TO REMEMBER

The "active" (*parasmaipada*) termination of a Sanskrit verb, indicating that the agency of the verb functions for the benefit of an "other" (*para-*), is represented in Tibetan by the same sort of causative/emphatic auxiliary construction formed by the present tense of an agentive verb together with the present-tense auxiliary verb བྱེད་.

Distributed Verbs with a Distributed Auxiliary

10

Page 486, Line 17

Recall (see ཤེས་རབ་སྙིང་པོ་ note 16) that multiple verbs occurring at the end of a sentence can distribute to the agents, objects, etc., of a sentence. Here, a similar situation is seen with the verbs གཞག་ and མཆི་ that distribute to their verbal object, ལག་, with the additional feature of being in an auxiliary construction (a negated optative) that likewise distributes to both verbs. Similar distributed auxiliary constructions are seen in the following verses as well.

WHAT TO REMEMBER

Just as two or more verbs may be applied to the same subject, object, etc., with the verbs being given sequentially, so too can any modifying auxiliary verbs.

11

Translation Hint

Page 487, Line 13

The Tibetan expressions ཞལ་སྔ་/ཞལ་སྔར་/ཞལ་སྔ་ནས་ are common translations of the Sanskrit honorific suffix *-pāda*, which designates a person as someone who embodies the unbroken oral lineage of the teachings. Hence, it can be variously translated as "embodied lineage," "embodiment of the lineage," "exalted presence," "eminent," etc.

12

Translation Hint

Page 488, Line 8

The phrase རྗེས་མ་གནང་བར་ is a locative-absolute construction and is not part of an auxiliary construction.

13

Translation Hint

Page 489, Line 11

Recall that the syllable ཉིད་ can function as a postpositional emphatic adverb ("really" or "really just"). See དེབ་ཐེར་དམར་པོ་ note 18.

Chapter One of Aśvaghoṣa's *Fifty Verses on the Guru*

In Sanskrit: *Ārya bhagavatī-prajñā-paramitā-hṛdaya*
In Tibetan: *'Phags pa bcom ldan 'das ma shes rab kyi pha rol tu phyin pa'i snying po*

Homage to the Bhagavān Vajrasattva!

Having bowed properly to the lotus feet of the guru—
The one who serves as the cause for the attainment of the state of glorious Vajrasattva—
The teachings on that [are] what is said in many stainless tantras, [so]
Listen respectfully to this concise abbreviation! // 1 //

The tathāgatas who dwell in the worldly realms of
The ten directions respectfully pay homage
Throughout the three times to the vajra master
Who has obtained the supreme empowerment. // 2 //

The supremely faithful, throughout the three times,
[Before] a maṇḍala, together with a flower, and palms pressed together,
[Should] serve and honor the supreme teacher and
Should venerate his feet with their head. // 3 //

As for [a teacher who is] a householder or a novice,
In order to avoid the world's criticism,
Arrange [a representation of] the holy Dharma and so forth, in front [of one's teacher], and then
Those holding the vows of conduct (*vrata*) should honor [them] in their mind. // 4 //

Prepare his seat, rise [in his presence], and
Respectfully attend to his needs and so forth.
Those holding the vows of conduct should do all [of these things];
Hence, abandon actions [that are forms of] inappropriate veneration. // 5 //

Since the commitments (*samaya*) of both
Guru and disciple would equally degenerate,
An intrepid person, initially, should investigate
The relationship between master and disciple. // 6 //

An intelligent student should not take
As a guru one who lacks compassion,
Who is angry, cruel, conceited, or greedy,
As well as [one who is] uncontrolled or boastful. // 7 //

[Instead,] steady, calm, intelligent,
Patient, honest, without deceit or guile,
Knowledgeable in the practices of mantra and tantra,
Compassionate and skilled in the treatises, // 8 //

Thoroughly knowledgeable in the ten principles,
Skilled in the activity of drawing maṇḍalas,
Knowledgeable in the practice of explaining mantra,
Thoroughly pacified and [with] calmed senses. // 9 //

Having thought about a protector such as this, and
Having become a disciple, if one despises [him],
Since one despises all the buddhas [by doing so],
That [person]will only ever obtain suffering. // 10 //

That one who disparages the master,
That great fool dies
From plagues, life-threatening illnesses,
Obstructive spirits (*vighna*), fevers, and poison, [and] ... // 11 //

Moreover, having been killed by a king, fire, poisonous snakes,
Water, ḍākinīs, thieves,
Obstructive spirits, or demons (*vināyaka*),
[These] sentient beings go to [one of] the hells. // 12 //

[You] should never completely upset
The mind of any of [your] teachers;
If [such] a fool has done so,
He will definitely roast in hell. // 13 //

There, in those hells—such as the Avīci and so forth—
Being taught as suitably terrifying,
It has been well explained, dwell
Those who were disparaging towards their master. // 14 //

Therefore, with all [your] effort,
[You] should never disparage
The vajra master, the one with great wisdom,
Who does not boast at all of his virtue. // 15 //

With respect, [you] should give gifts
To the guru that are agreeable.
Then forms of harm, such as diseases and so forth,
Will not [come back] again and [will not] arise. // 16 //

If one's commitment master
Should make use of even what is [usually] not given—
One's children, spouse, and even one's life—
Then what need is there to speak of fleeting wealth. // 17 //

Because of such [things], even buddhahood itself,
Which is difficult to find even in countless
Millions of eons, is granted
In this very life to one who strives. // 18 //

Always protect your pledges.
Always worship the tathāgatas.
Always make offerings to the guru as well,
For he is like all the buddhas. // 19 //

One who desires that which is inexhaustible
Should give to the guru just those [things]—
Whatever is pleasing in even the slightest way and
Whatsoever is most special. // 20 //

The offering of such [to the guru] serves as making
Continual offerings to all the buddhas.
The offering of such is the accumulation of merit, and
From that accumulation comes the supreme attainment (*siddhi*). // 21 //

Therefore, the disciple—one who deploys compassion
And is endowed with the qualities of ethics and patience—
Does not consider [their] master
To be different from Vajradhara. // 22 //

When one should not step over even [a teacher's] shadow out of fear
For the negative karmic consequences equivalent to having destroyed a stūpa,
What need is there to speak of not stepping over
Such things as [one's teacher's] shoes, seat, or carriage. // 23 //

The wise, with a joyous mind,
Should strive [to adhere to] and be attentive to the guru's words.
Being unable [to do it] with [good] reason,
[You should] excuse [yourself] for that inability. // 24 //

From the guru one attains
*Siddhi*s, high status, and bliss.
Therefore, with all [your] effort,
You should not transgress the guru's commands. // 25 //

With mental composure, always consider
The property of the guru like [one's own] life,
The guru's beloved like the guru [himself],
[And members of] his entourage like relatives. // 26 //

You should not sit on a bed, precede [the guru],
Have on a headdress,
Put [your] feet on your seat, place
[Your] hands on your waist, or rub [them]. // 27 //

When the guru gets up,
You should not [remain] sitting or lying down.
In these duties [you] should always
[Quickly] rise up, be skillful, and do [them] perfectly. // 28 //

[You] should not expel spit and so forth,
Nor point or extend [your] feet toward [his] seat,
Nor wander about, nor speak in an argumentative manner
In the presence of your teacher. // 29 //

[Do not] rub one's limbs, dance,
Sing, or play musical instruments.
Do not engage in many extended conversations
Within range of his hearing. // 30 //

[When] paying homage, [you should] get up from your seat.
[When] sitting, [you] should do so with respect.
[When] going down a path—at night, [when crossing] water, or in frightful areas—
When [you] have received authorization, [you] should walk in front. // 31 //

Within the teacher's sight,
The intelligent person does not twist [his] body,
Does not lean against a pillar, etc., and
Does not pull on his finger joints. // 32 //

[You should] wash [the guru's] feet, wash his body, and
Dry and massage [him], etc.
[You] should do [that] with a preliminary prostration, and
Similarly, at the end; [only then] should [you] do as [you] please. // 33 //

When [you] say his name or express [his words to others],
[You] should do so with "[his] exalted presence" at the end of his name;
In order that others will do so with respect,
Also speak [of the teacher] with special words. // 34 //

Making a request for instructions to the teacher,
Say "[I] will do [this] in accordance with [your] words," and
With palms pressed together and without distraction,
[You] should listen to the teacher's commands. // 35 //

[When] laughing, or coughing, etc.,
[You] should cover [your] mouth with [your] hand.
Having completed [your] tasks, [you] should inform
[Your teacher] with gentle words. // 36 //

When wishing to listen [to teachings] etc., remain calm
In front [of him], be restrained in the proper manner
Of clothing, etc., and with knee planted [on the ground] and
Palms pressed together, make three requests. // 37 //

In all acts of service and veneration,
[Your] mind should be without [any] pride.
With modesty, fear, and restraint,
[You] should remain in the manner of a new bride. // 38 //

In the presence of the teacher, you should abandon
All activities of showing off, etc.
Furthermore, regarding [other] activities such as that,
Having investigated [them] yourself, [you] should cast [them] off. // 39 //

If the teacher is residing in that area,
Without being given permission, [you] should not
[Do] consecrations [of statues], [make] maṇḍalas, [perform] fire offerings,
Collect disciples, or give explanations [of teachings]. // 40 //

Whatever [you] obtain from consecrating [statues] and so forth,
All of that [you should] offer to your teachers.
That [guru] having taken what has been offered,
[You] should do as you please with regard to [everything] else. // 41 //

The guru's disciples are not [to be treated] as [one's own] disciples.
[One's own] disciples, moreover, are not [be treated as one's own disciples] in the guru's presence.
[You] should stop those who serve and venerate [you],
Stand up [in your presence], and prostrate [to you]. // 42 //

Whatever [one] offers to the master and
Whatever the guru bestows as well,
Be respectful with regard to that, and with both hands
The intelligent [student] should accept [it]. // 43 //

Because of making effort at one's own proper conduct and
Being mindful and unforgetful,
[When] one's own relatives transgress [proper] conduct,
With joy [you] should mutually stop [each other]. // 44 //

A sick person [can] show respect for the actions
Of the teacher, even without permission [to not rise, etc.];
Although having done that which is proscribed,
For one endowed with a virtuous mind, [it] does not become an ethical transgression. // 45 //

What need to speak of many [things] here?
[You] should do whatever makes the guru happy.
Abandoning all activities that displease [him],
Make effort at those [two things], and hence practice [in that way]. // 46 //

Having understood that Vajradhara, himself,
Said, "*Siddhi*s follow from the master,"
You should thoroughly please the guru
With all things. // 47 //

A student whose mind is pure
Goes for refuge to the Three Jewels;
One who is a follower of a guru
Should be given [this] in order to recite [it]. // 48 //

Then, by giving [him] mantra and so forth,
[And] having made [him] a pure vessel for the excellent doctrine,
[He] should recite and really hold
The fourteen root [tantric] commitments. // 49 //

Thus, by means of whatsoever limitless virtue [produced] from composing this
Faultless [text]—producing benefit for disciples without exception
Who follow a teacher—that has been accumulated by me,
May all transmigrators quickly become conquerors! // 50 //

The *Fifty Stanzas on the Guru* composed by the great master Aśvaghoṣa is finished. It was translated, edited, and finalized by the Indian Abbot Padmākaravarman and the senior editor-translator, the monk Rinchen Sangpo.

The Fourteenth Dalai Lama's *Yoga of the Inseparability of the Guru and Avalokiteśvara, A Source of All Powerful Attainments*

The tantra (*rgyud*) class of Tibetan literature can be roughly divided into three categories: "root" tantras and their exegeses, ritual and meditational practice texts, and pedagogical/theory texts. The text presented here falls into the second category. This text, a "means of attainment" (*sādhana; sgrub thabs*) practice text, contains a "guru yoga" specifically focusing on the figure of Avalokiteśvara—that is, a meditation in which one's spiritual teacher is visualized in the aspect of Avalokiteśvara.

In terms of the classification scheme of tantras, this practice belongs to the first of the four-fold classification schemes of tantric practices, action tantra (*kriyā-tantra; bya rgyud*). Nonetheless, this simple "yoga" of Avalokiteśvara displays many of the generic elements found in the sādhanas of different lineages and practices. The basic structure of a sādhana has two parts: the preliminary practices, followed by the main practices. In this text, the preliminary practices consist of two parts:

I. Motivational Preliminaries
  A. Taking Refuge
  B. Generating Bodhicitta
  C. Cultivating the Four Immeasurables

II. Physical Preliminaries of Purification
  A. Blessing the Ground
  B. Blessing the Offerings

These are followed by the main practices of an action tantra sādhana, consisting of the four branches of repetition:

I. Other-base
  A. Visualization of the Deity in Front

B. Seven-limb Prayer
1. Making Prostrations
2. Making Offerings
3. Confession
4. Rejoicing
5. Requesting the Guru to Teach
6. Entreating the Guru to Stay
7. Dedication of Merit

C. Maṇḍala Offering

D. Blessing by the Guru

E. Prayer of the Graduated Path

II. Self-base
A. Visualizing Oneself as the Deity

III. Moon
A. Visualization of a Moon-disc at the Heart

IV. Sound
A. Visualization of the Letters of the Mantra around the Moon-disc

When combined with the subsequent practices of the three concentrations—abiding in fire, abiding in sound, and bestowing liberation at the end of sound—the *sādhana* constitutes the complete practice of deity yoga leading to the attainment of buddhahood as formulated in action tantra.

In terms of a reading challenge, as with other texts in this section, a certain amount of content knowledge is presumed.[1] In addition, the text presents reading challenges in terms of both the genre and the author's compositional style (mid-twentieth century), containing a number of colloquial expressions, elaborate poetic metaphors, and compressed and omitted grammar.

---

[1] See, for example, HH the Dalai Lama and Jeffrey Hopkins, *Tantra in Tibet* (Ithaca: Snow Lion Publications, 1987).

བླ་མ་དང་སྨྲུན་རས་གཟིགས་དབྱེར་མེད་ཀྱི་རྣལ་འབྱོར་ དངོས་གྲུབ་ཀུན་འབྱུང་ཞེས་བྱ་བ་བཞུགས་སོ།།

①རྒྱལ་ཀུན་སྙིང་རྗེའི་རང་བཞིན་བཙུ་དྲུག་ཆ།②
ཡོངས་རྫོགས་བྱིན་རླབས་བདུད་རྩིའི་འོད་དཀར་ཅན།
བླ་མ་སྤྱན་རས་གཟིགས་ལ་གུས་བཏུད་ནས།
དེ་ཡི་རྣལ་འབྱོར་ཟབ་མོའི་ཚིག་སྤེལ།

དེ་ལ་འདིར་བྱིན་རླབས་དང་། དངོས་གྲུབ་ཐམས་ཅད་ཀྱི་རྩ་བ་བླ་མ་ལ་རག་ལས་པར་མདོ་རྒྱུད་དུ་མ་ནས་ལན་གཅིག་མ་ཡིན་པར་བསྔགས་པ་བཞིན་རང་ལ་ལམ་ཕྱིན་ཅི་མ་ལོག་པར་སྟོན་པའི་བླ་མ་དང་ལྷག་པའི་ལྷ་ངོ་བོ་དབྱེར་མེད་དུ་བྱས་ནས་གསོལ་བ་འདེབས་པ་ཉིད་གདན་གྱི་མདུན་མའི་གཞི་རྟེན་གཅིག་པུར་གལ་ཆེ་ཞིང་། དེ་ཡང་རང་གང་ལ་མོས་པའི་ཡི་དམ་གྱི་ངོ་བོར་མོས་ཚོག་③ཀྱང་། ཐེག་པ་ཆེན་པོའི་ལམ་གྱི་སྲོག་ལྟ་བུ་ནི། བྱམས་སྙིང་རྗེ། བྱང་ཆུབ་ཀྱི་སེམས་རིན་པོ་ཆེ་ཁོ་ན་ཡིན་ཅིང་། སྙིང་རྗེ་ཆེན་པོ་ཐོག་མཐའ་བར་གསུམ་དུ་གལ་ཆེ་བར་གསུངས་པས། རང་གི་རྩ་བའི་བླ་མ་དང་། སྙིང་རྗེའི་ལྷ་མཆོག་འཕགས་པ་སྤྱན་རས་གཟིགས་ཟུང་འབྲེལ་གྱི་རྣལ་འབྱོར་ཉམས་སུ་ལེན་པར་འདོད་པའི་རྣལ་འབྱོར་པས་ཡིད་དུ་འོང་བའི་གནས་སུ་མཆོད་རྫས་སོགས་ལེགས་པར་འདུ་བྱས་ལ། སྟན་བདེ་བ་ལ་འཁོད་དེ། དགེ་སེམས་ཁྱད་པར་ཅན་གྱི་ངང་ནས་སྐྱབས་འགྲོ་སེམས་བསྐྱེད་ཚད་མེད་པ་བཞི་བསྒོམ་པ་སྔོན་དུ་བཏང་།

ཐམས་ཅད་དུ་ནི་ས་གཞི་དག །གསེག་མ་ལ་སོགས་མེད་པ་དང་། །
ལག་མཐིལ་ལྟར་མཉམ་བཻཌཱུར་ཡའི།④ །རང་བཞིན་འཇམ་པོར་གནས་གྱུར་ཅིག

ལྷ་དང་མི་ཡི་མཆོད་པའི་རྫས། །དངོས་སུ་བཤམས་དང་ཡིད་ཀྱིས་སྤྲུལ། །
ཀུན་བཟང་མཆོད་སྤྲིན་བླ་ན་མེད། །ནམ་མཁའི་ཁམས་ཀུན་ཁྱབ་གྱུར་ཅིག

ཨོཾ་ན་མོ་བྷ་ག་ཝ་ཏེ། བཛྲ་སཱ་ར་པྲ་མརྡ་ནེ། ཏ་ཐཱ་ག་ཏཱ་ཡ།
ཨརྷ་ཏེ། སམྱཀྶཾ་བུདྡྷཱ་ཡ། ཏདྱ་ཐཱ། ཨོཾ་བཛྲེ་བཛྲེ། མཧཱ་བཛྲེ།
མཧཱ་ཏེ་ཛ་བཛྲེ། མཧཱ་བིདྱཱ་བཛྲེ། མཧཱ་བོ་དྷི་ཙིཏྟ་བཛྲེ།
མཧཱ་བོ་དྷི་མཎྜོ་པ་སཾ་ཀྲ་མ་ཎ་བཛྲེ། སརྦ་ཀརྨ་ཨཱ་ཝ་ར་ཎ་བི་ཤོ་དྷ་ན་བཛྲེ་སྭཱ་ཧཱ།[5]

ཞེས་ལན་གསུམ་བརྗོད།[6]

དཀོན་མཆོག་གསུམ་གྱི་བདེན་པ་དང་། སངས་རྒྱས་དང་བྱང་ཆུབ་སེམས་དཔའ་ཐམས་ཅད་ཀྱི་བྱིན་གྱིས་བརླབས་དང་ཚོགས་གཉིས་ཡོངས་སུ་རྫོགས་པའི་མངའ་ཐང་ཆེན་པོ་དང་། ཆོས་ཀྱི་དབྱིངས་རྣམ་པར་དག་ཅིང་[7] བསམ་གྱིས་མི་ཁྱབ་པའི་སྟོབས་ཀྱིས་དེ་བཞིན་ཉིད་དུ་གྱུར་ཅིག ཅེས་ས་གཞི་དང་། མཆོད་རྫས་བྱིན་གྱིས་བརླབས།

དེ་ནས།

བདེ་ཆེན་ལྷུན་གྲུབ་ཆོས་སྐུའི་མཁའ་དབྱིངས་སུ།
སྣ་ཚོགས་ཀུན་བཟང་མཆོད་སྤྲིན་འཁྲིགས་པའི་དབུས།
སེང་གེས་བཏེགས་པའི་འོད་འབར་ནོར་བུའི་ཁྲིར།
ཆུ་སྐྱེས་ཉི་ཟླ་རྒྱས་པའི་གདན་སྟེང་དུ།

སྙིང་རྗེའི་གཏེར་ཆེན་འཕགས་མཆོག་འཇིག་རྟེན་དབང་།
རྣམ་པ་ངུར་སྨྲིག་འཆང་བའི་ཟློས་གར་ཅན།

རྩ་བའི་བླ་མ་གསུམ་ལྡན་རྡོ་རྗེ་འཛིན།
    རྗེ་བཙུན་བློ་བཟང་བསྟན་འཛིན་རྒྱ་མཚོའི་དཔལ།

དཀར་དམར་མདངས་གསལ་དགྱེས་པའི་འཛུམ་ཞལ་ཅན།
    ཕྱག་གཡས་ཐུགས་ཀར་ཆོས་འཆད་ཕྱག་རྒྱ་ཡིས།
གླེགས་བམ་རལ་གྲིས་མཚན་པའི་པད་དཀར་དང་།
    གཡོན་པ་མཉམ་གཞག་རྩིབས་སྟོང་འཁོར་ལོ་བསྣམས།

གུར་ཀུམ་མདངས་ལྡན་ཆོས་གོས་རྣམ་གསུམ་དང་།
    བསེ་མའི་གསེར་མདོག་པཎ་ཞྭ་མཛེས་པར་གསོལ།
ཕུང་ཁམས་སྐྱེ་མཆེད་ཡུལ་དང་ཡན་ལག་རྣམས།
    རིགས་ལྔ་ཡབ་ཡུམ་སེམས་དཔའ་སེམས་མ་དང་།

ཁྲོ་བོའི་རང་བཞིན་དཀྱིལ་འཁོར་འཁོར་ལོར་རྫོགས།
    སྣ་ལྔའི་འོད་ཕྲེང་འཁྲུགས་པའི་གུར་ཁྲིམ་དབུས།
ཞབས་གཉིས་མི་ཕྱེད་རྡོ་རྗེའི་སྐྱིལ་ཀྲུང་ཚུལ།
    གང་འདུལ་སྒྱུ་འཕྲུལ་དྭ་བའི་སྤྲིན་ཕུང་འགྱེད།

ཐུགས་ཀར་ཡེ་ཤེས་སེམས་དཔའ་སྤྱན་རས་གཟིགས།
    ཞལ་གཅིག་ཕྱག་བཞིའི་དང་ཟུང་ཐལ་མོ་སྦྱར།
འོག་མས་ཤེལ་ཕྲེང་པདྨ་དཀར་པོ་བསྣམས།
    རིན་ཆེན་རྒྱན་དང་དར་གྱི་ན་བཟའ་མཛེས།

རི་དྭགས་ལྤགས་པས་ནུ་མ་གཡོན་པ་བཀབ།
ཟླ་བའི་ཡང་ཆོ་པད་ཟླར་སྐྱིལ་ཀྲུང་བཞུགས།
དེ་ཡི་ཐུགས་ཀར་ཏིང་འཛིན་སེམས་དཔའ་ནི།
ཧྲཱིཿཡིག་དཀར་གསལ་འོད་ཟེར་ཕྱོགས་བཅུར་འཕྲོ།

བླ་མའི་གནས་གསུམ་རྡོ་རྗེ་གསུམ་གྱིས་མཚན།
ཐུགས་ཀའི་ཧཱུྃ་ཡིག་ལས་འཕྲོས་འོད་ཟེར་གྱིས།
རབ་འབྱམས་མཆོག་གསུམ་མ་ལུས་སྤྱན་དྲངས་ཏེ།
ཐིམ་པས་སྐྱབས་གནས་ཀུན་འདུས་ངོ་བོར་འགྱུར།

ཅེས་བླ་མ་སེམས་དཔའ་གསུམ་བརྩེགས་ཀུན་འདུས་ནོར་བུའི་ལུགས་སུ་གསལ་གདབ།

གསལ་རྫོགས་མཚན་དཔེས་མཛེས་པའི་མཐོང་གྲོལ་སྐུ།
སྙན་འཇེབས་དྲུག་ཅུའི་དབྱངས་ལྡན་འགག་མེད་གསུང་།
ཟབ་ཡངས་མཁྱེན་བརྩེ་དཔག་པར་དཀའ་བའི་ཐུགས།
གསང་གསུམ་རྒྱན་གྱི་འཁོར་ལོར་གུས་ཕྱག་འཚལ།

བདག་པོས་བཟུང་དང་མ་བཟུང་མཆོད་པའི་རྫས།
དངོས་བཤམས་ཡིད་སྤྲུལ་ལུས་དང་ལོངས་སྤྱོད་དང་།
དུས་གསུམ་བསགས་པའི་རྣམ་དཀར་དགེ་ཚོགས་ཀུན།
ཀུན་བཟང་མཆོད་སྤྲིན་རྒྱ་མཚོར་དམིགས་ནས་འབུལ།

མ་རིག་འཐིབ་པོའི་སྨག་གིས་ཡིད་ནོན་པས།
བཅས་རང་ཁ་ན་མ་ཐོའི་སྡིག་ལྟུང་སོགས།
ཡོག་པར་འཕྲུན་པའི་ནོངས་པ་ཅི་མཆིས་པ།
འགྱོད་སྡོམ་དྲག་པོས་དམིགས་མེད་ངང་དུ་བཤགས།

དཔལ་ལྡན་བླ་མའི་རྣམ་པར་ཐར་པ་དང་།
ཐེག་གསུམ་སྐྱེ་འཕགས་རང་གཞན་ཐམས་ཅད་ཀྱི།
དུས་གསུམ་རྣམ་དཀར་དགེ་བའི་ཕུང་པོ་ལ།
སྙིང་ནས་བསམ་པ་ཐག་པས་རྗེས་ཡི་རངས།

སྣ་ཚོགས་གདུལ་བྱའི་ཁམས་ཀྱི་རྗེས་སོང་བའི།
དམ་ཆོས་སྐབས་གསུམ་ལྷ་ཡི་རོལ་མོའི་སྒྲ།
ཟབ་ཞིའི་དབྱངས་སུ་འཁྲོལ་བས་ཡིད་ཅན་ཀུན།
ཤེས་ཉོན་སྒྲིབ་པའི་གཉིད་ལས་སློང་དུ་གསོལ།

སྲིད་ཞིའི་མུ་མཐའ་བྲལ་བའི་མངོན་རྟོགས་ལ།
འགྲོ་ཀུན་བདེ་བའི་དབུགས་འབྱིན་མ་ཐོབ་བར།[8]
ཞབས་ཟུང་ཨེ་ཝཾ་མི་ཤིགས་སྐྱིལ་མོ་ཀྲུང་།
གཞོམ་མེད་རྡོ་རྗེའི་ཁྲི་ལ་བརྟན་པར་བཞུགས།

རྣམ་དཀར་ལེགས་བྱས་བགྱིས་དང་བགྱིད་འགྱུར་ཀུན།
རྗེ་བཙུན་བླ་མས་འབྲལ་མེད་རྗེས་འཛིན་ཅིང་།

ཀུན་བཟང་སྤྱོད་མཆོག་སྨོན་ལམ་ཡོངས་འགྲུབ་ནས།
འགྲོ་ཀུན་དོན་དུ་རྫོགས་བྱང་ཐོབ་ཕྱིར་བསྔོ།

ས་གཞི་སྤོས་ཀྱིས་བྱུགས་ཤིང་མེ་ཏོག་བཀྲམ།
རི་རབ་གླིང་བཞི་ཉི་ཟླས་བརྒྱན་པ་འདི།
སངས་རྒྱས་ཞིང་དུ་དམིགས་ཏེ་དབུལ་བར་བགྱི།
འགྲོ་ཀུན་རྣམ་དག་ཞིང་ལ་སྤྱོད་པར་ཤོག

བདག་གཞན་ལུས་ངག་ཡིད་གསུམ་ལོངས་སྤྱོད་དུས་གསུམ་དགེ་ཚོགས་དང་།
རིན་ཆེན་མཎྜལ་བཟང་པོ་ཀུན་བཟང་མཆོད་པའི་ཚོགས་དང་བཅས།
བློ་ཡིས་བླངས་ནས་བླ་མ་ཡི་དམ་དཀོན་མཆོག་གསུམ་ལ་འབུལ།
ཐུགས་རྗེའི་དབང་གིས་བཞེས་ནས་བདག་ལ་བྱིན་གྱིས་བརླབ་ཏུ་གསོལ།

ཨི་དཾ་གུ་རུ་རཏྣ་མཎྜལ་ཀཾ་ནི་རྱཱ་ཏ་ཡཱ་མི།

ཞེས་ཡན་ལག་བདུན་པ་མཎྜལ་དང་བཅས་པ་འབུལ།

རྗེ་བཙུན་བླ་མའི་ཐུགས་ཀའི་ཧྲཱིཿཡིག་ལས།
བདུད་རྩི་འོད་ཟེར་སྣ་ལྔའི་རྒྱུན་བབས་དེ།
རང་གི་སྤྱི་བོ་ནས་ཞུགས་སྡིག་སྒྲིབ་སྦྱང་།
མཆོག་ཐུན་དངོས་གྲུབ་མ་ལུས་ཐོབ་པར་གྱུར།

ཅེས་བརྗོད་ཅིང་བསམས་ལ།

ཨོཾ་ཨཱཿགུ་རུ་བཛྲ་དྷ་ར་ཝཱ་གཱིནྡྲ་སུ་མ་ཏི་ཤཱ་ས་ན་དྷ་ར་ས་མུ་དྲ་ཤྲཱི་བྷ་དྲ་སརྦ་སིདྡྷི་ཧཱུྃ་ཧཱུྃ།

ཞེས་མཚན་སྔགས་གང་འགྲུབ་བཟླ། དེ་ནས་འདོད་བྱའི་དོན་ལ་གསོལ་བ་འདེབས་པ་ནི།

འཕྲལ་དང་ཡུན་གྱི་བདེ་བ་མ་ལུས་པའི།
གཞིར་གྱུར་མ་ནོར་ལམ་སྟོན་དྲིན་ཅན་རྗེ།
རབ་འབྱམས་སྐྱབས་ཀྱི་ཕུང་པོར་ངེས་རྙེད་ནས།
བསམ་སྦྱོར་དག་པས་བསྟེན་པར་བྱིན་གྱིས་རློབས།

ནོར་མཆོག་བྱེ་བས་བསླུན་མིན་དལ་འབྱོར་རྟེན།
ཐོབ་ཀྱང་མི་བརྟན་ནམ་འདོར་ཆ་མེད་པས།
འདི་སྣང་བྱ་བས་ནམ་ཡང་མི་གཡེང་བར།[9]
དམ་ཆོས་སྒྲུབ་པས་འདའ་བར་བྱིན་གྱིས་རློབས།

བཟོད་དཀའ་ངན་འགྲོའི་འཇིགས་ལས་སྐྱོབ་པའི་ཕྱུལ།
མཆོག་གསུམ་གདན་གྱི་སྐྱབས་སུ་ལེགས་བཟུང་སྟེ།
དཀར་ནག་ལས་འབྲས་ཇི་བཞིན་སེམས་པ་ཡིས།
སྡིག་སྤོང་དགེ་སྒྲུབ་ནུས་པར་བྱིན་གྱིས་རློབས།

སྲིན་མོའི་བསླུ་བྲིད་ཇི་བཞིན་ལྷ་དབང་གི།
ཕུན་ཚོགས་ཀུན་ཀྱང་བསླུ་བའི་ཆོས་ཅན་དུ།
མཐོང་བའི་ངེས་འབྱུང་དྲག་པོས་རྒྱུད་བསྐུལ་ནས།
བསླབ་གསུམ་ཉམས་ལེན་བྱེད་པར་བྱིན་གྱིས་རློབས།

ཐོག་མེད་དུས་ནས་དྲིན་གྱིས་ལེགས་བསྐྱངས་པའི།
སྲིད་ཞིའི་རྒྱུད་པས་མནར་བའི་མར་གྱུར་འགྲོའི།
ངང་ཚུལ་བསམ་ནས་སེམས་མཆོག་རབ་བསྐྱེད་དེ།
སྤྱོད་པ་རྒྱ་མཚོར་སློབ་པར་བྱིན་གྱིས་རློབས།

རབ་དྭངས་གཡོ་མེད་མཉམ་གཞག་མི་ཡོང་ངོགས།
མཐའ་བྲལ་གདོད་ནས་སྟོང་པའི་ངོ་མཚར་འབུམ།
འགོག་མེད་བཀྲ་བའི་ཞི་ལྷག་ཟུང་འབྲེལ་གྱི།
རྣལ་འབྱོར་རྒྱུད་ལ་སྐྱེ་བར་བྱིན་གྱིས་རློབས།

མཚན་ལྡན་རྡོ་རྗེ་འཛིན་པའི་བཤེས་གཉེན་གྱི།
དྲིན་ལས་ཚེས་ཟབ་སྔགས་ཀྱི་སྒོར་ཞུགས་ནས།
དངོས་གྲུབ་རྩ་བ་དམ་ཚིག་སྡོམ་པ་རྣམས།
ཚུལ་བཞིན་བསྲུང་བར་ནུས་པར་བྱིན་གྱིས་རློབས།

གཉིས་མེད་བདེ་སྟོང་ཡེ་ཤེས་མཚོན་དོན་གྱིས།
ཀུན་བྱེད་ལས་རླུང་རྒྱུ་བ་རབ་བཅད་ནས།
སྐུ་ཐུགས་ཟུང་འཇུག་བདེ་ཆེན་ཕྱག་རྒྱ་ཆེ།
ཚེ་འདིར་མངོན་དུ་འགྱུར་བར་བྱིན་གྱིས་རློབས།

(ཞེས་མདོ་སྔགས་ཀྱི་ལམ་ཡོངས་རྫོགས་རྒྱུད་ལ་སྐྱེ་བའི་གསོལ་འདེབས་དང་བཤར་སྒོམ་བྱས་མཐར་བླ་མ་སྙིང་ཞུགས་དང་འབྲེལ་བར་ཡིག་དྲུག་གི་བཟླས་པ་བྱ་བ་ནི།)

དེ་ལྟར་གསོལ་བ་བཏབ་པས་བླ་མ་མཆོག
   དགྱེས་བཞིན་བྱོན་དེ་རང་གི་ཚངས་བུག་བརྒྱུད།
འདབ་བརྒྱད་སྙིང་དབུས་མི་ཤིགས་ཐིག་ལེར་ཐིམ།
   དེ་ཉིད་སླར་ཡང་པད་ཟླར་བླ་མའི་སྐུ།

སེམས་དཔའ་སུམ་བརྩེགས་སྟར་བཞིན་གསལ་བ་ཡི།
   ཐུགས་ཀའི་ཧྲཱིཿམཐར་ཡིག་དྲུག་སྔགས་ཕྲེང་གིས།
བསྐོར་ལས་བདུད་རྩིའི་རྒྱུན་བབས་ནད་གདོན་དང་།
   སྡིག་སྒྲིབ་ཀུན་བྱང་ལུང་རྟོགས་ཡོན་ཏན་རྒྱས།

སྲས་བཅས་རྒྱལ་བའི་བྱིན་རླབས་མ་ལུས་ཐོབ།
   སླར་ཡང་འོད་འཕྲོས་སྣོད་བཅུད་སྐྱོན་སྦྱངས་ཏེ།
སྣང་གྲག་རིག་གསུམ་འཕགས་པའི་གསང་གསུམ་དུ།
   འཁྱེར་བའི་རྣལ་འབྱོར་མཆོག་ལ་གནས་པར་གྱུར།

(ཅེས་བརྗོད་ཅིང་བསམ་ལ། ཡིག་དྲུག་ཅི་ནུས་སུ་བཟླ། མཐར་ཡི་གེ་བརྒྱ་པས་བརྟན་པར་བྱས་ལ།)

འདིས་མཚོན་ལེགས་བྱས་[10] ཟླ་གཞོན་འབུམ་གྱི་གཟེས།
   བློ་གཏེར་རྒྱལ་བའི་ཆོས་ཚུལ་ཀུནྡའི་ཚལ།
བཤད་སྒྲུབ་གི་སར་དགོད་པས་ས་ཆེན་ཁྱོན།
   ཞིས་པ་སྒྲུབ་པས་སྲིད་མཐར་མཛེས་གྱུར་ཅིག

ཕུན་ཚོགས་དགེ་ལེགས་བྱེ་བས་རབ་བརྗིད་པའི།
དགའ་ལྡན་ཆབ་སྲིད་ནོར་བུའི་རྒྱལ་མཚན་ཆེ།
མི་ནུབ་སྲིད་གསུམ་ནླ་ན་སྒྲེང་བ་ཡིས།
ཕན་བདེའི་འདོད་པ་འབུམ་དུ་འཛོ་གྱུར་ཅིག

རྒྱ་ཆེན་དབྱིག་འཛིན་སྐྱེག་མོའི་[11]ཁྲིན་ཡངས་པོར།
དུས་ཀྱི་རྒྱུད་པའི་མུན་ཚོགས་ཐག་བསྲིངས་ནས།
བདེ་སྐྱིད་སྣང་བ་དར་བའི་དགེ་མཚན་ཆེར།
ཡིད་ཅན་རྣམ་པར་རྩེན་པས་སྐྱེམས་གྱུར་ཅིག

མདོར་ན་སྐྱེ་བའི་ཕྲེང་བར་མགོན་ཁྱོད་ཀྱིས།
འབྲལ་མེད་མཉེས་བཞིན་རྗེས་སུ་བཟུང་བའི་མཐུས།
ཀུན་གྱི་དབང་ཕྱུག་ཟུང་འཇུག་རྒྱལ་ས་ཆེར།
འབད་མེད་བདེ་བླག་ཉིད་དུ་སོན་གྱུར་ཅིག

(ཅེས་བསྔོ་བ་བྱ་ཞིང་། གཞན་ཡང་བཟང་པོ་སྤྱོད་པའི་སྨོན་ལམ་སོགས་བསྔོ་བ་སྨོན་ལམ་ཅི་རིགས་པའི་མཐར།)

སྲས་བཅས་རྒྱལ་བའི་རྨད་བྱུང་ཐུགས་རྗེའི་མཐུས།
ཕྱོགས་དུས་ཀུན་དུ་མི་མཐུན་རྒུད་ཚོགས་ཞི།
སྲིད་ཞིའི་དགེ་ལེགས་ཡར་ངོའི་ཟླ་བ་ལྟར།
འཕེལ་རྒྱས་དགེ་མཚན་དར་བའི་བཀྲ་ཤིས་ཤོག

ཅེས་ཤིས་པ་བརྗོད་པས་མཐའ་བརྒྱན་པར་བྱའོ།

ཞེས་པ་འདི་ཡང་དད་སྟོབས་ལྷག་བསམ་དགེ་བ་བཀའ་བློན་ལས་རྩིས་ཤན་ཁ་བ་འགྱུར་མེད་བསོད་ནམས་སྟོབས་རྒྱལ་ནས། ངོས་དང་སྤྱན་རས་གཟིགས་དབྱེར་མེད་ཀྱི་བླ་མའི་རྣལ་འབྱོར་ལམ་ཡོངས་རྫོགས་ཀྱི་བཤར་སྒོམ་མདོར་བསྡུས་ཚང་ཞིང་། མཚན་སྔགས་དང་། ཡིག་དྲུག་གི་བཟླས་པ་ཡང་བྱས་ཆོག་པ་ཆ་ཚང་ཁྱེར་བདེ་ཞིག་དགོས་ཞེས་བདོག་པའི་རྟེན་དང་བཅས་ནན་དུན་ཆེན་པོས་བསྐུལ་བར།⑫ རང་གིས་རང་ལ་འདི་ལྟ་བུའི་བླ་མའི་རྣལ་འབྱོར་སྦྱར་བ་མི་རིགས་ཀྱང་། དད་པ་བྱས་ན་ཁྱི་སོར་རིང་བསྲེལ་འབྱུང་བ་ལྟར།⑬ སློབ་མའི་ངོས་ནས་མོས་གུས་བྱུང་ན་སོ་སྐྱེ་ལས་ཀྱང་སངས་རྒྱས་ཀྱི་བྱིན་རླབས་འབྱུང་བས། དད་ལྡན་འགའ་ཤས་ལ་དོན་དུ་འགྱུར་བ་སྲིད་སྙམ་སྟེ། པད་དཀར་འཆང་བའི་མིང་འཛིན་ཤཱཀྱའི་དགེ་སློང་ངག་དབང་བློ་བཟང་བསྟན་འཛིན་རྒྱ་མཚོས་སྦྱར་བའོ།། །།

Annotations to the Fourteenth Dalai Lama's *Yoga of the Inseparability of the Guru and Avalokiteśvara, A Source of All Powerful Attainments*

① **_Sādhana_ Texts (General Features)**

Page 509, Line 5

In general, *sādhana* texts consist of mnemonic-style instructions for practice. The stages of practice are presumed to be known in advance and hence tend to not be specified or even explicitly indicated in the text (they are added for clarity in the translation here). The same holds true for key terms and their signifance.

WHAT TO REMEMBER

Some texts are written in such a manner as to explicitly require previous knowledge of the subject matter (e.g., tantra, medicine, Pāṇinian grammar, etc.) in order to be intelligible.

② **Astrological References**

Page 509, Line 5

Tibetan culture is deeply self-referential, with medicine, astrology, and many other fields interwoven into philosophy. The most obvious example of this is the system of calendrical calculations derived from the *Kālacakra Tantra*, in which a theoretical system of prognostication is combined with the practical needs of an agricultural calendar.

Another use of astrological terms is as tantric metaphor. Such is seen here in the reference to "the sixteen lunar digits" (བཅུ་དྲུག་ཆ་) of the visible moon. A full moon consists of all sixteen parts—that is, an appearance of the moon in which all sixteen parts are "complete" (ཡོངས་སུ་རྫོགས་པ་). The moon, moreover, is symbolic in tantric physiology as the biological constituent ("the white drop") that dwells at the crown of the head and is a metaphor for embodied compassion—hence the connection to Avalokiteśvara, the bodhisattva who is considered the embodiment of the compassion of all the buddhas.

WHAT TO REMEMBER

The use of the astrological terms in Buddhist texts occurs both in presentations of calendrical systems and as metaphors in tantric physiology.

Differentiating Senses of the Verb ཚོག་

3

Page 509, Line 13

Someone who has read extensively in Tibetan will eventually notice that English and Tibetan have a high rate of correspondence between grammatical constructions and that they even share some idiomatic expressions. The languages are, of course, distinct, and when sentences between those two languages diverge—as previously noted (see བར་དོ་འཕྲང་སྒྲོལ་ note 11)—they give rise to what is known as a "translation divergence." Sentences involving the verb ཚོག་ often give rise to such translation divergences.

In its most common usage, the verb ཚོག་ is a Class IV verb of containment that takes its qualifier marked by a syntactic particle (ཀྱིས་, གྱིས་, etc.). One way of understanding the meaning of the verb ཚོག་ is to think of it as meaning "to be fulfilled" in the sense of sufficiency or adequacy. In English, however, the corresponding concept is rendered either as an indirect construction ("It is sufficient to do ...") or as a passive construction ("Doing ... is sufficient"). It should be noted that the verb ཚོག་ also appears in a Class II form ("to be permissible") and takes a second verb as its qualifier (similar to the verb དགའ་). In this instance, there is no explicit grammar (i.e., མོས་པས་ཚོག་ or མོས་པར་ཚོག་) to differentiate between the two forms, so context determines the reading.

WHAT TO REMEMBER

The verb ཚོག་ means "to be fulfilled" in the sense of sufficiency or adequacy. In English, this can be rendered as an indirect construction ("It is sufficient to do ...").

④ Names of Precious Substances

Page 509, Line 21

As with the pantheon of beings (see བླ་མ་ལྔ་བཅུ་པ་ note 6), a common set of precious substances reoccurs throughout Indian and Tibetan literature. Sometimes these names are translated, while other times (such as here) they are merely transliterated (see ཤེས་རབ་སྙིང་པོ་ note 2). They occur commonly in descriptions of pure realms and other paradises.

WHAT TO REMEMBER

The most common list of "seven precious substances" (རིན་པོ་ཆེ་སྣ་བདུན་) is:

གསེར་	*Suvarṇa*: Gold
དངུལ་	*Rajata*: Silver
བཻ་ཌཱུར་ཡ་	*Vaiḍūrya*: Lapis Lazuli
སྤུག་	*Musāragalva*: Agate or Coral
རྡོའི་སྙིང་པོ་	*Aśmagarbha*: Emerald
ཤེལ་	*Sphaṭika*: Crystal
མུ་ཏིག་དམར་པོ་	*Lohitamukti*: Ruby

⑤ The Meaning and Translation of Mantras

Page 510, Line 7

In tantric literature, particularly those passages drawn from the "root" texts, the vocabulary is considered to be "loaded" with meaning, and as a result, subsequent commentaries often highlight the special significance of every syllable of every word. With regard to mantras in particular, it is important to remember that, with the exception of intentionally "nonsensical" syllables, the individual components of mantras are typically legitimate Sanskrit words with literal meanings.

Here, for example, the mantra to be recited has two parts. The first is the salutation: *Oṃ namo Bhagavate, vajrasāra pramardane, tathāgatāya, arhate, saṃyaksambuddhāya!* which can be translated as "Oṃ! Homage to the Bhagavān, the invincible destroyer [of ignorance], the Tathāgata, the Arhat, the perfectly and completely enlightened one!"

The second part: *Tadyathā, Oṃ vajre vajre mahāvajre, mahāteja-vajre, mahāvidya-vajre, mahābodhicitta-vajre, mahābodhi-maṇḍopasaṃkramaṇa-vajre, sarvakarmāvaraṇa-viśodhana-vajre svāhā!* can be translated as: It is thus, "*Oṃ*, vajra, vajra, great vajra, great sharp vajra, great knowledge vajra, great bodhicitta vajra, vajra of going over to supreme great enlightenment, vajra of the purification of all karmic obstructions, *svāhā*!" (where "*oṃ*" and "*svāha*" are merely auspicious syllables surounding a mantra).

As for the meaning of such mantras, some are simply intended as objects of complex visualization meditations, while others are mnemonic in one fashion or another, with words or syllables referring to structural elements or aspects of practices. The exact meaning of any particular mantra is usually only ever explained in the commentaries on that practice.

WHAT TO REMEMBER

The individual components of mantras are often legitimate Sanskrit words with literal meanings and can be read as such, but they are typically left untranslated.

The Vocabulary of Practice Instructions

6

Page 510, Line 9

Texts intended for ritual observances and practice have a distinctive way of phrasing instructions. Although one might expect instructional statements to be phrased in the imperative ("Do X!"), they are instead phrased in the generic third person ("One does X"). Here, for example, ཞེས་ལན་གསུམ་བརྗོད། would be translated as "One recites [the above statements] three times."

WHAT TO REMEMBER

Texts intended for ritual observances and practice are phrased in the generic third person ("One does X").

⑦

Translation Hint

Page 510, Line 12

As previously noted (see བློ་རིག་ note 25), the syntactic particle དང་ is used to connect noun phrases, while the syntactic particles ཅིང་, ཤིང་, and ཞིང་ are typically used to connect sentences, although it would be more accurate to say that they are used conjunctively following verbs. The phrase encountered here is one such example, in which the syntactic particle ཅིང་ joins two phrasal verbs: རྣམ་པར་དག་ and བསམ་གྱིས་མི་ཁྱབ་. By doing so, both verbs thus serve as clauses connecting སྟོབས་ to ཆོས་ཀྱི་དབྱིངས་. Hence, the entire phrase ཆོས་ཀྱི་དབྱིངས་རྣམ་པར་དག་ཅིང་བསམ་གྱིས་མི་ཁྱབ་པའི་སྟོབས་ཀྱིས་" can be read as "through the force of the inconceivable and utterly pure dharmadhātu ..."

⑧

Locative Absolute: As a Conditional Time Phrase

Page 513, Line 17

Recall that a locative-absolute construction is a complete or partial sentence that expresses a condition in which something takes place or some type of accompanying circumstance—in both negative and positive senses (see ཤེར་སྙིང་རྣམ་བཤད་ note 9 and གྲུབ་མཐའ་རིན་འཕྲེང་ note 17). Just as the negative sense can denote an accompanying condition of absence, such a condition can also be temporal, as it is here. Consequently, this construction can be translated as "until" or "so long as X has not occurred."

WHAT TO REMEMBER

A locative-absolute construction, when formed with a verb without negation, indicates a negative condition, either contextually ("without") or temporally ("until [such a time as]" or "so long as X has not occurred").

⑨

Double Negatives

Page 515, Line 12

While English takes negation strictly—such that a double negative results in a positive statement—in Tibetan, multiple instances of negation are often used solely for emphasis.

Here, for example, in the phrase ནམ་ཡང་མི་གཡེང་བར་ (lit. "without never being distracted"), the adverb ནམ་ཡང་ ("never") is not negated by the negative verb but is merely used for emphasis. Hence, the passage would be translated as "without ever being distracted."

WHAT TO REMEMBER

In Tibetan, multiple instances of negation (particularly with adverbs) are often used simply for emphasis and do not necessarily negate each other.

Translation Hint 10

Page 517, Line 18

Since the verse ends with a performative statement ("may it be the case"; see སྨོན་ཚིག་ note 30), the opening of the verse—as with many concluding statements—is likely the restatement of what has just been explained as a causal condition for a situation that one hopes will be fulfilled in the future. Such statements are typically translated as "by having done X ..."

Poetic Metaphors from the Sanskrit Tradition 11

Page 518, Line 6

The phrase དབྱིག་འཛིན་ literally means "bearing a treasure" but is, in fact, a translation of the name of an offering goddess (སྒེག་མོ་), Vasundharā, a poetic name for the Earth. In the Sanskrit poetic tradition—and in the Tibetan literary tradition that inherited it—such metaphors are quite common though not always familiar to a Western audience. Fortunately, glossaries of such terms, such as *The Treasury of Amarasiṃha* (*Amarakośa; 'Chi ba med pa'i mdzod*), exist to aid in the identification of such metaphors, although they are not the most easily accessed resources, often being thematically rather than alphabetically organized.

WHAT TO REMEMBER

Poetic metaphors, often derived from the Sanskritic tradition, are common in more sophisticated Tibetan literature. Although reference materials can be difficult to use, familiarity with their content is recommended. Hence, students should read through the classic texts of Indian poetics, such as *The Treasury of Amarasiṃha* (*Amarakośa; 'Chi ba med pa'i mdzod*), Daṇḍin's *Mirror of Poetics* (*Kāvyādarśa; Snyan ngag me long*), Kālidāsa's *Cloud Messenger* (*Meghadūta; Sprin gyi pho nya*), and others.

12

Translation Hint

Page 519, Line 4

The colophon consists of a single, long sentence, although one can begin with this locative-absolute construction.

13

Translation Hint: Popular Stories

Page 519, Line 5

There are a number of popular stories in Tibet centered around Buddhist themes. The reference here is to one of the more popular ones concerning a merchant who promised his mother that he would bring her a relic from India—a tooth of the Buddha. When he forgets, he instead quickly grabs a tooth from the corpse of a dog by the road and presents that to her. The story relates that due to the profound degree of her faith, the dog's tooth begins to produce secondary relics (*ring bsrel*).

Translation of The Fourteenth Dalai Lama's *Yoga of the Inseparability of the Guru and Avalokiteśvara, A Source of All Powerful Attainments*

Homage to the Bhagavān Vajrasattva!

> Having respectfully paid homage to my guru, Avalokiteśvara—
> The possessor of the white light of the elixir of the blessings of the complete
> Full-moon-like nature of the compassion of all the conquerors—
> I [shall now] compose a ritual of the profound yogic practice of that [bodhisattva, Avalokiteśvara].

Thus, here, relying on the guru [who is] the root of all consecrations and attainments, having taken [one's] own particular deity to be inseparable from the guru who unmistakenly teaches the path to us in accordance with what is praised—not [just] one time—in the many sūtras and tantras, [one should understand that] this supplication is of utmost importance as the sole foundation of [one's] final concern. And furthermore, although it is sufficient to have faith in the essential nature of the tutelary deity—whichever one [you] have faith in—[something,] for instance, as the vitality of the Mahāyāna path is solely loving compassion and the precious mind of enlightenment. Hence, since it is said that great compassion is of the utmost importance throughout all three [phases of practice]—the beginning, middle, and end—a yogi who wishes to take up the practice of the yoga of the inseparability of their own root guru and the supreme deity of compassion, Ārya Avalokiteśvara, [should] have properly gathered the ritual offering substances, etc., in a pleasant location. Then, sitting on a comfortable seat, and from within a state of an especially virtuous state of mind, [one] prepares [oneself by] going for refuge, generating bodhicitta, and meditating upon the four immeasurables.

[These three activities constitute the motivational preliminaries.]

[The Physical Preliminaries of Purification]

In all [directions], may the surface of the earth
Become a place that is smooth [with] the nature
Of lapis lazuli, like the palm of the hand, and
Free of gravel, and so forth.

May the divine and human [-made] offering substances—
Actually prepared and mentally emanated—
[Like] unsurpassed clouds of offerings [like those] of Samantabhadra,
Thoroughly pervade the realm of space.

Oṃ namo Bhagavate, vajrasāra pramardane, tathāgatāya, arhate, saṃyak-sambuddhāya! Tadyathā, Oṃ vajre vajre mahāvajre, mahāteja-vajre, mahāvidya-vajre, mahābodhicitta-vajre, mahābodhi-maṇḍopasaṃkramaṇa-vajre, sarvakarmāvaraṇa-viśodhana-vajre svāhā!

[One] recites [this] three times.

[One] consecrates the ritual offering substances and [their] supporting foundation [by saying], "Through the force of the truth of the Three Jewels of refuge, the blessings of all buddhas and bodhisattvas and the great power of those who have fully perfected the two collections [of merit and wisdom], and the inconceivable and utterly pure dharmadhātu, may all of these offerings be hereby transformed into suchness!"

[First Visualization, of the Deity in Front]

Then,

In the expanse of space of the dharmakāya of spontaneous great bliss,
In the midst of billowing clouds of offerings [like those] of Samantabhadra
[of] various [kinds],

On a throne of jewels radiating light that is supported by lions,
On top of a seat of broad lotus, sun, and moon [disks],

[Is] the great treasury of compassion, the Noble Supreme Lokeśvara,
Assuming the form of [one] wearing saffron-type [clothes, i.e., monks' robes],
[Your] root guru, possessing the three [sets of vows], Vajradhāra,
The glorious, Venerable Losang Tenzin Gyatso.

Having a clear white complexion with a tinge of red [and] a pleasant smiling face,
With [his] right hand at his heart [in] the mudra of explaining the Dharma,
[He holds the stem of] a white lotus adorned with a book and sword, and
[His] left [hand] is set in meditative equipoise, carrying a thousand-spoked wheel.

With the three kinds of saffron-colored religious robes [of a monk],
[He] is beautifully attired with a paṇḍita's hat the color of refined gold.
[His] aggregates, elements, sensory spheres, objects, and limbs
Are perfect as the circle of a maṇḍala with its natural wrathful protectors, ...

Five families [of buddhas] and their consorts, and male and female bodhisattvas.
[In] the center of a mansion, [under] a tent shimmering with a halo of five [-colored] variegated light rays,
[With his] two feet [in] a full vajra cross-legged posture,
[He] sends forth a heap of clouds of a net of illusory emanations [in order to] tame whoever [needs taming].

At [his] heart [is] the wisdom-being (*jñānasattva*), Avalokiteśvara,
With one face, four arms, and the palms of one pair [of hands] joined.
[His] lower [two hands] carry a crystal rosary and a white lotus.
[He] is adorned with jeweled ornaments and silk clothing.

An antelope skin is draped over [his] left shoulder;
[He is in] the fullness of youth, seated cross-legged on a lotus.
At [his] heart, the concentration-being (*samādhisattva*) [is]
A radiant white syllable *HRĪḤ*, emitting light rays in the ten directions.

The three places of the guru [crown, throat, and heart] are marked with the three vajras [a white *OṂ*, a red *ĀḤ*, and a blue *HŪṂ*, respectively].
The light rays that radiate out from the syllable *HŪṂ* at [his] heart
Invite the Three Jewels [from] countless [realms] without exception.
By dissolving [into him], [he] becomes the collected essence of the places of refuge.

[In this way, one] clearly visualizes the guru in the manner of a jewel who completely subsumes the three stacked beings [the commitment-being (*samayasattva*), the wisdom-being, and the concentration-being].

[The Seven-limb Prayer]
[<u>Prostrating</u>]

[I] pay homage to the wheel of the adornments of three secrets—
[Your] body, which liberates upon being seen, and which is adorned with the vivid and complete major and minor marks [of a buddha];
[Your] speech, which is sweet-sounding and euphonious, endowed with the sixty [types of] melodies, and unobstructed; and
[Your] mind, which is profound, vast, wise, compassionate, and difficult to fathom.

[<u>Offering</u>]

[All] material offerings [either] possessed or not possessed by me,
[Those] actually prepared, [those] mentally emanated, [my] body, resources, and

All collections of wholesome virtues that have been amassed throughout
the three times—
Having visualized [them] as an ocean of clouds of offerings [like those] of
Samantabhadra, [I] offer [them to you].

[Confessing]

Because my mind is oppressed by the darkness of obscuring ignorance,
Transgressions [of vows] and natural [offenses], unseemly ethical
transgressions, infractions [of vows], and so forth
—Whatsoever faults I may have from straying in error—
With regret and a strong vow [to not repeat them], in a state without
objectifying [them], [I] confess [them all].

[Rejoicing]

From the depths of my heart, with an earnest intention, [I] rejoice
In the heap of pure virtue [amassed in] the three times
Of all [deeds of] the glorious thoroughly liberated gurus and
Ordinary and noble beings of the three vehicles, myself, and others.

[Requesting]

[I] supplicate [you] to [cause to] awaken from the sleep of afflictive
obstructions and obstructions to omniscience,
All sentient beings, by resounding as the voice of the peaceful and the
profound,
The sound of divine music of the three realms [that is] the holy Dharma
That accords with the dispositions of various trainees.

[Entreating]

Until all transmigrators obtain the breath of joy
In the realization that is free from the extremes of worldliness or pacification,
[May you] firmly establish [yourself] upon the unconquerable vajra throne
[With your] pair of feet cross-legged [in] the indestructible [state of] *evaṃ*.

[Dedicating]

All wholesome actions that I have done well and will do
I dedicate for the purpose of obtaining perfect enlightenment for the sake of all transmigrators,
Having completely accomplished [my] aspirational prayers—the supreme deed of Samantabhadra—
And [for the purpose of] being cared for by the venerable gurus, without [ever] being separated [from them].

[Maṇḍala Offering]

Mt. Meru, [with] a base annointed with incense and arrayed [with] flowers,
[And] the four continents adorned by the sun and moon—this
[I] visualize as a buddhafield and offer [it to you].
May all transmigrators find enjoyment in [this] utterly pure [buddha]field!

I offer to [my] gurus, tutelary deities, and the Three Jewels—having brought [them] to mind—
The collection of virtues [amassed over] the three times, the enjoyments of body, speech, and mind of myself and others, and
A pure maṇḍala of precious [jewels], together with the collection of offerings of Samantabhadra.
Having accepted [these] through the power of [your] compassion, [I] request [you] to consecrate me.

Idaṃ guru ratna maṇḍalakaṃ niryatayami!

Saying [that], [one] offers the Seven-limb Prayer together with the maṇḍala.

[Blessing by the Guru]

From the *HRĪḤ* syllable at the heart of [my] venerable guru,
Flow streams of nectar and variegated five[-colored] light rays.
Entering from the crown of my head, [they] purify [me of all] ethical transgressions and obstructions.
May [I] come to attain [all] supreme and mundane siddhis without exception.

[One] recites [that] and thinks:

Oṃ āḥ guru vajradhara vāgindra sumati śāsanadhara samudra śrībhadra sarvasiddhi hūṃ hūṃ

Recite the name-mantra [also, as many times] as can be done.

[Prayer of the Graduated Path]

Then, making a petition for the purpose of [their] desired objective:

O foremost, kind teacher of the unmistaken path, who serves as the foundation
Of [all] temporary and everlasting bliss without exception,
Having developed confidence [in you] as the totality of countless refuges,
Bless [me] to rely [on you] with pure thoughts and actions.

Although [I] have obtained a stable basis of leisure and fortune, with which ten million precious jewels cannot compete,

Since [it] is unstable and [the time of its] loss is indefinite,
Without ever being distracted by the appearing objects [of] this [life],
Bless [me] to transcend [it all] by practicing the holy Dharma.

Well apprehending as the final refuge, the Three Jewels—
The gift that provides refuge from the frights of bad transmigrations [that are so] difficult to endure—and
Through properly contemplating the effects of positive and negative actions,
Bless [me] to be able to abandon ethical transgressions and accomplish [only] virtues.

Having been motivated by the strong renunciation that sees
As deceptive objects even all the marvels
Of the lord of the gods, just like the deceptive seduction of a siren,
Bless [me] to take up the practice of the three trainings.

Bringing forth the supreme mind [of enlightenment], having contemplated the state
Of transmigrators who were [my] mothers [and] who are tortured by the misfortunes of mundane existence and pacification
[And] who nourished [me] with kindness from beginningless time,
Bless [me] to train in the ocean of practices.

Bless [me, such that] in my continuum is born the yoga
That is the union of calm abiding and special insight, by means of which is unobstructedly reflected
A hundred thousand splendors of emptiness from beginningless time free from [all] extremes
[In] the face of the mirror of an utterly clear and unwavering meditative equipoise.

Having entered the door of exceptionally profound mantra through the
great kindness
Of a spiritual friend [who is] a fully qualified tantric master,
Bless [me, such that I] will be able to protect properly
[My] vows and commitments—the root of siddhis.

Having thoroughly severed the all-creating wind of karmic action
With the sharp sword [of] the wisdom of nondual bliss and emptiness,
Bless [me, such that] in this lifetime [I may] manifest
The great seal of great bliss [that is] the union of exalted body and exalted
mind.

Saying [this], at the end of making a request for the complete paths of sūtra and tantra to be be born in [your] continuum and performing reviewing meditation, in connection with [visualizing] the guru entering [your] heart, [one] should recite the six-syllable mantra [*oṃ mani padme hūṃ*].

[Visualizing Oneself as the Deity]
[Visualization of the Moon-Disk at the Heart]

By supplicating in this way, [my] supreme guru
Accordingly appears pleased, passes through my Brahmā (cranial)
aperture, [and]
Dissolves into the indestructible drop at the center of [my] eight-petalled
heart [cakra].
That itself, moreover, [has] the body of [my] guru on a lotus and moon [disk].

[Visualization of the Letters of the Mantra around the Moon-Disk]

At the edges of the *HRĪḤ* syllable at [my] heart, [which] clearly appears as
before
[With] the three stacked beings, the garland of the six-syllable mantra

Encircles [it, and] from [that] a stream of elixir flows out [and] thoroughly purifies
[All] diseases and harmful influences, ethical transgressions and obstructions, [and] increases [my] realizations and good qualities.

[I] obtain [all] the blessings of the conquerors as well as [their] sons without exception;
Furthermore, light rays purify the faults of the environment and [its] inhabitants. Thus,
[I] come to abide in the supreme yoga, which carries
[All] three— appearances, sounds, and thoughts—into the three secrets of a noble one.

([This should be] recited and meditated upon; then, [one] repeats the six-syllable mantra [*oṃ mani padme hūṃ*] as [many times as one] is able. At the end [of that], it is stabilized with the one hundred-syllable [mantra: *oṃ vajrasattva samaya, manupālaya, vajrasattva tvenopatiṣṭha, dṛḍho me bhava, sutoṣyo me bhava, supoṣyo me bhava, anurakto me bhava, sarva siddhiṃ me prayaccha, sarva karma su ca me, cittaṃ śreyaḥ kuru hūṃ, ha ha ha ha hoḥ, bhagavān sarva tathāgatavajra, mā me muñca, vajrī bhava mahā samaya sattva, aḥ hūṃ phaṭ*.])

[Dedication]

[By] having well illustrated [the practice] with this [presentation], [then] with the radiance of a hundred thousand full moons [and]
By arranging the stamens of explanation and accomplishment [in] the jasmine garden of the way of the Dharma of
The victorious treasury of awareness, may the extent of [this] vast earth
Be beautified to the end of existence by the accomplished auspiciousness.

By raising above the three worlds, the unvanishing
Jeweled banner of the Ganden government

That radiantly gleams with a million good virtues and marvelous [qualities],
May [it] yield satisfaction for a hundred thousand wishes for prosperity
and happiness.

Having banished the gloom of the unfortunate era
[That hangs] over the vast expanse of [this] great offering goddess,
Vasundharā (lit. "treasure-bearer," i.e., the earth),
May [all] sentient beings take pride, by delighting sentient beings,
With the great marks of virtue that spread the appearances of bliss and
happiness.

In brief, in [my] sequence of lives, O Protector, through the power
Of [your] affectionate care, as you please, [and] without being separated
[from you],
May [I] arrive, easily and effortlessly,
In that great kingdom that is [a state of] union [as] a powerful lord over all
[saṃsāra and nirvāṇa].

([One] should make [one's] dedication saying [this], and furthermore, at the end of whatsoever dedicatory prayers are appropriate, such as the *Aspirational Prayer of the Deeds of Samantabhadra* (*[Samanta]bhadra-caryā-pranidhāna*), and others.)

[Conclusion]

Through the power of the marvelous compassion of the Conqueror
together with [his] children,
[May all] accumulated nonconducive misfortunes thoughout all of time
and [in all] directions be pacified, [and]
Like the waxing moon, may [all] virtue and goodness in the mundane
world or [in a state of] peace
Flourish and grow brighter, and [may] there be the auspiciousness of the
spreading of its virtuous signs.

[You] should adorn the end [of this] with auspicious pronouncements.

[Colophon]

As for this, moreover, [I] was entreated with great sincerity together with [his] personal support (i.e., monetary offerings) from [the man of] great faith, unusual attitude, and virtue, the Assistant Cabinet Minister, Shankawa Gyurmé Sonam Topgyel, saying [he] needed an easy-to-carry complete ritual [for] performing a complete concise reviewing meditation for fully perfecting the path of the guru yoga of the inseparability of myself and Avalokiteśvara, together with a name-mantra, as well as a recitation of the six-syllable [mantra]. Although composing a guru yoga such as this by myself about myself is inappropriate, if it produces faith, then like relics arising from a dog's tooth, when veneration has arisen from the side of the student, since blessings of the Buddha [can] also arise from an ordinary being, thinking that it is possible that [it] would be meaningful to a few of the faithful, [this] was composed by the holder of the name "Holder of the White Lotus" (Padmapāṇi, i.e., Avalokiteśvara), the Buddhist monk, Ngawang Losang Tenzin Gyatso.

Long-life Prayer for His Holiness the Dalai Lama

The Tibetan genre of "long-life" prayers (*zhabs brtan*; literally, "firm feet") is rooted in the story of the passing away of the Buddha—specifically, in the story in which his disciple Ānanda failed to request him to live longer. Hence, the idea of requesting enlightened beings to "remain in saṃsāra for the benefit of living beings" sparked an entire genre of literature in Tibet,[1] of which this text is an excellent example.

In terms of literary form and style, "long-life" prayers are written in verse with a fixed number of syllables and typically contain allusions and metaphors drawn from both classical Indian Buddhism and the larger realm of generic Indian cosmology. In terms of a reading challenge, this text contains precisely such poetical allusions and metaphors as well as sociopolitical references to its historical context. As such, it contains vocabulary that may not be immediately recognized. When coupled with the terse syntax imposed upon it by the nine-syllable-per-line verse structure, a text such as this can prove challenging, requiring one to recognize brief sentences and noun-verb patterns.

An alternate version of this same text in འཁྱུག་ཡིག་ script is provided in appendix 4.

[1] For more on this genre, see José Cabezón 1996, 344–57.

སྲིད་ཞིའི་གཙུག་ནོར་[v]གོང་ས་[v]སྐྱབས་མགོན་[v]རྒྱལ་དབང་
ཐམས་ཅད་མཁྱེན་གཟིགས་ཆེན་མཆོག་བསྟན་འགྲོའི་མགོན་དུ་
ཞབས་ཟུང་བརྟན་ཅིང་། རླབས་ཆེན་བཞེད་དོན་ལྷུན་འགྲུབ་ཆེད་
མཆོག་གསུམ་རྒྱ་མཚོའི་ཐུགས་རྗེ་བསྐུལ་བའི་
གསོལ་འདེབས་འཆི་མེད་གྲུབ་པའི་དབྱངས་སྙན་
ཞེས་བྱ་བ་བཞུགས་སོ།།

([v]གོང་ས་མཆོག་ལ་གསོལ་བཏབ།)

ཨོཾ་སྭ་སྟི།

རབ་འབྱམས་རྒྱལ་བའི་གསང་གསུམ་མ་ལུས་པ། །
གང་འདུལ་ཅིར་ཡང་འཆར་བའི་སྒྱུ་འཕྲུལ་གར། །
སྲིད་ཞིའི་དགེ་ལེགས་ཀུན་འབྱུང་ཡིད་བཞིན་ནོར། །
དངོས་བརྒྱུད་དྲིན་ཅན་བླ་མའི་ཚོགས་རྣམས་ལ། །

བདག་ཅག་གདུང་ཤུགས་དྲག་པོས་གསོལ་འདེབས་ན། །
གངས་ཅན་མགོན་པོ་བསྟན་འཛིན་རྒྱ་མཚོ་ཡི། །
སྐུ་ཚེ་མི་ཤིགས་བསྐལ་བརྒྱར་རབ་བརྟན་ཅིང་། །
བཞེད་དོན་ལྷུན་གྱིས་འགྲུབ་པར་བྱིན་གྱིས་རློབས།

ཆོས་དབྱིངས་ཀུན་གསལ་ཁྱོན་དང་མཉམ་འཇུག་པའི། །
རྡུལ་བྲལ་བདེ་ཆེན་ཡེ་ཤེས་སྒྱུ་མའི་སྤྲིན། །

གྲངས་མེད་རྟེན་དང་བརྟེན་པའི་དཀྱིལ་འཁོར་དུ།
ཤར་བའི་ཡིད་དམ་ལྷ་ཚོགས་ཐམས་ཅད་ལ། །

བདག་ཅག་×།[1] །གངས་ཅན་མགོན་པོ་×། །
སྐུ་ཚེ་×། །བཞེད་དོན་×། །

སྤངས་རྟོགས་ཡོན་དན་ལྷུན་རྫོགས་འཕྲིན་ལས་ཀྱི།
སྣང་བ་འགྲོ་ཁམས་རྒྱ་མཚོར་རྟག་རྟེན་པས།
པན་མཛད་སྤོབས་བཅུ་མངའ་བ་ལྷ་ཡི་ལྷ། །
རབ་འབྱམས་དུས་གསུམ་རྒྱལ་བ་ཐམས་ཅད་ལ། །

བདག་ཅག་×། །གངས་ཅན་མགོན་པོ་×། །
སྐུ་ཚེ་×། །བཞེད་དོན་×། །

འཇིག་རྟེན་གསུམ་ལས་གང་གིས་ངེས་སྒྲོལ་ཞིང་། །
མཆོག་ཏུ་ཞི་བ་རྣམ་བྱང་ནོར་བུའི་གཏེར།
ཟག་མེད་མི་གཡོ་ཀུན་བཟང་དགེ་བའི་དཔལ། །
ཐེག་གསུམ་དམ་པའི་ཆོས་ཀྱི་ཚོགས་རྣམས་ལ། །

བདག་ཅག་×། །གངས་ཅན་མགོན་པོ་×། །
སྐུ་ཚེ་×། །བཞེད་དོན་×།

སྲིད་པའི་འཕྲུལ་འཁོར་འཇོམས་ལ་ཆེས་དཔའ་བའི། །
བདེན་དོན་མངོན་སུམ་འཛལ་བའི་ཡེ་ཤེས་ཅན། །
རྣམ་ཐར་རྡོ་རྗེའི་གྲོང་ལས་མི་ཕྱེད་པ།
རིག་གྲོལ་འཕགས་པའི་དགེ་འདུན་ཐམས་ཅད་ལ། །

བདག་ཅག་×། །གངས་ཅན་མགོན་པོ་×། །
སྐུ་ཚེ་×། །བཞེད་དོན་×། །

མཁའ་སྤྱོད་ཞིང་དང་གནས་ཡུལ་དུར་ཁྲོད་དུ། །
བདེ་སྟོང་ཉམས་བརྒྱར་རོལ་པའི་རྩེད་འཇོ་ཡིས།[2] །
རྣལ་འབྱོར་ལམ་བཟང་སྒྲུབ་ལ་གྲོགས་མཛད་པའི། །
གནས་གསུམ་དཔའ་བོ་མཁའ་འགྲོའི་ཚོགས་རྣམས་ལ། །

བདག་ཅག་×། །གངས་ཅན་མགོན་པོ་×། །
སྐུ་ཚེ་×། །བཞེད་དོན་×། །

རྡོ་རྗེ་འཆང་གི་བཀའ་རྟགས་ཕྱག་རྒྱའི་མདུད། །
མི་འབྲལ་རལ་པའི་ཐོད་དུ་ཉེར་བཀོད་ནས།
བསྟན་དང་བསྟན་འཛིན་སྐྱོང་བའི་མཐུ་རྩལ་ཅན། །
ཡེ་ཤེས་སྤྱན་ལྡན་བསྟན་སྲུང་རྒྱ་མཚོ་ལ། །

བདག་ཅག་གདུང་ཞུགས་དྲག་པོས་གསོལ་འདེབས་ན། །
གངས་ཅན་མགོན་པོ་བསྟན་འཛིན་རྒྱ་མཚོ་ཡི། །

སྐུ་ཚེ་མི་ཤིགས་བསྐལ་བརྒྱར་རབ་བརྟན་ཅིང་། །
བཞེད་དོན་ལྷུན་གྱིས་འགྲུབ་པར་བྱིན་གྱིས་རློབས།

དེ་ལྟར་བསླུ་མེད་སྐྱབས་ཀྱི་མཆོག་རྣམས་ལ།
ཤུགས་དྲག་སྙིང་ནས་གུས་པས་གསོལ་བཏབ་མཐུས། །
མི་ཟད་སྙིགས་མའི་ཟུག་རྔུས་རབ་མནར་བའི། །
བདག་སོགས་གངས་ལྗོངས་འགྲོ་བའི་མགོན་གཅིག་པུ།

ངག་དབང་བློ་བཟང་བསྟན་འཛིན་རྒྱ་མཚོ་མཆོག
གསང་གསུམ་མི་ཤིགས་མི་འགྱུར་མི་ནུབ་པར།[3] །
གཞོམ་ཞིག་ཡོངས་བྲལ་རྡོ་རྗེ་སྙིང་པོའི་ཁྲིར།
བསྐལ་པ་རྒྱ་མཚོར་གཡོ་མེད་རྟག་བརྟན་ཤོག །

རབ་འབྱམས་རྒྱལ་བ་ཀུན་གྱི་མཛད་པའི་ཁུར། །
སྙིང་སྟོབས་ཕྲག་པར་བཟུང་བའི་རླབས་ཆེན་གྱི། །
འཕྲིན་ལས་ཀུན་ཕན་ནོར་བུའི་སྙིང་པོ་ཅན། །
བཞེད་པ་ཇི་བཞིན་ལྷུན་གྱིས་འགྲུབ་གྱུར་ཅིག །

དེ་མཐུས་རྫོགས་ལྡན་སྐལ་བཟང་ནམ་མཁའི་སྒྲོ། །
ལུས་ཅན་ངལ་བསོའི་དཔྱིད་དུ་རྟག་གྲོལ་ཞིང་།
ཐུབ་བསྟན་ཕྱོགས་དུས་ཀུན་དུ་རབ་དར་བའི།
དགེ་མཚན་སྲིད་ཞིའི་རྩེ་མོར་རྒྱས་གྱུར་ཅིག །

ཕྱག་ན་པདྨོའི་བྱིན་རླབས་བདུད་རྩིའི་རྒྱུན། །
བདག་སོགས་སྙིང་གི་ཟུངས་སུ་རྟག་སྨིན་ཅིང་།
བཀའ་བཞིན་སྒྲུབ་པའི་མཆོད་པས་རབ་བསྙེན་ནས། །
ཀུན་བཟང་སྤྱོད་མཆོག་རྒྱ་མཚོ་མཐར་སོན་ཤོག །

རྨད་བྱུང་སྲས་བཅས་རྒྱལ་བའི་བྱིན་རླབས་དང་། །
རྟེན་འབྲེལ་བསླུ་བ་མེད་པའི་བདེན་པ་དང་།
བདག་གི་ལྷག་བསམ་དག་པའི་མཐུ་སྟོབས་ཀྱིས།
སྨོན་པའི་དོན་ཀུན་བདེ་བླག་མྱུར་འགྲུབ་ཤོག །

ཅེས་པ་འདི་ཡང་བདག་སོགས་ལྷ་དང་བཅས་པའི་འགྲོ་བ་ཡོངས་ཀྱི་རྣམ་འདྲེན་མཚུངས་ཟླ་མ་མཆིས་པ་༸གོང་ས་༸སྐྱབས་མགོན་རྒྱལ་བའི་དབང་པོ་ཐམས་ཅད་མཁྱེན་ཅིང་གཟིགས་པ་ཆེན་པོ་རྗེ་བཙུན་ངག་དབང་བློ་བཟང་བསྟན་འཛིན་རྒྱ་མཚོ་སྲིད་གསུམ་དབང་བསྒྱུར་མཚུངས་པ་མེད་པའི་སྡེ་དཔལ་བཟང་པོ་མཆོག་གི་༸ཞབས་ཟུང་སྲིད་མཐར་བརྟན་ཅིང་། རླབས་ཆེན་བཞེད་རྒྱ་མ་ལུས་ལྷུན་གྱིས་འགྲུབ་པའི་ཆེད་④སླུ་མེད་མཆོག་གསུམ་རྒྱ་མཚོའི་ཐུགས་རྗེ་བསྐུལ་བའི་བདེན་ཚིག་གསོལ་འདེབས་མངོན་བརྗོད་དང་། སྐན་དངགས་ཀྱི་རྒྱུན་གྱིས་མ་བཅིངས་པ་འདི་ལྟ་བུ་ཞིག་གསར་དུ་འབྲི་དགོས་ཞེས་གདན་ས་ཆེན་པོ་འབྲས་སེ་དགའ་གསུམ་དང་།⑤ བཀའ་ཤག །དྲུང་རྩིས་ཀྱིས་མཚོན་རྩེ་ཤོད་དྲུང་རིགས་སེར་སྐྱ་སྤྱི་ཚོགས། བོད་ལྗོངས་ལྷ་སྡེ་མི་སྡེ་ཡོངས་བཅས་ནས་མ་གྲོས་ལྷག་བསམ་གཅིག་མཐུན་གྱིས་ཕྲན་ཡོངས་འཛིན་ཆེ་བ་ཤར་ཆོས་གླིང་སྤྲུལ་སྐུ་ཐུབ་བསྟན་ལུང་རྟོགས་རྣམ་རྒྱལ་འཕྲིན་ལས་དང་། ཡོངས་འཛིན་ཆུང་བ་ཁྲི་བྱང་སྤྲུལ་སྐུ་བློ་བཟང་ཡེ་ཤེས་བསྟན་འཛིན་རྒྱ་མཚོ་གཉིས་ལ་ལྷ་རིག་དང་། རིན་ཆེན་གཉིས་པའི་རྟེན་བཅས་ཇི་ལྟར་བསྐུལ་མ་མཛད་པ་བཞིན།

ཕྲན་གཉིས་ནས་ཀྱང་སྨྲོ་བ་མཆོག་ཏུ་བདེགས་ཏེ་དད་གུས་ལྷག་བསམ་རྩེ་གཅིག་པའི་སྒོ་ནས་གསོལ་བ་བཏབ་པ་དེ་དེ་བཞིན་དུ་འགྲུབ་པར་གྱུར་ཅིག། ༎

Annotations to *Long-life Prayer for His Holiness the Dalai Lama*

Translation Hint ①

Pages 541 & 612, Line 4

Recall that the abbreviation of repetitious phrases can be indicated with a simple symbol such as X (see བར་དོ་འཕྲང་སྒྲོལ་ note 6).

Translation Hint ②

Pages 542 & 613, Line 10

Subtle differences in syntax can be critical in understanding how to read a sentence. Here, for example, one can see the difference between the author having written བདེ་སྟོང་ཉམས་བརྒྱར་རོལ་པའི་རྗེད་འཛེ་པས། vs. བདེ་སྟོང་ཉམས་བརྒྱར་རོལ་པའི་རྗེད་འཛེ་ཡིས།. In the former case, འཛེ་ functions as a verb in what appears to be a reason clause ("because of being mesmerized [by] a playful display in hundreds of states of bliss and emptiness"). In the latter case, however—as it reads here—འཛེ་ is functioning as a verbal adjective in an instrumental phrase attached to the verb གྲོགས་མཛད་.

Translation Hint ③

Pages 543 & 614, Line 10

The locative-absolute construction applies to all three verbs.

Translation Hint ④

Page 544, Line 14; Page 615, Line 16

The first major phrase in this sentence—a reason clause—ends at this point with ཆེད་ ("in order that," "for the sake of").

⑤ Sections of the Tibetan Government

Page 544, Line 16; Page 615, Line 19

The pre-1959 Tibetan government (known as the "Ganden Potrang Government") was composed of a hierarchy of lay and monastic officials forming an extensive secretariat.

WHAT TO REMEMBER

The structure of the Tibetan government was a hierarchy with several divisions:

ད་ལའི་བླ་མ་	*Dalai Lama*: The head of the government; a reincarnation lineage
རྒྱལ་ཚབ་	*Regent*: An appointed position of someone who ruled in the stead of the Dalai Lama when the latter had passed away or was still a minor
བློན་ཆེན་	*Prime Minister*: Position immediately subordinate to the Dalai Lama
སྤྱི་ཁྱབ་མཁན་པོ་	*Lord Chamberlain*: The senior monastic official in the government; a third-rank official who was in charge of the monasteries in general and of the Potala Palace, its staff, and official parks in particular
ཡིག་ཚང་	*Chancellery*: Council that oversaw monastic affairs subordinate to the Lord Chamberlain, consisting of four Secretaries (*drung yig chen po*) who were fourth-rank (*rim bzhi*) officials
བཀའ་ཤག་	*Kashag*, or *Council of Ministers*: A council of senior ministers (third rank)—three lay and one monastic—who held the title of Shapé (*zhabs pad*); they were the main administrative body of the government
རྩི་ཁང་	*Finance Ministry*: Headed by four Finance Ministers (*rtsi dpon*), it was responsible for governmental accounting and taxation of estates
སྤྱི་ཚོགས་/ཚོགས་འདུ་	*National Assembly*: An ad hoc general assembly—co-chaired by the Chancellery and Finance Ministers—of abbots (*mkhan po*) and former abbots (*mkhan zur*) of the three great monasteries (*gdan sa gsum*) of the Lhasa Valley, lay and monastic officials in Lhasa, representatives of major incarnation lineages and other monasteries, the Regent of Ganden (*dga' ldan khri pa*), captains (*ru dpon*) and lieutenants (*brgya dpon*) of the army, taxation officers (*tsho pa*), and clerks (*drung gtogs*)
རྩེ་ཤོད་	*secretariat*: a general term for monastic and lay government officials

Translation of the *Long-Life Prayer for His Holiness the Dalai Lama*

The Melodious Song for the Attainment of Immortality, A Petition of Supplication,
Invoking the Compasssion of the Ocean of the Three Supreme Ones,
in order that the Crown Jewel of [Both] Mundane Existence and Pacification,
His Holiness, [Supreme] Refuge and Protector, Lord of Conquerors,
Supremely Precious All-knowing and All-seeing One May Have a Long Life
As The Protector of Transmigrators, and [in order that]
the Goals [of His] Aspirations [like] Great Waves
Will Be Accomplished.

(Homage to His Supreme Presence!)

Oṃ svastī!

To the assembly of kind gurus, [both] actually [present] and of the lineage,
Wish-fulfilling jewels, [who are] the source of virtue and goodness in
mundane existence and pacification,
[Who embody] the three secrets [of body, speech, and mind] of countless
conquerors, without exception,
In the dance of illusions [i.e., the world], [and] who appear in whatever
[ways are necessary] to tame whichever trainees,

[To you,] as we petition with strong devotion,
[Please] bless the life of the Protector of the Land of Snows, Tenzin Gyatso,
That [it] will remain invulnerable and steadfast for a hundred eons, and
That the aims of [His] aspirations will be spontaneously accomplished!

To all assembled gods and tutelary deities who appear
In countless maṇḍalas of residences and residents,

[Which are merely] illusory clouds of exalted wisdom and great bliss, free from dust [and]
Which have entered into [a state of] equality with the utterly clear expanse of the dharmadhātu,

[To you,] as we petition with strong devotion,
[Please] bless the life of the Protector of the Land of Snows, Tenzin Gyatso,
That [it] will remain invulnerable and steadfast for a hundred eons, and
That the aims of [His] aspirations will be spontaneously accomplished!

To all the conquerors [throughout] the three times [and in] countless [realms],
Gods of gods, possessors of the ten powers, [and] bringing benefit [for all]
By means of the appearances of abandonment, realization, good qualities, [and] spontaneously and perfect enlightened activities
That are constantly at play in the ocean of the realms of transmigration,

[To you,] as we petition with strong devotion,
[Please] bless the life of the Protector of the Land of Snows, Tenzin Gyatso,
That [it] will remain invulnerable and steadfast for a hundred eons, and
That the aims of [His] aspirations will be spontaneously accomplished!

To the collection of the holy Dharma of the three vehicles
[With] the gloriousness of [its] uncontaminated, unshakable, excellent, [and] virtuous,
Treasury of jewels of thorough purification, supreme pacification,
And [bestowing] definite liberation from the three [realms of the] mundane world by whatsoever [means],

[To you,] as we petition with strong devotion,
[Please] bless the life of the Protector of the Land of Snows, Tenzin Gyatso,
That [it] will remain invulnerable and steadfast for a hundred eons, and
That the aims of [His] aspirations will be spontaneously accomplished!

To the entire Saṅgha of āryas—knowing and liberated—
[Those who] remain inseparable from the vajra-city of liberation,
Endowed with the exalted wisdom that directly comprehends the ultimate truth
[And] who are heroic in vanquishing the machinery of mundane existence,

[To you,] as we petition with strong devotion,
[Please] bless the life of the Protector of the Land of Snows, Tenzin Gyatso,
That [it] will remain invulnerable and steadfast for a hundred eons, and
That the aims of [His] aspirations will be spontaneously accomplished!

To the assembly of *vira*s and *ḍākinī*s of the three realms,
Who assist *sādhaka*s [i.e., "those who strive to accomplish"] of the excellent path of yoga,
By means of a mesmerizing display of delighting in hundreds of states of bliss and emptiness
In the [twenty-four] places, [thirty-two] countries, and [eight] charnel grounds, and realms of sky-traveling adepts (*khecarī*),

[To you,] as we petition with strong devotion,
[Please] bless the life of the Protector of the Land of Snows, Tenzin Gyatso,
That [it] will remain invulnerable and steadfast for a hundred eons, and
That the aims of [His] aspirations will be spontaneously accomplished!

To the ocean of protector-deities, endowed with the eye of wisdom,
Possessed of the power and skill of protecting the teachings and [those who] hold the teachings,
Having had the knotted seal that signifies the word of Vajradhara
Inseparably placed upon [their] matted crowns,

[To you,] as we petition with strong devotion,
[Please] bless the life of the Protector of the Land of Snows, Tenzin Gyatso,

That [it] will remain invulnerable and steadfast for a hundred eons, and
That the aims of [His] aspirations will be spontaneously accomplished!

Thus, by the power of [my] respectful prayer from [the depths of] my heart [and with] great strength,
To the supreme unfailing refuges,
O sole protector of transmigrators of the Realm of Snow [Tibet]—myself and others—
Who are afflicted with the pangs of the unbearable degenerate era (*kaliyuga*),

O Supreme Ngawang Losang Tenzin Gyatso,
With [your] three secrets indestructible, unchanging, and never declining,
May [you] remain steadfast and immovable for oceans of eons
Upon the utterly indestructible vajra-heart throne.

Possessing the jewel-like essence of benefitting all [with] enlightened activities
In great waves while bearing on [his] shoulders, [with] fortitude,
The burden of the activities of all limitless conquerors,
May [these actions] be spontaneously accomplished in accordance with [his] aspirations.

By the power of that, may the door to the sky of the good fortune of the era of perfection (*kṛtayuga*)
Be eternally opened to the springtime during which the embodied [may] recover from weariness, and
May the signs of virtue that [indicate that] the teachings of the Subduer have spread throughout all directions and times
Extend to the peak of saṃsāra and nirvāṇa.

May the stream of elixir of the blessings of Padmapāṇi
Continuously ripen as strength of heart [in] myself and others, and
Having served [him] with the offering of [our own] attainments in
accordance with [his] words,
May [we] arrive at the far [shore] of the ocean of supreme practices of
Samantabhadra.

By the blessings of the conquerors together with [their] marvelous
children, and
The incontrovertible truth of dependent arising, and
The power of my pure exceptional attitude,
May all the aims of [my] prayers be easily and quickly accomplished.

[Regarding] this [prayer], moreover, in order that the pair of feet of the Guide of the entirety of transmigrators—myself and others, including the gods—the Incomparable One, His Holiness, Supreme Protector, Powerful Conqueror, All-seeing and All-knowing, Venerable, Ngawang Losang Tenzin Gyatso, Lord of the Three Worlds, Devotee of the Incomparable One, Glorious One, Beneficient One, Supreme One, remain stable until the end of existence, and that [his] many aspirations without exception—[like] great waves—may be spontaneously accomplished, [this] petition of true words invoking the oceanic compassion of the infallible Three Jewels has been proclaimed. And, in accordance with the supplication that was made, together with a [gift of] support [for the request] of an ornate silk scarf (*kha btags*) and a monetary offering, to the two of us (*phran*)—the Senior Tutor [to His Holiness, the Dalai Lama], Eastern Dharma [Successor to the Throne of Ganden], Ling Tulku, Tupten Lungtok Namgyel Trinlé, and the Junior Tutor [to His Holiness, the Dalai Lama], Trijang Tulku, Losang Yeshe Tenzin Gyatso—by the three great seats [of learning] Drepung, Sera, and Ganden, and the Tibetan Cabinet ("Kashak"), secretariat (*rtse shod*) represented by the Secretary and Finance Minister, [lesser] orders [of officials] (*drung rigs*), and the General Assembly of monks and lay people, together with the entirety of groups of monks and groups of humans, without any disagreement (*ma gros*) and being of one thought, [saying] "[we] need [you to] newly compose a [prayer] such as this that is unrestrained by [formal] poetic ornamentation."

From the two of us, as well, [this] is offered up as a supreme expression [of all], and from the single-pointed special intention of faith and respect, may that [prayer] be accomplished accordingly!

Appendix 1: Yangjen Gaway Lodrö's *Grammar Verse* and Summary

As noted in the preface (*xii*), a part of education in literary Tibetan involves developing familiarity with basic rules of spelling and euphony, knowledge of which can provide a means of detecting typographical errors and omissions. To that end, this section of the *Reader* contains an annotated translation and summary of an eighteenth-century mnemonic poem about grammar written by the same author of the *Lamp Illuminating the Three Bodies*. It is short and useful enough that memorization is recommended.

ཡི་གེའི་སྦྱོར་སྦྱང་ཉེར་མཁོ་རབ་གསལ་མེ་ལོང་།

The Mirror Clarifying the Important Points of the Application of Letters

༄༅།། ན་མོ་གུ་རུ་བྷེ།

Homage to the Guru!

རྒྱལ་ཀུན་ཡབ་གཅིག་མཁྱེན་པའི་གཏེར། །ངག་དབང་ལྷ་མོ་དབྱངས་ཅན་མ། །
བདག་སྙིང་པདྨའི་དབུས་བཞུགས་ཏེ། །ཐོགས་མེད་སྨྲ་བའི་སྤོབས་པ་སྩོལ། །

O Goddess Sarasvatī, Powerful of Speech,
Treasury of the Knowledge that is the Sole Father of all the Conquerors,
Come, abide in the center of the lotus at my heart, and
Bestow upon me the eloquence of unobstructed speech!

དབྱངས་ཡིག་ཨི་ཨུ་ཨེ་ཨོ་བཞི། །གསལ་བྱེད་ཀ་སོགས་སུམ་ཅུ་ཡིན། །

The four vowels are *i*, *u*, *e*, and *o*; the thirty consonants are *ka* and so forth.

ག་ང་ད་ན་བ་མ་འ། །ར་ལ་ས་རྣམས་རྗེས་འཇུག་བཅུ། །ད་དང་ས་གཉིས་ཡང་འཇུག་གོ། གདབམའ་སྔོན་འཇུག །

The ten suffixes are *ka*, *nga*, *da*, *na*, *ba*, *ma*, *'a*, *ra*, *la*, and *sa*. *Da* and *sa* are the two secondary suffixes. The [five] prefixes are *ga*, *da*, *ba*, *ma*, and *'a*.

གོ་ངོ་དོ་ནོ་བོ་མོ་འོ། །རོ་ལོ་སོ་རྣམས་རྫོགས་ཚིག་སྟེ། །
སློར་སྡུད་ཟླ་སྡུད་ཅེས་ཀྱང་བྱ། །རྗེས་འཇུག་རང་འདྲའི་མཐའ་ལ་སྦྱར། །
The [ten] terminating particles are *go*, *ngo*, *do*, *no*, *bo*, *mo*, *'o*, *ro*, *lo*, and *so*. They are also called "final particles" and "complementing particles." They are affixed to the end of their similar suffix particles.

ན་ར་ལ་གསུམ་རྗེས་སུ་ནི། །ད་དྲག་ཡོད་ཚེ་ཏོ་ཞེས་སྦྱར། །
When, at the end of the three letters *na*, *ra*, and *la*, there is an elided *da*, it takes [the terminating particle] *to*.

སུ་རུ་ར་དང་དུ་ཏུ་ན། །ལ་དོན་རྣམ་པ་དྲུག་ཡིན་ཏེ། །
རྣམ་དབྱེ་གཉིས་པ་བཞི་པ་དང་། །བདུན་པ་དེ་ཉིད་དུས་ལ་འཇུག །
Su, *ru*, *ra*, *du*, *tu*, and *na* are the six types [of particles with the same] meaning as *la*. At the time of [declining words in] the second, fourth, and seventh [case], the case-marking particles are affixed.

ས་སུ་ག་བ་ད་དྲག་ཏུ། །ང་ད་ན་མ་ར་ལ་དུ། །
འ་དང་མཐའ་རྟེན་མེད་པའི་མཐར། །རུ་དང་ར་གཉིས་ཅི་རིགས་སྦྱར། །
After [the suffix] *sa* [is] *su*; after [the suffixes] *ga*, *ba*, and *da* [is] *tu*. [After] *nga*, *da*, *na*, *ma*, *ra*, and *la* [is] *du*; [after] *'a* and at the end of [words] lacking a final consonant, *ru* or *ra* is affixed as is appropriate.

གི་ཀྱི་གྱི་འི་ཡི་ལྔ་པོ། །རྣམ་དབྱེ་དྲུག་པ་འབྲེལ་སྒྲ་སྟེ། །
ད་བ་ས་ཀྱི་ག་ང་གི །ན་མ་ར་ལའི་རྗེས་སུ་གྱི། །
འ་དང་མཐའ་རྟེན་མེད་མཐར་འི། །རྐང་པ་སྐོང་ཚེ་ཡི་འཐོབ་བོ། །
The five, *gi*, *kyi*, *gyi*, *'i*, and *yi*, are the connective particles of the sixth case. Following *da*, *ba*, and *sa* [use] *kyi*; after *ga* and *nga* [use] *gi*. After *na*, *ma*, *ra*, and *la*, use *gyi*; [in place of] *'a* or where there is no final consonant at the end [use] *'i*. When it is neccessary to fill a line of verse, it takes *yi*.

གི་ཀྱི་སོགས་མཐར་ས་སྦྱར་ཆེ། །རྣམ་དབྱེ་གསུམ་པ་བྱེད་པའི་སྒྲོ། །
When [these same particles] *gi*, *kyi*, etc., are affixed with a *sa* suffix, they form the instrumental particles of the third case.

ཀྱང་ཡང་འང་གསུམ་རྒྱན་སྡུད་དེ། །ག་ད་བ་སའི་རྗེས་སུ་ཀྱང་། །
ང་ན་མ་འ་ར་ལ་ཡང་། །མཐའ་རྟེན་མེད་མཐར་འང་དང་ཡང་། །
Kyang, *yang*, and *'ang* are the three ornamental conjunctive particles. Following *ga*, *da*, *ba*, and *sa* suffixes, use *kyang*; following *nga*, *na*, *ma*, *'a*, *ra*, and *la*, use *yang*. At the end of words lacking a final consonant, *'ang* or *yang* is used.

དེ་ཏེ་སྟེ་གསུམ་ལྷག་བཅས་ཏེ། །ད་དེ་ན་ར་ལ་ས་ཏེ། །
ག་ང་བ་མ་འ་རྣམས་དང་། །མཐའ་རྟེན་མེད་མཐར་ས་སྟེ་འཐོབ། །
De, *te*, and *ste* are the three continuative [or semifinal] particles. After *da*, use *de*; after *na*, *ra*, *la*, and *sa*, use *te*. After *ga*, *nga*, *ba*, *ma*, *'a*, and words lacking a final consonant at the end, use *ste*.

གམ་ངམ་དམ་ནམ་བམ་མམ་འམ། །རམ་ལམ་སམ་རྣམས་འབྱེད་སྡུད་སྒྲ། །
རྗེས་འཇུག་རང་འདྲའི་མཐའ་ལ་སྦྱར། །ད་དྲག་ཅན་མཐར་ཏམ་སྦྱར་རོ། །
Gam, *ngam*, *dam*, *nam*, *bam*, *mam*, *'am*, *ram*, *lam*, and *sam* are the disjunctive particles. They are affixed at the end of their similar suffixes. In the case of words ending in an elided *da*, affix *tam*.

ནས་དང་ལས་གཉིས་འབྱུང་ཁུངས་དང་། །དགར་དང་སྡུད་པ་ལ་ཡང་འཇུག །
The two particles *nas* and *las* are placed to indicate the ablative case as well as the singling out of particulars and inclusion [in a sequence, for example].

ཀྱེ་དང་ཀྭ་ཡེ་འབོད་སྒྲ་སྟེ། །ཕལ་ཆེར་མིང་གི་ཐོག་མར་སྦྱོར། །
Kye and *kwa-ye* are vocative particles. Mostly, they are affixed prior to names.

ནི་སྒྲ་དགར་དང་བརྣན་པའོ། །
The particle *ni* [is used] to single something out or to mark a topic.

གང་སུ་ཅི་ཇི་སྤྱི་སྒྲ་སྟེ། །དཔེ་དང་གཞན་ལ་ཇི་སྦྱོར་ཞིང་། །
དོན་ལ་ཅི་དང་གང་ཟག་ལ། །སུ་འཐོབ་གང་ནི་ཀུན་ལ་སྦྱར། །

Gang, *su*, *ci*, and *ji* are generic terms. *Ji* is affixed to exemplars and others, *ci* is used for meanings, and persons take *su*. *Gang* is applied to all.

པ་དང་ཅན་ལྡན་བདག་པོའི་སྒྲ། །ག་ད་བ་ས་ན་མ་པ། །ང་འ་ར་ལ་མཐའ་མེད་པ། །བདག་པོའི་སྒྲ་ལ་པ་ཉིད་དོ། །

Pa, *can*, and *ldan* are particles [forming] possessive nouns. For words [ending in] *ga*, *da*, *ba*, *sa*, *na*, *ma*, *pa*, *nga*, *'a*, *ra*, *la*, and lacking a final consonant, [use] *pa* for possessive nouns.

མ་མི་མིན་མེད་དགག་པའི་སྒྲ། །མ་མི་གཉིས་ནི་ཐོག་མ་དང་། །མིན་མེད་གཉིས་པོ་རྗེས་ལ་སྦྱར། །

Ma, *mi*, *min*, and *med* are negation particles. Both *ma* and *mi* precede [what they modify,] and *min* and *med* are affixed after.

ཚིག་འཕྲད་ཅིང་ལ་སོགས་པ་ནི། །ག་ད་བ་དང་ད་དྲག་མཐར། །ཅིང་ཅེས་ཅེ་འོ་ཅེ་ན་ཅིག ང་ན་མ་འ་ར་ལ་དང་། །
རྗེས་འཇུག་མེད་པའི་མིང་མཐའ་རུ། །ཞིང་ཞེས་ཞེ་འོ་ཞེ་ན་ཞིག ས་མཐར་དམིགས་བསལ་ཞེས་མ་གདོགས།
(ཤེས་སྦྱར་ན་བློའི་ཤེས་པར་འཁྲུལ་བ་འབྱུང་བས་མི་བྱ་གསུང་།) །ཤིང་ཤིག་ཤེ་འོ་ཤེ་ན་འཐོབ།

Regarding phrase [terminators] such as *cing* and so forth: after *ga*, *da*, *ba*, and elided *da*, use *cing*, *ces*, *ce 'o*, *ce na*, and *cig*; after *nga*, *na*, *ma*, *'a*, *ra*, *la*, and words lacking a final consonant at the end, use *zhing*, *zhes*, *zhe 'o*, *zhe na*, and *zhig*. *Sa* at the end is considered an exception and is not included [among those]. (If one applied *shes*, then since it could be confused for the word *shes* [that refers to a type] of awareness, it is said to not be used.) Instead, it takes *shing*, *shig*, *she 'o*, and *she na*.

ཁ་ཅིག་ལྷན་ཅིག་ཐབས་ཅིག་དང་། །ལན་ཅིག་སོགས་ཀྱི་ཅིག་སྒྲ་དེ། །
མིང་གི་ཆ་ཤས་ཡིན་པས་ན། །ཚིག་འཕྲད་གྲངས་སུ་མ་ནོར་གཅེས། །

Although the syllable *cig*—which is used in words like "someone" (*kha cig*), "simultaneous" (*lhan cig*), "together" (*thabs cig*), "one time" (*lan cig*), and so forth—is part of [other] words, it is said there is no fault in including it in the enumeration of phrase [terminators].

ཚིགས་བཅད་རྐང་བའི་མཐའ་ལ་ནི། །ཉིས་ཤད་ངེས་པར་འཐོབ་པ་ཡིན། །ག་མཐར་ཚིག་ཤད་ང་ཡི་མཐར། །
ཤད་ཀྱི་གོང་དུ་ཕྱི་ཚེག་དགོས། (ང་ཡིག་གི་རྐང་པ་ཤད་དང་མི་འདྲེ་བའི་ཆེད་ཡིན།)

At the end of a line of verse, two *shad* markers are carried over. After a *ga*, only one *shad* [is used]; after a *nga*, a final *tsheg* is needed in front of the *shad*. (It is for the sake of distinguishing lines that [end in] the letter *nga* from the *shad* [that follows it].)

ཚིགས་ལྷུགས་ལ་ནི་རྫོགས་ཚིག་མཐར། །ཉིས་ཤད་རྣམ་གྲངས་སོ་སོ་དང་། །དོན་ཚན་ཕལ་ཆེར་མཐའ་དང་ནི། །
བོད་པའི་སྐབས་ལའང་ཚེག་ཤད་བྱ། །སྡེ་ཚན་ཆེན་མོ་རྫོགས་པ་དང་། །ལེའུའི་མཚམས་སུ་བཞི་ཤད་འཐོབ། །

In prose, a terminating particle [is placed] at the end. A double *shad* [is placed] [after] individual lists and at the end of most topic sections; in the context of vocatives, however, use a single *shad*. The completion of major sections and at chapter boundaries take four *shads*.

རྐང་པ་སྐོང་དང་མི་སྐོང་ལས། །འོ་འུ་འམ་གྱི་ཚིག་པར་ཡང་། །འཐོབ་ཚུལ་སྐབས་དང་སྦྱར་བར་བྱ། །
On such occasions [arising] out of [the need] to fill or shorten a line of verse, in accordance with the methods of application [previously described], one should affix the particles *'o*, *'u*, and *'am*.

དེ་ལྟར་རྗེས་འཇུག་དབང་གིས་ནི། །རྣམ་དབྱེ་ཚིག་འཕྲད་མི་འདྲ་བའི། །ཁྱད་པར་ཞིབ་ཏུ་ཤེས་པར་བྱ། །
Thus, one should know in detail, the particularities of the different cases and [their] particles [determined] through the force of [their] suffixes.

ཚིག་གི་འདབ་མས་མ་བསྒྲིབས་པའི། །གནད་བསྡུས་འབྲས་བུ་གཡུར་ཟ་བ། །
བློ་གསལ་དོན་གཉེར་དགའ་སྟོན་དུ། །དབྱངས་ཅན་དགའ་བའི་བློ་གྲོས་སྤེལ། །མངྒ་ལཾ།།
[This text] has been composed by Yangjen Gaway Lodrö as a festival for [those] seeking meaning with a clear mind, filling [them] with the fruits of the concise points unobstructed by foliage. May good fortune abound.

Summary

The first (nominative; ངོ་བོ་ཙམ་བརྗོད་པ་) case is left unmarked or is occasionally marked by ནི་ to indicate the subject or object of a verb or topic. The seven particles (སུ་, རུ་, ར་, ཏུ་, དུ་, ན་, and ལ་) that are used to indicate the second (accusative; ལས་སུ་བྱ་བའི་སྒྲ་), fourth (dative; དགོས་ཆེད་ཀྱི་སྒྲ་), and seventh (locative; རྟེན་གནས་ཀྱི་སྒྲ་) cases are deployed as follows:

- སུ་ — after ས་
- རུ་ and ར་ — added to suffixless syllables, or after/replacing the འ་ suffix
- ཏུ་ — after ག་, བ་, or secondary ད་
- དུ་ — after ང་, ད་, ན་, མ་, ར་, or ལ་
- ན་ — used particularly for the seventh (locative) case
- ལ་ — universally applicative

The five particles used to indicate the sixth (genitive; འབྲེལ་སྒྲ་) case are:

- གི་ — after ག་ or ང་
- ཀྱི་ — after ད་, བ་, or ས་
- གྱི་ — after ན་, མ་, ར་, or ལ་
- འི་ — instead of འ་ or appended to syllables with no suffix
- ཡི་ — to fill out verse

The five particles used to indicate the third (instrumental; བྱེད་སྒྲ་) case are likewise:

- གིས་ — after ག་ or ང་
- ཀྱིས་ — after ད་, བ་, or ས་
- གྱིས་ — after ན་, མ་, ར་, or ལ་
- ས་ — instead of འ་ or appended to syllables with no suffix
- ཡིས་ — to fill out verse

The two particles used to indicate the fifth (ablative; འབྱུང་ཁུངས་ཀྱི་སྒྲ་) case are ལས་ and ནས་, while the eighth (vocative; བོད་སྒྲ་) case is occasionally left unmarked (i.e., implied by context) or is indicated by expressions such as ཀྱེ་ or ཀྭ་ཡེ་.

Appendix 2: Index to Grammatical Annotations to the Texts

Part A. Running List of Annotations by Text

Annotations to Selection 1: *The Heart Sūtra*

1. Introduction to a Canonical Text
2. Transliteration of Sanskrit in Tibetan Letters
3. Opening Homage in a Canonical Text
4. Formulaic Opening to a Sūtra
5. Sanskrit Proper Names
6. Syntactic Particle དང་ and Postpositional Phrases
7. Recognizing Class IV Verbs
8. Complements and Qualifiers
9. Sanskrit Word *evaṃ* and the Tibetan འདི་སྐད་[ཅེས་] and དེ་སྐད་[ཅེས་]
10. Relative and Correlative Pronouns
11. Auxiliary Verbs: Optative Construction
12. The Syntactic Particles ཀྱང་, etc., Eliding Case Markers
13. Verbal Participles: Past Passive Participles
14. Omitted Verbs
15. The ་་་ནས་་་་བར་དུ་ ("From ... Up To ...") Construction
16. Distributed Verbs within a Single Sentence
17. Types of Clause Connectives
18. Translation Hint
19. Auxiliary Verbs: Causative Construction—བྱེད་, མཛད་, and བགྱིད་
20. The Alternate Reason Clause Marker –ས་ན་
21. Sanskrit Word *sādhu* and the Tibetan ལེགས་སོ་[ཞེས་བྱ་བ་]
22. Tibetan Modular Sentence Structures
23. Translation Hint

Annotations to Selection 2: Jñānamitra's *Explanation of the Heart Sūtra*

1. Opening of a Canonical Commentary
2. Case Marker ཀྱི་ as Syntactic Particle
3. Translation Hint
4. Formulaic Commentarial Structures
5. Closing Quotation Marker ཞེས་[བྱ་བ་]
6. Discrete Lists and the Particle སོགས་
7. Translation Hint: Canonical Text Titles
8. Commentarial Style: Rhetorical Questions
9. Locative Absolute
10. First-Person Statements
11. Agglutinative Sixth Case as a Syntactic Particle
12. Agent Nouns from Verbs
13. Translation Hint
14. Commentarial Style: Glossing
15. Run-on Sentences without Punctuation
16. Commentarial Style: Paraphrased Restatement
17. The Verb དམིགས་
18. Translation Hint
19. Translation Hint
20. Technical Terms of Grammar
21. Auxiliary Verbs: Exhortative
22. Auxiliary Verbs: Subjunctive
23. Translation Hint
24. Verbal Participles: Gerundives
25. Omitted Verb of Predication, ཡིན་
26. The Either-Or Construction
27. Translation Hint
28. Closing Quotation Marker སྙམ་[པ་/དུ་]
29. Translation Hint

30. Multiple Verbal Modifiers
31. Translation Hint
32. Translation Hint
33. Differences between Root Texts and Commentaries
34. Translation Hint
35. Commentarial Syntax: Use of ཀྱི་, etc., to Mark Apposition
36. Use of ནི་ to Disambiguate Grammar
37. The Negation of Verbal Collocations and the Verb ཟ་

Annotations to Selection 3:
The Sūtra Called "The Wise and the Foolish"

1. Translation Hint
2. Idiomatic Expressions
3. Semimodal Expressions with Passive Participles
4. The Alternate Gerund Marker ལས་
5. Tibetan Numbers: Cumulative vs. Adjectival
6. The Vocative in Supplications
7. Conditional Marker ན་
8. Translation Hint
9. Translation Hint
10. Semimodal Expressions in the Active Voice
11. Simple Infinitives: Purposives
12. The Tibetan འདི་སྐད་དུ་
13. Translation Hint
14. Auxiliary Verbs: The Precative Construction
15. Translation Divergences
16. Auxiliary Verbs: Nonreflexive Causative
17. Auxiliary Verbs: Imperfective
18. Simple Infinitives: Indirect Statements
19. Non-case Usage of the Particle ཀྱིས་ as a Verbal Emphatic
20. Translation Hint

21. Verbal Collocations and Modifiability
22. Translation Hint
23. Auxiliary Verbs: Exhortative (Honorific)
24. Translation Hint
25. Translation Hint
26. Auxiliary Verbs: Imperative
27. Auxiliary Verbs: Past Causative

Annotations to Selection 4: Tsongkhapa's
Three Principal Aspects of the Path

1. Reading Verse (General Features)
2. Translation Hint
3. Translation Hint
4. Auxiliary Verbs: First Person Emphatic Future
5. Translation Hint
6. -འི་ Case Marker as Syntactic Particle
7. Verb Tense in Classical Tibetan: A Discussion
8. Descriptive Verbs
9. The Verb ལགས་ and Indirect Statements Conveying Meaning
10. Translation Hint
11. Auxiliary Verbs: Honorific Imperative
12. Translation Hint
13. Translation Hint
14. Translation Hint
15. Translation Hint
16. Ubiquitous Technical Terms of Buddhist Epistemology
17. Translation Hint

Annotations to Selection 5:
Paṇchen Sönam Drakpa's *New Red Annals* (selection)

1. Reading Historical Narrative (General Features)
2. Enumerated Phenomena
3. Recognizing Proper Names
4. Tibetan Dates and Calendrical System
5. Annotations and Script Size
6. The Use of Sanskrit Letters as Tibetan Shorthand
7. Sanskrit Words in Tibetan Script
8. Tibetan Contractions
9. Chinese Words in Tibetan
10. Translation Hint: Nested Sentences
11. Tibetan Numbers: Set Multipliers
12. The Postpositional Phrase ཡན་ཆད་
13. Translation Hint: Numeric Expressions
14. Translation Hint: Chinese Words in Tibetan
15. The Verb གྲགས་ Marking Evidentiality
16. Translation Hint: Abbreviated Lists of Names
17. Auxiliary Verbs: The Concessive Verb མོད་
18. The Syllable ཉིད་ as Emphatic Verbal Suffix
19. The Syllable སྟེ་ as an Appositional Marker
20. Auxiliary Verbs: The Perfective Construction
21. Indirect Constructions with ཡོད་

Annotations to Selection 6: Purbujok's
"Introductory Path of Reasoning"

1. Reading Monastic Textbooks (General Features)
2. Text Titles
3. Initial Verse of Expression of Worship
4. Omitted Verbs of Existence: ཡོད་

Annotations to Selection 7: Jampel Sampel's
Presentation of Awarenesses and Knowers

7. Translation Hint
8. Verbal Collocations with བྱེད་
9. Translation Hint
10. Translation Hint: Text Titles as Agents
11. Verbal Adjectives vs. Clause-Connective Constructions
12. The Completed Action Auxiliary Verb ཟིན་
13. Canonical Text Titles
14. The Non-case Syntactic Particle ལ་
15. Canonical Quotations
16. Translation Hint
17. Translation Hint
18. Distributed Grammar—Multiple Sentences in Clauses
19. The Syllable ཉིད་ as Restrictive Verbal Suffix
20. Translation Hint
21. Translation Hint
22. Translation Hint
23. The Word དུས་ as a Verbal Suffix
24. Translation Hint
25. Hierarchy of the Syntactic Particles ཅིང་/ཞིང་ and དང་
26. Translation Hint: Recognizing Requisite Grammar
27. The Syllable ཚེ་ as a Verbal Suffix
28. Tibetan Numbers: Abbreviations
29. Compressed Grammar in Philosophical Verse
30. The Performative Construction

Annotations to Selection 8: Könchok Jikmé Wangpo's *Precious Garland: A Presentation of Tenets*

1. Reading Original Compositions (General Features)
2. Poetic Metaphor
3. Translation Hint
4. The Particle ས་ Following Verbs

5. Topical Outlines
6. Multiple Verbs in a Clause Construction
7. Identifying Text Titles and Citations
8. Abbreviations of Proper Names
9. Translation Hint: Contextual Meanings
10. Translation Hint: Buddhist Technical Terminology
11. Lists and the Syntactic Particle དང་
12. Translation Hint: Non-Buddhist Text Quotations
13. Translation Hint
14. Specifically and Generally Characterized Phenomena
15. Translation Hint
16. Non-Adverbial Qualifiers
17. Locative Absolute
18. Translation Hint
19. Lists and the Particle སོགས་
20. Auxiliary Verbs: The Perfective Construction
21. Tibetan Numbers: Reduplication
22. Rhetorical Questions with ནམ་ etc.
23. Translation Hint
24. Tibetan Numbers: Combinations of Types
25. The Use of བར་དུ་ to Designate a Duration of Time
26. Non-case Use of གྱིས་ etc., to Mark Adverbial Qualifiers
27. The Honorific Precative Construction with མཛོད་
28. Translation Hint: Adverbial Qualifiers
29. Translation Hint
30. Translation Hint: Time
31. Translation Hint
32. Translation Hint
33. The Adverbial Phrase Marker ཕྱིན་ (and ཕྱིན་ཆད་)
34. Translation Hint: Semantic Range of མཚན་ཉིད་(པ་)
35. The Nominalization of Verbs and Sentences
36. The Verb གདོགས་ as Phrase Marker

37. Translation Hint
38. Idiosyncratic Constructions with the Verb ལྟོས་
39. The Lexical Suffix ཅན་ as Frozen Verb
40. Translation Hint: Three Modes of a Correct Logical Sign
41. Translation Hint
42. The Numeric Prefix ཕ་
43. Translation Hint
44. The Adverbial Phrase Marker ཚོད་ལ་
45. The Use of སྒྲ་ to Indicate a Term marked for Discussion
46. ཡང་ as a Conjunctive and Disjunctive Particle
47. Translation Hint

Annotations to Selection 9: Yangjen Gaway Lodrö's
Lamp Illuminating the Presentation of the Three Bodies that are the Bases [of Purification]

1. Sanskrit Homages
2. Translation Hint
3. Sanskrit Abbreviations
4. Translation Hint
5. Run-on Sentences and Authorial Style
6. The Word རང་བཞིན་
7. Translation Hint
8. Auxiliary Verbs: Deontic Construction
9. The ་་་ནས་་་བར་དུ་ ("From ... Up To ...") Construction
10. The Use of བར་དུ་ to Designate an Intermediate Duration
11. Translation Hint
12. Translation Hint
13. Future Active Participles
14. Auxiliary Verbs: Completed Action Verb ཚར་
15. Reduplication of Adjectives
16. Translation Hint

17. Translation Hint
18. Translation Hint
19. Major Texts Commonly Cited
20. Idiomatic Expressions
21. Recognizing Paraphrases
22. Translation Hint
23. Locating Canonical Quotations
24. Translation Hint
25. Translation Hint
26. Numerical Expressions: Half-numbers
27. Translation Hint
28. Translation Hint
29. Auxiliary Verbs: Causative Constructions and Negated Past-Tense Verbs
30. Idiosyncratic Usage Paradigms of the Verb འགྲེས་

Annotations to Selection 10: The Fourth Paṇchen Lama's
Prayer for Release from the Dangerous Bardo

1. Simple Infinitives: External Action
2. The Verbal Suffixes ཀ་/ཀོ་/ཁ་/ག་
3. Recognizing Scriptural References
4. Translation Hint: The Syllable ཆ་
5. Translation Hint
6. Repeated Passages and Scribal Abbreviations
7. Translation Hint
8. Translation Hint
9. Tantric Metaphors and "Twilight Language"
10. Auxiliary Verbs: The Subjunctive Construction in Protasis
11. Translation Divergences with the Verb ཆོག་

Annotations to Selection 11: Chapter One of Śāntideva's *Engaging in the Deeds of a Bodhisattva*

1. High Classical Philosophical Verse
2. Translating Gendered Pronouns
3. Indirect Statements with ཡིན་ and མིན་ and Evidentiality
4. The Perfective Construction in Apodosis
5. The Tibetan Translations and Sanskrit Originals
6. Proper Nouns: Indian Flora and Fauna
7. Translation Hint
8. Filler Syllables in Verse
9. Translation Hint
10. Translation Hint

Annotations to Selection 12: Aśvaghoṣa's *Fifty Verses on the Guru*

1. Auxiliary Verbs: Honorific Imperative
2. Translation Hint
3. Verbal Collocations with བྱེད་
4. Sanskrit Middle Voice (*ātmanepada*) in Translation
5. Instruments with Nominative Verbs
6. References to the Indian Cultural Pantheon
7. Auxiliary Verbs: Subjunctive Causative
8. Translation Hint
9. Sanskrit Active Voice (*parasmaipada*) in Translation
10. Distributed Verbs with a Distributed Auxiliary
11. Translation Hint
12. Translation Hint
13. Translation Hint

Annotations to Selection 13: The Fourteenth Dalai Lama's *Yoga of the Inseparability of the Guru and Avalokiteśvara, A Source of All Powerful Attainments*

1. *Sādhana* Texts (General Features)
2. Astrological References
3. Differentiating Senses of the Verb ཚོག་
4. Names of Precious Substances
5. The Meaning and Translation of Mantras
6. The Vocabulary of Practice Instructions
7. Translation Hint
8. Locative Absolute: As a Conditional Time Phrase
9. Double Negatives
10. Translation Hint
11. Poetic Metaphors from the Sanskrit Tradition
12. Translation Hint
13. Translation Hint: Popular Stories

Annotations to Selection 14: *Long-life Prayer for His Holiness the Dalai Lama*

1. Translation Hint
2. Translation Hint
3. Translation Hint
4. Translation Hint
5. Sections of the Tibetan Government

Part B. Index of Annotations

Appendix 3: A Comparative Table of Various Scripts

The basic Tibetan script—attributed to Thonmi Saṃbhota—appears to have been derived from the North Indian family of scripts and, in particular, is a style based on the simple Gupta letters of the fifth and sixth centuries. Nontheless, the Tibetans themselves displayed considerable innovation in variant scripts. For example, among the variety of scripts in use in the Tibetan cultural region, the more prominent ones are "U-jen" ("possessing a headline") and certain various flavors of "U-mey" ("without a headline"):

"U-jen" (དབུ་ཅན་): ཀ་ཁ་ག་ང་ཅ་ཆ་ཇ་ཉ་ཏ་ཐ་ད་ན་····

"U-mey" (དབུ་མེད་)

- "Dru-tsa" (འབྲུ་ཚ་): ཀ།ཁ།ག།ང།ཅ།ཆ།ཇ།ཉ།ཏ།ཐ།ད།ན།
- "Bam-yik" (བམ་ཡིག་): ཀ།ཁ།ག།ང།ཅ།ཆ།ཇ།ཉ།ཏ།ཐ།ད།ན།
- "Kyuk-yik" (འཁྱུག་ཡིག་): ཀ།ཁ།ག།ང།ཅ།ཆ།ཇ།ཉ།ཏ།ཐ།ད།ན།

Below are a series of charts to aid in learning and reading these scripts.

Basic alphabet:

དབུ་ཅན་	འབྲུ་ཚ་	བམ་ཡིག་	འཁྱུག་ཡིག་
ཀ་	ཀ།	ཀ།	ཀ།
ཁ་	ཁ།	ཁ།	ཁ།
ག་	ག།	ག།	ག།
ང་	ང།	ང།	ང།
ཅ་	ཅ།	ཅ།	ཅ།

ཆ་	ཆ།	ཆ།	ཆ།
ཇ་	ཇ།	ཇ།	ཇ།
ཉ་	ཉ།	ཉ།	ཉ།
ཏ་	ཏ།	ཏ།	ཏ།
ཐ་	ཐ།	ཐ།	ཐ།
ད་	ད།	ད།	ད།
ན་	ན།	ན།	ན།
པ་	པ།	པ།	པ།
ཕ་	ཕ།	ཕ།	ཕ།
བ་	བ།	བ།	བ།
མ་	མ།	མ།	མ།
ཙ་	ཙ།	ཙ།	ཙ།
ཚ་	ཚ།	ཚ།	ཚ།
ཛ་	ཛ།	ཛ།	ཛ།
ཝ་	ཝ།	ཝ།	ཝ།
ཞ་	ཞ།	ཞ།	ཞ།
ཟ་	ཟ།	ཟ།	ཟ།
འ་	འ།	འ།	འ།
ཡ་	ཡ།	ཡ།	ཡ།
ར་	ར།	ར།	ར།
ལ་	ལ།	ལ།	ལ།
ཤ་	ཤ།	ཤ།	ཤ།
ས་	ས།	ས།	ས།
ཧ་	ཧ།	ཧ།	ཧ།
ཨ་	ཨ།	ཨ།	ཨ།

ཨི་	ཨི།	ཨི།	ཨི
ཨུ་	ཨུ།	ཨུ།	ཨུ་
ཨེ་	ཨེ།	ཨེ།	ཨེ
ཨོ་	ཨོ།	ཨོ།	ཨོ
་	་	་	་
།	།	།	།
༄༅	༄	༄༅	༄

Unique Conjuncts

ཀྵ་	ཀྵ།	ཀྵ།	ཀྵ་
ཀྵི་	ཀྵི།	ཀྵི།	ཀྵི
ཀྵུ་	ཀྵུ།	ཀྵུ།	ཀྵུ་
ཀྵེ་	ཀྵེ།	ཀྵེ།	ཀྵེ
ཀྵོ་	ཀྵོ།	ཀྵོ།	ཀྵོ
ཀྵྲ་	ཀྵྲ།	ཀྵྲ།	ཀྵྲ
ཀྵཱ་	ཀྵཱ།	ཀྵཱ།	ཀྵཱ
ཀྵྲུ་	ཀྵྲུ།	ཀྵྲུ།	ཀྵྲུ་
ཀྵཱུ་	ཀྵཱུ།	ཀྵཱུ།	ཀྵཱུ་
ཧྨ་	ཧྨ།	ཧྨ།	ཧྨ་
ཧྨྃ་	ཧྨྃ།	ཧྨྃ།	ཧྨྃ་
ཧྨི་	ཧྨི།	ཧྨི།	ཧྨི
ཧྨུྃ་	ཧྨུྃ།	ཧྨུྃ།	ཧྨུྃ་

Standard Conjuncts

ཀྱ་	ཀྱ།	ཀྱ།	ཀྱ་
ཁྱ་	ཁྱ།	ཁྱ།	ཁྱ་
གྱ་	གྱ།	གྱ།	གྱ་
ཕྱ་	ཕྱ།	ཕྱ།	ཕྱ་
བྱ་	བྱ།	བྱ།	བྱ་
མྱ་	མྱ།	མྱ།	མྱ་
ཧྱ་	ཧྱ།	ཧྱ།	ཧྱ་

ཀྲ་	ཀྲ།	ཀྲ།	ཀྲ་
ཁྲ་	ཁྲ།	ཁྲ།	ཁྲ་
གྲ་	གྲ།	གྲ།	གྲ་
དྲ་	དྲ།	དྲ།	དྲ་
པྲ་	པྲ།	པྲ།	པྲ་
ཕྲ་	ཕྲ།	ཕྲ།	ཕྲ་
བྲ་	བྲ།	བྲ།	བྲ་
སྲ་	སྲ།	སྲ།	སྲ་
ཧྲ་	ཧྲ།	ཧྲ།	ཧྲ་

ཀླ་	ཀླ།	ཀླ།	ཀླ་
གླ་	གླ།	གླ།	གླ་
བླ་	བླ།	བླ།	བླ་
ཟླ་	ཟླ།	ཟླ།	ཟླ་
རླ་	རླ།	རླ།	རླ་
སླ་	སླ།	སླ།	སླ་

ཀ་	ཀ།	ཀ།	ཀ།
ཁ་	ཁ།	ཁ།	ཁ།
ང་	ང།	ང།	ང།
ཇ་	ཇ།	ཇ།	ཇ།
ཉ་	ཉ།	ཉ།	ཉ།
ཏ་	ཏ།	ཏ།	ཏ།
ད་	ད།	ད།	ད།
ན་	ན།	ན།	ན།
པ་	པ།	པ།	པ།
མ་	མ།	མ།	མ།
ཙ་	ཙ།	ཙ།	ཙ།
ཛ་	ཛ།	ཛ།	ཛ།

ཀྲ་	ཀྲ།	ཀྲ།	ཀྲ།
ཁྲ་	ཁྲ།	ཁྲ།	ཁྲ།
མྲ་	མྲ།	མྲ།	མྲ།

ཀ་	ཀ།	ཀ།	ཀ།
ཁ་	ཁ།	ཁ།	ཁ།
ང་	ང།	ང།	ང།
ཙ་	ཙ།	ཙ།	ཙ།
ཛ་	ཛ།	ཛ།	ཛ།
ཏ་	ཏ།	ཏ།	ཏ།
ད་	ད།	ད།	ད།
པ་	པ།	པ།	པ།

ལྦ་	ལྦ།	ལྦ།	ལྦ་
ལྷ་	ལྷ།	ལྷ།	ལྷ་

སྐ་	སྐ།	སྐ།	སྐ་
སྒ་	སྒ།	སྒ།	སྒ་
སྔ་	སྔ།	སྔ།	སྔ་
སྙ་	སྙ།	སྙ།	སྙ་
སྟ་	སྟ།	སྟ།	སྟ་
སྡ་	སྡ།	སྡ།	སྡ་
སྣ་	སྣ།	སྣ།	སྣ་
སྤ་	སྤ།	སྤ།	སྤ་
སྦ་	སྦ།	སྦ།	སྦ་
སྨ་	སྨ།	སྨ།	སྨ་
སྩ་	སྩ།	སྩ།	སྩ་

སྐྱ་	སྐྱ།	སྐྱ།	སྐྱ་
སྒྱ་	སྒྱ།	སྒྱ།	སྒྱ་
སྤྱ་	སྤྱ།	སྤྱ།	སྤྱ་
སྦྱ་	སྦྱ།	སྦྱ།	སྦྱ་
སྨྱ་	སྨྱ།	སྨྱ།	སྨྱ་

སྐྲ་	སྐྲ།	སྐྲ།	སྐྲ་
སྒྲ་	སྒྲ།	སྒྲ།	སྒྲ་
སྨྲ་	སྨྲ།	སྨྲ།	སྨྲ་
སྤྲ་	སྤྲ།	སྤྲ།	སྤྲ་

ཕྱོཿ	ཕྱོཿ	ཕྱོཿ	ཕྱོཿ
ཕྱྭོཿ	ཕྱྭོཿ	ཕྱྭོཿ	ཕྱྭོཿ

Bam-yik Letters with Vowels

ཀི།	ཀུ།	ཀེ།	ཀོ།
ཁི།	ཁུ།	ཁེ།	ཁོ།
གི།	གུ།	གེ།	གོ།
ངི།	ངུ།	ངེ།	ངོ།
ཅི།	ཅུ།	ཅེ།	ཅོ།
ཆི།	ཆུ།	ཆེ།	ཆོ།
ཇི།	ཇུ།	ཇེ།	ཇོ།
ཉི།	ཉུ།	ཉེ།	ཉོ།
ཏི།	ཏུ།	ཏེ།	ཏོ།
ཐི།	ཐུ།	ཐེ།	ཐོ།
དི།	དུ།	དེ།	དོ།
ནི།	ནུ།	ནེ།	ནོ།
པི།	པུ།	པེ།	པོ།
ཕི།	ཕུ།	ཕེ།	ཕོ།
བི།	བུ།	བེ།	བོ།
མི།	མུ།	མེ།	མོ།
ཙི།	ཙུ།	ཙེ།	ཙོ།
ཚི།	ཚུ།	ཚེ།	ཚོ།
ཛི།	ཛུ།	ཛེ།	ཛོ།
ཝི།	ཝུ།	ཝེ།	ཝོ།
ཞི།	ཞུ།	ཞེ།	ཞོ།

ཇི།	ཇུ།	ཇེ།	ཇོ།
གི།	གུ།	གེ།	གོ།
ཡི།	ཡུ།	ཡེ།	ཡོ།
རི།	རུ།	རེ།	རོ།
ལི།	ལུ།	ལེ།	ལོ།
ཤི།	ཤུ།	ཤེ།	ཤོ།
པི།	པུ།	པེ།	པོ།
ཞི།	ཞུ།	ཞེ།	ཞོ།

ཀྱི།	ཀྱུ།	ཀྱེ།	ཀྱོ།
ཁྱི།	ཁྱུ།	ཁྱེ།	ཁྱོ།
གྱི།	གྱུ།	གྱེ།	གྱོ།
ཕྱི།	ཕྱུ།	ཕྱེ།	ཕྱོ།
པྱི།	པྱུ།	པྱེ།	པྱོ།
མྱི།	མྱུ།	མྱེ།	མྱོ།
ཧྱི།	ཧྱུ།	ཧྱེ།	ཧྱོ།

ཀྲི།	ཀྲུ།	ཀྲེ།	ཀྲོ།
ཁྲི།	ཁྲུ།	ཁྲེ།	ཁྲོ།
གྲི།	གྲུ།	གྲེ།	གྲོ།
ཏྲི།	ཏྲུ།	ཏྲེ།	ཏྲོ།
པྲི།	པྲུ།	པྲེ།	པྲོ།
ཕྲི།	ཕྲུ།	ཕྲེ།	ཕྲོ།
བྲི།	བྲུ།	བྲེ།	བྲོ།
སྲི།	སྲུ།	སྲེ།	སྲོ།
ཧྲི།	ཧྲུ།	ཧྲེ།	ཧྲོ།

ཀྱི།	ཀྱི།	ཀྱི།	ཀྱི།
གྱི།	གྱི།	གྱི།	གྱི།
བྱི།	བྱི།	བྱི།	བྱི།
མྱི།	མྱི།	མྱི།	མྱི།
ཧྱི།	ཧྱི།	ཧྱི།	ཧྱི།
པྱི།	པྱི།	པྱི།	པྱི།

རྐི།	རྐི།	རྐི།	རྐི།
རྒི།	རྒི།	རྒི།	རྒི།
རྔི།	རྔི།	རྔི།	རྔི།
རྗི།	རྗི།	རྗི།	རྗི།
རྙི།	རྙི།	རྙི།	རྙི།
རྟི།	རྟི།	རྟི།	རྟི།
རྡི།	རྡི།	རྡི།	རྡི།
རྣི།	རྣི།	རྣི།	རྣི།
རྦི།	རྦི།	རྦི།	རྦི།
རྨི།	རྨི།	རྨི།	རྨི།
རྩི།	རྩི།	རྩི།	རྩི།
རྫི།	རྫི།	རྫི།	རྫི།

རྐྱི།	རྐྱི།	རྐྱི།	རྐྱི།
རྒྱི།	རྒྱི།	རྒྱི།	རྒྱི།
རྨྱི།	རྨྱི།	རྨྱི།	རྨྱི།

ལྐི།	ལྐི།	ལྐི།	ལྐི།
ལྒི།	ལྒི།	ལྒི།	ལྒི།
ལྔི།	ལྔི།	ལྔི།	ལྔི།

ཀྱི།	ཀྱུ།	ཀྱེ།	ཀྱོ།
ཁྱི།	ཁྱུ།	ཁྱེ།	ཁྱོ།
གྱི།	གྱུ།	གྱེ།	གྱོ།
པྱི།	པྱུ།	པྱེ།	པྱོ།
ཕྱི།	ཕྱུ།	ཕྱེ།	ཕྱོ།
བྱི།	བྱུ།	བྱེ།	བྱོ།
མྱི།	མྱུ།	མྱེ།	མྱོ།

ཏྲི།	ཏྲུ།	ཏྲེ།	ཏྲོ།
ཐྲི།	ཐྲུ།	ཐྲེ།	ཐྲོ།
དྲི།	དྲུ།	དྲེ།	དྲོ།
ནྲི།	ནྲུ།	ནྲེ།	ནྲོ།
པྲི།	པྲུ།	པྲེ།	པྲོ།
ཕྲི།	ཕྲུ།	ཕྲེ།	ཕྲོ།
བྲི།	བྲུ།	བྲེ།	བྲོ།
མྲི།	མྲུ།	མྲེ།	མྲོ།
ཤྲི།	ཤྲུ།	ཤྲེ།	ཤྲོ།
སྲི།	སྲུ།	སྲེ།	སྲོ།
ཧྲི།	ཧྲུ།	ཧྲེ།	ཧྲོ།

ཀླི།	ཀླུ།	ཀླེ།	ཀློ།
བླི།	བླུ།	བླེ།	བློ།
ཟླི།	ཟླུ།	ཟླེ།	ཟློ།
རླི།	རླུ།	རླེ།	རློ།
སླི།	སླུ།	སླེ།	སློ།

[illegible]	[illegible]	[illegible]	[illegible]
[illegible]	[illegible]	[illegible]	[illegible]
[illegible]	[illegible]	[illegible]	[illegible]
[illegible]	[illegible]	[illegible]	[illegible]
[illegible]	[illegible]	[illegible]	[illegible]
[illegible]	[illegible]	[illegible]	[illegible]

Dru-tsa Letters with Vowels

ཀི།	ཀུ།	ཀེ།	ཀོ།
ཁི།	ཁུ།	ཁེ།	ཁོ།
གི།	གུ།	གེ།	གོ།
ངི།	ངུ།	ངེ།	ངོ།
ཅི།	ཅུ།	ཅེ།	ཅོ།
ཆི།	ཆུ།	ཆེ།	ཆོ།
ཇི།	ཇུ།	ཇེ།	ཇོ།
ཉི།	ཉུ།	ཉེ།	ཉོ།
ཏི།	ཏུ།	ཏེ།	ཏོ།
ཐི།	ཐུ།	ཐེ།	ཐོ།
དི།	དུ།	དེ།	དོ།
ནི།	ནུ།	ནེ།	ནོ།

པི།	པུ།	པེ།	པོ།
ཕི།	ཕུ།	ཕེ།	ཕོ།
བི།	བུ།	བེ།	བོ།
མི།	མུ།	མེ།	མོ།
ཙི།	ཙུ།	ཙེ།	ཙོ།
ཚི།	ཚུ།	ཚེ།	ཚོ།
ཛི།	ཛུ།	ཛེ།	ཛོ།
ཝི།	ཝུ།	ཝེ།	ཝོ།
ཞི།	ཞུ།	ཞེ།	ཞོ།
ཟི།	ཟུ།	ཟེ།	ཟོ།
འི།	འུ།	འེ།	འོ།
ཡི།	ཡུ།	ཡེ།	ཡོ།
རི།	རུ།	རེ།	རོ།
ལི།	ལུ།	ལེ།	ལོ།
ཤི།	ཤུ།	ཤེ།	ཤོ།
སི།	སུ།	སེ།	སོ།
ཧི།	ཧུ།	ཧེ།	ཧོ།

ཏི།	ཏུ།	ཏེ།	ཏོ།
ཨི།	ཨུ།	ཨེ།	ཨོ།
ཀི།	ཀུ།	ཀེ།	ཀོ།

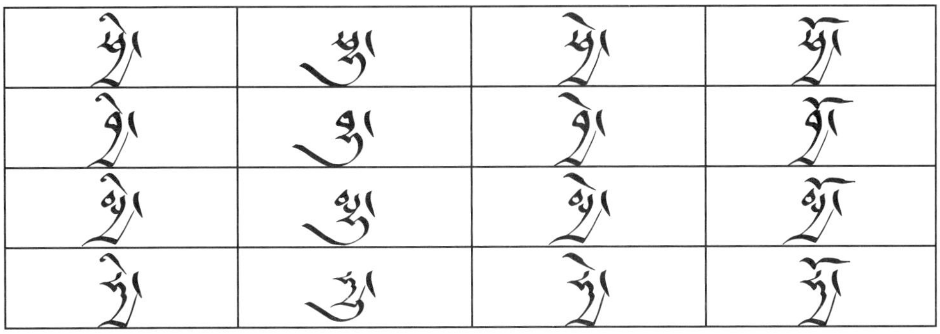

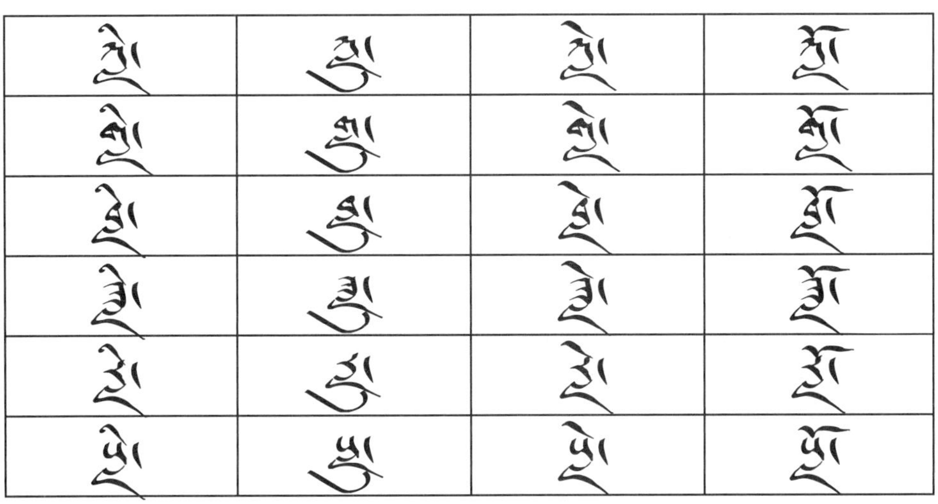

རྐི།	རྐུ།	རྐེ།	རྐོ།
རྒི།	རྒུ།	རྒེ།	རྒོ།
རྔི།	རྔུ།	རྔེ།	རྔོ།
རྗི།	རྗུ།	རྗེ།	རྗོ།
རྙི།	རྙུ།	རྙེ།	རྙོ།
རྟི།	རྟུ།	རྟེ།	རྟོ།
རྡི།	རྡུ།	རྡེ།	རྡོ།
རྣི།	རྣུ།	རྣེ།	རྣོ།
རྦི།	རྦུ།	རྦེ།	རྦོ།
རྨི།	རྨུ།	རྨེ།	རྨོ།
རྩི།	རྩུ།	རྩེ།	རྩོ།
རྫི།	རྫུ།	རྫེ།	རྫོ།

རྐྱི།	རྐྱུ།	རྐྱེ།	རྐྱོ།
རྒྱི།	རྒྱུ།	རྒྱེ།	རྒྱོ།
རྨྱི།	རྨྱུ།	རྨྱེ།	རྨྱོ།

ལྐི།	ལྐུ།	ལྐེ།	ལྐོ།
ལྒི།	ལྒུ།	ལྒེ།	ལྒོ།
ལྔི།	ལྔུ།	ལྔེ།	ལྔོ།
ལྕི།	ལྕུ།	ལྕེ།	ལྕོ།

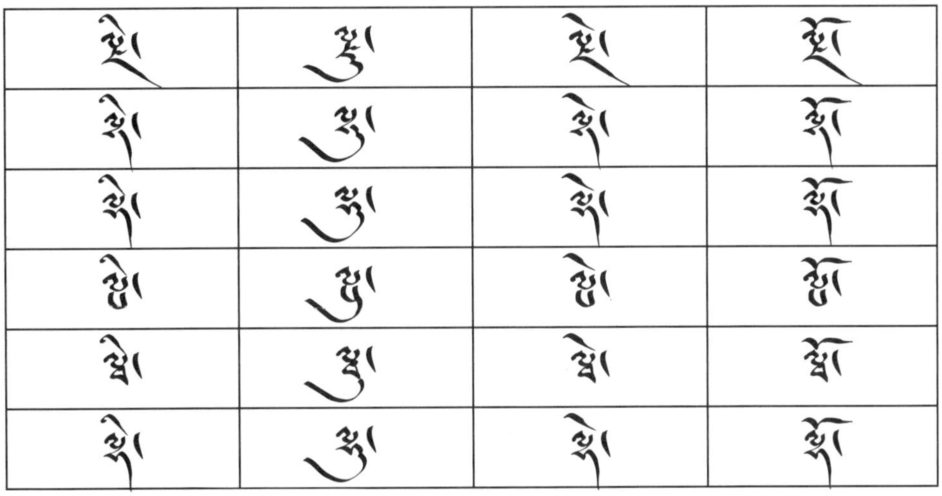

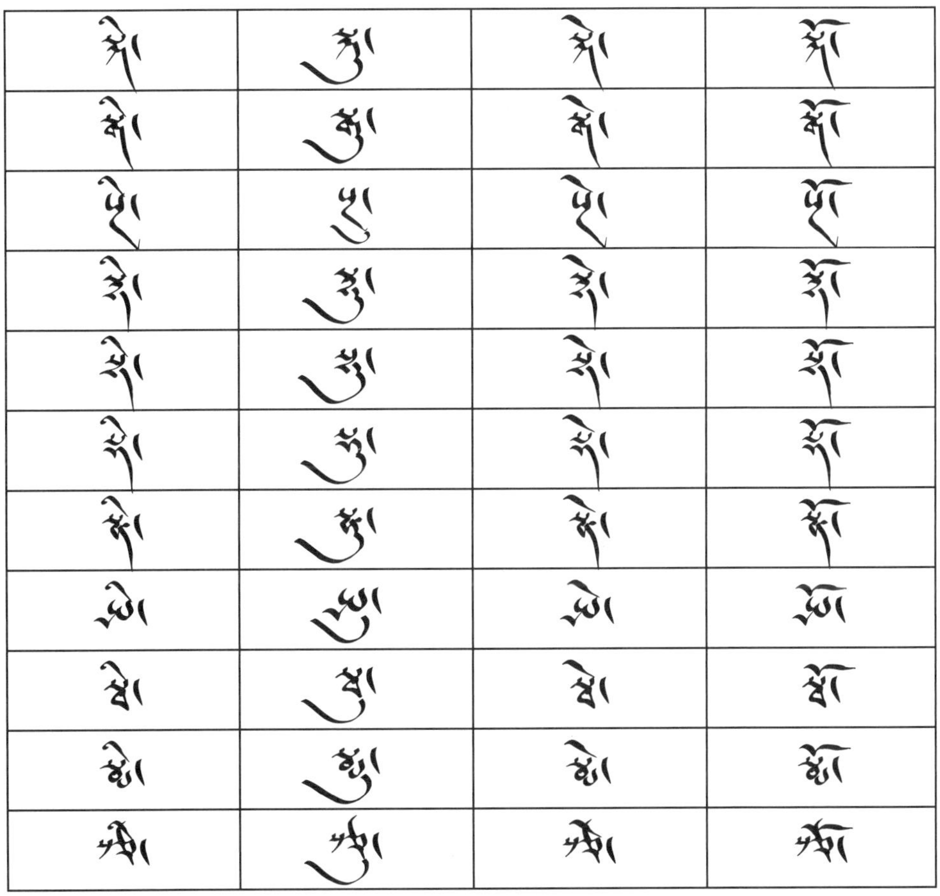

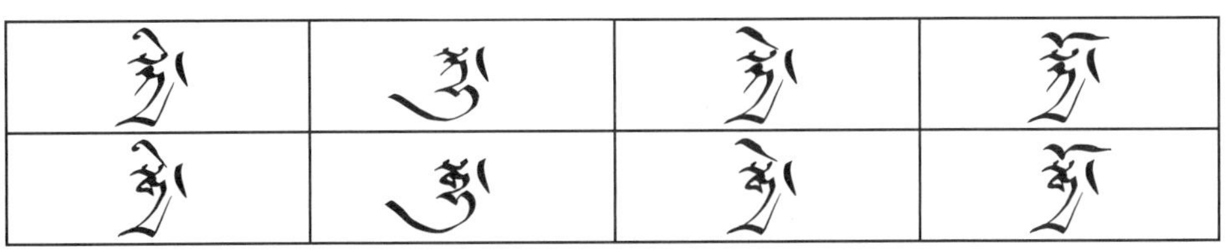

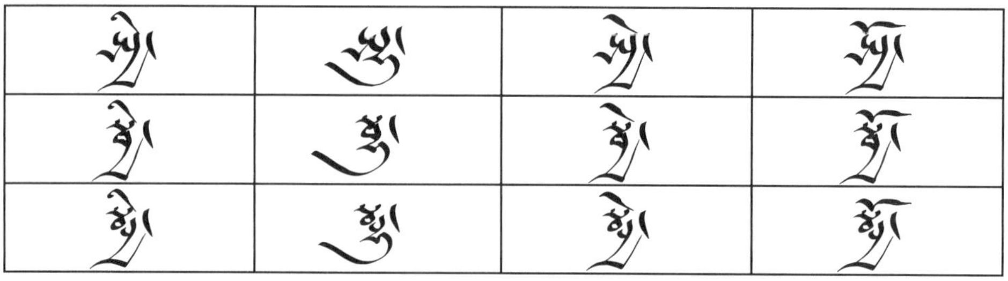

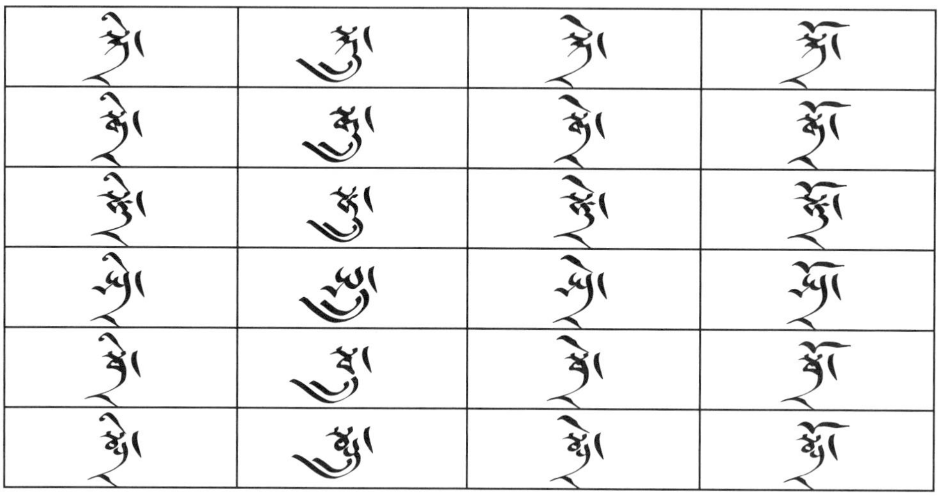

Kyuk-yik Letters with Vowels

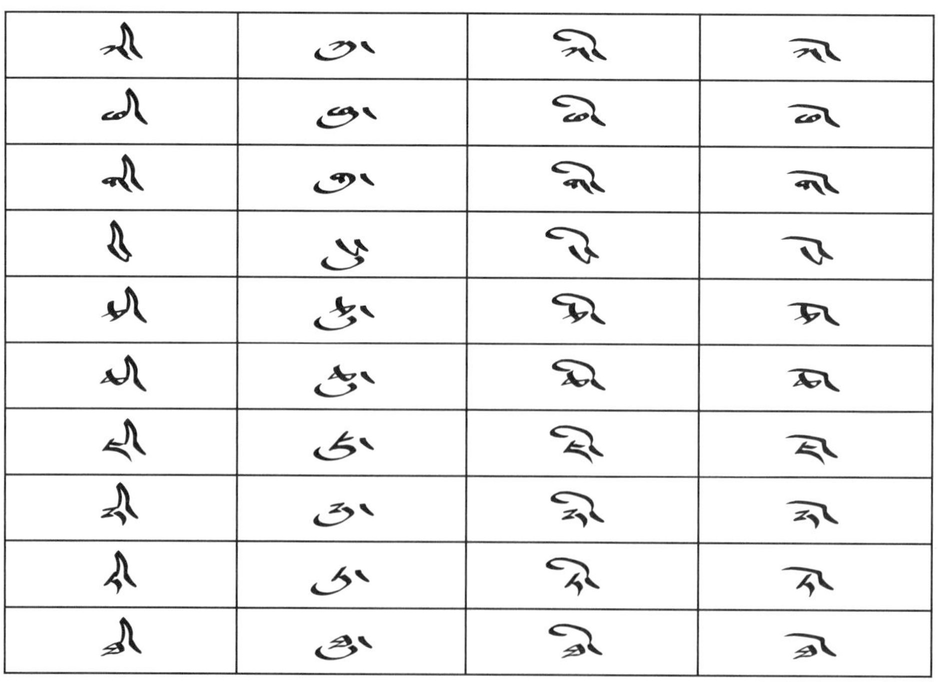

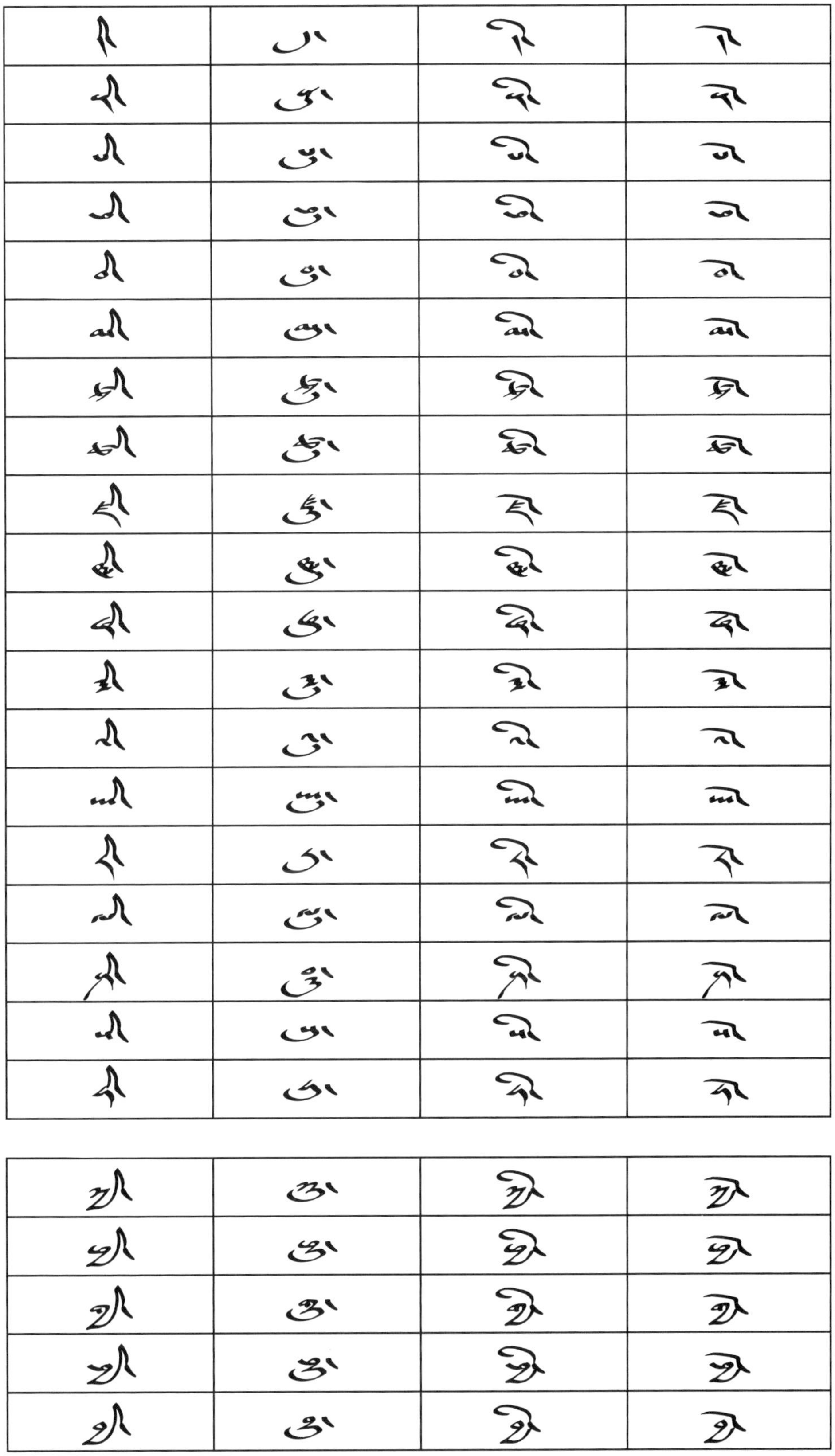

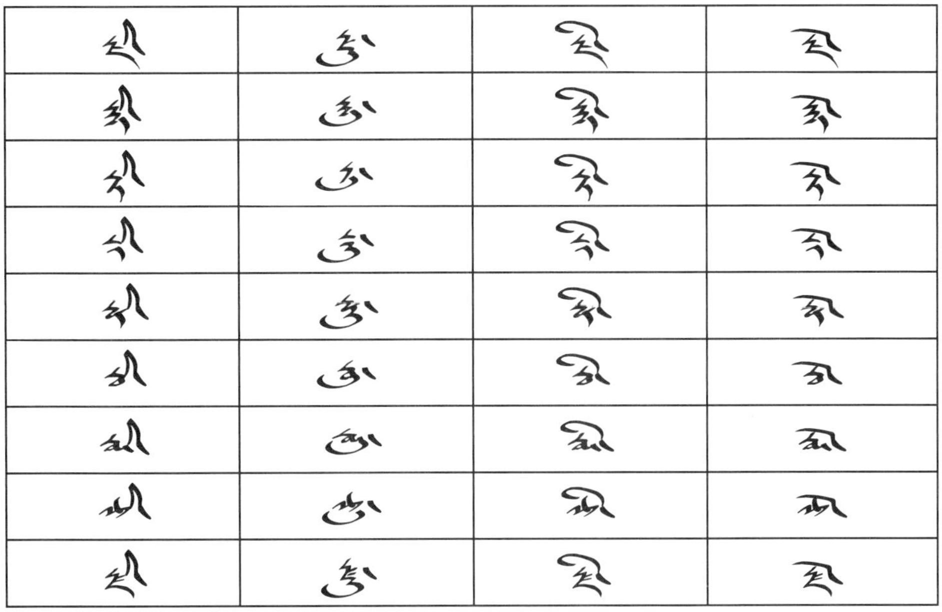

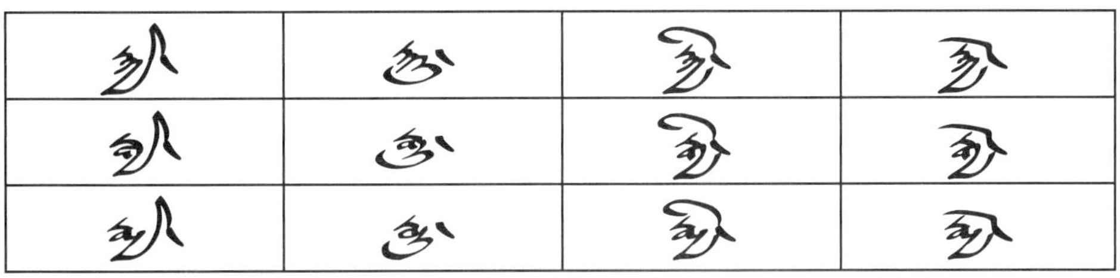

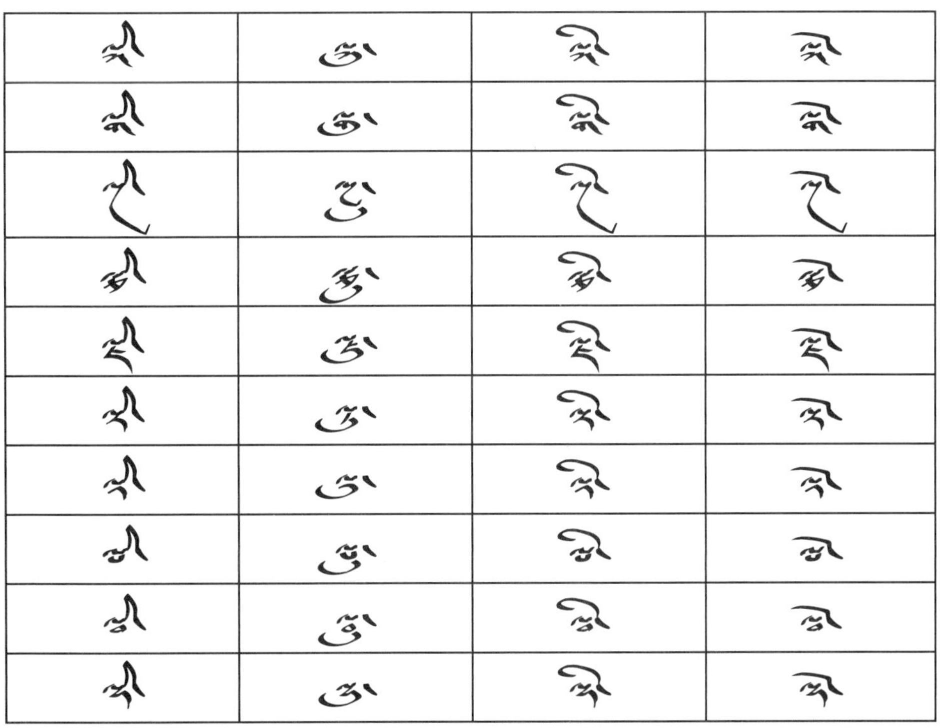

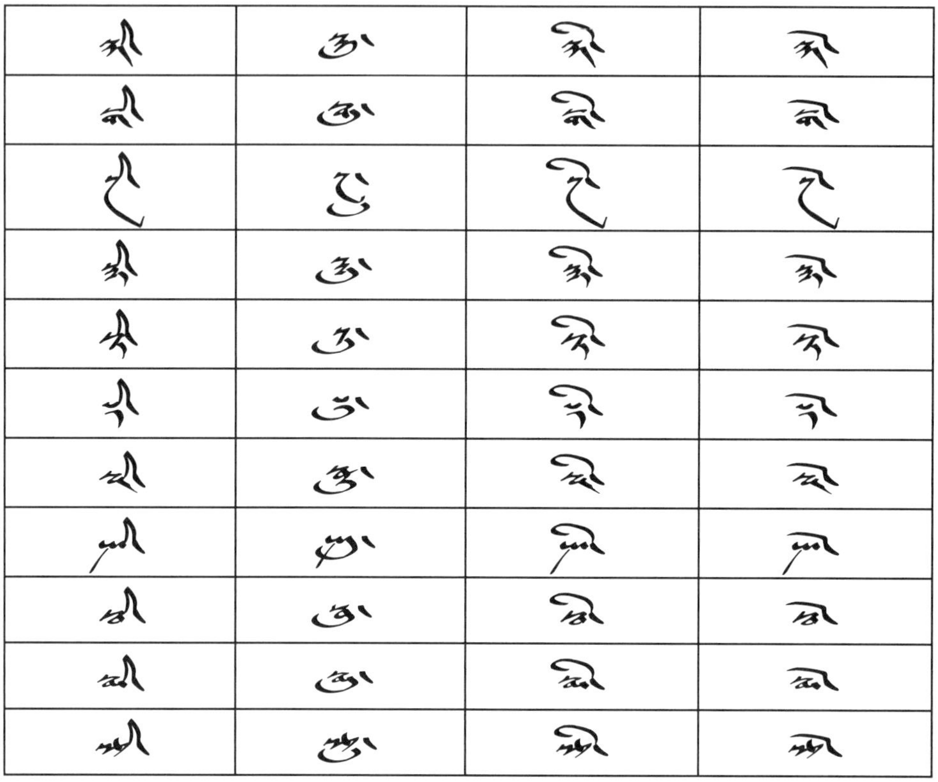

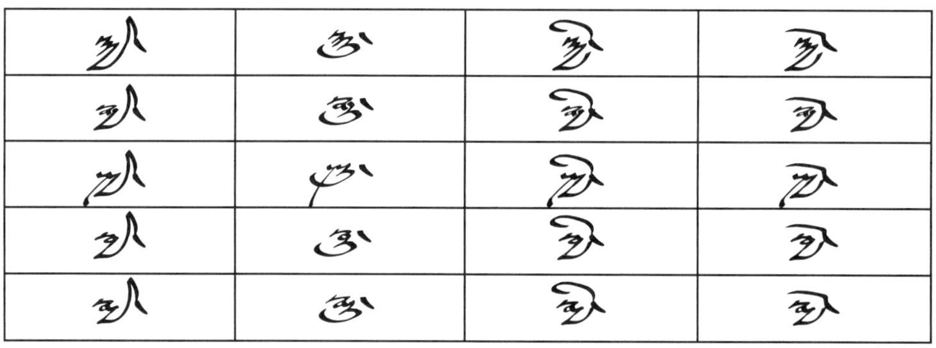

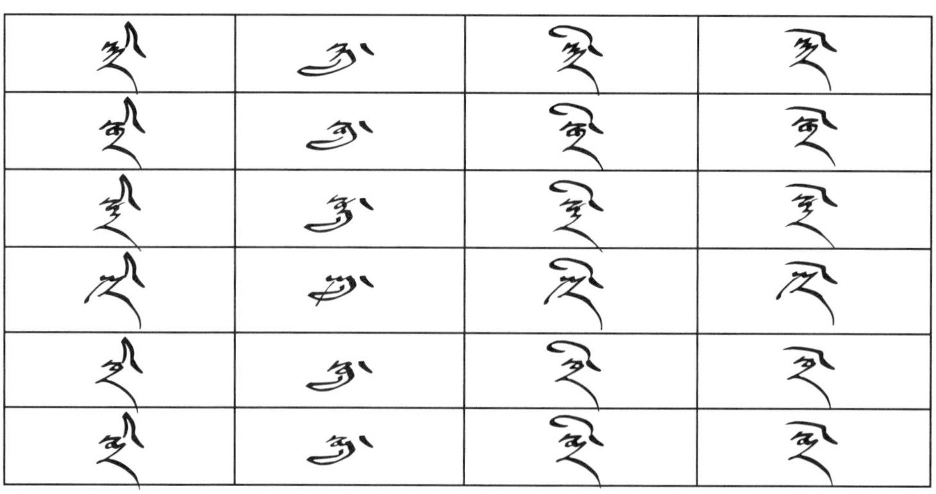

Appendix 4: Texts in Alternate Scripts

Although the most common Tibetan script—"U-jen" ("possessing a headline")—is the easiest to read and most amenable to woodblock printing, manuscripts and other documents are often found in one of the more stylistic "U-mey" ("without a headline") forms. Dru-tsa script, for example, is traditionally used for official documents, while Bam-yik script is often found in manuscripts as well as being popular in Bhutan and Kham (eastern Tibet). Kyuk-yik script is a form of cursive handwriting typically found in personal correspondence or marginalia, although entire texts may be written in the script as well, and like personal handwriting, Kyuk-yik can be idiosyncratic in nature.

Thus, as an introductory excercise in exposure to these scripts, this appendix contains three duplicate texts:

(1) Tsongkhapa's *Three Principal Aspects of the Path* in Dru-tsa Script
(2) Chapter One of Śāntideva's *Engaging in the Deeds of a Bodhisattva* in Bam-yik Script
(3) the *Long-Life Prayer for His Holiness the Dalai Lama* in Kyuk-yik Script

Any student wishing an additional challenge can substitute the alternate script version of these texts for their U-jen versions when progressing through the selections in this *Reader*. When doing so, students should attempt to read the text by consult the reference charts in appendix 3 and only under extreme circumstances make reference to the U-jen versions of the texts. In this way, through trial-and-error, the specific letter forms and combinations will be learned and memorized for future use.

༄༅། ལམ་གྱི་གཙོ་བོ་རྣམ་གསུམ། [1]

རྗེ་བཙུན་བླ་མ་རྣམས་ལ་ཕྱག་འཚལ་ལོ།

རྒྱལ་བའི་གསུང་རབ་ཀུན་གྱི་སྙིང་པོའི་དོན། །རྒྱལ་སྲས་དམ་པ་རྣམས་ཀྱིས་བསྔགས་པའི་ལམ།
སྐལ་ལྡན་ཐར་པ་འདོད་རྣམས་[2] ཀྱི་འཇུག་ངོགས་དེ། [3] ཇི་ལྟར་ནུས་བཞིན་བདག་གིས་བཤད་པར་བྱ། [4] ༡
གང་དག་[5] སྲིད་པའི་བདེ་ལ་མ་ཆགས་ཤིང་། །དལ་འབྱོར་དོན་ཡོད་བྱ་ཕྱིར་བརྩོན་པ་ཡིས།
རྒྱལ་བ་དགྱེས་པའི་ལམ་ལ་ཡིད་རྟོན་པའི། [6] སྐལ་ལྡན་དེ་དག་དང་བའི་ཡིད་ཀྱིས་ཉོན། ༢
ངེས་འབྱུང་དག་པ་མེད་པར་སྲིད་མཚོ་ཡི། །བདེ་འབྲས་དོན་གཉེར་ཞི་བ་ཐོབ་ཐབས་མེད།
སྲིད་པ་ལ་བརྣབ་པ་ཡིས་ཀྱང་ལུས་ཅན་རྣམས། །ཀུན་ནས་འཆིང་ཕྱིར་ཐོག་མར་ངེས་འབྱུང་བཙལ། [7] ༣
དལ་འབྱོར་རྙེད་དཀའ་ཚེ་ལ་སྐབས་མེད་པ། [8] ཡིད་ལ་གོམས་པས་ཚེ་འདིའི་སྣང་ཞེན་ལྡོག
ལས་འབྲས་མི་བསླུ་འཁོར་བའི་སྡུག་བསྔལ་རྣམས། །ཡང་ཡང་བསམས་ན་ཕྱི་མའི་སྣང་ཞེན་ལྡོག ༤
དེ་ལྟར་གོམས་པས་འཁོར་བའི་ཕུན་ཚོགས་ལ། །སྐད་ཅིག་ཙམ་ཡང་འདོད་བློ་མི་སྐྱེ་ཞིང་།
ཉིན་མཚན་ཀུན་ཏུ་ཐར་པ་དོན་གཉེར་བློ། །བྱུང་ན་དེ་ཚེ་ངེས་འབྱུང་སྐྱེས་པ་ཡིན། [9] ༥
ངེས་འབྱུང་དེ་ཡང་རྣམ་དག་སེམས་བསྐྱེད་ཀྱིས། །ཟིན་པ་མེད་ན་བླ་མེད་བྱང་ཆུབ་ཀྱི།
ཕུན་སུམ་ཚོགས་པའི་བདེ་རྒྱུར་མི་འགྱུར་བས། །བློ་ལྡན་རྣམས་ཀྱིས་བྱང་ཆུབ་སེམས་མཆོག་བསྐྱེད། ༦
[10] ཤུགས་དྲག་ཆུ་བོ་བཞི་ཡི་རྒྱུན་གྱིས་ཁྱེར། །བཅོས་དཀའ་ལས་ཀྱི་འཆིང་བ་དམ་པོས་བཅིངས།
བདག་འཛིན་ལྕགས་ཀྱི་དྲ་བའི་སྦུབས་སུ་ཚུད། །མ་རིག་མུན་པའི་སྨག་གིས་ཀུན་ནས་བསྒྲིབས། ༧
མཐའ་མེད་སྲིད་པར་སྐྱེ་ཞིང་སྐྱེ་བ་རུ། །སྡུག་བསྔལ་གསུམ་གྱིས་རྒྱུན་ཆད་མེད་པར་མནར།
གནས་སྐབས་འདི་འདྲར་གྱུར་པའི་མ་རྣམས་ཀྱི། །རང་བཞིན་བསམས་ནས་སེམས་མཆོག་བསྐྱེད་པར་མཛོད། [11] ༨
གནས་ལུགས་རྟོགས་པའི་ཤེས་རབ་མི་ལྡན་ན། །ངེས་འབྱུང་དང་བྱང་ཆུབ་སེམས་ལ་གོམས་བྱས་ཀྱང་།
སྲིད་པའི་རྩ་བ་བཅད་པར་མི་ནུས་པས། །དེ་ཕྱིར་རྟེན་འབྲེལ་རྟོགས་པའི་ཐབས་ལ་འབད། ༩
གང་ཞིག་[12] འཁོར་འདས་ཆོས་རྣམས་ཐམས་ཅད་ཀྱི། །རྒྱུ་འབྲས་ནམ་ཡང་བསླུ་བ་མེད་མཐོང་ཞིང་།
དམིགས་པའི་གཏད་སོ་གང་ཡིན་ཀུན་ཞིག་པ། །དེ་ནི་སངས་རྒྱས་དགྱེས་པའི་[13] ལམ་ལ་ཞུགས། ༡༠

སྣང་བ་འདི་ཀ་ནི་རྨི་ལམ་སྒྱུ་མ་ཡི། །ཡོད། །སྟོང་པ་ཙམ་ཡིན་ཉམས་བདེ་སྐྱོ་བ།[14] གཉིས།
རྗེ་ཡེ། །ཡེ་ཡིར། སྣང་བ་ཡི། །སྐྱེ། །[15] སྐྱེ་བ་འཆི་བའི། །སྡུག་བསྔལ་རྟོགས་པ་ཡི། ༡༡
ཀུན་ཞིག་ཏུ་ཡིན་རྟོག་མེད་པར་བཞག་སྟེ། དེ་ཀ་ནི་ལམ་མི་སྐྱེ་འཕྲོ་བ་ཆུ་ཡི། །ཀུ།
ཡི་ཞིག་ལ་ཡུལ་ཀྱི་རྟོག་སྟོང་།[16] ཐག་རྟོག་ག །ཀྱི་སྟོང་བ་ནི། །སྐྱེ། །རྟོགས་པ་དག་པ། ༡༢
གཞག་ཡང་། །སྣང་བ་ཡོད། །འཆར་ཡེ་མེད་ལ། ། སྟོང་པ་ཡི། །འཆར་ཡེ་མེད་ལ་ཞི། །སྟོང་པ་ཉི། །
རྒྱུ། །ཡུལ་ཞེན་བུར་ཆ་རབ་བཞི། །རྒྱ་ལ་ཞེན་ཀ། འཆར་རྟོག་སྣང་བ་ཐོག་པར་མེད་རྒྱུར་རོ། ༡༣
། །སྣང་ཞིང་ཀྱི་ནི་རྩོ་བོ་ནི་ལ་ཡུལ་ཀྱི། གཀ། །ཉམས་ལ་ཡང་ལེན་རྗེ་བཞིན་རྟོགས་པ་ནི་ཀྱི།
། །ཞིག་པ་འཛིན་ཏེ་བ་རྟོག་རྒྱལ་སྟོང་པ་འཛིན། །ཀུན། གཏན་ཀྱི་གཏན་ལ་ཕྱུང་། །ཆུ་བ་ལ་ཞེན་ནོ།[17] ༡༤

ཞེས་པ་འདི་ནི་ཡུལ་ཇི་བ་ཞིག་འདི་སྐྱེ། །སྐྱེ་བཟང་རྒྱལ་བ་འདི། །ཐབས་ཀྱི་ཀ་ཚོ་ཡིན་ཡིད་གྱི་བ།
རྒྱལ་པ་བ་ལ་གསོལ་བ་འདོ། ། |

༄༅། །བྱང་ཆུབ་སེམས་དཔའི་སྤྱོད་པ་ལ་འཇུག་པ་ལས།

ལེའུ་དང་པོ།

སངས་རྒྱས་དང་བྱང་ཆུབ་སེམས་དཔའ་ཐམས་ཅད་ལ་ཕྱག་འཚལ་ལོ།

[1]བདེ་གཤེགས་ཆོས་ཀྱི་སྐུ་མངའ་སྲས་བཅས་དང་། །ཕྱག་འོས་ཀུན་ལ་ཡང་གུས་པར་ཕྱག་འཚལ་ཏེ།
བདེ་གཤེགས་སྲས་[2]ཀྱི་སྡོམ་ལ་འཇུག་པ་ནི། །ལུང་བཞིན་མདོར་བསྡུས་ནས་ནི་བརྗོད་པར་བྱ། །༡་༡།

སྔོན་ཆད་མ་བྱུང་བ་ཡང་འདིར་བརྗོད་མེད། །སྡེབ་སྦྱོར་མཁས་པ་བདག་ལ་ཡོད་མིན་ཏེ།[3]
།དེ་ཕྱིར་གཞན་གྱི་དོན་བསམ་པ་བདག་ལ་མེད། །རང་གི་ཡིད་ལ་བསྒོམ་ཕྱིར་ངས་འདི་བརྩམས། །༡་༢།

དགེ་བ་བསྒོམ་ཕྱིར་བདག་གི་དད་པའི་ཤུགས། །འདི་དག་གིས་ཀྱང་རེ་ཞིག་འཕེལ་འགྱུར་ལ།
བདག་དང་སྐལ་བ་མཚུངས་པ་གཞན་གྱིས་ཀྱང་། །ཅི་སྟེ་འདི་དག་མཐོང་ན་དོན་ཡོད་འགྱུར། །༡་༣།

དལ་འབྱོར་འདི་ནི་རྙེད་པར་ཤིན་ཏུ་དཀའ། །སྐྱེས་བུའི་དོན་སྒྲུབ་ཐོབ་པར་གྱུར་པ་ལ།
གལ་ཏེ་འདི་ལ་ཕན་པ་མ་བསྒྲུབས་ན། །ཕྱིས་འདི་ཡང་དག་འབྱོར་པར་ག་ལ་འགྱུར། །༡་༤།

ཇི་ལྟར་མཚན་མོ་མུན་ནག་སྤྲིན་རུམ་ན། །གློག་འགྱུ་ཐང་ཅིག་རབ་སྣང་སྟོན་པ་ལྟར།
།དེ་བཞིན་སངས་རྒྱས་མཐུ་ཡིས་བརྒྱ་ལམ་ན། །འཇིག་རྟེན་བསོད་ནམས་བློ་གྲོས་ཐང་འགའ་འབྱུང་། །༡་༥།

།དེ་ལྟས་དགེ་བ་ཉམ་ཆུང་རྟག་པར་ཏེ། །སྡིག་པ་སྟོབས་ཆེན་ཤིན་ཏུ་མི་བཟད་པ།
།དེ་ནི་རྫོགས་པའི་བྱང་ཆུབ་སེམས་མིན་པ། །དགེ་གཞན་གང་གིས་ཟིལ་གྱིས་གནོན་པར་འགྱུར། །༡་༦།

འཕྲུལ་པ་བྱ་ལ་དང་དབང་ཐོབ་པ་ལ་ཛ་བ་ཡི། །ཐབ་འབྲས་སྡུལ་པ་ཀྱིས་ནི་ཡ་ཐག་པ་དང་གཞིགས་པ། །
གི་པ་ནི་ཅ་ལོ་སྣོ་ཚིགས་སྡུལ་པ་ཀྱིས། །ཡོ་ལ་ཚེགས་ཡོ་བྲག་ནི་བྱ་ཐབ་པ་དགེ། ། ༡༡༧ །

ཕྱི་མ་ཡི་སྡུག་བསྔལ་འཇིགས་གཞི་ཞལ་ཀོ་སྟེ། །ཕ་ལས་ཚད་མི་ཡོ་བལ་བ་དགོ་པ། །
ཡོ་ལ་འཇིགས་གཞི་བྱོ་པ་དགོ་པ་པ་ཀུ། །བྱང་ཆུབ་སེམས་པ་ནི་སྡག་ཏུ་གནད་ལི་སྔ། ། ༡༡༨ །

བྱང་ཆུབ་སེམས་པ་སྐྱེས་བུ་དང་ན་སྒྲ་སྟེ་ཀི་པ། །གཞོན་ཡོ་འཚིན་དང་འབྱུལ་པ་ཡོ་ཟུ་ལ་ཐ་ག་སྡུལ་པ། །
ཡོ་ཀི་ཉིགས་པ་སྡུལ་པ་ཀྱིས་ཕྱུ་པ་ཞིབ་འཛིན་ལྡ་ཞི། །ཀྱིན་རྟོན་ལྷ་ལི་དང་འཚམ་པ་ཕ་པ་འཕྲུག་ལྡང་ཀུ་ང་ཉུར། ④ ། ༡༡༩ །

ག་པ་དང་ཉུར་ཀྱི་ཡི་སྡུལ་པ་ལ་ཚེགས་སྟུ་ཉུར། །ལི་ག་ཚ་ལྡུ་པ་གི་བྲུ་ཡ་ན་པ་ཐུལ་ཡོ་གི་སྐྱ། །
རིན་ཆེན་རིན་ཐ་ཡོ་པ་དང་འཇུར་འབ་ན། །བྱང་ཆུབ་སེམས་པ་ཞིབ་ལྡ་བ་དང་བ་འཚན་ཟུ་ཡ། ། ༡༢༠ །

ཀྱུ་ཡོ་གི་པ་ཐ་ག་ཚིག་ཕྱུ་ཅ་ལོ་ཁྲི་པ། །ལོ་ག་པ་པ་དང་ཡི་ཡ་ཕྱུ་འཚོག་པ་ན་རིན་ཆེ་བ་པ། །
ཀྱུ་ཡོ་གི་ག་ན་པ་ཡ་ཁྲུལ་བ་དང་གི་པ་སྡུལ་པ། །རིན་ཆེན་བྱང་ཆུབ་སེམས་པ་ལོ་ག་པ་འཚན་པ་དང་འཛུ། ⑤ ། ༡༢༡ །

སྐྱེ་བོ་གཞན་ཀུན་ཏུ་ཡི། ⑥ བཞིན་དུ་ནི། །ཐུབ་ཏུ་འགྲོ་ན་པ་ཟ་པ་དང་ཉུར་བ་ནི། །
བྱང་ཆུབ་སེམས་པ་ཀྱི་ལྷ་ན་ཕྱི་སྟག་པ་དང་ཡ། །ཐུབ་ཏུ་གི་ན་པ་པ་ལི་ཟ་གི་ཞལ་བ་དང་ཉུར། ། ༡༢༢ །

སྡིག་པ་ཕྱིན་ཆད་ལི་བཟ་བྱུ་པ་ན་ཡ། །པ་ག་ལ་འཚན་ན་པ་གཉིས་པ་པ་ཆེན་པོ་སྒྲ་ར། །
ག་ལ་འཚན་ན་པ་ཡུ་ཀྱི་སྡེ་ལ་ཉུར་བ། །ལ་བ་ག་ཚད་སྡུལ་པ་ཀྱིས་ཚེ་བ་ལི་འཕྲེན། ། ༡༢༣ །

།པ་ནི་ཡུ་པ་ལ་ཟུ་གི་ལི་བཞིན་སྡིག་ཆེན་སྡུལ་པ། །སྒྲ་ཚིག་ག་ཚིག་ཀི་པ་ཡ་བ་དང་ཕྱིག་པ་དགེ། །
།ཡི་ཡ་ན་ཡི་ན་པ་ག་ཕྱུ་ལོ་པ་ག་བྱ་ལ་པ་ལི་ག་ན་ཁྲི་བྱུ་ན་པ་པ་ན་དང་བ་ཟ་ཡ། ⑦ ། ༡༢༤ །

བྱང་ཆུབ་སེམས་ནི་མདོར་བསྡུ་ན། རྣམ་པ་གཉིས་སུ་ཤེས་བྱ་སྟེ།
བྱང་ཆུབ་སྨོན་པའི་སེམས་དང་ནི། བྱང་ཆུབ་འཇུག་པ་ཉིད་ཡིན་ནོ། ། ༡།༡༥ །

འགྲོ་བར་འདོད་དང་འགྲོ་བ་ཡི། བྱེ་བྲག་ཇི་ལྟར་ཤེས་པ་ལྟར།
དེ་བཞིན་མཁས་པས་འདི་གཉིས་ཀྱི། བྱེ་བྲག་རིམ་བཞིན་ཤེས་པར་བྱ། ། ༡།༡༦ །

བྱང་ཆུབ་སྨོན་པའི་སེམས་ལས་ནི། འཁོར་ཚེ་འབྲས་བུ་ཆེ་འབྱུང་ཡང་།
ཇི་ལྟར་འཇུག་པའི་སེམས་བཞིན་དུ། བསོད་ནམས་རྒྱུན་ཆགས་འབྱུང་བ་མིན། ། ༡།༡༧ །

གང་ཚེ་མཐའ་ཡས་སེམས་ཅན་ཁམས། ཡོངས་སུ་བསྒྲལ་བར་བྱ་བའི་ཕྱིར།
མི་ལྡོག་པ་ཡི་སེམས་ཀྱིས་སུ།[8] སེམས་དེ་ཡང་དག་བླངས་གྱུར་པ། ། ༡།༡༨ །

དེ་ཕྱིན་ཆད་ནི་གཉིད་ལོག་གམ། བག་མེད་གྱུར་ཀྱང་བསོད་ནམས་ཤུགས།
རྒྱུན་མི་ཆད་པར་དུ་མ་ཞིག ནམ་མཁའ་མཉམ་པར་རབ་ཏུ་འབྱུང་། ། ༡།༡༩ །

འདི་ནི་འཐད་པ་དང་བཅས་པར། ལག་བཟང་ཞུས་པ་ལས་ཀྱང་ནི།
དམན་མོས་སེམས་ཅན་དོན་གྱི་ཕྱིར། དེ་བཞིན་གཤེགས་པ་ཉིད་ཀྱིས་གསུངས། ། ༡།༢༠ །

སེམས་ཅན་རྣམས་ཀྱི་ཀླད་ནད་ཙམ། བསལ་ལོ་སྙམ་དུ་བསམ་ན་ཡང་།
ཕན་འདོགས་བསམ་པ་དང་ལྡན་ན། བསོད་ནམས་དཔག་མེད་ལྡན་གྱུར་ན། ། ༡།༢༡ །

སེམས་ཅན་རེ་རེའི་མི་བདེ་བ། དཔག་ཏུ་མེད་པ་བསལ་འདོད་ཅིང་།
རེ་རེའང་ཡོན་ཏན་དཔག་མེད་དུ། བསྒྲུབ་པར་འདོད་པ་སྨོས་ཅི་དགོས། ། ༡།༢༢ །

[illegible]
[illegible] །༡༢༣།

[illegible]
[illegible] །༡༢༤།

[illegible] ⑨
[illegible] །༡༢༥།

[illegible]
[illegible] །༡༢༦།

[illegible]
[illegible] །༡༢༧།

[illegible]
[illegible] །༡༢༨།

[illegible]
[illegible] །༡༢༩།

[illegible]
[illegible] །༡༣༠།

ཕན་འདོགས་པ་ལན་ལྡོན་གང་ཡིན་པ། །ཡང་རེ་ཞིག་བསྔགས་པར་འོས་པ་ན། །
མ་བཅོལ་ལེགས་པར་བྱེད་པ་ཡི། །བྱང་ཆུབ་སེམས་དཔའ་སྨོས་ཅི་དགོས། །༡།༣༡།

འགྲོ་བ་ཉུང་ཟད་རྣམས་ལ་ནི། །སྐད་ཅིག་ཟས་ཙམ་སྦྱིན་པར་བྱེད་པ་ཡང་། །
བརྙས་བཅས་ཉི་མ་ཕྱེད་ཀྱི་ལྟོ་བར་བྱེད་པ་ཡང་། །དགེ་བ་བྱེད་པ་ཡིན་ཞེས་སྐྱེ་བོས་བཀུར། །༡།༣༢།

སེམས་ཅན་གྲངས་མེད་ལ་ཡུན་རིང་དུ། །དེ་བཞིན་གཤེགས་པའི་བདེ་བ་བླ་ན་མེད། །
ཡིད་ལ་འདོད་པ་ཐམས་ཅད་རྫོགས་པར་བྱེད་པ། །རྟག་ཏུ་སྦྱིན་པ་པོ་ཞིག་སྨོས་ཅི་དགོས། །༡།༣༣།

གང་ཞིག་དེ་འདྲ་རྒྱལ་སྲས་སྦྱིན་བདག་ལ། །གལ་ཏེ་ངན་སེམས་སྐྱེ་བར་བྱེད་པ་དེ། །
ངན་སེམས་བསྐྱེད་པའི་གྲངས་བཞིན་བསྐལ་པར་ནི། །དམྱལ་བར་གནས་པར་འགྱུར་ཞེས་ཐུབ་པས་གསུངས། །༡།༣༤།

འོན་ཏེ་གང་ཞིག་ཡིད་རབ་དང་བྱེད་ན།[10] །དེ་ཡི་འབྲས་བུ་དེ་བས་ལྷག་པར་འཕེལ། །
རྒྱལ་སྲས་རྣམས་ལ་བཙན་ཏེ་སྡིག་པ་ནི། །མི་འབྱུང་དགེ་བ་ངང་གིས་འཕེལ་བར་འགྱུར། །༡།༣༥།

གང་ལ་སེམས་ཀྱི་དམ་པ་རིན་ཆེན་དེ། །སྐྱེས་པ་དེ་ཡི་སྐུ་ལ་ཕྱག་འཚལ་ཞིང་། །
གང་ལ་གནོད་པ་བྱས་ཀྱང་བདེ་འབྲེལ་བ། །བདེ་བའི་འབྱུང་གནས་དེ་ལ་སྐྱབས་སུ་མཆི། །༡།༣༦།

བྱང་ཆུབ་སེམས་དཔའི་སྤྱོད་པ་ལ་འཇུག་པ་ལས། བྱང་ཆུབ་སེམས་ཀྱི་ཕན་ཡོན་བཤད་པ་ཞེས་བྱ་བ་སྟེ་ལེའུ་དང་པོའོ། །

[illegible]

[illegible]

[illegible]

[illegible]

[illegible]

ཞེས་བྱ་བ་བཞུགས་སོ།

([illegible])

ཨོཾ་སྭསྟི།

[illegible]

[illegible]

[illegible]

[illegible]

[illegible]

[illegible]

[illegible]

[illegible]

[illegible]

[illegible]

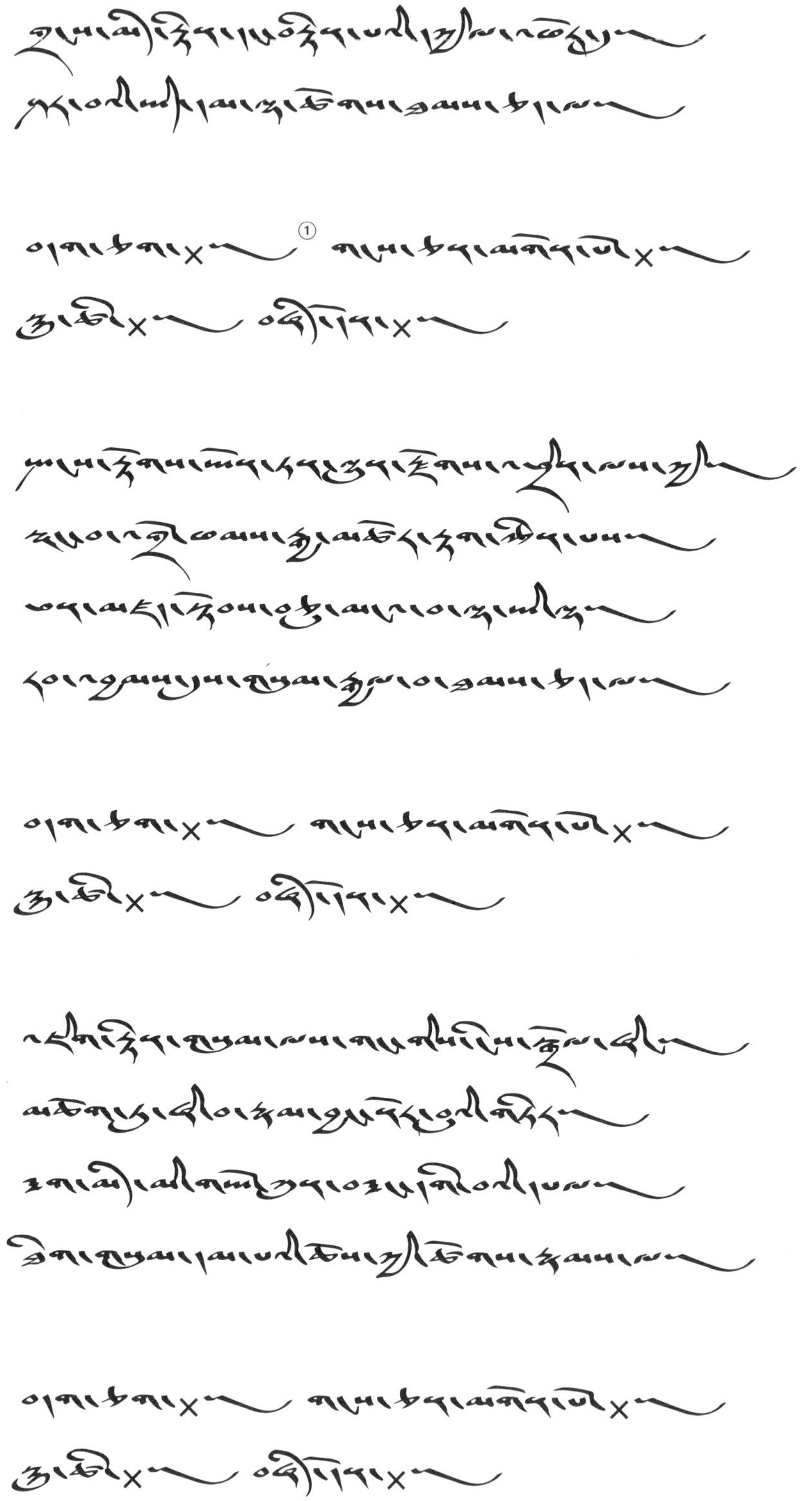

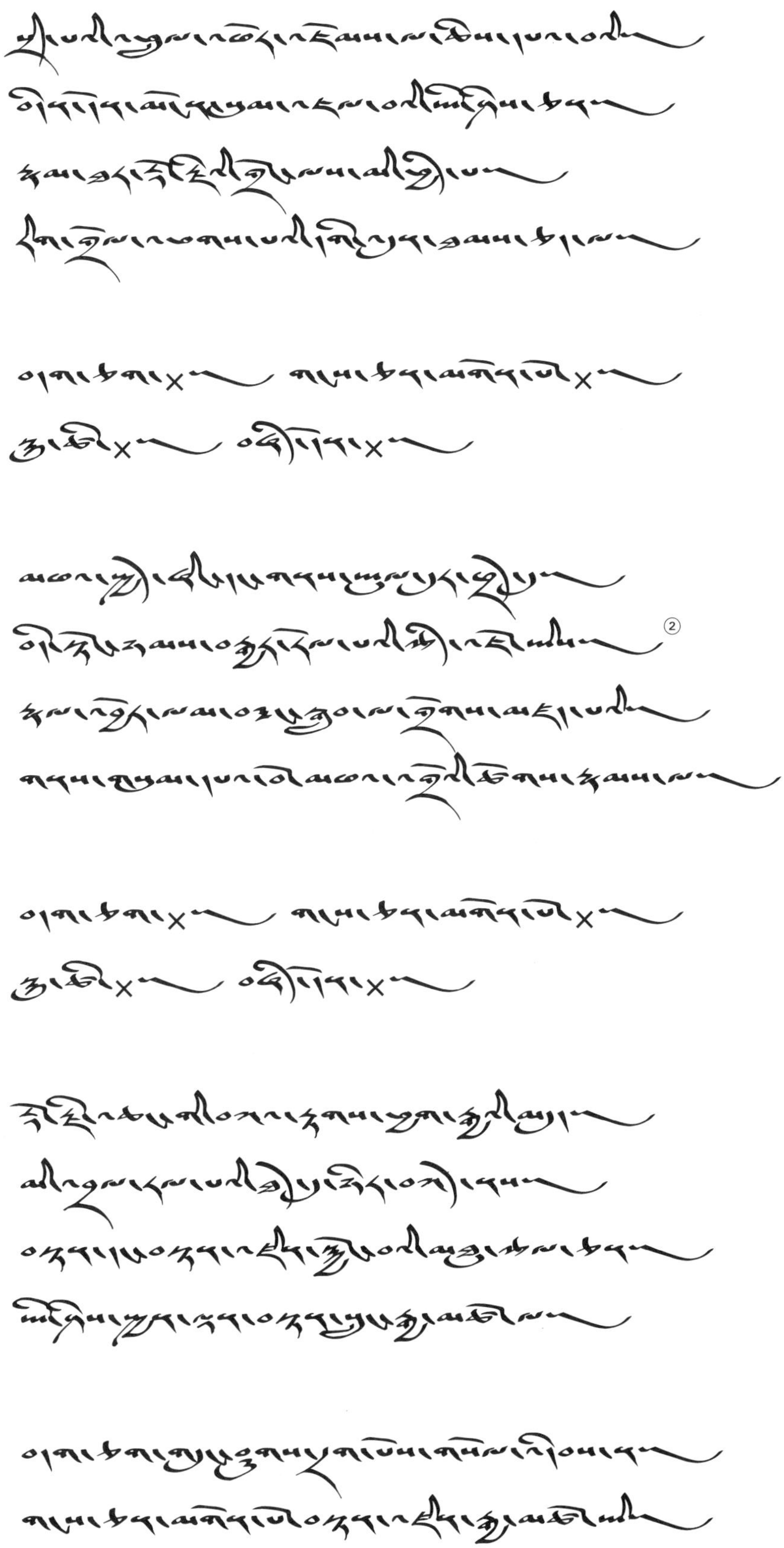

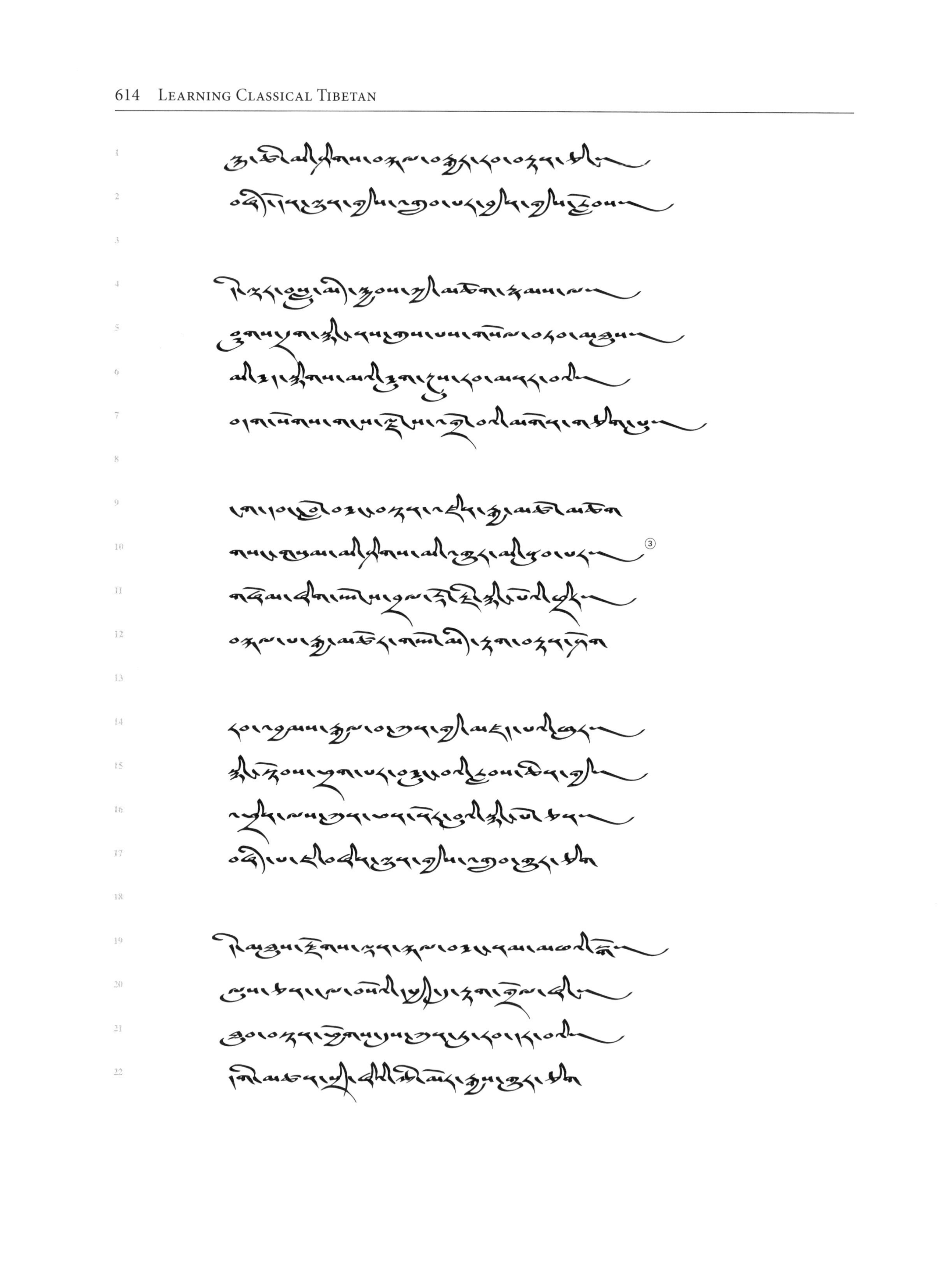

③

[illegible]
[illegible]
[illegible]
[illegible]

[illegible]
[illegible]
[illegible]
[illegible]

[illegible]
[illegible]
[illegible]
[illegible]
[illegible]
[illegible] ④ [illegible]
[illegible]
[illegible]
[illegible] ⑤ [illegible]
[illegible]
[illegible]
[illegible]

[illegible]

[illegible]

[illegible]

[illegible]

[illegible]

Appendix 5: Sample Debate Drill

While engaging with this material, it is important to keep in mind that the texts presented here represent aspects of a living tradition of philosophical inquiry and meditative practice embedded in a rigorous education system. What follows here is a sample debate for recitation and memorization that can enable a student to develop a sense of the "flavor" of this tradition by engaging with the pedagogical system as a living entity.

Here "C" stands for "challenger" (*rigs lam pa*; "proponent of the path of reasoning") in the debate and "D" stands for "defender" (*dam bca' pa*; "holder of a thesis"). Passages in square brackets represent passages that would normally be assumed (and hence, omitted) in a spoken debate, but they are included here for clarity. It may also be helpful to review the specifics of the debate structure (རིགས་ལམ་ notes 7, 10, 14, and 16).

Tibetan Version

C: དྷཱིཿ་ཇི་ལྟར་ཆོས་ཅན།
ཁ་དོག་དང་དམར་པོ་གཉིས་ལ་ཁྱད་པར་གཞག་རྒྱུ་མེད་པའི་ཕྱིར།

D: རྟགས་མ་གྲུབ།

C: ཁ་དོག་དང་དམར་པོ་གཉིས་ལ་ཁྱད་པར་གཞག་རྒྱུ་ཡོད་པ་ཐལ།

D: འདོད།

C: ཁ་དོག་དང་དམར་པོ་གཉིས་ལ་ཁྱད་པར་ག་རེ་ཡོད།

D: དོན་གཅིག་རེད།

C: ཁ་དོག་ཡིན་ན་དམར་པོ་ཡིན་པས་ཁྱབ་པར་ཐལ།

D: [ཁ་དོག་ཡིན་ན་དམར་པོ་ཡིན་པས་ཁྱབ་པར་]འདོད།

C: ཆོས་དུང་དཀར་པོའི་ཁ་དོག་ཆོས་ཅན། དམོར་པོ་ཡིན་པར་ཐལ།

D: [ཆོས་དུང་དཀར་པོའི་ཁ་དོག་དམོར་པོ་ཡིན་པ་] ཅིའི་ཕྱིར།

C: ཁ་དོག་ཡིན་པའི་ཕྱིར། ཁྱབ་པ་ཁས།

D: [ཆོས་དུང་དཀར་པོའི་ཁ་དོག་ཁ་དོག་ཡིན་པ་] རྟགས་མ་གྲུབ།

C: ཆོས་དུང་དཀར་པོའི་ཁ་དོག་ཆོས་ཅན། ཁ་དོག་ཡིན་པར་ཐལ། དཀར་པོ་ཡིན་པའི་ཕྱིར།

D: [ཆོས་དུང་དཀར་པོའི་ཁ་དོག་དཀར་པོ་ཡིན་པ་] རྟགས་མ་གྲུབ།

C: ཆོས་དུང་དཀར་པོའི་ཁ་དོག་ཆོས་ཅན། དཀར་པོ་ཡིན་པར་ཐལ། ཆོས་དུང་དཀར་པོའི་ཁ་དོག་དང་གཅིག་ཡིན་པའི་ཕྱིར།

D: ཆོས་དུང་དཀར་པོའི་ཁ་དོག་དཀར་པོ་ཡིན་པར་འདོད།

C: ཚར། ཆོས་དུང་དཀར་པོའི་ཁ་དོག་ཆོས་ཅན། ཁ་དོག་ཡིན་པར་ཐལ།

D: [ཆོས་དུང་དཀར་པོའི་ཁ་དོག་ཁ་དོག་ཡིན་པར་] འདོད།

C: ཚར། ཆོས་དུང་དཀར་པོའི་ཁ་དོག་ཆོས་ཅན། དམར་པོ་ཡིན་པར་ཐལ། ཁ་དོག་ཡིན་པའི་ཕྱིར།

D: ཆོས་དུང་དཀར་པོའི་ཁ་དོག་དམར་པོ་ཡིན་པར་འདོད།

C: ཚར། ཆོས་དུང་དཀར་པོའི་ཁ་དོག་ཆོས་ཅན། དམར་པོ་མ་ཡིན་པར་ཐལ།

D: ཅིའི་ཕྱིར།

C: དཀར་པོ་ཡིན་པའི་ཕྱིར།

D: [དཀར་པོ་ཡིན་ན་དམར་པོ་མ་ཡིན་པས་] མ་ཁྱབ།

C: དཀར་པོ་ཡིན་ན་དམར་པོ་མ་ཡིན་པས་ཁྱབ་པར་ཐལ། དཀར་པོ་དང་དམར་པོ་གཉིས་ཀྱི་གཞི་མཐུན་མེད་པའི་ཕྱིར།

D: [དཀར་པོ་དང་དམར་པོ་གཉིས་ཀྱི་གཞི་མཐུན་མེད་པ་] རྟགས་མ་གྲུབ།

C: དཀར་པོ་དང་དམར་པོ་གཉིས་ཀྱི་གཞི་མཐུན་མེད་པར་ཐལ། དཀར་པོ་དང་དམར་པོ་གཉིས་འགལ་བ་ཡིན་པའི་ཕྱིར།

D: དཀར་པོ་དང་དམར་པོ་གཉིས་ཀྱི་གཞི་མཐུན་མེད་པར་འདོད།

C: ཚར། དཀར་པོ་ཡིན་ན་དམར་པོ་མ་ཡིན་པས་ཁྱབ་པར་ཐལ།

D: [དཀར་པོ་ཡིན་ན་དམར་པོ་མ་ཡིན་པས་ཁྱབ་པར] འདོད།

C: ཚར། ཆོས་དུང་དཀར་པོའི་ཁ་དོག་ཆོས་ཅན། དམར་པོ་མ་ཡིན་པར་ཐལ།

D: [ཆོས་དུང་དཀར་པོའི་ཁ་དོག་དམར་པོ་མ་ཡིན་པར] འདོད།

C: ཚར། ཆོས་དུང་དཀར་པོའི་ཁ་དོག་ཆོས་ཅན། དམོར་པོ་ཡིན་པར་ཐལ། ཁ་དོག་ཡིན་པའི་ཕྱིར།

D: [དཀར་པོ་ཡིན་ན་དམར་པོ་ཡིན་པས] མ་ཁྱབ།

C: ཚར། ཁ་དོག་ཡིན་ན་དམར་པོ་ཡིན་པས་མ་ཁྱབ་པར་ཐལ།

D: [ཁ་དོག་ཡིན་ན་དམར་པོ་ཡིན་པས་མ་ཁྱབ་པར] འདོད།

C: རྩ་བའི་དམ་བཅའ་ཚར། ཁ་དོག་དང་དམར་པོ་གཉིས་ལ་ཁྱད་པར་ག་རེ་ཡོད།

D: མུ་གསུམ་ཡོད། དམར་པོ་ཡིན་ན་ཁ་དོག་ཡིན་པས་ཁྱབ།
ཁ་དོག་ཡིན་ན་དམར་པོ་ཡིན་པས་མ་ཁྱབ།

English Version

C: Dhīḥ! [Let us debate] the subject, in just the way [Mañjuśrī debated]:
Because a distinction between the two, color and red, cannot be posited.

D: The reason is not established.

C. It follows that a distinction between the two, color and red, can be posited.

D: I accept it.

C. What is the distinction between the two, color and red?

D. They are equivalent.

C. It follows that whatever is a color is necessarily red.

D: I accept [that whatever is a color is necessarily red].

C: It [absurdly] follows that the subject, the color of a white religious conch, is red.

D: Why [is the color of a white religious conch red]?

C: Because of being a color. You asserted the pervasion [that whatever is a color is necessarily red].

D: The reason [the color of a white religious conch is a color] is not established.

C: It follows that the subject, the color of a white religious conch, is a color because of being white.

D: The reason [the color of a white religious conch is white] is not established.

C: It follows that the subject, the color of a white religious conch, is white because of being one with the color of a white religious conch.

D: I accept that the color of a white religious conch is white.

C: Finished! It follows that the subject, the color of a white religious conch, is a color.

D: I accept [that the color of a white religious conch is a color].

C: Finished! It follows that the subject, the color of a white religious conch, is red because of being a color.

D: I accept that the color of a white religious conch is red.

C: Finished! It follows that the subject, the color of a white religious conch, is not red.

D. Why?

C. Because of being white.

D: There is no pervasion [that whatever is white is necessarily not red].

C: It follows that whatever is white is necessarily not red because a common locus of the two, white and red, does not exist.

D: The reason [a common locus of the two, white and red, does not exist] is not established.

C: It follows that a common locus of the two, white and red, does not exist because those two are contradictory.

D: I accept that a common locus of the two, white and red, does not exist.

C: Finished! It follows that whatever is white is necessarily not red.

D: I accept [that whatever is white is necessarily not red].

C: Finished! It follows that the subject, the color of a white religious conch, is not red.

D: I accept [that the color of a white religious conch is not red].

C: Finished! It follows that the subject, the color of a white religious conch, is red because of being a color.

D: There is no pervasion [that whatever is a color is necessarily red].

C: Finished! It follows that whatever is a color is not necessarily red.

D: I accept [that whatever is a color is not necessarily red].

C: Your base thesis is finished! What is the distinction between the two, color and red?

D. There are three possibilities. Whatever is red is necessarily a color. Whatever is a color is not necessarily red. [And there exist things that are neither red nor color.]

Appendix 6: Sample Syllabi for the Use of this Reader

The materials comprising this *Reader* were used over several years while teaching Classical Literary Tibetan at Columbia and Yale Universities. What follows are two sample syllabi for the use of this book in a Tibetan language course as either a six-semester course or as an abbreviated four-semester course. The course structure described below presumes four hours per week of in-class meetings utilizing Joe Wilson's *Translating Buddhism from Tibetan* (TBFT), the author's *A Tibetan Verb Lexicon* (TVL), and this *Reader*.

Six Semester Course Syllabus

First Semester

Week 1: Introduction to the Tibetan language, Tibetan script, pronunciation rules, & normative romanization (Wylie). Wilson, *TBFT*, chapters 1–3.

Week 2: Simple vocabulary, syllable formation rules, and corresponding pronunciation changes. Difference between words and particles (lexical and syntactic). Basic sentential grammar. Introduction to parts of speech. Wilson, *TBFT*, chapters 4–7.

Week 3: Forming Words. Syntax. Lexical Particles. Noun Phrases. Numbers. Wilson, *TBFT*, chapters 8–9.

Week 4: More on Numbers. Case-marking Particles. Verbs and Requisite Syntax. Complements vs. Qualifiers. Verbal Collocations. Wilson, *TBFT*, chapters 10–15; Hackett, *TVL*, "Introduction."

Week 5: Case-marking Particles. Verbs and Requisite Syntax. Complements vs. Qualifiers. Verbal Collocations. Wilson, *TBFT*, Appendixes 4 and 5.

Week 6: Locative Absolute. Sixth-Case Connectives. Wilson, *TBFT*, Appendixes 5 and 7; Hackett, *TVL*, "Introduction."

Week 7: Clause Connectives. Continuative Particles. Auxiliary Verbs. Wilson, *TBFT*, Appendix 4; Hackett, *TVL*, "Introduction."

Weeks 8–10: *Reader*, Selection 1, *Heart Sūtra.*

Weeks 10–14: *Reader*, Selection 2, Jñānamitra's *Explanation of the Heart Sūtra.*

Week 15: Review and Exams.

Second Semester

Weeks 1–4: *Reader*, Selection 2, Jñānamitra's *Explanation of the Heart Sūtra.*

Weeks 5–8: *Reader*, Selection 3, *Sūtra Called "The Wise and Foolish."*

Weeks 8–9: *Reader*, Appendix 4 (Selection 4), Tsongkhapa's *Three Principal Aspects.*

Weeks 10–14: *Reader*, Selection 5, Paṇchen Sönam Drakpa's *New Red Annals.*

Week 15: Review and Exams.

Third Semester

Weeks 1–3: *Reader*, Selection 6, Purbujok's "Introductory Path of Reasoning."

Week 4: *Reader*, Appendix 7, "Grounds and Paths."

Weeks 4–14: *Reader*, Selection 8, *Precious Garland: A Presentation of Tenets.*

Fourth Semester

Weeks 1–14: *Reader*, Selection 8, *Precious Garland: A Presentation of Tenets.*

Fifth Semester

Weeks 1–13: *Reader*, Selection 9, *Lamp Illuminating the Three Bodies.*

Weeks 13–14: *Reader*, Selection 10, *Prayer for Release from the Dangerous Bardo.*

Week 15: Review and Exams.

Sixth Semester

Weeks 1–5: *Reader*, Selection 7, *Presentation of Awarenesses and Knowers.*

Weeks 6–7: *Reader*, Appendix 4 (Selection 11), *Engaging in the Deeds of a Bodhisattva.*

Weeks 8–9: *Reader*, Selection 12, *Fifty Verses on the Guru.*

Weeks 10–12: *Reader*, Selection 13, *Yoga of the Guru and Avalokiteśvara.*

Weeks 13–14: *Reader*, Appendix 4 (Selection 14), *Long-life Prayer for HHDL.*

Week 15: Review and Exams.

Four Semester Course Syllabus

First Semester

Same as above.

Second Semester

Same as above.

Third Semester

Weeks 1–12: *Reader*, Selection 9, *Lamp Illuminating the Three Bodies.*

Weeks 13–14: *Reader*, Selection 10, *Prayer for Release from the Dangerous Bardo.*

Week 15: Review and Exams.

Fourth Semester

Weeks 1–3: *Reader*, Selection 6, Purbujok's "Introductory Path of Reasoning."

Weeks 4–5: *Reader*, Selection 11 (or Appendix 4), *Engaging in the Deeds of a Bodhisattva.*

Weeks 6–7: *Reader*, Selection 12, *Fifty Verses on the Guru.*

Weeks 8–10: *Reader*, Selection 13, *Yoga of the Guru and Avalokiteśvara.*

Weeks 11–12: *Reader*, Selection 14 (or Appendix 4), *Long-life Prayer for HHDL.*

Weeks 13–14: *Reader*, Selection 8, Excerpts from *Precious Garland: A Presentation of Tenets.*

Week 15: Review and Exams.

Appendix 7: Key Concepts in "Grounds and Paths" (*sa lam*)

In the very first text encountered in this *Reader—The Heart Sūtra*—the subject of the path to enlightenment was briefly touched upon. While the perfection of wisdom (*prajñāpāramitā*) literature explicitly teaches the eight subjects of "Clear Realization" (*abhisamaya*), it is the commentary by Maitreya—his *Ornament for the Clear Realizations* (*Abhisamayālaṃkāra; Mngon rtogs rgyan*)—that is said to make explicit the Buddhist "path" structure contained within those discourses. In this presentation, the Buddhist path is laid out as two intertwining progressions consisting of five paths (*marga; lam*) and ten grounds (*bhūmi; sa*).

In a course of advanced studies, this text—together with Haribhadra's *Clear Meaning* commentary—is studied in combination with additional Tibetan commentaries. In summarized form, however, this material is approached through two types of textbooks: presentations of "Grounds and Paths" (*sa lam*) and presentations of the "Seventy Topics" (*don bdun bcu pa*). Since the "Seventy Topics" textbooks form more of a topical guide to Maitreya's text, it is less relevant here.

There are two distinct ways of presenting the grounds and paths to enlightenment. The first is as it accords with the Middle Way Consequence School (*prāsaṅgika-madhyamaka; thal 'gyur pa'i dbu ma pa*)—that is, the interpretation of Middle Way philosophy following Candrakīrti. In this system, there is only one object to be realized—the emptiness of intrinsic existence—and consequently only one vehicle leading to enlightenment. The second manner of presenting grounds and paths is as it accords with the Middle Way Autonomy School (*svātantrika-madhyamaka; rang rgyud pa'i dbu ma pa*), or the philosophical system following Bhāvaviveka's interpretation of Nāgārjuna. In this system, objects have intrinsic existence on a conventional level. Consequently, the three different "vehicles" of *śrāvaka*s, *pratyekabuddha*s, and *bodhisattva*s are asserted as distinct since they each take a different object as their object of meditation and have different realizations in the fruition of their respective paths. It should be noted that the vast majority of "Grounds and Paths" texts are composed from this latter perspective—primarily to highlight the distinctive features of the bodhisattva path as well as the detailed differences between the three vehicles as described in the lower tenet systems. As an introduction to the basic vocabulary of the topic, sets of key terms and their definitions from these presentations are given here, organized thematically.

For a detailed explanation of these terms, refer to Elizabeth Napper's *Kön-chog-jig-may-wang-po's Presentation of the Grounds and Paths* (n.d.) and Jules Levinson's *The Metaphors of Liberation* (1994).

According to Svātantrika

སྐྱེས་བུ་གསུམ།

མཚོན་བྱ་	མཚན་ཉིད་
སྐྱེས་བུ་ཆུང་ངུ་ཁྱད་པར་ཅན་གྱི་ལམ།	རང་ཉིད་ཁོ་ནའི་དོན་དུ་ཚེ་ཕྱི་མའི་འཁོར་བའི་མངོན་མཐོ་ཙམ་གཙོ་བོར་དོན་དུ་གཉེར་བའི་ཆ་ནས་བཞག་པའི་བསམ་པ།
སྐྱེས་བུ་འབྲིང་གི་ལམ།	འཁོར་བའི་ཕུན་ཚོགས་ལ་བློ་ལོག་པའི་སྒོ་ནས་རང་ཉིད་ཁོ་ནའི་དོན་དུ་ཐར་པ་གཙོ་བོར་དོན་དུ་གཉེར་བའི་ཆ་ནས་བཞག་པའི་བསམ་པ།
སྐྱེས་བུ་ཆེན་པོའི་ལམ།	སྙིང་རྗེ་ཆེན་པོའི་གཞན་དབང་དུ་གྱུར་པའི་སྒོ་ནས་སེམས་ཅན་གཞན་གྱིས་སངས་རྒྱས་ཐོབ་ཕྱིར་དུ་རྣམ་མཁྱེན་དོན་དུ་གཉེར་བའི་ཆ་ནས་བཞག་པའི་བསམ་པ།
སྐྱེས་བུ་ཆུང་འབྲིང་ཐུན་མོང་གི་ལམ།	སྐྱེས་བུ་གསུམ་ཀའི་ཉམས་སུ་བླང་བྱ་ཡང་ཡིན་འབྲིང་གི་ལམ་རང་རྒྱུད་ལ་སྐྱེ་བ་ལ་རང་ཉིད་ལ་ཐོག་མར་བློ་སྦྱོང་དགོས་པའི་བསམ་པ།
སྐྱེས་བུ་ཆེ་འབྲིང་ཐུན་མོང་གི་ལམ།	སྐྱེས་བུ་ཆེ་འབྲིང་གཉིས་ཀའི་ཉམས་སུ་བླང་བྱ་ཡང་ཡིན། ཆེན་པོའི་ལམ་རང་རྒྱུད་ལ་སྐྱེ་བ་ལ་རང་ཉིད་ལ་ཐོག་མར་བློ་སྦྱོང་དགོས་པའི་བསམ་པ།

ས་ལམ་གཉིས།

མཚོན་བྱ་	མཚན་ཉིད་
ས་ལམ་གཉིས་ཀྱི་ནང་ཚན་དུ་གྱུར་པའི་ས།	རང་གི་འབྲས་བུར་གྱུར་པའི་ཡོན་ཏན་དུ་མའི་གཞི་རྟེན་བྱེད་པའི་ལམ་ཞུགས་ཀྱི་མངོན་རྟོགས།
ལམ།	རང་འབྲས་བྱང་ཆུབ་ཏུ་བགྲོད་པའི་གོ་སྐབས་ཕྱེ་ཤུལ་དུ་གྱུར་པའི་ལམ་ཞུགས་ཀྱི་མཁྱེན་པ།
ཚོགས་ལམ།	ཆོས་མངོན་རྟོགས།
སྦྱོར་ལམ།	དོན་མངོན་རྟོགས།
མཐོང་ལམ།	བདེན་པ་མངོན་རྟོགས།
སྒོམ་ལམ།	རྗེས་ལ་མངོན་རྟོགས།
མི་སློབ་ལམ།	ཉོན་སྒྲིབ་སྤངས་པའི་ཆ་ནས་བཞག་པའི་མཁྱེན་པ།

ཉན་ཐོས་ཀྱི་ལམ།

མཚོན་བྱ་	མཚན་ཉིད་
ཉན་ཐོས་ཀྱི་ཚོགས་ལམ།	རང་འབྲས་སྦྱོར་ལམ་མ་སྐྱེས་གོང་གི་ཉན་ཐོས་ཀྱི་ཆོས་མངོན་རྟོགས།
ཉན་ཐོས་ཀྱི་སྦྱོར་ལམ།	རང་འབྲས་ཉན་ཐོས་ཀྱི་མཐོང་ལམ་མ་སྐྱེས་གོང་གི་ཉན་ཐོས་ཀྱི་དོན་མངོན་རྟོགས།
ཉན་ཐོས་ཀྱི་མཐོང་ལམ།	རང་འབྲས་ཉན་ཐོས་ཀྱི་སྒོམ་ལམ་མ་སྐྱེས་གོང་གི་ཉན་ཐོས་ཀྱི་བདེན་པ་མངོན་རྟོགས།
ཉན་ཐོས་ཀྱི་མཐོང་ལམ་མཉམ་བཞག་ཡེ་ཤེས།	རང་ཡུལ་དུ་གྱུར་པའི་གང་ཟག་གི་བདག་མེད་ལ་རྩེ་གཅིག་ཏུ་མཉམ་པར་བཞག་པའི་ཉན་ཐོས་ཀྱི་བདེན་པ་མངོན་རྟོགས།
ཉན་ཐོས་ཀྱི་མཐོང་ལམ་བར་ཆད་མེད་ལམ།	ཉོན་སྒྲིབ་ཀུན་བཏགས་ཀྱི་དངོས་གཉེན་དུ་གྱུར་པའི་ཉན་ཐོས་ཀྱི་བདེན་པ་མངོན་རྟོགས།

མཚོན་བྱ་	མཚན་ཉིད་
ཉན་ཐོས་ཀྱི་མཐོང་ལམ་རྣམ་གྲོལ་ལམ།	ཉོན་སྒྲིབ་ཀུན་བཏགས་སྤངས་པའི་རྣམ་གྲོལ་ལམ་དུ་གྱུར་པའི་ཉན་ཐོས་ཀྱི་བདེན་པ་མངོན་རྟོགས།
ཉན་ཐོས་ཀྱི་མཐོང་ལམ་རྗེས་ཐོབ་ཡེ་ཤེས།	ཉན་ཐོས་ཀྱི་མཐོང་ལམ་བར་ཆད་མེད་ལམ་དང་རྣམ་གྲོལ་ལམ་གང་རུང་མ་ཡིན་པའི་ཉན་ཐོས་ཀྱི་མཐོང་ལམ་ཡང་ཡིན་རང་འདྲེན་བྱེད་ཀྱི་རྣམ་གྲོལ་ལམ་རྫོགས་རྗེས་སུ་བྱུང་བའི་ཆ་ནས་བཞག་པའི་ཉན་ཐོས་ཀྱི་བདེན་པ་མངོན་རྟོགས།
ཉན་ཐོས་ཀྱི་སྒོམ་ལམ།	ཉན་ཐོས་ཀྱི་རྗེས་ལ་མངོན་རྟོགས།
ཉན་ཐོས་ཀྱི་སྒོམ་ལམ་མཉམ་བཞག་ཡེ་ཤེས།	རང་ཡུལ་དུ་གྱུར་པའི་བདག་མེད་ལ་རྩེ་གཅིག་ཏུ་མཉམ་པར་བཞག་པའི་ཉན་ཐོས་ཀྱི་རྗེས་ལ་མངོན་རྟོགས།
ཉན་ཐོས་ཀྱི་སྒོམ་ལམ་བར་ཆད་མེད་ལམ།	རང་གི་ངོས་སྐལ་གྱི་སྤང་བྱ་སྒོམ་སྤང་ཉོན་སྒྲིབ་ཀྱི་དངོས་གཉེན་དུ་གྱུར་པའི་ཉན་ཐོས་ཀྱི་རྗེས་ལ་མངོན་རྟོགས།
ཉན་ཐོས་ཀྱི་སྒོམ་ལམ་རྣམ་གྲོལ་ལམ།	རང་འདྲེན་བྱེད་ཀྱི་བར་ཆད་མེད་ལམ་གྱི་ངོས་སྐལ་གྱི་སྤང་བྱ་སྒོམ་སྤང་ཉོན་སྒྲིབ་སྤངས་པའི་རྣམ་གྲོལ་ལམ་དུ་གྱུར་པའི་ཉན་ཐོས་ཀྱི་རྗེས་ལ་མངོན་རྟོགས།
ཉན་ཐོས་ཀྱི་མི་སློབ་ལམ།	ཉན་ཐོས་ཀྱི་ལམ་གྱི་བགྲོད་པ་མཐར་ཕྱིན་པའི་མངོན་རྟོགས།

རང་རྒྱལ་གྱི་ལམ།

མཚོན་བྱ་	མཚན་ཉིད་
རང་རྒྱལ་གྱི་ལམ།	རང་རྒྱལ་གྱི་ཐར་པར་བགྲོད་པའི་གོ་སྐབས་ཕྱེ་ཤུལ་དུ་གྱུར་པའི་རང་རྒྱལ་གྱི་མངོན་རྟོགས།
རང་རྒྱལ་གྱི་ཚོགས་ལམ།	རང་འབྲས་རང་རྒྱལ་གྱི་སྦྱོར་ལམ་མ་སྐྱེས་གོང་གི་རང་རྒྱལ་གྱི་ཆོས་མངོན་རྟོགས།

མཚོན་བྱ་	མཚན་ཉིད་
རང་རྒྱལ་གྱི་སྦྱོར་ལམ།	རང་གི་ཉེར་ལེན་དུ་གྱུར་པའི་ཚོགས་ལམ་རྫོགས་རྗེས་སུ་བྱུང་ཞིང་རང་འབྲས་རང་རྒྱལ་གྱི་མཐོང་ལམ་མ་སྐྱེས་གོང་གི་རང་རྒྱལ་གྱི་དོན་མངོན་རྟོགས།
རང་རྒྱལ་གྱི་མཐོང་ལམ།	རང་གི་ཉེར་ལེན་དུ་གྱུར་པའི་རང་རྒྱལ་གྱི་སྦྱོར་ལམ་རྫོགས་རྗེས་སུ་བྱུང་ཞིང་རང་གི་འབྲས་བུར་གྱུར་པའི་རང་རྒྱལ་གྱི་སྒོམ་ལམ་མ་སྐྱེས་གོང་གི་རང་རྒྱལ་གྱི་བདེན་པ་མངོན་རྟོགས།
རང་རྒྱལ་གྱི་མཐོང་ལམ་མཉམ་བཞག་ཡེ་ཤེས།	རང་ཡུལ་དུ་གྱུར་པའི་ཆོས་ཀྱི་བདག་མེད་རགས་པ་ལ་རྩེ་གཅིག་ཏུ་མཉམ་པར་བཞག་པའི་རང་རྒྱལ་གྱི་བདེན་པ་མངོན་རྟོགས།
རང་རྒྱལ་གྱི་མཐོང་ལམ་བར་ཆད་མེད་ལམ།	ཤེས་སྒྲིབ་རགས་པ་ཀུན་བཏགས་ཀྱི་དངོས་གཉེན་དུ་གྱུར་པའི་རང་རྒྱལ་གྱི་བདེན་པ་མངོན་རྟོགས།
རང་རྒྱལ་གྱི་མཐོང་ལམ་རྣམ་གྲོལ་ལམ།	ཤེས་སྒྲིབ་རགས་པ་ཀུན་བཏགས་སྤངས་པའི་རྣམ་གྲོལ་ལམ་དུ་གྱུར་པའི་རང་རྒྱལ་གྱི་བདེན་པ་མངོན་རྟོགས།
རང་རྒྱལ་གྱི་སྒོམ་ལམ།	རང་གི་ཉེར་ལེན་དུ་གྱུར་པའི་རང་རྒྱལ་གྱི་མཐོང་ལམ་རྫོགས་རྗེས་སུ་བྱུང་ཞིང་། རང་གི་འབྲས་བུར་གྱུར་པའི་རང་རྒྱལ་གྱི་མི་སློབ་ལམ་མ་སྐྱེས་གོང་གི་རང་རྒྱལ་གྱི་རྗེས་ལ་མངོན་རྟོགས།
རང་རྒྱལ་གྱི་སྒོམ་ལམ་མཉམ་བཞག་ཡེ་ཤེས།	རང་ཡུལ་དུ་གྱུར་པའི་ཆོས་ཀྱི་བདག་མེད་རགས་པ་ལ་རྩེ་གཅིག་ཏུ་མཉམ་པར་བཞག་པའི་རང་རྒྱལ་གྱི་རྗེས་ལ་མངོན་རྟོགས།
རང་རྒྱལ་གྱི་སྒོམ་ལམ་བར་ཆད་མེད་ལམ།	རང་གི་ངོས་སྐལ་གྱི་སྤང་བྱ་སྒོམ་སྤང་ཤེས་སྒྲིབ་རགས་པའི་དངོས་གཉེན་དུ་གྱུར་པའི་རང་རྒྱལ་གྱི་རྗེས་ལ་མངོན་རྟོགས།
རང་རྒྱལ་གྱི་སྒོམ་ལམ་རྣམ་གྲོལ་ལམ།	རང་འདྲེན་བྱེད་ཀྱི་བར་ཆད་མེད་ལམ་གྱི་ངོས་སྐལ་གྱི་སྤང་བྱ་སྒོམ་སྤང་ཤེས་སྒྲིབ་རགས་པ་སྤངས་པའི་རྣམ་གྲོལ་ལམ་དུ་གྱུར་པའི་རང་རྒྱལ་གྱི་རྗེས་ལ་མངོན་རྟོགས།
རང་རྒྱལ་གྱི་མི་སློབ་ལམ།	གཟུང་བ་ཕྱི་རོལ་དོན་དུ་འཛིན་པའི་རྟོག་པ་མ་ལུས་པར་སྤངས་པའི་རང་རྒྱལ་གྱི་མཁྱེན་པ།

བྱང་ཆུབ་སེམས་དཔའི་ས་ལམ།

མཚོན་བྱ་	མཚན་ཉིད་
ཐེག་ཆེན་གྱི་ལམ།	ཐེག་ཆེན་གྱི་བྱང་ཆུབ་ཏུ་བགྲོད་པར་བྱེད་པའམ། དེར་བགྲོད་ཟིན་པ་གང་རུང་གིས་བསྡུས་པའི་ཐེག་ཆེན་གྱི་མཁྱེན་པ།
བྱང་སེམས་ཀྱི་ལམ།	ཐེག་ཆེན་གྱི་ཐར་པར་བགྲོད་པའི་གོ་སྐབས་ཐེ་ཤུལ་དུ་གྱུར་པའི་བྱང་སེམས་ཀྱི་མངོན་རྟོགས།
བྱང་སེམས་སོ་སྐྱེའི་ལམ།	སོས་སྐྱོད་ཀྱི་སས་བསྡུས་པའི་བྱང་སེམས་ཀྱི་མཁྱེན་པ།
ཐེག་ཆེན་གྱི་ཚོགས་ལམ།	ཐེག་ཆེན་གྱི་ཆོས་མངོན་རྟོགས།
ཐེག་ཆེན་སྦྱོར་ལམ།	བྱང་སེམས་ཀྱི་དོན་མངོན་རྟོགས།
ཐེག་ཆེན་གྱི་མཐོང་ལམ།	ཐེག་ཆེན་གྱི་བདེན་པ་མངོན་རྟོགས།
ཐེག་ཆེན་གྱི་མཐོང་ལམ་བར་ཆད་མེད་ལམ།	རང་གི་ངོས་སྐལ་གྱི་སྤང་བྱ་བདེན་འཛིན་ཀུན་བཏགས་ཀྱི་དངོས་གཉེན་དུ་གྱུར་པའི་ཐེག་ཆེན་གྱི་བདེན་པ་མངོན་རྟོགས།
ཐེག་ཆེན་གྱི་མཐོང་ལམ་རྣམ་གྲོལ་ལམ།	ཤེས་སྒྲིབ་ཀུན་བཏགས་སྤངས་པས་རབ་ཏུ་ཕྱེ་པའི་ཐེག་ཆེན་གྱི་བདེན་པ་མངོན་རྟོགས།
ཐེག་ཆེན་གྱི་མཐོང་ལམ་རྗེས་ཐོབ་ཡེ་ཤེས།	ཐེག་ཆེན་གྱི་མཐོང་ལམ་རྣམ་གྲོལ་ལམ་ལས་ལངས་པའི་མཁྱེན་པ་ཡང་ཡིན། རང་རྒྱུད་ལྡན་གྱི་གང་ཟག་གི་རྒྱུད་ལ་མངོན་གྱུར་དུ་འབྱུང་བའི་ཐེག་ཆེན་གྱི་བདེན་པ་མངོན་རྟོགས།
ཐེག་ཆེན་གྱི་སྒོམ་ལམ།	ཐེག་ཆེན་གྱི་རྗེས་ལ་མངོན་རྟོགས།
ཐེག་ཆེན་གྱི་སྒོམ་ལམ་མཉམ་བཞག་ཡེ་ཤེས།	རང་གི་ཡུལ་དུ་གྱུར་པའི་བདག་མེད་གསུམ་གང་རུང་ལ་རྩེ་གཅིག་ཏུ་མཉམ་པར་བཞག་པ་ཡང་ཡིན། རང་རྒྱུད་ལྡན་གྱི་གང་ཟག་གི་རྒྱུད་ལ་མངོན་གྱུར་དུ་འབྱུང་བའི་ཐེག་ཆེན་གྱི་རྗེས་ལ་མངོན་རྟོགས།
ཐེག་ཆེན་གྱི་སྒོམ་ལམ་བར་ཆད་མེད་ལམ།	རང་གི་ངོས་སྐལ་གྱི་སྤང་བྱ་བདེན་འཛིན་ལྷན་སྐྱེས་ཀྱི་དངོས་གཉེན་དུ་གྱུར་པའི་ཐེག་ཆེན་གྱི་རྗེས་ལ་མངོན་རྟོགས།
ཐེག་ཆེན་གྱི་སྒོམ་ལམ་བར་ཆད་མེད་ལམ་ཆུང་ངུའི་ཆུང་ངུ།	རང་གི་ངོས་སྐལ་གྱི་སྤང་བྱ་བདེན་འཛིན་ལྷན་སྐྱེས་ཆེན་པོའི་ཆེན་པོའི་དངོས་གཉེན་དུ་གྱུར་པའི་ཐེག་ཆེན་གྱི་སྒོམ་ལམ་བར་ཆད་མེད་ལམ།

མཚོན་བྱ་	མཚན་ཉིད་
ཐེག་ཆེན་གྱི་སྒོམ་ལམ་རྣམ་གྲོལ་ལམ།	རང་འདྲེན་བྱེད་ཀྱི་བར་ཆད་མེད་ལམ་གྱི་ངོས་སྐལ་གྱི་སྤང་བྱ་བདེན་འཛིན་ལྷན་སྐྱེས་ལས་གྲོལ་བའི་ཐེག་ཆེན་གྱི་རྗེས་ལ་མངོན་རྟོགས།
ཐེག་ཆེན་གྱི་མི་སློབ་ལམ།	སྒྲིབ་གཉིས་ཟད་པར་སྤངས་པའི་མཐར་ཐུག་གི་མཁྱེན་པ།
བྱང་སེམས་འཕགས་པའི་ས།	སྟོང་ཉིད་མངོན་སུམ་དུ་རྟོགས་པའི་ཤེས་རབ་དང་། སྙིང་རྗེ་ཆེན་པོས་ཟིན་པའི་བྱང་འཕགས་ཀྱི་མཁྱེན་པ།

མཚོན་བྱ་	དབྱེ་བ་
བྱང་སེམས་འཕགས་པའི་ས།	རབ་ཏུ་དགའ་བ། དྲི་མ་མེད་པ། འོད་བྱེད་པ། འོད་འཕྲོ་བ། སྦྱང་དཀའ་བ། མངོན་དུ་གྱུར་པ། རིང་དུ་སོང་བ། མི་གཡོ་བ། ལེགས་པའི་བློ་གྲོས། ཆོས་ཀྱི་སྤྲིན།

Three [Types of] Beings [of Different Capacities]

Term	Definition
path of a special being of small capacity	a thought posited from the viewpoint of seeking mainly mere high status within a future cyclic existence for one's own sake alone
path of a being of middling capacity	a thought posited from the viewpoint of mainly seeking liberation for the sake of oneself alone, from the viewpoint of having turned the mind away from the marvels of cyclic existence
path of a being of great capacity	a thought that is posited by way of seeking [to attain] an exalted knower of all aspects for the sake of other sentient beings' attaining buddhahood from the point of view of having come under the influence of great compassion

Term	Definition
path common to beings of small and middling capacity	that which is (1) an object of practice by beings of all three capacities and (2) is a thought in which it is initially necessary to train the mind in order to generate in one's continuum a path of a being of middling capacity
path common to beings of middling and great capacities	that which is (1) an object of practice by beings of both middling and great capacities and (2) is a thought in which one must train initially the mind in order to generate in one's continuum a path of a being of great capacity

General Definitions of Grounds and Paths

Term	Definition
ground—within the set of "Grounds and Paths"	a clear realization of one who has entered the path that acts as a basis of the many [good] qualities that are its fruit
path	an exalted knower of one who has entered a path that serves as a passageway allowing the opportunity of progressing to that enlightenment which is its result
path of accumulation	a clear realization of the Dharma ("doctrine")
path preparation	a clear realization of the meaning
path of seeing	a clear realization of the truth
path of meditation	a subsequent clear realization
path of no more learning	an exalted knower that is posited from the perspective of having abandoned the afflictive obstructions

Śrāvaka Paths

Term	Definition
śrāvaka path of accumulation	a śrāvaka's clear realization of the Dharma generated prior to the path of preparation that is its own effect

Term	Definition
śrāvaka path preparation	a śrāvaka's clear realization of the meaning generated prior to the śrāvaka path of seeing that is its own effect
śrāvaka path of seeing	a śrāvaka's clear realization of the truth that is generated prior to the śrāvaka path of meditation that is its effect
śrāvaka path of seeing that is an exalted wisdom of meditative equipoise	a śrāvaka's clear realization of the truth that is in one-pointed equipoise on the subtle selflessness of the person, which is its object
śrāvaka path of seeing that is an uninterrupted path	a śrāvaka's clear realization of the truth that serves as the actual antidote to the artificial afflictive obstructions
śrāvaka path of seeing that is a path of release	a śrāvaka's clear realization of the truth that serves as a path of release that abandons the artificial afflictive obstructions
śrāvaka path of seeing that is an exalted wisdom of subsequent attainment	a śrāvaka's clear realization of the truth that is posited from the viewpoint of (1) being a śrāvaka path of seeing that is neither an uninterrupted path nor a path of release of a śrāvaka path of seeing, and (2) arising after the completion of the path of release that induces it
śrāvaka path of meditation	a subsequent clear realization
śrāvaka path of meditation that is an exalted wisdom of meditative equipoise	a śrāvaka's subsequent clear realization that is set in one-pointed meditative equipoise on the selflessness that is its object
śrāvaka path of meditation that is an uninterrupted path	a śrāvaka's subsequent clear realization that serves as an actual antidote to the afflictive obstructions that are to be abandoned by a path of meditation and that are its own corresponding objects of abandonment
śrāvaka path of meditation that is a path of release	a śrāvaka's subsequent clear realization that serves as a path of release having abandoned the afflictive obstructions that are to be abandoned by a path of meditation and that are the corresponding objects of abandonment by the uninterrupted path inducing it

Term	Definition
śrāvaka path of no more learning	a clear realization of one who has completed the progress of a śrāvaka's path

Pratyekabuddha Paths

Term	Definition
pratyekabuddha path	a pratyekabuddha's clear realization that serves as a passageway opening the opportunity of progressing to a pratyekabuddha's liberation
pratyekabuddha path of accumulation	a pratyekabuddha's clear realization of the Dharma generated prior to the pratyekabuddha path of preparation, which is its effect
pratyekabuddha path preparation	a pratyekabuddha's clear realization of the meaning that arises after the completion of the path of accumulation, which is its substantial cause, and that is generated prior to the pratyekabuddha path of seeing, which is its effect
pratyekabuddha path of seeing	a pratyekabuddha's clear realization of the truth that arises after the completion of the pratyekabuddha path of preparation, which serves as its substantial cause, and that precedes the generation of the pratyekabuddha's path of meditation, which becomes its effect
pratyekabuddha path of seeing that is an exalted wisdom of meditative equipoise	a pratyekabuddha's clear realization of the truth that is in one-pointed equipoise on the coarse selflessness of phenomena that is its object
pratyekabuddha path of seeing that is an uninterrupted path	a pratyekabuddha's clear realization of the truth that serves as the actual antidote to the coarse obstructions to omniscience
pratyekabuddha path of seeing that is a path of release	a pratyekabuddha's clear realization of the truth that serves as a path of release that abandons the coarse obstructions to omniscience

Term	Definition
pratyekabuddha path of meditation	a pratyekabuddha's subsequent clear realization that arises after the completion of the pratyekabuddha path of seeing, which serves as its substantial cause, and that occurs prior to the generation of the pratyekabuddha path of no more learning, which is its effect
pratyekabuddha path of meditation that is an exalted wisdom of meditative equipoise	a pratyekabuddha's subsequent clear realization that is set in one-pointed meditative equipoise on the coarse selflessness of phenomena that is its object
pratyekabuddha path of meditation that is an uninterrupted path	a pratyekabuddha's subsequent clear realization that serves as an actual antidote to the coarse obstructions to omnisciences that are to be abandoned by a path of meditation and that are its own corresponding objects of abandonment
pratyekabuddha path of meditation that is a path of release	a pratyekabuddha's subsequent clear realization that serves as a path of release having abandoned the coarse obstructions to omniscience that are to be abandoned by a path of meditation and that are the corresponding objects of abandonment by the uninterrupted path that induces it
pratyekabuddha path of no more learning	a pratyekabuddha's exalted knower that has abandoned all conceptual consciousnesses conceiving apprehended objects to be external objects

Bodhisattva Grounds and Paths

Term	Definition
Mahāyāna path	a Mahāyāna exalted knower that is included either within that which causes progress to the Great Vehicle enlightenment or within having progressed to that [Mahāyāna enlightenment]

Term	Definition
bodhisattva path	a bodhisattva's clear realization that serves as a passage-way opening the opportunity for progressing to the Mahāyāna liberation
path of a bodhisattva common being	a bodhisattva's exalted knower that is included within the levels of engagement through belief
Mahāyāna path of accumulation	a Mahāyāna clear realization of doctrine
Mahāyāna path preparation	a bodhisattva's clear realization of the meaning
Mahāyāna path of seeing	a Mahāyāna clear realization of the truth
Mahāyāna path of seeing that is an uninterrupted path	a Mahāyāna clear realization of the truth that serves as the actual antidote to the artificial conception of true existence which is its corresponding object of abandonment
Mahāyāna path of seeing that is a path of release	a Mahāyāna clear realization of the truth that is distinguished by having abandoned the artificial obstructions to omniscience
Mahāyāna path of seeing that is an exalted wisdom of subsequent attainment	that which is (1) an exalted knower of one who has risen from the path of release of a Mahāyāna path of seeing and (2) a Mahāyāna clear realization of the truth that manifestly occurs in the continuum of persons who possess it in their continua
Mahāyāna path of meditation	a Mahāyāna subsequent clear realization
Mahāyāna path of meditation that is an exalted wisdom of meditative equipoise	that which is (1) a one-pointed meditative equipoise on any of the three selflessnesses [of persons, of duality, or of true existence] that is its objects, and (2) a Mahāyāna subsequent clear realization occurring manifestly in the continuum of the person who possesses it in their [mental] continuum

Term	Definition
Mahāyāna path of meditation that is an uninterrupted path	a Mahāyāna subsequent clear realization that serves as the actual antidote to the innate conception of true existence which is its corresponding object of abandonment
small of the small uninterrupted path of a Mahāyāna path of meditation	an uninterrupted path of the Mahāyāna path of meditation that is the actual antidote to the great of the great innate conceptions of true existence which is its corresponding object of abandonment
Mahāyāna path of meditation that is a path of release	a Mahāyāna subsequent clear realization that involves having been liberated from the innate conception of true existence that is the corresponding object of abandonment by the uninterrupted path inducing it
Mahāyāna path of no more learning	a final exalted knower that has exhaustively abandoned the two obstructions
ground of an ārya bodhisattva	an ārya bodhisattva's exalted knower that is conjoined with the wisdom directly realizing emptiness and with great compassion

Term	Divisions
ground of an ārya bodhisattva	(1) Very Joyful, (2) Stainless, (3) Luminous, (4) Radiant, (5) Difficult to Overcome, (6) Manifest, (7) Gone Afar, (8) Immovable, (9) Good Intelligence, (10) Cloud of Dharma

According to Prāsaṅgika

མཚོན་བྱ་	དབྱེ་བ་
ཐེག་ཆེན་གྱི་ས།	རང་གི་འབྲས་བུར་གྱུར་པའི་ཡོན་དན་དུ་མའི་གཞི་རྟེན་བྱེད་པའི་ཐེག་ཆེན་ལམ་ཞུགས་ཀྱི་མངོན་རྟོགས།

མཚོན་བྱ་	དབྱེ་བ་
ཐེག་ཆེན་གྱི་ལམ།	ཐེག་ཆེན་གྱི་མངོན་རྟོགས།
བྱང་སེམས་སོ་སྐྱེའི་ལམ།	མོས་སྤྱོད་ཀྱི་སར་བསྡུས་པའི་བྱང་སེམས་ཀྱི་མངོན་རྟོགས།
ཐེག་ཆེན་གྱི་ཚོགས་ལམ།	ཐེག་ཆེན་གྱི་ཆོས་མངོན་རྟོགས།
ཐེག་ཆེན་སྦྱོར་ལམ།	བྱང་སེམས་ཀྱི་དོན་མངོན་རྟོགས།
བྱང་སེམས་འཕགས་པའི་ས།	སྟོང་ཉིད་མངོན་སུམ་དུ་རྟོགས་པའི་ཤེས་རབ་དང་། སྙིང་རྗེ་ཆེན་པོས་ཟིན་པའི་བྱང་འཕགས་ཀྱི་མཁྱེན་པ།
དོན་དམ་པའི་བྱང་སེམས་འཕགས་པའི་ས།	གྲོགས་སྙིང་རྗེ་ཆེན་པོས་ཟིན་ཅིང་ངོ་བོ་ཟག་པ་མེད་པའི་བྱང་སེམས་འཕགས་པའི་མཉམ་བཞག་རྣམ་པར་མི་རྟོག་པའི་ཡེ་ཤེས།
ཐེག་ཆེན་གྱི་མཐོང་ལམ།	ཐེག་ཆེན་གྱི་བདེན་པ་མངོན་རྟོགས།
ཐེག་ཆེན་གྱི་མཐོང་ལམ་མཉམ་བཞག་ཡེ་ཤེས།	སྟོང་ཉིད་ལ་གཉིས་ནང་ནུབ་པའི་ཐེག་ཆེན་གྱི་བདེན་པ་མངོན་རྟོགས།
ཐེག་ཆེན་གྱི་མཐོང་ལམ་བར་ཆད་མེད་ལམ།	ཐེག་ཆེན་གྱི་མཐོང་ལམ་མཉམ་བཞག་ཡེ་ཤེས་གང་ཞིག བདེན་འཛིན་ཀུན་བཏགས་ཀྱི་དངོས་གཉེན་བྱེད་པ།
ཐེག་ཆེན་གྱི་མཐོང་ལམ་རྣམ་གྲོལ་ལམ།	ཐེག་ཆེན་གྱི་མཐོང་ལམ་མཉམ་བཞག་ཡེ་ཤེས་གང་ཞིག བདེན་འཛིན་ཀུན་བཏགས་སྤངས་པས་རབ་ཏུ་ཕྱེ་པ།
ཐེག་ཆེན་གྱི་མཐོང་ལམ་རྗེས་ཐོབ་ཡེ་ཤེས།	སྟོང་ཉིད་མངོན་སུམ་དུ་མ་རྟོགས་པའི་ཐེག་ཆེན་གྱི་བདེན་པ་མངོན་རྟོགས།
ཐེག་ཆེན་གྱི་སྒོམ་ལམ།	ཐེག་ཆེན་གྱི་རྗེས་ལ་མངོན་རྟོགས།
ཐེག་ཆེན་གྱི་སྒོམ་ལམ་མཉམ་བཞག་ཡེ་ཤེས།	སྟོང་ཉིད་ལ་གཉིས་སྣང་ནུབ་པའི་ཐེག་ཆེན་གྱི་རྗེས་ལ་མངོན་རྟོགས།
ཐེག་ཆེན་གྱི་སྒོམ་ལམ་བར་ཆད་མེད་ལམ།	རང་གི་ངོས་སྐལ་གྱི་སྤང་བྱར་གྱུར་པའི་སྒྲིབ་གཉིས་གང་རུང་གི་དངོས་གཉེན་བྱེད་པ།
ཐེག་ཆེན་གྱི་སྒོམ་ལམ་རྣམ་གྲོལ་ལམ།	ཐེག་ཆེན་གྱི་མཐོང་ལམ་མཉམ་བཞག་ཡེ་ཤེས་གང་ཞིག རང་འདྲེན་བྱེད་ཀྱི་བར་ཆད་མེད་ལམ་གྱི་ངོས་སྐལ་གྱི་སྤང་བྱར་གྱུར་པའི་སྒྲིབ་གཉིས་གང་རུང་ལས་དངོས་སུ་གྲོལ་བ།

མཚོན་བྱ་	དབྱེ་བ་
ཐེག་ཆེན་གྱི་སྒོམ་ལམ་རྗེས་ཐོབ་ཡེ་ཤེས།	སྟོང་ཉིད་མངོན་སུམ་དུ་མ་རྟོགས་པའི་ཐེག་ཆེན་གྱི་རྗེས་ལ་མངོན་རྟོགས།
ཐེག་དམན་གྱི་མཐོང་ལམ་མཉམ་བཞག་ཡེ་ཤེས།	སྟོང་ཉིད་ལ་གཉིས་ནང་ཉུབ་པའི་ཐེག་དམན་གྱི་བདེན་པ་མངོན་རྟོགས།
ཐེག་དམན་གྱི་མཐོང་ལམ་བར་ཆད་མེད་ལམ།	ཐེག་དམན་གྱི་མཐོང་ལམ་མཉམ་བཞག་ཡེ་ཤེས་གང་ཞིག བདེན་འཛིན་ཀུན་བཏགས་ཀྱི་དངོས་གཉེན་བྱེད་པ།
ཐེག་དམན་གྱི་མཐོང་ལམ་རྣམ་གྲོལ་ལམ།	ཐེག་དམན་གྱི་མཐོང་ལམ་མཉམ་བཞག་ཡེ་ཤེས་གང་ཞིག བདེན་འཛིན་ཀུན་བཏགས་སྤངས་པས་རབ་ཏུ་ཕྱེ་པ།
ཐེག་དམན་གྱི་མཐོང་ལམ་རྗེས་ཐོབ་ཡེ་ཤེས།	སྟོང་ཉིད་མངོན་སུམ་དུ་མ་རྟོགས་པའི་ཐེག་དམན་གྱི་བདེན་པ་མངོན་རྟོགས།
ཐེག་དམན་གྱི་སྒོམ་ལམ།	ཐེག་དམན་གྱི་རྗེས་ལ་མངོན་རྟོགས།
ཐེག་དམན་གྱི་སྒོམ་ལམ་མཉམ་བཞག་ཡེ་ཤེས།	སྟོང་ཉིད་ལ་གཉིས་སྣང་ཉུབ་པའི་ཐེག་དམན་གྱི་རྗེས་ལ་མངོན་རྟོགས།
ཐེག་དམན་གྱི་སྒོམ་ལམ་བར་ཆད་མེད་ལམ།	ཐེག་དམན་གྱི་སྒོམ་ལམ་མཉམ་བཞག་ཡེ་ཤེས་གང་ཞིག རང་གི་དངོས་སྐལ་གྱི་སྤང་བྱར་གྱུར་པའི་བདེན་འཛིན་ལྷན་སྐྱེས་ཀྱི་དངོས་གཉེན་བྱེད་པ།
ཐེག་དམན་གྱི་སྒོམ་ལམ་རྣམ་གྲོལ་ལམ།	ཐེག་དམན་གྱི་སྒོམ་ལམ་མཉམ་བཞག་ཡེ་ཤེས་གང་ཞིག རང་འདྲེན་བྱེད་ཀྱི་བར་ཆད་མེད་ལམ་གྱི་དངོས་སྐལ་གྱི་སྤང་བྱར་གྱུར་པའི་བདེན་འཛིན་ལྷན་སྐྱེས་ལས་དངོས་སུ་གྲོལ་བ།
ཐེག་དམན་གྱི་སྒོམ་ལམ་རྗེས་ཐོབ་ཡེ་ཤེས།	སྟོང་ཉིད་མངོན་སུམ་དུ་མ་རྟོགས་པའི་ཐེག་དམན་གྱི་རྗེས་ལ་མངོན་རྟོགས།
ཐེག་དམན་གྱི་མི་སློབ་ལམ།	ཐེག་དམན་གྱི་མངོན་རྟོགས་གང་ཞིག བདེན་འཛིན་ས་བོན་དང་བཅས་པ་ཟད་པར་སྤངས་པ།

Term	Definition
Mahāyāna ground	a clear realization of one who has entered a Mahāyāna path that serves as a basis of the many good qualities that are its effect
Mahāyāna path	a Mahāyāna clear realization
path of a bodhisattva common being	a bodhisattva's clear realization that is included within the grounds of activites through belief
Mahāyāna path of accumulation	a Mahāyāna clear realization of the Dharma ("doctrine")
Mahāyāna path preparation	a Mahāyāna clear realization of the meaning
ground of an ārya bodhisattva	an ārya bodhisattva's exalted knower that is conjoined with both the wisdom directly realizing emptiness and great compassion
ultimate ground of an ārya bodhisattva	an ārya bodhisattva's nonconceptual exalted wisdom of meditative equipoise whose entity is uncontaminated and which is conjoined with great compassion, its accompanier
Mahāyāna path of seeing	a Mahāyāna clear realization of the truth
Mahāyāna path of seeing that is an exalted wisdom of meditative equipoise	a Mahāyāna clear realization of the truth for which all dualistic appearances with regard to emptiness have vanished
Mahāyāna path of seeing that is an uninterrupted path	that which (1) is an exalted wisdom of meditative equipoise of a Mahāyāna path of seeing and (2) serves as an actual antidote to the artificial conceptions of true existence
Mahāyāna path of seeing that is a path of release	that which (1) is an exalted wisdom of meditative equipoise of a Mahāyāna path of seeing and (2) is distinguished by having abandoned the artificial conceptions of true existence
Mahāyāna path of seeing that is an exalted wisdom of subsequent attainment	a Mahāyāna clear realization of the truth that does not realize emptiness directly
Mahāyāna path of meditation	a Mahāyāna subsequent clear realization

Term	Definition
Mahāyāna path of meditation that is an exalted wisdom of meditative equipoise	a Mahāyāna subsequent clear realization for which all dualistic appearances with regard to emptiness have vanished
Mahāyāna path of meditation that is an uninterrupted path	that which (l) is an exalted wisdom of meditative equipoise of a Mahāyāna path of meditation and (2) serves as a direct antidote to whichever of the two obstructions is its corresponding object of abandonment
Mahāyāna path of meditation that is a path of release	that which (l) is an exalted wisdom of meditative equipoise of a Mahāyāna path of meditation and (2) is directly released from whichever of the two obstructions that is the corresponding object of abandonment of the uninterrupted path inducing it
Mahāyāna path of meditation that is an exalted wisdom of subsequent attainment	a Mahāyāna subsequent clear realization that does not realize emptiness directly

Hīnayāna path of seeing that is an exalted wisdom of meditative equipoise	a Hīnayāna clear realization of the truth for which dualistic appearances with respect to emptiness have vanished
Hīnayāna path of seeing that is an uninterrupted path	that which (1) is an exalted wisdom of meditative equipoise of a Hīnayāna path of seeing, and (2) serves as an actual antidote to artificial conceptions of true existence
Hīnayāna path of seeing that is a path of release	that which (1) is an exalted wisdom of meditative equipoise of a Hīnayāna path of seeing, and (2) is thoroughly distinguished by having abandoned the artificial conceptions of true existence
Hīnayāna path of seeing that is an exalted wisdom of subsequent attainment	a Hīnayāna clear realization of the truth that does not realize emptiness directly

Term	Definition
Hīnayāna path of meditation	a Hīnayāna subsequent clear realization
Hīnayāna path of meditation that is an exalted wisdom of meditative equipoise	a Hīnayāna subsequent clear realization for which dualistic appearances with respect to emptiness have vanished
Hīnayāna path of meditation that is an uninterrupted path	that which (l) is an exalted wisdom of meditative equipoise of a Hīnayāna path of meditation and (2) serves as the actual antidote to the innate conception of true existence that is its corresponding object of abandonment
Hīnayāna path of meditation that is a path of release	that which (l) is an exalted wisdom of meditative equipoise of a Hīnayāna path of meditation and (2) is directly released from the innate conception of true existence that is the corresponding object of abandonment of the uninterrupted path that induces it
Hīnayāna path of meditation that is an exalted wisdom of subsequent attainment	a Hīnayāna subsequent clear realization that does not realize emptiness directly
Hīnayāna path of no more learning	that which (1) is a Hīnayāna clear realization and (2) has abandoned exhaustively the conception of true existence together with its seeds

Bibliography

Contraction and Short-hand References

Bacot, Jacques. 1912. "L'écriture cursive tibétaine." *Journal Asiatique* [Jan-Fév. 1912]: 5–78.

Dzongkha Development Commission / *rdzong kha gong 'phel lhan tshogs*. 2011. *bsdu yig gser gyi a long: A Handbook of Abbreviations*. Thimphu: Royal Government of Bhutan.

Prats, Ramon. 1991. "On 'Contracted Words' and a List of Them Collected from a Bon-po Work." *East and West* 41 (1/4): 231–237.

Rta-mgrin-tshe-dbang. 1999. "Skung yig ngo sprod mdor bsdus." *Tibetan Studies* (Beijing) 73 (3): 109–26.

Wenyi Gu and Xueli Shi. 1995. *Ngo mtshar ba'i gangs can 'phrul ldan skung yig be'u bum*. Lanzhou: Kan-su'u mi rigs dpe skrun khang.

Enumerated Lists of Phenomena (chos kyi rnam grangs)

Das, Sanjib Kumar. 2009. *Basic Buddhist Terminology (Tibetan-Sanskrit-Hindi-English)*. Sarnath, Varanasi (India): Kagyud Relief and Protection Committee.

Dkon mchog 'jigs med dbang po. 1971. "Chos kyi rnam grangs shes ldan yid kyi dga' ston." 7: 465–532. In *The Collected Works of Dkon-mchog-'jigs-med-dbaṅ-po*. Delhi: Ngawang Gelek Demo. Reprinted as *Chos kyi rnam grangs*. Zi ling (A mdo): Mtsho sngon mi rigs dpe skrung khang (1983).

Mgon po dbang rgyal. 1986. *Chos kyi rnam grangs shes bya'i nor gling 'jug pa'i gru gzing*. Chengdu: Sichuan Peoples' Publishing House.

Negi, J. S. 2006. *Dharmasaṅgraha-Kośaḥ (Tibetan-Sanskrit Dharma Terms with Categories)*. Sarnath, Varanasi (India): Central Institute of Higher Tibetan Studies.

Tashi Zangmo and Dechen Chime. 2007. *Dharmasamgrahah (Excellent Collection of Doctrine) of Ācārya Nāgārjuna*. Sarnath, Varanasi (India): Central Institute of Higher Tibetan Studies.

Language References

Wilson, Joe B. 1993. *Translating Buddhism From Tibetan*. Ithaca: Snow Lion Publications.
Magee, William A. et al. 1993. *Fluent Tibetan*. Ithaca: Snow Lion Publications.

Tibetan-English Dictionary References

Das, Sarat Chandra. 1902, 1969. *Tibetan-English Dictionary*. Calcutta: Bengal Secretariat Book Depot. Reprinted Kyoto: Rinsen Book Company.
Hackett, Paul G. 2019. *A Tibetan Verb Lexicon*. Ithaca: Snow Lion Publications.
Hopkins, Jeffrey, and Paul G. Hackett. 2016. *The Uma Institute for Tibetan Studies Tibetan-Sanskrit-English Dictionary*. Dyke, VA: UMA Institute for Tibetan Studies. http://uma-tibet.org/.
Tsepak Rigzin. 2003. *Tibetan-English Dictionary of Buddhist Terminology*. Dharamsala: Library of Tibetan Works and Archives.

Tibetan-Sanskrit Dictionary References

Fukuda, Yoichi, and Ishihama Yumiko. 1989. *A New Critical Edition of the Mahāvyutpatti*. 2 vols. Tokyo: The Toyo Bunko.
Negi, J. S. 1993–2005. *Tibetan-Sanskrit Dictionary*. 16 vols. Sarnath, Varanasi (India): Central Institute of Higher Tibetan Studies.

Cited Works

Agwangdamba. 1980. "Byang chub sems dpa'i spyod pa la 'jug pa'i mchan bu tshig gsal me long." 1: 1–149. In *Works of Agwangdamba (Ṅag-dbaṅ-bstan-pa)*. New Delhi: Sharada Rani.
Beckwith, Christopher. 1993. *The Tibetan Empire in Central Asia*. Princeton: Princeton University Press.
Brunnhölzl, Karl. 2010. *Gone Beyond*. 2 vols. Ithaca: Snow Lion Publications.
———. 2012. *Groundless Paths*. Ithaca: Snow Lion Publications.

Cabezón, José. 1996. "Firm Feet and Long Lives: The Zhabs brtan Literature of Tibetan Buddhism." In *Tibetan Literature: Studies in Genre*. Edited by José Cabezón & Roger Jackson. Ithaca: Snow Lion Publications, 344–57.

Dreyfus, Georges. 1987. "Some Considerations on Definition in Buddhism." Masters Thesis. University of Virginia.

———. 1997. *Recognizing Reality: Dharmakīrti's Philosophy and Its Tibetan Interpretations*. Albany: State University of New York Press.

Haarh, Erik. 1969. *The Yar-luṅ Dynasty*. Copenhagen: Gad's Forlag.

HH the Dalai Lama and Jeffrey Hopkins. 1987. *Tantra in Tibet*. Ithaca: Snow Lion Publications; reprinted with revisions as *The Great Exposition of Secret Mantra, Volume I: Tantra in Tibet*. Boulder: Snow Lion Publications, 2016.

Hopkins, Jeffrey. 1983. *Meditation on Emptiness*. Boston: Wisdom Publications.

———. 1983. "The Tibetan Genre of Doxography: Structuring a Worldview" in Cabezón, José, and Roger Jackson, eds. 1996. *Tibetan Literature: Studies in Genre*. Ithaca: Snow Lion Publications, 170–86.

———. 2003. *Maps of the Profound*. Ithaca: Snow Lion Publications.

Klein, Anne. 1986. *Knowledge and Liberation*. Ithaca: Snow Lion Publications.

———. 1991. *Knowing, Naming, and Negation*. Ithaca: Snow Lion Publications.

Kun bzang chos grags a.k.a. Mkhan po kun dpal. 1970. *Byang chub sems dpa'i spyod pa la 'jug pa'i tshig 'grel 'jam dbyangs bla ma'i zhal lung bdud rtsi'i thig pa*. Nepal: s.n.

Lamrim Translation Committee. 2000–2008. *The Great Treatise on the Stages of the Path to Enlightenment*. 3 vols. Ithaca: Snow Lion Publications.

Lati Rinbochay, and Elizabeth Napper. 1980. *Mind in Tibetan Buddhism*. Ithaca: Snow Lion Publications.

Lati Rinbochay, and Jeffrey Hopkins. 1985. *Death, Intermediate State and Rebirth in Tibetan Buddhism*. Ithaca: Snow Lion Publications.

Levinson, Jules B. 1994. "The Metaphors of Liberation: a study of Grounds and Paths According to the Middle Way Schools." PhD dissertation. University of Virginia.

Lopez, Donald. 1988. *The Heart Sūtra Explained*. Albany: State University of New York Press.

———. 1996. *Elaborations on Emptiness*. Princeton: Princeton University Press.

Napper, Elizabeth. n.d. *Kön-chog-jig-may-wang-po's Presentation of the Grounds and Paths: Beautiful Ornament of the Three Vehicles: Five Paths of the Three Vehicles and the Ten Bodhisattva Grounds of the Great Vehicle*. Dyke, VA: UMA Institute for Tibetan Studies. http://uma-tibet.org/.

Paṇ chen bsod nams grags pa. 1982–1988. "Shes rab kyi pha rol tu phyin pa'i man ngag gi bstan bcos mngon par rtogs pa'i rgyan 'grel pa dang bcas pa'i rnam bshad snying po rgyan gyi don legs par bshad pa yum don gsal ba'i sgron me" a.k.a. "Phar phyin spyi don." In *The Collected Works (Gsuṅ 'bum) of Paṇ-chen Bsod-nams-grags-pa*. vol. 3. Mundgod Karnataka (India): Drepung Loseling Library Society.

Perdue, Daniel. 1992. *Debate in Tibetan Buddhism*. Ithaca: Snow Lion Publications.

Rogers, Katherine. 2009. *Tibetan Logic*. Ithaca: Snow Lion Publications.

Śāstrī, Hara Prasad. 1916. *Hājāra bacharēra purāṇa Baṅgālā bhāshāya Bauddhagāna ō dōhā*. Kolkata: Baṅgīya-Sāhitya-Parishat; see also: Bhattacharya, Vidhushekhara. "Sandhabhasa," *Indian Historical Quarterly* 4(1) [1928]: 287–296.

Ser smad thos bsam nor bu'i gling. 1990. *Ser-smad Thos-bsam-nor-gliṅ gi yig cha, zur bkol: Supplementary Texts for the Study of the Perfection of Wisdom at Sera Mey Tibetan Monastic University*. Bylakuppe (India): Computer Center of Sera Mey Tibetan Monastic University.

Siderits, Mark et al. 2011. *Apoha*. New York: Columbia University Press.

Sonam Rinchen, and Ruth Sonam. 2003. *The Heart Sūtra*. Ithaca: Snow Lion Publications.

Sopa, Geshe Lhundup, and Jeffrey Hopkins. 1990. *Cutting Through Appearances: the Practice and Theory of Tibetan Buddhism*. Ithaca: Snow Lion Publications.

Sparham, Gareth. 1999. *The Fulfillment of All Hopes: Guru Devotion in Tibetan Buddhism*. Boston: Wisdom Publications.

———. 2006–2012. *Abhisamayālaṃkara with Vrtti and Ālokā*. 4 vols. Fremont, Calif.: Jain Publishing Co.

———. 2008–2013. *Golden Garland of Eloquence (Legs bshad gser phreng) by Tsong-kha-pa*. 4 vols. Fremont, Calif.: Jain Publishing Co.

Tenzin Dorjee. 1989. "Namgyal Dratsang: A 413 Year-old Monastery." *Tibet Journal* 14 (3): 33–46.

Thupten Jinpa, and Jaś Elsner. 2000. *Songs of Spiritual Experience*. Boston: Shambhala Publications.

Tubb, Gary A., and Emory R. Boose. 2007. *Scholastic Sanskrit: A Manual for Students.* NY: American Institute of Buddhist Studies.

Vekerdi, J. 1952. "Some Remarks on Tibetan Prosody." *ACTA Orientalia Hungaricae* 2 (2/3): 221–233.

Whitney, William Dwight. 1889. *A Sanskrit Grammar*. Oxford: Clarendon Press.

Wolff, Dieter, and David Marsh. 2012. *Diverse Contexts - Converging Goals in CLIL in Europe*. Frankfurt: Peter Lang GmbH.

Wylie, Turrell. 1959. "A Standard System of Tibetan Transcription." *Harvard Journal of Asiatic Studies* 22: 261–267.